D0984318

Fit for Service

The Training of the British Army
1715–1795

FIT FOR SERVICE

The Training of the British Army, 1715–1795

J. A. HOULDING

CLARENDON PRESS · OXFORD

OXFORD
UNIVERSITY PRESS

Great Clarendon Street, Oxford OX2 6DP

Oxford University Press is a department of the University of Oxford.
It furthers the University's objective of excellence in research, scholarship,
and education by publishing worldwide in

Oxford New York

Athens Auckland Bangkok Bogotá Buenos Aires Calcutta
Cape Town Chennai Dar es Salaam Delhi Florence Hong Kong Istanbul
Karachi Kuala Lumpur Madrid Melbourne Mexico City Mumbai
Nairobi Paris São Paulo Singapore Taipei Tokyo Toronto Warsaw
with associated companies in Berlin Ibadan

Oxford is a registered trade mark of Oxford University Press
in the UK and in certain other countries

Published in the United States
by Oxford University Press Inc., New York

British Library Cataloguing in Publication Data
Data available
ISBN 0-19-822647-0

1 3 5 7 9 10 8 6 4 2

Printed in Great Britain
on acid-free paper by
Biddles Ltd., Guildford and King's Lynn

If my soldiers began to think,
not one would remain in the ranks.
                FREDERICK THE GREAT

Preface

The peacetime training of the eighteenth-century British Army was not good. In their private correspondence intelligent and experienced field officers, in close touch with the corps, often gave vent to their frustration with the prevailing system under which they laboured, and with its fruits. Lt.-Col. Caroline Frederick Scott of Hopson's 29th of Foot, writing from Limerick in July 1750, put his view of the situation in a concerned if satiric vein. As he wrote to his friend Col. Robert Napier, the Adjutant-General,

In my Leisure Hours, I dress out a line of battle of our Army in this Kingdom and had begun a March from Dublin in the Stile of my Brother Quarter Master, Monsr. de Puysegur, but when I had truly look'd att the Names, officers, Heads, and limbs, etc., of people, the almighty task was too hard for me to go on with, and I dropped my supposed March before we had proceeded half way to our intended purpose, which did Spoil a most Elegant March from Dublin to Corke.[1]

Lt.-Col. James Wolfe of Honywood's 20th of Foot, writing from Southampton in September 1755, was more direct. As he wrote to his father, Lt.-Gen. Edward Wolfe,

I have but a very mean opinion of the infantry in general. I know their discipline to be bad, & their valour precarious. they are easily put into disorder, & hard to recover out of it; they frequently kill their Officers thro' fear, & murder one another in their confusion . . . our Method of training & instructing the Troops, is extreamly defective, & tends to no good end; we are lazy in time of Peace & of course want vigilance & activity in War—our military Education is by far the worst in Europe, & all our concerns are treated w^h contempt, or totally neglected.[2]

Both had more to say. That 'our ignorance is as great as our presumption, & both are in excess', Wolfe thought obvious; and he regretted that 'the People of this Country' would not

---

[1] Cumb. Pprs, Box 44, no. 98.
[2] Public Archives of Canada M.G.18, L5, vol. 3, pt 2, pp. 390–1.

'suppose or acknowledge, that subordination in an Army is necessary to its success—they have no idea of a free born English Soldier's marching, working or fighting, but when he thinks proper.' 'It will cost us very dear, some time hence', he concluded.[3] Scott in Limerick had little better to say of 'the Darling Children of Saint Patrick', among whom were working 'the blessed effects of Long Peace and Plenty, as if the chance of War, or day of Rebellion would never come no more'; and like Wolfe he concluded that, when war did come, 'no people in the World will be more frightened, than Those who now Govern this Kingdom.'[4] 'We are in imminent danger of being cut to pieces in our first encounter', Wolfe could speculate; and 'meanwhile we can only look on & marvel at the insensate Stupidity which tollerates this laxity in our Affairs.'[5]

Writing in 1775 Col. Edward Harvey, as Adjutant-General at the Horse Guards, could take a larger view of the situation; but his frustration was the more evident for that. 'I am too sensible of ye relaxation of discipline & of the want of System in the Brit. Service', he wrote; but there was little he could do. 'Too many concurrent Circumstances contribute to this Misfortune.'[6]

In the following discussion of the training of the eighteenth-century army we have addressed ourselves primarily to these 'many concurrent Circumstances', the operation of which, by and large, described the limits of the possible. Among the majority of the regiments, horse and foot, the training that it was possible to carry on in peacetime was insufficient; among the remaining minority it was only just barely sufficient. The problem was essentially one of time and opportunity. Both were lacking, since 'many concurrent Circumstances' restricted the former and almost denied the latter. To determine and then to discriminate among these circumstances we have had to build up a most detailed picture of the peacetime service of the corps—and indeed training could not otherwise have been described without our having first of all reconstructed the

---

[3] R. H. Whitworth (ed.), 'Some Unpublished Wolfe Letters, 1755–58', *JSAHR* 58 (1975), 73, 68; and Public Archives of Canada, ibid.

[4] Cumb. Pprs, Box 44, no. 99, p. 3; and Box 44, no. 98.

[5] R. Wright, *The Life of Major General James Wolfe . . . Illustrated by his Correspondence* (1864), 349; and McCord Museum MS 1290, 15 Sept. 1755, fo. 2.

[6] WO 3/5, p. 97.

'timetable' according to which the service was conducted. We need to know how much time the regiments devoted to their various peacetime duties, how much time was left for training, and where lay the opportunities for the most effective and valuable sorts of training.

The peacetime army was not well trained because (as we shall see) it was much preoccupied and much afflicted. Serious and detailed study of the army's preoccupations has not before been attempted; and in consequence most of what we have written here is taken from primary—indeed mostly from archival—sources. The central archives have proved to be our most useful source.[7] When used in great masses, certain classes of War Office documents held at the PRO—the Marching Orders (WO 5) in particular, not before used in this fashion—yielded a vast store of data, so much in fact that we were put under the necessity of reducing to statistics what could not handily be expressed in a more palatable fashion. More statistics were drawn from the Inspection Returns (WO 27) and from the printed annual *Army Lists*, used in conjunction—again an approach not previously tried. These researches have uncovered the 'many concurrent Circumstances' affecting training, of which officers complained; and the statistics have laid bare the bones of the training problem while providing us with the all-important timetable of peacetime service. Most of this material is put forward in Chapters I and II. The phases into which we have divided the training of the regiments (Chapters IV–VII) derive quite naturally from the timetable of service, used together with the Inspection Returns, senior and staff officers' correspondence, and related documents.

Some historians have commented upon the often ill-trained and ill-prepared state of regiments; but none having analysed

[7] This is by default. During the period under consideration each regiment was responsible for its own training, and hence for its tactical skill and drill proficiency. The central authorities administered and cajoled from afar. It is the papers of the central authorities that survive; and most unfortunately, those belonging to the corps themselves—orderly books, regimental record books, etc.—have not. Before the Victorian army with its regimental depots, the papers of the regiments (like all the rest of their possessions) went where the regiments went. Thus, the eighteenth-century records of the old 28th Foot, for example, 'were unfortunately lost in the Peninsular War'; and all those of the old 14th Foot 'were lost in a ship wreck off Guadeloupe on Christmas Day 1838.' (Letters to the author from RHQ, The Gloucestershire Regiment, and from RHQ, The Prince of Wales's Own Regiment of Yorkshire, respectively.)

time and opportunity, the true reasons for these flaws have not been adduced. The purchase system (by which officers bought their commissions) and a lack of drill regulations (by which regularity, uniformity, and diligence might have been served) have most often been cited as responsible. The first of these, as we shall see, is irrelevant to the issue; and the second is utterly mistaken. We have in fact found the regiments well officered, led by men who were ambitious and, for the most part, dependent upon long service and merit for their advancement. We have found too that the army's drill was always closely regulated, practised in accordance with a lengthy series of drill regulations and orders issued from time to time by authority, throughout the period. And there were other important advantages, favourable to the army's peacetime training. From the beginning of our period the corps were subject to annual inspection and review by general officers attached for the purpose to the London and Dublin staffs: their training was enquired into minutely and was reported upon to the Hanoverian Kings, each of whom took the closest interest; and by these means drill regularity was assured and enforced. Additionally, there was a flourishing military literature in the English language, catering to all aspects of training and drill; and where native authors failed to deal with certain topics, English translations of foreign treatises were to be had.

We have described and analysed at length, below, each of these several significant advantages. Like the army's preoccupations, these have nowhere been dealt with before in detail; and failure to do so would be not only to distort the training milieu in which the army found itself, but to do an injustice to the army too often rendered and not by any means deserved.

But withal, we have found the army to be the victim of time and opportunity, insufficiently trained upon the outbreak of war to meet a regular enemy in the field. Where training-time was restricted and where proper opportunities were come by only with difficulty, and erratically, peacetime training became a thing not so much of artful design, but of expediency. Only when war came did expediency give way to necessity; and it was always at the eleventh hour that the best training was done in the British Army.

It has been my good fortune to enjoy the co-operation and assistance of many people and institutions during the course of my research.

I must acknowledge, with the deepest respect, the gracious permission of Her Majesty The Queen to quote from the Cumberland Papers in the Royal Archives, as recently published on microfilm.

I am very much in the debt of the Archivists, Librarians, and staffs of the following institutions: the Department of Manuscripts, the Reading Room, and the Map Room, at the British Library; the Historical Manuscripts Commission, Chancery Lane; the Library of the Royal United Services Institute; the Reading Room of the National Army Museum, Chelsea; the Library, St. Andrews University; the Institute of Historical Research, Senate House, University of London; King's College Library, University of London; Trinity College Library, University of Dublin; the Library of Congress, in Washington DC; the Public Archives of Canada; the McCord Museum, McGill University, Montreal; and the County Record Offices in Berkshire, Buckingham, Cornwall, Kent, Nottinghamshire, and in Ipswich and East Suffolk. I wish to thank collectively the Regimental Secretaries, Archivists, Curators, and Officers Commanding at dozens of Regimental Museums and Associations throughout the United Kingdom. I am especially grateful to the staff of the Round Room at the Public Record Office, in Chancery Lane, who showed me every kindness.

Many individuals rendered signal services, notably Mrs Sylvia Smither at King's College London; Brigadier Bernard Rigby CBE, of The Cheshire Regiment; Maj. L. H. Colbeck at the Royal Canadian Military Institute, Toronto, where Col. C. P. Stacey lent his good offices; Maj. R. Bartelot, at the Royal Military Academy, Woolwich; Lt.-Col. E. C. T. Wilson VC; Dr Piers Mackesy, of Pembroke College, Oxford; Professor I. R. Christie, of University College London; Professor O. Kennedy, of the Ontario Agricultural College, Guelph; Professor Leo Johnson, of the University of Waterloo, Ontario; Dr D. G. Paz, of Clemson University, South Carolina; Dr Douglas Marshall, of the William Clements Library, Ann Arbor; Dr A. J. Hayter, of The University College at Buckingham; Mr

James Barker, of Toronto; Mr George Houlding QC, of Brantford; and Mr James Hayes, of Hong Kong.

I am grateful to The Canada Council for the award of a
Doctoral Fellowship, without which this study—presented
originally as a doctoral dissertation in the Department of War
Studies at King's College London—could not have been
undertaken.

Finally, I wish to thank Dr Ian Roy at King's, for whose
scholarly guidance, always helpful criticisms, and abundance
of patience I shall always be most deeply indebted.

Two final notes need to be made. Firstly, the training of the
Ordnance corps—the Royal Artillery and Royal Engineers—
has not been dealt with here. Our subject is the training of the
'army' proper, of which these technical services, regarded as
ancillary, were not a part. 'The People of the Train'—who
were the responsibility of the Master-General, not of the
general officers—were specialists, technicians, steeped in
geometry, mathematics, and physics; their cares were little
understood by the officers of the army, their professions were
remote, and they were often despised as mechanical fellows for
their pains. The specialist training of the artillery and engineers,
which in tactics embraces the wide fields of gunnery, fortification, and siegecraft, requires its own specialist treatment, and
could in no way be attempted here.

Secondly, we have been at pains to avoid technical terms and
jargon, in so far as that is possible in a study such as this.
Jargon, the arcana of the profession, was beloved of eighteenth-
century officers—and of none more so than the tacticians and
authors of drillbooks. Much in training is concerned with the
minutiae of military life; and there is much that cannot be
clearly understood—the tactical and administrative subdivisions into which the regiments were broken down, for instance, or the several elements composing the drill regimen
taught in the corps and dealt with in the regulations—without
the introduction of some technical terms. But we have taken to
heart the example of von der Goltz who, throwing up his hands
in despair while pouring over these old drillbooks, concluded
of the eighteenth century that 'a real strategist of that period

believed that he could lead no more than three men over the gutter without a logarithm table.'[8]

Brantford, Ontario   J.A.H.
May 1979

---

[8] Freiherr von der Goltz, *Von Rossbach bis Jena und Auerstadt: Ein Beitrag zur Geschichte des preussischen Heeres* (Berlin, 1906), 361, quoted in J. Luvaas (ed.), *Frederick the Great on the Art of War* (New York, 1966), 17.

Contents

Maps

Notes and Abbreviations

Public Record Office. To save space, I have not entered 'PRO' each time I quote from documents located there. The following letter references refer only to papers in the PRO, which comprise the bulk of my footnotes:

DATES

2. All dates given herein (before the 1752 changeover to the New Style, Gregorian calendar) are Old Style, except that the year is taken as beginning not on 25 March but rather on 1 January. Dates of events and papers from Flanders and Germany are given in New Style throughout, as I found them, unless noted otherwise.

SPELLING AND PUNCTUATION

3. All quotations from eighteenth-century sources, whether printed or in manuscript, are given in their original spelling, grammar, and punctuation. I have occasionally fleshed out abbreviations, but have noted that liberty with square brackets [ ].

PLACE OF PUBLICATION

4. The place of publication of all books is London, unless noted otherwise.

REGULATIONS

5. For simplicity's sake, I have adopted the custom of describing each set of drill regulations, collectively, by the date of their first issue by authority. Eighteenth-century titles being cumbersome and—when dealt with in great numbers—confusing, a shorthand description is

preferable. When a new regulation drillbook is first described in the text, therefore, it is referred to by its proper eighteenth-century title; but it is referred to subsequently by its date of issue. Thus, *The Duke of Marlborough's New Exercise of Firelocks and Bayonets; Appointed by His Grace to be used By all the British Forces, and the Militia* (n.d. [*c.*1708]), becomes and remains the *1708 Regulations*.

In that part of our Bibliography devoted to the regulations, entries are made not alphabetically but chronologically, so that this system of describing the regulations can be cross-referenced.

REGIMENTAL RANK AND DESIGNATION

6. Since the later nineteenth century the bureaucrats, reformers, cheeseparers, and other 'fertile geniuses', as the Duke of Cumberland was wont to refer to them, have had a field day with the old regiments, disbanding some, amalgamating others, naming and renaming, ranking, renumbering, and un-numbering. This most lamentable process continues apace, to the point where the modern researcher on the trail of regiments must carry about with him genealogical tables; and confusion is easy.

One must lay down a convention. I have, therefore, referred to all regiments of foot by the numerical ranks that they held in the 1795 List; and all regiments disbanded before that date have been referred to by the numerical rank they held while in service. Only in 1751 were official designations made of the numbers by which the regiments ranked in seniority; prior to (and for about a decade after) that date, the regiments were known by the names of their proprietary colonels. Until the later-1750s I have in most cases, therefore, referred to a regiment both by its rank and its colonel's name (e.g. Primrose's 24th of Foot). I have seldom used the special titles granted some regiments before or during our period (e.g. Royal North British Fuziliers); and have never used the county titles, first adopted in 1782.

I have followed much the same practice with the cavalry regiments, though omitting colonels' names. The eight regiments of Horse are always a source of confusion. The 1st Horse I have referred to constantly as The Blues. The 2nd, 3rd, and 4th Horse (all of which served in Britain throughout the century) became the 1st, 2nd, and 3rd Dragoon Guards in 1746; and with that the 5th–8th Horse (all of which served in Ireland throughout the century) were re-ranked as the 1st–4th Horse. In 1788, finally, these last became the 4th–7th Dragoon Guards. These corps are all referred to in the text by the rank and title they held at the date for which the reference is made.

Most of the regiments of foot consisted of one battalion only. Where a regiment had more than one battalion (as in the case of the 1st Foot), it is referred to in the normal convention as the 1/1st Foot, or 2/1st Foot.

I use the terms 'regiment' and 'corps' interchangeably; and sometimes (for the foot) use the terms 'regiment' and 'battalion' interchangeably.

The 1st–10th Marine Regiments of the 1739–48 war are always referred to as such, and never by the numerical rank that they held temporarily in the line.

Since the 41st Foot (the Invalid Regiment, until 1787) and the two dozen or so Independent Companies (usually composed of Invalids) are of no significance in the history of training and tactics, they are only mentioned in passing, and are excluded from calculations of the army's size and strength.

I have relied upon J. B. M. Frederick, *Lineage Book of the British Army. Mounted Corps and Infantry, 1660–1968* (Cornwallville, New York, 1969), as the standard reference.

Chapter I

The Friction of Peace: Time, Roles, and Dispositions

We shall in this chapter concern ourselves primarily with time. Between the initial adumbration of tactical theory and drill regulations and their ultimate, often intense and fleeting expression in wartime tactical situations, there stretched those often lengthy periods during which the army, it is supposed, had available the time in which to prepare itself to translate theory into practice.

It is hardly a unique observation to say that between theory and practice there stretches training-time—it is rather like saying that in peacetime armies prepare for war. But however axiomatic the statement, how true is it of the British Army of the eighteenth century? We have here an axiom which we must test, if we are to consider the training link between theory and practice. To test the axiom we must measure the amount of time actually available to the army for training, and not simply count the years between the conclusion of a peace ('une Paix Chrétienne, universelle, et perpétuelle', as the first article of each successive eighteenth-century treaty had it) and the next outbreak of war. When we do actually examine the way in which the army spent its time we discover that from the training point of view there is both time gained and a very great deal of time lost. Indeed so much time is time lost, it turns out, that our hitherto all-too-lightly accepted axiom must be quite dismissed; and with that dismissal our understanding of the training and tactics of the eighteenth-century army must, to a considerable extent, be altered. Thus, having measured the activities of Handasyde's 16th of Foot from the spring of 1737 to the spring of 1743, we discover that the regiment spent 63 per cent of its time totally dispersed in billets or upon the march, another 17 per cent of its time operating against the smugglers and owlers, and 2 per cent suppressing and then overawing rioters; only 13 per cent of its time was spent fully concentrated and stationary, and another 5 per cent at a lower level of concentration.

Meanwhile, Peers' 23rd of Foot was traced from the spring of 1738 until embarking for the wars in Flanders in the summer of 1742. During that period the regiment spent 62 per cent of its time either marching or dispersed and 23 per cent of its time operating against smugglers. Like Handasyde's, Peers's spent only 13 per cent of its time fully concentrated and stationary, and another 2 per cent at a lower level of concentration. Neither Handasyde's by 1743, then, nor Peers' by 1742 was prepared to perform complicated tactical evolutions. Neither had spent so much as one-seventh of its time in England in sufficient concentration to permit even the rudiments of the 'firings' to be practised. Neither regiment is an exceptional case, but quite typical of the army in general.[1]

For philosophical purposes Clausewitz assumed the existence of an archetypical or ideal form of war—namely ultimate, 'absolute war'—towards which violence, viewed in the metaphysical, would tend. He was quick to point out, however, that when passing from conceptual to real war we leave behind us the realm of certitude and pass over into that in which sheer chance operates, introducing a host of unforeseen difficulties, unpredictable reactions, untimely events; and where politics intrudes, describing and thus limiting the ends for which violence was originally introduced and for which it is kept in motion. Absolute war could be no more than a postulate in Clausewitz's day since the carrying on of military violence was, then, hobbled by an inertia which was the result of the accumulation of considerable 'friction'.

Military historians—not to mention retired generals in their memoirs, *limogés* in their apologias, even 'armchair strategists' ('cabinet practitioners', as the eighteenth century styled them), accumulating their terrible 'ifs'—are all rather given to employing the phrase 'friction of war'; and where the subtleties of Clausewitz's argument have frequently been done less than justice, still the notion of friction in war is well-enough understood. So let us suppose, then, that there can be a 'friction of peace'. Let us suppose that, as it is the business of an army in

---

[1] Quite detailed statistics, such as those just given, have been assembled here for all regiments serving in England and Wales; the figures, their source and method of computation are to be found in Appendix A (pp. 396–408). The value of these statistics in assessment of training will be made clear later.

war to fight, to exert pressure, it is the business of an army in peacetime to prepare for war, to train. All of those things—friction-producing agents—that act upon the army in peacetime so as to interfere with training for war are part of the 'friction of peace'. No army is able, of course, to devote itself fully to training in peacetime, just as no army can advance unhindered, can be fully violent, in wartime. The training of the peacetime British Army in the eighteenth century was hampered by certain basic structural features, and also by a variety of petty friction each bit trivial in itself but cumulatively quite significant. Altogether this structural and this petty friction described the nature of the peace in which the army found itself. In this chapter we shall consider the major, structural factors that operated in peacetime, those creating the greatest friction of peace, almost unchanging throughout the century. In the following chapters we shall consider some of the minor characteristics, varying from corps to corps, which added to the friction of peace.

If we may generalize broadly, the British Army in the eighteenth century may be said to have had three roles to play. The first of these was its war role, which is self-defining and which, as we shall see, was most important for our purposes because it was while carrying out this role that the army accomplished its most essential tactical training. That this was so was due to the nature of the other two roles, which were essentially peacetime roles: these were the police role, and the garrison role.

The police role of the army is described in detail in two of the subsections that follow in this chapter. The army, acting in aid of the civil power, was for much of its time involved in the suppression of smuggling, riot, and disorder in general, come war or peace; since the age was a turbulent one and because police forces as such were either non-existent or at best nascent, the regular army had an essential social role to play. But the playing of the police role—either actively in the pursuit of felons or, much more commonly, in the maintenance of a simple passive presence—required that individual regiments be very widely dispersed and preoccupied for lengthy periods of time. Training, in consequence, suffered very considerably.

A garrison is simply a body of troops stationed in a territory or a stronghold to defend it, or to hold it down. Thus, regiments in the Highlands of Scotland until the mid-1750s; regiments in Ireland until perhaps 1720 and then again at the end of the century; regiments in Minorca, Gibraltar, and the West Indies throughout the century; and regiments in Nova Scotia and later in the Canadas were, all of them, clearly garrisons. The Guards in London and Westminster were a garrison too. Garrison duty was usually passive; but since the army was widely distributed about the Empire and because its individual regiments were often being shifted from one place to another, garrison duty meant continually subjecting units to new sets of circumstances which mightily affected their training and proficiency. Units in North America were often so widely dispersed and ill supplied as to be in no condition for active service, and were months beyond the inspection of the War Office. Units in the West Indies fell apart, as fever and boredom did their work. Gibraltar and Minorca, each with as many marching regiments of foot as were usually to be found in the whole of England, were dismal places, hard to recruit, and often in a sorry state where training was concerned.

We shall then in the bulk of this chapter describe the rotation and dispersal of the army about the British Isles and the overseas Empire, note the size of the army, describe the conditions prevailing on the most important stations, note the units involved together with their status and the duration of their spells of duty and dispersal, and consider the police duties of the army in general.

(a) DISTRIBUTION AND ROTATION ABROAD

Throughout our period the dominions of the Crown—and hence its defence responsibilities—were extensive on the North American continent and among the sugar islands of the Caribbean. To the old New England and Southern colonies on the mainland others were added as the century progressed. Thus Georgia was established as a buffer against the Spaniards in the Floridas, and a regular regiment was raised there in 1737–8 to add to Spanish discomfiture; meanwhile, Acadia to the north had been taken at Utrecht, and from 1717 a regular regiment there kept a weather-eye on the French (be they subjects of Louis XV or of King George). The whole of New France with her immense attendant Louisiana territory—an area so vast as quite to dwarf the English Atlantic colonies—passed to the British Crown at the Peace of Paris; but much of this North American empire was lost again, in its turn, twenty years later at Versailles. The fortunes of the individual Caribbean islands are too involved to be catalogued here, but the trend in those seas was towards ever-increasing dominion. Elsewhere, in the other New Worlds, the West African enclaves of Gorée, Gambia, and the Senegal were (somewhat fleetingly) parts of the Empire, and even distant Manila wore the Great Union momentarily. In India, although very few troops of the regular army were employed there during the century, a British presence was assured if its extent remained uncertain.

In the Old World too the century saw an increase in territory beyond the British Isles, for both Minorca and Gibraltar became British possessions after the Treaty of Utrecht. Gibraltar was retained throughout the century, while Minorca was lost twice. Not just England, but Ireland and Scotland too drew in great numbers of troops; both rebelled against English rule during our period but, neither being 'abroad', these we shall treat separately below. Nor should we forget the Channel Islands, those original imperial dominions of the English Crown, which had often enough to be garrisoned later in the century.

So the 'first British Empire', though in many respects utterly different from the second, was huge, and the responsibility for its defence was a major burden. That burden was borne in two different ways. Before the considerable shift in how Englishmen appreciated the notion and hence in how they approached the fact of empire, a change which chrystallized at about the time of the accession of George III and resulted in the 'rationalization' of imperial administration and the introduction of the modern policy of imperial defence, the overseas subjects of the Crown were, by and large, left to their own devices as regards defence during peacetime. Both they and the Crown were content with this arrangement, for a number of reasons. Firstly, the standing army was still in its infancy at the beginning of the century, and was regarded in many quarters with profound suspicion. Particularism, social and political—as powerful a force in Cornwall as in Massachusetts, oftentimes—could better assert itself at a distance from Whitehall, and Whitehall's army was not wanted meddling in much of the Empire. A few Independent Companies, usually of Invalids, would serve for mainland America;[2] and only the threat of war or of slave insurrection would suffice to make the colonials wish to see redcoats. Otherwise, the traditional English device of local self-help —the raising of militia—was deemed a sufficient defence. In the opinion of most influential Englishmen the 'first Empire' existed as a joint-stock trading enterprise; and in consequence permanent defence (which meant expense, and an extension of government, evils both) was best left to the navy, and to the workings of the Navigation Acts and the mercantile laws in general.

Nevertheless even before the mid-century shift there were already major garrisons about the Empire. Gibraltar and Minorca, neither colonies nor factories, were regarded as strategic positions to be held by garrisons of considerable size. In peacetime there were often as many marching regiments of foot at Gibraltar as there were in England, and the same was true of Minorca (see Appendix B). The Mediterranean garrisons, like Ireland, served also as handy places in which to hide away regiments from the prying eyes of cheeseparers, or of back-benchers ever ready to invoke the 'no standing army' issue. Troops at Minorca contributed as effectively to the defence of Massachusetts as did troops at Boston, since Mahon was nearer Toulon; and Mahon was the only secure base for the navy between Lisbon and Leghorn. Gibraltar, although its strategic value was debatable, had a fine anchorage and became rather quickly an object dear to the hearts of the mob. Acadia was also an exceptional case, since most of the population of that place was French, Roman Catholic, and hence deemed sullen; and those few islands in the West Indies where troops

---

[2] Sir John St. Clair, upon seeing the 'picked men' of the New York Independent Companies, those drafted into two special companies sent to aid Braddock's 1755 expedition, observed of them that they 'had neither Legs to get upon the Heights nor to run away thro the Valleys', adding that they 'seem to be draughted out of Chelsea'. F. T. Nichols, 'The Organization of Braddock's Army', *William & Mary Quarterly*, 3rd Ser. 4 (1947), 128–9. St. Clair was not exaggerating, as any perusal of the Inspection Returns (WO 27) on the poor wretches serving in the Independent Companies in Britain will show.

The history of the limited appearance of regulars in America before 1755 can conveniently be traced in J. Shy, *Toward Lexington. The Role of the British Army in the Coming of the American Revolution* (Princeton, 1965), 19–44.

were stationed were likewise exceptional, for there the white populations were too small to form any adequate militia,[3] and fear of slave insurrection was deservedly great.

Characteristic of the second, 'rationalized' phase of empire, after 1760, was the notable increase in the number of troops serving throughout the Empire in peacetime. Inherent in the sweeping designs of the elder Pitt during the Seven Years War (or the 'Great War for Empire', as Gipson so appropriately called it) was the concept of a bigger, imperial army, necessary to patrol the walls of a world-wide empire taken by the sword. What was taken from others must needs be held; and so rapacious were the British during the Seven Years War that it could be only a matter of time before the French and the Spaniards, having bound up their wounds and nursed their grievances, should seek to restore the Balance of Power. So defence had truly become an imperial necessity after 1763; and although a part of the Empire was lost after 1783, and even though the commitment of regulars to India remained limited (the three armies of the presidencies of the East India Company were almost sufficient for any duties required in the sub-continent, since taken together they numbered some 115,000 men by 1782),[4] the army was to remain an imperial garrison from the early 1760s until the mid-twentieth century.

By the close of the reign of George II and in the years that followed, the army was being transformed. What had been a small, ill-constituted, haphazardly organized force whose main aim had been to second punitive fleet operations or to accompany English guineas on to the Continent to stiffen the backs of (or to stampede into action) an odd assortment of allies, was becoming a new-model imperial army, bigger and better organized to outward appearances. But at no time during the century, neither before nor after the mid-century water-shed, were the land forces available for the peacetime policing and defence of the Empire—let alone the British Isles—suffi-

[3] For a summary of the dismally trained and pathetically inadequate militia main-tained in the English Caribbean islands, see R. Pares, *War and Trade in the West Indies, 1739–1763* (Oxford, 1936), 234–40.

[4] On the armies of the East India Company, 1757–98, see R. Callahan, *The East India Company and Army Reform, 1783–1798* (Harvard, 1972), 1–14. With 115,000 troops in 1782 and 155,000 by 1805, Callahan rightly reminds us (p. 6) that 'The Company controlled one of the largest standing armies in the world.'

ciently strong for the task. Only during peak war years was the size of the army at all equal to the pretensions of the British Crown; and even then the statement must be qualified by a consideration of the security that the navy afforded, since in any strict comparison with the land forces of the other Great Powers those of Britain look small indeed.

A sketch of the fluctuations in the army's size, throughout our period, will provide a scale against which peacetime imperial commitments, and hence dispersal, can be measured. Thus from a mere twenty-eight battalions in 1702 the army had been expanded, by the height of the War of the Spanish Succession, to seventy-three battalions of marching Foot and six battalions of Foot Guards,[5] a figure not to be equalled again for fifty years, and greatly reduced with the coming of peace in 1712. By 1714 the peacetime standing army consisted of six troops of Household cavalry, eight regiments of Horse, six regiments of Dragoons, six battalions organized as three regiments of Foot Guards,[6] and thirty-one battalions organized as thirty 'marching regiments of Foot'.[7] This represented a drastic reduction, and the surviving standing force was pathetically small; Britain by Utrecht had emerged as a Great Power, and if she wished to retain that status in the councils of Europe she would be obliged to bear the expense of a more sizable military establishment. How inadequate was this establishment was soon made clear, for upon the outbreak of the Jacobite rebellion in 1715 fourteen regiments of dragoons and fifteen of foot had hastily to be raised just to handle internal defence.[8] Not all of

[5] R. E. Scouller, *The Armies of Queen Anne* (Oxford, 1966), 97.

[6] The Foot Guards regiments, properly, were not organized into fully fledged individual battalions until later in the century, although each had sufficient companies on its establishment to form two battalions (and three in the 1st Foot Guards). When the three regiments camped together in Hyde Park—e.g. in 1722 (WO 55/348, pp. 37–41)—they were issued battalion-guns on a scale of seven battalions. The number of field officers and adjutants is also confusing. On this problem, see R. E. Scouller, ibid. 97 n. 1; the *1740 Army List* (rpt. by the *JSAHR*, 1931), 12–15; and the subsequent *Army Lists* themselves. See also J. B. M. Frederick, *Lineage Book of the British Army: Mounted Corps and Infantry, 1660–1968* (Cornwallville, N.Y., 1969), 65, 92–3, 271, whose approach I have followed here.

[7] 'Marching' regiments of Foot, or regular line infantry regiments with no fixed and permanent quarters, as distinct therefore from the sedentary Foot Guards.

[8] Sir J. Fortescue, *A History of the British Army*, ii (1899), 3–7 (cited hereafter as Fortescue). In 1715 were raised (or re-raised), the 7th–14th Dragoons (which corps survived), and Newton's, Tyrrell's, Churchill's, Rich's, Molesworth's, and Stanhope's Dragoons (which were disbanded by 1718). Similarly the foot regiments later to be

these new corps survived for long, but by 1718 the size of the army had at last been stabilized. From the reductions following the suppression of the Jacobites to the outbreak of war with Spain in 1739, the standing British Army consisted of some six troops of Household cavalry, eight regiments of Horse, fourteen regiments of Dragoons, six battalions organized as three regiments of Foot Guards, and forty-one battalions organized as forty marching regiments of Foot (one more regiment of Foot, Oglethorpe's 42nd of one battalion, was added in 1737). Although no part of the Army establishment and only recently regimented, there were also standing throughout the same period four companies of Artillery.[9] There were in addition a handful of Independent Companies of Invalids distributed among the fortifications of Great Britain and the Plantations, and a full Regiment of Invalids usually to be found about Portsmouth.

Although there were periodic but short fluctuations in its strength as the exigencies of European affairs or of the Jacobite menace might dictate, the army during this period numbered less than 35,000—which made it a paltry force indeed. Although the combined populations of Great Britain and Ireland may have numbered 8,500,000 by 1730, nevertheless His Sardinian Majesty could boast of an army equal in size to that of King George I. At the same time the population of the lands of the Crown of Prussia was less than 2,250,000 souls, yet the Prussian Army totalled some 56,575 troops in 1720, 66,861 in 1729, 75,124 in 1738, and 83,446 at the time of Frederick William I's death.[10] Prussia may indeed have been an aberration, but she was still only the tenth state in Europe in extent of territory, the twelfth in size of population—figures which suggest that the

---

ranked as the 6th, 14th, 22nd, 28th, 29th, 30th, 32nd, 33rd, and 34th were all re-raised in 1715; while Stanwix's, Dubourgay's, Lucas's, Pocock's, Hotham's, and Grant's Foot were raised that same year, but were also disbanded by 1718.

[9] The best work of reference on the raising, length of service, amalgamations, and disbandment of British regiments is J. B. M. Frederick, op. cit. I have followed Frederick throughout, supplementing it occasionally with the printed annual *Army Lists*. Useful also is N. B. Leslie, *The Succession of Colonels of the British Army From 1660 to the Present Day* (*JSAHR* Special Publ. No. 11, 1974). On the artillery, I have used M. E. S. Laws, *Battery Records of the Royal Artillery, 1716–1859* (Woolwich, 1952).

[10] R. Ergang, *The Potsdam Führer* (New York, 1941), 63.

size of the British Army was as much an aberration, in the age of *raison d'état*, as was that of Prussia. The British Army was to remain disproportionately small, indeed, until at least 1763, given the vast extent of the Empire, the strategic necessity to commit troops to both Continental and colonial campaigns, and the need for considerable numbers to ship on board the fleet as marines.

It was then with these paltry numbers that England, Scotland, Ireland, the Mediterranean garrisons, and the overseas empire had to be policed, garrisoned, and defended. During the period 1716–39 an average of one-quarter of the regiments of marching Foot was to be found serving abroad; another quarter was in Britain and the remaining half in Ireland. But with such wide commitments, and with so few regiments, it was obvious that the army must grow if it was to perform its tasks; and although it did continue to grow it was never to do so quickly enough to keep pace with its ever-expanding peace-time role.

During wartime, new regiments were always being raised and existing units augmented; and most of these accretions were pruned away with the coming of peace. We say 'most' because with the conclusion of each war fought during the century there was always an absolute increase in the number of units making up the standing army. We described the size of the army to 1739 above. During the wars of 1739–48 there were added a further two regiments of Horse (both raised as fencible corps during the '45 Rebellion, but one of which became part of the regular army upon being converted into Dragoons in 1746), plus ten full regiments of Marines, twenty-three battalions of marching Foot (two of which were attached to old marching regiments,[11] while the other twenty-one were organized as sixteen new regiments), plus a further thirteen battalions of foot whose exact status—since they were raised in England only to assist in the suppression of the Jacobite rebels, but ranked nevertheless in the regular army list—is a matter of some controversy.[12]

---

[11] These were the 2/5th and 2/35th, raised for Irish duty as the forces in that kingdom were depleted. Bruce's 60th and Folliott's 61st, both serving in Ireland, likewise raised second battalions.

[12] On these 'fencible corps' see C. C. P. Lawson, *A History of the Uniforms of the*

Following the reductions at the war's end, the army from 1748 to 1755 was made up of four troops of Household cavalry, The Blues, four regiments of Horse, three regiments of Dragoon Guards (converted from Horse in 1746), fourteen regiments of Dragoons, six battalions in three regiments of Foot Guards, and forty-nine battalions in forty-eight marching regiments of Foot. Two more of Foot, Shirley's 50th and Pepperell's 51st, were raising from the very end of 1754. The artillery meanwhile, having grown from four companies in 1739 to twelve by 1748, stood on ten companies from 1749 until 1755 when it too joined in the general expansion of the forces which began in that year. The ten Marine Regiments had been totally disbanded after Aix-la-Chapelle, but in 1755 independent Marine Companies were raised, a different but now a permanent establishment.[13] From 1749 to 1755, rather as had been the case from 1716 to 1739, one-quarter of the corps of marching Foot was on foreign garrison duty, half was in Ireland, and the rest in Britain. During this period there were always more battalions of marching Foot in Scotland than there were in England; and there were as many in Gibraltar, and as many in Minorca, as there were in England. There were more battalions in Scotland than in the whole of the Americas; more battalions in Minorca than in North America (see Appendix B).

The largest increase in the size of the army—slightly greater even than the one that occurred during the War of the Spanish Succession—took place during the Seven Years War; and of the new-raised corps more survived the 1763 peace than any other in the century. At the height of the Seven Years War there were on the infantry establishments alone some 133 battalions in 126 marching regiments, plus seven battalions of Foot Guards and two corps of Rangers.

The peacetime establishment after 1763 reflected the new design for imperial defence, the peacetime standing army averaging some 45,000 men during the second half of the century. From 1764 until the renewal of war in 1775 the army was composed of four troops of Household cavalry plus The Blues, four regiments of Horse, three of Dragoon Guards, thirteen of

---

British Army, ii (1963), 25–7; and C. T. Atkinson, 'Jenkins' Ear, The Austrian Succession and the Forty-Five', *JSAHR* 22 (1943–4), 283–5, 293.

[13] J. B. M. Frederick, op. cit., *passim*; and M. E. S. Laws, op. cit. 15–35.

Dragoons, five regiments of the new Light Dragoons, seven
battalions formed as three regiments of Foot Guards, seventy-
one battalions in sixty-nine regiments of Foot, and fifty Marine
Companies administered in three 'divisions' from Chatham,
Portsmouth, and Plymouth. The ten artillery companies of
1755 had become thirty by 1764. More than one-third of the
Foot was serving abroad during the years between the Peace
of Paris and the crisis of 1774–5.

During the American War for Independence, seven battalions in the three regiments of Foot Guards and 111 battalions
in 105 marching regiments were on the establishments of the
regular army, as were thirty regiments of cavalry. Reductions
consequent on the 1783 peace left the army with seven battalions of Foot Guards and seventy-four battalions of Foot[14]
ready for service upon the outbreak of war in 1793; and an
average of between one-third and one-half of the regiments of
Foot was serving abroad. Inclusive of Household cavalry[15]
there were also standing by 1793 some thirty regiments of
cavalry; and the Royal Artillery counted forty-two companies
exclusive of the Invalid gunners in the forts.[16] Although it strays
beyond our period, finally, some idea of the vast increases
necessitated by the Napoleonic Wars may be gained from the
consideration that there were 186 battalions of infantry in the
army by 1814 and 100 companies of Foot Artillery alone at the
time of Waterloo.[17]

Continually growing as the century progressed, then, the
army will be seen to have been considerable in size only at peak
war years. During the periods of peace a significant part of the
foot which survived the war-end disbandments was, as we have
seen, sent abroad: between 1716 and 1739 an average of one-
quarter of the foot was serving abroad; between 1748 and 1755
one-quarter of the foot was still doing so; between 1763 and
1775 more than one-third of the foot was serving outside of the

[14] The 41st Foot, previously composed of invalids and doing duty about Portsmouth,
was in 1787 converted to a regular line regiment.

[15] From the two troops of Horse Guards and two troops of Horse Grenadier Guards
were formed in 1788 the 1st and 2nd Regiments of Life Guards; the Household
cavalry had previously stood as independent Troops.

[16] M. E. S. Laws, op. cit. 79–81.

[17] Ibid. 162–5; and Sir C. Oman, *Wellington's Army, 1809–1814* (New York, 1912),
178–89.

British Isles; and between 1783 and 1793 more than one-third of the foot was, on average, serving abroad. The world-wide deployment in peacetime of what was so significant a part of the forces, therefore, were it to be maintained in a proper state of training and *au courant* with tactical developments on the Continent and at home, must needs be done with considerable care. But in fact the opposite was the case.

Under the material conditions prevailing in the eighteenth century, any extended stay on a distant station was bound to have the most serious effects upon a unit. The greatest of the several problems affecting corps so situated was the replacement of dead men and deserters—for where were recruits to be found on Minorca or Gibraltar, let alone in the West Indies or Acadia? Recruiting parties sent home cost a great deal, and took time to effect their business. In consequence, the sweepings of English society (whether inveigled by recruiters or condemned to it by the law), were dispatched abroad to the regiments.[18] Since recruits for units on foreign stations were scarce, commanding officers preferred not to discharge worn-out men, and consequently the regiments left overseas for extended periods began to age, and to decline in efficiency.[19] Regiments aged quickly where little could be done to infuse new blood, in the shape of recruits, in a steady trickle. Thus the 2nd Foot, seen at Gibraltar in April 1772, was quite typically reported as 'very much worn Out' and 'the worst in the Garrison'; the men were 'in general Old, & mostly worn Out'.[20] The 2nd had been there less than five years. In March 1777 the 12th Foot, at Gibraltar, was reported a 'very fine Regiment,

---

[18] An example of how desperate the problem was came after the suppression of the '45 Rebellion. In July 1746 some 250 rebel prisoners were shipped to Antigua as replacements for Dalzell's 38th Foot; another 100 were sent to Trelawney's 49th in Jamaica, and 200 each went to Shirley's 65th and Pepperell's 66th at Louisbourg. Atkinson, 'Jenkins' Ear', 296.

[19] The Adjutant-General, in a lengthy letter to the Secretary at War of 8 Dec. 1767, noted these problems. He was particularly disturbed by the tendency in corps serving abroad not to discharge old and worn-out men, but rather to retain them 'while they can Crawl'; recruiting difficulties was the cause. Such corps were becoming ever more aged and infirm; and the Adjutant-General feared that, in case of sudden war, then 'the Greatest National Inconveniencys must Arise' because the regiments would have immediately to discharge great numbers of invalids even before they could set about augmenting to wartime strengths. Peacetime regimental establishments abroad, therefore, became increasingly illusory as corps remained unrotated. WO 3/1, pp. 129–36.

[20] WO 27/25.

but growing Old'; of the 366 rank and file with the corps only sixty had seen less than seven years' service.[21] Likewise in May 1788 a reviewing officer described the 11th Foot, then serving with the Gibraltar garrison, as 'very indifferent . . . the men being chiefly low, Stunted and a very large proportion of them elderly; & in their present State, would be totally unequal to active Service in the Field.' The 11th had been in Gibraltar for five years; and of its 364 men only forty-two were recruits—a very low percentage, pointing the age of the corps.[22]

The drafting of men from one regiment into another—lifting them from one unit not likely to see action immediately and transferring them into another unit already in the field, or about to go on service—was resorted to, in consequence, a process which did neither unit any short-term good. The evils of drafting are well-enough understood, and the important features will be discussed below; we need do no more at this stage than provide a couple of illustrations.[23] In May 1775, when he reviewed the 54th Foot at Cork, Lt.-Gen. Lord Blayney found them 'not by any means a good Regiment nor fitt for service', having been 'much drafted for the late Embarkation'.[24] The efficiency of the 54th had been destroyed in order to flesh out other corps being sent, too late, to overawe a Boston already in arms. In May 1787 the 44th Foot was seen at Hilsea Barracks, lately returned from the Canadas. Only 132 men were able to appear under arms, since '134 of their best men' had been drafted into other regiments still in Canada upon the 44th's sailing for home; and the few men whom the 44th had received in exchange were 'indifferent', and must soon be discharged. The 44th was wholly unfit for service.[25]

With men drafted, ageing, or regiments below strength, discipline began inevitably to fall off in corps on long foreign service—the cumulative effect of boredom, long periods of dispersal,[26] and a relaxation of punishments and fatigues for

[21] WO 27/39.

[22] WO 27/62. The average number of recruits generally with the corps is treated in detail here, on pp. 125–32.

[23] For the more detailed discussion, see pp. 120–25.

[24] WO 27/35.

[25] WO 27/59.

[26] Typically, when in October 1768 Maj.-Gen. John Clavering saw the newly returned 15th Foot at Stroud, he found them wanting 'both Steadiness and Precision' in

fear of driving the men to desertion. The customary practice
of letting the men eke out their pay by working away from the
corps part-time, during off hours, increased. Working away
from quarters—such as the routine hauling of firing and provisions, the repair of fortifications, and the guarding of military
installations—was doubtless another way of filling idle hours;
and like the constant use of the private men as coolies on the
road-gangs in Scotland this was a commonplace of army life.[27]
That this cannot have contributed to drill proficiency goes
without saying; but on distant and dreary stations such as
Minorca and Newfoundland it may at least have provided the
men with labour for variety and pay for drink, and so have kept
them with the colours. Soldiers might meanwhile contract
alliances and, when at last the regiment departed from a
foreign station, considerable numbers (as in the case of the 44th
Foot just noted) might be allowed to volunteer as drafts to fill
up the newly-arriving unit; and in this way the military
efficiency of such men would continue to decline.[28] Worse
could happen on some stations: the rigours of the winters in
Nova Scotia took a heavy toll of the 40th Foot, stationed there
from 1717, the Board of Ordnance hardly aware of it. The
Caribbean heat could prostrate, or sap the will; more surely,
its diseases would kill great numbers. Describing the fate that
was the lot of Dalzell's 38th of Foot, in garrison on Nevis,
Montserrat, Antigua, and St. Kitts, Pares wrote that the West
Indies were 'the grave of English soldiers, and the planters
would not have the regiments recruited among their own
servants, so the numbers began to fall.' How dramatically the
numbers 'began to fall' is easily illustrated. In 1738 the 38th

the performance of all their manoeuvres; but this was understandable, 'Considering the
Regiment's long Services in America, and having been Situated in a Country where
only a small part of the year could be appropriated to the Discipline of the men.' The
15th had gone to North America in 1758, and returned home in 1768. WO 27/12.

[27] For examples of this, see F. T. Nichols, art. cit. 128; and see J. T. Findlay, *Wolfe in
Scotland in the '45 and from 1749-1753* (1928), 188-9.

[28] Thus in May 1788 the 29th and 31st of Foot were seen at Pershore and Andover
respectively, both recently home from Canada. The 29th had been in North America
since 1776; and the 31st had arrived there that same year, but from the West Indies.
The 29th was in ruins, all of its arms either bad or wanting, and so under strength that
'only 28 file' appeared under arms at a regimental review. The condition of the 31st
was similar. WO 27/61. Both had been drafted heavily before sailing for England, to
fill out corps in Canada. J. Shy, op. cit. 358-62.

Foot numbered 700 men, while by 1745 it numbered only 492; in the interim, 960 recruits had been sent out to the regiment, and it had only once been on active service—and that a trivial affair.[29] The 31st Foot, lately returned from the West Indies, was luckier than the 38th had been: seen at Sittingbourne in June 1773, the 31st could muster 299 men (the establishment called for 440), half of whom had worn-out firelocks; the corps was reported unfit for service—but more than half of the men were still alive.[30] Gibraltar was an unhealthy station too, although hardly comparable to the Indies. Garrison returns for 1740, for example, show that the regiments there were losing 17 per cent of their men to sickness—a rate unchanged by 1748.[31] When in March 1742 Graham's 43rd and Houghton's 45th of Foot were ordered to the Mediterranean garrisons they were given the chance of drawing lots for Gibraltar; and when in August 1748 deserters lodged in the Savoy were drafted for the Mediterranean they too were given the chance of lots. When in 1725 Tyrrell's 17th and Handasyde's 22nd were embarked for Minorca, it was remarked upon that the establishments of both corps were nearly complete—'it being very disagreeable to the common soldiers to go into garrison abroad, which in consequence entails much desertion.'[32] Minorca, if healthier than Gibraltar, was a depressing, boring place, measuring only 12 miles by 30. The Duke of Argyll said in 1742 that a long term of service at Port Mahon 'was equivalent to a punishment, and that his only surprise was that the troops had not mutinied both at Minorca and Gibraltar.'[33]

Long service overseas, then, did little good to the units so employed. Neglect was no doubt the worst evil from which the distant units suffered; and the more distant the units, given the

---

[29] R. Pares, op. cit. 258. On the pitiful situation of regiments in the West Indies see Pares, pp. 257–64. P. Mackesy, *The War for America, 1775–1783* (1964), 526, calculates that 11 per cent of the men in twelve regiments sent from the British Isles to the West Indies between 1776 and 1780, *died on passage.*

[30] WO 27/27.

[31] Atkinson, 'Jenkins' Ear', 287–8, 298. In 1740 Kirke's 2nd Foot had lost 124 men, while Hargrave's 7th had lost 102, Columbine's 10th had lost 138, Clayton's 14th had lost 144, and Fuller's 29th had lost 129. In 1748, Fowke's 2nd needed 101 men, Hargrave's 7th needed 114, Reade's 9th needed 153, and Tyrawley's 10th needed 134. The establishments called for 780 other ranks per regiment. WO 24/273.

[32] C. T. Atkinson, 'The Army Under the Early Hanoverians', *JSAHR* 21 (1942), 143.

[33] Fortescue, ii. 45.

clumsiness of bureaucracy and the slowness and expense of communications, the greater the neglect. And for the army, there was no such thing as salutary neglect in the eighteenth century. In 1768 the 8th Foot arrived in the Canadas, and was distributed with four companies at Niagara, three at Detroit, one at Oswego, and two at Michilimackinac—spread over a distance of some 700 miles, by inland waterways. Seventeen years later when the 8th came home to England it consisted of 150 'very Old Men'. Five hundred officers and men had gone out; and the 1785 establishments called for 392 NCOs and men.[34] When reviewed at Plymouth in May, 1787, two years after coming home, the corps had recruited to a strength of 311 men; but the reviewing officer reported that since the 8th had 'been many years in the Back Settlements of Canada', it would require 'two or three years to get rid of their Old Men, & to form Non Commission'd Officers.'[35] The regiment was not fit again for service until 1789. A system of rotation or, failing that, at least frequent replacement, was obviously essential, so that the burden could be shared and its evils mitigated. This was recognized, and on at least one occasion (in 1729) the Board of General Officers urged the question upon the King.[36] But, incredibly, no such rotation took place before 1749. Until then, regiments were sent abroad and left to rot. Only fortuitous events, such as a crisis in British relations with the Bourbons or the discovery of some new Jacobite plot, saved units from perpetual exile.[37] In the flurry and confusion always incident to Britain's last-minute preparation for war, some regiments might be fortunate enough to be recalled (in both senses of the word); and their replacements had at least the knowledge that a state of war was either imminent or actual, to sharpen their

[34] WO 27/56; WO 24/446, /534; and P. R. N. Katcher, *King George's Army, 1775–1783. A Handbook of British, American and German Regiments* (Reading, 1973), 32.

[35] WO 27/59.

[36] Fortescue, ii. 46. In 1730 the King asked the Governor of Gibraltar for a detailed report on the condition of the corps there, since a 'rotation for foreign service' was to be planned 'to relieve soldiers of despair of ever returning home'. Atkinson, 'Early Hanoverians', 145. No rotation was introduced, however: the expense involved was deemed too great.

[37] Thus in 1718, when Byng's squadron sailed for the Mediterranean to deal with the Spanish fleet then harrying Sicily, the opportunity was taken to embark the 9th, 18th, 30th, and 35th, from Ireland, to relieve the Minorca garrison (7th, 12th, 27th, and 39th), which corps had been in that island since 1713. This was an almost unique occurrence. Atkinson, 'Early Hanoverians', 142.

new-found exile. But in some cases not even war, invasion threats, or the rebels at Derby were enough to release a regiment from foreign garrison duty. Some regiments were lucky. At the end of the War of the Spanish Succession, two companies were drafted from Handasyde's 22nd of Foot and sent, as Independent Companies, to garrison Port Royal in Jamaica; the whole of the 22nd had, at least, been spared.[38] Lucky too were Hayes's 34th and Newton's 39th of Foot, sent from Ireland via England to reinforce the besieged Gibraltar garrison early in 1727. The 34th and 39th remained at Gibraltar until late in 1730, when they were ordered to Jamaica to deal with slave insurrection; but luckily both were recalled to Ireland in 1731, and remained there in peace, having narrowly escaped the imprisonment of Gibraltar and the disease of the Caribbean.[39]

For many other units it was to be a different story. During that same half-century before the introduction of rotation of number of corps spent incredibly long periods on foreign service, without relief. In June 1730, for example, Kirke's 2nd of Foot embarked from England for Gibraltar, and stayed there for nineteen years before being relieved in 1749 and sailing for Ireland.[40] In 1725 Tyrrell's 17th of Foot was sent out to Minorca, and was not relieved for twenty-four years when, in 1749, the corps was brought home to Ireland. In 1725 too the luck of the 22nd Foot ran out, when the corps was dispatched to Minorca for a twenty-four-year stay.[41] Otway's 9th of Foot served in Minorca from 1718 until 1746, was transferred to Gibraltar temporarily, and returned to Ireland in 1749; the regiment had been continuously on foreign service for thirty-one years.[42] Cosby's 18th of Foot joined the Minorca garrison in 1718, with Byng, and returned to England only in 1742.[43] Yet these were all merely quarter-century stints, and so not extraordinary. In August 1717 Philipp's 40th of Foot was formed from Independent Companies then serving in the

[38] Fortescue, ii. 42–6.

[39] R. Cannon, *Historical Record of the Thirty-Ninth, or The Dorsetshire Regiment of Foot* (1853), 10–12.

[40] R. Cannon, . . . *Second Foot* (1838), 35; Anon., *The Quarters of the Army in Ireland in 1748* (Dublin, 1748), 18; and *Quarters . . . in 1749* (Dublin, 1749), 23.

[41] R. Cannon, . . . *Seventeenth Foot* (1848), 16–17, and . . . *Twenty-Second Foot* (1849), 6–7. See also Anon., *Quarters . . . in 1748*, p. 18, and *Quarters . . . in 1749*, p. 23.

[42] Fortescue, ii. 45 n. 1; WO 24/273 and 282.

[43] Ibid. 45 n. 4; WO 5/35, p. 461.

Americas, and was sent to garrison Newfoundland and Nova Scotia. There the corps remained until 1765 when, at long last, it was relieved and sent to Ireland. The 40th had been continuously on foreign service for forty-eight years; it was under its fifth colonel before it ever laid eyes upon the British Isles. The record, however, belongs to the 38th Foot, for that unlucky corps rotted in the West Indies from 1716 until 1765. Replaced after half a century, the 38th was allowed less than nine years' respite in Ireland, when in mid-1774 it was packed off to Boston, a place by then even less hospitable than the West Indies. Before a year was out the luckless 38th was to be shattered storming the entrenchments on Breed's Hill, just across Boston harbour.

The whole of the horse and the Guards were stationed permanently in the British Isles, during peacetime; and so it was the marching Foot that suffered from the capriciousness of foreign garrison duty. As we have observed there was no pattern of rotation, and almost no relief for regiments abroad, until the mid-century. Thus of the forty-one battalions composing the marching regiments from 1718 to 1739 (we exclude the 42nd here, raised in Georgia and serving there from 1737), an average of eight were always to be found in the Mediterranean garrisons. Only the 1726–8 war with Spain caused some movement in these garrisons, in effect merely ending the exile of some units to impose exile on others.[44] For the West Indian and Nova Scotian corps there was to be no relief at all. Therefore, one-quarter of the marching Foot of the British Army was left to rot, unrelieved, on distant foreign stations for the whole of the period.

The rapid expansion of the army, beginning in 1739, led to some reinforcing of the overseas garrisons, but few of the units already in those garrisons were relieved during the war. In 1749 however, the Duke of Cumberland initiated the first (and indeed the only) system of regular rotation of the regiments in Europe; it functioned until 1755, and not for the rest of the century was so regular a system attempted again. To set the stage for his system the old Gibraltar and Minorca garrisons

---

[44] R. Cannon, . . . *Thirty-Ninth Foot* (1853), 9–10; Cumb. Pprs, O.B.Ex. 1/21, 34, 38, 55; Anon., *Quarters . . . in 1744*, p. 15, *Quarters . . . in 1745*, p. 14, *Quarters . . . in 1748*, p. 18, *Quarters . . . in 1749*, p. 23. See also Appendix B.

were completely replaced in 1749: the four regiments that had
until then been serving in Minorca (the 17th, 22nd, 26th, and
43rd) were relieved by two corps from Britain (12th and 31st)
and two from the army in Brabant (33rd and 37th); and
similarly the four Gibraltar regiments (the 2nd, 7th, 9th, and
10th) were replaced by four from Brabant (the 8th, 19th, 32nd,
and 36th). Beginning in 1751, one each of these units at
Minorca and Gibraltar was rotated annually back to Britain,
from where their replacements were drawn. By late 1754,
therefore, the whole of these new Mediterranean garrisons had
been fairly replaced.[45] In the Americas during this period, however, there were no rotations; the 38th and 40th continued
there, and so too did the new 45th, 47th, and 49th of Foot.[46]
With the coming of war in 1755 the system ceased to function.

The influence of the Duke of Cumberland lingered beyond
the end of the 1756–63 war, however. His system had been
found useful and workable; there were now many corps in the
Americas and—although the system was not restored to the
letter—peacetime rotation was now extended beyond Britain
and the Mediterranean to include Ireland, North America,
and the West Indies too. Thus after half a century of neglect
there were to be periodic attempts made at large-scale reliefs,
and occasional (although unsuccessful) attempts at regular
rotation; and this was to continue through the rest of our
period.

The new imperial system of reliefs worked from 1763 until
1775, when war once again interfered. Thus in 1763 a restored
Minorca was garrisoned by the 3rd and 67th from Portugal,
the 57th from Gibraltar, and the 11th, 33rd, and 37th from
Germany. In 1771 the 3rd, 11th, and 67th were relieved by the
2/1st, 51st, and 61st, all from England, the rest of the Minorca
garrison having by then already been relieved.[47] Gibraltar
regiments too were being periodically relieved. After the 1763
peace fifteen battalions were left in North America;[48] and early
in 1764 the Secretary at War outlined a plan for a 'general

---

[45] R. Cannon, . . . *Twenty-Third Foot* (1850), 75; Anon., *Quarters . . . in 1748*, p. 18,
Quarters . . . in 1750, p. 27, *Quarters . . . in 1751*, p. 27, *Quarters . . . in 1752*, p. 27.

[46] On the chronological build-up of units in the Americas, from 1754, see Ch. vi, n. 63.

[47] R. Cannon, . . . *Sixty-Seventh Foot* (1849), 9–10.

[48] J. Shy, op. cit. 269; WO 24/446; and J. R. Alden, *General Gage in America* (Baton
Rouge, 1948), 128.

fixed rotation' between the British Isles and that station. 'The plan called for the replacement of five regiments in North America in 1765, five in 1766, and three in 1768'; and this proved to be only a shade too ambitious since, with Irish troubles intervening, the timetable was put off although thirteen regiments had been rotated by 1769.[49] Rotation continued into the 1770s, the last regiment crossing the Atlantic in 1773. Regiments in the West Indies, similarly, were being rotated with others in the British Isles between 1764 and 1774.

The post-1763 rotations, however, were never so successful as had been that of Cumberland; and considering the difficulties of communications not just on a Mediterranean, but on an Atlantic scale too, this is understandable. The Carib War and the American War for Independence interfered; and hence during the period 1763–93 many corps—like the 8th Foot which we noted earlier, left in central Canada from 1768 until 1785—spent long periods on foreign service, suffering the same ills (if not for such extraordinarily lengthy periods) as had the corps serving abroad before 1749. The 45th Foot, for example, was in 1746 hastily dispatched from Gibraltar to Louisbourg; and for the next twenty years the regiment remained in North America, returning home after four years' service at Gibraltar followed by twenty across the Atlantic. The 16th Foot shipped from Ireland to New York in 1767, and served in America for fifteen years before returning home.[50] The 14th Foot spent nine years in Jamaica, from 1782 to 1791; and the 67th Foot too spent nine years in the West Indies, sailing from Ireland in 1785 and returning home in 1794.[51] Several other regiments saw equally lengthy service abroad during these decades; and the Inspection Returns submitted on all of these corps, upon their return to the British Isles, show clearly that the effects of long foreign service were as harmful after 1763 as they had been before the appearance of rotation and reliefs. A great many of these corps, especially after 1783, suffered too-lengthy spells on foreign duty simply because it was their misfortune not to get caught up in the nets periodically

---

[49] J. Shy, ibid. 274; and see this work for maps showing the distribution of the army in America late in 1760, early in 1763, in 1766, in 1772, and early in 1775. See also Appendix B, here.

[50] G. W. H. Peters, *The Bedfordshire & Hertfordshire Regiment* (1970), 30.

[51] R. Cannon, . . . *Fourteenth Foot* (1845), 37–8, and . . . *Sixty-Seventh Foot* (1849), 10.

cast by the War Office and the Horse Guards, since from 1783 until the renewal of war in 1793 considerable reliefs were going on annually to and from all stations. As in the period of the Duke of Cumberland's administration there was again in operation, from 1787 onwards, another regular annual rotation system— now embracing Britain, Gibraltar, Ireland, and (if not quite so regularly) the West Indies and the Canadas. This system usually involved the rotation of three regiments from Britain to Ireland, three from Ireland to overseas stations, and three from abroad back to Britain. In 1787 for example, three from Britain (the 43rd, 64th, and 70th) crossed to Ireland, three from Ireland (the 4th, 5th, and 26th) sailed for the Canadas, and three from the Canadas (the 29th, 31st, and 34th) returned to Britain; and so the system proceeded, the most ambitious attempted in the century if—unlike that of Cumberland—not wholly regular.[52] Sir William Fawcett, the Adjutant-General in London, described the rotation in a note of 6 October 1791 written to the colonel of a corps in England:[53]

the 8th (or King's) Regt of Foot, under your Comm^d will be one of the three Regiments, destined according to the established rule of Rotation to go to Ireland, early in the next Spring. . . . The other two Regiments will be the 33rd & 44th which are to go with Your's to Ireland, to replace the 46th, 51st, and 61st, on that Estabt. which are to be sent from thence to Gibraltar to relieve the 2nd, 25th, and 59th on that Station.

During this period, too, corps did duty on Jersey and Guernsey; but those few now serving in India were, needless to say, left to the fate that had once been the lot of the old 38th of Foot from 1716 until 1765.

Regiments serving abroad suffered, as we have seen—and as we shall see repeatedly below—from the effects of distance, mismanagement, disease, privation, dispersal, and dearth of recruits. That the material technology of the century was ill equipped to deal with many of these problems is true enough; but it is true too that little or no attempt was made to alleviate the cumulative effects of long service abroad, where help could be rendered, until the Duke of Cumberland took matters in hand and set the example at mid-century. Training in the

[52] WO 5/66–8, *passim.*
[53] WO 3/10, p. 77.

corps long abroad was left to the industry of local governors or regimental officers, who in most cases could not for long periods overcome the friction of foreign service. Some efforts were made by the central authorities after the mid-century to improve training in the corps abroad, as we shall see; but rotation was really the only effective palliative. As we noted earlier, however, the army was at no time large enough to handle efficiently all of the duties imposed upon it in peacetime. Rotation or replacement for those units stretched out over the Empire helped to mitigate a burden which was simply too great for so few regiments; but for all intents and purposes, we must conclude that at least one-fifth and often as much as one-quarter of the marching foot of the British Army, strewn abroad, was in a perpetually low state of interior economy and training and was, consequently, either unfit for service or capable of only modest exertion. This conclusion will be all the more apparent once the condition of those units safely home in Britain and Ireland is considered, which we shall do in the following subsections.

(b) DISTRIBUTION AND ROTATION IN GREAT BRITAIN

When serving in Britain, the army conformed to a set of patterns which varied hardly at all throughout the century, and which collectively had the most profound impact upon the training of the regiments. The dictates of physical and social geography generally and, most specifically, population densities in the various regions, economic fluctuations and their accompanying social unrest, an as yet unimproved and archaic road-network, together with a general lack of quarters sizeable enough to house large numbers of troops, and also the vagaries of crisis—international disputes and wars, rebellion, local riots and disorders—these were the most significant factors contributing to the formation and maintenance of this set of patterns.

Whereas geography provided the framework—the points of embarkation around Britain's shores, the crossings between England, Wales, and Scotland, the main march-corridors the army used once arrived within Britain, and to some extent the duty areas that these corridors linked—it was primarily the more immediate requirements of civil society that provided the motor-mechanism, setting the army in motion along the corridors, determining its distribution and dispersal about and within the duty areas and along the coasts, rotating the regiments from one place to another, and deciding the duration of their stay.

It was the result of these patterns that the army, when serving in Britain, was always on the move from one area to the next, always very widely dispersed, and in consequence ill-trained and unprepared for war. Since the effect of these patterns on the training of the regiments was so marked and so primary, we must consider them here in detail.

Although the number of soldiers in Great Britain was always comparatively large—that is, compared with the numbers serving anywhere else in the Empire—the actual number of regiments 'entertaining' them was small, since regimental establishments in Britain were considerably greater than those of sister units in Ireland.[54] Since many of the regiments serving abroad were sent out from Britain while many of those replaced abroad returned directly to Britain, it is quite clear that this small number of corps made each of them much more mobile, relatively, than any of their counterparts in Ireland. The Irish Parliament disliked sending its regiments abroad, at least during the earlier part of the century; the Irish administration would pay for its own (and for part of Britain's) defence, but it disliked paying to defend New York. Peacetime mobility for units on the British establishment was therefore considerable— and not only between Britain and the Empire, but also between England and Scotland. Only during the 1760s and 1770s were units in Ireland as mobile, Irish-American rotation having been introduced.

There were patterns to this mobility, discernible at various levels. Mobility in and out of Britain (and once the regiments

---

[54] For charts of regimental establishments, see Appendix C. The size of the peacetime Irish establishment was fixed and permanent: 12,000 men from 1699 to 1769, and 15,000 from 1769 until the Union. The size of the peacetime British establishment varied: it stood at around 17,000 from 1720 to 1739, at about 19,000 from 1748 to 1755, and was cut to 17,000 again from 1763. See Sir J. Fortescue, *The British Army, 1783–1802* (1905), 18; F. G. James, *Ireland in the Empire, 1688–1770: A History of Ireland from the Williamite Wars to the Eve of the American Revolution* (Harvard, 1973), 175; and C. M. Clode, *The Military Forces of the Crown: Their Administration and Government*, i (1869), 398 (cited hereafter as Clode). For the disparity in the number of units on the two establishments, see Appendix B.

arrived, within Britain) was great; but the regiments arrived and departed at a set of points whose number was limited. Regiments moving between England and Scotland passed from one command into the other at either Carlisle or Berwick or, occasionally, at Coldstream—the Cheviots of the Border, and the barren Pennines stretching south from Northumberland and Cumberland, effectively canalizing traffic into the Lancashire or Durham road corridors. By sea, regiments arrived at Plymouth, Portsmouth, or Bristol (Bideford, when weather made the Bristol Channel dangerous); less often, regiments landed in the Dee, near Chester, at Liverpool, in the Clyde, or at the Thames ports. Regiments sailing from Britain embarked at Plymouth, Portsmouth (and the Isle of Wight), or Bristol; less often from the Thames reaches at Greenwich, Woolwich, Dartford, or Gravesend, or from the Medway embarkation places, Chatham and Rochester; and much less commonly units sailed from Newcastle, Liverpool, and the Clyde ports. This then is a first pattern, the one that operated at Britain's frontiers.

For the regiments once arrived in Britain, there was another pattern: there were areas in which the density of troops was always great, and other areas where a red coat would have been a rare sight indeed. Wales saw very little of the army: during our survey periods (Appendix A) there was never, at any one time, so much as a whole regiment in that country. Small detachments from regiments stationed in England were usually to be found only at Carmarthen, Aberystwyth, and Aberdovey, and only occasionally at Wrexham, Harlech, Pembroke, and Milford Haven. The main billeting towns just across the border in England were, north to south, Chester, Malpas, Whitchurch, Oswestry, Shrewsbury, Church Stretton, Ludlow, Leominster, Hereford, and Ross; and it was from these places, and from bigger Bristol and Worcester, that the small detachments moved into Wales. There were only four main routes used for marching into Wales, running along the lines Montgomery–Llanidloes–Aberystwyth (that is, up the Vale of Powys cut by the Severn, and then skirting the southern slopes of the Pumlumon Fawr); from Monmouth, up the valley of the Usk by Abergavenny and Brecon to Llandovery, then north via Tregaron or south via Llandeilo along the cut of the Tywi

Map 1. Great Britain

stream; New Radnor (or Hay on Wye)–Builth Wells–Tregaron –Aberystwyth, a difficult route across spurs of the southern Cambrians; and south of the Brecons along the easy line of the Glamorgan coast, that is Chepstow–Caerleon–Caerphilly– Neath–Swansea–Llanelli–Carmarthen–Narberth–and on to Haverfordwest, Pembroke, or Millford Haven. The whole of north Wales, then, almost never saw the British Army.

The same was true for most of north Devon and south-west Somerset, since soldiers almost never strayed north of the line Bude–Okehampton–Crediton–Tiverton–Milverton. Again, almost as deserted of troops as Wales was that great section of the six northern counties cut by the Pennine Chain: the area bounded on the north by Hadrian's Wall; to the east by the line Newcastle–Darlington–Ripon–Leeds; across the south by the line Leeds–Bradford–Rochdale–Wigan; and bounded on the west by the line Wigan–Lancaster–Kendal–Penrith– Carlisle. East–west crossings north of the Leeds–Wigan line were seldom attempted; when they were made, the soldiers followed the stages Clitheroe–Skipton–Ripley, between Preston to the west and either Boroughbridge or Ripon to the east. Otherwise, the British Army followed the ancient route of the legionaries, from Newcastle via the stages Hexham and Halt-whistle and so to Carlisle. But even that well-worn path was a difficult one: Field-Marshal Wade attempted it, in earnest, late in November 1745, as the Rebels moved upon Carlisle; but he had to give it up and return to Newcastle with a sick and exhausted force, wind and snow having prevented his crossing.

The Pennines and the Welsh Cambrians were rugged, bleak, and exposed; they were sparsely inhabited, there were few roads and almost no towns with facilities to house and feed troops. North Devon, with its Exmoor, was difficult country and little inhabited too. There was not only considerable logistical difficulty presented by these regions, but little occasion for a military presence anyway. How difficult such country was can be judged not only from Wade's experience but from the fact that during all of the periods surveyed (Appendix A) there were only four occasions on which cavalry was sent into Wales, and each time in aid of the civil power; and significantly, on three of those occasions the troopers marched dismounted.[55]

[55] WO 5/41, pp. 144, 356–8; 5/42, pp. 82, 152; and 5/59, pp. 136, 154.

Indeed, the orders that sent three troops of the 2nd Dragoons from Worcester in March 1753, to suppress rioters at Aberystwyth and environs, pointed out that to 'go to those Places, Mounted, is almost Impracticable'.[56]

Save for the periods of Jacobite outbreaks and suppression, much of Scotland was left empty of the regular army, the more rugged and inhospitable areas being left to Independent Companies like those from which the Black Watch was regimented. Most troops were quartered between the Border and the Highlands, and along the east coast north of the Forth and around Rattray Head. Farther north, the line of the Great Glen and its forts of 'the Chain'—Fort William, Fort Augustus, and Fort George at Inverness—was the only other regular station for troops in the country, save for isolated police barracks like Ruthven and Bernara. There were seldom regulars north of the Great Glen and, except in times of rebellion, cavalry seems never to have penetrated the Highlands. Save for the posts at which the few recruiting additional companies lay (Inveraray, Dunkeld, and Taybridge), there was maintained between the Great Glen forts and the cities of the Lowlands only a fleeting and irregular presence as detachments moved to rotate with others along Wade's roads, cut through the Grampians for the purpose. Most of Scotland, like Wales, was rugged and barren, and large numbers of soldiers could neither be subsisted nor moved without great difficulty and expense.

The rest of Britain, other than these areas, was quite familiar with the army. From the great concentration of troops at London and Westminster to the more thinly quartered areas like Monmouth or much of Lincolnshire, the map of quarters was a leopard-spot map. And yet another pattern emerges, that of duty areas. A regiment once arrived in Britain could expect to do various kinds of duty in any of a number of geographical areas; it must be emphasized, however, that at no time during the century was there any fixed rotation pattern or timetable connecting these areas. Regiments were shunted from one area to another in a haphazard fashion, and officers can seldom have known where in Britain their unit would be sent next. Only the relatively small number of regiments in Britain, the thorough dislike of most officers for service in the

[56] Wo 5/41, pp. 356–8.

wilds of Scotland, the need to keep cavalry horses fed on good English grass, and fear that lengthy residence in one place might encourage liaisons between the men and the locals, thus encouraging desertion, ensured that a regiment would not remain too long in any one part of Britain. The frequency of war, of Jacobite scares and European crises which failed to become wars (as in 1722, 1734, and 1787), militated against any long-term planning of regular rotation in Britain. Not only major, widespread hunger riots caused by slender harvests (as in 1766), and those innumerable local crises and tumults which occurred in an economy subject to violent short-term fluctuations; but also recurring regional economic crisis which resulted from long-term shifts in trade patterns or technological change —as in the Cornish stannaries or the West-country cloth industry—meant that units in one region might always be on call in another. And then the 'political', industrial, or other violent riots which periodically swept the big towns would always throw any fixed plan into confusion.

There was thus a large number of specific geographic areas in each (or in most) of which one or more regiments were to be found; but there was no orderly pattern to these assignments. We have already described the situation in Wales (where the small detachments were simply on call to the Revenue service, or maintaining a usually passive police presence) and in north Devon and the great empty area of the Pennines; and we shall add a few notes on Scotland below. It remains then to list (however briefly) the duty-areas in England, which long study of the Marching Orders (WO 5) has led us to isolate.

There were fifteen of these areas:

1. Cornwall and south Devon invariably quartered a regiment of foot, usually headquartered at Exeter, or often at Plymouth later in the century. The duty in this area was the most onerous in England, since the regiment was broken into small detachments stretching from Penzance to Ottery St. Mary. The area was the most notorious centre of unrest and riot in England, the tinners in particular being given to disorder in the 1720s, 1730s, and 1740s; and the officers of Customs and Excise were always in need of military assistance since smuggling was endemic on those coasts.

Owing to the difficult nature of the terrain and the great numbers of soldiers required to aid the civil power, horse (a regiment of horse usually had only about a quarter to half as many men as one of foot[57]) was almost never employed in this area. Only during the years 1788–90 do we find horse doing the duty here, and that at a time when the army was under strength, overworked, and overextended.[58]

2. 'Dorset', or the area including the towns and villages between Exeter and the New Forest (stretching to Salisbury, often the headquarters of a regiment in this area), and from the Channel coast up into south Somerset and south Wiltshire, always had a regiment. Of horse more often than of foot, the unit usually spent only a few months on the Dorset duty, since riots were uncommon and the 'coast duty' (i.e. patrols against smugglers), was less taxing here than elsewhere along the Channel.

3. The city of Bristol and the area stretching out to include the weaving towns between the Mendips and Salisbury Plain, and then northwards towards Marlborough and into the southern Cotswolds, was always occupied by a regiment of foot. Huge Bristol had to be watched, and its food supplies assured. Places like Trowbridge, Bradford on Avon, and Chippenham were chronic centres of riot, while Frome, Devizes, Marshfield, and the villages about Stroud were very busy communications centres. The duty here varied, but the suppression of riot throughout the area was common. After London and Dublin, Bristol was the largest city in the Empire, and it was consequently subject to all of the disorders of such sprawling places.[59]

4. The very large area within the rectangle formed by Gloucester–Ludlow–Warwick–Oxford (an area sometimes extended to include Coventry on the one side, and Hereford and Ross on the other) usually provided quarters for two regiments of horse. This was a quiet area, but occasionally detachments were dispatched towards Bristol, the Welsh coast, or to the

---

[57] For regimental establishments see Appendix C.

[58] WO 5/67, pp. 9, 146–285, *passim*.

[59] A fact noted by Maj.-Gen. James Murray when he reviewed the 35th Foot there in August 1771; this corps was full of recruits, and Murray reported Bristol 'a very bad quarter for so Young a Regiment, It is productive of all the Vice, and bad Consequence, Which Wapping would be.' WO 27/21.

Midlands industrial towns, if the civil power in those places was hard pressed.

5. The sprawl of towns around Birmingham, Stourbridge, Wolverhampton, and Coventry provided fairly transient quarters usually for a regiment of horse, and often for one of foot. There were no particular duties in this area but, as these towns grew with the progressing capitalist economy of manufacture, the horse tended to stay longer and action in aid of the civil power occurred more frequently.

6. Manchester and the surrounding area usually supported a cavalry regiment whose duties were little more arduous than suppressing the occasional riot, or finding detachments to check disorder at Liverpool or north towards Preston. It was very common for a cavalry regiment, having marched south from a tour of duty in Scotland, to settle in at Manchester for some months as its first station in England. Like the industrial centres south of it, Manchester's reputation declined with the rise of local industry and population. Both south from this area and north from the Birmingham area, noted above, a few troops or companies were sometimes extended to include Burton, Stoke-on-Trent, and Macclesfield among their quarters.

7. As the century progressed, the growth of Liverpool and increased attention to the smuggling of Irish goods through the Isle of Man led to the establishment of a regiment of foot partly on the island, partly at Liverpool, and partly doing coast duty about Whitehaven—a regiment thus much dispersed. Before the mid-century the area had been little frequented by the army. Often enough, Man itself was policed by companies detached from the foot in Ulster, and so only irregularly was the island a problem for the army on the British establishment.

8. The Border area usually occupied the time of one foot regiment, or of two if we include Newcastle and Gateshead. The few companies at Carlisle were often extended down to Maryport, Cockermouth, and Whiteheaven, on the coast duty; the many companies at Newcastle often detached to Sunderland, and there was a barrack at Tynemouth from early in the century. The GOC North Britain often drew detachments from Berwick to patrol the East Lothian and Berwickshire coasts. There was persistent agricultural unrest in Durham and

Northumberland, and a few companies close at hand at Newcastle and Gateshead were a comfort to magistrates. The Newcastle mob—notably on the waterfront, where wages fluctuated considerably—had occasionally to be suppressed.

9. York, like Manchester, usually quartered a cavalry regiment for a few months as it passed into or from Scotland. Detachments were regularly quartered at Leeds; and Beverley, Bridlington, Scarborough, and Whitby often housed further detachments out of York on the coast duty.

10. A regiment of horse (and often one of foot, too) was usually headquartered at either Stamford or Peterborough, or occasionally at Norwich. From these places, many detachments were found to serve throughout Norfolk and Suffolk, mostly patrolling against smugglers; and places as far inland as Oundle, Huntingdon, and Bury St. Edmunds served as quarters on the southern and western borders of this area.

11 Essex usually maintained a cavalry regiment, occasionally in company with detachments of foot. Colchester and Chelmsford were the main quartering centres in this area, and Ipswich across the county line was often used for this purpose.

12. A cavalry regiment always patrolled the Sussex coast, making detachments as far north as the Surrey border to choke off the inland smuggling arteries.

13. Kent usually supported all or part of a regiment of horse, again on the coast duty; and at least one and usually two regiments of foot were normally to be found in the county. One of these foot units was generally quartered along the Straits of Dover from Rye to Margate, the other along the Thames shore. Canterbury was a constantly used headquarters centre, as was Chatham with its defensive Lines and, later in the century, its big barracks; and Dover Castle always quartered a few companies.

14. London and Westminster were, of course, the province of the Household Cavalry and Foot Guards. Only in wartime (or occasionally in detachments as escorts to the Sovereign, in peacetime), did the Guards leave the capital; and the regular regiments of the line quartered in the outlying villages round the metropolis only when ordered in briefly for royal inspection. The privileges of London's 'Liberties' (the Rolls in Chancery Lane, for example, were exempt from army quartering)

created great problems, making of the capital a leopard-spot quartering map just like the wider kingdom.[60]

15. The very large area including Northamptonshire, the west Midlands, and extending as far north as Sheffield, occasionally but rather infrequently supported in its northern end (that is, from Leicester up to Nottingham and Sheffield) a regiment of horse or of foot; while The Blues constantly patrolled a beat in the southern part of the area, so constantly in fact that they very seldom left these parts in peacetime.

These, then, were the regular duty areas. In addition to these, four other regions should be mentioned which, although not duty areas, were nevertheless areas reserved for special purposes. The first was the countryside round about Lincoln city, stretching from Grantham north to Doncaster, and from Mansfield on the western side to Horncastle towards the coast. This was an area very seldom occupied and, when it was, it served only to provide quarters for a foot regiment that could not be accommodated elsewhere. There were three other areas which, though not duty areas, were almost constantly in use. The first of these was the Portsmouth hinterland, usually including Havant, Bishops Waltham, Petersfield, Liphook, Alresford, and Alton; these were the transient quarters for a regiment of foot waiting to embark on board transports or the fleet for overseas duty, or for service as marines. The second area consisted of the swathe of towns and villages in the southern parts of Buckinghamshire, Bedfordshire, Hertfordshire, and in Middlesex, forming an arc around northern London. Here, places like High Wycombe, Uxbridge, Aylesbury, Dunstable, Barnet, Baldock, and St. Albans were constantly used to quarter regiments—notably of cavalry—destined

---

[60] Typical were the quarters of the Foot Guards late in 1726. The 1st Foot Guards had nine companies distributed about Holborn and the parish of St. Andrew Holborn, two companies in Clerkenwell, two in St. Giles Cripplegate, one each in Spitalfields, Whitechapel, and St. Sepulchre without Newgate, one company in Shoreditch and Folgate, another in East Smithfield and St. Katherines, and a further ten companies lying across the river in the Borough of Southwark. The Coldstream, meanwhile, lay with nine companies in the Tower and another nine up-river at the Savoy. The 3rd Foot Guards were spread throughout the City and Liberty of Westminster (WO 5/27, pp. 60–1). This sort of in-town dispersal was common in most places: e.g. 'Worcester' quarters meant the central city and the parishes of SS John, Peter, Michael, and Martin; 'Salisbury' quarters usually included that city plus Milford, Fisherton, and Harnham.

for London inspections. The last of these areas, finally, was the small area extending from Windsor west to Newbury and south to Winchester, an area in which regiments normally quartered for only a short time while doing guard-duty at Windsor, resting after returning home from overseas, or preparing for inspection at Reading or nearer London.

Because of the paucity of archival material on the day-to-day activities of the army in Scotland we shall have to deal with that country rather quickly, adding here only a few generalizations (and a list of dispositions) to the details already given.

The number of regiments normally serving in Scotland was very small (see Appendix B), and these were mostly to be found in the Lowlands. In 1716 and 1746, however, in the aftermath of the great Jacobite risings, immense concentrations of troops were to be found in the northern kingdom;[61] and their dispositions, reflecting as they do the main centres of population and lines of communication, point at the same time the main quartering and duty regions into which the geographic and demographic patterns naturally divided the country, as they did England and Wales. There were five distinct areas of occupation both in 1716 and 1746:

1. The first such area was the Great Glen, the great fault cut between the Grampians and the almost impenetrable north-western Highlands. Here the foot was based chiefly at Inverness and in smaller numbers at Fort William (and at Fort Augustus by 1746); while single additional companies were normally out at Ruthven and well to the south at Inveraray.

2. The north-east coastal plain, from Inverness round Rattray Head and then south to Aberdeen where the Dee comes down from the Eastern Grampians, formed another area of occupation. Aberdeen was the main quarter here, with smaller numbers at Banff and Elgin; while Nairn, Forres, Garmouth, Cullen, and Peterhead held detachments.

---

[61] Early in 1716 there were in Scotland more than 12,000 soldiers, serving in seven regiments of British dragoons (1,700 all ranks), ten battalions of British foot (4,500 all ranks), and eleven battalions of Dutch foot (6,000, all ranks). Late in 1746 there were in Scotland some 13,000 soldiers (all of whom were British) serving in five regiments of dragoons and sixteen battalions of foot, plus nine additional companies. See J. Baynes, *The Jacobite Rising of 1715* (1970), 200–1, and C. S. Terry (ed.), *The Albermarle Papers: Being the Correspondence of William Anne, Second Earl of Albemarle . . . 1746–48*, i (Aberdeen, 1902), 201–7, 226, 274–7, from which these figures and the following dispositions are principally drawn.

3. The third region consisted of the lowlands of Fife and Strathmore, stretching from the Ochil Hills north of the Forth and along the narrow coastal plain to Aberdeen. The main quartering towns were Montrose, Dundee, and Perth, while smaller numbers might be found at Dunkeld and Cupar; detachments lay at Brechin and Arbroath, and two additional companies usually lay at Dunfermline and up in the hills at Taybridge.

4. Much of the Lowlands, broadly speaking, composed the fourth and chief area of occupation: that is, the area stretching out from the line Dumbarton–Glasgow–Stirling (from Forth to Clyde), south to the line Stranraer (or Ayr)–Lanark–Dunbar, bounded all along its southern edge by the Southern Uplands. The main quarters here were Glasgow, Stirling, and Edinburgh, while smaller numbers might be based at Dumbarton, and detachments found at Ayr, Stranraer, Dalkeith, Haddington, and Musselburgh.

5. The last area consisted of the plain of the Tweed and the line of the Border. Troops at Carlisle and Berwick were on call here, so that the area was thinly quartered; but Dumfries, Swinton, Foulden, and Duns were often used.

As we observed earlier these quartering regions, despite the extraordinary circumstances prevailing in 1716 and 1746, reflect the geographical realities of eighteenth-century Scotland —most especially the difficulties of movement and quartering inland from the coastal plains anywhere to the north of the Highland line. The normal routine of peacetime duty in the country, where it can be traced, conformed to this area pattern. We can, for example, follow the movements of Bury's 20th of Foot in Scotland, 1749–53; its movements and the areas where it served were typical. Early in 1749 Bury's arrived at Stirling, and stayed there until March when the corps moved to Glasgow. From 5 June until the end of the summer, half of the regiment fanned out from there to do road work. In October 1749 the 20th marched to Perth, and the following spring was again employed on road work. In September 1750 the regiment moved to Dundee, and a few weeks later went on to Banff. Late in September 1751 the 20th marched to Inverness, and in May 1752 moved to Fort Augustus. By April 1753 Bury's had finished its spell of patrolling out of the Chain forts, and was again at

Glasgow. In September 1753, finally, the regiment marched south into England.[62]

The big cities of the Lowlands and the coastal plains were, like their English counterparts, subject to riot and disorder, and the coasts themselves were much frequented by smugglers. The Lowlands were in consequence as thickly quartered and as often patrolled as were most parts of southern England. Many of the Lowland towns had barracks, and in Scotland quartering upon private houses was legal. Edinburgh and Stirling had their old castles, which housed troops. But the Highlands, as we noted earler, were another story. Before the later 1740s and the pacification which ended even the possibility of another Jacobite rising, the army had been engaged in pushing roads into the Highlands as arteries to feed the forts along the Chain. But these forts normally held few troops,[63] and after the 1750s all save Ardersier were allowed to fall into disrepair. The Highlands themselves, despite Wade's road-building of the 1720s, were too thinly settled to support sizeable forces, and the rugged country made the use of cavalry impracticable; the rule of law there was in consequence left to small detachments of regulars, to the Whig militia, to Independent Companies, and to the watches.

Along with the pattern of duty areas in England, there also existed a pattern of main march-corridors. Units seldom remained in any one area for more than several months before they were set in motion again, or sent abroad. Movement about the kingdom (save in Wales, and across the Pennines), was easily managed, since there were roads almost everywhere; but naturally some routes were more heavily travelled than others, and we can isolate nine major corridors or road-systems which were most commonly used. These were, briefly: (1) the London–Dartford–Canterbury route, along the busy artery between the south shore and the North Downs; (2) the London–Newbury–Devizes–Bristol route, an easy route well worn since ancient times; (3) the busy London–Guildford–Petersfield–Portsmouth route; (4) the route from Plymouth

---

[62] J. T. Findlay, op. cit. 143–298, *passim*.

[63] On the outbreak of the '45, the forts were almost empty, as were the few smaller posts. R. C. Jarvis, *Collected Papers on the Jacobite Risings*, i (Manchester, 1971), 8–9, 25–47. Curiously, there is no decent study of the surveying and road-building of the 1720s and 1730s; J. B. Salmond, *Wade in Scotland* (1934), regularly cited, is thin.

which reached Exeter by skirting to the south of Dartmoor, then went north via Bridgwater to Bristol, and then passed on to the Midlands manufacturing towns via a general series of roads lying in the easy Vales of Berkeley and Gloucester, and along the Severn east of the Mendip Hills; (5) the route from Walsall north via Stoke-on-Trent, Warrington, and Preston, to the Border at Carlisle (another series of roads following the Cheshire and Lancashire Plains, before ascending the slopes between the Pennines and the Lake District peaks along the route Lancaster–Kendal–Penrith); (6) the great north–south artery along the line London–Northampton–Nottingham–Rotherham–Leeds; (7) the Chester to Gloucester routes, either via Whitchurch, Shrewsbury, Ludlow, Hereford, and Ross, or via Whitchurch, Wellington, Bewdley, and Worcester; (8) the whole complex of the Great North Road; and (9) the Worcester to Worksop route via Birmingham, Lichfield, Burton-on-Trent, Derby, and Mansfield.

These were the main movement corridors; but as we noted earlier, roads were everywhere. The road-system of eighteenth-century England was complex but there were almost no long, single-surfaced highways. There was, rather, an intricate web of smaller parish roads (often no more than tracks), weaving from every village to each of its neighbours, with the best heading towards the market town. Given this road-system, there existed a very great number of small villages functioning largely as secondary halts or stages along the routes between the bigger towns, stages essential to the economy of an age moving at the speed of a horse, a wagon, or of drove cattle. As Braudel observed of such places, 'the cities could not do without them, any more than the traveller along a road could do without somewhere to change his horses or lay his head. The life of these intermediary places was linked to the arithmetic of distances, the average speed of travellers along the roads.'[64] Conforming to the dictates of the 'arithmetic of distances', the stages used by the army in England appear, when plotted on a map, as regular as beads on a necklace. Most of the villages along the march-corridors had for centuries served as halting-places and, though most were small, they were nevertheless

---

[64] F. Braudel, *The Mediterranean . . . in the Age of Philip II*, trans. S. Reynolds, i (1972), 282.

well supplied with inns and stables for the relief of travellers. It was possible for the Quartermaster-General, therefore, to choose from a number of parallel routes when moving troops along the corridors noted above, since there were always alternate routes and stages along the corridors, given the complexity of the village and road network. Thus on the busy north–south route running down the Vale of York and then along the banks of the Trent between Durham and Newark, the following places were all very frequently used stages, north to south: Bishop Auckland, Darlington, Bedale, Northallerton, Thirsk, Ripon, Boroughbridge, Knaresborough, Wetherby, Tadcaster, Sherburn, Ferrybridge, Pontefract, Doncaster, Blyth, Bawtry, East Retford, and Tuxford. That is to say, there were eighteen stages to choose among for a march which usually required only seven of them. Another example is the complex of roads in the Vale of Berkeley between Gloucester and Bristol, again heavily travelled. A marching unit (of horse or foot, for both invariably covered the same amount of ground on a day's march) spent no more than one or two nights on the 30 miles between those two cities; but the Quartermaster-General could choose from among seven stage towns, namely Thornbury, Chipping Sodbury, Wickwar, Wotton under Edge, Dursley, King's Stanley, and Stroud.

The fact that most of the stages or halting-places were small exacerbated another problem always encountered in the movement of forces in England. During the course of the seventeenth century it had come to be regarded as one of the fundamental rights of Englishmen that troops (lewd, licentious, unbridled fellows by definition) could not be quartered upon private householders without prior consent and payment. By the beginning of the eighteenth century this right had been recognized in law, and any infringement was henceforth an offence punishable under the Mutiny Acts. In consequence— since barracks were virtually unknown, and great numbers of troops (whatever their character) had to be sheltered—'the Government had to make shift for their dangerous charges by visiting them upon the other criminal class—inn-keepers.'[65]

---

[65] R. E. Scouller, *The Armies of Queen Anne* (Oxford, 1966), 164. On the issue in general, with a few interesting notes on practice in Scotland, see S. M. Pargellis, *Lord Loudoun in North America* (New Haven, 1933), 188–9. Scouller, 164–70, discusses the

The troops, then, were billeted in 'public houses'—specific-ally, 'inns, livery stables, alehouses, victualling houses, and all houses selling brandy, strong waters, cyder, or metheglin by retail to be drunk on the premises, and in no other', as the Mutiny Acts had it.[66] The innkeepers, however, raised con-tinual complaints, largely over the small sums received in pay-ment for their unwanted guests; humble petitions were fre-quent and, in parts of Sussex and other places off the beaten track, 'it had become a practice with the publicans, as a class, to take down their sign-boards and throw up their licenses upon the approach of troops.'[67]

The absence of any extensive or adequate barrack facilities greatly influenced the quartering pattern of the Army in Britain.[68] As the army grew in size through the century a few new barracks were built and a few old buildings were bought for the purpose by the Board of Ordnance (which body was charged with their erection, maintenance, and administration, and with the supply of furniture, utensils, candles, and heating); but the building of barracks was never intended to keep pace with the growth of the army, since building was expensive and, as Marshal Wade put it, 'the people of this kingdom have been taught to associate the idea of Barracks and Slavery so closely together that, like darkness and the Devil, though there be no manner of connection between them, yet they cannot separate them.'[69] Before the great building boom which began in 1793

problem in the three kingdoms in some detail (for the 'rights of Englishmen' did not extend to Irishmen, and of course few rights at all were accorded the Scots *vis-à-vis* the army). Good Victorian that he was, Clode, i. 229–38, discussed the legal technicalities and niceties of quartering, and the ensuing financial complications; while J. Shy, op. cit. 163–91, considers the thorny problem of quartering the army in America where, as in Ireland, the 'rights of Englishmen' were sometimes deemed inoperative.

[66] Quoted in R. E. Scouller, op. cit. 165.

[67] Clode, i. 237. The publicans had good cause to be wary. Late in May 1756, Kingsley's 20th of Foot marched across southern England from Canterbury to Devizes, following the stages Wye–Lenham–Tonbridge–Westerham–Leatherhead–Woking–Bagshot–Hartley Row and Hartfordbridge–Basingstoke–Newbury and Speen–Bur-bage. WO 5/43, p. 245. The lieutenant-colonel of the 20th, writing home from Basingstoke, observed: 'We have ruined half the public houses upon the march, because they have quartered us in villages too poor to feed us without destruction to them-selves.' Beckles Willson, *Life and Letters of James Wolfe* (New York, 1909), 292.

[68] Clode, i. 221, believed that in 1697 there was barrack accommodation in England for 5,000 men; even including the Savoy, the Tower of London and the major fortifica-tions, this figure seems excessive in the extreme.

[69] Clode, ii. 223.

the barracks in existence were few and generally ruinous, since funds were not provided. Typical of the many reports submitted, in consequence, was that made by the 64th Foot when quartered in Dover Castle—itself a major and extensively used facility: 'they complain of a Want of all kinds of Barrack Utensils, & very small allowance of Wood & Candles, the Men not having sufficient Quantity to dress their Provisions. No Pump for the Tank, for getting Water, & . . . are obliged to draw Water from a Well of 350 Feet deep, with very great Labour.'[70] These complaints were made as late as 1785 and indicate how little progress had been made, for Dover Castle had much to recommend it in comparison with places like Limerick, Ruthven, Glasgow, or Hilsea. In 1740 Hilsea Barracks at Portsmouth were in too bad a state of repair to house all of the men of Wolfe's 1st Marines, supposed by authority to be quartered there.[71] Hilsea remained one of the biggest barracks in the country throughout our period (the biggest was at Fort George Ardersier, with room for 1,600 men by 1764), even though Hilsea was built on low, wet ground, surrounded by salt springs, and consequently unhealthy. The Norfolk Militia, sent there in 1759, found the place infected with smallpox, and dysentery and typhus were known there too.[72] There were large barracks at Chatham from at least the 1750s, and by the 1780s Chatham had the most extensive facilities in England. Tynemouth Barrack near Newcastle was in use from at least 1766, and so was that at Plymouth Dock from at least 1774. We hear of barracks at Winchester during the 1775–83 war, at Liverpool from 1787, at Scarborough from 1788, and at Deal from 1789. Berwick had good barracks within its walls from 1721, with room for 600 men;[73] and regular soldiers had always been quartered in strong places like Dover Castle, Plymouth Citadel, the Tower of London, the Savoy, Stirling Castle, Fort William, Fort Augustus, Inverness Castle, and in the smaller defensive works like Deal and Landguard Forts. The barracks in Fort George Ardersier, building from 1753, were extensive and 'good'; but at the other extreme were the

[70] WO 27/54.
[71] WO 5/33, p. 442.
[72] J. R. Western, op. cit. 383–4.
[73] I. MacIvor, *The Fortifications of Berwick-upon-Tweed* (1972), 19–22, 29.

barracks of the Royal Artillery at Woolwich regarded as one of the best in Britain—and utterly foul.[74]

It has been estimated that by 1792 some 20,000 men (including Ordnance troops and Invalids) could be quartered in all of the forts and barracks in Britain and the Channel Islands; but only during the years 1793—4 did government begin that major barrack-building programme which was still proceeding after Waterloo, and which was to provide the regular facilities used by the Victorian army.[75]

Because troops could be quartered only in certain types of buildings, then; because most stages were small places, with few inns, and because it took time to cover ground at the pace of a walking horse or man, it took what seems to us an inordinately long time for a regiment to carry out a march. The quarters in the halting-places being limited in capacity and number, whole regiments could not possibly be moved from one place to another as single units; they had, rather, to march in from two to four 'divisions', each setting off upon the intended route one day ahead of the next. Marching, it was invariably the custom to rest on two days out of every seven ('halting-days', usually Thursdays and Sundays), and this again added to the time spent by a unit strung out upon a march. Thus in May 1738, for example, Montague's 11th of Foot set out for Berwick, from Exeter; it quartered at twenty-nine stage-towns in between, marched in three divisions which remained halted on Thursdays and Sundays, and rested for a full week at Newcastle and Gateshead. The regiment, therefore, took fifty-one days to complete a march of about 430 miles.[76] Another long march, from Portsmouth to Carlisle and environs, was made by Holmes's 31st of Foot beginning on 13 July 1752. Holmes's quartered at twenty-five places in between, marched in three divisions and observed the usual halting-days, and rested for seven days at Newbury and another seven at Preston (they had just returned from Minorca, and were allowed these rests to refresh themselves after the fatigues of the voyage home).

---

[74] O. F. G. Hogg, *The Royal Arsenal: Its Background, Origin and Subsequent History*, i (1963), 316–27; and I. MacIvor, *Fort George* (Edinburgh, 1970), 15–16, 33–5.

[75] Fortescue, iv. 903–7. The whole question of barracks in Britain has hardly been explored, and we know now little more than Fortescue did.

[76] WO 5/33, pp. 114–15.

Holmes's whole march, therefore, took fifty-two days to complete.[77] The same rules applied to short marches as to long. In July 1732 Cadogan's 4th of Foot was ordered from Bristol to Exeter via the stages Axbridge–Bridgwater–Wellington–Cullompton; marching in three divisions and observing halting-days, it took Cadogan's nine days to carry out this move.[78] An ordinary traveller could easily have arrived in Exeter on the third day out. These few examples, it must be stressed, are wholly typical.

Many other factors slowed the movement of troops upon the march or broke up units once they had arrived at new quarters. Thus the units were kept dispersed or long on the roads, and so generally even more time was wasted. The effects of bad weather, of ruined roads and broken bridges, and of riot, war, crisis, and rebellion, need hardly be detailed. When the annual fairs and racing meets were held in the towns and big villages, any troops quartered there had to be dispersed into tiny billets in the villages of the surrounding countryside. Several companies of Harrison's 15th of Foot, for example, were cleared out of Chester at fair time in September 1728; and the whole of Sabine's 23rd of Foot was dispersed from Newcastle in May 1732, the crowds come to the local horse races being given precedence.[79] Likewise, soldiers had to be cleared from towns where assizes were being held (unless, of course, the gaol or the court needed protection from the mob); hence in July 1728 the army was cleared from seventeen towns because of the coming assizes.[80] Similarly, if the county militia mustered in a town where regulars occupied the billets, the regulars had to clear out; hence, three troops of the 1st Dragoons were, in 1764, literally sent to Coventry when the militia arrived in Warwick city.[81] Again, local elections meant that the troops had temporarily to be removed, as happened to the whole of Barrell's 4th of Foot when at Bristol, in November 1742; or later, when elections were held at York in October 1774, four troops of the 2nd Dragoons were removed to Leeds, and the other two sent to

[77] WO 5/41, pp. 231–2.
[78] WO 5/30, pp. 313–14.
[79] WO 5/28, p. 177; and 5/30, p. 299.
[80] List in WO 5/28, p. 154. There are innumerable examples of gaols and court buildings needing military protection, throughout WO 5.
[81] WO 5/53, p. 99.

Wakefield.[82] Stragglers, and large numbers of sick men, were often left behind: thus in January 1766 the 'recovered men' of the 22nd and 35th of Foot, who had been left in a party of sick men at Carrisbrooke Castle, were from time to time setting out for Chatham to rejoin their regiments.[83] This list contains but a few random examples of the dozens of burdens under which the army laboured all the time. We might conclude by noting one or two of the many 'Acts of God' which, like those of Whitehall, spared neither men nor beasts. In January 1753 the move of three troops of the 3rd Dragoons from Colchester was cancelled because of the arrival of 'letters from Ipswich, Earnestly begging, the Troops now Quarter'd at Colchester may not be removed to Ipswich the small Pox much raging at Colchester';[84] and from September 1753 to May 1754 a troop of the 2nd Dragoons had to be kept detached from the regiment, the troop-horses being infected with glanders.[85] The lieutenants-colonel, majors, and adjutants of the regiments—not to mention the NCOs—the men most responsible for the training, discipline, and good order of their regiments, must have oftentimes been called upon to exercise the most considerable patience.

We have, thus far, looked at the patterns of density, mobility, duty areas, routes, and marches, in Britain. We shall now turn to the pattern of rotation in Britain. Specific details and the actual units involved, during the periods of years singled out for our surveys, can be found in Appendices A and B.

As we noted earlier, there was never any fixed rotation pattern between the main duty areas in Britain; but there was often a pattern of sorts operating between England and Scotland. Since the cavalry regiments, unlike the foot, left Britain only in time of war, their service pattern was much more stable than that of the foot. Until the 1780s there were almost invariably two cavalry regiments serving in Scotland, while only one regiment did duty in that country thereafter, at any one time. During the survey periods 1726–9, 1737–43, and 1751–6, a cavalry regiment served in Scotland for one or two years (usually about eighteen months), after which it could expect

[82] WO 5/35, p. 498: and 5/58, pp. 487–8, 500.
[83] WO 5/54, p. 36.
[84] WO 5/41, p. 343.
[85] WO 5/41, pp. 491, 503, 516; and 5/42, p. 87.

to remain in England until the ten regiments ahead of it had completed their tours on the same duty. Wars and crises could alter this pattern, of course, as is evident with the 6th and the 7th Dragoons, 1741–2, the 7th Dragoons, 1753–6, and the 2nd Dragoon Guards, 1754–6 (see Appendices A and B). During our three later survey periods (1764–7, 1772–6, and 1786–90) a cavalry regiment served for only one year in Scotland, before returning to England and waiting for all the rest to take their turn.

Foot serving in Britain enjoyed no such security.[86] War and the shifting patterns of imperial duty, as we have seen, affected the foot erratically. The period of the 1720s, for example, was one of great mobility for the foot in Britain, stimulated by Jacobitism and the aggression of the Spanish court. On average, however, some three or four regiments of marching foot were serving in Scotland and five or six in England, at any one time. Much the same was true of the later 1730s to earlier 1740s, for the foot: the regiments serving in Britain were in constant motion, so that there was again no rotation pattern between the two kingdoms; but new-raised replacements kept the strength in Scotland at an average of four or five regiments.

The most interesting period of rotation in Britain is that between 1751 and 1755, since during those years—and they are the only years during the century when such a system operated —the pattern in Great Britain was fixed. The hand of the Duke of Cumberland, as always when so efficient a system was in operation, is evident. As we have seen, the old Gibraltar and Minorca garrisons were replaced at the end of the War of the Austrian Succession, four regiments going to each place. By 1751 the whole of the army had been similarly settled into peacetime quarters, and the Duke's fixed rotation could begin. In 1751 there were seven marching regiments in Scotland, and four in England; and so their numbers remained until 1755 although the whole of them, by that year, had successfully been rotated on to different stations and replaced by newcomers. The system worked as follows (and we illustrate its functioning with examples drawn from 1753): each year, a regiment from Minorca (Johnson's 33rd) and one from Gibraltar (Leighton's 32nd) sailed home to England, landed at Plymouth or Ports-

---

[86] The Foot Guards, always relatively stationary, are excluded from this discussion.

mouth, and then marched north for Scotland; meanwhile, the two regiments in Scotland thus replaced (Bocland's 11th and Bury's 20th) moved south into England; and to complete the rotation two regiments embarked from England, one (Guise's 6th) for Gibraltar and the other (Rich's 4th) for Minorca. Thus the Duke had not only set up a fixed rotation in Britain, but had drawn in the two major overseas garrisons.[87] The 1755 crisis put the system into abeyance. During this period there had always been seven battalions of marching foot in Scotland, and four in England, what with the 'pacification' proceeding.

During the period 1764–7 there were always four regiments of foot in Scotland, one being replaced annually from England. The situation in England was capricious, however, for full imperial rotation was at long last being attempted, although the great disturbances of 1766 in both England and Ireland did not contribute to its smooth functioning. On average, seven regiments of marching foot were in England at this time.

Finally, during the periods 1772–6 and 1786–90 rotation between England and Scotland was carried on frequently, but according to no plan; the concentration of the authorities was now on imperial rotation, as we have seen, and this in itself guaranteed mobility within Britain, if not regularity. On average during the earlier 1770s, four or five marching battalions were to be found in Scotland, and ten in England; while during the later 1780s the average figure was five for Scotland and twelve for England.

(c) DISTRIBUTION AND ROTATION IN IRELAND

A rather different pattern prevailed in Ireland. After Westminster, it was the Dublin Parliament that voted the largest amount of money to maintain the regular army; and the number of troops maintained on the Irish establishment (12,000 men from 1699 to 1769, and 15,000 from 1769 until 1801) was the second largest in the Empire, accounting for more than one-third of the standing peacetime army. As James put it, 'from the standpoint of the British government the existence of the army in Ireland, paid for out of Irish taxes, constituted perhaps Ireland's greatest contribution to the wel-

---

[87] It is possible that the Duke planned to include Ireland in his infantry rotation scheme. Cumb. Pprs, Box 44, no. 140, fo. 3.

fare of the empire',[88] while at the same time the Irish army not only defended Ireland from invasion and maintained order and the laws, but provided the Anglo-Irish ruling classes with a large and rich field for careers and patronage.

Were it not for the facts that the size of the army in Ireland was fixed by English statute of 1699, that there was no Irish Mutiny Act until 1781 (the English Mutiny Acts extending to Ireland), and that none of the Catholics and only a relatively small percentage of the Irish Protestants—of whom two-thirds were Presbyterian and, therefore, suspect like the Catholics and subject to the Test Act until 1780—could lawfully serve as private men in the Irish army, one might confidently assert that the regiments on the Irish establishment and the regiments on the British formed two distinct armies, united only in their allegiance to the same Sovereign in whose service they were mustered and paid. It is nevertheless true that, until the end of the century, it was difficult for the War Office to meddle with the army in Ireland. The army there was a charge on the Irish Exchequer;[89] it had its own resident head of state (the Lord-Lieutenant), its own Commander-in-Chief, general officers and staff in Dublin,[90] its own Paymaster-General, its own Board of Ordnance (and from 1755 to 1801 there was a corps of Royal Irish Artillery[91]), and its own rates of pay.[92] The Lord-Lieutenant when resident in Dublin, and for the rest of the year the Lords Justices, controlled all troop dispositions in Ireland, and for that matter the disposition of all cornetcies and ensigncies.[93] The C.-in-C. in Britain had only indirect powers in

[88] F. G. James, op. cit. 177.

[89] During the Spanish Succession war, Ireland had paid for its regiments serving in Europe; but increasingly after 1712 the Dublin Parliament disliked paying for Irish corps serving abroad. On this, see ibid. 177–8.

[90] In 1748 and 1749 e.g. the C.-in-C. of the army in Ireland was Gen. Gervase Parker; beneath him, forming the 'staff', there was one lieutenant-general (Richard, Viscount Molesworth), three lieutenants-general serving as majors-general (Henry Hawley, Phineas Bowles, and James, Lord Tyrawley), and eight general officers (the first a full general, the next five lieutenants-general, and the last two majors-general) serving as brigadiers-general, namely Lord Mark Kerr, Sir John Cope, James St. Clair, Philip Bragg, Alexander Irwin, Richard St. George, Henry de Grangues, and Sir John Mordaunt. The Adjutant-General was Lt.-Col. Thomas Butler. Anon., *Quarters . . . in 1748*, 10, and *Quarters . . . in 1749*, 22.

[91] F. Forde, 'The Royal Irish Artillery, 1755–1801', *Irish Sword*, 11 (1973), 32–8.

[92] Sir J. Fortescue, *The British Army, 1783–1802* (1905), 18–19; and Rex Whitworth, *Field Marshal Lord Ligonier: A Story of the British Army, 1702–1770* (Oxford, 1958), 40.

[93] Rex Whitworth, op. cit. 40; and J. Hayes, 'The Social and Professional Back-

Ireland. For most of the century his powers in Ireland rested on the influence of his person; and where training and drill were concerned it was only towards the later part of the century that the War Office in London could take for granted its control of these matters in both kingdoms. The Duke of Cumberland, the most respected, powerful, and influential captain-general during the century, could lay down the law on training and drill not only in Britain but in the garrisons from Nova Scotia to Minorca; yet his orders on that head were often ignored in Ireland, where at best they were viewed only as guidelines.[94] To illustrate this independence with but one example: late in 1748, just as Richbell's 39th of Foot was embarking at Bristol for Ireland, a subaltern in the corps was insubordinate with the lieutenant-colonel, who consequently put him under arrest. A report was sent to Cumberland. Once landed on the Irish establishment, however, the lieutenant-colonel had to drop the whole affair since (as he was informed by the Speaker of the Irish Commons), 'the Duke had no Command here, And that the Lords Justices were quite independent of him.'[95]

Of primary importance was the fact that the standing army in Ireland had considerably fewer men in its ranks than had the army on the British establishment, while at the same time the Irish army was composed of many more regiments of foot than were to be found in Britain, and of as many regiments of horse. During the 1720s and 1730s an average of twenty-two marching battalions were to be found in Ireland, while only ten served in Britain; during the later 1740s and earlier 1750s Ireland supported on average twenty-five marching battalions, while there were only eleven in Britain; during the 1760s and early 1770s an average of twenty-five marching battalions served in Ireland, as against an average of only thirteen in Britain; while during the later 1780s and earlier 1790s there were some twenty-seven marching battalions serving in Ireland, compared with an average of sixteen in Britain. Of the regular cavalry

---

ground of the Officers of the British Army, 1714–63', unpubl. London M.A. thesis, 1965, 17–18 (cited hereafter as J. Hayes, 'Officers').

[94] See Cumb. Pprs, Box 44, nos 98 and 99, where the situation in Ireland is clearly shown; and cf. Box 43, no. 294, Blakeney to Cumberland, Port Mahon, 15 Aug. 1749. The Duke had to rely on toadies for much of his news of Irish army affairs, an excellent example of which is Box 44, no. 99.

[95] J. Hayes, 'Officers', 18–20.

there were always ten regiments in Ireland and twelve in Britain during peacetime, until 1763, when new-raised corps lifted these numbers to twelve and fourteen respectively.[96] The consequence of this disparity was that corps in Ireland—notably the foot—were kept on establishments very much weaker than those of regiments in Britain.[97] As we noted earlier there was always with the conclusion of a peace an absolute increase in the number of units kept on in the standing army; but the several establishments were kept as low as possible by cheeseparing legislators, and establishments never expanded at the same rate as the number of standing corps. Since it was the custom to keep up at reasonable strengths those regiments serving on the British establishment, in the Mediterranean garrisons and the Plantations, it followed that Ireland was crammed full of regiments at scarcely more than cadre strength. Ireland, therefore, served a useful twofold purpose: the number of units in the army could be kept high by being removed from the attention of the backbenchers in the English Commons; and at the same time great numbers of regimental officers serving on a full-time basis and gaining experience, rather than rusting on half-pay, could be maintained. This was all to the good of the Service.

Irish corps could be kept weak because the eighteenth century (until 1798) was one of the most quiet in the history of that troubled country;[98] and the army in Ireland was regarded not principally as a garrison but rather as a strategic reserve which could be drawn upon by Britain in time of emergency. In any such emergency regiments were brought over to Britain, transferred on to the British establishment, and recruited or drafted up to that strength. Meanwhile, the vacancies thus created in the Irish establishment were filled either by new regiments raised there or by the augmenting of those that remained. With the return of peace the ex-Irish corps (or substitutes from elsewhere) were returned to Ireland, their establishments reduced, and most or all of the new-raised units disbanded.

These changes in establishment caused endless headaches,

[96] See Appendix B for annual variations.

[97] See Appendix C for examples of Irish regimental establishments.

[98] How quiet it was is shown by the fact that, in the summer of 1745 with most of the army holding the Mediterranean garrisons or campaigning in Flanders, the forces in Ireland had been reduced to only four battalions of foot and six regiments of cavalry.

administrative and otherwise. In the spring of 1734, for example, in response to the recent Franco-Spanish declaration of war upon Austria, eight battalions of foot were brought over from Ireland to beef up the defences of Britain, should the conflagration spread. These had come over on the Irish establishment strength of ten companies per regiment, each company consisting of a captain, a lieutenant, an ensign, two sergeants, two corporals, a drummer, and thirty-three private men; and each regiment had now to recruit ten sergeants, ten corporals, ten drummers, and 260 private men, in order to fill up to the British establishment strength. The twelve battalions remaining in Ireland were augmented at the same time, taking in thereby an additional 290 men each. Remaining in Britain until January 1736, these eight regiments had each in 1735 to find an additional 110 private men, since the British establishment was augmented generally that year. Thus the reinforcement of the army in Britain with eight Irish battalions involved the recruiting of 6,680 men on both sides of the Irish Sea; and all of these were turned loose when, early in 1736, the Irish units went home again, and establishments were reduced.[99]

The authorities were obliged to accept the Irish cadre system if sufficient officers, NCOs, and seasoned privates capable of being formed into NCOs were to be kept on hand, immediately available in skeletal regiments which could be fleshed out speedily upon any emergency. There was always the possibility, however, that years of training could be thrown away by such an operation, if it was done too quickly. When in the autumn of 1754 it was deemed necessary speedily to check the French in the distant Ohio country, two regiments of foot were taken from the Irish establishment for the purpose. Those chosen, Halkett's 44th and Dunbar's 48th, were at weak Irish strengths: each was made up of ten companies, a company consisting of a captain, a lieutenant, an ensign, two sergeants, two corporals, a drum, and twenty-nine private men. The total strength of each regiment was 374 officers and men.[100] Halkett's and Dunbar's had to be filled up quickly to the strength of regiments on the British establishment, for active service, each of which was

[99] Atkinson, 'Early Hanoverians', 146–7; WO 24/161.
[100] Cumb. Pprs, Box 44, no. 124. See also Anon., *Quarters . . . in 1752* (Dublin, 1752), and WO 24/313.

made up of ten companies, a company consisting of a captain, a lieutenant, an ensign, three sergeants, three corporals, two drums, and seventy privates, for a total regimental strength of 815 officers and men.[101] Halkett's and Dunbar's, then, each stood in need of ten sergeants, ten corporals, ten drums, and 410 privates.[102] To save time the two regiments were assembled at Cork, and drafts from other regiments were sent to them there. Thus, 100 men were taken from Bocland's 11th and another 100 from Bury's 20th, both in England; and in addition seventy-eight men from each of four regiments in Ireland (the 2/1st Royals, Pole's 10th, Anstruther's 26th, and Bragg's 28th) were drafted, and sent on to Cork.[103] Thus Halkett's and Dunbar's each received 256 drafts, and stood in need of only 185 men more, apiece. These were provided by 350 men enlisted from the unregimented companies of Virginia Provincials, when arrived in America.[104] The rapid mobilization of two Irish regiments meant, therefore, that four others should each lose one-fifth of their already skeletal strength, and that two good English regiments should be significantly weakened. Then, a large number of Provincials—better than militia, but still ill trained at the regular discipline—was dumped among them. Halkett's and Dunbar's, clearly, had been completely altered during this process: from trained but under-strength regiments they had been converted into jumbled associations of uneven quality. But given a little time, fine regiments could have been built up around their old original Irish cores. This was the purpose of the cadre system.

Although cavalry regiments on the Irish establishment remained much smaller than their British counterparts throughout our period, the practice of keeping the battalions of Irish

[101] WO 24/303.

[102] WO 24/313.

[103] K. L. Parker, 'Anglo-American Wilderness Campaigning, 1754–1764: Logistical and Tactical Developments', unpubl. Columbia University Ph.D. thesis, 1970, 75–7. The confusion in the six regiments so drafted was considerable, their state of training and efficiency reduced, and recruiting parties had now to set out in search of raw replacements. When ordered to make this draft Bury's 20th, for example, was lying with five companies at Bristol, four at Exeter and one at Tiverton; and to save time the 100 drafts were stripped from the companies at Bristol. A detachment of fifty men had then to be skimmed from the companies at Exeter and Tiverton and sent 'to Levell the Comps.' at Bristol. Then recruiting parties were sent out. WO 27/42, pp. 53–4, 68, 176.

[104] F. T. Nichols, art. cit. 131.

foot at cadre strength ceased in 1770. Several factors made possible this change, which was salutary. The setting up of a large garrison in North America from 1763, together with an increase in the number of regiments regularly sent to do West Indies duty or to man the Mediterranean strongholds, plus a general reduction in the strength of regiments on the post-1763 British establishment, were all contributory; but most important in forcing the change was the adoption in 1765, as noted earlier, of a rotation scheme between the British Isles and the Americas. From 1765 until 1773 regiments relieved one another across the Atlantic; and the small size of the Irish regiments compared with those serving in the Americas (297 officers and men in an Irish corps, as against 497 in America), meant that to continue with the good policy of rotation, units arriving in Ireland had immediately to draft away or discharge half their men (unless they had already left them behind to feed the weak newcomer to America), while those leaving Ireland had to double their strength almost overnight by receiving drafts. This being quite unworkable, it was finally arranged by the King and the Lord-Lieutenant, at the instance of the Adjutant-General in London,[105] to augment the Irish establishment in 1769 from 12,000 men (where it had been fixed since 1699) to 15,000. Henceforth the foot in Ireland, Britain, and the Americas stood on similar regimental establishments.[106]

Reference to Appendix B will show that in spite of the fact that from 1764 Irish regiments were rotating through the Americas, they were much more likely to remain at home for long periods than were the regiments in Britain, in peacetime. Irish regiments suffered less from dispersal on to foreign stations and the consequent deterioration in discipline, efficiency, interior economy, and strength which plagued such a large proportion of those going abroad from the British establishment. Similarly, the pattern and incidence of rotation within Ireland itself was quite unlike that prevailing in Britain. In Ireland the standing army was neither subjected to the abuse, nor did it stir the same fears, that it aroused in England. Although Ireland was quiet for most of the century the supremacy

---

[105] J. Shy, op. cit. 274–7.
[106] WO 27/20–75, for Irish regimental establishments, and WO 24/449–578 for those of corps elsewhere.

of the Anglican ruling classes in that country rested ultimately (as in 1690, so in 1798) upon the army—and the ruling classes knew this only too well. Quartering therefore did not create in Ireland the legal and political problems that it occasioned in England; and hence the dispositions of the army in Ireland more closely resembled those of the army in Scotland than the leopard-spot dispositions of England.

Many of the towns in Ireland were provided with barracks by the later 1720s, and most of the big towns were certainly well provided by the 1740s. Billeting seems to have been much less commonly resorted to than was the case in Britain, save by troops upon their march, suppressing or overawing the disorderly, or by detachments patrolling the isolated smugglers' coasts. As Map 2 shows, the army was widely dispersed about the country in these quarters: in 1752, typically, its 250 companies of marching Foot, twenty-four troops of Horse, and thirty-nine troops of Dragoons were distributed among sixty-nine towns and forts. But as the map also shows, there were two sorts of quarters in Ireland: there were, firstly, the numerous small posts, often little better than police stations, strewn everywhere; and secondly there were the half-dozen big towns where two or three regiments were usually headquartered. It was the cavalry regiments in Ireland that were most dispersed about the small places, since cavalry, with its superior mobility, was the arm best adapted to the patrolling duties necessary when aiding the civil power. For most of the cavalry in Ireland the scattered state of its quarters inevitably meant a decline in training and drill proficiency: some units, like the 8th Horse, were kept in good order only through the most dedicated and careful management;[107] but dispersed with two troops at Clonmell and one each at Cappoquin, Mallow, Charleville, and at Carrick on Suir, as was the 8th in 1734—'a spread of a 100 miles and more over terrible roads'[108]—efficiency could hardly be maintained. Although the cavalry was widely dispersed in Britain, too, it was not kept in that condition for such lengthy periods as was the Irish horse. Half of the foot in Ireland suffered from being distributed in quarters as widely dispersed

---

[107] On the situation of the 8th Horse in Ireland, 1720–42, see Rex Whitworth, op. cit. 41–56.
[108] Ibid. 45.

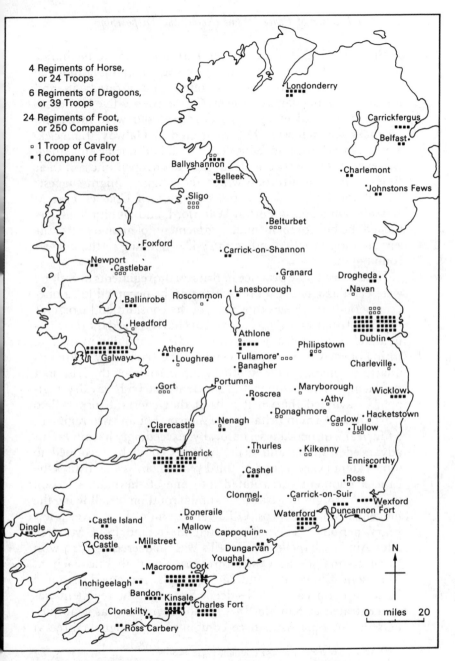

Map 2.   Quarters of the Army in Ireland for 1752

as those in which the bulk of the Irish horse was to be found; but if half of the foot regiments were dispersed in this fashion the rest were headquartered—and often concentrated—in and about the six big garrison towns. Of the twenty-five battalions of foot in Ireland in 1752, for example, four were in Dublin barracks and ten were headquartered at Galway, Limerick, Cork, Waterford, and Kinsale.[109] It should not be imagined, however, that the regiments in these towns spent most of their time in the concentration which these figures might suggest; for all these places (with the exception of Charles Fort at Kinsale, Duncannon Fort at Waterford, and Dublin itself) detached the bulk of their small complements of men to patrol the surrounding beaches and countryside, billeting in the villages round about.

In contrast to the practice in Britain, the regiments in Ireland were each assigned a set of quarters to be occupied for a one-year period; there was thus none of the constant and irregular shifting of quarters or duty areas that characterized the distribution and rotation of the army in Britain. Annually, in the late spring of early summer, the whole of the Irish army shifted its quarters from one set to another; and in so doing the Irish foot regiments—if to a much lesser extent the Irish cavalry regiments—avoided the worst evils of that constant dispersal to which most corps in Britain were subject. For an Irish regiment a full year's dispersal was, naturally, exceedingly harmful to its advanced training and drill; but this could be recouped to some extent every second or third year when, as was always the case, a regiment was rotated into one of the main garrison towns. We might illustrate this annual rotation by following the movements of one corps, O'Farrell's 22nd of Foot, over a few years' period.[110] Having returned to Ireland from Minorca after Aix-la-Chapelle, O'Farrell's was quartered in 1749 with three companies at Cork, three at Youghal, one each at Macroom, Clonakilty, and Inchigeelagh, and one distributed between Kilmeedy and Needeen. For 1750, the regiment was concentrated at Kinsale. In 1751 the regiment was again dispersed, this time with three companies at Youghal, three at

---

[109] Anon., *Quarters . . . in 1752* (Dublin, 1752), 8–20.

[110] Anon., Quarters . . . in *1749* (Dublin, 1749), 29; *Quarters . . . in 1750*, 11; *Quarters . . . in 1751*, 11; and *Quarters . . . in 1752*, 13.

Cashel, two at Dungarvan and two at Nenagh, thus stretching over some 60 miles from Youghal to Nenagh. Then, in 1752, O'Farrell's was again quartered together, at Limerick. The rest of the Irish foot followed a similar quartering pattern.

A very large garrison was always maintained in Dublin barracks and a regiment could be sure of spending a year in the great city, every few years. The big Dublin garrison was, indeed, always the largest peacetime concentration of regular regiments of infantry and cavalry in the British Isles; in size it was rivalled only by the Gibraltar and Minorca garrisons in the Empire as a whole. Dublin's Phoenix Park was the largest exercising-ground at the disposal of the peacetime British Army; and as we shall see it was often the scene of some extraordinary mock battles, and on one occasion of advanced tactical experimentation.

Granting that the Irish regiments were sure of a kind of peacetime permanence unknown among their sister regiments across the Irish Sea, there was much in their situation—their weak establishments especially—that was not to be envied. Even the supposed advantages and comforts of the barracks in the big towns could be illusory, as is often indicated in the inspection reports. When Lt.-Gen. Lord Blayney saw the 27th Foot at Limerick in June 1774, for example, he reported that 'the Lower Barrack of Limerick which now contains 7 Companies of this Regiment, have been condemned near Twenty Years, The Stairs, floors, windows and Doors very bad, Officers were obliged at their own expence to Plaister the Cieling, as the Barrack master would not do it without an order from the Board, the Barrack being condemned.'[111] Blayney's report shows up the inefficiency of the Irish Board of Ordnance; and inefficiency seems to have been an almost permanent feature of Dublin Castle's administration of the army.[112] Meanwhile, duties quite as onerous as those that took up the time of so many of the corps in Britain, and wide dispersal, were equally harmful in Ireland. When in 1777 the 11th, 30th, and 32nd of Foot arrived from typical dispersed quarters to begin a tour on the Dublin duty, the commanding

[111] WO 27/32.
[112] This is the burden of the lengthy report on the army in Ireland, 1749–50, in Cumb. Pprs, Box 44, no. 99, pp. 1–46.

officers of these corps 'represented to the Commander in Chief, that as the Companies of their respective regiments had been widely distributed into County Cantonments', they would require from a month to six weeks 'to establish their regiments in a uniformity of Discipline' before they could possibly be inspected.[113] Even corps concentrated in Dublin were not free from trouble: in 1771, for example, the six regiments forming the Dublin garrison had to be reviewed singly, rather than in brigade as was customary, since 'it was found Necessary that part of the Garrison should remain upon Duty, to prevent Riots and Disturbances in the Town'.[114] Rural hunger riots, notably in 1766, 1771, and 1772, led to considerable dispersal from regular quarters.[115] Mounting rural discontent in the 1790s caused the most widespread dispersal, as the gentry pressed to have troops stationed everywhere to protect their persons and property from violence. By 1797–8, in consequence, Sir Ralph Abercromby, the newly arrived C.-in-C., found that dispersal had left the army with 'little or no order or discipline'; the practice was 'really ruinous to the service. The best regiments in Europe could not long stand such usage'. In summary, Abercromby wrote that the Irish army was 'in a state of licentiousness which must render it formidable to everyone but the enemy'.[116] Not long after he penned those words the French landed in the country, and a long and bloody mass rising erupted. The army in 1798 was ill prepared for it, and the fumbling of the authorities did not improve the situation. The Irish army had been in the same sort of disorder by 1750, a situation which an intelligent field officer described as 'the blessed effects of Long Peace and Plenty'. Laxity was 'quelque chose de règle en Irelande', as he put it.[117]

Interesting comparisons, then, may be drawn between the army in Britain and in Ireland. That the laxity of Irish army administration should have far exceeded that prevailing in England is not surprising. Neither the favour of the King nor that of the prestigious British C.-in-C. could well be courted from Ireland, and neither the Lord-Lieutenant nor the Irish

---

[113] WO 27/37, 11th Foot.
[114] WO 27/23, 24th Foot.
[115] WO 27/23, 42nd Foot, and 27/26, 18th Light Dragoons.
[116] Quoted in T. Pakenham, *The Year of Liberty* (1972), 59, 61.
[117] Cumb. Pprs, Box 44, no. 98.

C.-in-C. was so well worth the courting. Although a significant minority of the regimental officers were drawn from the Irish ruling classes, most of the officers found service anywhere in the country, outside Dublin, to be dull. The low-establishment, cadre character of their regiments, which inevitably meant a huge influx of drafts and recruits were the regiment to go abroad on active service, can have provided scant incentive to ensure a high standard of training.[118] Nevertheless, among the foot, the occasionally high levels of individual unit concentration in the garrison towns, and the frequent opportunities in Dublin quarters for brigade manoeuvres and mock battles (of which more below) were excellent advantages nowhere to be met with in Britain.

(d) IN AID OF THE CIVIL POWER

In a society essentially rural, where social mobility was limited, where norms and obligations were notions rooted in the traditional rights and customs of the community, and where property, wealth, and power were the possession of a numerically weak ruling class, it was ideally in the balance of paternalism and deference that both civil order and social hierarchy were maintained and reinforced. Charity and the Poor Laws, manorial and corporate controls, the pulpit, wages, rents and tenures, and—*in extremis*—the stocks and the gibbet, these were the glue of the social fabric. Such at least was the ideal; but the economic realities of a century and a half of commercial capitalism (to be followed, within our period, by the colder winds of 'improving' agriculture, by early industrial capitalism, and by the hard logic of *laissez-faire*) had made archaic many features of the paternalist ideal. Paternalism and deference were manifestly personal relations, functioning man to man in

[118] How scant was illustrated in 1750, when four of these weak regiments of foot were brought together at Limerick to be reviewed. Their weakness led several officers to suggest that the regiments pair off, each pair combining to form a single battalion on the day of review because there were so few private men on their establishments. At this suggestion other officers protested vehemently, one summarizing by arguing quite properly 'that it was an Unsoldierlike manner of Drawing up, that we were each a Regiment, by His Majestys orders our number so small; that haveing each our Compleat Colours, officers, and Every thing that Constitutes a Regiment, it was not our business to consider whither our plattoons were few, or of many files; but to Endeavour to make the few men each Regiment is Composed of, as fit for Service, and capable of teaching new levys, in case of an augmentation.' Cumb. Pprs., Box 44, no. 99, p. 13.

small, and especially in market or agrarian, communities; and to these the onset of modernity was inimical.

The increasing weakness during the later-seventeenth and eighteenth centuries of the old paternalist socio-economic model is evident. Concurrent with a later stage in the slow readjustment of social relations, consequent upon these realities, was the half-century of the Whig supremacy—that period during which political stability, the rule of law, and the means of both acquiring property and protecting its privileges, were secured. It has lately been argued that the chief resource of the Whig ruling élite in the Lockean state had become, by the eighteenth century, the criminal law and its courts, now 'critically important in maintaining bonds of obedience and deference, in legitimizing the status quo, in constantly re-creating the structure of authority which arose from property and in turn protected its interests'.[119] The unprecedented increase in the number of capital statutes—without doubt 'one of the great facts of the eighteenth century'[120]—provided authority with one awesome and standard recourse: 'the example of terror'.[121] But this was flexible terror, invoked arbitrarily and tempered with mercy; and (so the argument runs) it was in the common extension of mercy through pardons and the commutation of sentences—these obtained by the élite in the interest of tenants and others under their 'protection'—that the social hierarchy was reinforced, the patronage powers of the ruling class greatly extended, and social deference strengthened. Despite these formulations, however, the ominipresence of the new standing army argues, *ipso facto*, the inadequacy of the law in achieving the ends thus prescribed for it; and it is less in the burgeoning of the statute book and more especially in the intrusion of an impersonal and outside agent—the new standing army—into the towns and throughout the countryside, come quartering or in aid of the civil power, that the measure of that decline is to be taken. Come war or peace, the army served as the guardian of the civil order. That too is one of the great facts of the eighteenth century.

---

[119] D. Hay, 'Property, Authority and the Criminal Law', in D. Hay, P. Linebaugh, E. P. Thompson, et al., *Albion's Fatal Tree* (1975), 25.

[120] Ibid. 18.

[121] E. P. Thompson, *Whigs and Hunters* (1975), 197.

Equally evident is the turbulence of the age, the 'extreme precariousness between the forces of law and order and those of crime and anarchy in eighteenth-century England'.[122] Violence and brutality were endemic; we have come to regard Hogarth not as a caricaturist so much as a social commentator of sensitivity, with a deep sympathy. It is not however with the callousness of the age, nor with the wide spectrum of everyday petty violence or common crime that we are especially concerned here (although the latter in particular provides graphic illustration of the size and nastiness of that criminal underworld of which Englishmen, of whatever class, went in fear[123]); rather, it is with those forms of violence that the local civil authorities—JPs, magistrates, sheriffs, constables, keepers, and watchmen—most apprehended, and were least capable of dealing with on their own. Although we shall note below a number of other duties that the army performed in aid of the civil power it was of course the riot that was the main problem for the civil power and, where it failed to avert or to contain it, for the army.

Riot was a calamity in any community since it weakened the local social fabric: hence the common anxiety on the part of the civil authorities 'either to anticipate the event, or to cut it short in its early stages, by personal presence, by exhortation and concession'.[124] Indeed in certain types of civil disorder—food riots in particular—traditional patterns of behaviour employed both by the crowds and by the authorities have been discerned: physical restraint was common, there were mutually recognized phases of action and of escalation and often a 'consensus of support in the community' which was 'endorsed

---

[122] L. Stone, 'Whigs, Marxits, and Poachers', in *New York Times Review of Books* (5 Feb. 1976), 25.

[123] There is no better catalogue of the range and variety of crime than that shown in G. Howson's fine biography, *Thief-Taker General: The Rise and Fall of Jonathan Wild* (1970).

[124] E. P. Thompson, 'The Moral Economy of the English Crowd in the Eighteenth Century', *Past & Present*, 50 (1971), 120–2. Thompson's description of 'the old moral economy of provision' and the 'pattern of social protest which derives from a consensus as to the moral economy of the commonwealth in times of dearth', is sensitive and appealing; but it is also an example of sociological model-building which suffers much from not having taken into consideration the activities of radical agents (i.e. troops) effecting the model from without.

by some measure of licence afforded by the authorities'.[125] But where restraint failed, as was frequently the case, other patterns of behaviour are noticeable: as Professor Plumb observed, 'burning, looting, and destruction by the mob were commonplaces of life'; 'no nation rioted more easily or more savagely than England—from 1740 to 1830 angry mobs, burning and looting, were prevalent as disease, and as frequent in the countryside as in the great towns'.[126] One researcher has estimated that between 1740 and 1775 there were 159 major riots in England alone, and his estimate is a conservative one.[127] Given this scale of disturbance, there were a great many occasions on which the army had to be called in to the aid of the civil authorities, where that authority was on its own unable 'to carry the laws into execution'. Riots—from the formal, structured protest-riot which was the common mechanism for the expression of popular opinion or the dramatization of grievances, to the brutal and desperate rioting which occasionally broke out for economic reasons (or, often enough, out of sheer bigotry, or in blind response to the manipulation of the credulous by the sly)—were all too frequent, and the civil authorities all too often impotent. Yet England was a nation where any increase in the authority of the central government in local, internal affairs, was disliked; and she was equally a nation in which the protection of property (and the rights and liberties it conferred) was deemed the paramount responsibility of the courts and the law.

It is generally appreciated that for a significant segment of the political nation in eighteenth-century England the standing army, a creature of the central executive and an intrusive agent in the provinces, was an object of extreme jealousy; while among the public at large it was almost universally reviled. There were many for whom the centralizing tendencies of all the Stuarts, the myths that issued out of the experience of Cromwell and Putney, the example of James II's 'papist' army, and the sudden appearance in their midst of a big standing

---

[125] Ibid. 78–9, 107–20, where Thompson traces various 'patterns of behaviour' in the major English crowd actions, notably those of 1740, 1756, 1766, 1795, and 1800.

[126] J. H. Plumb, *England in the Eighteenth Century* (1963), 13; and *The First Four Georges* (1966), 15.

[127] W. A. Smith, 'Anglo-Colonial Society and the Mob, 1740–1775', unpubl. Claremont Ph.D. thesis, 1965, 29–30.

army in 1697 and again after 1712, were all facts of consequence which augured ill for the future, and summoned
frightening visions of praetorians. A standing civil police force
was a concept even more obnoxious than that of a standing
army, and in eighteenth-century England police forces, as
such, were non-existent; both police and army threatened the
ancient social order, rooted in paternalism, by which authority
and law had been maintained in the countryside and both, of
course, were now necessary as that social order waned. But with
so jaundiced a view of Whitehall's military arm, with such en-
trenched regionalism, and with so unhappy a historical experience of standing forces, great care was taken to scrutinize and
often to impede the activities of those forces in civil society.[128]

Since the Glorious Revolution the use of troops in civil
affairs had been closely watched not only by the responsible
Minister, a Secretary of State, but by public opinion in general;
and by the beginning of our period there had developed an
official course of conduct guaranteeing the control of the
military by the civil power. In the event of disorder greater than
what could be handled on the scene by traditional means, it was
usual for the local JPs to report the situation to a Secretary of
State in London, asking for military assistance to maintain
order and the laws. The Secretary at War, acting at the instance
of the Secretary of State, then dispatched from the War Office
marching orders to the officer commanding the troops nearest
to the scene, who set off for the trouble spot upon receipt of
these. Once arrived, the troops were employed at the discretion
and under the immediate direction of the local magistrates—
for whatever their common law obligations, soldiers could not
stir to preserve the peace unless acting in the presence of the
magistrates; and once order had been restored it was usual for
the troops to remain quartered in the vicinity for some time
afterwards. This was, admittedly, a time-consuming procedure; but it was a bold officer or magistrate who circumvented
it, however pressing the situation. Very occasionally, the local

---

[128] The complex legal and constitutional issues involved in the use of the military in
aid of the civil power are best discussed in Tony Hayter, *The Army & The Crowd in Mid-
Georgian England* (1978), *passim*, and esp. pp. 9–19, 48–74; and in Sir L. Radzinowicz,
A History of English Criminal Law and its Administration from 1750, iv (1957), 124–7,
141–50. W. J. Shelton, *English Hunger and Industrial Disorders* (Toronto, 1973), is useful,
if myopic.

civil power or an officer with soldiers billeted near by might on their own initiative move troops to, or closer to, a riot area; but they drew the line at direct intervention or force without the sanction of the War Office and legal direction.[129]

The incidence of such aid varied considerably from one part of the Empire to the next. The question hardly occurs with Gibraltar and Minorca since both were strongholds and sparsely settled. In the West Indies slave insurrection was the only real danger to society, and this was guarded against by maintaining a presence, not by much vigorous activity. In the North American colonies the situation differed from that prevailing in Britain. There the army was only rarely used in aid of the civil power during the century, since the local authorities were usually loath to call it in. The army was too widely scattered in North America, too thin on the ground to be readily available; and the militia (unlike that in England) often acted in its stead. Unlike the English and Irish mobs, there were many more Americans with firearms;[130] and there were far fewer riots in America: the mobs of Boston and New York made up only a tiny fraction of the population, and attempts by historians to distinguish a current of popular violence in America, out of the English mob tradition, ring hollow.[131] The events in Boston, 1768–75, were quite extraordinary; and they were so precisely because the regular army there seemed to be acting as a coercive force, against which resistance was justifiable. Such a view was possible in the colonies, where the experience of regulars acting in aid of the civil power was a rarity; it was hardly a view likely to gain currency with the English masses, whose acquaintance with the redcoats was more intimate.

In Ireland, the army came to the support of the civil power as often, no doubt (for we have few records) as it did in England,

[129] On certain occasions after the mid-century the Secretary at War took it upon himself to employ troops, in times of riot, without first obtaining the Secretary of State's authorization (on which see Tony Hayter, op. cit. 56, 64–71, and *passim*). Hayter notes that, for practical purposes, riot control was the War Office's business: (pp. 56–7) 'The effect of constant calls for help over the years was to make the Secretary at War into a sort of police chief or minister of the interior.' See also W. J. Shelton, op. cit., *passim*, in this regard.

[130] J. Shy, op. cit. 36–44, 191–231, 376–418.

[131] As does R. M. Brown, 'Violence and the American Revolution', in S. G. Kurtz and J. H. Hutson (eds), *Essays on the American Revolution* (N. Carolina, 1973), 81–121.

and perhaps more often. King William had brought over an army to rescue the Protestant Irish in 1690.

His venture completed, the king had returned to England; the army had remained. The complete Protestant victory of 1692 made future rebellion improbable and ushered in one of the longest periods of peace in Irish history. Yet, in the last analysis, the Irish state in the early eighteenth century rested upon British military power.[132]

Most contemporaries thought that troops were as essential to the maintenance of the Irish state later in the century. There, Lord North wrote in 1775, 'they depend so much upon the protection and assistance of the military force, who are in constant employment under the command of the civil magistrate for the carrying on every part of the internal police of the kingdom, which could not be carried on without it.'[133] Ireland, like England, was prey to many local and many widespread disturbances. Thus there were serious provincial riots in 1766, 1771, 1772, and 1797. Dublin was huge and, like London, had a very large garrison whose purpose was patently to overawe and occasionally to repress the mob—as it did in 1771, for example. By 1797 half of the army in Ireland was not in its regular quarters but dispersed in penny-packets to protect the frightened gentry, peasant discontent being by then so widespread. The 1780s and 1790s had seen mounting discontent over taxes and land tenures, and the army seems to have been acting against the disaffected without always waiting for the call of the magistrates. The dreadful events of 1798 were partly the response of a peasantry tired of being roughly handled by Whiteboys, Volunteers, and gentry who believed that the rule of dragoons and that of law were one and the same.

The Highlanders of Scotland, until the close of George II's reign, were regarded as a dangerous and unruly people. The Whig clans were often suspect, and deservedly so;[134] and the other clans were deemed to be disaffected and rebellious, as in-

---

[132] F. G. James, op. cit. 181.

[133] Quoted in J. Brooke, *King George III* (1972), 310.

[134] Cope got no support from the 'loyal' clans of the central Highlands on his march from Stirling for Fort Augustus in August 1745. Indeed, when Argyll was sounded for his 'assistance, advice and countenance', he replied with only 'Assistance, advice and countenance—magna sonantia verba'. Marching north through Athol country, Cope got no provisions but was, rather, robbed of what little he had. See R. Jarvis, op. cit. i. 12–19.

deed they were. The Jacobite clans hoped to rise in 1708, and did so in 1715, in 1719, and in 1745; and French and Spanish troops had come ashore to assist them. Not only were many of the clansmen Catholic in their religion and Jacobite in their sympathies, but they were a primitive people whose tribal social organization was utterly archaic, whose language and customs were not understood, and whose feuds and raids were hardly to be tolerated. Finally broken in 1746 and in the severe repression that followed, the Highlands after the accession of George III were, from the point of view of the army, a dull backwater where little time had to be spent any more in aid of the civil power, let alone in support of the Whig 'happy establishment'. Before the Seven Years War there had been some considerable difference between Highland and Lowland service. In the Lowlands the army aided the civil power much as it did in England: riots were common enough in the big Lowlands towns, as in those further south across the border. The Glasgow Riots of 1725, the Porteous Riots in Edinburgh in 1736, were major affairs.[135] In the Highlands meanwhile, the army settled in garrison at Forts George, Augustus, and William, and at the police barracks of Bernara, Inversnaid, and Ruthven in Badenoch; moving along the military roads laid out mostly in the 1720s and 30s, the small army amidst a hostile population treated it, if it dared, as it treated the Acadiens of Nova Scotia during the same period.

With England, because our sources are copious, we can be more precise. Rioting was part of the fabric of English society. Given hardships—unemployment, poor harvests, high prices and falling wages, and that decline of the old paternalist economy of supply already quite noticeable early in the century; given too the fact that there was no regular police force, and that central government was unrepresentative and unresponsive to the needs of the masses; there had developed within this context a 'mob tradition' which served Englishmen as an

extra-legal channel by which to make their grievances known and felt by government . . . Since concern for English rights and liberties was a concept deeply imbedded in the society, it came to be tacitly ac-

---

[135] See W. A. Smith, op. cit. 92–3, on the Glasgow Riots, and 94–101 on the Porteous Riots.

cepted by that society that mob violence in defence of those rights or in protest against some major grievance was in itself a legitimate, if not a legal right of freeborn English subjects.[136]

Rioting was a 'right' all too commonly exercised, so far as the army was concerned: officers generally agreed with Barrington that civil affrays imposed 'a most Odious Service which nothing but Necessity can justify'.[137] We can follow the course of one typical outbreak in order to illustrate the problem confronting the army. During the 1730s the big cloth industry of the west Wiltshire weaving towns was suffering from unsettling changes in manufacture, a lowering of wages, and a generally unprosperous period of business.[138] By late 1738 orders were falling off, and this seems to have been the last straw for the mass of weavers. Attempts by loosely organized 'brotherhoods' to bargain with the clothiers failed and, finally, a lowering of wages at the end of November by a Melksham clothier set off rioting: his shop and mill were sacked, and the near-by Chippenham JPs sent post-haste to London for military assistance. In consequence, on 1 December a large detachment was ordered to be found by Harrison's 15th of Foot, then at Bristol, and sent to Chippenham: from that town the soldiers were to be disposed 'in such Place or Places as shall be desired by the Civil Magistrates'. Since the Melksham clothiers were noted for the low wages they paid, reductions there were taken, elsewhere, as a bad sign; and so rioting began soon after at Chippenham, Bradford, and Trowbridge 'to prevent a fall in wages from spreading'.[139] Late on the evening of 1 December there arrived at the Secretary of State's office further accounts of the 'Outrages committed by the Weavers', and of the spreading riots—'their Number continuing to Encrease, insomuch that there is good reason to apprehend much greater Mischief than has been Committed'; and so further orders were sent 'by Express at 12 o'Clock the same Night' from London, directing that two troops of Campbell's 2nd Dragoons at Salisbury (the corps was then lying with two troops at Salisbury, two at

---

[136] W. A. Smith, op. cit. 1.

[137] E. P. Thompson, art. cit. 121.

[138] J. de L. Mann, 'Clothiers and Weavers in Wiltshire during the 18th Century', in L. S. Pressnell (ed.), *Studies in the Industrial Revolution: Essays Presented to T. S. Ashton* (1960), 66–96, *passim*.

[139] Ibid. 72.

Dorchester, and one each at Blandford and Sherborne) should likewise march immediately for Chippenham to assist the detachment from Harrison's.[140] Then on 9 December the troop of Campbell's at Sherborne was ordered to Westbury 'to Aid & Assist [the magistrates] in Suppressing the riotous Weavers & other disorderly persons who have already committed great Outrages & from whom the Civil Magistrates apprehend mor mischief'; the same day, the troop at Blandford was ordered to Warminster for the same purpose.[141] By then it seems that the foot had been distributed between Chippenham, Melksham, Bradford, and Trowbridge. By mid-February the weavers had at last been 'suppressed and dispers'd'; and the good people of Westbury, 'not under any further Apprehensions of Mischief', were petitioning for the removal of the troops lately sent to deliver them from the great outrages of the weavers.[142] No doubt mischief was now apprehended from the dragoons. All that remained was to hang three of the ringleaders from Salisbury gallows, two troops of Campbell's being detailed to keep a weather-eye on the crowd, assembled for the occasion.[143]

These weavers' riots were on a considerable scale, for a local affair; but the army's involvement was none the less typical of the aid it rendered to the civil power. Despite the constitutional issues raised and the social weaknesses pointed thereby, the local civil power was constantly obliged to call upon the army in order to preserve property and the public peace, and to uphold the laws: any detailed study of the Marching Orders, and of the dispositions and quartering patterns resulting from these, makes it quite clear that the army was employed 'to an enormous extent'[144] in this capacity throughout the century. The following survey—not of the constant minor affrays but *only* of the *more serious* instances of such activity, and limited to the west-country counties from Cornwall round to the Severn—underlines this conclusion; and it should be stressed that comparable surveys may be made anywhere else in the country.

Cornwall and south Devon were much afflicted with dis-

[140] WO 5/33, pp. 100–86, *passim*.
[141] Ibid., pp. 187–8.
[142] WO 5/33, p. 201.
[143] Ibid, p. 207.
[144] T. Hayter, op. cit. 34.

order, especially during the first half of our period. The tin mines of those counties, long the main source of supply for the whole of Europe and the Levant, entered a period of prolonged slump from about 1700 with the arrival in Dutch merchantmen of higher-quality Asian tin; not until the 1760s did the English stannaries revive, and in the meantime the plight of the tinners had been severe. Smuggling, the stranding of vessels, and, most especially, hunger riots and price regulating by mobs had in consequence become endemic.[145] During the autumn of 1726, on through the winter of 1727–28, and into the following spring there were repeated hunger riots in this area, led by the tinners; and the 15th and later the 16th of Foot were repeatedly drawn in.[146] From the spring of 1737 to the summer of 1738 the 11th, and later the 16th, of Foot were often engaged with the tinners—notably so early in October 1737 when the whole of the 11th was aiding the civil power in several Cornish towns.[147] In 1738 and 1740 Modbury mobs on three occasions plundered the cargoes of ships, and troops were required. So serious was the situation by 1740 that the exportation of grain was halted, during the winter, with detachments of the 8th Foot in the ports aiding the civil power in 'Compelling all Ships to a Strict Embargo'.[148] The troops had only occasionally to suppress rioters here during the 1750s, notably in the spring and summer of 1753, when half of the 23rd Foot was so employed[140]; and during the mid-1760s the tinners seem again to have been assured of supply, since only in that area of east Devon about Ottery St. Mary and Cullompton did hunger riots occur—where, late in the summer of 1766, hungry mobs were demolishing the flour mills, regulating the markets, and 'compelling the Farmers to sell their provisions at a fixed Price', activities which obliged the 3rd Dragoons to come to the

---

[145] Serious hunger riots occurred not just here but over wide areas of England in 1727, throughout the 1730s, in 1740, 1752–3, 1756–7, 1766 (the worst year of all), 1772–4, and again in 1783 and 1795. Depending upon localities, most of these outbreaks required the presence of troops to protect mills, markets, granaries, wagons, barges, and mealmen, and to break up roving bands of price regulators or of the starving.

[146] WO 5/27, pp. 48–316, *passim*; and 5/28, pp. 3–255, *passim*.

[147] WO 5/32, pp. 257–505, *passim*; 5/33, pp. 48–109, *passim*; 5/34, pp. 73–112, *passim*.

[148] WO 5/33, pp. 48, 91; and 5/34, pp. 85–6, 275.

[149] WO 5/41, pp. 395–509, *passim*.

assistance of the civil power.[150] There had meanwhile been industrial disorder in the region; and in an economy subject generally to violent short-term advances and retreats it could hardly have been otherwise. In the summer of 1765, for example, units of the 4th Foot had to deal with the Tiverton weavers, who had 'entered into Combinations & Agreements not to work, or suffer any work to be done for several of the Inhabitants of the Town . . . & continue assembling and meeting at their Clubb houses'.[151] From early in 1773 until late that summer, the 23rd, and later the 33rd, Foot had to deal with a new wave of hunger riots by the tinners throughout Cornwall and south Devon: they had once again become 'very Riotous and Outrageous in plundering the Maltsters, Millers and Farmers', and had 'commited many Robberies on the High Roads'.[152]

Quite as troubled as the Cornish stannaries was the cloth industry centred in the weaving towns of west Wiltshire and over the Somerset border. Late in 1726—when the whole of the 10th and 11th Dragoons had to be dispatched to ten of the main weaving towns in the area round about Trowbridge and Melksham, where 'great Numbers of Weavers and other disorderly persons' were rioting[153]—there began that series of industrial disorders that was to last until the end of our period, as the cloth industry slowly shifted to the north. We noted above the riots that swept the area late in 1738; and for several weeks during the spring of 1752 the weavers were again rioting sporadically ('which will be attended with the most fatall Consequences', warned the clothiers), and the 2nd Dragoon Guards and 2nd Dragoons had to suppress them.[154] During the great hunger riots of 1766 the Wiltshire weavers were caught up again: in the summer and autumn of that year elements of four regiments (the 3rd and 4th Dragoons, 13th and 43rd Foot) were aiding the civil power in virtually all the Wiltshire

[150] WO 5/54, pp. 270–318, *passim*.

[151] WO 5/53, pp. 432–3. By Sept. 1766 the Tiverton weavers had resorted to sending 'threatening and incendiary letters' to leading citizens, which brought the soldiers to town once again. WO 5/54, pp. 303–4.

[152] WO 5/58, pp. 44–383, *passim*.

[153] WO 5/27, pp. 76–101, *passim*. The towns occupied were Frome, Westbury, Bradford, Trowbridge, Lacock, Melksham, Devizes, Chippenham, Marlborough, and Calne.

[154] WO 5/41, pp. 153–258, *passim*.

and Somerset weaving towns, in some of which places starvation was real and the violence extreme.[155] There was a final wave of rioting through these towns early in 1789, but only two troops of the 4th Dragoons were required on this occasion.[156]

Bristol, and its hinterland, was often a scene of disorder too. In October 1738 'a great number' of coal-heavers had rioted in that city and, to head off further trouble, the 15th Foot occupied the city and the parishes round about.[157] In the spring and summer of 1753 there were 'great Riotts and Disturbances at Bristol and the Neighbourhood', occasioned once again by dearth. The Bristol coal-heavers had attempted to seize a grain ship lying in the port; other colliers were robbing the corn at Shepton Mallet market and planning to do the same at Wells. Most of the 2nd and 4th Dragoons marched for these places, in aid of the civil power.[158] The Bristol turnpike trust suffered from prolonged trouble before and about the mid-century; and there were frequent turnpike riots in nearby Somerset, Gloucestershire, and Herefordshire during the 1720s, '30s, and '40s. Typically, a detachment of the 16th Foot went to the aid of the civil power at Ledbury in April 1737 to 'suppress any Riotts Disorders and unlawfull Assemblys' in order to 'preserve the Turnpikes'.[159] Disorders affecting Bristol could come from farther afield too. Late in 1756 and again in 1757 hunger rioters in parts of Herefordshire, Monmouth, and Gloucestershire were interfering with Wye and Severn navigation; barges carrying grain were being stopped, leaving Bristol to run 'great Risque of being Starved'. The whole of the 20th Foot and part of the 3rd Foot were sent in.[160]

To this survey of west-country rioting should be added a larger, more widespread instance; and mention of London

---

[155] WO 5/54, pp. 276–416, *passim*. Mobs traversing Wiltshire were said to be gutting houses, firing mills, murdering mealmen, and instilling 'the greatest Terrors'; and 'the Magistrates of that Neighbourhood having represented that there is reason to apprehend they shall be totally incapable to put the Laws in execution without the Assistance of a Military Force', the troops were set in motion. WO 5/54, pp. 310–11.

[156] WO 5/67, pp. 102–3.

[157] WO 5/33, p. 165.

[158] WO 5/41, pp. 408–69, *passim*.

[159] WO 5/32, pp. 394–7, and W. Albert, *The Turnpike Road System in England, 1663–1840* (Cambridge, 1973), 26–8. See also WO 5/28, p. 340; 5/33, pp. 4, 52, 357; 5/41, pp. 427–8; and 5/42, p. 172.

[160] WO 5/43, p. 484; and 5/44, pp. 23–4.

should also be made. Thus the year 1766 saw not merely a local but, as noted earlier, a great sweep of hunger rioting from Devon and Gloucester eastwards across much of southern England, the Midlands, and East Anglia. These riots were so serious and widespread as to lead government to take the unprecedented step of sending to every regiment of horse and foot, and to every Invalid and Independent Company, in England, orders authorizing them to assist the civil power 'in case of any Riots or disturbances that may happen at, or in the Neighbourhood of your Qua^{rs}'—that is, even before such riots may have broken out.[161] In the event, troops had to take serious action to suppress rioters in much of twelve counties (namely Derbyshire, Warwickshire, Worcestershire, Gloucestershire, Wiltshire, Devonshire, Dorsetshire, Berkshire, Rutland, Huntingdon, Norfolk, and Suffolk), and lesser action in eight more; while of the several corps involved, there were nine (2nd Dragoon Guards; 3rd, 4th, 6th, and 11th Dragoons; 15th Light Dragoons; and 8th, 13th, and 43rd Foot) that saw considerable activity, and three more went into the southern ports to enforce an embargo hastily laid on the export of grain.[162]

London, of course, was unique. There were in London major riots in 1733 over the Excise, in 1736 over the Gin Tax, [163] in 1753 over Jewish naturalization,[164] over the silk industry in 1765, and in 1768–9 over the well-known series of issues that linked industrial disputes and the figure of John Wilkes.[165] The 1780 Gordon Riots were the worst the metropolis ever suffered; and before they were over some 12,000 regulars and militia were in the streets of London, 285 persons had been killed, and 173 wounded. Most of these disorders in the capital were handled by the Guards, assisted occasionally by London mil-

---

[161] WO 5/54, p. 318. The best study of the 1766 hunger riots is W. J. Shelton, op. cit. 1–151; and on the use of troops in 1766 see T. Hayter, op. cit. 114–27.

[162] Embargo was enforced along the Cornwall coasts by the 4th Foot, in Sussex by the 2nd Dragoons, in Kent by the 1st Dragoons, and in Suffolk and Essex by the 2nd Dragoon Guards, already mentioned. WO 5/54, pp. 353–4.

[163] G. Rudé, *Paris and London in the 18th Century. Studies in Popular Protest* (1970), 201–21.

[164] W. A. Smith, op. cit. 103–8.

[165] J. Brooke, op. cit. 113–16. George III took a personal interest in the suppression of the 1765 riots, and again in 1768 and 1780. 'The King exercised personal control over the use of the army, and . . . directed what were virtually military campaigns against rioters in London.' *Ibid.* 310.

itia; but regiments of the line had to be brought in during the 1765 riots (2nd Dragoon Guards, 10th and 11th Dragoons, 15th Light Dragoons), and again during the May 1768 riots when seven such regiments (The Blues, the 2nd, 3rd, and 6th Dragoons, the 15th and 16th Light Dragoons, and the 25th Foot) were moved into the villages surrounding the metropolis, although they were not employed in the event. By the end of the first week of June 1780, there were in London in addition to the Guards and nine militia battalions all of nine regular regiments (3rd Dragoon Guards, 3rd, 4th, and 11th Dragoons, 16th Light Dragoons, and the 2/1st, 2nd, 18th, and 52nd Foot), the presence of which George III 'highly approved', as he informed Amherst, 'for I am convinced till the Magistrates have ordered some Military Execution on the Rioters this Town will not be restored to Order.'[166] These figures, of course, represent a most significant part of the whole of the regular forces in the kingdom.

These were the most common types of riot that occasioned the use of the army, in the regions noted and elsewhere in the country. But there were many other situations, some riotous and some not, that could not be controlled by the civil authorities without military assistance; and if only to underline their frequency and variety it is worth noting some of them. Thus there were industrial riots severe enough to require the movement of troops to Liverpool and Wrexham in 1789; similar events took place at Nottingham and Leicester in 1787 and at Coventry in 1772, where the ribbon-makers were rioting over wage reductions.[167] In August 1789 a detachment of the 1st Dragoons had to march to Leeds, where the workers had smashed some spinning machines lately introduced in the wool manufactory—an early instance of that practice.[168] As early as the summer of 1739, four companies of the 24th Foot had to suppress rioting weavers at Manchester, as that industry moved north. In the autumn of 1751 and again the following spring there were industrial riots at Stafford, Shrewsbury, Walsall,

---

[166] For all troop movements in response to the 1765 riots, see WO 5/53, pp. 312–27. The King's letter is in Kent RO Amherst MSS 074/64, George III to Amherst, Queen's House, 6 June 1780. On the 1760s riots in London, see W. J. Shelton, op. cit. 155–202; and T. Hayter, op. cit. 128–45.

[167] WO 5/67, pp. 180–2; 5/66, pp. 448–74, *passim*; and 5/58, p. 25.

[168] WO 5/67, pp. 189–90.

Birmingham, and Burton upon Trent, serious enough to involve the 7th Dragoons; and late in 1752 rioting recurred in these places, bringing in more soldiers.[169] Enclosure of land and the erection of parish workhouses set off many local disturbances with which troops had to deal.[170] So too did the gaoling of the leaders of popular disturbances: a detachment of the 10th Dragoons had to guard Ely gaol during the summer of 1740, for example, and a troop of The Blues had to defend a 'temporary gaol' in Coventry in 1773, since rioters had 'pulled down' the old one.[171] Only rarely was the army called in to enforce the game laws: but with 'blacking' going on widely during the 1720s no less a corps than The Blues was sent in mid-1727 to assist the Ranger and keepers of Whittlewood Forest, near Stony Stratford, where the poachers had been bold of late.[172] The army was regularly employed on the transfer of felons either to the ports for transportation, or to some local gallows. There were many other activities, more often pursued. Quarantine had sometimes to be imposed at various of the ports: thus in July 1729 a detachment of the 16th Foot was sent from Bristol 'to oblige the Ship called Newton shortly expected from Zant, to perform Quarantine in Portshute Pill' (i.e. Portishead or Pill).[173] Shipwreck offered opportunities for great gain, and the army was often turned out to protect stranded ships and cargoes. In August 1738 a detachment of the 15th Foot aided the civil power in 'apprehending several Rioters concerned in plundering a Cargo of Tobacco from Virginia, in the Pye Sloop Stranded near Cardiff'; early in 1742 a ship stranded near Lower St. Columb in Cornwall, and a detachment had to be sent to prevent 'the Tinners from Plundering the said Ship'; and the tinners also attempted to loot the 'treasure chest' from a wrecked Hanover–Lisbon packet in 1765.[174]

Mutinous sailors, soldiers, and pressed men had to be dealt

---

[169] WO 5/33, p. 291; and 5/44, pp. 67–103, 204–332, *passim*.

[170] WO 5/42, p. 25; 5/53, pp. 416–27, 450, 487; and 5/54, pp. 53–4.

[171] WO 5/34, p. 140; and 5/58, p. 154. See also 5/59, p. 24.

[172] WO 5/27, pp. 205–6.

[173] WO 5/28, p. 341. Zante, one of the Ionian Islands long under Venetian control, a source of wood and wine. See also 5/41, p. 88. The great Marseilles plague of 1720 was not officially declared ended until January 1723; 93,000 were dead of it.

[174] WO 5/33, p. 149; 5/35, p. 126; 5/53, p. 292. Wrecking—the looting of wrecked vessels and goods—was most common in Cornwall, the Scillies, the Welsh coast, the Wirral Peninsula of Cheshire, and on the east coast of Kent, but the army was only

with by the army—an unpleasant task. The militia riots of 1757 were widespread, and mob violence was particularly dangerous in Yorkshire, Gloucestershire, and Bedfordshire—in which latter county as many as twenty-one troops of cavalry from The Blues, and from the 1st, 4th, and 10th Dragoons were required to restore order.[175] In April 1755 a navy press set off rioting in Whitehaven, and the 18th Foot had to send in a company—an example of a not uncommon occurrence. In October 1741 a detachment from the 45th Foot was sent to guard recruits belonging to the 38th Foot, penned up in Tilbury Fort and doubtless having second thoughts about joining the regiment in the West Indies. In 1755 and 1756 there were frequent mutinies of recruits and pressed seamen on board the men-of-war and transports at Chatham, Gravesend, and riding at Spithead: detachments of the 8th, 11th, and 20th of Foot had to go on board these ships to 'be Aiding & Assisting to the Officers of the Ships, in preventing or Suppressing any Mutiny'.[176] In November 1786 elements of the 7th Dragoons and 55th Foot were sent to patrol around Sandwich and Margate, since 'a Number of Foreign Soldiers on board a Dutch East India Man, now lying in the Downs, have mutinied, and after plundering the Ship of several valuable Articles, have made their escape on Shore'.[177] Most of the Black Watch mutinied at Finchley in May 1743, and set off home for Scotland; a troop of Horse Grenadier Guards and the better part of two regiments of Horse and two of Dragoons had to hunt them down.[178]

We must not, finally, forbear from including a duty that fell to the lot of a subaltern and twenty troopers of Churchill's 10th Dragoons, who in December 1738 were sent from Norwich in aid of the civil power at Bury—

It having been represented by the Mayor & other Magistrates of Bury St. Edmunds by several Affidavits, giving an Account of the Extravagant Behaviour of Captain Joshua Draper, who appears

---

infrequently called in; its incidence has either been exaggerated, or the wreckers were too quick at their business to attract the army.

[175] On the militia riots, see T. Hayter, op. cit. 98–113; and J. R. Western, *The English Militia in the Eighteenth Century* (1965), *passim*.

[176] WO 5/42, p. 284; 5/35, p. 51; and 5/42, pp. 215, 220–2.

[177] WO 5/66, p. 306.

[178] WO 5/35, pp. 600–2. J. Prebble, *Mutiny. Highland Regiments in Revolt, 1743–1804* (1975), 13–87, gives a fine reconstruction of the Black Watch mutiny.

thereby to have threatened to set fire to the Houses of Divers Persons, and to Shoot others, and has Secured himself in such a Manner in his house by nailing up the Windows & providing himself with Arms, that it is represented impossible for the Constables to apprehend him, and therefore they have desired to have such a Military assistance as Shall be thought proper.[179]

To conclude then, although it is quite clear that the army was the guardian of civil order in eighteenth-century England (failing the gentry and local town authorities to maintain the peace), it is equally clear that the army spent very little of its time in the actual mayhem of riot and disorder.[180] This need not be surprising, and may perhaps be the measure of the success of the army in its police role. The point of police activity is to prevent rather than have to suppress riot and felony; and the army, which if small was nevertheless ominipresent, played a police role simply by maintaining a presence. Figures for such a passive role cannot be assembled; but a study of the dispositions that units assumed upon their arrival in the duty areas indicates that policing was clearly a factor of major consideration when the Marching Orders were drawn. At the end of the subsection below we trace in detail the dispositions of units in one of our duty areas—dispositions which make this conclusion clear. Radzinowicz, the legal historian, noting the great barrack-building programme which commenced at the end of the century, makes no bones about this 'concentration of the army' as the 'police force of industrial England'.[181] By the time of the Luddite and other industrial disorders we are, of course, dealing with an economy, with a social structure, and above all with social prejudices unlike those that held sway for most of the eighteenth century: the standing army was now recognized as a necessity if social order was to be maintained, rather than as itself a grave threat to society. But the fact remains that, however tacitly, the army was the instrument of social coercion from the beginning of our period.

---

[179] WO 5/33, pp. 189–90.

[180] As Appendix A illustrates. It will also be noted there that cavalry was used more often than the foot in suppressing riots, as on some other police activities; mounted men on powerful horses could break up crowds and pursue and disperse fugitives much more easily than could the foot; they could do so moreover without having to open fire.

[181] Sir L. Radzinowicz, op. cit. iv. 115–24.

(e) THE COAST DUTY

Army operations against smugglers, since they were conducted only in assistance to magistrates or Revenue officers, should properly be considered as but one other variety of aid to the civil power. However, because of the great demands the 'coast duty' made upon the army's time, and the wide dispersal that the performance of the duty made necessary, we shall deal with it separately here.

We know that wherever there were coasts, there were smugglers; and we can safely assert that smuggling was one of the occupations that, next to agriculture, employed the greatest number of eighteenth-century Englishmen. In consequence, the army was kept very busy indeed. But beyond those bald assertions it is at present impossible to advance specific figures as to the real numbers of smugglers involved, the quantities of various goods run, the value of the 'trade', its fluctuations, or as to the efficiency of the preventive forces.[182] We are able, however, to detail the amount of time the army spent pursuing the smugglers and patrolling against them; and the amount of time so spent—indeed time wasted from the point of view of training—is quite staggering, as the figures in Appendix A illustrate.

Some description of the Revenue Service, and of the character (if not the volume) of smuggling, is thought necessary before we proceed. Smuggling and 'owling'[183] were ancient occupations; and the collection of duties had always, through English history, been the work of tax-farmers who bought the privilege from the Crown. Only as recently as 1671 had the collection of customs, and from 1683 the collection of excise, passed to the

---

[182] W. A. Cole, in his 'Trends in 18th-Century Smuggling', in W. E. Minchinton (ed.), *The Growth of English Overseas Trade in the Seventeenth and Eighteenth Centuries* (1969), 121–43, considers the major difficulties that the lack of statistics on smuggling present to the economic historian; and illustrates the sort of roundabout (not to say primitive) approaches necessary where such estimates (not to say guestimates) are to be arrived at. Hoh-Cheung and L. H. Mui, in their ' "Trends in Eighteenth-Century Smuggling" Reconsidered', in *Economic History Review*, 2nd Ser. 28 (1975), 28–43, conclude that Cole's technique is unworkable. Tea, wool, and brandy were the goods most frequently run; and testimony given to Parliamentary Committees indicates that at least as much tea and brandy was run as was lawfully imported. See C. Winslow, 'Sussex Smugglers', in D. Hay, P. Linebaugh, E. P. Thompson, et al. op. cit. 123–5 and *passim*.

[183] 'Owling' was, specifically, the illegal exportation of wool, so essential to the cloth industry, which had long been the staple of English trade, and which remained the single most important industry in Britain until well beyond our period.

newly created Revenue Service.[184] For the people living along the coasts this change was one of considerable importance, both economic and legal: for smuggling was widely felt to be a legitimate activity time out of mind and, in many coastal areas (Sussex, Kent, and Cornwall notably), it was important to the livelihood of the poor, a traditional and indeed a popularly esteemed calling.[185] Whereas for centuries past the rich smuggler-entrepreneurs with their hundreds of moonlighters, and the thousands of petty traffickers, middlemen, fences, and sailors, had had few qualms about dodging the private farmers and their employees, they were faced after the Restoration by Revenue men who were officers of the Crown. Old attitudes could hardly be expected to change overnight and, with smuggling and other forms of tax-evasion so common and ingrained a feature of life, a marked degree of hostility was shown to these new intruders from the central government.[186] The antagonism between the smugglers and the Revenue officers was greatly exacerbated by other developments concurrent with the creation of the Revenue Service. The tightening of mercantilist laws, the wars of William and Anne, the huge new standing forces, the general expansion of bureaucracy and of the trend towards the 'rationalisation' of administration—not to mention new and sophisticated methods of financing ever-increasing state expenditure, all these developments made the

[184] E. Hoon, *The Organization of the English Customs System, 1696–1786* (Newton Abbot, 1968), 6–7. E. Carson, *The Ancient and Rightful Customs* (1972), 49–61, outlines the organization of the Board, the Port of London's Revenue officials, and the officers in the Outports. See also H. Atton and H. Holland, *The King's Customs* (1908), esp. i. 102–445.

[185] For some good general notes on the social composition of the gangs, the economic importance of the trade, and the attitude with which it was viewed locally, see C. Winslow, *art. cit.* 149–60.

[186] E. Carson, op. cit. 56–61. This antagonism has been likened to a 'guerrilla war', and it was frequently bloody. The Customs Solicitor, in 1744, could describe the smugglers as 'a standing army of desperadoes, who must pay themselves'. Though the smugglers were often popular heroes, they were as often feared, since they supported their traffic by robbery and extortion and kept large areas intimidated. Where support or silence was not forthcoming, the big gangs survived by intimidation: thus in 1747 a notorious gang threatened to burn down Goudhurst in Kent and to kill the inhabitants; they were only driven off after a fire-fight with the local militia, called out by the gentry. Folkestone in 1744 was described by its Customs officer as being 'like a frontier town in a state of war'. Dover and Rye were visited by gangs who shot up the streets in broad daylight. C. Winslow, art. cit. 119–20, 123, 133.

need for efficient tax collection more urgent.[187] Thus, more
duties were levied on new sorts of goods between 1702 and 1714
than in all the years since the Restoration.[188] It was natural that
the young but growing standing army, the most voracious of the
new creatures of the expanding centralized state, should soon
be turned to supplying its own maw.

The smugglers, whose chief trade was across the Channel
with the French, across the North Sea with the Flemings and
the Dutch, and across the Irish Sea, faced three lines of defence
when closing the English coast. The first two lines were ineffective. The smugglers' boats—usually shallow-draught vessels, speedy, heavily armed—had first to evade the Revenue
cruisers (very few in number) or the occasional man-of-war
(fewer still, in peacetime). Next, they must unload their contraband along some beach, where the second line of defence was
run up against—the 'riding officers' of the Revenue Service,
each of whom patrolled a beat or stretch of the coast, alone save
for his horse and pistols. Since the smugglers went in gangs and
were usually well armed, and since the local country-people
were sure to be hostile, lone riding officers presented very little
threat. The last line of defence, both near the coast and in detachments inland, was the army. The smugglers' advantages
were their gang strength, the friendship or the silence of the
locals,[189] the great stretches of coast so thinly protected, the
connections of the big smuggler-entrepreneurs, the comparatively mild attitude of the courts and juries,[190] and perhaps most
importantly, the silence and surprise of their passing. It is quite
clear from all accounts that at night the coasts were wholly in
the hands of the smugglers, unless soldiers were present. The
Riding Officers, although appointed in ever-increasing num-

---

[187] See P. G. M. Dickson and J. Sperling, 'War Finance, 1689–1714', in *The New Cambridge Modern History*, vi (*The Rise of Great Britain and Russia, 1688–1725*), ed. J. S. Bromley) (Cambridge, 1970), 284–315. On the burgeoning Revenue bureaucracy, a field of lush rake-offs and rich patronage, see J. H. Plumb, *Political Stability*, 121–4, 127.

[188] E. Hoon, op. cit. 26.

[189] Turning 'evidence' was dangerous, in tight-knit communities; see H. Atton and H. Holland, op. cit. i. 212–16, for the grisly fate of an 'evidence' who saw too much at Poole, in 1747.

[190] The laws were draconian, but the courts seldom used their full rigour. See ibid. 102–405, *passim*, and P. Muskett, 'Military Operations Against Smugglers in Kent and Sussex, 1698–1750', *JSAHR* 52 (1974), *passim*.

bers by the Board of Customs from early in the century, were simply too few to deal with the gangs: as a local Customs overseer, the Collector at Weymouth, wrote to the Board in 1717, the smugglers 'are grown to such a head that they bidd deffiance to all Law and Government . . . [and] beat, knock down & abuse whoever they meet in their way soe that travelling by night neer the coast & the peace of the country are become very precarious'[191]—sentiments echoed repeatedly for the rest of the century.

The standing army being so recent a creation, and still the object of jealously and bitter attack, it only slowly took up a full-time role as the auxiliary of the Revenue Service. During the first three decades of the century the local Revenue officers at the Outports had more and more occasion to beg of their superiors on the Board increased numbers of riding officers and tidesmen, but even after substantial increases their numbers remained quite insufficient. The smugglers were too numerous, the quantity and value of the goods run too great. Lone riding officers, even when supported by two or three volunteers, could effect little against armed gangs.[192] For the gangs were not dealing with trifling quantities, and their own profits and investments were high, as random examples amply illustrate. Thus in October 1763 a gang loaded a ton of tea near Poole, and drove off the riding officers. In April 1766 a gang of forty men loaded 5,000 lb. of tea on to a fifty-horse pack-train, in broad daylight, near Exeter; the same gang had recently driven a train of thirty horses, loaded down with contraband, directly through the centre of Exeter city, bidding defiance to any Revenue men who came too near.[193] In 1731, over 54,000 lb. of tea and 123,000 gallons of brandy had been seized by the Revenue men in Suffolk, Essex, Kent, and Sussex; the quantity successfully run can be imagined.[194] In 1783 a Cawsand lugger of 300 tons, mounting twenty-six guns, was frequently landing goods between the Needles and Christchurch Head; in one night she landed 300 casks of spirits and over 10 tons of tea. A report from the Revenue officers at Cowes noted that a Folke-

[191] E. Carson, op. cit. 63–4.

[192] For such calls for reinforcements, see ibid. 63–4, 67–73, and P. Muskett, art. cit., *passim.*

[193] E. Carson, op. cit. 77, 80.

[194] P. Muskett, art. cit. 101. See also W. A. Cole, art. cit., *passim.*

stone vessel of about 270 tons and twenty-two guns, was frequenting the same area; the report continued, 'they carry about 60 to 80 men and each trip smuggle from 2000 to 3000 casks and 8 or 10 tons of tea. If they go to Guernsey they return once a fortnight, if to Dunquerque, once in three weeks.'[195] These ships were armed because their owners had been wise enough to take out letters of marque. These few examples should, then, illustrate the major investments, great profits, and numerous hands involved in the trade; meddling Revenue men were hardly well received.

Since the later seventeenth century the number of soldiers acting in assistance of the Revenue on the coast duty had been growing, very slowly, as the demands of the Revenue Service brought increasing pressure. By 1730 large numbers of troops were so employed; and by then also a large number of separate areas, in some cases corresponding to the duty areas noted earlier, were being regularly patrolled. This was a pattern which was to continue throughout the century.[196] The most heavily patrolled areas were six in number, each usually under the care of at least one regiment. These six areas were as follows:

1. The coasts of Cornwall and Devon, stretching from Bude Bay on St. George's Channel, round Land's End, and down the Channel coast to Lyme Regis and the Dorset border, were heavily trafficked by the smugglers. The particular stretches of those coasts most constantly patrolled by the army were those running from Port Isaac past Padstow to St. Ives; next, the stretch from Penzance down-Channel to East Looe; and finally the strip between the Great Mew Stone in Wembury Bay and the lesser Mew Stone off Dartmouth. Inland, detachments large and small were to be found everywhere, but Redruth, Helston, Tregony, St. Austell, Modbury, Kingsbridge, and Ottery St. Mary were most regularly employed as the headquarters of the detachments.

2. The Dorset and Hampshire coasts, notably about Weymouth, and from Poole to Lymington, were constantly patrolled, even though the shorter distances to be covered here

---

[195] E. Carson, op. cit. 82–3.

[196] These areas showed up in the plotting of troop movements and dispositions for Appendix A, where the method is explained.

made the duty less onerous than in Cornwall or elsewhere. Inland, the larger detachments were regularly to be found at Wimborne Minster, Ringwood, Bere Regis, Cerne Abbas, and Beaminster.

3. Every square foot of the Sussex coast had constantly to be patrolled. The whole coast, from Chichester to Rye, was frequented by the smugglers, and there were detachments far inland to choke off run goods. No particular section of the Sussex coast can be singled out, for the army was thick along the whole of it. Inland, places like West Dean, Petworth, Arundel, Storrington, Lewes, and Battle, quartered the largest detachments.

4. The Channel coast of Kent was almost as heavily patrolled as that of Sussex, notably in the Romney Marsh stretch between Lydd, Romney, and Folkestone. Although the Thames estuary was another major smuggling artery, the army was less active on the Kent shore than on the Essex side; Revenue cutters probably accounted for this, forcing some of the waterborne contraband trade heading for London to take to the less-peopled north shore.

5. Essex, like Cornwall, was a scene of considerable smuggling activity. The topography of inland Essex, like most of the rest of gently rolling East Anglia, made it an easy area for cavalry to patrol, easing the manpower required. Colchester or Ipswich was usually the headquarters of the cavalry regiment doing the coast duty in Essex, although Chelmsford was frequently used also. The whole of the Essex coast from the Crouch to the Stour was constantly patrolled; and detachments at Colchester, Witham, Braintree, Maldon, Chelmsford, and Billericay were all admirably placed to choke off some of the incoming traffic.

6. Norfolk and Suffolk were, like Essex, well sited for the reception of smuggling craft on their coasts, and were broad enough inland to make the movement of goods fairly safe. The flatness of the country suited it for cavalry. From Ipswich north all the way around the coast, past Lowestoft and Yarmouth to King's Lynn (and indeed as far as Boston across The Wash), the whole coast was used for smuggling. This was an immense area to patrol; and the detachments, consequently, tended to operate out of small and numerous posts rather than from the shore-

bases typical of Sussex. Thus Framlingham, Halesworth, Southwold, Beccles, Bungay, North Walsham, Holt, Walsingham, Lynn, Long Sutton, Holbeach, and Spalding, all served this purpose.

There were four other areas in which the army operated regularly against smugglers, but never so intensively as in those areas described above. The Welsh coast from Harlech to Aberystwyth was one such. Another was the stretch along the Solway Firth from Whitehaven to Carlisle, with detachments on the Isle of Man (that 'warehouse of Frauds', as the Whitehaven Customs men described it), after its sovereignty was re-vested in the Crown in 1765, to choke off this main entrepôt for run Irish goods. Lastly, the troops were deployed along two stretches of the North Sea coast: the first running from the Humber to about the Tees, an area seeing but little illicit traffic, and patrolled from York city; and the second, just north of Berwick along the Berwickshire and East Lothian coasts, where the patrols were directed by the GOC North Britain.

The detachments frequently, in all of these areas, had to fight regular little actions with the armed gangs; and upon occasion their French and Irish confrères had likewise to be driven back to their boats. Violence was the rule. Typical was the report made by the Customs officers at Fowey who, in the spring of 1766, reported it worth their lives to interfere with the smugglers—'one Gang having lately consisted of thirty six and another of twenty eight Men with each a Horse Load of Tea or Brandy, and that two of the said Officers in assisting the Officers of Excise at St. Austle and Mevagizey, had lately an Engagement with Six of these Ruffians, and were all much beaten and bruised with Sticks and Stones.' Intelligence had been received furthermore, 'that the said Smugglers carry Fire Arms, and have given out Threats, that if ever they meet with any of H.M.'s Officers, they would kill them'; troops were needed immediately so that 'a Stop' might be 'put to these daring Fellows', and so elements of the 4th Foot were dispatched to their aid.[197] Nor was the army always victorious: one night in December 1740 Thomas Carswell, the riding officer at Hastings, together with four troopers of the 2nd Dragoons, impounded a ton of smuggled tea discovered by

[197] WO 5/54, pp. 169–70.

them in a barn. They loaded the tea in a wagon and set off, but were pursued by twenty men, mounted and armed.

Carswell pulled up, and warned this gang to keep off on pain of being shot. They told him to "fire and be damned" and the dragoons got off a volley. "On which their horses whirled round a little to the left, and the gang pushing in nearer, discharged a great many blunderbusses and other firearms, by which Mr. Carswell was shot dead, Corporal Finlater received eleven bullets or slugs in his head, shoulder, elbow, and right side of his back, and James Crabtree received a ball in his right arm. Thereupon the smugglers rushed in and seized the dragoons arms and confined them prisoners and made the dragoons turn round with the tea and carry the same back to the Bull ale house at Hurst Green".[198]

Actions like the above, although they must generally have gone in favour of the army, were typical occurrences on the coast duty.

Save for the more rugged Devon and Cornwall, cavalry was more often employed on the coast duty than was foot, because of their superior mobility. But cavalry could be scarce in wartime, and then other measures had to be adopted. In 1744 for example, three of the under-strength regiments of Marines were ordered to aid the riding officers in the Romney Marsh—provoking a Revenue officer to write that 'I do not know how to proceed, considering they are foot soldiers and therefore not of that service to the officers in the customs as dragoons would be'.[199] It was also the practice to distribute the soldiers in tiny detachments all along the coast, backed up by somewhat larger detachments farther inland to pinch off the trade that the advanced posts missed. General Henry Hawley objected to this method of deployment as early as the 1740s, and called for the establishment of inland quarters near the waterways and other frequented routes; his plan would have reduced the dispersal to which the corps on the coast duty were subject, but it was not implemented.[200]

How very widely dispersed a regiment on the coast duty usually was, is easily illustrated. In May 1739 some 263

[198] P. Muskett, art. cit. 105–6, quoting the Crown Brief on the case. There are several other accounts of these encounters in this article.

[199] Ibid. 107. Perhaps authority considered their amphibious character a qualification for duty in the marshes.

[200] Ibid. 108–10.

officers and men (three-quarters of the regiment) belonging to the 4th Dragoons were distributed among forty-two towns and villages in Norfolk and Suffolk, averaging six soldiers in each place. The 4th was thus dispersed utterly—and they remained like this for more than a year.[201] In October 1753 half of the 1st Dragoons were distributed among fifteen Norfolk and Suffolk villages, while the rest were quartered a very considerable distance apart at Colchester and Norwich. The 1st remained dispersed, in these quarters, for a year.[202] In May 1766 the Scots Greys took up coast duty quarters in Sussex. Their quarters and distribution were typical (see Map 3). Two troops were headquartered at Lewes, from which place detachments were sent out as follows: thirty-four troopers to patrol about Lewes, four to Shoreham by Sea, six to Brighthelmstone, two to Rottingdean, and four to Newhaven. Similarly, two troops were headquartered at Chichester, from where the following detachments were sent out: twenty-six troopers to act about Chichester, eight to Arundel, ten to Havant, four to Angmering, and two to Ferring. The fifth troop was headquartered at Hastings, and of its men seven remained there, two went to Winchelsea, eight to Rye, four to Battle, and four to Wadhurst. The last troop was disposed at Eastbourne and Pevensey, with fifteen men between those two places, six at Bexhill, and four at Seaford.[203] These figures refer only to troopers; and since in 1766 there were twenty-eight troopers on the strength of a troop of Dragoons,[204] the Greys were in consequence totally dispersed by these postings, stretched in penny-packets over 80 miles of coast. The corps remained so disposed for a year; and it must be stressed that this example, like the others given here, is absolutely typical. The effects of such dispersal need hardly be pointed out. The effects of even longer periods of coast duty can be imagined. The 3rd Dragoons were on the coast duty, similarly dispersed, from October of 1751 until May of 1756 continuously. During one part of that period, in May 1753, three troops headquartered at Colchester had detachments on patrol in Essex and Suffolk, while the other three troops were doing the coast duty in Kent! Nor was this sort of dispersal, on both sides of the Thames estuary, irregular. From October 1754

[201] WO 5/33, pp. 241–2.   [202] WO 5/41, pp. 514–15.
[203] WO 5/54, pp. 187–9.   [204] WO 24/434.

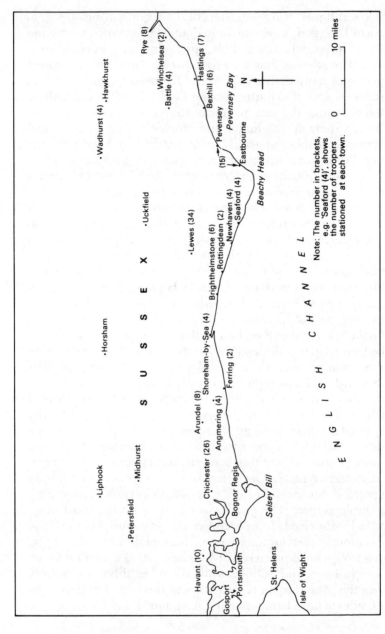

Map 3. The Coast Duty. Anti-Smuggling Dispositions of the 2nd Dragoons, Summer 1766–Summer 1767.

to May 1755, the regiment was strewn all the way from Winchelsea to (and including) the Isle of Wight.[205] The 6th Dragoons in 1751, meanwhile, had three troops based on Colchester operating against the smugglers, while the other three were in Kent; and the 6th was dispersed upon the coast duty until 1754. The 6th Dragoons served in Essex and Kent in 1751, in Kent and Sussex in 1752, in Sussex and Dorset in 1753, and in Dorset in 1754—all the while on the coast duty.[206]

Such was the most common duty of half of the cavalry in the eighteenth-century British Army. The other half, in Ireland and Scotland, seems to have been similarly engaged. In 1776, when much of the army had been sent to America, the Duke of Argyll as GOC North Britain wrote to the government to point out that there were no more than 600 soldiers left under his command; 'The revenue will suffer very considerably', wrote the Duke, 'for want of military assistance, so frequently called for by the officers of customs and excise.'[207] In Ireland, one of the 'curses' of duty was 'the requirement for patrolling remote coasts and deserted boglands for smugglers and lawbreakers. This meant long and tedious isolation for small bodies of troops.' We know that the 8th Horse was constantly employed on such duties;[208] and the Inspection Returns show that patrols against smugglers remained a constant feature of Irish duty throughout the century. The dispersal and patrol pattern in Scotland and Ireland was probably similar to that in England.

Having discussed the use of the army in aid of the civil power, and particularly upon the coast duty, we shall conclude with a detailed and representative account of such operations in one of our duty areas, namely Cornwall and south Devon, during the course of one of the series of years selected for study in Appendix A.

In May 1736 Montague's 11th of Foot marched from Worcester to Exeter, to take up the duty of Cornwall and south Devon. Upon arrival at Exeter, 150 men were detached and quartered in Cornwall as follows: twenty-two at Penzance,

---

[205] WO 5/41, pp. 54–5 and *passim*, to WO 5/43, p. 214.
[206] WO 5/40, p. 413 and *passim*, to WO 5/42, p. 157.
[207] J. Brooke, op. cit. 310. On the Revenue Service and Scotland, see H. Atton and H. Holland, op. cit. 154–202, and E. Carson, op. cit. 118–28.
[208] Rex Whitworth, op. cit. 41–5.

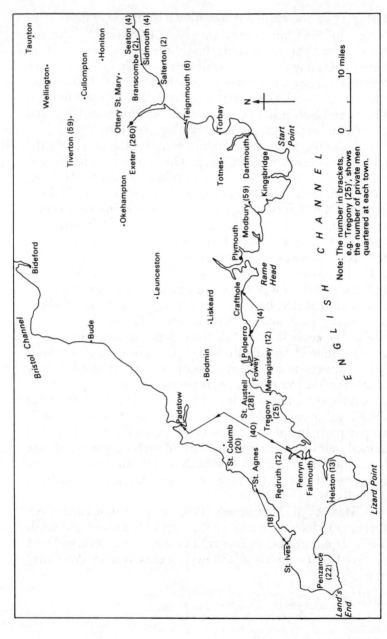

Map 4.   Distribution and Dispersal. Dispositions of the Private Men of Handasyde's 16th of Foot in the Cornwall and South Devon Duty Area, July 1738–June 1740.

thirteen at Helston, twelve at Redruth, eighteen at St. Ives and St. Agnes, twenty at St. Columb, twenty-five at Tregony, twelve at Mevagissey, and twenty-eight at St. Austell. These detachments, representing about one-quarter of the strength of the regiment, were to act in aid of the local authorities in suppressing any smuggling or riotous disturbances, should these occur, and when called upon to do so; and they were to be relieved occasionally by like detachments from Exeter.[209] The regiment remained distributed thus until May of 1737, when riots being apprehended along the east Dorset coast, a detachment equal in strength to two companies had to be sent to Poole and Wimborne Minster, from Exeter. This detachment was not recalled until the end of June, so that for over a month Montague's was strung out from Penzance to Poole, a good 175 miles.[210] Then in September 1737, the Secretary having received intelligence that 'very great Riots & Disorders have been committed at Penryn in Cornwall by the Tinners'—this hard upon news from the Mayor of Falmouth that the tinners there were about 'to rise in a tumultuous manner & to go to Falmouth where they Threatned to commit great Outrages'—the whole of the regiment still remaining at Exeter set out for Penryn, Falmouth, and Padstow, to suppress the tinners there and anywhere else in Cornwall where the civil power might call for their assistance. In mid-October this task had been accomplished, and the troops lately marched from Exeter (save for a detachment of about forty men left to watch Penryn, Padstow, and Falmouth), returned to that city. There were now some 200 men of Montague's detached in Cornwall, a third of the regiment.[211] The winter was quiet, but late in March and early in April 1738 a company-size detachment had to be sent from Exeter to Modbury, to 'preserve the Ships & Cargos belonging to the Merchants from being plundered by the Populace', and another had to be sent to Tiverton where riots were apprehended. By May, however, all these detachments were being called in to Exeter, as they were replaced by the new regiment now coming in to take up the duty of the area; and early in July 1738 Montague's set off for Scotland, there to take up new quarters.[212]

---

[209] WO 5/32, pp. 257, 405–6.
[211] WO 5/32, pp. 495–7, 505.

[210] WO 5/32, pp. 444, 453, 459–60.
[212] WO 5/33, pp. 48, 60, 97–8, 109, 114–15.

Montague's 11th was replaced by Handasyde's 16th of Foot, which had come down from Berwick and had been doing duty at Bristol (with detachments in Wales) since August of 1737. Early in May 1738 Handasyde's had sent from Bristol 150 men to replace the detachments of Montague's still in the nine places in Cornwall first quartered by that corps, together with another forty men to replace those of Montague's watching the tinners at Penryn, Padstow, and Falmouth. A further detachment, equal to a company, replaced Montague's men at Modbury, where the populace was still restive, and yet another detachment of company size took over the policing of Tiverton. Then early in July the remainder of Handasyde's 16th marched from Bristol and installed itself in the quarters vacated by Montague's 11th, at Exeter.[213] It would seem that the Devon smugglers had grown more bold of late, for soon after their arrival at Exeter small detachments had to be settled in at Seaton, Branscombe, Sidmouth, Salterton, and Teignmouth.[214] So Handasyde's remained until January of 1740, with half of its strength dispersed upon the coast duty, and overawing the disorderly. In that month (war having been declared against Spain in October 1739) approximately half of the regiment was drafted and turned over to Moreton's 6th Marines, then raising in Somerset.[215] In June Handasyde's concentrated at Exeter and, like Montague's before them, set off for new quarters.

Meanwhile, the war with Spain had brought about the transfer of units from the Irish to the British establishment. Eight regiments of foot landed in England in 1739, five of them at Bristol in the summer—no doubt to the momentary terror of the tinners and owlers. One of these, Onslow's 8th of Foot, had been quartered in various Somerset towns since its landing, recruiting up to the British establishment strength; and in May of 1740 it sent over 200 of its men to replace all the detachments of Handasyde's in Devon and Cornwall. Late in June, the remainder of the regiment marched to Exeter and replaced the departing 16th. Like its two predecessors, Onslow's was already busy with the coast duty, and was soon to be caught up

---

[213] WO 5/33, pp. 91–9, 108, 110, 129.
[214] WO 5/33, pp. 138–9.
[215] WO 5/33, pp. 418, 420.

in major grain riots.[216] Onslow's 8th of Foot remained on the Cornwall and south-Devon duty, disposed as its predecessors had been, until it too was replaced in its turn in May of 1742.[217]

Altogether then, the amount of time spent by the army in the actual suppression of riot and disorder, and in operations against smugglers, was considerable. In England, where the surviving records are sufficient to permit accurate calculations, the foot spent 3 per cent of its time on these duties during the period 1726–9, 13 per cent of its time during the period 1737–43, 12 per cent during the years 1751–6, 14 per cent during the years 1764–7, 10 per cent during the years 1772–6, and 8 per cent during the period 1786–90. During the same periods, respectively, the cavalry devoted 1, 11, 26, 17, 13, and 27 per cent of its time to these duties.[218] Some corps in particular were very heavily involved. Thus the 45th Foot spent 43 per cent of the full year following March 1741 on the coast duty, and the 4th Dragoons had to devote 29 per cent of their time to patrols against smugglers between April 1739 and June 1742. Between August 1751 and April 1753 the 4th Foot spent half of its time on these duties, as did the 14th Foot between April 1751 and April 1752. The 3rd Dragoons spent 52 per cent of their time, 1751–6, operating against smugglers. Later in the century, the 2nd Dragoon Guards spent 38 per cent of their time from late 1764 to early 1767 on these duties. The 3rd Foot spent 35 per cent of its time, 1772–5, on vigorous police activity, while the 1st Dragoon Guards likewise lost 22 per cent of their time between 1773 and 1776. The 38th Foot spent 25 per cent of its time chasing smugglers between 1786 and 1789. The 3rd Dragoons, the 4th Dragoons, and the 11th Light Dragoons each lost 33 per cent of their time during the period 1786–90 on these duties, and the 10th Light Dragoons spent 37 per cent of their time operating against smugglers between March 1786 and May 1790.

These figures do not tell the whole story; for as we noted earlier, it is clear that the wide dispersal of individual regiments was partly the result of the need to maintain a passive police presence.[219] As Appendix A illustrates, there were very few

[216] WO 5/34, pp. 80–1, 85–6, 126–8, 227–8.

[217] WO 5/35, pp. 219–20.

[218] See Appendix A for these (and similar) figures.

[219] T. Hayter, op. cit. 23–4, reproduces an interesting exchange of letters between the Secretary at War and the Quartermaster-General, on this subject in Britain generally.

regiments of foot that spent so much as a third of their time fully concentrated and stationary; and among the horse few spent as much as one-tenth of their time concentrated and stationary.

(f) DISPERSAL AND TACTICAL ORGANIZATION

The movements and dispositions of the peacetime army are of the utmost significance, since at the conclusion of every movement the regiments, as we have seen, were likely to be dispersed. We need to define the term 'dispersal' as it is used here in our analysis of training; and must therefore describe the several relevant 'divisions' into which the regiment was normally broken for administrative and tactical purposes. We shall consider the infantry first, then the cavalry.

Firing and manoeuvring were, of course, the two essentials of tactical training; both were performed in a variety of ways and by units of various sizes. The basics of both firing and manoeuvring—namely elementary discipline, carriage, individual loading and firing (the 'manual exercise'), firing at targets, firing in unison with other men in rank and file upon command (the 'platoon exercise'), riding, swordsmanship, marching in proper pace and cadence, and bayonet drill—could be taught to the smallest handful of men. A few files were sufficient even for the practice of the platoon exercise. Given a dutiful NCO, these simple skills—merely the 'first Rudiments or Ground Work of a Soldier', as Lt.-Col. John LaFaussille described them[220]—could be practised endlessly with profit by the smallest of detachments; and the soldiers' proficiency at these basics was little affected by dispersal. If tactical training of any greater complexity was to be attempted, however, certain proportions of the battalion had to be concentrated; and naturally, the more men concentrated, the more advanced could be the level of training.

The regiment was, strictly speaking, an administrative unit; shorn of its staff and with its administrative subdivisions temporarily ignored, it assumed its tactical aspect and was drawn up as a 'battalion' with various tactical subdivisions. The regiment was made up of only one type of administrative unit—the company—and during the century the number of companies

[220] Cumb. Pprs, Pt 4, II, fo. 3.

per regiment varied between eight, nine, ten, and twelve, according to the vagaries of finance and voted establishments. One of these companies was always composed of grenadiers and (during the Seven Years War in the Americas, and again permanently after 1771–2), another was a light company; while the rest were the regular 'battalion-companies' whose men, in their simple tricornes, were usually referred to as 'hatmen' to distinguish them from the grenadiers and light in-fantrymen and to avoid clumsy terms like 'battalion-company men'. In peacetime the battalion was the largest independent unit in which tactical training was conducted (brigades, lines, and wings were *ad hoc* formations, very seldom formed during peacetime and operating only under the command of general officers); and virtually all eighteenth-century tactical theory, training schemes, and regulations were based on the battalion —notably so in the British Army, where such professional and expensive goings-on as the great annual manoeuvres of the Prussian Army or the formation of vast camps of exercise, as in the French Army, were almost unheard of.

Although there were several different tactical divisions into which the battalion might be divided, it was the 'grand-division' and the 'platoon' that were most important during the century; and since the grand-division was the largest commonly used tactical unit below the level of the full battalion itself, it was, from the earlier decades of the century, the most important unit in the battalion so far as advanced training and tactics were concerned.[221] Hence it is the ideal unit by which dispersal can be measured.

The solid core of soldiers making up the bulk of the regiment were the hatmen of the battalion-companies. Although the whole regiment deployed together in battalion, the grenadier company (and later the light company too) usually played a more individual tactical role than did the battalion-companies, covering and supporting the solid line of hatmen rather than wholly blending with them or conforming with their every

---

[221] The practice of training and fighting in four grand-divisions began to be widely adopted in the army during the War of the Spanish Succession (the drill used in the regiments in Flanders, by 1708, will be found in a MS book in the Cornwall RO, DD.R.H.388, discussed here on p. 176–7; and it had become standard practice by the 1720s, as is clear from all succeeding treatises, regulations, orders, and inspection reports, etc.—dealt with at length in Ch. III.

manoeuvre. Indeed it was a very common practice, on campaign, to detach these flank companies from their parent regiments and to form them into élite provisional grenadier and light battalions.[222] Thus when we consider the size of the grand-division, the grenadiers (and later the light infantrymen) may be ignored.

The grand-division was always composed of one-quarter of the hatmen: a battalion deployed in line always formed four grand-divisions which often served as fire-units and, much more commonly, as manoeuvre-units.[223] Within each of the grand-divisions the hatmen were told off into a varying number (two to four) of platoons; and although the platoons on occasion might act as manoeuvre-units it was most common for them simply to deliver fire. The number of platoons into which a grand-division was divided was determined, before the *1764 Regulations*, by the number of hatmen available; thus Lt.-Col. Humphrey Bland, writing in 1727, observed that a platoon was seldom composed of less than thirty men (the fire of fewer men would have been inconsequential), or of more than forty-eight men (it was not at that time thought possible for an officer to control effectively the fire of a larger body).[224] After 1764 the grand-divisions were simply chopped in half, each half acting both as a fire-unit and as a manoeuvre-unit. Since the regimental establishments varied, it was almost never the case before 1764 that the administrative unit (the company) and the tactical unit (the platoon) coincided; platoons were almost invariably smaller than companies. The officers and men of the companies, consequently, divided themselves between the platoons, and usually the most senior captain took command of each grand-division. After 1764 it was generally (but not always) the case that the company and the smallest fire-unit—the halves of the grand-divisions—coincided.

[222] First formed in the British Army in Flanders in 1742. 'The Observations His Majesty makes of the Grenadiers being so often separated from their Corps is very just,' wrote Lt.-Gen. Jasper Clayton in March 1743, 'and not formerly practised in the British Troops, and may be attended by the consequences of not being in the same good Order when joyn'd again to their Corps for want of propper inspection by their Feild Officers.' BL Add. MS 22, 537, fo. 228.

[223] The reader is referred to the figures on pp. 318–21, where the several tactical subdivisions into which the battalion was told off, as described here, are shown in diagram form.

[224] Humphrey Bland, *Treatise of Military Discipline* (1743), 66.

The platoons in the grand-divisions were small, easy (it was supposed) for the officers to control in the noise and confusion of battle. However, there was an added complication which, until 1764, increased considerably the difficulties for all concerned. Before that year the many platoons in the battalion line were organized not only in the four grand-divisions, which were essentially manouevre-units, but also into three 'Firings' (so called because all the platoons in one Firing fired at once). The platoons making up a Firing were not contiguous, but rather were scattered all down the battalion line. The three Firings, therefore, did not correspond with the four grand-divisions. After 1764 the system of Firings was abolished in favour of less complex and more flexible arrangements, although the new system too required constant practice if it was to be carried out.

It followed, therefore, that a concentration in peacetime of a part of the regiment sufficient to form a grand-division (generally two or three companies, depending upon establishments), made possible more advanced training than any single company could practise. It also followed that, before 1764, a single grand-division was not by any means a unit large enough with which to practise, with any worthwhile degree of realism, the various complicated methods of giving fire—not to mention the advanced manoeuvres; plenty of officers and NCOs were needed to conduct platoon fire, and there were too few of these available in a single grand-division to simulate platoon fire. Two grand-divisions was the lowest level of concentration at which sufficient numbers of officers were likely to be available to form three scratch Firings. After 1764 and the demise of the system of three Firings, the new 'alternate fire' which replaced it, although simpler, required in its way too that two grand-divisions be present for realistic training; and the increasing complexity of battalion manoeuvres taught after the mid-century placed new emphasis upon concentration. We have, therefore, an excellent basis for a definition of 'dispersal': where there are too few companies gathered together in one place to form two grand-divisions, they may be said to be dispersed. 'Concentration', on the other hand, occurs in three ascending stages: at the level of two grand-divisions, of three, and of four. Since the battalion almost always fought as a unit, and since it was for the full battalion that tactical theory and drill regulations were scored, training at the level of four grand-divisions was of course the most valuable training experience a regiment could enjoy. The presence of the flank company (or companies) would also add to the realism of the experience. Three grand-divisions would be that much less effective in simulating the condition of the battalion on the battlefield. Two would only barely suffice.

We must also add the obvious proviso that any concentration of companies sufficient to form two or more grand-divisions must, if they are to be considered as capable of carrying on tactical training, be stationary. A regiment spent a good deal of time strung out along the roads, simply marching from one set of billets to another. As we have seen, regiments of foot marched in three or four sections, each one a day's distance from the next. A marching regiment was therefore fully occupied in covering ground, and was quite dispersed while doing so.

Whereas the infantry regiment formed in battalion for tactical purposes, the cavalry regiment (which we shall now turn to briefly, the general rules advanced for the estimation of concentration and dispersal applying equally well here) normally formed two or three squadrons, depending upon the number of troops composing the regiment and—to a degree unknown in the infantry, which manoeuvred much more slowly—upon the immediate tactical situation. It is however clear that in wartime, after Marlborough's campaigns, the British cavalry regiment generally operated in three squadrons, and in peacetime too a full regiment practised most often in three squadrons.[225] As with the foot, basic skills could be learned by small detachments; but the troops had to concentrate at the level of one, two, or three squadrons if the more intricate and important manoeuvres were to be learned both by the men and by the horses. (The fact that both horses and men had to be trained added a

---

[225] Throughout the century the Horse and Dragoon regiments trained and fought in three squadrons or, much less commonly, in two: e.g. the British Dragoon regiments in Flanders commonly formed in three squadrons, 1742–8 (Kent RO Amherst MS 05/4); and Lt.-Gen. Henry Hawley, an old and experienced cavalryman, based his MS 'Plans of Evolution . . . for Squadrons', submitted to the Duke of Cumberland *c.* 1750 on three squadrons (BL King's MS 239). Three squadrons was the standard disposition, as is clear from all the treatises, regulations, orders, inspection returns, etc.— as described at length in Ch. III.

dimension not to be found in the infantry's training, of course.)
Cavalry had also to be very intensively trained because, once
set in motion, it was difficult to recall and could soon become
dispersed. The squadron in the cavalry regiment, then, can be
taken to correspond with the foot's grand-division, since it
stood in about the same relation to the cavalry regiment as a
training and tactical unit as did the grand-division in the infantry battalion. Dispersal in the cavalry occurred, therefore,
when there were fewer troops gathered together and stationary
than were necessary to form one squadron out of the three most
commonly formed by a regiment. Concentration, on the other
hand, occurs in three ascending stages: at the levels of one, two,
and three squadrons. Just as with the foot, training was more
sophisticated and effective the greater the number of squadrons
concentrated.

We have throughout this chapter been attempting to account
for the too little time that regiments spent in concentration;
and we have noted here (as we shall do elsewhere) the ill
effects on training and overall efficiency that dispersal and pre-
occupation with civil police activities produced. Dispersed
about the Empire, dispersed when arrived upon foreign stations, dispersed upon the coast duty, dispersed either in active
assistance to the civil power or in the maintenance of a police
presence, strung out upon the march, ill housed, and often
wretchedly cared for, the army in general knew that any opportunity for advanced training in peacetime was a luxury.
But of course the central authorities (specifically the King, the
Commander-in-Chief, the Board of General Officers, the
Adjutant-General, and the Quartermaster-General) and the
commanding officers actually with the corps were fully aware
that training had to progress. What was possible, however, was
of the most limited nature. When in May 1728 the lieutenant-
colonel of Harrison's 15th of Foot was given leave by the War
Office to march his six companies at Ringwood, Romsey,
Bishops Waltham, Alton, Fareham, and Chichester, 'to Relieve [the six] at Winchester & Southampton, as often as You
shall see Occassion, for the better Conveniency of Disciplining
the Men),[226] this was an exceedingly unusual indulgence.

[226] WO 5/28, pp. 43–5, 114.

Harrison's had just taken up these Hampshire quarters after spending almost two grinding years dispersed on the Cornwall and south-Devon duty; and fifteen days after receiving these orders the regiment marched to concentrate at Lewisham, Eltham, Peckham, Camberwell, and Deptford, where it had another two weeks to train in preparation for a review upon Blackheath by George II.[227] This was little enough, considering the duty on which the corps had been employed for the past two years, and considering also that the training now permitted them, in concentration, was against their being seen by the King. Late in June 1742 the three troops of the 6th Dragoons quartered at Market Harborough, Kettering, and Welling-borough were ordered to join the other three at Northampton, 'there to remain, in order for the whole Regiment to be several Times exercised.' They were allowed 'there to remain' for all of four days, before being broken up again; and this concentra-tion, too, was in favour of a coming royal review at Hampton Court.[228] The regiment had spent most of the past year dis-persed in England and in Scotland. In October 1786, more reasonably, the two companies of the 23rd Foot detached at Sunderland were ordered to be rotated with two from the regiment then lying at Tynemouth Barracks—'the said Com-panies to be relieved . . . as often as you shall judge proper for equalizing the Discipline of the Regimt.'[229]

Even less-favoured treatment was shown to some corps, al-though it was better than none at all. In April 1742, some 120 new recruits belonging to Handasyde's 16th of Foot (the 16th had lost half of its men as drafts for the 1740 Cartagena ex-pedition) were to march from 'their respective quarters of their respective companies' (i.e. two companies at Nantwich, one each at Macclesfield, Congleton, Liverpool, Bolton, and Lancaster, two at Manchester, and one distributed between Northwich, Middlewich, and Moulton) to Manchester, there to be dis-ciplined together before being returned to their companies. On 14 July 1755 two dismounted men from each troop of the 11th Dragoons were ordered sent to Faversham 'in Order to attend the Drills'; they were to be rotated frequently with other men

---

[227] WO 5/28, pp. 130–3, 145, 150.   [228] WO 5/35, p. 385, 391–5.
[229] WO 5/66, p. 296.   [230] WO 5/35, pp. 35, 39–41, 73, 192.

from their troops, so that the whole might learn the new manual and platoon exercises authorized that year by the Duke of Cumberland. The reason for training in such small detachments was that the 11th was then busily employed on the Kent coast duty, widely dispersed with troops at Faversham, Sittingbourne, and Ashford, and with single troops divided between Sandwich and Deal, Margate and Ramsgate, Folkestone and Hythe.[231] The corporals of The Blues, in April 1765, were likewise assembled in St. Albans and there taught the new manual and platoon exercises, issued late in 1764; once trained, they could return to the regiment and instruct their men in this drill.[232] But this was all little enough, and rare.

The situation may have been slightly better in Scotland, at least during the weeks preceding the springtime reviews of the regiments. On 11 March 1756 the GOC North Britain, Lt.-Gen. Humphrey Bland, wrote as follows to the Secretary:

> As the weather is now very favourable, and that the Season Approaches for assembling the Regiments in North Britain at their Respective Head Quarters for Exercise, I must desire Your Lordship will be so good as to Honour me with His Royal Highness's Pleasure on this Head, as I think, considering the Number of Recruits and young men in the Several Corps here, the sooner the Regiments can be assembled as above, it will be so much the better.[233]

Bland's letter refers only to the assembling of corps for drill before their spring reviews. The circumstances affecting training that year were, in any event, extraordinary: Bland was a noted tactician, Cumberland was C.-in-C. and devoted to perfecting the army's discipline, and a new manual and platoon had just been issued—and war was about to be declared by France. There were in Scotland, at the time of Bland's writing, the 2nd Dragoon Guards and 7th Dragoons, together with Yorke's 9th, Folliott's 18th, Beauclerk's 19th, Holmes' 31st, and Leighton's 32nd of Foot; and they were, wrote Bland, in a 'dispersed Situation, the Cantonments of each Regiment as now occupied being Fifty or more miles in Extent'. All of which is to say that the army in Scotland was in the same situation as

---

[231] WO 5/42, pp. 336, 354.

[232] WO 5/53, p. 238. The Blues being a regiment of Horse, they had no sergeants but 'Corporals of Horse' instead.

[233] Cumb. Pprs, Box 46, no. 183.

that in England, most of Ireland, and the Americas.

The effects of lengthy dispersal, and of duties not related to the purely military role of the army, are made apparent in the reports submitted by the reviewing general officers who saw each of the corps annually. We need mention only a few examples here, as many others will be noted in due course in the following chapters. Thus, in November 1754, Lt.-Gen. James Cholmondeley reviewed Howard's 3rd of Foot, part of which was at Berwick and the rest at Newcastle. The 3rd's timing was very poor in its platoon exercise and firings, and it marched and manoeuvred badly, this in spite of the fact that more than three-quarters of the 686 rank and file had seen at least five years' service. Wrote Cholmondeley, 'Upon Observing their Faults, I was told that the Regiment had been Working at the Roads all Summer.'[234] A year later, in October 1755, Maj.-Gen. James Stuart saw Folliott's 18th of Foot, likewise dispersed between Berwick, Newcastle, and Carlisle. The regiment was neither perfect in its drill nor fit for service, since most of its men were relatively new recruits, many of the officers and NCOs were away recruiting, and 'the companies being separated in different Garrisons'.[235] In June 1775 the 28th Foot was reviewed at Limerick, where it was found to be ill disciplined. The commanding officer 'mentioned a variety of circumstances that hurt the appearance of the Regiment.—It had been lately Separated and so harrassed guarding wrecks and attending custom house Officers, that 10 Men could not be got together in the Spring for Exercise.'[236]

The exigencies of peace—notably the need for police activity, the lack of barracks and of sizeable quarters, and the peculiar rotation patterns—all combined to reduce severely the training-time available to the peacetime army. Other factors, often petty in themselves, but (where they affected individual corps) cumulatively quite significant, exercised a further baneful influence, as we shall see below.

[234] WO 27/3.
[235] WO 27/4. The 18th had landed early in April at Liverpool from Ireland, and had since been recruiting up to the strength of foot on the British establishment. WO 5/42, pp. 257, 269.
[236] WO 27/35.

Chapter II

The Condition of the Corps: Men and Arms

(a) OFFICERS

From the 1718 reductions until the major war augmentations of 1739–40, there were normally in the British Army some 500 regimental officers serving with the horse and 1,450 with the foot, for a total of 1,950.[1] Periodic crises during the long Walpole–Fleury peace saw the total number of officers go as high as 2,250, but 1,950 was the normal figure during these years. This number was to increase steadily as the century progressed, and spectacularly so in wartime. At the height of the 1739–48 war there were over 500 officers with the horse, 2,100 with the foot and nearly 400 with the marines, totalling some 3,000 officers. The army from Aix-la-Chapelle until the new 1755 augmentations consisted of over 450 officers with the horse and nearly 1,650 with the foot, all told 2,100; and by the height of the Seven Years War these figures had swollen to 600 cavalry officers and nearly 4,000 infantry officers, for a total of nearly 4,600—the largest number ever to serve at one time before 1795. From the 1763 reductions until the augmentations of 1771 there were nearly 550 officers serving with the horse and over 2,000 with the foot, for a total of 2,600; and from 1771 until 1776 another 200 infantry officers raised the total to 2,800. By the height of the 1775–83 war there were some 400 officers serving with the horse and nearly 3,700 with the foot, for nearly 4,100 all told; and from the mid-1780s until the opening of the war against Revolutionary France in 1793 there were, finally, more than 550 officers with the horse and nearly 2,400 with the foot, for a total of more than 2,900.

---

[1] These figures—taken mostly from the establishments in WO 24, and from the *Army Lists*—include all officers below the rank of proprietary colonel, i.e. all the officers normally serving with the regiments. Only officers with the horse and foot, both Guards and Line, are included, as are officers of Marines during the 1740s when those units were still counted part of the army; otherwise, officers with the Independent Companies, Marine Companies, on the half-pay list and, of course, those serving in the Ordnance corps, are excluded. Our figures encompass, therefore, almost all the officers below general rank serving in the army proper, as then understood.

According to the most informed estimate some two-thirds of the commissions held in the British Army at any one time were had by purchase, the remainder having been obtained by a variety of non-purchase methods.[2] The workings of this system of promotion are well-enough understood, and we need do no more here than provide a sketch;[3] it is with the results of the system as reflected in the career patterns of the officers, and only incidentally with its social and political origins and significance, that we need especially to deal.

The first two Georges disliked the buying and selling of commissions; the practice however was already customary at the time of the Hanoverian succession and it had created a huge vested interest, so that George I and his son were obliged to regulate what they could not abolish. This they did with some success: Royal Warrants of 1720 and 1722 fixed prices of all commissions,[4] obliged an officer to sell only to another officer holding the rank immediately below his own, and retained for the Crown the right of selecting and approving an officer's successor.

All commissions from colonelcies downwards were subject to purchase; general rank alone was attained strictly by seniority or merit.[5] A young man bought his ensigncy or cornetcy and then, as vacancies appeared, bought his way up the ladder. Purchase vacancies appeared when an officer retired, sold out, or transferred into another regiment. When he did so he received the regulated price of his commission from government, and in addition (since commissions were desirable and so

[2] J. H. Bassett, 'The Purchase System in the British Army, 1660–1871', unpubl. Boston University Ph.D. thesis, 1969, 40. By 1810 in the bigger wartime army, as many as four-fifths of all commissions were had by non-purchase methods (mostly through vacancies filled by seniority). M. Glover, *Wellington's Army in the Peninsula, 1808–1814* (Newton Abbot, 1977), 82–9.

[3] For a fine account which illustrates in detail the many subtleties involved in eighteenth-century promotion, which we cannot enter into here, see I. F. Burton and A. N. Newman, 'Sir John Cope: Promotion in the Eighteenth-Century Army', *English Historical Review*, 78 (1963), 655–68. Very useful too is M. Glover, op. cit. 76–89.

[4] The 1720 tariff was revised by warrants of 1766, 1772, 1773, and 1783. These were in practice only guidelines, prices varying considerably.

[5] The purchase of colonelcies was fairly common in the army before 1714; but it was an abuse that George I and George II were determined to stamp out. They had done so by 1760, by discouraging the purchase of colonelcies and by filling any death-vacancies that occurred with colonels appointed by the Crown. J. Hayes, 'The Purchase of Colonelcies in the Army, 1714–63', *JSAHR* 39 (1961), *passim*.

usually traded at prices much greater than those laid down in the Warrants) he received the unofficial over-regulation price from his successor; the successor meanwhile paid the regulated price to government.[6] An officer selling was usually required to offer his commission to that officer in his regiment with the most seniority in the rank immediately below his; if that senior officer of the next lower rank lacked the funds or the inclination to purchase, then the commission was offered to the next senior, and so on. The purchaser got the rank but not the seniority of the officer from whom he purchased, thus becoming the most junior of the regiment's officers in his new rank. It will be noted that a vacancy set off a chain reaction within a regiment since nobody could move up the ladder without at the same time selling, thus requiring a chain of purchasers. A vacant captaincy, for example, meant four vacant ranks—the captaincy, the captain-lieutenancy,[7] a lieutenancy, and an ensigncy. A vacant lieutenant-colonelcy meant six vacancies, as each below moved up a step. Likewise, everyone within each rank in the regiment moved up one notch in seniority after a purchase was transacted. There was much activity whenever a vacancy occurred, therefore, since it involved everyone in the regiment at or below the rank become vacant; and if at any rung along the ladder no applicant could readily be found, it was the obligation of all the officers interested in the promotion to find one.[8] Seniority, clearly, was all-important to officers.[9]

When an officer wished to leave active service he either sold out entirely or retired on to half-pay. If he sold out, he received the value of his commission as a retirement fund; and since most officers got at least one promotion without purchase—a

---

[6] Army agents usually handled the trading in commissions, because the over-regulation prices paid by purchasers were illegal, and the agents (one of whom handled most of the financial affairs of each regiment, as the private agent of the proprietary colonel) were best placed to cover this part of the business. J. H. Bassett, op. cit. 61.

[7] The captain-lieutenant (since the colonel was seldom present) commanded the colonel's company; he was regarded as the 'youngest captain though in reality he is only the first lieutenant, the colonel being himself captain'. Capt. G. Smith, *An Universal Military Dictionary, a Copious Explanation of the Technical Terms . . . of an Army* (1779), 50.

[8] J. Hayes, 'Officers', 41–60, for a good description of the process.

[9] Hence the importance of brevet rank—that is, a higher rank in the army than that held in the regiment, usually awarded either for long service, or to officers who had served in a capacity (but not actual rank) higher than that actually held. It conferred no pay but gave seniority, and thus claim to subsequent vacancies in regiments other than one's own.

process described below—they not only got their money back but in this way made a capital gain.[10] If an officer wished to retire from active service, but keep some part of his pay and retain his investment without selling, he went on to the 'half-pay list'. Here he kept himself 'on reserve' as it were, ready to return on active service if called and hence given half pay as a retaining fee. Officers from regiments raised during the wars and reduced with the coming of peace also went on to the half-pay list, for the same reason. All three Georges, ever solicitous of the interests of their old officers, frequently provided non-purchase vacancies for half-pay officers when these arose in established regiments, and likewise appointed numbers of them to new-raised corps.

The purchase system was simple enough and it offered several advantages. Fortescue rightly thought it secure, economical, and convenient.[11] It was secure because government held the purchase money as a bond against an officer's good behaviour; if he were 'cashiered' his investment was forfeit. It was economical because an officer's pay 'little exceeded the interest on the price of his commission.' It was convenient for all concerned too, since traffic in commissions, the rule of moving up one step at a time, and the device of retiring on half pay all ensured a steady flow of promotion. The system had its abuses, naturally enough. Infants might be gazetted cornets or ensigns, and in this way get a head start in the seniority which sped an officer's first promotion. Occasional jobbery, or frauds by army agents heavily involved as commission brokers, sometimes made it possible for an officer to skip a step on the promotion ladder. High over-regulation prices might induce an officer selling to ignore the next officer in seniority, who otherwise would rightfully have been given first chance to buy. But, save for the first, these practices were thought less than honourable and so were exceptional, not least because sharp practice harmed the chances not just of one but of most of a regiment's officers; and the Hanoverian Kings paid such close attention to the granting of commissions that frauds were seldom successful.

As we noted above, at least one-third of all vacancies were

[10] J. H. Bassett, op. cit. 155.
[11] Sir J. Fortescue, *The Last Post* (Edinburgh, 1934), 13–19. Quoted in R. E. Scouller, op. cit. 71–2.

filled without purchase. Non-purchase vacancies were for the most part those that appeared because of the death of an officer or, infrequently, through his being cashiered. As with purchase promotions, when a non-purchase promotion occurred it too affected the senior officer in each successive rank below the vacancy, each of them getting a free step up the ladder. In wartime, when new corps were raised and old ones augmented, many non-purchase vacancies also appeared. The recipients of free promotions were a varied lot. A death vacancy usually went to the senior officer of the next-lowest rank; but the King could, and often did, appoint to these vacancies from the half-pay list—as he did in the 39th Foot in 1747, for example, upon the death in harness of that corps's major.[12] Sons of deserving officers and sons of impecunious officers' widows often got these posts. In wartime it was common for large numbers of senior NCOs to be given ensigncies or lieutenancies; four NCOs in the 64th Foot and three in the 33rd, among others, were commissioned subalterns in 1756, for example.[13] Young men of good family but without other resources often took service in the capacity of 'volunteers', carrying firelocks on their shoulders and marching in the ranks with the private men; it was their hope that, by distinguishing themselves in action, they might be given an ensigncy in the regiment. Many officers who later reached high rank began their careers as volunteers. But if, as Hayes notes, the granting of commissions without purchase made it 'possible for a man with little money to climb in the service by non-purchase vacancies to the rank of major or even lieutenant-colonel',[14] still free commissions were not an unmixed blessing. Where the normal rule had it that there could be no purchase without a sale, the corollary here was that a commission obtained without purchase could not normally be sold. Free commissions represented one-third of all promotions, contributed notably to the steady flow of seniority and promotion, and raised officers who lacked money and 'interest' and who otherwise would have mouldered without hope on a subaltern's pay; but the fact that they could not normally sell meant that the half-pay list was often the only

---

[12] J. Hayes, 'Officers', 43–6.
[13] WO 27/5 and 6.
[14] J. Hayes, 'Officers', 43–6.

resource of officers promoted in this fashion, when they grew grey in the service.

A system so organized was bound to produce a body of officers whose social origins were diverse and whose career expectations were varied; and such was indeed the case. The British officer corps, after 1715, was a social mélange.[15] Broadly speaking, there were four groups from which officers were recruited. First came the nobility and the landed gentry, titled and untitled, whose sons—younger sons, generally—made up at least one-quarter of the regimental officers and well more than half of the proprietary colonels and general officers.[16] Because of their birth they possessed 'interest' and, in most cases, money; and it was these three advantages that marked them out from other officers and gave them the highest promotion prospects. The second group provided the great majority of the regimental officers: these were men drawn from the lesser gentry, from the cadet branches of good families now involved in the professions or in trade, from the clergy, and even from the surviving yeomen farmers. Their distinguishing characteristics were the lack of birth, money, and interest of the first group and, consequently, of the prospects of high rank open to their betters. An officer of this class described most of his fellows exactly when he referred to himself as 'a private Gentleman without the advantage of Birth and friends'.[17] Nevertheless, considerable numbers of this group—as of the third group below—were the protégés of the great, were under their 'protection', and so their impecunious condition did not doom their chances of advancement.[18]

The third group is less easy to categorize, since it was drawn

---

[15] 'Officer corps' is a term used advisedly, for convenience only, since (just as J. Childs has observed of the later seventeenth-century army, in *The Army of Charles II* (1976)) there was during our period no officer corps in Britain, but rather an officer class. Even the notion of an 'officer class' is (and was at the time) recognized as something of a fiction. Neither the caste exclusiveness of the Prussian officer corps which was relaxed in favour of non-nobles only *in extremis*, nor the cosmopolitan and often quite professional nature of the Austrian officer corps, nor the increasing élitism and entrenchment among the *noblesse d'épée* which makes possible the use of the term to describe the French officer corps, is recognizable in the British Army.

[16] J. Hayes, 'Officers', 80–1. In general, I follow Hayes's system of classification here.

[17] Ibid. 80. See also I. F. Burton and A. N. Newman, art. cit. 667–8.

[18] An interesting collection of letters illustrating the workings of 'interest' in getting commissions and promotions, is in M. Balderston and D. Syrett, *The Lost War. Letters from British Officers during the American Revolution* (New York, 1975).

socially from a wide spectrum stretching across the first two groups, and it included a significant minority of foreigners, chiefly Huguenots. Most of its members were without lands or much money, but were nevertheless gentlemen well-enough born and educated—the Huguenots being a case in point. It was a distinct group in that it was composed of what would later be referred to as 'army families', families whose sons traditionally served in the army and—especially among the majority with little wealth—had by the end of the Seven Years War developed a new 'professional' outlook and a 'service mentality'. Establishing dynasties between 1715 and 1739, theirs was a new professionalism, the product of the institutionalized standing army;[19] and it was quite unlike the older mercenary professionalism of the Kirkes or Douglasses which had characterized the later seventeenth-century army and had all but died out during the first decade of the eighteenth.

The fourth group, greater in numbers than is generally realized, consisted of subaltern officers of advanced age and experience promoted from among the non-commissioned officers. These were men who had enlisted as private soldiers and, by diligence and luck, had become outstanding senior NCOs. As many as 200 of them were commissioned during the 1739–48 war, and perhaps as many again got commissions during the Seven Years War. Like the long-service subalterns with few prospects of advancement, they were particularly useful in new-raised corps where a leavening of old soldiers thoroughly acquainted with training and discipline was essential.[20]

It will be appreciated from what we have said so far about the mechanics of the purchase system and the social and financial

---

[19] The Churchills, Lascelleses, Howards, Duroures, Handasydes, and, of course, the Campbells and other Scottish families, stand out. These families had their naval equivalents—the Knowles family, for example, or the Hyde Parkers.

[20] J. Hayes, 'Officers', 100: e.g. late in 1756 new second battalions were added to each of fifteen old marching regiments. The officers of the new 2/3rd Foot were typically drawn from many places: thirteen came from active service in other marching regiments, and one each came from the Marines, the Engineers, the Scots-Dutch brigade, and the half-pay list. Of the rest, six were lads given first commissions as ensigns while the quartermaster and four lieutenants were sergeants of the 1/3rd commissioned as officers. C. Knight, *Historical Records of The Buffs, East Kent Regiment (3rd Foot)* . . . *1704–1914*, ii (1935), Pt 2, 733–4. The 2/3rd was regimented in 1758 as the 61st Foot, by which time six of the corps's subalterns were ex-sergeants. Of these, one had served twenty-five years before being commissioned, three had served nineteen years each before being commissioned, one had served thirteen years, and the last had served

advantages of the officer corps, that for the majority of the officers it was always relatively easy to acquire a first commission; but thereafter it was only those officers possessed of birth, wealth, and interest who could be fairly sure of advancement into the higher ranks. For most officers—those with the least advantages—the army promised 'nothing but the certainty of long years of wearisome regimental service and a limited preferment which would stop at the rank of lieutenant-colonel if they were favoured by fortune, or at captain or major if they were not.'[21] Most of these officers, by the same token, relied on the army for their livelihood: the subalterns lived on their pay, eked it out with the odd windfall, and hoped for the day when command of a company would provide a modest addition derived from the proprietary rights of a captaincy. Long service was the rule (as we shall see in more detail); and it is clear that the majority of officers—since they were long-serving, since they lived off their pay and meagre supplements, since they had neither interest nor private fortune, since their advancement was slow, and since merit was their chief or sole advantage—were career officers, and consciously so. The value of experience and merit, given the social and financial circumstances of most officers, was a much more important aspect of the promotion system than is usually credited. All commissions came from the King; and only to the Lord-Lieutenant in Dublin and to the commanders-in-chief of forces serving in the field abroad was some part of this most jealously guarded of royal prerogatives delegated. The Lord-Lieutenant could appoint to ensigncies and cornetcies only, while field commanders could appoint or promote to vacancies created by death or disease; and all such appointments were subject to the royal sanction. Any proprietary colonel with political influence, whose judgement in military affairs was respected by the King, was easily able to advance the careers of able officers in the regiment of which he held the command. Whenever a vacancy appeared it was the proprietary colonel whose recommenda-

---

eleven years (WO 27/5). Likewise the new 64th Foot (lately 2/11th) had among its subalterns four ex-sergeants; of these, one had served twenty-two years before being commissioned, another had served seventeen years, and the others had served twelve years. Ibid.

[21] J. Hayes, 'Officers', 158.

tions to the sovereign—especially so in the cases of George I and George II—were those most likely to get a good hearing. Colonels who were at all interested in the affairs of their own regiments knew which officers possessed merit and deserved advancement, and which did not; and when a vacancy occurred, the colonel, in recommending, could simply pass over any officer lacking reputation or capacity. In 1747, for example, when the majority of Richbell's 39th of Foot fell vacant, the two senior captains were so ignored; the first was a rogue and the second incapable and, despite the fact that the first moved heaven and earth for the promotion neither Richbell nor his lieutenant-colonel, nor any others of the officers in the 39th would have either of the two succeed.[22] The Duke of Cumberland, as Captain-General from 1745 to 1757, paid scant regard to interest and looked out for the deserving; and the Duke of York later acted in the same fashion, whenever possible. Since there was considerable mobility between the regiments and since non-purchase vacancies were common (especially in wartime),[23] not only experienced officers with interest and money but, equally, those with experience but without these other advantages, often profited by zeal and merit.

There were always, of course, officers possessed of the birth and influence of a Lord George Lennox who, second son of the Duke of Richmond, got his ensigncy at the age of thirteen, in 1751, and seven years later—aged twenty—was lieutenant-

---

[22] Ibid. 43–6.

[23] The officer turnover in eight sample regiments of foot during the 1775–83 war—corps with a typical cross-section of service—illustrates wartime mobility. Of these regiments (the 5th, 11th, 22nd, 23rd, 29th, 38th, 64th, and 66th of Foot), six arrived in North America before or in 1775, while the 11th and 66th spent the whole of the war quietly in Ireland. The 5th, 22nd, 23rd, 38th, and 64th were all heavily engaged; the 22nd and 38th finished the war at New York in 1783, and the 5th and 64th in the West Indies. Most of the 23rd had been interned at Yorktown; and the 29th sat out the war in Canada where it saw little or no action after 1776.

Seven of these regiments each had twenty-nine regimental officers in 1775, while the 5th (with one vacancy) had twenty-eight. Of the twenty-eight officers with the 5th in 1775, only nine were still with the corps in 1783; similarly, only twelve of the 11th's original complement were still with that corps in 1783, while in that same year only five of the 22nd's remained, only four of the 23rd's, only ten of the 29th's, only six of the 38th's, only four of the 64th's, and only eight of the 66th's. Death in action, disease, incapacitating wounds, retirement, promotion to general rank, and exchanges into other corps had by 1783 accounted for 173—75 per cent—of the 231 officers who had been with these corps in 1775, at the same time providing an equal number of vacancies which were filled by promotions, exchanges, and new appointments. *Army Lists.*

colonel commanding the 33rd Foot. Lord George got his first full colonelcy in 1762, aged twenty-four. Equally there were in every corps officers like Peter Franquefort of the 19th Foot who, by 1740, had given a total of forty-six years to the service. Franquefort had obtained his ensigncy in 1694, and it had taken him thirty-eight years to move up two steps to become a captain; eight years later, when the Spanish war broke out, he was still only a captain. Lennox and Franquefort represent extremes, however; if we are to appreciate fully the workings of the purchase system, and to judge the career service and experience of the officer corps in general some detailed sets of statistics must be assembled. Three such sets are, therefore, advanced here: in Table 1 the overall length of time that officers had spent in the service, since obtaining their first commissions, is determined; in Table 2 the length of time spent by officers in their present commissions, as held at selected years, is considered; and in Table 3 the number of years that officers could expect to remain in each commission—that is, on each rung of the ladder—is calculated. The officers serving with the regiments—that is, from subalterns to the lieutenants-colonel, inclusive—are dealt with first, after which the proprietary colonels are considered in their turn. It will be seen that these figures clearly support the general impression of career service described above.[24]

Table 1, our first set of figures from our sample regiments,[25] concerns the overall length of time that officers had spent in the

[24] These sets of figures are taken from statistical bores made at selected years in the printed annual *Army Lists*, from the officers' commission histories compiled for each regiment appearing in WO 27, and from the register-books in WO 25. Our survey covers the years 1739–95, there being insufficient evidence upon which representative statistics could be drawn for the two earlier decades covered by this study. Several short lacunae in the materials make it impossible, in many instances, to give all three sets of our statistics for the same year; and not all of our survey regiments were on hand in each of the years selected for bores.

For convenience, the captain-lieutenant is counted among the captains here and henceforth; such was contemporary practice.

[25] These were eleven of horse and twenty-nine of foot, chosen carefully so that their service records during our period would reflect closely the distribution pattern of the army at home and abroad. The regiments of horse were: The Blues, 2nd, and 4th Horse; the 2nd Dragoon Guards; the 2nd, 3rd, 5th, 7th, and 14th Dragoons; and the 15th and 17th Light Dragoons. The foot were the Coldstream Guards, plus the 1/1st, 2nd, 4th, 5th, 6th, 8th, 11th, 12th, 15th, 17th, 19th, 22nd, 27th, 28th, 32nd, 33rd, 38th, 39th, 42nd, 43rd, 45th, 46th, 51st, 54th, 58th, 63rd, 64th, and 69th of Foot.

service since obtaining their first commissions, as young cornets or ensigns. The figures in Table 1 point the long service described earlier; and when read in conjunction with Table 2[26]

TABLE 1
Average Number of Years' Service From First Commission

YEAR	HORSE				FOOT			
	Lts-Col.	Majs	Capts	Lts	Lts-Col.	Majs	Capts	Lts
1740	35	31	26	20·5	35	30·5	27	19
1754	28	27	13·5	8·5	22	18	15·5	10
1759	21	20	11·5	6	15	19	14	5
1768	24	21	14	9·5	23	24	15	10
1773	19	18	14	8·5	29	20·5	16	10
1777	25	19·5	15	9	30	23·5	17	10
1785	28·5	26	15	7	26·5	22	17·5	7·5
1789	27·5	26	17	9	23	26·5	16	8·5
1791	28	23	13·5	8	30	29	18	9

—figures giving the average number of years spent by officers in their presently held commissions, accounting therefore for only their most recent service—they jointly shed a good deal of light upon career patterns, and upon the service experience that officers brought with them when promoted from one rank to the next.

TABLE 2
Average Number of Years Spent by Officers in Their Present Commission

YEAR	HORSE					FOOT				
	Lts-Col.	Majs	Capts	Lts	Crts	Lts-Col.	Majs	Capts	Lts	Ens
1740	14	8·5	8·5	8	6	8	3	8	7·5	3·5
1758	3·5	2·5	3	3	3	3	2	4	3	1·5
1766	7	5	6	5·5	3·5	5	4	5·5	5·5	4
1774	5	4	5	4	3	8	3·5	6	6	3
1780	6	2·5	4·5	3	2	5	3	4·5	3·5	1·5
1787	9·5	7	7	4	3	8	5	9	6	3·5
1793	10·5	5	5	3·5	2·5	9	6	8	5·5	3

Table 3 illustrates the 'rates of promotion'—the number of years that officers could expect, upon average, to remain in one rank before advancing to the next—obtaining in the officer corps.

These figures are all largely self-explanatory, illustrating the pattern of service described earlier; but a few comments might, nevertheless, be made here. Thus it will be noted that early in 1740 the lieutenants-colonel of horse had seen, on average,

[26] Figures on the length of service in cornetcies and ensigncies, since they were the first ranks obtained, are essentially the same in Tables 1 and 2; and do not of course apply in Table 3.

TABLE 3
Average Number of Years Served Before Attainment of Present Rank

	HORSE				FOOT		
YEAR	Lts-Col.	Majs	Capts	Lts	Lts-Col.	Majs	Capts	Lts
1740	21	22	17	14	27	26	19	11·5
1759	18·5	17·5	9	3	13	17	10	2
1767	16	14·5	8	4	17	19	9	6
1775	21	9	11	6	20	18	10	4
1786	20	18	9	3	21·5	18	7	2
1792	21	19	10	5	23	24	10	4

some 35 years of army service since first obtaining their cornet-cies; and the lieutenants-colonel of foot had likewise seen an average of 35 years of service since first taking a pair of colours, as obtaining an ensigncy was described. This was long service indeed, and it was matched in the lower commissioned ranks. For all ranks above the humble cornet and ensign, none of these statistics for such sheer long service were again to be equalled during the century. In 1740 too it had taken the lieutenants-colonel of horse an average of 21 years' service before being promoted to that rank; majors of horse had taken an average of 22 years to reach their majorities; while lieutenants-colonel of foot had, in 1740, spent an average of 27 years in the army be-fore reaching that rank, and similarly the foot majors had achieved their majorities only after an average of 26 years' service.

The figures for 1740 were all high, the result of the long peace that had followed upon the Utrecht settlement; the army's size had been stable since the reductions that followed the 1715 Rebellion; and the officer corps as a whole, when the Spanish war broke out late in 1739, was a very experienced, long-serving body. In the horse, none of the figures just given was to be equalled again during the century; while in the foot it was only by the later 1780s that such figures were once again achieved. The influence of prolonged peace and of only the most limited augmentations had already set a trend in career-service experience. The slightly lower promotion rate evident in the horse in these statistics for 1740, as compared with the foot, was exceptional; during the rest of the century the service statistics and promotion rates were to be generally alike in the two arms.

The campaigns and augmentations of 1739–48 undid all

this, and by the early 1750s the army was much 'younger'—that is, the great majority of officers had much less experience of the service. By the mid-point of the Seven Years War promotion rates had sped up dramatically, reflecting not only wartime conditions—what with casualties, new-raising, and augmentations occurring—but also the expanded 'imperial' role of the army, with its greater number of corps and consequent need for more officers. The mid-Seven Years War figures set a trend for the rest of the century, reflecting the importance of the large size of the force kept standing, and its imperial commitments, to the career patterns and upward mobility of officers.

If in wartime speedy promotion tended to water down noticeably the experience of officers in their present commissions, nevertheless with the settled conditions of peacetime the figures once again always begin to rise: in 1774 for example, on the eve of the American Rebellion which would become a world war, the experience of the officers of foot in their present commissions—and it was the foot that would bear almost the entire burden of the war—was for most ranks greater than it had been at any time since the 1739 war. Our final figures for the early 1790s, just before the opening of hostilities against Revolutionary France and the great expansion of the army which then began, show the officer corps to have again accumulated more experience of the service than had been the case upon the outbreak of war in either 1756 or 1775; and among the field officers of foot there was more experience of service than had been the case since 1712.

Another trend in career patterns, already noted above, is apparent in the statistics: field rank—the lieutenant-colonelcies especially—was being attained after periods of service proportionately shorter than those spent on the lower rungs of the ladder. This illustrates the more speedy promotion rates obtaining among that minority of officers—the first of the four groups described above from which the officer corps was recruited—possessed of birth, wealth, and interest. Indeed it was common for the lieutenants-colonel to have no more service experience than had the majors.

All the above statistics illustrate strikingly the influence of war, with its concomitant expansion of the forces and consequent increase in the number of officers serving with the regiments, upon the service experience of the officer corps in general; but it must be recalled that expansion was a short-lived phenomenon, and its effects must not be overrated. With the coming of peace the great majority of all new officers found themselves relegated to the half-pay list, as their units were broken.[27] In most of the new-raised regiments, furthermore, half of the officers—all the field officers and captains, and half of the lieutenants—were old soldiers either appointed from other corps or taken up from the half-pay list. Entirely typical were Manners's 56th, Anstruther's 58th, and Montague's 59th of Foot, all raw regiments raising from late December 1755; each was staffed with experienced officers at all ranks save for the ensigns, who were mostly young fellows, and save for a handful of junior lieutenants (one in the 59th, and four each in the 56th and 58th). In terms of experience of the service the lieutenants-colonel of the 56th, 58th, and 59th had by the autumn of 1756 served for twenty-eight, twelve, and twelve years respectively since obtaining their first commissions; the three majors had served twenty-four, ten, and eighteen years respectively; the captains of these regiments had served an average of 12·5, 11, and 12 years respectively; and the lieutenants (including the new men) had behind them an average of 3·5, 4·5, and 6·5 years respectively.[28] Compared with the rest of the foot in the army the service experience of these officers was no less than the average. Not even the practice of 'raising for rank' was likely to flood the officer corps with incompetents, since this was rarely attempted after the '45 Rebellion, its disadvantages being too well appreciated.[29]

What is striking about the statistics is the closely comparable service records of the captains and subalterns among all the regiments of each arm, in any period surveyed; the essentially similar service experience of each regiment's body of officers is apparent. There were no favoured units, in so far as service

---

[27] On the near-panic casting about for exchanges into older more established corps, which the merest hint of a peace would set off in new-raised regiments, see J. Shy, op. cit. 71–9, where several examples of this are given.

[28] WO 27/4.

[29] 'Raising for rank' involved granting to noblemen, or occasionally to a city corporation, the right to raise a new regiment largely at their own expense. When the corps approached full strength it was then taken on to the regular establishment and paid for henceforth by the state. The practice had only one real advantage: it produced a few

with the company or troop was concerned; and since dispersal in penny-packets was the common lot of the army, this essential homogeneity of service experience among the officers of company or troop grade contributed not a little towards bringing a fairly even experience to the training of widely separated units. The Dublin garrisons of 1773, new and old, conveniently illustrate this point. Among the old garrison which was replaced late in the spring of that year and sent out into county cantonments the average length of service of the captains and subalterns in their present commissions, together with the dates at which they had obtained their present ranks, are shown in Table 4.

TABLE 4

Old Garrison, 1773

9th Foot			17th Foot			27th Foot		
Capts	3	(1764–72)	Capts	5·5	(1760–72)	Capts	5	(1764–72)
Lts	4·5	(1760–72)	Lts	4	(1761–72)	Lts	5	(1758–72)
Ens	1	(1771–2)	Ens	1·5	(1771–2)	Ens	3	(1762–72)

28th Foot			45th Foot			46th Foot		
Capts	7	(1761–72)	Capts	6	(1755–71)	Capts	5·5	(1757–72)
Lts	5·5	(1761–72)	Lts	10	(1754–72)	Lts	4·5	(1761–72)
Ens	2·5	(1769–72)	Ens	4	(1763–72)	Ens	1·5	(1770–2)

The same figures for the new Dublin garrison which came in from county cantonments and replaced the old, in the spring of 1773, are given in Table 5. The average service in their present commissions of all of the captains in the old garrison was 6 years, and it was 5·5 for all the captains of the new; among the lieutenants of the old garrison the average was 6 years' service, and it was 6 years also among the lieutenants of the new; and where the old garrison's ensigns had served 2 years, on average, the new garrison's ensigns had served for 3 years. Among all twelve regiments only five groups—the captains of the 9th and

---

new units much more quickly than regular recruiting could, since the raiser's tenants were most often obliged to take service in his regiment. This made it a system especially successful in Scotland. Its main disadvantages were two in number: the mopping up of several hundred men, usually in one district, denied the old, well-trained corps the recruits they needed; and a considerable number of the officers in the new corps were nominated not by the usual methods but by the gentleman doing the raising (who himself normally got the full colonelcy of the corps, and thus the profits of proprietor and the advantages of patronage). The raiser would naturally nominate from among friends and relations, usually possessed of little or no experience but all as a body made officers overnight (hence 'raising for rank').

TABLE 5
New Garrison, 1773

	5th Foot			42nd Foot			54th Foot	
Capts	3·5	(1765–72)	Capts	5	(1758–70)	Capts	8	(1755–72)
Lts	6	(1758–72)	Lts	8·5	(1759–71)	Lts	6·5	(1759–72)
Ens	2	(1770–2)	Ens	4	(1761–72)	Ens	3·5	(1761–72)

	55th Foot			62nd Foot			63rd Foot	
Capts	7	(1760–72)	Capts	4·5	(1759–72)	Capts	5	(1761–72)
Lts	5	(1755–72)	Lts	5	(1761–72)	Lts	5	(1760–72)
Ens	2	(1769–72)	Ens	3	(1768–72)	Ens	3	(1762–72)

54th, the former rather 'youngish' and the latter rather more experienced; the lieutenants of the 42nd and 45th, both rather more experienced than the norm; and the ensigns of the 9th, who were a bit young again—stand out; and of these only the lieutenants of the 45th were at all exceptional.

This general similarity was always the rule in the army. There were exceptions, but these were usually exceptions proving the rule. In 1740 for example, the promotion rates and dates of purchase among the captains and lieutenants of Dalway's 39th of Foot diverge noticeably from what was then normal through the rest of the army. The 39th's ten lieutenants had obtained their lieutenancies after only 3·5 years' service as ensigns, on average, where the average figure for the army was 11·5 years; and half of the corps's lieutenants had served for only one year as ensigns, before obtaining promotion. The dates of the lieutenants' (and of the captains') commissions indicate what was occurring in the regiment. Six of the lieutenants had obtained their lieutenancies in 1731 and 1732, within less than a year of one another; and six of the eight captains had obtained their captaincies in 1730 and 1731, within eighteen months of one another. There had been, quite clearly, a great wave of selling out and transfers among the captains and lieutenants serving with the corps during the period 1730–2. Why this was so is easily determined: after several years of easy service in Ireland the 39th had, among others, been sent late in 1726 to join the Gibraltar garrison, under Spanish attack. The 39th had stayed on at Gibraltar when, late in the autumn of 1730, it was ordered to proceed to Jamaica to deal with slave insurrection; and only in the spring of 1732 was the corps freed from this unexpected duty, coming home to Ireland. The officers of the 39th had been dismayed neither by the shells of the Spaniards nor by the boredom of the Gibraltar garrison duty which followed. It was, rather, the likely prospect of death from tropical disease that had set them scrambling to sell or exchange, and this resulted in a massive intake of new men and promotion of old, those willing to risk yellow fever for rank.

Considering these several sets of statistics we cannot do other than conclude that the British army was, during our period, led by an officer corps of the most considerable experience, made up of men who, by and large, entered the service for life and got on by steady, competent service. This was careerism. Long service does not in itself, of course, imply any outstanding merit; but within the context of the several attributes of careerism and in light of the slow rates of promotion, a thorough acquaintance with their business and, surely, a capable performance of it must be conceded these men. Considering also the disadvantageous conditions in which the peacetime army always found itself serving, nothing but competence and sound proficiency among the regimental officers could have kept the majority of the regiments fit for service.

This conclusion is lent additional weight by the fact that the men appointed to the proprietary colonelcies of the corps were likewise, in the great majority of cases, soldiers of long experience of the service. The colonelcies were valuable, much-sought-after plums, and their disposal was a matter of weight in the patronage system by which high political interest was maintained. But however well born, however well possessed of interest, and however powerful politically were the officers—usually general officers—appointed, the fact remains that all but a mere handful of the colonels appointed during the eighteenth century were men of long years of service in the army. All three Georges regarded colonelcies as rewards for deserving officers of long service, and viewed with distaste the fact that patronage had also, upon occasion, some part to play in their disposal. The role of patronage was, however, firmly restricted by them—especially by George II—with results most clearly expressed in the following statistics. There were 293 colonels appointed during the years 1714–63. Of these, 18 had served over 45 years each on appointment; 63 had seen from 35 to 44 years of service, upon appointment; another 78 had served between 25 and 34 years, on appointment; and a further

90 had already served between 15 and 24 years, on appointment. More than half of the colonels had, therefore, served for at least a quarter-century before being given their colonelcies; and fully five-sixths of the colonels had, upon appointment, between 15 and 50 years of service behind them. Only 44 of the colonels—15 per cent—had seen less than 15 years' service on appointment, and of those most had served more than 10 years.[30] The conclusion is inescapable that only officers of long service and experience—many with experience of active operations—could, in the great majority of cases, aspire to a colonelcy while the first two Georges commanded the army. The same pattern prevailed (albeit with some further nod to political interest) during the first four decades of George III's reign, which takes us to the end of our period.

(b) MEN[31]

Where the great majority of the officers serving with the regiments were, as we have seen, men of no inconsiderable experience of the service, this was not the case among the non-commissioned officers, musicians, and private men over whom they exercised command. At no time during our period were men available in numbers sufficient to keep the corps recruited up to the strengths called for in the regimental establishments, while in the meantime considerable numbers of the men actually serving with the corps were mere recruits, as yet insufficiently trained to be masters of their business. It was with this chronic, two-pronged manpower problem—too few recruits to complete to the establishments, too many recruits

---

[30] J. Hayes, 'Officers', 115–17, 224. See also J. Hayes, 'Lieutenants-Colonel and Majors-Commandant of the Seven Years' War', *JSAHR* 36 (1958), 3–13, 38–9, where the author concludes (p. 12) of the thirty-three commandants of the corps that were the last to be raised during the 1756–63 war, that they too were mostly 'well qualified for their command'. He adds of the mid-century army, that 'there was in existence at this time a well-balanced, practised, professional body of officers' which could be drawn on to train and lead new-raised units.

[31] By 'men' we refer collectively, here and henceforth, to the NCOs (sergeants and corporals), musicians (drummers, trumpeters, hautbois, fifers, and pipers), and private soldiers. A soldier with one year's service or less was generally deemed to be not yet sufficiently trained or disciplined to be trusted to perform all of the tasks and duties normally within the province of the 'compleat soldier'; and we follow this approach here, describing as recruits those men who had served for only that length of time or less. The basic-training scheme and timetable according to which recruits were brought along is described at length in Ch. IV.

among the men already with the corps—that the regiments had continually to contend; and both aspects of the problem, the latter especially, often caused the most severe difficulties for individual corps.

It is with the effects of the manpower problem most especially, rather than with its causes, that we are concerned here. Before dealing with the broad statistical dimensions of the problem and examining in detail the condition of the regiments that suffered most acutely from the problem, however, we offer a brief survey of the practices employed in the endless effort to keep the regiments up to strength.

Men were always needed; and while men already trained, or recruits accustomed at least to the initial or 'material' phase of the normal basic-training regimen (on which, see Chapter IV below) were much to be preferred, the rawest of lads fresh from the plough were always useful too, given the manpower problem. Several means were employed to obtain both sorts of men. The army got its recruits either by voluntary enlistment (which accounted for the majority) or by force. The best-known method of filling the regiments was, of course, the routine peacetime and wartime 'beating up' for volunteers carried on by the recruiting parties—a subaltern, one or two NCOs, and a drummer (to 'beat')—dispatched to likely or favourite areas direct from the regiments.[32] Recruiting parties were to be found touring the counties at all times and were especially common in winter, after the harvest, when idle hands were most likely to be found. It was by these parties that the majority of recruits were obtained, whether the parties were beating up for the old established corps or seeking greater numbers for newly raising regiments. Special Recruiting Acts were passed on occasion in wartime offering high bounties and short-term enlistments

[32] This activity was authorized by 'beating orders' (e.g. WO 26/29, p. 108), obtained from the War Office. Corps were authorized 'by Beat of Drum or otherwise to raise so many Men . . . as are or shall be wanting'; and magistrates, JPs, and constables were required 'to be assisting . . . in providing Quarters, impressing Carriages & otherwise as there shall be occasion'. The enlistment oath signed by every recruit and witnessed in the presence of a JP laid down the following qualifications for a soldier: he must be a Protestant, he must 'have no Rupture' and not be 'troubled with Fits', he must be 'in no ways disabled by Lameness . . . but have the perfect Use' of his limbs, and he must not be a runaway 'Indented Apprentice or Militia Man'. That—along with a height requirement of 5′ 6″ which was regarded only if recruits were plentiful and the need not pressing—was sufficient qualification for a red coat. T 1/572, fo. 100.

(usually for three years or for the duration of hostilities) to all who would come forward; but since normal enlistments before 1795 were for life, this practice, though productive of men in the short term, was not in the long run cost-efficient and so was infrequently used.[33] The other well-known method of obtaining men was by duress. Insolvent debtors could escape prison and persons capitally convicted could sometimes escape the noose if they volunteered to serve, but these were few in number.[34] Most of those obtained by duress were not criminals but came rather from the next category in the current scale of values—that is, 'all such able-bodied, idle, and disorderly persons who cannot upon examination prove themselves to exercise and industriously follow some lawful trade or employment';[35] and these the JPs and the constables took up and pressed into service. The Press Acts, which were in operation only during the years 1704–12, 1745–6, 1755–7, and 1778–9, hardly provided the most willing or able of recruits; and the main purpose of impressment was never simply to take up the rogues, vagabonds, and others socially undesirable but rather *pour encourager les autres*—to drive others to volunteer for fear of being pressed.[36]

Normal beating up, short-term listing, bounties, and the press produced in the great majority of cases raw men only, and these were good enough for the corps serving at home; but among the regiments serving abroad and among those told off

[33] Clode, ii. 24–7.

[34] A typical example of recruiting after this fashion appears in the Inspection Returns on the 1/60th Foot, which was reviewed at Spanish Town, Jamaica, in December 1783. The battalion was described as composed partly of 'Foreigners', partly of 'Draughts received from the 92nd Regiment' since disbanded, and partly of 'British and Irish sent from the Jails in England'. WO 27/52. See also Sir C. V. F. Townshend, *The Military Life of Field Marshal George, First Marquess Townshend, 1727–1807* (1901), 79, for a variation on this theme—pardoning deserters 'tho Condemn'd on Condition they afterwards go to the West Indies to serve his Majesty in the Troops there.'

[35] 18 Geo. II, c. 12, quoted in Clode, ii 17.

[36] Clode, ii. 10–18, described the origins of impressment and the laws governing it; and he noted that the 'great principle of supply' during the eighteenth century 'was that of conscription limited to the Criminal and Pauper classes', not necessarily distinguishable to Clode. The most detailed of recent discussions are for Queen Anne's reign: R. E. Scouller, op. cit. 102–25, gives the history of the Press Acts of 1704–12, while A. N. Gilbert, 'Army Impressment During the War of the Spanish Succession', *Historian*, 38 (1976), 689–708, describes their actual operation in London and Kent. Scouller reminds us that impressment carried out under these Acts was 'the only form of conscription . . . to be imposed for the Standing Army prior to the First World War'.

for service abroad, both in wartime and in peacetime, it was trained or partially trained men who were most wanted. The means most commonly employed towards this end was the device of the 'additional company', one or two of which were added to the strength of each foot regiment serving outside the British Isles in wartime.[37] The additional companies were not meant for active service and remained in Britain or Ireland; it was their purpose to serve as recruiting and training depots for their parent regiments overseas, which drew on them from time to time as circumstances required; and numbers of these companies were often temporarily brigaded (notably at Chatham, Stirling Castle, and at Charles Fort Kinsale), for an introduction to advanced drill.[38]

It was usually difficult to find sufficient men even at the best of times; but at peak war years and in sudden emergencies true dearth was experienced both by the regular recruiting parties and the additional companies, as competition from the militia and from new-raising regular regiments (not to mention the navy, the marines, and the artillery) made itself felt. On such occasions, therefore, since neither the additional companies nor the regular recruiting parties were able to reinforce their distant parent regiments quickly enough or with sufficient numbers, other schemes had to be put into play in order to obtain numbers of men who would arrive in the theatres with at least the basics of training behind them. One such scheme—resorted to in 1760–1, and again in 1793—was the augmenting of already existing Independent Companies and the rapid rais-

---

[37] Additional Companies were not used during the Spanish Succession war, appearing first in 1727 when they were raised in corps on, or taken on to, the British establishment to prosecute the conflict with Spain centred upon the siege of Gibraltar. These were disbanded at the end of 1729 (WO 24/127, and WO 5/27, *passim*). Additional companies were raised again in 1744 and were retained until 1748, in the regiments serving in the Low Countries (WO 24/231). Late in 1755 additional companies were being raised again, and were mostly used as cadres upon which new regiments were built in 1756 (WO 5/42 and 43, *passim*). In late 1775 and early 1776 additional companies were again established to recruit for battalions serving in the Americas (WO 5/59, *passim*), and from 1779 for all battalions (WO 24/496). Only for the 1775–83 war have I seen references to additional companies in battalions on the Irish establishment; and these companies, although joined to Irish corps, were often recruiting in Britain (WO 4/95, pp. 116–17, and WO 5/59, *passim*). After 1793, 'recruiting troops' appeared in the cavalry for the first time.

[38] An excellent series of letters on the role and training of these companies is in WO 4/98, pp. 249–54.

ing of dozens more. Independent Companies (so called because they were unregimented) were always to be found about the British Isles and the plantations[39] doing jobs too simple (such as manning the fortifications in Britain), or too small (such as policing Bermuda), to require the services of marching regiments; and though composed for the most part of elderly and infirm Invalids they served, on these occasions, as organized and trained cadres into which sound but raw recruits might be put for processing.[40] The best of these new companies, when partially trained, were brigaded, forming new regiments quickly thereby;[41] and the rest served as a pool of replacements.[42]

Normal beating up, new-raising, the gaols, and the press all failed to provide men on the scale indicated at the outset of this discussion; and, although they were helpful, neither the additional companies nor the expanded Independent Companies were sufficient for the task. This left but one other method of obtaining men—lifting them from one unit not likely to see action immediately and transferring them into another unit already in the field, or about to go on service. This practice, known as 'drafting', was the most commonly used expedient for obtaining quickly large numbers of trained or partially trained men. Drafting was a commonplace, much more so than is usually credited; and since most (though by no means all) drafts were taken from corps serving in the British Isles and sent to corps under embarkation orders, or already serving abroad, it played a significant role in alleviating the manpower problem overseas

[39] Early in 1739, for example, there were thirty-one in Britain (four at Hull, four at Plymouth, three each at Pendennis Castle, Tynemouth, Landguard Fort, and on Jersey, two each at Chester, Carlisle, Sheerness, Tilbury Fort, and on Guernsey, and one in the Scillies). In the plantations there were seven more (four at New York, two in Jamaica, and one in Bermuda). Strength varied from 35 to 100 men, depending on the duty.

[40] Rex Whitworth, op. cit. 346–9; and Fortescue, iv, Pt. 1. 80.

[41] The quality of these regiments was none of the best. Calcraft, the army agent, described two such (Stuart's 97th and Grey's 98th, sent on the 1761 Belle Isle expedition) as 'a corps and sort of men you never saw in Europe and if you had would never wish to see elsewhere'. Rex Whitworth, op. cit. 349.

[42] Writing home from the army in Germany in May 1761, Lt.-Gen. George Howard was casting about for replacements for the British grenadier companies. Standards had fallen off, he admitted—so much so that he felt, like Kite, that 'if there is here and there a good Independent, born to be a great man and fit for a Cap, he may be sent.' NAM Townshend Pprs., 6806/41/5, Soest, 26 May 1761, fo. 1.

—but in so doing it was drafting that, next to the simple and normal dearth of men, contributed most effectively to perpetuating the manpower problem among most of the regiments at home. Because it had so serious an effect on the corps, drafting deserves to be illustrated in some detail, and its variety indicated.

The most common type of drafting, as we noted above, was that practised among the old established regiments embarking for (or already upon), foreign service. Late in 1743, for example, the 4th, 14th, 16th, 18th, 36th, 44th, 46th, and 48th of Foot, all in Britain, each gave up 100 men—one-seventh of their rank and file—as drafts for the battalions in Flanders.[43] These were sizeable numbers, but this was a light draft. We noted earlier the drafts made to fill up the 44th and 48th, when those corps went on active service from Ireland in 1755: each got 256 drafts by taking 100 men each from the 11th and 20th in England, and seventy-eight each from the 2/1st, 10th, 26th, and 28th in Ireland.[44] Losses on this scale—one-quarter of their men, from the Irish corps—had they occurred in the field, would have rendered the units *hors de combat*; as it was, from the point of view of training the drafted corps were no longer fit for service. Typically, therefore, when in May 1775 the 54th Foot was reviewed at Cork it was reported 'not by any means a good Regiment nor fitt for service' since it, like several other Irish corps, had recently been 'much drafted for the late Embarkation' of reinforcements to Boston.[45] Typical again was the 17th Foot, seen at Dover in May 1788; having in October past lost 150 men as drafts, the corps was now composed chiefly of recruits unable to perform any part of the regulation drill.[46] Drafting among the old corps moving between the British Isles and foreign stations could be as harmful to units coming home as to those departing since, as we noted earlier, it was a common practice to leave men behind to fill up newly arriving corps.

This was only the beginning of the damage that drafting could inflict on the old-established corps: they were, for example,

[43] Atkinson, 'Jenkins' Ear', 289.
[44] See above, pp. 49–50.
[45] WO 27/35.
[46] WO 27/61.

drafted to form experienced cadres around which new regiments might be built. When in 1737 Oglethorpe's 42nd Foot was raising for service in Georgia, the 25th Foot at Gibraltar was drafted to the tune of 240 men for Oglethorpe's cadre, thus reducing the 25th to 'a skeleton'.[47] Similarly, when at the end of 1739 six new regiments of marines were raised, one-third of the private men from each of eighteen old marching battalions then serving in Britain were drafted to fill these new units; this was an exceedingly hard blow, especially since half of these old corps had only just arrived in Britain from Ireland and were themselves employing every means to recruit up to British establishment strength.[48] Early in 1741 a further four new marine regiments were raised, and so too were seven new regiments of foot; and for these fifty men were drafted from each of fourteen regiments then in Britain, a bearable draft this time.[49]

Another blow regularly delivered was the drafting of a regiment's additional companies. When the 50th–59th of Foot were raised in Britain early in 1756, the additional companies of sixteen old battalions (together with further drafts made from the bodies of those battalions) were used as cadres around which the new units were built. The 50th Foot, for example, was raising at Norwich from mid-January; and to that place early in February went the four additional companies, plus further drafts, taken from the 7th Foot at Dover and from the 30th Foot around Croydon. Similarly, the 52nd Foot raising at Coventry got at the same time the four additional companies, plus drafts, from the 8th Foot at Canterbury and from the 33rd Foot lying about Gravesend.[50]

We have already seen how the Independent Companies were drafted, in emergencies, to fill up the regular regiments. The process occasionally worked in reverse. Midway through

[47] Atkinson, 'Early Hanoverians', 140, 147.

[48] Atkinson, 'Jenkins' Ear', 286–7. The corps so drafted were the following (those italicized being lately landed Irish corps): 12th, 23rd, *34th*—into Wolfe's 1st Marines; 4th, *24th*, *31st*—into Robinson's 2nd Marines; *6th*, 13th, *19th*—into Lowther's 3rd Marines; *21st*, *27th*, *36th*—into Wynyard's 4th Marines; 3rd, 11th, *32nd*—into Douglas' 5th Marines; *8th*, 15th, 16th—into Moreton's 6th Marines.

[49] Ibid. 288.

[50] WO 5/43, pp. 73–4, 78–9, 163. No sooner had the 52nd's drafts arrived at Coventry than detachments were told off to aid the local civil power in 'Safely Securing such Men as shall be Impressed for His Majesty's Service', the irony of which may not have been lost on them.

1734, for example, when six such companies were formed for Jamaica, 108 men were taken from each of the six regiments then serving at Gibraltar. This draft took away one-sixth of the strength of the corps there (the 2nd, 7th, 10th, 14th, 25th, and 29th); and considering the difficulty of recruiting for Gibraltar this was a draft which could only slowly be made good.[51]

A very common practice was to draft the whole of the rank and file from new-raised units and send them into other corps; and indeed some units were raised for no other purpose than to be repeatedly milked in this fashion. The 93rd Foot, for example, raised in 1760 and disbanded in 1763, was several times 'turned out into the Barrack Yard, and all the Best men picked out of it', as its major complained; 'All my Schemes and all my Pains about your Regiment is gone to the Devill', he informed his colonel.[52] From mid-1793 to mid-1795 many new corps were 'ab initio, expressly rais'd for the purpose of being draughted', after which the unit was re-raised 'upon the Ashes of the First', as the Adjutant-General described the process.[53] One such was the 114th Foot which, in June 1795, was marched to Chelmsford and there broken up into eight equal parts which were drafted into the 3rd, 14th, 19th, 33rd, 38th, 53rd, 63rd, and 88th of Foot.[54] With the French war going badly by 1795 the largest such draft of the century was set in motion late that summer, when one-quarter of all the foot regiments were in effect simply turned into a recruiting pool for the rest. In that year all the regiments numbered above the 100th (there were 131 at the time) were drafted into those below that rank, the ultimate aim being to raise the establishment of each of the 100 surviving regiments to 1,000 rank and file. The first twenty-two corps were built up to this strength in 1795, according to the following scheme. The 17th, 32nd, 39th, 56th, and 67th were sent from Britain to Ireland, where they joined the 93rd and 99th; and there the whole of the 104th, 105th, 106th, 111th, and 113th of Foot, already in Ireland, were drafted into these corps. Meanwhile the new second battalions of the 2nd and 29th of Foot were drafted into the 92nd and 94th, both serving in Guernsey; and the 66th at Gibraltar, together with

[51] Atkinson, 'Early Hanoverians', 146.   [52] J. Hayes, 'Officers', 182–5.
[53] WO 3/14, pp. 4–5, 16.   [54] WO 3/13, pp. 252–3.

the 6th, 35th, 64th, and 70th, all just home from the West Indies and on their way to Gibraltar, were soon filled up by the drafting of all the young corps already in that garrison. In Britain itself eight regiments were built up to the new strength by the drafting of full battalions (Table 6).

TABLE 6

Corps built up	Corps drafted
8th Foot	1/84th Foot
31st Foot	2/25th Foot
37th Foot	89th Foot
38th Foot	88th Foot
43rd Foot	Londonderry Regt
44th Foot	Royal Glasgow Regt
48th Foot	Dublin Regt
55th Foot	Loyal Sheffield Regt

It will be noted that the 88th and 89th, designed to survive in the master plan, were temporarily crushed in order to feed other units, and that the 2/84th survived where the older 1/84th was drafted. The vagaries of logistics accounted for this; and other problems intervened too. It was thought wise that the 'draughtable Sheffield Regt.', raised and quartered in the town after which the corps was named—'a very bad, disaffected Place', in the opinion of the Adjutant-General— should be marched to Doncaster to be drafted there, in case any of the men (or of the Sheffield citizenry) should find such usage objectionable.[55]

The major drafting policy of 1795 was launched in response to the crisis situation in which the army found itself early in the struggle with Revolutionary France.[56] Wholly drafting new corps was one thing, given such a situation; but doing the same to old-established corps was quite another, indicating a major failure in the recruiting system. This occurred during the American War of 1775–83, when the logistics of supplying replacements to units serving in the West Indies and North America proved beyond the means of anyone. Of the seventy-

[55] The 1795 drafting can be traced in WO 3/14, pp. 127–80, *passim.*
[56] The critical condition of the army, *c.*1795, is the theme of R. Glover, *Peninsular Preparation. The Reform of the British Army, 1795–1809* (Cambridge, 1963). In order to describe the Duke of York's reforms, Glover exaggerates considerably when describing the supposed ill-trained nature of the regiments, as will become apparent here in later chapters.

nine battalions of marching foot to serve there, eleven—one-
-seventh of them—were wholly drafted, their men distributed
among other units while their officers and NCOs returned
home to rebuild the corps anew. Two (the 18th and 59th)
were wholly drafted in 1775; three (the 6th, 50th, and 65th)
were drafted in 1776; another (the 14th) was drafted in 1777;
three more (the 10th, 45th, and 52nd) suffered the same fate in
1778 (as did the 16th Light Dragoons); another (the 26th)
went in 1779; and the last (the 16th) was drafted in 1782.
When one of these corps, the 10th Foot, was reviewed in England two years after coming home to rebuild, it was still in very
poor condition: it had not recruited so much as half its authorized establishment, and 75 per cent of the men it did have were
as yet no better than recruits. The 10th in addition was suffering
from an 'unaccountable Desertion', its old NCOs come home
in the surviving'cadre were 'almost totally worn out', and it
was not yet trained sufficiently to be fit for service.[57] In this
condition the 10th was typical of all regiments heavily drafted,
and obliged to rebuild with recruits. Indeed so insidious was
the whole process of drafting that, when he reviewed the 19th
Foot at Dublin in May 1779, Lt.-Gen. Lancelot Baugh reported the regiment to be in excellent order, adding of the 19th
that, 'not having Suffered by being Drafted, the Men are remarkably tall, well made, and Set up and think well of themselves, a Circumstance that will insure their good behaviour on
all occasions.'[58]

These then were the practices employed to alleviate the
manpower problem, and by which the problem was exacerbated. The statistical dimensions of the problem reveal its very
considerable extent, which the practices just described suggest;
and two sets of figures describe the normal dimensions of the
problem, against which the more severe cases may be measured.[59] Firstly, during the years from the mid-century down to
1795 the combined effect that death, desertion, discharges,
drafts, and periodic augmentations had upon the regiments of

[57] WO 27/45.
[58] WO 27/44.
[59] The figures in the following paragraphs were calculated from the voted annual
strengths of the regiments, which appear in the Establishment warrants (WO 24); from
the reports on the numbers of men in individual regiments, and their periods of
service, which appear in the Inspection Returns (WO 27); and from the regimental

foot serving in the British Isles was to oblige them to recruit an average of 1·5 per cent of their strength every month in peacetime, and 2·1 per cent per month in wartime; while the cavalry regiments recruited an average of ·9 per cent of their strength each month in peacetime, and 1·5 per cent per month in wartime. Annual intakes on this scale represent the most considerable numbers of recruits. Secondly, during the same period, the regiments of foot serving in the British Isles were able to recruit to an average strength of 90 per cent of their authorized establishments in peacetime, and to 83 per cent in wartime; while the cavalry regiments averaged 95 per cent of their authorized establishments in peacetime, and 94 per cent in wartime.

Three broad patterns or cycles in the manpower problem are worthy of note. To begin with, it will have been observed in the figures just given that the horse was much more stable than the foot: there were always fewer recruits serving with the cavalry, and cavalry regiments were always kept up quite close to their establishment strengths. This stability was the result of four factors: the cavalry regiments were only rarely subject to drafting; the cavalry suffered very little from desertion because the troopers (who were cut from a somewhat better cloth than were foot soldiers) were better paid and had a busier and less boring regimen than the foot, and consequently were subjected to a much less brutal discipline; mounted regiments were not shunted about abroad in peacetime, and so escaped some of the evils described in the previous chapter; and lastly, the number of new mounted corps raised in wartime was never great, in proportion to the number already existing, thus keeping that arm from being watered down as much as was the foot in wartime. It was largely due to the fact that the foot, conversely, was prey to all these factors, that there were always many more recruits with the foot corps than with the mounted units; and these same factors caused the actual strengths of the foot regiments to lag more noticeably behind their authorized establishments than was the case in the cavalry.

As would be expected, it is clear too that in wartime there was a falling off in effective strengths and an increase in the

returns which give detailed effective strengths (as opposed to the strengths in the stuffed muster rolls) and which appear in the Monthly Returns (WO 17). Evidence surviving before the mid-century is too scanty to permit detailed calculations.

proportion of recruits with the regiments; and this is a second pattern in the manpower problem. Table 7 illustrates quite clearly the war–peace cycle, averaging the strengths of all the regiments serving in both Britain and Ireland.

TABLE 7			
	Average Number of Recruits as a Percentage of Actual Strengths (%)		Average Actual Strengths as a Percentage of Establishments (%)
1750–4	Cavalry	9	Cavalry 95
	Infantry	16	Infantry 93
1755–63	Cavalry	17	Cavalry 94
	Infantry	25	Infantry 86
1767–74	Cavalry	13	Cavalry 95
	Infantry	20	Infantry 90
1775–85	Cavalry	19	Cavalry 95
	Infantry	27	Infantry 80
1786–93	Cavalry	12	Cavalry 93
	Infantry	22	Infantry 88

A third pattern is observable, finally, in the variations between the two kingdoms. Whereas there was never any noticeable difference between the cavalry regiments serving in Britain and those in Ireland, either in proportions of recruits in their ranks or in actual strengths as percentages of their establishments, the contrary was true among the foot. There were dissimilar recruiting rates in the foot in the two kingdoms throughout the period; and (for reasons not yet understood) the manpower problem became less severe in Ireland about 1773, and more severe in Britain. During the years 1750–73 there were proportionately more recruits in the foot regiments serving in Ireland than in those in Britain; and at the same time the actual strength of Irish corps, as percentages of their establishments, was generally less than that of their British counterparts. This whole pattern reversed itself around 1773, and henceforth it was the British corps that found themselves understrength and bringing along more recruits.

These general long-term trends tend to distort what was often, over shorter periods and at the level of individual corps, a very irregular pattern. Two sets of figures illustrate these variations, and are shown in Charts 1 and 2. The charts illustrate the manpower patterns in the foot regiments in Britain and in Ireland during the same years 1768–74 and 1784–90, years which are especially interesting because they immediately preceded, and followed upon, a long and bloody war. Chart 1 shows a general stability in the foot regiments serving in Britain, 1768–74, while in Ireland the years 1770–1 stand out, showing a notable increase in the proportion of recruits in service and a significant falling off in the actual strength of regiments in relation to establishments. What these patterns illustrate is the 'levelling' of the establishments of the British and Irish foot, put into effect in 1770, as we saw earlier: in that year the Irish regimental establishments were raised by nearly 50 per cent, and it took

CHART 1 : 1768–74

(The upper figure shows the average strengths of the battalions, as a percentage of establishments; the lower shows the average percentage of recruits in the battalions)

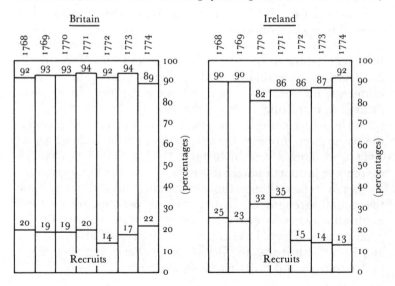

the Irish corps two years to recruit up to their new numbers.[60] Chart 2 shows quite clearly the harmful effects of the 1775–83 war upon the foot, and illustrates the length of time taken to rebuild. It also shows how very considerable a part of the army's strength consisted of recruits during most of the 1780s, notably among those corps brought home to Britain.[61]

CHART 2: 1784–90

(The upper figure shows the average strength of the battalions, as a percentage of establishments; the lower shows the average percentage of recruits in the battalions)

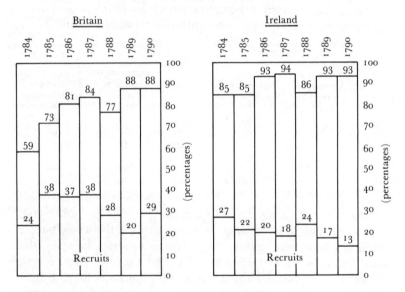

[60] In 1770 the establishment of a marching regiment in Ireland was increased from 297 to 442 men, while at the same time the establishment of a marching regiment in Britain was reduced from 497 to 442 men, to facilitate the equalizing of establishments. During 1771 a light company of forty-four men was being formed in each British battalion, and during 1772 the Irish battalions followed suit. On the formation of these companies (usually dated, mistakenly, in 1770), see WO 4/88, pp. 5–6; WO 55/416, pp. 269–70; and WO 27/21–6, *passim*.

[61] From 1784 until 1788 the establishment of battalions both in Ireland and Britain was at 392 men, while from 1788 onwards it was at 430 men. How heavily the foot had suffered is indicated—as Chart 2 shows—by the fact that in 1784 the average battalion in Britain stood on only 59 per cent of its full establishment, and that 24 per cent of these men were recruits. By 1786 these figures had been raised to only 81 per cent and 37 per cent respectively.

The annual Dublin garrisons, old and new, always serve as interesting barometers—and as a view in microcosm—of the state of the manpower problem. In 1769 for example, the manpower situation in the regiments composing the old garrison which broke up late that spring and dispersed into county cantonments, and in the regiments that came in from dispersed quarters to form the new garrison, was typical of that prevailing in the army in general; and it illustrates too the occasional irregularities always to be met with. As in Table 7, the figures in Table 8 indicate firstly the number of recruits in each regiment expressed as a percentage of the regiment's actual strength, and secondly the actual strength of each regiment expressed as a percentage of the authorized establishment.[62]

TABLE 8

| | Old Garrison, 1769 | | | New Garrison, 1769 | |
	Average no. of recruits (%)	Percentage of Establishment (%)		Average no. of recruits (%)	Percentage of Establishment (%)
45th	29	88	27th	50	84
49th	25	94	28th	27	94
50th	17	96	42nd	32	94
51st	22	90	46th	26	95
56th	4	91	53rd	25	88
63rd	14	91	54th	20	91

Of the corps forming the old garrison in 1769, the 50th, 51st, and 56th had been serving in Ireland since the 1763 peace, while the 49th had arrived from North America in 1764, the 63rd from the West Indies in 1765, and the 45th from North America in 1766. All these corps, save perhaps for the last-arrived 45th, had had ample time to recruit; and all save the 45th had a lower proportion of recruits on their strength, and stood on a higher percentage of the establishment strength than was the average condition that year among all the foot regiments in Ireland. The 56th had been out of the British Isles for only two years since its raising in 1756, a fact which accounts for the low percentage of recruits in its ranks.[63] The new garrison, meanwhile, presents a rather different picture, especially as regards recruits. None of these corps had been long

[62] WO 27/17, *passim.*
[63] R. Cannon, . . . *Fifty-Sixth Foot* (1844), 10–15.

in Ireland: the 27th, 28th, 42nd, and 46th had arrived home from North America in 1767, while the 53rd and 54th had come to Ireland from the Gibraltar garrison in 1768. Wastage abroad made good by energetic recruiting since coming home accounts for the relatively high proportion of recruits with these units, all of which (save the 54th) had a higher proportion of recruits in their ranks than the Irish average for that year. That 50 per cent of the men with the 27th Foot were recruits was due to that corps's heavy losses at Martinique and Havana, followed by drafting before leaving America.

The new Dublin garrisons of 1771 and 1774 once again point trends quite clearly (Table 9).[64]

TABLE 9

	New Garrison, 1771			New Garrison, 1774	
	Average no. of recruits (%)	Percentage of Establishment (%)		Average no. of recruits (%)	Percentage of Establishment (%)
5th	33	76	24th	17	91
28th	16	88	35th	6	88
34th	42	82	40th	16	95
44th	46	90	49th	14	92
49th	27	89	53rd	10	93
62nd	39	80	57th	14	92

The large number of recruits and the marked lag behind establishments, in 1771, show the heavy recruiting going on in the Irish foot as it was endeavouring to meet the new higher establishments set in 1770. The large numbers of men (of whom relatively few were recruits) with the regiments in 1774 shows the results of four years of stability following the 1770 augmentations, and shows too the fruits of eleven years of peace. As usual there were exceptional cases. The 34th Foot had come home in 1769 after seven years' hard service in the West Indies, West Florida, and the Louisiana country; and just before sailing for Ireland half the corps had been drafted to flesh out units newly arriving in America. The 62nd too had only recently come home from the West Indies; and the 5th— although it had been in Ireland for more than a decade—had lately been drafted to fill up departing corps.

---

[64] WO 27/23, *passim*, for 1771; and WO 27/32, *passim*, for 1774.

As Table 7 indicates, it was normal for 16–27 per cent of the men in a regiment of foot to be recruits, as it was for 9–19 per cent of those in a cavalry regiment; and our sample Dublin garrisons show that there were always a few corps containing even larger proportions of recruits. Wherever the normal figures were surpassed the regiments so situated were normally rendered unfit for service. This was one of the hard realities of the service in the eighteenth century: sound corps were struck down repeatedly and capriciously as the rigours of duty, the immediate needs of corps less fortunately situated, the press of peculiar circumstances or the simple operation of chance came into play. The manpower problem—too few recruits to complete to the establishments, too many recruits among the men already with the corps—was a permanent feature in the life of the army, against which the corps were obliged continually to struggle. Failure to recruit every month at the rates described meant that strengths would begin to lag ever more noticeably behind establishments, necessitating eventually a large-scale transfusion from other corps; and any such transfusion inevitably meant a commensurate increase in the number of recruits somewhere else in the army. This was a permanent situation because the material condition of the century ensured that there were always running sores in the army—the 38th Foot, for instance, rotting in the West Indies from 1716 to 1765, where men died almost as fast as they were shipped out—and that there would occasionally be bleeding wounds difficult to staunch by any means. Examples of corps suffering acutely from the manpower problem are legion; and it will be sufficient here to conclude with but a few individual cases and finally with a general case illustrating the problem at its worst and, hence, the bounds beyond which the manpower problem could not be alleviated.

The fumbling of bureaucracy often contributed to the fate of regiments already put in distress by the press of service, as in the cases of the 69th Foot in 1788 and the 53rd Foot in 1791. The 69th came home from West Indian campaigning at the 1783 peace and, informed (erroneously) that it would be disbanded, discharged most of its men. Not until 1784—by which time 'the remains were old and worn out objects for the Chelsea Pension' —was a beating order issued to the 69th, so that the corps had 'not only lost that time in Recruiting but all the Men from the Reduction of the Army that were fit for Service were reinlisted into other Regiments, and Recruits became very scarce from these Circumstances.' As late as 1788 some 36 per cent of the men with the regiment were recruits; and not until 1789 was it deemed fit once more for active service.[65] The 53rd, meanwhile, came home to England in August 1789 after thirteen years' service in the Canadas, and by June 1790 the corps had recruited up to 78 per cent of the establishment strength. Then a year of troubles began for the still-rebuilding regiment. Between June 1790 and June 1791 the 53rd discharged 100 worn-out men and sickly recruits, and took in 150 new men; but since five of these months, from July to November, were spent by the 53rd serving as marines on board the fleet (the corps was then quartered about Plymouth for the following two months 'where the Season of the year and the Climate . . . precluded a possibility of bringing forward our Recruits'), and because the corps was then (late in February) sent off on the long march for new quarters at Glasgow, it had proved impossible to train the regiment. When seen by a reviewing officer at Glasgow in June 1791, the 53rd was naturally unfit for service; the regiment was up to strength but 50 per cent of its men were recruits whom the War Office had not given the field officers the time to train.[66]

Other corps found themselves with large numbers of recruits and with similar training problems. In the early months of 1755 the 5th and 7th of Foot, among others, came over from Ireland and landed at Bristol and Bideford respectively. Put upon the British establishment and quartered so as to recruit up to that strength, both were reviewed in the spring. The 5th (seen at Salisbury) had by 3 May recruited to 64 per cent of the new establishment, with 49 per cent of its men recruits; the 7th (seen at Bristol) had by 12 May reached 55 per cent of the new establishment, and 48 per cent of its men were recruits. Both were reported 'too full of Recruits to be as yet fit for Service', as were several other ex-Irish regiments similarly situated; and

[65] WO 27/63. Major Yorke thought it 'a Duty I owe to myself & the Officers' to point all of this out to Maj.-Gen. Charles Lyon, when he reviewed the 69th at Dublin in 1788.

[66] WO 27/39. Major Mathews was 'mortified' by all of this, and he requested that the reviewing officer would point out the circumstances to the C.-in-C.

these corps would remain unfit for service for more than a year to come. Their condition, as Irish corps newly arrived upon the British establishment, was not extraordinary, this being as we have seen the common lot of Irish corps upon mobilization before the equalization of establishments in 1770.[67]

A few other examples should complete the picture. When in 1767 the 45th Foot was seen in Ireland, after twenty years of American service and but one year at home, it stood on only 57 per cent of the establishment and some 48 per cent of its men were 'Recruits who are not yet taught their exercise'. The 45th was unfit for service.[68] In 1786, when the 27th Foot was seen at Limerick, 60 per cent of its men were 'weakly Recruits . . . who had not sufficiently the use of their Arms'; and of these 'a Considerable number' were 'too Small and slight for any Service'. The 27th too was unfit.[69] The 37th Foot, seen at Fort George Ardersier not long after coming home from Minorca, was described in 1773 as being made up of 'Mostly growing Boys', without 'strength enough for any very hard service'.[70] In 1790 the 31st Foot, at Tynemouth, stood on 78 per cent of the establishment and 27 per cent of its men were raw: it 'consists chiefly of Young Men, and numerous Recruits,' said a reviewing officer, 'and in this State no Corps can be reported fit for immediate active Service.'[71] Every year there were always several corps in this condition.

The figures in the tables above show that war put a strain on the manpower problem by increasing the demand for soldiers. As long as a good part of the army was campaigning in theatres close to home—Germany, the Low Countries, the Iberian peninsula, and the Mediterranean—and as long as that part of the army committed to distant theatres—North America and the West Indies—was not kept excessively large for several successive campaigns, and had between itself and the British Isles open and assured lines of communication, then the strain on manpower could be accepted and the worst effects kept at bay. Only once during our period did these conditions, which were essentially strategic and logistical, not obtain; and the result for the army was catastrophic. We refer of course to the

[67] Both are in WO 27/3.   [68] WO 27/11.
[69] WO 27/58, Pt 1.   [70] WO 27/27.
[71] WO 27/66.

war of 1775–83, in which seventy-nine regular battalions—
two-thirds of the total number in service at the height of the
war—were deployed in the Americas.

During the 1775–83 war, government attempted to subdue
a rebellion by conquering a map; the venture was risky in the
first place and, when the Bourbons intervened and sent their
fleets into the Atlantic and Caribbean, it was doomed to failure.
Almost from the outset it was accepted in London that there
would be too few troops available with which to prosecute such
a war; great numbers of German troops were hired and loyalist
corps were raised, therefore, without which the war could not
have been undertaken.[72] But if government put faith in auxil-
iaries there were some soldiers, aware of the army's chronic
manpower problem, who saw from the start the futility of using
force in such a venture; and none was better placed than
Edward Harvey who, as Adjutant-General, was daily made
aware of the problem and knew where such an attempt must
lead. It was Harvey's professional opinion, voiced as early as
30 June 1775, 'that attempting to Conquer A[merica] Intern-
ally by our Ld. Forces, is as wild an Idea, as ever controverted
Com^n Sense'—a 'Truth' which, he was certain, 'will be in the
end Apparent.'[73] On 6 July, referring to the massive reinforcement sent to a beleaguered Gage at Boston, Harvey stated the
position once again:

'It is expected yt ye last of the Troops from Ire^d wou'd reach Bost^n ab^t ye
10th of June. Probably soon after, they will get Elbow Room, as the
Troops will not be contented to eat Salt Beef in yt D——'d Oven. News
is expected ab^t ye 3rd Week of this Month, yt G[age] has freed himself
from ye B.kade, *but what then?*'[74]

Three weeks later, on 31 July, Harvey observed that in London
'The *Ton* is Vigour & Conquest'; but he added, 'Where's the
Means?', and answered his own question by saying 'Not by

---

[72] The decisive influence of Bourbon naval operations has most recently been demonstrated by P. Mackesy, op. cit., and by J. R. Dull, *The French Navy and American
Independence* (Princeton, 1976). D. Syrett, *Shipping and the American War. A Study of
British Transport Organization, 1775–1783* (1970): N. Baker, *Government and Contractors.
The British Treasury and War Supplies, 1775–1783* (1971); and R. A. Bowler, *Logistics and
the Failure of the British Army in America, 1775–83* (Princeton, 1975), discuss in depth
some of the logistical difficulties.

[73] WO 3/5, pp. 36–7.

[74] WO 3/5, p. 40. My italics.

Land, by Brit. Troops. The Fund is not Suff¹, take my word for
it. A Driblet is going over. What then?'[75] This was practical and
informed opinion: the Adjutant-General's appreciation of the
military situation was sharp, and was proved correct when it
became impossible to keep the army in the Americas up to
strength, let alone to augment it very considerably. Twelve
regiments, as we noted earlier, became so weak that they had
to be wholly drafted into the others, themselves understrength;
and as the regiments straggled home after the 1783 peace the
extent of the manpower collapse was immediately apparent.
It had in fact been evident from 1778. Before that year the manpower patterns in the foot in the British Isles had continued
rather as they were during the years preceding the war (as in
Chart 1 above): that is, the average strength of a regiment had
been about 90 per cent of the authorized establishment, while
on average about 17 per cent of the men in each corps were
recruits. These figures began to slide in 1776, and the slide
became quite noticeable by 1777. In 1779 27 per cent of the
men in the average regiment of foot in the British Isles were
recruits, while the average strength of the regiments had fallen
to 85 per cent of the establishments. By 1781, 29 per cent of the
men were recruits and, very alarmingly, strengths had fallen
to only 71 per cent of the establishment. By 1784, as the regiments were coming home, the figures were 26 per cent recruits
and 71 per cent of the establishment; and henceforth they
followed the patterns shown in Chart 2 above.

These figures were appalling; and the conditions that they
reflect may be seen in a summary of the manpower situation in
ten regiments quartered in Britain in 1784, randomly selected
from those that came home to Britain in 1783 (Table 10).[76]
Most of these regiments had been reduced to small hard cores
of veterans; but because their numbers were so weak, and because there were so many units similarly situated and now all
competing for great numbers of men, it would take several
years to rebuild. The 23rd Foot, for example, had in its ranks
only eleven recruits when seen in May of 1784; but its 'ranks'
contained only 103 private men, scarcely enough to fill three

---

[75] Ibid., p. 49. On 29 July, refering to the news of Bunker Hill, Harvey frankly told
a friend that 'Honʳ is gam'd in N.A. with too much Blood.'

[76] WO 27/51, *passim*.

TABLE 10

	Average no. of recruits (%)	Percentage of Establishment (%)	
22nd	16	49	(seen at Chatham, 18 June)
23rd	8	30	(seen at Doncaster, 14 May)
24th	50	68	(seen at Edinburgh, 7 July)
27th	59	33	(seen at Kidderminster, 7 June)
28th	22	55	(seen at Claydon, 22 May)
38th	17	60	(seen at Stafford, 5 June)
40th	24	52	(seen at Plymouth Dock, 27 Aug.)
43rd	27	48	(seen at Hilsea, 2 Aug.)
62nd	42	59	(seen at Dundee, 20 Sept.)
63rd	10	40	(seen at Bury St. Edmunds, 3 May)

companies. The 27th Foot, in June 1784, had only ninety-nine private men left in its ranks—and of these nearly eighty were recruits, making its plight even worse than that of the 23rd.

Regiments continued to straggle home in this condition until as late as 1788, since some were left behind in garrison in the Canadas and the West Indies; there was little that the recruiting parties could do, and there were only a few sound corps from which drafts could be sent out. As Chart 2 shows, it was not until 1786 that most of the regiments serving in Ireland were restored to order, and not until 1789 that corps in Britain were back up to scratch. Thus had Harvey's expectations been fulfilled: and thus the limits of the possible were delineated, and the effects of crossing over those limits were brought home. The manpower problem was always difficult enough in peacetime; by pushing the system beyond endurable limits in an ill-advised pursuit of political goals which were probably unattainable, the military power of Britain was rendered almost negligible for most of the 1780s, indeed almost up to the outbreak of the French Revolution. Until nearly the end of the 1780s much of the British Army consisted of recruits, in very under-strength regiments. No doubt the Revenue suffered.

(c) MUNITIONS

The condition of the arms carried in the regiments was frequently bad—often atrocious; and both the quantity and quality of the ammunition and ancillary equipment were, in general, worse. Since this munitions situation not only was to have a baneful effect upon the training of the corps in general but was, in many cases, to render individual units unfit to take the field, its salient features must be considered here.

The quarter-century of conflict preceding the Utrecht settlement had seen violence carried to an unprecedented scale, creating for the munitions makers a seller's market. The agents and surveyors of the Ordnance had encountered shortages (both real and artificially created), high prices, monopoly, and competition from allies in the foreign munitions markets; and the result was that, by Utrecht, the army and the Ordnance held a variety of non-standardized and often shoddy weapons.[77] In order to avoid any repetition of the unwarranted expense and confusion which had characterized British munitions procurement during these years, the Board of Ordnance instituted in 1715 the 'Ordnance system of manufacture' whereby, instead of purchasing completed firearms as heretofore, the separate component parts were contracted for among several manufacturers. These parts—locks, barrels, brass furniture, and so forth—were delivered to the Tower and to Dublin Castle from where, as occasion required, they were sent to private gunsmiths for roughstocking and setting up. By this system a quantity of parts and firearms sufficient to cater to the army's normal requirements was kept on hand in stores, and the gunmakers were deprived of the opportunity to fleece the Treasury in time of crisis.[78] Additionally, the Ordnance was able by this system to enforce sealed patterns, supplying these to the parts makers and final 'setters-up'; and from 1722 the

[77] Of the many monographs dealing with most aspects of arms technology, only the most useful are listed here. The best background survey on the course of arms evolution before Blenheim is G. R. Mork, 'Flint and Steel: A Study in Military Technology and Tactics in 17th-Century Europe', *Smithsonian Journal of History*, 2 (1967), 25–52; while H. C. B. Rogers, *Weapons of the British Soldier* (1972), 51–89, and H. L. Blackmore, *British Military Firearms, 1650–1850* (1967), 17–39, give the best available background material dealing specifically with British arms. The confused arms situation, *c.*1700–15, is described in H. C. B. Rogers, op cit. 83–9, in H. L. Blackmore, op cit. 38–44, and in C. Walton, *History of the British Standing Army, 1660–1700* (1894), 425–36. D. Chandler, *The Art of Warfare in the Age of Marlborough* (1976), *passim*, contains some useful material.

[78] The system is best described in H. L. Blackmore, op. cit. 39–42; in A. D. Darling, *Red Coat and Brown Bess* (Ottawa, 1970), 15–19; and in D. W. Bailey, *British Military Longarms, 1715–1815* (1971), 9–12. Blackmore is considered the standard reference on 'Brown Bess', but Darling and Bailey—used in conjunction—are preferable. Darling deals with his subject in great detail, but, writing as a collector, tends to impose a system of classification on individual members of a family of arms not designed or thought of after any such fashion. Bailey is full of good sense and is a useful antidote to the usual approach, which is that of arms collectors.

colonels of corps—who were still free to take from government the cash value of their regiments' arms, rather than taking from the royal armouries the actual arms themselves, and to contract on their own for cheaper replacements elsewhere—were obliged to purchase firearms built after the established pattern.[79] The Ordnance system survived well into the nineteenth century and, although low peacetime budgeting occasionally forced the government to import large quantities of foreign arms in times of crisis, it was generally successful.

The standard pattern Ordnance-issue flint firelock, the Land Pattern Musket or, more familiarly, the 'Brown Bess', appeared in three successive variants during our period.[80] The first of these was phased in slowly, issued as corps found it necessary to replace older sets of arms, and as the custom of private purchase by colonels fell into disuse. Until about 1730 the majority of the regiments were carrying a variety of pre-Land Pattern firelocks, but these—'structurally a combination of Dutch features from earlier muskets and more modern ideas taken from sporting weapons and from French military arms'—were of the same calibre as the Land Pattern firelocks, and were comparable ballistically.[81] Contemporary Englishmen thought the Land Pattern firelocks to be the best service firearm available in Europe, a view with which most modern authorities agree; they were certainly better than the Prussian pieces and were stronger (if heavier and less easy to handle) than those of the French.[82] But despite the fact that the evolution of military-firearms design had by the third decade of the century placed

[79] A. D. Darling, op. cit. 16–19. Chandler, *Warfare*, 79, gives a good example of the activities of a colonel's agent (of the 16th Foot), searching London for contract arms in 1717.

[80] These were the Long Land Pattern, which flourished *c.*1720–90, but was being phased out from 1768; the Short Land Pattern, made standard issue throughout the army in 1768, but versions of which had been carried by the dragoons since *c.*1720; and the India Pattern, manufactured originally for the East India Company's forces and in construction somewhat inferior to the Short Land Pattern, commandeered into service in 1793 and manufactured in great numbers for the regular army until 1815. A fourth variant, the New Land Pattern, was introduced in 1802: it slowly superseded the other patterns during the Napoleonic Wars. Variations between (and within) these several patterns are best treated in H. L. Blackmore, op. cit., D. W. Bailey, op. cit., and A. D. Darling, op. cit., all *passim*. Land Pattern muskets were all of ·75 bore.

[81] D. W. Bailey, op. cit. 13. The best survey of pre-Besses and proto-Besses is in H. L. Blackmore, op. cit. 42–4, and plates 5, 10–13.

[82] E.g. Lord George Townshend recalled that during service with Wolfe's army at Quebec in 1759 'the Superiority of our Musquets over the French Arms were generally

a generally fine weapon in the hands of the British Army, advantage was dissipated by a Board of Ordnance which conformed rigidly to the peacetime policy of parsimony, of which the army was the principal victim. It was the firm policy of the Ordnance to issue new sets of arms only *in extremis*—that is, either when a regiment would no longer accept the risk of loading its current set with blank cartridges, let alone with ball, or when an already ill-armed unit was about to embark upon active wartime service. The average life expectancy of a set of firelocks was about eight to ten years, after which they should have been returned to stores for salvage and rebuilding; but since the Ordnance preferred to wait until one or the other of the two above-mentioned eventualities had actually arisen, before acting, a great many corps were always exceedingly ill armed. This deserves some illustration, since the situation was always common and often incredible.

A typical set of arms was that belonging to the 3rd Dragoons, seen at Rochester in 1754. The 3rd—'a Good Regiment'— 'want much to be Supplied with a New Sett of Arms', it was reported. The corps's firelocks had been issued in small lots each year from 1744 through 1747; and although a last lot had been received in 1751 most were now in bad condition. Another typical set of arms was that belonging to the 31st Foot, serving in England in 1773. The 31st had been completely rearmed in 1762 and now, eleven years later, 173 of its firelocks were reported still in good condition while 162 were in 'bad' shape.[83] There were always a great many corps armed in this fashion. What 'bad' meant, the following examples illustrate. Some two-thirds of the firelocks belonging to the 61st Foot, when in garrison in 1777 at St. Philip's Castle, Minorca, were 'bad'— that is, they 'would not last two Days firing from the Works in

acknowledged both as to the Distance they carried & the Frequency of the Fire, driving them from Their Bushes— & holding them at a great Distance as Circumstances required.' This suggests a better quality of powder, not of arms (Kent RO Amherst MSS 073/22). The best study of the eighteenth-century French Army's regulation longarms is the series of booklets published collectively as J. Boudriot, *Armes à feu françaises* (Paris, 1961–3). Cahier 10, 'Le fusil modèle 1717 et le système 1728–1734', is most useful on the establishment of sealed patterns and royal arsenals for the production of government firearms, with which early British practice can be compared. On the Prussian firelocks, see P. Paret, *Yorck and the Era of Prussian Reform* (Princeton, 1966), 14–15, 97, 271–3.

[83] WO 27/3 and 27.

case of a Siege'. The firelocks of the new 71st Foot, when seen at Edinburgh in 1759, were mostly 'bad' too: while the corps was being reviewed 'some few Mistakes happen'd, occasion'd by some of the Mens Pieces going off as they Presented.' Like those of the 71st, the firelocks of the 11th Foot, seen in 1774, must have inspired fear in the men: during a review 'some Firelocks [were] going off when loading—and some upon the Men's Shoulders'. At a 1785 review the 22nd Foot, otherwise well drilled, declined to put on a display of volley fire: 'None could be perform'd, on account of the very bad state of the Arms', reported the reviewing officer, who concluded that the 22nd would be fit for service only 'when supplied with Arms'.[84]

When news of this sort reached the Ordnance the records show that, in the majority of cases, there would be two or three years of heel-dragging before action was taken. Thus the arms of Bury's 20th of Foot were, in 1753, reported to be mostly worn out; and although the corps was 'well Deciplin'd' it could not be considered fit for service until 'Supply'd with Sufficient Arms'. It took the Ordnance two years to issue a new set to the 20th.[85] When seen at Kilkenny in mid-1774, the firelocks of the 17th Foot were all 'clean, but bad'; the reviewing officer was informed that these arms had been 'received in 1768 and reported to be thin and defective when received'. The Ordnance had turned a blind eye for six years. A year later, in June 1775, the 17th was still carrying these defective arms.[86]

---

[84] WO 27/38, 6, 30, and 54 respectively. The Ordnance, cheeseparing, occasionally took advantage of corps so situated by palming off upon them second-rate stores. In mid-1787 the 44th Foot's firelocks had been 'Received new very lately'; but they were 'not good, being the Arms bought in Holland during the [last] War' (WO 27/59). In 1785 most of the firelocks of the 58th Foot were in 'good' condition, but a reviewing officer reported that 'the Regiment ought to have a complete set of New Arms' because those they had were 'not the usual Arms of the Infantry, being some Inches shorter than the common, and not all of a length, having been delivered from the Garrison Stores at Gibraltar' (WO 27/54). Late in 1756 the 23rd Foot, home from the Minorca disaster, was rearmed with 'Firelocks of different kinds'; and the 23rd, accordingly, was in Feb. 1757 as yet unable to go through the arms exercises or the firings (WO 27/4). In late 1754–early 1755 two corps new-raising in America, Shirley's 50th and Pepperell's 51st of Foot, were sent inferior firelocks. Shirley's got 1,000 with 'single Bridle Locks, Nose bands & Wood Ram[ro]ds', and Pepperell's 1,000 old 'Dutch with Noseband & wood Rammers'. The locks were reported 'wore out and the Hammers soft' [i.e. giving a poor spark] R. Chartrand, 'The 50th (Shirley's) and 51st (Pepperell's) Regiments of Foot', *Military Collector & Historian*, 27 (1975), 172–4.

[85] WO 27/3.

[86] WO 27/32 and 35. On the morning of 17 June 1775 the 52nd Foot, which had been

With several corps armed after this fashion the army was apt to find itself, on the eve of war, ill prepared to take the field. Random surveys for 1755 and 1774 show this to be true. Of six regiments (the 7th, 8th, 11th, 12th, 20th, and 37th of Foot) seen in England between April and October 1755, for example, the 20th had just been rearmed and the 11th (whose firing had been 'indifferent . . . probably occasion'd by the badness of their arms'), was expecting 'new ones hourly'. The arms of the other four corps were all bad: those of the 7th had last been issued as long ago as 1739, and those of the 37th in 1742; and while the drill of the 8th was 'Excessively well perform'd' and that of the 12th was 'Extream Fine', neither could be considered fit for service until rearmed.[87] It was the same story in 1774. Of six regiments randomly selected (the 17th, 34th, 35th, 55th, 57th, and 63rd of Foot) among those seen in Ireland between May and July of that year, all were exceedingly ill armed. The firelocks of the 17th, as we noted above, had been defective in manufacture. All the firelocks of the 35th, issued eight years previously, were bad, while of those belonging to the 55th two-thirds were bad. Among the other three corps only the firelocks of the new light companies (raised and armed in 1772) were any good, while all the rest were unfit: thus 351 out of 390 stand of arms in the 34th were bad, as were 351 out of 390 stand in the 57th, and 328 out of 377 stand in the 63rd.[88] None of these corps could fight with firelocks in this condition, and training with such weapons was both dangerous and difficult.[89]

Cavalry pistols—in ·56 calibre for the Horse and ·65 calibre

in America for nine years, was issued a new set of arms, badly needed, on Boston Common—and went into action with them that afternoon at Bunker Hill. This was no doubt the Ordnance's record for eleventh-hour issues.

[87] WO 27/3, *passim*.

[88] WO 27/32, *passim*. A 'stand' of arms consisted of a firelock and a bayonet which fitted it. Bayonets were made to a pattern by contractors and, when a firelock was set up, bayonets were sent out with the other parts; since they, like the barrels to which they were attached, varied slightly in dimensions, pairs were matched by the setters-up, creating a 'stand'.

[89] Much of the problem could have been averted if government had made provision for an armourer on the establishment of each corps. The Prussian regiments each had one for this purpose. In 1756 Jeffrey Amherst, like a few other colonels, himself paid the salaries of two such to serve with his 15th Foot; and this bore fruit, his lieutenant-colonel reporting in 1757 on the excellent musketry of the corps due in part to 'the good Order our Arms are kept in, oweing I think in great measure to our own Gun Smiths . . . a thing so necessary that I am amaz'd there is not an establishment for an adequate

for the Dragoons—were manufactured according to the Ordnance system too, although surviving examples indicate that colonels contracted more frequently among the private gunmakers than did their fellow colonels of foot. Pistols were merely an accessory arm in the cavalry and were little used or abused, although the light dragoon corps (raised from 1759) spent much time practising skirmishing tactics with them. Since they were so little used they were not subjected to much hard service, and it is rare to find a report on a cavalry corps with bad or faulty pistols.[90]

Not only worn-out firearms but ammunition too presented a problem for the corps. Powder (which was manufactured at both private and government mills, and issued from the Royal Laboratory at Woolwich), was issued in sizeable quantities.[91] From 1715 to 1755 the marching battalions in Britain each got in peacetime sufficient powder for 45,000 firelock charges (priming included) per annum; from 1764 to 1768 the issue was down to 31,500 charges per battalion p.a.; during the peacetime years between 1769 and 1786 the issue was back up at 42,000 charges p.a.; and from 1786 to the end of our period the scale was 35,000 charges per battalion p.a. In Ireland, from 1769, each battalion in 'county cantonments' got powder for 35,000 charges p.a., while those in the Dublin garrison (where mock actions were normal training routine) each got 60,000 p.a. These variations reflected both changes in the establishment strengths of the battalions and government efforts to cut costs; but the issue, though not princely, was enough to provide every infantryman with powder enough to fire from 60 to 120 charges

number in every Corp' (Kent RO Amherst MSS 013/4). Instead, the Ordnance periodically sent out officers of the Royal Artillery 'to examine the Arms of those Regiments who were upon the late Reviews [in this case, of 1734] reported to be out of Order'. SP 41/12, Secretary at War to Gen. Evans, 4 Jan. 1739/40.

[90] The army's horse pistols are best dealt with in H. L. Blackmore, op. cit. 40, 47, 63–4, and plates 8 and 18. L. H. Gordon, 'The British Cavalry & Dragoon Pistol', *CJAC* 5 (1967), 111–18, and 6 (1968), 10–13, is well illustrated; and the text, if skimpy, indicates the main points in the development of cavalry pistols through our period.

[91] The statistics on the quantities of powder, flints, and ball which appear in the next two paragraphs have been collected from the following sources: WO 3/26, pp. 165–6; WO 4/130, pp. 382–4, 4/83; p. 364, 4/87, p. 60 (plus 4/88, 89, 92, 93, 94, 125, and 137, *passim*); WO 55/348, pp. 10, 16, 55/411, pp. 140–1, 163–4, 55/416, pp. 127, 155, 174, 193; Notts. RO Staunton of Staunton MSS, DDS. 49/10; Berks. RO, D/E.Ll.05, fo. 45; *Standing Orders and Regulations for the Army in Ireland* (Dublin, 1794), 95–6; and Capt. G. Smith, *An Universal Military Dictionary* (1779), 36–7, 58, 254.

annually, the variation again depending upon establishments.[92] Flints were issued in the same proportion to the foot—that is, an average of about 1,400 per battalion p.a. during the peace years from 1715 to 1755, and in varying quantities thereafter; this was sufficient to provide each infantryman with two flints per year (four in Ireland) and, since these could be reversed when worn and new striking faces knapped, that was just sufficient to fire off the 60–120 charges of powder. The quantities of powder and flint issued to the cavalry were more varied, since establishments in the Horse, Dragoons, and other mounted types were not alike, and because establishment strengths within one type varied too. Issues were sizable, however, since not only muskets or carbines but pistols too had to be provided for. Until 1726 the ordinary dragoon regiment got enough powder per annum for about 7,000 charges for their firearms and, from 1726 to the century's end, enough for about 24,500 charges per year in peacetime.[93] In Ireland the dragoons got enough for about 17,500 charges per regiment per year. The heavy Horse regiments each got enough powder for about 14,000 charges per year throughout the century in peacetime. Flints were issued at the rate of about three carbine flints per man and three pistol flints per man, each year, to cavalrymen of all types.

The government, then, cannot be said to have stinted on the quantity of its annual peacetime issues of powder and flints. Quality was, however, sometimes another matter, as we shall see below. It was rather upon lead shot that government fixed, to save money. Each year in peacetime, from the outset of our period until as late as 1785, the annual issue of shot to each battalion of foot in Britain, Ireland, and the overseas garrisons and plantations, was a fixed 1 cwt.—sufficient, depending upon establishment strengths, to provide each infantryman with from two to four musket balls per year. Only in 1786 was the annual issue of shot increased—by 800 per cent, so massive an increase as to point the sudden and extraordinarily late awareness of the evils of cheeseparing. In the horse, an average of two

---

[92] See the tables of regimental establishments in Appendix C, for variations. In wartime much larger quantities of ammunition were issued, so that it was then possible to carry on adequate musketry training, unlike in peacetime.

[93] Early in 1726 each dragoon regiment in Britain had its annual powder supply raised from two to six barrels, in belated recognition of the fact that, as dragoons, they had often to practise the firings on foot. WO 55/348, pp. 10, 16.

pistol balls and from six to ten longarm balls were issued each year to each dragoon, and an average of three pistol balls and from seven to thirteen longarm balls went to each trooper of Horse and to each dragoon guard. Peacetime musketry drill—firing blank cartridges or 'squibs'—was possible; target practice—firing ball cartridge for effect—was not, until 1786.[94]

The quality and quantity of the ammunition issued were subjects of continual and often bitter complaint. When in 1768 the officers of the 2/1st Foot, serving in Scotland, complained that 'the Allowance of Ammunition [is] not sufficient for the Exercise and Discipline of the Regiment', they were echoing a general complaint.[95] Reviewing general officers often took it upon themselves to speak on this subject for the corps they had seen: thus, after Maj.-Gen. Alexander Mackay had seen the 4th, 11th, and 67th of Foot, serving in England in 1773, he reported that 'the Powder given to the Troops is in General very bad, the Flints remarkably so; And the Quantity of Ball so small,' he added, 'that it is impossible to practice the men to fire at Marks, as should be done constantly.'[96] These complaints were so much wasted ink. A year after Mackay sent in his remarks another reviewing officer, Maj.-Gen. William Howe, saw the 4th Foot once again, and they, like all the rest, were still ill supplied; he reported that the 4th needed 'practice in firing Ball', and added that the 4th's light company (whose very business was accurate skirmishing), had 'not been practiced in firing Ball'.[97] When Howe saw the 3rd Foot that summer, he found it poorly trained; and among other things, he reported, the corps loaded too slowly, 'presents too high without Aim . . . & *have not fired Ball for some years*.'[98] When Pulteney's 13th of Foot was reviewed in England in 1753, 'the several Fireings cou'd not be perform'd for Want of Powder'—another complaint which was not at all unusual, although the firings were the most important part of the drill of the foot.[99] The quality of

[94] Musketry and target practice are described here, pp. 262–3, 279–80.
[95] WO 27/12.
[96] WO 27/27, 67th Foot.
[97] WO 27/30.
[98] Ibid. My italics.
[99] WO 27/3. When in 1773 the 11th Foot applied for its yearly supply, the Board of Ordnance 'sent only Six Months powder . . . Alledging the Regt had no right to the Powder for the first Six Months because the Application had not been made in proper time.'

flints, likewise, was often wretched: they were either too chalky or had in them too much iron. The colonel of the 46th Foot, serving in the war of 1775–83, 'lamented that the valour of his men was often "rendered vain by the badness of the pebble stone".'[100]

It was, therefore, fairly common to find a regiment of foot armed with old and worn-out firearms, and it was normal for the ammunition issued to all corps, horse and foot, to be inferior, in short supply, or both. These things were all to have a serious effect upon the training and readiness of the corps. There were in addition three other munitions-related problems which, since they too affected the training and firepower of the regiments, should also be considered.

Where the Prussians had shown the way from very early in the century by issuing to their infantry ramrods made of iron instead of wood, thereby speeding the rate of fire, the British were slow to follow this lead. It would appear that a combination of factors—economy, and difficulty in preparing a strong but tensile steel alloy—made for conservatism here.[101] Not until the 1750s were steel rods fitted by the Ordnance to all new Long Land firelocks, and not until 1770 were all new Short Land firelocks so equipped.[102] Several regiments in both Britain and Ireland had been issued firelocks fitted with iron ramrods during the 1720s (the earliest known case occurred in 1724), but these issues were not continued during the 1730s and earlier 1740s.[103] During the later 1740s and henceforth, firelocks returned to the armouries for repairs were usually fitted with steel rods at the same time; and from 1748 onwards corps were selected at random and irregularly—as stores and finances

---

[100] R. A. Bowler, op. cit. 150–1.

[101] Rods were made of both iron and steel, and their slow and erratic issue may have been due in part to varying metallurgy, producing varied results. Writing in 1726, Henry Hawley, then colonel of the 33rd Foot, had the following to say in favour of the standard wooden rods, and he probably echoed wide sentiment in the army: 'The iron rammers the Foot are coming into are very ridiculous . . . for if they have not some alloy of steel they stand bent and cannot be returned. If they have the least too much steel then they snap like glass.' He noted too that they rusted easily and got stuck in the tailpipes of the firelocks. 'I would stick to the wooded rammers,' he concluded. P. Sumner (ed.), 'General Hawley's "Chaos" ', *JSAHR* 26 (1948), 93.

[102] A. D. Darling, op. cit. 21; H. L. Blackmore, op. cit. 46–7; and D. W. Bailey, op. cit. 15.

[103] A. D. Darling, op. cit. 21, and H. L. Blackmore, op. cit. 47.

permitted—to have the whole of their arms converted.[104] By
the mid-1750s the general sentiment was clearly in favour of
metal rods;[105] and although as late as 1776 part of the army at
Boston still had wooden rods, most had gone by 1763.[106]

Although the self-contained paper cartridge—a short paper
tube, twisted and tied shut at each end and containing a ball
and a measured charge of powder—had been taken up by the
whole of the army during Queen Anne's reign, it was not until
the mid-1730s that the speedy practice of both loading *and*
priming from cartridges was adopted. Before then, the British
soldier carried on his right hip not only a case to hold his
cartridges but also a bottle-shaped flask known as a primer. The
flask contained finer-grained priming powder for sprinkling in
the pan of the lock, since fine grains took the spark and ignited
faster than did the more heavily granulated powder in the
main charge cartridges. Of the several drill regulations that appeared early in the century (in 1708, 1711, 1716, 1723, 1727–8,
and 1740, each of which is discussed in Chapter III below) only
the last provided for priming directly from the cartridge itself;
the others followed a sequence of loading motions which involved, first, the priming of the pan from the flask and only
then (once the flask had been put back in place, and the muzzle
of the piece brought up close to the soldier) was the cartridge
taken from its case, torn open with the teeth, the charge poured
down the barrel and the paper and ball stuffed down after it.
Like the use of the metal ramrod, the trick of priming direct

[104] E.g. early in 1748 the colonels of the 13th, 20th, 31st, and 36th of Foot were instructed that they should 'immediately send up to the Office of Ordnance 200 Firelocks
of each Regt. in Order to be fitted with Iron Rammers, and that when the same were
returned to the Respective Regiments they Should send up 200 more of each Regiment,
and continue so to do, till, all the Firelocks of these Corps should be compleated with
Iron Ram Rods' (WO 55/409, p. 75). Many similar orders went out during the 1750s
(e.g. WO 55/349, p. 79).

[105] Review reports and private publications show the changed sentiment. When the
3rd Foot was reviewed in England in 1754 the men were observed to 'Load very slow':
'it was an extream Cold day, and they have Wooden Rammers', said the reviewing
officer. As early as 1740, when the 6th Marines were raised, a subaltern in that regiment
complained of its being issued wooden ramrods. He thought them 'enough to dis-
concert the best battalion of Infantry that ever went into the field in the firings; I have
seen forty men at common exercise and there were twelve rammers broken in firing six
rounds, by which it is plain that they are very unfit to go into action with.' Lt. Terence
O'Loghlen, *The Marine Volunteer* (1766), quoted in C. Field, *Britain's Sea Soldiers. A
History of the Royal Marines and Their Predecessors*, i (Liverpool, 1924), 73.

[106] A. D. Darling, op. cit. 21.

from the self-contained cartridge sped up the rate of fire, and so was an important innovation. In this the British were about as up to date as the Bourbon armies but, once again, they lagged behind the Prussians.[107]

Wooden rammers and priming flasks slowed the rate of fire; and yet a third weak link in the munitions chain was the cartridge case, slung at the right hip from a belt worn over the left shoulder. These cases—made of leather, with a weather-proof flap, and containing a wooden block drilled to receive the paper cartridges—were contracted for by the colonels of corps with funds provided by government; and, since the colonels customarily profited by ordering shoddy cases (and by ordering them as infrequently as possible), they were often either in disrepair or absent altogether. If government practised economy on lead shot, it was on the cartridge cases that the colonels and their agents did likewise; and examples of this abuse are legion. Seven-eighths of the cartridge cases worn by the 42nd Foot in 1775, though new, were of bad construction, 'not being deep enough to Contain Cartridges with Ball'. The 42nd campaigned extensively in America from 1776 to 1783 and, when seen at Halifax, Nova Scotia, in 1784, all these cases had been 'wore out on Actual Service' and were beyond repair.[108] Only half of the men in the 33rd Foot had cartridge cases in 1775; the rest, it was reported, 'were lost in Germany'—twelve years earlier, in 1763.[109] The cases worn in Shirley's 50th and Pepperell's 51st, in 1755, were too small; and they contained blocks so small that the cartridges would not fit the holes, while there was not 'substance of the Wood to widen them sufficiently, the leather scanty and bad likewise'. The cases belonging to the

---

[107] British military dress and accoutrements, despite the plethora of works on these subjects for later periods, have nowhere been studied in detail for the period *c.* 1689–1735. I have seen no illustrations of primers or cartridges in these years, nor have I seen detailed illustrations of the cartridge cases of the same period. On the contrary, detailed studies of the dress and accoutrements of the French Army of this period have been made, and might provide grounds for comparisons. The French soldier carried a small cartridge case in which there were ten or twenty paper cartridges, each with a measured charge but without any shot; these charges were backed up by a large powder flask, used in case all of the cartridges were expended. A smaller flask contained the priming powder, while a small bag held the supply of ball. The self-contained cartridge became regulation in France *c.* 1725–30. See L. Rousselot's series of plates with accompanying texts, *L'Armée française* (Paris, 1962–7), plates *19, 79, 93*, and *99*.

[108] WO 27/37 and 52.

13th Foot in 1768 were all bad, not having been replaced since receiving them at Gibraltar, eleven years previously.[110] In 1778 the 36th Foot, having been in Ireland for three years since returning home from the West Indies, had among its men only 180 good cases; of the rest belonging to the regiment, 319 were 'bad' and 311 were missing altogether.[111] The effects of foreign service upon such shoddy materials, whether in wartime or peacetime, were serious. When the 29th and 31st of Foot came home from the Canadas in 1787, where they had been for nearly two decades, they were in poor condition. The 29th was thirty cases short and the rest were useless; and while the 31st had 150 good cases, all the rest were wanting.[112] Regiments in which the men had no cartridge cases, or no proper cartridge cases in which to keep their ammunition, were from the standpoint of training and active service at a serious disadvantage, since the musketry drill of the period was designed around the ready availability of ammunition—and that necessitated cases.[113] That this one item of equipment should have been so generally bad in the army is a sad comment on the care with which the regiments were maintained.

Finally, little need be said with regard to the edged weapons —the swords and sabres carried by the cavalry and the hangers worn by the foot—since these seldom presented difficulties. The heavy, straight-bladed, basket-hilted swords used universally by all types of British cavalry (save light dragoons) were ordered for all regiments in 1707, and the general pattern

---

[109] WO 27/35.

[110] WO 27/12 and R. Chartrand, art. cit. 172.

[111] WO 27/41.

[112] WO 27/61.

[113] Light infantrymen frequently loaded not with cartridge but with loose or patched ball carried in bullet bags, and carried large powder horns for charging and priming. They argued that cartridge cases and shoulder straps were an encumbrance, interfering with their rapid motions; but in fact the horns were more of an affectation than they were utilitarian. Lt.-Gen. the Earl of Cavan, after considering horns and bullet bags (in 1777), concluded correctly that their use 'must be confessed to be very dilatory and inconvenient': the soldier had to load from two places rather than the single self-contained cartridge; there was paper for wadding immediately available only with cartridges; the proper charge could not easily be measured; and priming from a horn could be dangerous if a weapon had hung fire, since the horn might blow up once in contact with the priming pan. Cavan, therefore, would 'not hesitate to pronounce, that a Man with Cartridges will fire at the least twice, before a Man who is provided as above, can fire once'. WO 27/37, 32nd Foot.

remained in use until 1788.[114] In the interim the only significant modification in general design occurred at about the mid-century, and consisted in the lengthening of the blade from 30–4 inches to 35–9 inches, and the gradual replacement of double-edged blades with single-edged—both changes reflecting the increased tactical emphasis on giving the point or thrust, rather than laying about with less-effective sideways cuts. Swords were no concern of the Ordnance but were bought by the colonels from private manufacturers: most blades were of Solingen or Toledo manufacture earlier in the century but later came increasingly from the Birmingham cutlers, while the hilts (which varied greatly in detail and quality) were made in England, in Ireland, and in Scotland especially. The light dragoons, meanwhile, carried a lighter, somewhat shorter weapon, without the large basket hilt and with a noticeably curved blade—the sabre. Before 1788 these were of regimental pattern, more so than the swords of the heavies, and they were built for slashing and cutting—the style of fighting expected of light horsemen.

The weapons of both types of cavalry, heavy and light, were standardized in 1788, after a sword or sabre from each regiment was sent to the Adjutant-General's office for testing; it was intended to 'fix upon one, for the general use of the whole'.[115] The result was the 1788 pattern light cavalry sabre (which was improved upon in 1796), and a slightly modified heavy sword with a half-basket hilt (again modified in 1796).[116]

Swords lasted a very long time: typical were those of the 10th Dragoons in 1754, all in good condition though acquired in 1740–1, and so too were those in the 11th Dragoons in 1754, even though many had gone into service with the corps as long

---

[114] The best detailed discussion (with fine illustrations), is A. D. Darling, 'The British Basket Hilted Cavalry Sword', *CJAC* 7 (1969), 79–96. See also A. N. Ingram, 'Mid-Eighteenth Century Cavalry Swords', *JSAHR* 29 (1951), 30–2, for some variations.

[115] WO 3/7, pp. 1–2.

[116] These improvements were the work of Gaspard Le Marchant, an expert swordsman who had made a study of military swordsmanship and had recently produced the army's first sword-drill manual (on which, see pp. 250–1). On the new pattern swords, see R. H. Thoumine, *Scientific Soldier: A Life of General Le Marchant, 1766-1812* (1968), 39–45, and J. d'Arlington, 'The Pattern 1796 Light Cavalry Sabre', *CJAC* 9 (1971), 127–34, which has fine illustrations.

ago as 1735.[117] It was in fact extremely rare to find defective swords in any corps at any time in the century, in so far as strength and serviceability were concerned.

The other edged weapon common in the army—the light, short-bladed, small-hilted sword known as a hanger—was carried by all British infantrymen until 1768 and by the grenadiers until 1784.[118] A survival of the sidearm carried by the foot during the previous century, it was at best no more than a secondary defensive weapon and, at worst, a useless encumbrance kept in service almost entirely for aesthetic and traditional reasons.[119] Throughout our period, orders had repeatedly to be sent out to oblige the soldiers actually to wear them; but only in peacetime were they much used, most general and field officers permitting the corps to put them in store when upon campaign.[120]

It is fair to say that the view most often advanced in the general histories of the age and, consequently, the impression most widely held among non-specialists, is that the British Army of the eighteenth century was officered by inexperienced and often indifferent amateurs; that its ranks were filled for the most part with men who, for a variety of reasons, were long-serving (and long-suffering) professionals; and that it was well armed. Our study of the condition of the corps shows, clearly, that these impressions are ill-found. The army was, in fact,

---

[117] WO 27/3.

[118] The most detailed discussion is A. D. Darling, 'The British Infantry Hangers', *CJAC* 8 (1970), 124–36.

[119] ''Tis soldierlike and graceful for the men to have swords', observed Col. Henry Hawley in 1726, admitting current taste; but he thought them nevertheless a useless hindrance, for 'when are they ever used in the field or in action?' Sumner, 'Chaos', 93.

[120] As early as October 1711, general orders given out in the 'Camp of Marcheinne' in Flanders ran as follows: 'Whereas Sev^l Regim^ts. have no Swords its expressly Ord^d that ye Sold^rs be provided wth them against ye taking ye feild.' BL Add. MS 29, 477, fo. 8. Even in the Highland regiments, where good broadswords were issued to the men largely in deference to their supposed national pride in such arms, they were neglected. The men of the Black Watch (42nd Foot), rid themselves of their swords as early as the Seven Years War, in America: as the lieutenant-colonel of that corps said, 'the Highlanders on several occasions declined using Broad Swords in America; that they all prefer'd Bayonets; and that Swords for the Battalion Men, tho' part of their dress and Establishment are incumbrances'. WO 27/35.

The several arms peculiar to the Highlanders, not mentioned above, are dealt with in A. D. Darling, 'Weapons of the Highland Regiments, 1740–1780', *CJAC* 8 (1970), 75–95.

officered by men of the most considerable experience, the great majority of whom got on by application; the bulk of the other ranks consisted of men of short service, of whom a significant proportion were generally recruits; and the arms carried in the regiments—especially in the foot—were frequently unserviceable and often unsafe, while the supply of ammunition in peacetime was quite insufficient for proper training. Such was the actual condition of the corps, dispersed about the British Isles and the overseas stations and garrisons.

Chapter III

The Drillbooks: Regulations by Authority and Private Publications

INTRODUCTION

The administrative machinery of the British Army in the eighteenth century was a masterpiece of the bureaucratic principle of 'multiple fission'.[1] Consisting of an elaborate but disconnected and confused profusion of offices, departments, and boards, most of these characterized by hazy jurisdictions and ponderous processes, and with the whole lacking any real centre of responsibility and hence of direction, this was an administrative 'system'—or rather more accurately, 'an entanglement of disoriented and diffused conditions'[2]—whose functioning was invariably attended by amateurism and inefficiency, and occasionally by incompetence.[3] There was, however, method in this absurdity, the army's administration illustrating the play of two considerations which contemporaries regarded as of overriding significance. These considerations were: firstly, the fear of an efficient and powerful standing force at the immediate disposal of any faction; and secondly, the desire that private and not public funds should, as far as possible, play a part and earn a return in the business of the service of the state.

To satisfy these considerations the military administration was almost entirely in civil hands, from the regimental agents at one end of the scale to the great Officers of State who shared political administration at the other. But if civil authority had engrossed the bulk of the administration of the army it had, nevertheless, conceded to the army the necessity of administer-

[1] R. Glover, *Preparation*, 15.
[2] A. D. Darling, op. cit. 6.
[3] This conclusion is generally held. R. E. Scouller, op. cit. xiii, for example, concludes of the administration that it was, 'if not quite like the Icelandic snakes, absolutely incapable, to present-day eyes, of functioning at all'; while S. G. P. Ward, *Wellington's Headquarters: A Study of the Administrative Problems in the Peninsula* (Oxford, 1957), 4, remarks upon 'the existence of the multitude of small offices and boards scattered over London which anyone who takes up an almanack of the day will be astonished to find constituted the government of the military force of this country.'

ing for itself certain specialist matters which could only be regarded as purely professional; the army had, after all, to be
professionally competent, capable of opposing in the field the
forces of the Bourbon Crowns. Among these specialist matters
came the preparation, dissemination, inspection, enforcement,
and periodic alteration of the regulations governing the training
and drill of the army—all of which were essentially the responsibility of a small body of officers who (since their activities
in these and certain other matters were complimentary) functioned as a central staff and were responsive to a competent
central authority. Here the Sovereign, in whose prerogative
were the command and allegiance of the army, played an
essential and active role. The army had always been 'peculiarly
the royal instrument';[4] and it was the army's great good fortune
that each of the Hanoverian Kings jealously guarded this
prerogative and actively pursued the duties and professional
interests which it entailed.[5] To assist him in these duties the
King at his own pleasure appointed deserving officers to serve
as his lieutenants and staff. As his staff, they reported to the
King and acted at his instance; and although at best they may
be regarded as forming no more than the embryonic general
staff of the nineteenth-century Horse Guards, still these
officers were referred to as the King's 'staff', they normally
worked in close concert, they frequently consulted one another
both officially and unofficially, and for half the century they
shared the same roof.[6]

As regards training and drill, this command and staff displayed an unwonted efficiency in comparison with the standards of practice elsewhere in the army's administration. That
part of the central London staff directly concerned with these

---

[4] R. E. Scouller, op. cit. 6.

[5] There is no monograph dealing with the royal command of the army; in lieu of
this, the best account of the attachment and close involvement of George I and George
II with the army's professional affairs is J. Hayes, 'The Royal House of Hanover and
the British Army, 1714–60', *Bul. John Rylands Library*, 40 (1957–8), 328–57. George
III's many biographers have unaccountably ignored that monarch's very close concern
with the army, details of which will appear repeatedly in the chapters that follow.

[6] From its completion *c.* 1760, the C.-in-C., the Adjutant-General, the Quartermaster-
General, the Board of General Officers, their secretaries and staffs (together with the
Paymaster-General, and the field officers of the Guards), all shared the new Horse
Guards building. Much correspondence, however, was dated from the shifting offices
elsewhere in the metropolis, and from private homes.

matters consisted, under the King, of the Adjutant-General and—if one had been appointed—the Commander-in-Chief; occasionally involved also were the Board of General Officers, general officers who had served as reviewing officers, and in some cases officers who had experimented with, or written privately upon, the subject and had established reputations as tacticians. Since these were the source of drill regulations, they deserve to be looked at more closely before we pass on to the regulations themselves.

The Sovereign from time to time delegated the actual carrying on of some part of his prerogative duties and powers, as supreme commander, to a much-trusted general officer, who was in consequence appointed commander-in-chief for a period determined by the Sovereign's good pleasure. The commander-in-chief was the highest-ranking officer in the army; and his responsibilities, which were largely administrative, were considerable. Of particular importance, he had the right of nominating officers to the King or to his ministers for all promotions and commands; he was on occasion called in as a military adviser to the Cabinet; he could (in co-operation with responsible ministers) organize the broad plan of troop movements and dispositions, both in peacetime and wartime; he ruled on all matters relating to the training, drill, and discipline of the army, and could initiate and enforce major reforms in this field. In performing these duties the commander-in-chief was assisted by the Adjutant-General and the Quartermaster-General, who were his principal staff officers, and he could be sure of the co-operation of the Secretary at War and the Master-General of the Ordnance. The commander-in-chief's orders were taken everywhere as commands, on the British establishment and abroad; and they were taken as directives on the Irish establishment where (since there was an Irish C.-in-C. in Dublin), his authority did not officially extend.[7]

The Adjutant-General was responsible for the maintenance of proper drill and discipline among the troops on the British establishment and in the overseas posts and garrisons—what

---

[7] On the role of the C.-in-C. see Clode, ii. 335–8, 689–714; R. E. Scouller, op. cit. 54–8; Rex Whitworth, op. cit., *passim*; and S. M. Pargellis, *Military Affairs in North America, 1748–1765: Selected Documents from the Cumberland Papers* (New York, 1936), ix–xii.

was 'proper' being laid down in the Regulations and Orders issuing from time to time through his office. To carry out these duties further he was responsible for co-ordinating the system of regular inspection or 'reviewing' of the regiments, by which it was ascertained if discipline was being enforced and the regulations and periodic orders were being complied with. The Adjutant-General's powers were largely executive—'He must be under some Commander, he can't from the nature of his Employment act merely from himself', as Gen. Thomas Gage put it; he was responsible to and acted at the behest of the Commander-in-Chief and the King.[8] Nevertheless although merely adjutant, in theory, in actual practice the office had a considerable influence in its own right on tactical doctrine and training; men such as Robert Napier, Edward Harvey, and Sir William Fawcett, all of whom held the appointment, were much regarded by officers. This was so largely because the Adjutant-General was not a politician like the Secretary at War, but rather a regular officer and usually a thorough professional; he commanded professional respect in army circles and frequently had much to do with the preparation or adoption (in consultation with other individuals or bodies) of new drill, organization, and equipment. He was continually handling small military matters for the King, and was in constant communication with officers of all ranks. He was in daily communication with the Secretary at War,[9] and (significantly) was frequently petitioned by officers and private citizens who either confused his powers with those of that Secretary, or who assumed for him an influence greater than he in fact had. Given his duties, and the close relationship with the regiments on the one hand and with the King and the C.-in-C. on the other, which the performance of his duties entailed, his was the finger closest to the pulse of the army. For all of these reasons, then, the Adjutant-General's office was a key link in what was in fact the most professional channel in the army's administration.

[8] C. E. Carter (ed.), *The Correspondence of General Thomas Gage*, ii (New Haven, 1933), 431–2, Gage to Barrington, 26 Aug. 1967. See also p. 413, Gage to Harvey, 21 Apr. 1767; and pp. 415–16, Gage to Barrington, 28 Apr. 1767, where the red-tape chain is clearly shown and with it the place of the Adjutant-General in the command structure.

[9] The Secretary at War was a responsible civil official, concerned with financing, quartering, and civil–military relations; and training and tactical matters were no concern of his.

The Board of General Officers concerned itself primarily with viewing, and approving as sealed patterns, the regimental clothing submitted to it annually by the agents of the proprietary colonels. Disputes between officers over recruiting, and matters concerning officers' pay, seniority, and (occasionally) their honour, were also considered by the Board. It sat first in 1705, and permanently from 1706. Under the presidency of a senior general officer nominated to the post annually, the Board sat irregularly as matters were brought before it; it was composed of a varying number of general officers (usually those immediately available in town), who were called upon by the president to attend and sit. Infrequently, the King ordered the Board to prepare or to consider drill regulations, since its members as senior officers formed a pool of considerable experience of the service.

Finally, about ten general officers were appointed annually by letters of service to review the regiments in Britain and Ireland (and, where possible, in the overseas garrisons) and to report on their condition—including, prominently, their state of training. By the end of each spring and summer reviewing season these reviewing officers had made a most intimate and immediate acquaintance with the corps and their state of training; and they were, consequently, occasionally consulted by the King, the C.-in-C., and the Adjutant-General on matters of training and drill. The reviewing officers were considered as 'on the staff' during the year in which they carried on their reviews; and sometimes (for example, William Howe in the 1774 Salisbury camp) they were given active command of formations brought together in camps of exercise for purposes of intensive training.[10]

Beyond the King's London staff there were two others, one in Edinburgh and the other in Dublin. Scotland was an area command, not a separate establishment as was Ireland; and for almost all purposes the small Edinburgh Castle staff's functions were executive, the GOC North Britain carrying out directives framed by the London staff. The details of troop movements and quartering, and the use of troops on the coast duty and otherwise in aid of the civil power in that kingdom

---

[10] For a detailed discussion of the reviewing system and the duties of the reviewing officers, see pp. 296–317.

were Edinburgh's business; but the initiative lay in London because of the presence there of the King and the C.-in-C., and on
all matters concerning training and drill regulations the London
staff governed Edinburgh Castle just as it governed the commands in the plantations and the Mediterranean garrisons.

In Ireland meanwhile, there was a large command and staff
structure nominally under the Lord-Lieutenant, closely paral-
leling that in London. The Irish Army's staff formed no part of
the jurisdiction of the staff in London and it governed the army
there in its own right, although for most purposes following the
English model, as was natural. Where training and drill were
concerned the Irish C.-in-C. might issue orders concerning details, but otherwise the Irish Army was obliged to follow all
such Regulations and Orders as were issued explicitly in the
King's name—which was not always the case, if they were entirely the pet project of the C.-in-C. in London. Regiments on
the Irish establishment were reviewed by general officers who,
though serving on the Irish staff and usually appointed reviewing officers by Dublin Castle, sent copies of their review reports
to the Adjutant-General in London for the use of the King and
the Horse Guards staff. The Lord-Lieutenant confined himself
to ceremonial duties in this regard, such as reviewing annually
the Dublin garrison.

These then were the agencies of uniformity, the source of all
official drill regulations issued 'by Authority'. Most of the
regulations prepared by one or more of these agents were issued
on the direct and explicit authority of the Sovereign as King's
Regulations, and as such they commanded immediate ob-
servance by all the regiments in the army no matter which
establishment they might find themselves serving upon. Occasionally the British or Irish C.-in-C. might issue regulations
on his own authority, as we shall see, thereby obliging only the
corps on the British or Irish establishments to conform. In
actual practice, whenever individual regiments left Britain, the
Mediterranean garrisons, or the Americas—for any or all of
which places the British C.-in-C. could, if he so chose, lay down
binding regulations—to go to Ireland, these regiments carried
such regulations with them and usually continued to follow
them when arrived upon that establishment; regiments departing from Ireland for other stations were obliged to conform to

the British standard upon landing. There was therefore a clear recognition of the authority derived by the British C.-in-C. from his close proximity to the King, enhanced (as it was for the Dukes of Cumberland and York) by their sharing in the blood royal or (as for Marlborough and Amherst) by their prestige through the army generally. Hence there was only an occasional divergence in the drill practised in the regiments commanded by the London and Dublin staffs; and the chance of any greater confusion was averted by the Adjutant-General in Ireland normally following the example of his London counterpart. Indeed, from the later 1780s the Adjutant-General in London had the full co-operation of the Irish staff, and London simply forwarded everything concerning drill.

In spite of the keen and considerable activity on the part of the central authorities in preparing, distributing, and keeping up to date the army's drill regulations, and despite their almost invariably successful efforts at enforcing a general adherence to the practice laid down in the regulations, there was an occasional tinkering with various elements of it—with odd movements in the manual of arms, especially, and with the methods of giving fire when in battalion line—by the commanders of regiments, and by the commanders of armies serving in the field. This is understandable enough: it was a particularist age, and the system of proprietary regimental 'ownership' and administration fostered such activities. But it must be emphasized that these improving 'fertile geniuses' (as the Duke of Cumberland derisively styled them) seldom strayed far from the regulations, and so their 'improvements' were more of a nuisance than an actual hindrance to the achievement of regularity. On a very few occasions, however, major departures were made from normal practice; and although certain of these departures were justified by peculiar conditions of service (and sometimes recognized as useful, and adopted by the central authorities), others were absurdities prejudicial not only to the military efficiency of the units concerned but also to the safety of other units with which they might be brigaded. In any event, as we shall see, the influence of the central authorities soon made itself felt: corps and field forces in which undue liberties had been taken were obliged to conform to standard practice.

Throughout the eighteenth century the drill practised in each regiment (be it of horse or foot) consisted of five main elements known as the 'manual exercise', the 'platoon exercise', the 'evolutions', the 'firings', and the 'manoeuvres';[11] and it was with any or all of these elements that each of the several Regulations and Orders issued by the central authorities dealt, whether in whole or in part.[12] Briefly, the 'manual exercise' was the long, slow, and detailed sequence of movements endlessly drilled into the private soldier whereby he learned, by the numbers, how to load and fire his firelock, to perform the bayonet drill, and to do a variety of ceremonial movements such as clubbing or saluting with his piece. The 'platoon exercise' was that essential core of the manual used in volley-firing, which, unlike the manual, was performed very quickly and to only a few words of command or to commands relayed by the drums.[13] The simple 'evolutions' were the short, precise movements done on the spot in rank and file, such as left-turns, about-turns, and opening and closing the rank- and file-intervals. Young soldiers had at the very least to be familiar with these first three elements, building-blocks the knowledge of which was essential for the performance of the final two elements of the drill. The 'firings' comprised the quite complicated systems and sequences according to which fire was given and controlled—standing,

[11] Often, however, officers used these terms interchangeably—to the great confusion of subsequent students—and frequently such terms as 'exercise', 'duty', 'evolutions', and 'discipline' were used collectively to refer to some or all of the five elements comprising the drill. The specific usage must be studied in its original context. It is a commonplace for historians to assume that, because two corps are described as performing their 'exercise' in different fashions, their full drill must have differed completely; most often, such descriptions refer in fact only to trivial irregularities in the manual and platoon exercises, whereas the regiments might fire and manoeuvre exactly alike, and do so moreover quite in accordance with the regulations.

To avoid confusion we shall use the term 'drill' henceforth as a collective, referring to all five elements at once; and when dealing with a specific element of the drill we shall describe it by its eighteenth-century name.

[12] Details incidental to the uniform performance of the drill elements (such as the exact manner of posting all ranks when drawing up the regiment, the proper intervals to be observed between ranks and files depending on the disposition adopted, the specific commands or signals, and the timing of responses, etc.) were also included in the Regulations and Orders, where appropriate.

[13] E.g. the manual exercise made regulation in 1728 was performed to sixty-four vocal commands and involved 185 separate motions for the soldier to perform. The platoon exercise of 1728 consisted of only four verbal commands, and sixty-three motions.

advancing, and retreating—by sections of the line told off into a varying number of fire-divisions, and groups of fire-divisions. Not only did the foot perform these first four elements of the drill but so too did the cavalrymen, dismounted; the troopers were expected to be quite as capable as the foot at the manual, platoon, and evolutions, since they might well have to fight dismounted, though it could scarcely be expected of them that they go through the firings with as much expertise as did the foot, whose proper province this was. The troopers in their turn, however, had to perform not only the foot evolutions but also a considerable number of evolutions on horseback; these consisted of simple facings and changes of front performed on the spot, at which not only the riders but the horses had to be schooled. Finally, there came the elaborate and extensive repertoire of close-order linear 'manoeuvres'; or rather, the two distinct sets of manoeuvres drawn up in accordance with the peculiar tactical roles of the two arms, cavalry and infantry.

Passing from one element of the drill to the next, the soldier acquired first, at the manual, poise, confidence, and a certain skill with his arms, while at the same time coming under the influence of military discipline; next he learned to use his arms in unison with other soldiers and as a response to command; then, well acquainted with his arms, he was taught the basic elements of carriage and regulated movement, individually and then with others in rank and file. Having passed through these first three elements of the training regimen the private soldier had acquired the three things most essential to the performance of his more advanced tactical role: knowledge of the use of his weapons, the ability to move in a regulated way, and a docile obedience. It was in training at the complicated and difficult firings and manoeuvres that he put these elementary skills to use in combination.

The division of its drill regimen into a system of five elements, taught progressively, was not by any means something foisted on the army by the theoreticians; it was rather the fruit of the evolution of seventeenth-century practice and practical experience. By the opening of the eighteenth century this division of the drill was so rooted in everyday practice that it was simply taken for granted as the established tradition of pro-

ceeding—that is to say, well before the beginning of our period
it had come to be regarded as a sound and practical approach
to training. The demise among the foot of the dual weapon-
system and its supersession by the battalion armed uniformly
with firelocks and bayonets (though technically and tactically
a development of great importance) merely simplified training
and drill; it did not alter the logic and practicality of training
according to the progressive drill regimen.[14] In an army subject
to the dispersal and neglect which characterized its peacetime
condition, with an officer corps formed by purchase and given
absolutely no common training experience before joining their
units, the existence of a single drill regimen as unquestioned and
ubiquitous custom was a circumstance of the most fundamental
importance.

By the earlier eighteenth century, therefore, there was
already a central command and staff structure, responsible for
the preparation and enforcement of drill regulations; and there
existed too a well-established regimen in accordance with which
the drill regulations were drawn up and according to which the
regiments were trained. It remains only to note certain characteristics of the drill regulations in general, before describing in
detail the genesis and the salient features of each of the particular sets of regulations that appeared during the eighteenth
century.

It was invariably the case that the drill laid down in the
regulations was confined to the level of the regiment and its
sub-units; the drill of larger bodies such as brigades, wings, or
lines was ignored. The Crown, traditionally, had been obliged
to farm much of the business of the management of its land
forces, and the resulting proprietary 'ownership' of regiments
still prevailing in the eighteenth century made of each a particularist and partly self-administering unit; each regiment had
its own staff, each shunned its neighbours and dealt directly
with the central authorities, and each was therefore so constituted as to be ideally suited to carry on its own training, at the
direction of the central authorities. Since the regiment was
normally subject to extended dispersal, regulations aimed

[14] The pikemen and musketeers of the seventeenth century had been brought along
according to an essentially similar progressive regimen. On this, see G. R. Mork, art.
cit., *passim*.

specifically at the regiment and its sub-units served the wholly necessary purpose of knitting the regiment together, providing an ideal guide to regularity among long-separated companies and troops. Nor were larger bodies than the regiment likely to be formed in peacetime; except in the most extraordinary circumstances it was politically inexpedient and financially undesirable ever to concentrate and encamp corps for the purpose of brigade manoeuvres. Additionally, the series of evolutions and manoeuvres in the drill regulations were designed in large part with a view to preparing each regiment to take its place amongst others in the greater line of battle; when eventually they were brigaded, therefore, the individual regiments required not so much new drill techniques as constant practice in conducting the drill at a time and pace that would conform with that of the line as a whole.

Until the large-scale remodelling and innovation that occurred on the very eve of, and during, the French Revolutionary and Napoleonic Wars, British drill regulations—whether issued as complete drills (that is, containing directions on all five drill elements), as partial drills (dealing with only some of the elements), as general orders touching on certain details of the drill and issued either to the army as a whole or, on occasion, to one arm only, or as standing orders treating specific details of drill in individual regiments or field armies—were invariably brief, laconic, devoted to describing only the mechanics of performing the drill, and seldom, if ever, attempting to discuss the theoretical origins or practical application of any of the several parts of the drill laid down. Until the 1780s, each set of regulations dealt most fully with the intricacies of the manual, the platoon, the evolutions, and the firings; only by the close of the century did pride of place go to the details of the manoeuvres. Only the manual, platoon, and evolutions could be practised effectively by the dispersed companies, troops, and detachments, so that lengthy technical instructions on these elements were appropriate and helped to ensure uniformity of practice. The firings, although they could be practised with profit only at the higher levels of concentration, were so technically difficult, demanding, and (until the 1770s) so highly esteemed, that they too were very carefully spelled out so as to admit of no confusion or deviation. As regards the fifth element, the manoeuvres, only the most important were treated in the regulations; and only from the mid-1760s onwards, by which time the theory and practice of military movement had advanced to the point where fast and flexible movement was possible, did detailed descriptions of the manoeuvres appear in the regulations. Essentially, it was only those manoeuvres regarded as most likely to be necessary in action, plus those few the mastery of which would provide groundwork upon which others could be based or extemporized, that were laid down in the regulations. These were the 'core' manoeuvres; and regularity at these few manoeuvres most likely to be performed in the line of battle, where regularity was supremely important, was the aim of the regulations. It was the essential duty of each regiment to master these; and the King, the British and Irish Cs.-in-C., the Adjutants-General, and the reviewing general officers saw to it that they did. And if regiments added to this the practice of several other manoeuvres—then well and good. It must be stressed here that, in addition to the few core manoeuvres laid down in whatever regulations were currently in force, there were always several times as many manoeuvres that regiments practised. These additional manoeuvres were taken from the army's store of 'customary' practice; and being customary, they were not specifically laid down in the regulations. The *1778 Regulations*, for example, laid down nine major manoeuvres that the battalions were obliged to master, thus ensuring regularity throughout the army at a solid core of common practice. Additionally, each battalion built up (so far as it could) a considerable body of 'customary' manoeuvres; these were derived from previous regulations, from the English-language treatises, from foreign regulations and treatises, from developments made in response to experience of active service, and from the 'fertile genius' of individual officers serving with their units. Altogether, these accumulated customary manoeuvres represented a very large, ever-increasing pool on which regiments drew as occasion, whim, or opportunity suited; and by 1782 a learned officer, John Williamson, could write that 'the number of different movements has been so multiplied, that some regiments can perform above two hundred.'[15]

---

[15] John Williamson, *The Elements of Military Arrangement, and of the Discipline of War; Adapted to the Practice of the British Infantry*, i (1782), 117. The figure is a considerable

That all regulations confined themselves to these technical basics, without elaboration, was due to the way in which interested contemporaries viewed regulation drillbooks and drill orders, and to what contemporaries expected from them. It was the purpose of regulations simply to lay down all the details of the drill that the units concerned were required to learn and to conform to, so that tactical regularity could be expected of these units when they came to be employed together in the field by general officers. Drill was kept up to date by the issue, periodically, of new or revised regulations; but it was not expected even of new regulations that they essay the theoretical or practical application of their contents. That was attended to in a different way.

The several things omitted from the regulations—theoretical justification·and commentary on new forms of drill, descriptions of the tactical situations in which particular manoeuvres should be employed, notes on the best methods by which elements of the drill might be taught—were not by any means regarded as inconsequential; rather, their inclusion in the regulations was deemed superfluous. That such an approach could be adopted meant that the central authorities, in forming drill regulations, knew that it could safely be taken for granted that there existed throughout the service at large a fulsome expertise in the living, accumulated custom of the service. Thus the means and techniques of training and appreciation of the efficacy and tactical relevance of particular aspects of drill were learned, not from regulations, but rather from this accumulated custom. This custom consisted of experience of active service against enemies as different in their tactics as the warriors of the North American tribes and the troopers of horse in the *maison du roi*, and in geographical conditions as varied as the plains of Flanders and the jungles of the West Indies; it consisted of experience acquired in the actual peacetime performance of the drill, especially of those elements endlessly repeated in the dispersed condition of the peacetime regiments; in knowledge acquired in the extensive training of the reviewing season and in the wartime camps of exercise; in knowledge acquired through theoretical and historical study; in know-

---

exaggeration, since every manoeuvre could be performed in half a dozen ways hardly distinguishable one from another.

ledge gained from the voluminous literature privately published, which was readily available and which covered all
aspects of military affairs both domestic and foreign; in the
simple fruit of reflection and, sometimes, of common sense; and
(at the century's end), in the new military academies just then
being established. In the knowledge and experience of the
officers and NCOs with the regiments—knowledge which they
inherited and passed on—lay the wealth that was the accumulated custom unwritten in the drill regulations but
bespoken on their every page.

Where opportunities for advanced tactical training were infrequent at the regimental level and almost unknown at higher
levels; and where the drill regulations were technical and brief
rather than expansive, the existence of a large body of privately
published literature devoted to all aspects of drill and tactics
was, naturally, of especial significance. Such a body of literature existed in English; and before dealing with individual
works in detail, we might consider the general characteristics
which distinguished this literature as a whole.

To begin with we should note of this literature that, though
often wide-ranging and occasionally excellent, it displayed
little of the intellectual brilliance and none of the polemicism
so characteristic, throughout the century, of the work of the
French theorists and tacticians.[16] There was instead a very
pragmatic bent to the great bulk of English-language military
texts and treatises; and this pragmatism extended even to the
choice of foreign works that were translated into English. Thus,
there was room for the regulations of the Prussian infantry, but
none for the seminal, though controversial, commentaries of
the Chevalier de Folard. This pragmatism was the result of
several factors, and only to the most limited extent does it
indicate stagnation or sterility; most significantly, it reflects the
physical dispersal of the small British officer corps, together
with the prejudices of a society which made no provision for the
discussion of the broader or topical aspects of military affairs
(as in the salons of Paris) or of the more technical and pro-

---

[16] A subject dealt with by J. Colin, *L'Infanterie au XVIIIᵉ siècle. La Tactique* (Paris,
1907); by R. Villate, 'Le mouvement des idées militaires en France au XVIIIᵉ siècle',
Revue d'histoire moderne, NS 10 (1935); and more recently by R. S. Quimby, *The Background of Napoleonic Warfare* (New York, 1957).

fessional military matters (as in the garrisons of Prussia), just as it reflects the mood of general national indifference or antipathy to military affairs and the consequent non-existence of facilities for advanced training in peacetime. This English approach also illustrates the fact that a sound appreciation of the supremacy of firepower over all other forms of combat had been a lesson well learned by the end of Marlborough's campaigns, and had been taken to heart in the army; hence the issue of shock- versus fire-tactics, which so stirred the French after 1714, was not significant in Britain.

Neither do the written efforts of British officers and tacticians reveal any lack of professionalism or of expertise: on the contrary, some exhibited a marked interest in theoretical and practical developments both at home and abroad; and foreign campaigns, regulations, and treatises were constantly referred to, and drawn on, by British authors. Many were critical of various aspects of current British practice; there were even a few who (in the vein of Saxe) set about an elaborate new modelling of the army. What we would describe on the one hand as factors of grand strategy, and on the other as sociopolitical theories, were likewise called forth on occasion by the military writers: thus, some supposed that the island power should convert the whole of its land forces into marines, and conduct amphibious operations only; while others, well grounded in the political philosophy of the age, saw in this naturally brave people, living in liberty under the balanced constitution of a limited monarchy, where monarchical honour was wedded to republican virtue, the material from which unconquerable armies of citizen militiamen might be formed. Less elaborately, but nevertheless radically, some authors called for the establishment of universal military service based on short-term conscription; others thought that a system of county regiments, supported by their home counties and vying with one another in recruiting, in training, and in the field, would be an excellent innovation; still others laid down schemes for new weapons, clothing, and accoutrements. There were also, naturally enough, a great many pedants who failed to rise above the pedestrian; there were not a few sharpers quick to cash in whenever the national interest was caught up in military affairs, as in 1745–6 for example; and there were even a few crackpots who (as ever) found their niche in the market.

Not only the training, drill, and tactics of the army were taken up by the military writers; ancillary topics provided scope for treatises and for commentary as well. Among these topics, those most closely related to training and drill (and those most commonly essayed) were the following: the mathematics, mechanics, and techniques of siegecraft, gunnery, and fortification; historical campaigns, in narratives with commentary; the service of partisans, or ranging companies; field fortification; encampments; the 'grand operations of war'—that is, the daily marches of an army, its grand tactics and major movements; and the service of marines and of the land forces on board the fleet. More immediately relevant topics, also commonly essayed, were the training and employment of light infantry, the drill employed in foreign armies, and weaponry.

Translations of foreign regulations and treatises, together with up-dated editions of the military classics of antiquity, made up an important part of the body of private publications to appear in English during the century. Caesar's *Gallic War* and *Civil War* appeared in numerous editions, as did the *Peloponnesian War* of Thucydides ('our historian', as Wolfe called him); and there were at least two eighteenth-century English editions of Polybius, Tacitus, Xenophon, Josephus, and Vegetius.[17] Translations of contemporary works, chiefly from the French and German, were commonplace: the main Prussian and French regulations appeared in English, as did the works of most distinguished foreign soldiers.

The volume and variety of these publications illustrates what was indeed a very active 'Military Literary World', as Lt.-Col. Caroline Scott styled it in 1750; and if less flourishing than Paris, the London military printers and booksellers were certainly as busy as their Amsterdam counterparts, and probably busier than any others in the Germanies or elsewhere. The most

---

[17] Roman antiquity was, of course, a subject of considerable interest in the military literary world, as it was in the civil; and Roman tactical formations were treated with as much veneration as were Roman architectural motifs. Engineer General William Roy published in 1793 his *Military Antiquities of the Romans in North Britain*, often cited today; and it was more than mere coincidence that Roy was chiefly responsible for siting the British Army's wartime encampments later in the century. We shall describe only one of these works below, in passing—Clarke's *Vegetius* of 1768—since it is representative of a body of literature not immediately germane, but not to be ignored.

useful of the English drillbooks, for the most part London-printed, were usually available elsewhere in the English-speaking world in reprint not long after their first impression: Dublin reprints were a commonplace; Edinburgh, York, and Exeter houses sometimes printed; and even the presses in the more advanced of the colonial towns like New York and Philadelphia occasionally brought out editions. If Scott found Limerick in 1750 to be a place affording 'nothing but bibles Missalls, Breviarys, Prayer books, and Child guides, by which our only Stationer (for he dont deserve title of bookseller) pleases protestants and papists', then that was just plain bad luck, for he would have been better served almost anywhere else.[18]

The tacticians, editors, translators, compilers, and officers who 'set up for an Author' (as Lt.-Col. John LaFaussille described himself and his colleagues in 1752)[19] appear to have served themselves fairly well, in serving their fellow officers at the presses. Their gain was not monetary. The Hanoverian Kings, all three of whom permitted several soldier-authors to dedicate their works to them, rewarded their efforts with the 'encouragement' due to zeal and merit. Lt.-Col. Humphrey Bland, for example, whose excellent treatise on military discipline appeared in 1727, was to gain royal favour, the comradeship of the Duke of Cumberland, and general rank. Capt. Samuel Bever, who brought out a guide for young officers in 1756, was rewarded with a majority, Lt.-Col. Campbell Dalrymple got the governorship of Guadeloupe for his brilliant essay of 1761, and Capt. Joseph Otway likewise 'got a Government' for his 1761 translation of Turpin de Crissé's treatise. Lt. John Clarke got a captaincy as a reward for his 1768 version of Vegetius. Most favoured of all, perhaps, was William Fawcett. When he began to publish his translations of foreign treatises and regulations during the mid-1750s, he was a mere subaltern; but so studious and so devoted to the service was he that 'encouragement' came his way, and he finished a long and brilliant staff career as a Knight of the Bath, a full General, and a member of the privy council. But this is not to imply that the aims of soldier-authors were mercenary. It is

[18] Cumb. Pprs, Box 44, no. 98.
[19] Cumb. Pprs, Pt. 4, II, fo. 1.

clear that, for most, the good of the service was the principal motive behind their endeavours, and a great many of them either published anonymously or simply forwarded their ideas or manuscripts to the office of the Adjutant-General, for his inspection and use.[20] Officers with good ideas, who wished to see these implemented in the service at large, could always expect a fair hearing from the Adjutant-General, and sometimes enlisted his aid in forwarding such projects.[21] On a few occasions the Adjutant-General lent his name as good backing for treatises; and on at least one occasion, in 1786, went so far as to send a circular to the commanding officers of all regiments recommending a forthcoming translation of Tielke's study of the Seven Years War, and canvassing for subscriptions from their officers.[22]

Of the fact that the bulk of this wide-ranging military literature, privately published, was widely read, and much of its topic matter taken to heart or directly implemented, there can be no doubt. The performance of drill and tactics put on by the regiments at their annual reviews repeatedly illustrates the fact that units were practising such material; and the behaviour of corps on campaign illustrates this further. The lists of subscribers appended to many of these publications are quite extraordinary. Capt. Bennett Cuthbertson's treatise on the management of a battalion, for example, first published at Dublin in 1768, was subscribed for by some 939 officers of the land forces and marines, ranging from the C.-in-C. Granby to the lowest '2nd surgeon'—exclusive of militia officers and private subscribers. Similarly, Maj. Robert Donkin's slight collection of remarks, published in 1777, was subscribed for by

[20] References to many such are to be found in WO 3. Typical of the tone normally adopted was Adjutant-General Edward Harvey's reply of July 1774, to Capt. Staunton of the 14th Foot. Staunton had submitted proposed instructions for the drill of a battalion of foot; and Harvey, who replied that he would soon take them under consideration, added that 'I am always glad to receive ye Opin[ion]s of Off^{rs} whose Zeal & Abilities make them give their attentn. to the Service, & think myself Hon^d wth this Mark of your attention.' WO 3/4, p. 124.

[21] E.g. in 1775 Maj. Charles Vallancey was corresponding with the Adjutant-General on behalf of himself and a group of officers who wished to establish a military academy in Dublin. Harvey lauded 'the Conduct of those Intelligent & Able Off^{rs}, who take pains yt their knowledge may be of use to ye younger part of the Army', but could not assist since he had no command in Ireland. WO 3/5, p. 38.

[22] WO 3/27, p. 3. The Adjutant-General raised 600 officers as subscribers for this very expensive work.

several hundred officers from subaltern through general rank. Thomas Simes's derivative, uninspired compilations, which appeared between 1768 and 1780, regularly drew several hundred officer-subscribers too. Fawcett's 1757 translation of the Prussian cavalry regulations drew nearly 500 officer-subscribers. Bland's treatise, the most successful of them all, sold several thousand copies between 1727 and 1762. When these figures are compared with those for the total number of officers serving in the army (see p. 99 above), these subscribers represent very sizeable proportions of the officer corps as a whole.

Whatever the topics taken in hand, the common inspiration most generally shared by the military authors in Britain was twofold: to assist an officer corps which otherwise had no formal training, and a large part of which often had little or no active experience of warfare, to acquire a sound understanding of the basics of the service; and secondly, to fill in with instruction and commentary the gaps that, as we have seen, were left open in the regulations. Fleshing out the bones of the regulations—describing the tactical situations in which certain manoeuvres were most appropriate, noting the easiest means by which the drill might be taught, giving the history and theory of the development of drill procedures, and providing realistic tactical commentary and example, the understanding of which would be of great assistance to the officer on the day when he came to translate drill into bloody practice, and which would also make it easier for him to appreciate the aim of the regulations—all this was most necessary. Since many of the treatises included large numbers of manoeuvres not, as we noted earlier, included afresh in each successive set of regulations, but which continued to be practised in the regiments as each individual corps thought appropriate, the private publications served as an all-important vehicle for preserving and passing on the accumulated custom of the service.

In doing all these things, the private publications gave life to the regulations issued by authority; this private literature served as a training curriculum for the young officer who otherwise in peacetime could have acquired no more than the simple experience of the practice of the troop or company, less often of the squadron or grand-division, and much less often of the full regiment itself. Meanwhile, the field and general officers were in their turn provided with badly needed drill and tactical instruction by the more advanced of the private treatises; for it was only when the bulk of the regiment was concentrated that the field officer had the opportunity of actually carrying on the drill of which he was expected to be master; and the vast majority of the general officers had even more need of such publications, almost never having in peacetime the opportunity to manoeuvre so much as a small brigade, let alone lines, wings, or armies.

1712–1748

When William of Orange landed in England he found there a small standing army which had had considerable and varied experience of active service, which was well-enough armed and equipped, and which was trained to a system of drill and tactics quite as up to date as those practised elsewhere in Europe.[23] William's landing was to set in train events which, during the ensuing quarter-century, were to add vastly to that experience, and were to establish for the army a European reputation. In the years between 1688 and 1712 the regiments of the growing British Army were to take part in successive major operations, and were to serve with or against every militarily significant state in western Europe; the close co-operation of English, Scots, and Dutch forces, during these years, was to be especially advantageous where drill and tactics were concerned;[24] and the evolution of British arms, unit organization, drill regulations, and training not only reflects this experience but indicates also what admirable foundations had already been laid in the system of drill used in the army immediately before William's landing.

During the last decades of the seventeenth century the situation in the army as regards arms, and hence formations and

[23] A good recent study is J. Childs, op. cit.
[24] Nowhere is the close relationship of the drill used in the Dutch, English, and Scottish armies more clearly illustrated than in the detailed MS treatise 'Schola Martis, or the Arte of War', compiled *c.*1728 by Brig.-Gen. James Douglass (BL Add. MS 27, 892, fos. 209–318). Douglass served in the Flanders wars from 1688 to 1714, for most of that period in regiments of the Scots-Dutch Brigade, in the Foot Guards of the pre-Union Scottish Army and latterly in the British Army.

tactics, had been one of considerable complexity.[25] Aware of this, the authorities had imposed drill regulations in order to provide the army with some settled core of common practice; and in this they succeeded admirably. The regulations issuing from Whitehall at this time were to serve as a lodestone, where so much else was flux; and by the beginning of the new century both the manner of organizing and the way of going about the drill and training of the regiments had been so firmly established that it was henceforth to remain the common practice. The regulations that William found in force in 1688, therefore, and those that followed in 1690 and 1701 were only the culminating publications in a series of official drillbooks which had been appearing with some frequency since mid-way through the reign of Charles II.[26] These differed one from another more in their format or style of presentation, and here and there in matters of minutiae, than in any of the essentials of the system of drill and tactics that they laid down; and where they varied it was on the stress placed upon the exercises for the matchlock, pikes, flint firelocks, plug bayonets, and grenades, as arms evolution replaced one with the other. Taken together, this long series of very detailed regulations had, by the time of Ryswick, cumulatively established a system of drill and a tradition of basic practice which was to leave the most marked imprint on the army of the early eighteenth century.

---

[25] The best survey of arms evolution before Blenheim is G. R. Mork, art. cit.

[26] In 1688 the army was following *An Abridgement of the English Military Discipline. Printed by Especial Command, for the Use of his Majesties Forces* (1686), which was a slightly up-dated edition of *An Abridgment of the English Military Discipline. Reprinted by His Majesties Special Command* (1682). This 1682 edition, however, contained many fine plates, unlike its successors; and it was itself a considerable improvement upon *An Abridgement of the English Military Discipline. By His Majesties Permission* (1678). The original of this series appeared mid-way through Charles II's reign, the earliest copy being *The English Military Discipline* (1672): it appeared again as *The English Military Discipline, or the way and method of exercising Horse & Foot, according to the practice of this present time* . . . (1680); the 'abridgements' (the first of which appeared in 1676), were however lengthy in themselves, despite the title, and were themselves the standard regulation drillbooks.

A new, though hardly altered, revision was prepared in 1690 as *The Exercise of the Foot; with the Evolutions* . . . *By Their Majesties Command* (1690). Another edition of this 1690 version appeared at London in 1696, but it was quite like the original and bore the same title; and like the 1690 version too (but with a cavalry exercise appended as a supplement) was *The Exercise of the Foot* . . . *To which is added, the Exercise of the horse, grenadiers of horse, and dragoons* (Dublin, 1701).

This survival is everywhere apparent when the drill and tactics of the army at the opening of our period are analysed. Nor is at surprising. If the weapon-system used in Marlborough's and Galway's battalions was a notable advance upon that employed in those of King William, nevertheless the battalion armed uniformly with firelocks and bayonets was of such recent origins that many of the tactical possibilities that it offered were, naturally enough, not immediately apparent and so remained only potential. By the time of Blenheim a new fire-tactics—the famous platoon-fire system—had established itself as the forte of the British foot; but almost everything else—the evolutions, manoeuvres, and marches of the army—had changed hardly at all by the end of Marlborough's campaigning, so strong was the tradition of basic practice already established. We are too easily dazzled by the brilliance of Marlborough's grand-tactical dispositions, the more so when these are contrasted with those of William; Marlborough's victories were the fruit of the military genius of the commander, and not of any radical departure in the drill and tactics (save for platoon-fire) of the individual corps under his command. We come closest to the mark when we conceive of Marlborough's battalions as essentially those passed on and trained up in the campaigns of William, differing only in that they were newly and uniformly armed, and able to lay down a most formidable and destructive fire; in so far as speed of movement, variety of manoeuvre, and suppleness are concerned, they were only marginally better than those of William, or no better at all. Any detailed analysis of the drill practised by the British foot just before and just after Marlborough's campaigns leads one to conclude that, if in some respects the soldiers and tacticians of the early eighteenth century were inventive, in most others they clung to what they already knew. Conservatism was at work, understandably enough at a time of technological change.

This conservatism is evident not only (as we shall see) in the major codifications of drill drawn up in 1727 and 1728; it is equally evident in the absence of any such works between 1690 and 1727. There was no new full drill regulation published for the army of Queen Anne, despite the fact that it was during her reign that the British Army rose to such sudden prominence;

and there was none published during the reign of George I, despite the fact that the first Hanoverian monarch was a soldier and would concern himself closely with the army's affairs. The absence of any new full drill regulations during these warlike decades illustrates how extraordinarily successful and adaptable was the series of Stuart regulations and their Williamite reissues; and indeed not until the end of the eighteenth century was there to appear again a set of regulations at once so informative, so detailed, and (with their pleasant discursive style), so immediately and easily comprehended and applied. The excellence of these wholly admirable Stuart drillbooks ensured the survival of the core of practice that they laid down; consequently, brief supplements which regularized the most recent active-service experience—and which owed their brevity to the fact that they implicitly (and sometimes explicitly[27]) left most of the core of the drill to the regulations of the 1680s and 1690s—were sufficient to transform the drill of the army at Landen into that of the army of Ramillies. Between 1690 and 1728, accordingly, little more than the manual and platoon exercises for the flint firelock and bayonet, together with the manner of carrying on the platoon-fire system and of telling off in four grand-divisions for certain manoeuvres, had to be set out in supplemental regulations. The part of the army that saw Flanders service under Marlborough became acquainted with, and thoroughly accomplished at, these revised or new elements of the drill while actually on the spot, in the theatre where drill modification was taking place. The rest of the army meanwhile—and especially the very many regiments stationed in Ireland—had all the new modifications taught them nearly contemporaneously with their development in Flanders. By the time of Utrecht the whole of the army that survived the reductions was as well acquainted with the Flanders modifications as it was accomplished at the surviving core of the practice of the 1680s and 1690s.

The first of the supplements to appear under Anne (and the only regulation of any sort to be printed during her reign or during that of her successor) was drawn up by 'an Officer in

---

[27] Most of the printed and MS regulations of the period *c.* 1702–27 refer their readers to 'King Wm.'s Book of Exercise' (i.e. the *1690 Regulations*, so called), for many of the details which they themselves abridge or omit.

Her Majesties Foot Guards' and entitled *The Duke of Marlborough's New Exercise of Firelocks and Bayonets; Appointed by His
Grace to be used By all the British Forces, and the Militia* (n.d. [*c.*
1708]).[28] This short booklet, which confined itself to the manual
and platoon exercises as they were now being practised in
Flanders, was the first in an endless succession of similar booklets devoted almost entirely to the intricacies of the manual and
platoon exercises. Although 'appointed' by Marlborough for
all the troops on the British establishment, the Duke's writ as
Captain-General did not run to the forces in Ireland; and consequently an effort more elaborate than the simple issuing of a
manual and platoon was required if the drill of the forces in that
kingdom was to be brought up to date with Flanders practice.
This effort was to be an exceedingly important one since, with
the majority of the regiments in the army always stationed in
Ireland after any peace, uniformity on that establishment
would go far towards effecting uniformity throughout the army.
This goal was soon accomplished, not through the office of
Captain-General but by another of those sources of regulation
which we noted earlier, namely the Irish Commander-in-
Chief.

The process is worth following since it sets the tone for much
that was to follow later in the century. Upon the death of Cutts
in 1707 his place as C.-in-C. at Dublin Castle went to Lt.-Gen.
Richard Ingoldsby, a soldier with considerable experience of
William's and Marlborough's campaigns; and upon arrival in
his new command from Flanders (where his own regiment, the
18th Foot, was serving under Marlborough), Ingoldsby found
the troops 'very defective in their discipline, especially the
foot'. In consequence, he applied to Marlborough and had a
captain and ex-adjutant of his own 18th Foot brought over to
Ireland where, from 1708 to 1710, the whole of the foot upon
that establishment was drilled by him to 'the discipline practised in Flanders'.[29] As early as September 1708 this officer,
Capt. Robert Parker, was writing from Dublin that 'I am here

---

[28] Henceforth, *1708 Regulations*. The date of publication has been torn from the only
extant copy; and though a date of 1712 is sometimes attributed, 1708 is much more
likely, given Parker's activities in Ireland and the fact that the manual and platoon
taught there is exactly the same as in this printed copy.
[29] D. Chandler (ed.), *Robert Parker and Comte de Mérode-Westerloo: The Marlborough
Wars* (1968), 7–8, 10, 75.

labouring hard wth ye two Regim^{ts} here in Town in showing them & ye Ajud^{ts} our fireings, the Gen^{ll} [Ingoldsby] is come from his progress & will See these Regim^{ts} perform in a day or two after which I shall be going for Corke and when ever the wether permitts I must be wth ye Regim^{ts} there & at Kinsale.'[30] Parker spent two years on this duty, 'in which time all the regiments of foot passed through my hands', as he wrote.[31] The system of drill he taught there, which was made regulation in that kingdom by Ingoldsby's command, was not printed, but rather copied in manuscript, and in that less-expensive form spread through all the regiments. The bulk of this regulation was devoted to the new platoon-fire system; included also were the manual and platoon exercises of the firelock almost exactly as laid down in the *1708 Regulations*. Finally, although considerable space was given to forming the square, and although several of the evolutions already long practised were also included, little space was given in this Irish drill to the evolutions and manoeuvres because these had of course not been much altered from the well-established practice of the 1680s and 1690s.[32] Nor does this drill, practised almost army-wide with the end of Parker's labours in 1710, seem to have been further improved upon in Flanders during the remainder of the Spanish Succession war; for a series of general orders, issued by Orkney late in 1711 to the regiments there, describe a drill which did not differ from that taught by Parker and Ingoldsby in Ireland.[33]

It was then with this system of drill—made up of the new manual and platoon exercises, of the new platoon-firings, with a modified system of telling off the fire- and manoeuvre-units, and with most of the old evolutions and manoeuvres—that the British Army emerged from almost a quarter-century of unbroken campaigning. And it was with this system that it

[30] BL Add. MSS 23, 642, fo. 35.

[31] Chandler (ed.), *Parker*, 75.

[32] Despite the fact that it was abridged and supplemental, this Parker–Ingoldsby drill, since it encompassed all five elements, must be regarded as the first full drill regulation to be issued by authority to the new firelock-and-bayonet army of the eighteenth century. A MS copy—'The Exercise of Firelok and Bayonet with the sevll. Fireings of the Foot . . . according to the method appointed by his Ex^{cie} Lieu^t Gen^{ll} Ingoldsby'—survives in the Cornwall RO (DD.R.H.388).

[33] The 1711 foot drill in Flanders appears partly in Orkney's general orders (BL Add.MS 29,477)—the thrd major supplement of Anne's reign.

entered the period of British military history under scrutiny here. Much had been learned. The army had been rearmed. The cavalry had definitely abandoned fire action in favour of the sword and become accustomed to practising shock tactics. The foot had developed a successful (if complicated) system of fire tactics and with it a keen perception of the supremacy of heavy fire over any other form of combat. In this view the British were considerably in advance of most Continental tacticians. Whereas Frederick II of Prussia was until mid-way through the Seven Years War an advocate of the bayonet attack as the best offensive tactic of the foot, it was rather the Prussian system of alternate divisional fire that was to interest the British during the 1750s.[34] But if the cavalry had learned to trust to weight and *l'arme blanche*, and if the foot had learned to rely upon the speed and volume of its fire, there had, by 1712, been almost nothing acquired at the regimental level as regards manoeuvre techniques that was not already known in 1697, and for the most part in 1688. The great antagonist France began, after 1712, to search for new means of introducing flexibility into the manoeuvres of her infantry. It remained to be seen what new measures the officers and tacticians in Britain would put forward in the quarter-century of peace that dawned with the settlement of Utrecht and the accession of the Hanoverian dynasty.

The army, reduced greatly in strength after 1712 and widely dispersed about Britain, Ireland, and the overseas stations, entered in 1712 upon the longest period unmarked by a general war that Britain was to experience between 1688 and 1815. The few operations in which some of the regiments were engaged—troops were employed in Scotland and the northern counties in 1715, where the Jacobite rebels were dealt with at Sheriffmuir and Preston; in Scotland again in 1719, when the few Jacobites who came out (together with 300 wretched Spanish troops) were dispersed at Glenshiel, events which led to Lord Cobham's punitive raid on Vigo, with ten battalions; and in 1727, when the Spaniards conducted a desultory siege of Gibraltar, requiring reinforcements from Ireland and England—were more

---

[34] For Frederick's conservative, though changing, views on the efficacy of fire, see Y. Gras, 'Les guerres "limitées" du XVIIIᵉ siècle', *Revue historique de l'armée*, 26 (1970), 31–2.

in the nature of brief flurries of activity than extended campaigns; and as regards technical military developments they were without significance.[35] As has so often been the case among armies recently victorious, the British Army that came home from Queen Anne's wars settled down resting on its laurels. The friction of peace thereupon began its work; and it is but a slight exaggeration to say that, when occasion offered, the regiments that managed to assemble set about training to fight the War of the Spanish Succession. In almost all essentials, the drill prescribed for, and practised by, the horse and foot throughout these decades was that used during Marlborough's later campaigns. Indeed during the years from 1712 until 1748 only one full-scale regulation drill was issued to the army; and only a handful of orders by authority and private publications appeared to supplement this regulation, none of which attempted anything more significant than to codify current practice or to quibble over details.

Because of their commanding influence in the army, two works stand out above the others that appeared during this period, and both were published within a year of one another. The first, Humphrey Bland's *Treatise of Military Discipline*, appeared in 1727 and was a private venture; the second, the *1728 Regulations*, was the first major drill regulation to be issued by authority since 1690.

The genesis of the *1728 Regulations* illustrates the operation of another of those channels for the introduction of drill alluded to above. Within four months of the death of his royal father, the new king, George II, 'having Observ'd in his Review of his Forces, that the Regiments do not use One and the same Exercise, and that every Colonel alters or Amends as he thinks fit', ordered the Board of General Officers to consult together and 'propose a proper Exercise for the Horse, another for the Dragoons and a third for the Foot, which when approv'd by his

---

[35] Fifteen regiments of horse and eleven of foot were employed in the '15 Rising, namely the 3rd Horse; the 1st, 2nd, 3rd, 4th, 6th, 7th, 10th, 11th, 13th, 14th, Stanhope's, Newton's, Churchill's, and Molesworth's Dragoons; and the 3rd, 8th, 11th, 14th, 16th, 17th, 21st, 25th, 26th, 36th, and Grant's Foot (corps listed by colonels names were disbanded by 1718). In 1719 the 11th, 14th, and 15th of Foot were at Glenshiel. On the Vigo expedition were the 3rd, 19th, 24th, 28th, 33rd, 34th, and 37th of Foot, plus a battalion from each of the three Foot Guards regiments. The corps taking part in the defence of Gibraltar were a battalion from the 1st Foot Guards, plus the 5th, 13th, 14th, 20th, 25th, 26th, 29th, 30th, 34th, and 39th Foot.

Majesty will be given out in Orders to be Observ'd respectively.'[36] The Board, in consequence of this order of 7 October 1727, directed at their meeting of 9 October that 'a Comittee of the General Officers of Dragoons Horse & Foot do Meet and Prepare Rules for Exercise.'[37] The committee acted with dispatch, since by 15 December the Board had approved ('after some small Alterations') the new exercises drawn up for both the Horse and the Dragoons; and on 20 December the Board 'Mett and Sign'd the Report of the Exercise, prepared for the Horse Dragoons & Foot.' King George II quickly gave his approbation, and the new drills thereby became regulation.[38]

That the Board and its committee acted with such dispatch indicates that considerable thought had already been given to the problem; and a Whitehall circular of the previous February had already directed that a uniform Dragoon exercise be prepared.[39] Likewise, the manual and platoon exercises that the Board proposed for the Foot had already in fact been published the previous April by Lt.-Col. Humphrey Bland; the Board had simply lifted the whole of it from Bland's book and made it regulation for the army. Indeed there were no departures from the norm, in fact nothing at all was really new in these drills drawn up and approved for the three arms late in 1727; the Board and its committee had merely drawn on, systematized, and made uniform current practice, and that practice was no

[36] WO 71/6, pp. 19–20. The King, it is clear, was referring only to a general tinkering with the manual and platoon, not to any great deviations between the corps. The Board however took the opportunity to draw up rules for the full five elements of the drill.

[37] Ibid. Thirteen of the fourteen members of the Board, which met on 9 October, were also colonels of regiments and represented all arms being considered. Under the presidency of Gen. the Duke of Argyll (3rd Horse), the Board was composed of Gens. Lord Cobham (2nd Horse) and Sir Charles Wills (1st Foot Guards); of Lts.-Gen. Thomas Whetham (12th Foot), Joseph Sabine (23rd Foot), William Evans (4th Dragoons), and George Wade (4th Horse); of Majs.-Gen. the Earl of Deloraine (16th Foot), Russell, Humphrey Gore (1st Dragoons), and Lord Mark Kerr (13th Foot); and of Brigs.-Gen. Charles Churchill (10th Dragoons), Edmund Fielding (41st Foot), and the Hon. William Kerr (7th Dragoons). This assembly not only represented all types of corps, but combined a formidable experience of the service, as was often the case with the Board.

[38] On the boards of 15 and 20 Dec. Wills, Cobham, Evans, Sabine, and Mark Kerr were not present, their places being taken by Gens the Earl of Cholmondeley (3rd Dragoons) and the Earl of Stair (6th Dragoons); and by Maj.-Gen. William Tatton.

[39] WO 26/17, circular, '16 Feb. 1726/7'. This was at the request of the colonels of the several regiments of dragoons.

more than the result of the experience accumulated in the wars from 1688 to 1712.

The new regulations were sent to the King's Printer, John Baskett, within two weeks of their having been approved by His Majesty; and the printer was ordered to run off and bind 300 copies immediately.[40] Baskett seems now to have slowed down what had been accomplished hitherto in record time; for although the Secretary at War was able on 25 March to distribute copies of 'the Book of Military Exercise which His Majesty hath been pleased to approve of' to the colonels of every regiment then serving in Britain, the Secretary on 22 March had had to threaten Baskett with the loss of his contract unless he set about his business more promptly.[41] Henceforth, however, notes from the Secretary at War to the senior secretary at the Treasury, desiring that the Treasury provide funds for further bulk printings of these *1728 Regulations*, are a commonplace in the letter-books of the Secretary at War.[42]

These three drills were reprinted and issued periodically from 1728 until 1743. During that time they were not revised in the slightest; and not until the pressure of events on active service began to be felt during the later 1740s was modification made. Each copy carried a printed royal warrant dated at Whitehall, 6 January 1728, directing that it was 'His Majesty's express Will and Pleasure' that these regulations 'be observed and followed without any Deviation'. Briefly, the 1728 Horse and Dragoon drillbooks laid down the manual and platoon exercises of the carbine (for the Horse) and of the firelock (for the Dragoons), and then proceeded to describe the simple evolutions to be performed by the troopers when acting in line, dis-

---

[40] WO 4/29, p. 133. It should be pointed out here that, in order to cut costs, it was the custom to issue only a few sets of regulations to each regiment. In 1728, for example, a single regiment of foot on the British establishment would alone have needed thirty-seven copies, were each of its officers to be provided with one (WO 24/133). From the few sets arriving at each corps, officers might copy into their manuscript commonplace books any material immediately relevant to their duties—or they might purchase printed copies at their own expense.

[41] WO 4/29, pp. 182–6.

[42] The last order for copies was made in 1743. For examples of these orders, see WO 4/34, p. 409 (300 copies, Apr. 1737) and WO 4/38, p. 263 (500 copies, Aug. 1743). Similar orders directed through the Treasury for bulk printings of material for the regiments appear in WO 4. These regulations were issued both singly (i.e. the drill for the Horse alone, or for the Dragoons) and bound up together. I have used one of these combined copies, namely the *Exercise For The Horse, Dragoons, and Foot Forces* (1739).

mounted. The evolutions and the essentials of manoeuvring for mounted regiments told off into two or three squadrons, came next. There were no significant differences between the drills to be followed by the two mounted arms. The manual and platoon exercises prescribed for the Foot were quite like those for the cavalry; and lastly came the evolutions, the various types of firings, and a very few manoeuvres which were wholly within the province of the infantry.

Late in April of 1727—that is, about two months after the circular calling for the establishment of a uniform Dragoon exercise, eight months before the drills settled upon by the Board were made regulation in January 1728, and eleven months before the *1728 Regulations* were first distributed— there was published the first edition of Humphrey Bland's *Treatise of Military Discipline*, the best known (both then and now) of all eighteenth-century military treatises in the English language. The author was in 1727 lieutenant-colonel of the 2nd Horse, had seen service under Marlborough, and was to serve again as a general officer under Cumberland in Scotland and Flanders; he was an officer of sound judgement, and an author who organized his ideas and his prose with the greatest clarity.

Bland's book was an instant success, and for over thirty years to come it served as the basic text or primer for the young officer who, having just bought his commission and being desirous to know the daily duties and routine of the service, could do no better (nor for that matter could he do any other, for where else was the young British officer to look for such guidance?) than turn to Bland.[43] The whole of the manual exercise of the foot in the *1728 Regulations* was copied word for word from Bland, and the platoon exercise, the rank- and file-

[43] Humphrey Bland, *A Treatise of Military Discipline; In Which is Laid down and Explained The Duty of the Officer and Soldier, Thro' the several Branches of the Service*, was first published in London and Dublin, in 1727. A 2nd edition followed immediately in the same year. The later editions (all London-printed), appeared as follows: 3rd edn, 1734; 4th edn, 1740; 5th edn, 1743; 6th edn, 1746; 7th edn, 1753. The 2nd–7th editions were simply reprints of the 1st, the term 'edition' in the eighteenth century only infrequently implying 'revised'. In 1759 an 8th, revised edition was published (the revision was the work of Sir William Fawcett, the noted tactician and soldier who had by then translated the Prussian regulations and was later to be made Adjutant-General); and in 1762 Fawcett's revision was reprinted as the 9th rev. edn of Bland.

I have used the 1743 edn (cited hereafter as Bland, *Treatise of Military Discipline*); and I have also used the 1762 rev. edn (cited hereafter as Bland, *Treatise of Military Discipline* (rev. edn, 1762)).

intervals, the wheelings, the essentials of the firings, of platoon fire, and other details, were paraphrased from Bland. Similarly the 1728 manual exercise of the Dragoons, and most of that for the Horse, were drawn from his Foot exercise. Unfortunately, we are unable to trace the process whereby much of Bland's text was transferred to the Board of General Officers, nor can we ascertain whether the February 1727 circular, mentioned above, influenced the process; the links are clear, nevertheless. Likewise, parts of Bland's book, and many shortened or simplified versions, were published in the American colonies for the use of the militia and Provincial corps.[44]

Granted its success, however, Bland's treatise, like the *1728 Regulations*, offered nothing that was new, tactically. Nor was it meant to be anything more than a description of the drill, training, and duties as practised at the time of writing, and so immediately useful. Bland himself in 1727, describing a part of his work, wrote that he would 'insert no more here than what was practised by the Foot during the late War in Flanders'; and that holds true for most of his text. He wrote the book because the old experienced officers of King William and Queen Anne were dying off, and a younger generation of officers unused to service was in need of a practical treatise based on experience; because, although British arms had of late gained a great reputation, there were available no English treatises more recent than that of Orrery (1677);[45] and because in his view neither alliances nor treaties could of themselves be suffi-

---

[44] E.g. Anon., *An Abstract of Military Discipline: more particularly with regard to the Manual Exercise, Evolutions, and Firings of the Foot. From Col. Bland* (Boston, 1743): this and others like it were printed at Boston in 1743, 1744, 1747, 1754, and 1755, and others were printed at New York in 1754, 1755, and 1759. Printed in the 1754 New York version were Governor William Shirley's orders that all corps of foot within the province were to conform to this drill. Bland's 'evolutions' were also published in the colonies, in company with a 1740 manual exercise devised by Col. William Blakeney (of whom more presently), appearing first as Anon., *The New Manual Exercise by General Blakeney. To which is added the Evolutions of the Foot by General Bland* (Philadelphia, 1746). This work, first printed by Benjamin Franklin, was reprinted in Philadelphia in 1747 and 1755, and in New York in 1754 and 1756.

The only such simplified version ever to appear in England was a précis of Fawcett's 1759 revision, designed for the Yorks militia. This was Capt.-Lt. George Thompson's *An Abstract of General Bland's Treatise of Military Discipline . . . With . . . the New Exercise, as practised by the Guards* (York, 1760). Thompson, a militia officer himself, thought Bland's the 'perfectest' drillbook 'in our Language'.

[45] Roger, Earl of Orrery, *A Treatise on the Art of War* (1677).

cient 'without the Ratio Ultima . . . it is a true Observation, that, First or Last, Force has been the Conclusive Argument of most Treaties, and those have been found the best, which have been supported by the best Troops.'

Bland devoted about two-thirds of his text to the intricacies of the manual and platoon exercises, the evolutions and the firings, all of which either was repeated by or—because he dealt with these subjects at greater length—supplemented the *1728 Regulations*. This was all most useful down to the mid-1740s. The final third of the book was given over to fine general comments on drill, shrewd tactical observations, and a long series of chapters dealing with everyday affairs separate from drill—such as garrison and camp duties, mounting guards, parading, regimental inspections and reviews, and the host of other routine matters none of which was to be found in the official regulations—and accordingly very useful.

Taken together, then, the *1728 Regulations* and the *Treatise of Military Discipline* described the drill practised in the British Army at the accession of George II. Neither work was in any way theoretical but rather immediate and practical; and although these were by far the most important drillbooks of this period, there were others which—although they too dealt essentially with current practice, scarcely breaking new ground—were widely read and illustrate further the nature of English military literature at this time. The most important of these was Brig.-Gen. Richard Kane's *Campaigns*, written just before 1736 and first published, posthumously, in 1745.[46] Although primarily a narrative military history, the short section that Kane devoted to the drill and tactics of a battalion reflects the trend of developments, in practice, by the mid-1730s; and

[46] Brig.-Gen. Richard Kane, *Campaigns of King William and Queen Anne; From 1689, to 1712. Also, A New System of Military Discipline, for a Battalion of Foot on Action; with the Most Essential Exercise of the Cavalry* . . . (1745), was reprinted with the addition of several excellent plates illustrating manoeuvres and firings (the 'Designs of experienced Officers', as his anonymous editor described them), as Brig.-Gen. Richard Kane, *Campaigns of King William and the Duke of Marlborough . . . The Second Edition* (1747). Parts of this work appeared again in 1757, although the anonymous author of this version so altered its format, and added so much new material, that it bore little resemblance to the original. This last work, by a 'Gentleman of the Army', was *A System of Camp Discipline . . . and other Regulations for the Land Forces . . . In which are included, Kane's Discipline for a Battalion in Action* . . . (1757). These works will be cited hereafter as Kane, *Campaigns*; Kane, *Campaigns (2nd Ed.)*; and Anon., *Camp Discipline & Kane* (1757), respectively.

within the limitations of its length it was both exceedingly realistic and in some respects more up to date than either Bland or the *1728 Regulations*. Kane was considerably experienced, having served throughout the wars of 1689–1712 in Ireland, on board the fleet, and in Flanders and Germany. Most of his service was with the 18th Foot (the corps whose drill Parker had taught in Ireland); hence the realism which infuses Kane's tactical observations. Indeed (as his editor wrote in 1747), Kane 'with great Contempt, read some Books, which pretended to Teach the whole Military Art; and often assured his Friends, that those mean Performances provoked him, to attempt something on the same Subject.'[47] He succeeded in his purpose, Wolfe for one thinking it 'a very pretty, concise discourse, to the great advantage and improvement of those persons for whom it was intended'.[48]

Of limited use on the theme of tactics, but an excellent introduction to the major operations of the unitary army and (with the inclusion of the full Standing Orders of his dragoon regiment) an important source on the training of the cavalry, was Lt.-Gen. Richard, Viscount Molesworth's *Short Course of Standing Rules*, a treatise printed in London in 1744 and again in Dublin in 1745.[49] Molesworth had seen much service in Flanders and Spain after 1702, and was an ADC to Marlborough at Ramillies and for some time thereafter. He was devoted to the service: he raised a regiment of dragoons in the '15, and in 1723 he was planning to write a history of the Duke of Marlborough—'which I propose as the chief affair of my life'[50] —and he had some interesting ideas on the formation of the

[47] Kane, *Campaigns (2nd Ed.)*, Editor's Preface.
[48] Beckles Willson, op. cit. 166.
[49] Lt.-Gen. Richard, Viscount Molesworth, *A Short Course of Standing Rules, for the Government and Conduct of an Army, Designed for, or in The Field. With Some useful Observations . . .* (1744), was published under the same title (though *Corrected and Amended by the Author*—which in fact it was not) in Dublin in 1745. Included in both printings was a lengthy appendix of 'Standing Orders for the Royal Dragoons of Ireland, Given in the Year 1738', which might be compared with 'The First Standing Orders of the Fifteenth Light Dragoons', dating from *c.*1789, and which Lt.-Col. J. B. R. Nicholson reprinted in *Tradition*, 10 (1965), 2–3; 11 (1965), 30–3; 12 (1965), 30–1; 13 (1966), 30–1; and 15 (1966), 28–9.
[50] This project did not come off, owing mainly to Duchess Sarah's obstinacy. As Molesworth complained, 'I have . . . in vain been dunning Her Grace for certain materials, which are necessary to my first setting out.' *HMC Clements MSS* (1913), pp. 354, 359, 405–6.

army.[51] His military career prospered (although during the
1720s promotion was slow, Molesworth complaining in 1724
that 'all colonels are immortalized by my being next heir to a
regiment'), since he became Irish C.-in-C. in 1751 and was
made Field-Marshal in 1757; but his success as a military
writer was mixed.[52] His *Short Course of Standing Rules* was hardly
profound: Lt.-Col. Caroline Scott of the 29th Foot ordered the
book in 1750 only 'to fill up my collection rather than of real
use';[53] and as anything more than an introductory guide for the
inexperienced, Scott judged it rightly.

   Another work which, like Molesworth's, was best suited to
informing the inexperienced was Brig.-Gen. Adam Williamson's *Maxims of Turenne*, published in London in 1740 and reprinted there in 1744.[54] Full of wise, if disjointed, commentary,
Williamson's book was (he said himself) best read by young
officers only after they had grounded themselves in the regulations and Bland's treatise. 'Let them put this book in their
pockets,' he wrote; 'it will take little more room than their
snuff-box, and if as often look'd into, will be of greater use to
them; for every paragraph is a lesson.'[55] Like Molesworth,
Williamson had joined the army in 1702 and had served
throughout Marlborough's campaigns. In 1722 he served
briefly as Adjutant-General, and was thereafter Deputy-
Lieutenant of the Tower. A brigadier in 1741, he was at the

   [51] Molesworth thought that recruiting would be eased if the authorities were 'to
nominate the several *Foot Regiments* in His Majesty's Service, from the several *Shires* in
Great Britain'. This would inspire the shires to vie with each other to keep the corps
bearing their names complete; it would prevent desertion ('Since, should any, in that
Circumstance, offer to go home, the whole Neighbourhood would be Piqued in Honour
to detect and restore them'); and finally 'so strong an *Emulation* would be raised between (for instance) the *Yorkshire*, *Nottinghamshire*, and *Derbyshire* Regiments, and so on,
that each would be cut to Pieces, before it would yield any Preference to its Neighbour'
(pp. 167–71).
   [52] C. Dalton, *George the First's Army*, i (1910), 85; and *HMC Clements MSS* (1913),
pp. 377, 405.
   [53] Cumb. Pprs, Box 44, no. 98.
   [54] Brig.-Gen. Adam Williamson, *Military Memoirs and Maxims of Marshal Turenne;
Interspersed with Others, taken from the Best Authors and Observation, with Remarks* (1740),
was (as its title indicates) a series of general maxims dealing with all aspects of active
operations, ably commented upon by Williamson. The work, like Bland's, was inspired
partly by declining experience in the army: 'A cessation of Arms for twenty-eight years
must unavoidably have been attended with the loss of most of our old Generals and
Officers, and their Posts fill'd with many who never served abroad' (p.v).
   [55] Ibid. vi.

time of his death a lieutenant-general. Like so many of the soldier-authors of the eighteenth century, Williamson was granted permission to dedicate his work to the King; and in 1740 he presented copies of his *Maxims of Turenne* both to George II and to the Duke of Cumberland.[56]

The *1728 Regulations*, and the treatises of Bland, Kane, Molesworth, and Williamson were the only major works concerning the training and drill of the horse and foot to appear in Britain before 1748. Of the more significant foreign treatises, only one—the *Mémoires* of Lt.-Gen. the marquis de Feuquières, first published in Paris in 1711—was translated for the benefit of the British officer corps;[57] and there is no evidence that the British profited by the translation, or were busy reading other foreign works. Not even Folard, whose major treatises appeared during the later 1720s, seems to have penetrated the British Army.

In sharp contrast to this shortage of major treatises, however, was the plethora of manual and platoon exercises—some issued by authority and others privately published—that appeared regularly from 1716 through 1746. The contrast is significant and, as we shall see, the concentration on these exercises is revealing of the condition of the peacetime army. Thus in 1716 a manual and platoon exercise was issued to the army generally; but it was exactly like that given out in general orders by Orkney in Flanders in 1711, and now simply reaffirmed.[58] Again, in 1723, a manual and platoon exercise exactly like that issued in 1716 was given out by Dublin Castle, and it was 'order'd to be used by all the Regim^ts in Ireland'.[59] In 1735 the exercise for the handling of grenades, as laid down in the *1728 Regulations*, was illustrated in a book of engravings published in

---

[56] J. C. Fox (ed.), *The Official Diary of Lieutenant-General Adam Williamson, Deputy-Lieutenant of the Tower of London, 1722–1747* (1912), 5–6, 103.

[57] Antoine de Pas, marquis de Feuquières, *Memoirs Historical and Military . . . Translated from the French with Preliminary Remarks . . . by the Translator*, 2 Vols (1735–36). The anonymous translator was careful to expunge French jingoism from this very important study on tactics and recent campaigns and, having thus rendered the work 'impartial', to fill it with the English equivalent.

[58] I have found only one copy of the 1716 exercise, in the MS commonplace book of an officer in Handasyde's 22nd of Foot (NAM MS, no. 6807/205, pp. 1–4). The 1711 Flanders manual is to be found in BL Add. MS 29, 477, fo. 9.

[59] NAM MS, no. 6807/205, pp. 11–14.

London.[60] Another engraver, Benjamin Cole, produced in 1745 a series of plates illustrating the several 'positions of a Soldier under arms' according to the manual exercise in the *1728 Regulations*; and Cole in 1746 brought out a fuller version, responding no doubt to the spur which Prince Charles Edward Stuart had given to public interest in military affairs.[61] These several exercises differed hardly at all, one from another.[62] In 1740 however, Colonel (later Lt.-Gen. Lord) William Blakeney devised a platoon exercise which was significantly shorter and simpler than that authorized by regulation; this was to be used in the training of a new, four-battalion marching regiment (Spotswood's, later Gooch's), to be raised in America for service in the forthcoming expedition to Cartagena. As adjutant-general to the expedition Blakeney went to America in June, 1740, to assist in raising this regiment; and since there would be little time for training Spotswood's in the intricacies of the regulation manual and platoon he drew up his own short, easier version.[63] This circulated in manuscript at this time in England where (according to a hostile critic) Blakeney was 'very much in vog among ye officers for his pretended tran-

[60] The engraving and publication were the work of Bernard Lens, in his *The Granadiers Exercise of the Grenade . . .* (1735). This was reprinted in 1744 and has since been reproduced, with an introduction, as part of the National Army Museum Historical Series (*The Granadiers Exercise 1735* [1967]). The 1728 grenade exercise on which Lens based his booklet was itself taken directly from Flanders practice of 1711 (BL Add. MS 29, 477, fo. 10).

[61] These works of Cole were, *The Gentleman Volunteer's Pocket Companion, describing the Various Motions of the Foot Guards, Drawn from an Officer long experienced in ye Military Disciplin . . .* (1745); and *The Soldier's Pocket-Companion, or the Manual Exercise of our British Foot as now practis'd . . .* (1746). These are a clear illustrative accompaniment to the manual of 1728.

[62] If we compare the platoon exercises laid down in the *1708 Regulations*, in Orkney's 1711 Flanders orders (BL Add. MS 29, 477, fo. 9), in the Parker–Ingoldsby Irish drill of 1708 (Cornwall RO DD.R.H. 388, fos. 1–3), in the *1716 Regulations* (NAM MS, no. 6807/205, pp. 1–2), in the Irish *1723 Regulations* (NAM MS, no. 6807/205, pp. 11–12), in Bland's 1727 *Treatise of Military Discipline* (pp. 19–25, 72–3), and in the *1728 Regulations* (pp. 6–49), we find that the words of command in the 1708 platoon and in the Parker-Ingoldsby platoon are identical, although the former version (which may contain misprints) consists of 68 motions for the soldier while the latter consists of 63; the Orkney platoon, the 1716, the 1723, the Bland, and the 1728 platoons, respectively, consist of 63, 64, 64, 63, and 63 motions; all are virtually identical, except that the versions in Bland and in the *1728 Regulations* make a slight change in two of the motions.

[63] On this unit, which was part of the regular army, see C. McBarron et al., 'The American Regiment, 1740–1746', *Military Collector & Historian*, 21 (1969), 84–6. On Blakeney's role in preparing Gooch's, see Pargellis, *Loudoun*, 13.

scendency in ye Manual Exorcise—and got a Regmt. of Foot for the same';[64] but Blakeney's exercise was never printed in Britain or Ireland although, as we have seen (Ch. III n. 44), it was frequently reprinted in the colonies for the militia and Provincials.[65]

Neither was the English militia spared the mania for the manual and platoon. To note but two examples among several: in 1717 William Breton published a lengthy manual and platoon together with a description of the evolutions and the firings, of which some was based on the regular army's current practice but much of which was cribbed from an outdated, anonymous work of 1689.[66] Much more useful was *The Militia-Man*, which came out in 1740; the anonymous author of this tome recommended that all schoolmasters in the 'Charity Schools' of England should learn the manual exercise, so that they might teach it to their pupils who would thereby acquire early in life a dexterity in the use of arms. 'The humour will spread, and the boys of other schools will take to the same sport, and the Exercise will become as common play as cricket or football.' The result would be to fill out the county militia battalions with eager 'veterans'.[67]

There is, finally, no evidence of any pamphlet discussion of

[64] The critic was Brig.-Gen. James Douglass, who obtained an early version 'at Court, from Coll. Blakney himself', before he sailed. Douglass kept the copy and appended his criticisms (BL Add. MS 27, 892, fo. 219). Blakeney was given a regiment (the 27th Foot) in 1737; he retained its colonelcy until his death in 1761.

[65] Blakeney served in Flanders under Marlborough, and saw service again in the 1739–48 war. In 1756, with four battalions, he held out for seventy days in St. Philip's Castle, Minorca, when Richelieu besieged the place with 16,000 troops. Blakeney was a veritable Uncle Toby, often developing drills during the 1740s. An adulatory biographer said of him that, during the long peace between 1712 and 1739, he 'had a Number of Things made of Pasteboard, which the Wags of those Days called Puppets, by the Movements thereof he could represent all the different Postures and Exercise of a Battalion.' Anon., *Memoirs of the Life and particular Actions, of . . . General Blakeney . . .* (Dublin and London, 1756), 16, 7–8.

[66] William Breton, *Militia Discipline. The Words of Command and Directions for Exercising . . .* (1717). The earlier work was that of Capt. J. S., *Military Discipline; or the Art of War . . . of Doubling, wheeling, Forming and Drawing up a Battalion or Army into any Figure, etc.* (1689), itself only a reprint of Part II of Capt. J. S., *Treatise of Fortification and Military Discipline . . .* (1688). This work was by 1688 already old-fashioned, full of elaborate pike drill reminiscent of the theory (hardly the practice) of the 1630s. A revised version of Breton's book was published in Boston, Mass., as late as 1733, by which time it would have been of more use to antiquaries than the militia.

[67] Anon., *The Militia-Man. Containing, Necessary Rules for both Officer and Soldier . . .* (1740).

drill and training; and save for a few short manuscript compilations, and the occasional plans and suggestions circulated in
correspondence between officers, it was from these relatively
few sources—and from customary practice—that young officers
entering the army during these long years of peace acquired
their understanding of the drill.[68]

The regulations and treatises that appeared during these
years were by no means innovative. Their purpose was essentially conservative, their goal modest: on the one hand to
codify and preserve the drill that the army had learned during
its lengthy and successful experience of Flanders, and on the
other to ensure that all the regiments should continue to practise this drill uniformly. Since all of the regiments that survived
the post-Utrecht reductions were by 1712 well acquainted with
'the discipline practised in Flanders', these regulations and
treatises, though few in number, should nevertheless have been
more than sufficient to accomplish such modest ends. But were
these ends accomplished? How successful were the drillbooks
at retaining or imposing uniformity, and at assisting the army
in keeping itself fully trained against the day when war might
be renewed? The answers to these questions are to be found
partly in the circumstances that occasioned the introduction of
certain of these drills, partly in the nature of the peacetime experience of the regiments, and partly in the army's record
during the campaigns of 1740–8.

It is important to remember that George II had ordered the
preparation of the *1728 Regulations* because 'every Colonel
alters or Amends as he thinks fit.' It is also worth remembering
that Bland, Williamson, and the others had drawn up their
works because a whole new generation, unused to the experience of Flanders from 1689 to 1712, had entered the officer
corps since Utrecht. But it was not simply the waning of the
memory of drill and tactics as practised under Marlborough,
nor the vagaries of purchase and regimental proprietary 'ownership' which throughout the century led to a particularist
spirit among the corps, encouraging 'alterations and amend-

[68] Hence, in his text for young officers, *The Cadet* (1756), p. viii, Capt. Samuel Bever
lamented the fact that most of his material had to be drawn from foreign sources: 'I
wish I could have added a few English Names to the List of Authors; but I am sorry to
say, that a disappointed Search for Books of this Kind in our Language, exonerates me
from the Guilt of Plagiarism from my Countrymen.'

ments', that made regulation necessary. Nor was it simply the presence of new officers that made the codification and regulation of established practice essential. It was rather that the multitude of factors operating in and upon the standing peacetime army—the factors we noted in Chapter I above—were cumulatively so powerful as to derange any wholly uniform system of drill. The speed with which the friction of peace acted upon the army is extraordinary. George II in 1727—that is, fifteen years after Queen Anne's wars had ended—was disturbed to discover variety in the army's exercise. But George I, as early as 1716, had observed the same thing in his forces. That King in 1716, as his son was to do after him in 1727, had had a uniform exercise drawn up for the army; and not only George II's observations on unauthorized 'alterations and amendments', but those made by George I himself in 1718, show that success in imposing the *1716 Regulations* was limited.[69] And the extraordinary thing about this was that the exercises of 1716, of 1723, of Bland, of the *1728 Regulations*, and the later engraving books and summaries differed hardly in the slightest from the exercises practised in the Flanders regiments by 1708, taught by Parker in Ireland from 1708 to 1710 and published by authority in 1708; and differed not at all from those given out in Flanders in 1711. So, despite the keen edge to which the army had been honed by 1712; despite the fact that the drill used in Marlborough's regiments had been carried from Flanders and introduced to the whole of the army in Ireland by 1710, and had been practised everywhere by 1712; despite the fact that the manual and platoon exercises in use by 1708 and 1711 had been repeatedly given out by authority in 1711, 1716, 1723, and 1728; despite, again, that a system of regular inspection of regiments had been introduced in 1716, and made annual from

[69] As the Secretary at War informed the Board of General Officers on 18 Sept. 1718 (and in so doing described succinctly the reasons for attempting to enforce regularity), 'The Genl. Officers, who have lately been upon the Review of ye Troops, have Represented to H.M. yt. ye Exercise of ye Severall Corps differs One from Another, by which means there can not but happen great Confusion, in case They should be exercised, when upon Detachmts. or in Brigades; H.M. is therefore pleased to Order ... ye Board ... to draw up a Methodicall Exercise to be practised throughout all His Forces, & proposes to Them ye Exercise of His Guards as a fitting Plan' (WO 4/21, p. 187). The Board's reply is lost; but since no new exercise was forthcoming it may be presumed that the 1716 exercise, as practised by the Foot Guards, was once more reaffirmed.

c. 1720;[70] despite the fact that by 1727 the army's firearms were very close to being built to a uniform design, and that from 1715 firearms production had been supervised under the Ordnance system of manufacture; and finally, despite the fact that several regiments had been marched into encampments in 1722 and 1723, there to drill together (on which more anon), none of these developments was powerful enough to overcome the friction of peace. Away from the wars, dispersed about the British Isles or about the Empire and suffering the effects of peacetime duty, the drill efficiency and regularity of the army began inevitably to slump. The system of drill and tactics laid down in the treatises and regulations before 1740, then, was a system to which the peacetime regiments could only aspire. The stiff nature of much of the drill and the clumsiness of the tactics prescribed, therefore, must in many units have seemed the very essence of fluidity and flexibility.

The army's drill efficiency deteriorated because, after twenty-five years of almost continual campaigning, the regiments were suddenly dispersed and left in that condition for a period as long and undisturbed as the previous quarter-century had been eventful. After 1712 there was to be relatively little opportunity for carrying on training even at the level of one or two grand-divisions or squadrons, let alone regiments. The officers, the tacticians, and the central authorities clung to what had been practised under Marlborough; but the regiments themselves were unable, for the most part, even to do this. Dispersed, their only resource was to devote themselves to those parts of the drill that a few troops or companies could practise with any profit—the simple evolutions, small-scale marches and manoeuvres and, with increasing frequency, the manual and platoon exercises. Firepower, the major tactical advance handed on to the army after 1712, was based on the successful performance of the complicated platoon-fire system; and since the smallest of units could practise at least the role of the individual platoon, the manual and platoon exercises became not just the main item in the peacetime training of the dispersed companies but a fetish which was carried to absurd lengths. Since so much time came to be devoted to the manual and platoon—and indeed this is understandable, for what else could

[70] See pp. 297–300.

isolated companies attempt with any real profit?—the net result was a deterioration in most other of the essential elements of the drill. Even the cavalry, who were without their horses for many months of the year, spent much of the time available firing away blank cartridges in three ranks, booted and spurred. As expediency became seeming necessity, so the manual and platoon became the commonplace of training; these exercises were issued repeatedly, as we have seen, and the treatises and regulations came increasingly to dwell on the intricacies of the manual to the near exclusion of everything else. Almost the whole of the *1728 Regulations*, for both the foot and the horse, was devoted to these exercises. There were some who deplored this development. Brig.-Gen. Richard Kane, writing just before 1736, thought the *1728 Regulations* 'a poor Performance', and was surprised that such a work 'should be skreen'd by Authority'; with its concentration on the manual and platoon, Kane wrote that these regulations allowed 'nothing relating to Action [to be] introduced into our Discipline'. Of the cavalry, he thought it 'preposterous . . . to see some of our English Jack-Boot-Men, with all their Accoutrements, perform an Exercise on Foot! Was this ever known to be of Use upon Action? Is it possible for young Gentlemen that never saw any thing of Action (of whom the Army in a short Time will be composed), to form an Idea of Action, out of this Book of Discipline?'[71] Col. (later Lt.-Gen.) Henry Hawley, writing in 1726, was equally nonplussed. 'If the Peace continues long, I may live to see the Foot of England carried in waggons from quarter to quarter, for what with their vast size and the idleness they live in, I'm sure they can't march.' He thought the foot should be employed on road-work, rather than strewn about in billets; 'this would keep Officer and soldier out of sloth and idleness, 'twould keep them in good discipline, another and better sort of discipline than what is now erroneously so called, having them out twice a week to act over that silly thing called Manual Exercise.' Hawley thought that the cavalry would likewise be better employed constantly patrolling the roads for highwaymen: thus 'the horses would be in better health, fitter for service, the men not grow so fat, know the use of their accoutrements, be kept sober and not such fops, with their curled locks

[71] Kane, *Campaigns*, 109–10.

and Holland stockings . . .'[72] Writing in 1740, Brig.-Gen. James Douglass denounced the practice too, arguing that the separation of the arms exercises into the slow manual and the speedy platoon was foolish, since the one was but the core of the other, practised at greater speed. 'If then you pass them under different denominations, the Souldiers in time of action, will plunge into horid mistakes greatly to ye prejudice of ye Service.' He concluded that 'ye superflous tearme Ploton exercise, ought never to be more heard off, but by all generals condemn'd as erroneous, and canceled out of all books of military exercise"[73] But theirs were voices crying in the wilderness, as is attested by the frequency with which manual and platoon exercises appeared, were practised, and fussed over.

This development was not without some fruits. By the mid-1720s the procedure of 'locking' the ranks was becoming common practice, a development which made for greater ease and concentration of fire, at the same time increasing its accuracy.[74] Metal ramrods began to be introduced at this time and during the 1730s the practice of priming the pans of firelocks from small flasks was abandoned in favour of speedier priming directly from the paper cartridge.[75] It is unquestionable that the rate of fire of the British foot was increased during this period from an average of two shots per minute to three, in sustained fire. And the clear perception of the overall efficacy of fire was not forgotten. Thus Kane was quite convinced that 'if a Body of Foot have but Resolution to keep their Order, there is no Body of Horse dare venture within their Fire.' Bland wrote that, 'If Foot could be brought to know their own Strength, the Danger which they apprehend from Horse would soon vanish; since the Fire of one Platoon, given in due Time, is sufficient to break any Squadron'; and again, 'one battalion of well-disciplin'd Foot [given secure flanks] may despise the Attacks of a whole Line of Horse, while they continue their Attacks on Horse-back, and oblige them to retire with considerable Loss.'[76]

---

[72] Sumner, 'Chaos', 93.

[73] BL Add. MS 27, 892, fos. 212–19.

[74] Bland, *Treatise of Military Discipline*, 72. On the origins and mechanics of 'locking' see p. 281 here, where basic training is dealt with.

[75] On which see pp. 146–8.

[76] Bland, *Treatise of Military Discipline*, 91, and Kane, *Campaigns*, 123–5.

The army, clearly, had taken Wynendaele to heart. But despite the endless attention devoted by the dispersed troops and companies to the arms exercises, Bland would have been hard put to find more than a handful of battalions of 'well-disciplin'd Foot' outside of London and Dublin. It was all very well for the Foot Guards' battalions, constantly in concentration in and about London and Westminster, to go through the whole of the complicated platoon-firings—'Hyde Park discipline', as many appropriately and derisively styled it. Companies might know their arms exercises; but since platoon fire was delivered according to a prearranged and intricate sequence by platoons and 'firings' told off here and there down the full battalion (as in Figs 1–4, pp. 318–20 below), expertise by individual companies at the simple manual and platoon did nothing to guarantee the successful performance of the platoon-fire system—let alone major manoeuvres—by the full battalion when at last it might be assembled. This was made abundantly clear by the performance of the army in the wars of 1739–48.

1748–1764

The generally poor performance of the army during the campaigns of 1739–48 (especially before 1746), made it clear that the old system of drill laid out in the *1728 Regulations* was in need of considerable revision. This was to be carried out piecemeal during the years 1748–64, a fifteen-year period which—in sharp contrast to the three decades preceding it—was to see the appearance of a number of regulations issued by authority and of a score of private publications some of which were excellent, and many of which illustrate a new spirit of professionalism loose in the army.

Although the Duke of Cumberland had considerable forces under his command in the Low Countries in 1748, negotiations for the peace were proceeding in earnest from the spring; there were consequently both sufficient forces available in concentration and plenty of opportunities to introduce and establish new drill procedures. Always deeply concerned with all matters concerning drill and regularity, the Duke now set in train the revision of the British drill with the preparation and dissemination, that summer, of the *1748 Regulations*, which all regiments of foot in the Low Countries were to 'Conform to & practice'.[77] These new regulations concerned themselves only with the firings, with forming the square and wheeling the battalion line upon its centre, and with fine points such as the disposition of officers and drums; and it was in the firings that the changes made were most significant, since the telling off of the fire-divisions and the ordering of the sequence according to which divisions were to give fire was now standardized on a method more easily practised than those laid down in the *1728 Regulations* and in Bland.[78] With the introduction of these changes, all the British foot except those units in Ireland was, by 1749, practising the manual and platoon exercises, the evolutions, and the majority of its manoeuvres after the old 1728 drill; while the firings and several of its manoeuvres were being carried on according to the new *1748 Regulations*.

The spread of the *1748 Regulations* illustrates once again the powers and limitations of authority. The Duke as Captain-General commanded the forces on the Continent and all the forces elsewhere except those in Ireland. With him in the Low Countries in 1748 were three battalions of Foot Guards and nineteen battalions of marching Foot; and by 1749 four of these battalions (the 8th, 19th, 32nd, and 36th) were at Gibraltar, four were in Minorca (the 12th, 31st, 33rd, and 37th), three Guards battalions and four marching battalions (the 13th, 20th, 21st, and 23rd) were in Britain, six battalions were in Ireland (the 1/1st, 25th, 28th, 42nd, 44th, and 48th), while the last, Loudoun's 64th, had been disbanded. Thus, by mid-1749,

[77] These regulations were issued in manuscript to the majors of brigade, whose business it was 'to give An Exact Copy of the Same' to the adjutants of each of the regiments in their brigades. There are copies in the Cumb. Pprs, Pt 4, II, fos. 61–2, and in the Kent RO Amherst MSS 05/6. Another copy (although easily overlooked, since it is untitled and undated) appeared in Anon., *Camp Discipline & Kane* (1757), 29–32. In the Kent RO Amherst MSS 05/5, the practice of these revisions (together with the rest of the drill current at the end of the war) is beautifully illustrated in the 'Review of the 2^d Batt^n of the 1st Regim^t of Foot Guards by H.R.H. the Duke ye 26th of Sept. 1748 N.S. at Eyndhoven'.

[78] The Duke was busy reviewing British and allied regiments in the Low Countries' camps throughout the spring and summer of 1748 (see Kent RO Amherst MSS 05/1–8; and J. O. Robson, 'Military Memoirs of Lt-Gen the Hon. Charles Colville', *JSAHR* 28 (1950), 77–80). The new system of telling off the fire divisions seems likely to have been taken from the drill used in the Hanoverian foot: see Amherst MSS 05/1, 'Review of the First Line of Hanover Infantry . . . at the Camp of Nestelroy the Second of July 1748 N.S.'; and note especially the telling off of the 1st bn., Hanoverian Foot Guards, and of the battalion of Druchtleben.

the full Minorca and Gibraltar garrisons were using the new system, and the Duke had made it general practice in Britain.[79] In Ireland meanwhile, the six battalions come home from the Low Countries continued to practise the new *1748 Regulations*;[80] and a seventh Irish corps (Hopson's 29th) was following these regulations too, since its lieutenant-colonel (a crony of the Duke, and of the Adjutant-General in London) claimed that he 'had received Verbal Orders from such high rank as was sufficient to him, to make Hopson's . . . Stick Close to these fireings and Evolutions.'[81] Otherwise, it was not until 1756 that the new system now printed, modified, and issued generally 'By His Majesty's Special Command', was adopted by the rest of the Irish foot.[82]

The drill of the cavalry was considered at this time too. On 5 May 1749 a board composed of colonels of Dragoon Guards and Dragoons met at the King's command in the Privy Garden, to consider and report on 'a Paper containing several Articles' relative to the organization, interior economy, and drill of their regiments. Their report was read at a meeting of 9 May and then laid before the King.[83] On the question whether they felt that there was 'any thing deficient or Superfluous in the present Discipline of the Dragoons', their reply was in the negative, and they had 'no Alterations to propose on that Head'.[84] That they should thus have replied is interesting, since the expertise of this board—with general officers of the experience of Honywood, Bland, Hawley, and Cope for members —was great; and six of the seven regiments that they represented had only recently been on active service against the French in the Low Countries. The Dragoon Guards and

[79] Cumb. Pprs, Box 43, no. 294.

[80] Ibid., Box 44, no. 99, pp. 10–18.

[81] Ibid., pp. 13–14.

[82] Proposals dated 15 Dec. 1750, in the Duke's papers, indicate that it was planned at the time to attempt to introduce the new system in Ireland. The plan was abandoned, presumably because the Duke's writ did not run across the Irish Sea. Cumb. Pprs, Box 44, no. 140, fo. 3.

[83] WO 71/9, pp. 65–74. Gen. Sir Philip Honywood (1st Dragoon Guards) acted as president of this Board, the members of which were Lts.-Gen. Henry Hawley (1st Dragoons), the Earl of Crawford (2nd Dragoons), Humphrey Bland (3rd Dragoons), Sir Robert Rich (4th Dragoons), Sir John Cope (7th Dragoons), and the Hon. Sir Charles Howard (3rd Dragoon Guards). These were seven of the eleven line cavalry corps then in Britain.

[84] WO 71/9, pp. 72–3.

Dragoons on the British establishment, therefore, continued to perform their drill according to the *1728 Regulations*; and indeed this is not surprising: changes in the manoeuvres and tactics of the mounted arm were few after Marlborough's campaigns, since before the appearance of true light horse the tactical role of the cavalry was well defined, its manoeuvres few, settled, and understood.[85]

Beginning in 1755, a series of regulations and orders appeared which continued the revision of the drill begun in 1748. The first of these—issued by the Adjutant-General in May 1755 to all regiments on the British establishment, by order of the Duke of Cumberland—was a collection of extracts from the general orders given out in the army in the Low Countries between 1745 and 1748.[86] Dealing for the most part with the myriad daily routine duties in the corps on campaign, in the cantonments, and upon the march, it was only in passing that training and drill were touched upon; nevertheless these orders, which were to be 'looked upon as Standing Orders, and as such to be transcribed in the Regimental Book of each Regiment', helped considerably in systematizing routine throughout the army, as had Bland's text. In 1755 there was also drawn up at the Duke's bidding a set of 'Standing Orders to be Observed by the Whole Corps of Dragoons'.[87] Although the horses, tack, and kit, and the routine duty of quarters, camps, and marches was included, much space in these dragoon orders was devoted to the mounted evolutions and manoeuvres, and to the dismounted evolutions and firings (after the *1748 Regulations*, now introduced officially among the dragoons).

These collections of standing orders were only preliminary, for in April 1756 there was issued 'By His Majesty's Special

---

[85] The manoeuvres practised by the Dragoon Guards and Dragoons, *c.*1750, will be found in BL King's MS 239. This is a finely bound, 54-folio MS book of well-executed plans of the mounted evolutions and manoeuvres; and in the finely drawn plan of the 'Review of the British Cavalry By His Royal Highness the Duke ye 9th of July 1748. Camp of Nestelroy, New Stile' (Kent RO Amherst MSS 05/4). There is nothing among these that differs from earlier practice.

[86] Reprinted by P. Sumner as 'Standing Orders for the Army—1755', in *JSAHR* 5 (1926), 191–9, and 6 (1927), 8–10 (cited hereafter as *1755 Standing Orders*). These were reprinted in Anon., *Camp Discipline & Kane* (1757), 57–70.

[87] Reprinted with notes by P. Sumner as 'Standing Orders For The Dragoons, circa 1755', in *JSAHR* 23 (1945), 98–106 (cited hereafter as *1755 Dragoon Orders*). It is clear from their style and content that Hawley had a hand in their preparation.

Command' an entirely new platoon exercise, to be observed henceforth (without 'the least Alteration in or Deviation from it') by all the regiments in Britain, Ireland, and the overseas stations and garrisons.[88] With notes on the posting of officers, NCOs, and drums in the battalion line, and retaining both the firings and the system of telling off the fire-units as laid down in the *1748 Regulations*, this new regulation represented the most significant official revision of the army's platoon exercise since the appearance of the 1708 arms drill. These *1756 Regulations* cut the platoon exercise to a mere twenty-four motions; they were much more easily learned than the sixty-three of the old *1728 Regulations* (still officially in use until now, but doubtless modified of late years according to the whims of the colonels and field officers of individual corps), and when mastered would have added noticeably to the rate of fire that the battalions could keep up—by an additional round every two minutes, at least, a factor to be of no small importance on the open battlefields of the Seven Years War. The new platoon exercise was practised by the sergeants and corporals of the 1st Foot Guards before being printed and issued to the whole of the King's forces, on 18 April 1756; and indeed the new drill was already being performed publicly by the NCOs of the 1st Guards on the 24th of April.[89]

The 1756 platoon was reprinted several times during the ensuing few years, but each time as part of a larger drillbook—the *1757 Regulations*—which now embraced all five elements of the drill. Prepared by the Duke of Cumberland, his Adjutant-General Robert Napier, and Lt.-Col. Alexander Dury of the 1st Foot Guards (of which corps Cumberland was colonel), this new drill, like the 1756 platoon before it, was being prac-

---

[88] This was *A New Exercise, To be observed by His Majesty's Troops on the Establishment of Great-Britain and Ireland* (1756).

[89] This was reported in the *London Evening-Post* of 27 Apr.; and that paper's report was copied by the *Gentleman's Magazine* (Apr. 1756). The reporter described the performance, which he watched in St. James's Park, as 'the Manual Exercise of the Prussians'; and (what with the easy availability of that magazine) historians have assumed ever since not only that he was correct, but (quite mistakenly) that he was referring to the full Prussian drill and not to just one element of it. It is quite possible that the Prussian platoon exercise (first privately published in English in 1754) was the inspiration of the 1756 English platoon; they resemble one another closely, although the English platoon exercise resembles that composed by Blakeney in 1740 quite as much as it does the Prussian platoon exercise.

tised in the months before its army-wide issue by the NCOs of the 1st Guards.[90] Once satisfied, the Adjutant-General on 25 June 1757 issued through his office this new full regulation drill which not only laid down the 1756 platoon exercise, together with the firings and the system of telling off the fire-units as first described in the *1748 Regulations*, but made regulation a new manual exercise, a new series of evolutions,[91] and added a few manoeuvres now to be practised as the regulation drill in all of the regiments.[92] Slightly shortened versions (i.e. without the new manoeuvres) of these *1757 Regulations* were issued thereafter;[93] and from 1758 marginal notations were included for the instruction of the dragoons, when performing the drill on foot.[94] These regulations, and the series of editions that

[90] Cumb. Pprs, Box 50, nos. 17, 211; and Box 52, no. 64.

[91] Of the greatest importance in the development of manoeuvre technique, the *1756 Regulations* significantly reduced the rank- and file-intervals (always learned as part of the simple evolutions), which had been used unchanged in the army since the days of King William, making possible for the first time true close-order drill at speed, on all occasions.

[92] There is no known extant copy of the *1757 Regulations*, as issued under the Adjutant-General's signature on 25 June 1757. There are however a great many contemporary references to them: e.g. in William Windham's *Norfolk Militia* (1760), 15 n. 2 (on which work, see p. 207; repeatedly by James Wolfe, as in his letter of 7 Feb. 1758 to Lord George Sackville (quoted in R. Wright, op. cit. 418–19); and in the Inspection Returns (WO 27) for the later 1750s. The 1758–60 editions of the *1757 Regulations*, if approached *without* awareness of the existence of the *1757 Regulations*, are difficult to interpret; and this has caused much confusion in the historical literature, often leading to the erroneous assumption—reinforced by the appearance at this time of translations of the Prussian regulations and by the unfortunate remark picked up from the press by the *Gentleman's Magazine*, noted above—of their derivation from the Prussian regulations. The full contents (save for some of the manoeuvres) can be deduced from the later editions.

[93] The 1756 edition was reprinted under the same title in New York in 1757, for the corps there; and in the same year it was reprinted in that catch-all, the anonymous *Camp Discipline & Kane* (1757), 71–8. Early in 1758 the first of the subsequent editions of the *1757 Regulations* (containing manual, platoon, evolutions, firings, and notes) appeared as *Manual Exercise As Ordered By His Majesty, For The Year 1758* (1758); later in the year another edition (with marginal notes for the dragoons' training) appeared as *New Manual Exercise, As Performed by His Majesty's Dragoons, Foot-Guards, Foot, Artillery, Marines, And by the Militia . . . Second Edition* (1758), thus including explicitly the other arms which had already been practising the drill since 1756. Copies were printed in Dublin and Limerick in 1758 with the Lord-Lieutenant's orders of 18 Mar. 1758 appended, ordering that these regulations be observed by all the foot and dragoons on that establishment. The latest copy I have seen was *The New Manual Exercise As Performed by His Majesty's Dragoons, Foot-Guards, Foot, Light Infantry, Artillery . . . Third Edition . . .* (Dublin, 1760), in which the new light infantry companies were included.

[94] On 7 June 1757 Ligonier wrote to Cumberland from London, where he was soon 'to see the adjut^s Serg^ts & Corp^ls of the dragoons . . . go through the new Exercise in

followed, up to 1760, were the culmination of Cumberland's programme of drill reform.

The same new spirit of energy manifest in the work of the central authorities during these years infused the world of private military writers. Several important treatises appeared at this time, and the period is a notable one for the translation of foreign drillbooks.

Of the private works that now appeared, three especially— although devoted to quite different subjects—stand out because of the breadth of vision and the occasional brilliance they displayed. Foremost among these was the *Art of War* by the comte Turpin de Crissé, first published in Paris, 1754, and in London in translation, 1761.[95] Turpin's lengthy essay, which was a detailed study of the practical carrying on of operations by an army in the field, was without doubt the best work available on that subject during the eighteenth century. Though he described war as he found it and was not inventive, Turpin's style was spirited and intelligent, commanding respect; never formal or dogmatic, his descriptions of tactical dispositions and the conduct of operations were bound only by general rules admitting considerable flexibility. These qualities were the fruit of profound study; and the sophistication of his analysis of active operations, his firm appreciation of the importance of retaining the initiative, and his grasp of the importance of intelligence, security, and terrain not only in grand and petty tactics but on overall strategic planning, derived from that study. The exceedingly clear format, the realism, and the vigour of the *Art of War* made it an immensely profitable work for both field and general officers.[96]

---

which Gen[ll] Napier [the Adjutant-General] tells Me they are very Perfect'. Cumb. Pprs, Box 52, no. 116. R. Whitworth, op. cit. 218, makes the common error of assuming that some new Prussian drill is being referred to in this letter.

[95] Lancelot, Count Turpin de Crissé, *An Essay on the Art of War. Translated from the French . . . by Captain Joseph Otway*, 2 Vols (1761), was published in German translation at Potsdam in 1756, which speaks well for it. Turpin (who was a colonel of French hussars from 1747 until 1761, and a lieutenant-general by 1792) was a prolific author on military subjects, including translation and commentary on the works of several captains both ancient and modern.

[96] E.g. John Forbes, James Wolfe, and Henri Bouquet all studied and recommended the work even before its translation. Forbes conducted his Fort Duquesne operations

Broader in vision, if less expert in detail, was Thomas More Molyneux's *Conjunct Expeditions*, published in 1759 in the wake of the 1757 and 1758 raids on Rochefort, Saint-Malo, and Cherbourg.[97] Presenting his work in two parts, Molyneux first wrote the history of the main amphibious operations from antiquity to the present, and having done so he drew lessons and analysed the evident implications. The general failure of most such expeditions, he concluded, resulted from several factors, the chief of which was that there had never been any attempt to learn from past mistakes; consequently no body of tactical doctrine had been developed, no proper equipment, and no special training procedures, so that nothing but continued ill success could be expected to attend future amphibious expeditions. Having concluded this, Molyneux set out in the second part of his treatise to correct this situation by laying down overall operational procedures and plans, by describing special equipment which experience had shown to be needed, and by suggesting what training and tactics were appropriate for such a form of warfare. He argued that amphibious warfare, properly conducted, could achieve important results; and that Britain—with her huge navy, small army, and geographical position—should by her nature pursue this form of warfare. Molyneux's was by far the most thoughtful of those works that took this strategic line, and his analytical approach made his argument convincing; likewise his lengthy technical treatment of the special *matériel* necessary for such operations and his suggestions on the technical handling of assault landings (though often ill-found) added to the solid impression the book created. It was in fact to be of the greatest use to the army and marines, so often called upon in the Seven Years War and in the American

---

in 1758 according to the tactical system known as the 'protected advance', as laid down by Turpin—who had it from Montecucculi. In his 1763–4 campaigns in the Ohio country, Bouquet practised a version of this too. George Washington (who became acquainted with the work while serving under Forbes) obtained a copy of the 1761 English translation, and recommended its study to fellow American officers at the time of the War for Independence. Beckles Willson, op. cit. 295; O. L. Spaulding, 'The Military Studies of George Washington', *AHR* 29 (1924), 677–8; and K. L. Parker, op. cit. 254–69, and 292–342, *passim*.

[97] Thomas More Molyneux, *Conjunct Expeditions: Or Expeditions that have been carried on jointly By the Fleet and Army, with a Commentary on a Littoral War* (1759). Molyneux, as an officer of the regular army, had been on Mordaunt's Rochefort raid of 1757, which had been ill conceived and badly carried out.

War of 1775–83 to take part in coastal raids and landing operations.[98]

The third of these most impressive works was Lt.-Col. Campbell Dalrymple's *Military Essay*, a long and detailed treatise, the overall aim of which was to 'new-model' the army.[99] Like Saxe, Dalrymple knew his Greek and Roman history; and he felt that any full-scale remodelling would have to be based on a system of recruiting that, like those of antiquity, turned not to mercenaries and pressed men but rather drew in 'citizens' educated from youth to valour, discipline, and self-sacrifice.[100] Nevertheless, although impracticable in this respect, the work was otherwise invariably realistic; and the great bulk of the work, which consisted of a detailed discussion of weapons, of clothing and accoutrements, and of basic and advanced training and drill, was always admirable and generally applicable in the British Army. Dealing equally with the horse and foot, he was most concerned that recruits in their training should be brought along with consideration; and he described in much detail the steps according to which basic training should be laid on. His ideas on advanced drill, similarly, were well-found. The *Military Essay* was a mine of useful information for regimental officers, experienced or otherwise; it was always interesting and often brilliant, a challenge to officers, and without doubt one of the half-dozen best treatises written in English during the eighteenth century.[101]

---

[98] Two other works, Lt. John MacIntire's *A Military Treatise on the Discipline of the Marine Forces, When at Sea: Together with Short Instructions for Detachments Sent to attack on Shore* (1763), and Joseph Robson's *The British Mars. Containing Several Schemes and Inventions . . . shewing more plainly, The great Advantage Britain has over other Nations, by being Masters at Sea* (1763), appeared at this time: they dealt with other aspects of amphibious operations and with marine service. MacIntire's book was a sound, practical text on the training of Marines (and of regular foot shipped as marines) in the drill peculiar to action afloat. Robson's book, on the other hand, was filled with a fascinating collection of crackpot inventions designed for use in assault landings and the siege operations that might follow.

[99] Campbell Dalrymple, *A Military Essay. Containing Reflections on the Raising, Arming, Cloathing, and Discipline of the British Infantry and Cavalry* . . . (1761). Dalrymple was lieutenant-colonel of the 3rd Dragoons in 1761.

[100] Dalrymple's suggestions—on the establishments of the foot, e.g., pp. 25–8—were sometimes taken from Saxe's *Reveries*, which appeared in English at this time (see p. 205; and the book was clearly inspired by Saxe's example.

[101] Dalrymple was to be quoted with regularity by most British writers, henceforth; and as early as May 1762 he was acknowledging 'the gracious manner' in which no less

Several other works appearing at this time added significantly to the store of drillbooks available. The sudden prominence of the Prussians after Mollwitz was reflected, during the 1750s, in the publication of the first of many subsequent English translations of their regulations.[102] Unlike the several regulations issued to the British Army, these official Prussian works dealt not only with the five elements of the drill but also with the complete interior management and discipline of the regiments, and with all of the routine duties of the officers. The most striking characteristic of these regulations—one no doubt already half expected by British readers, aware of the machine-like discipline prevailing in the Hohenzollern service—was their sheer thoroughness; concise, pithy, clear, and well organized, these regulations read like statute books. Several other works dealing in depth with various aspects of the Prussian service also became available at this time.[103]

The French, too, were well represented in English translations at this time; and the best of their works, Saxe's *Reveries*, owed its appearance in English to the on-going labours of Sir William Fawcett. The *Reveries*, of course, is one of the classics of military literature; and it can hardly be done justice in a few lines of summary. Infused throughout with an extraordinary spirit of innovation and reform—'nothing is so disgraceful as that slavish adherence to custom, which prevails at present',

an expert than the Duke of Cumberland had been 'pleased to receive my Book'. Cumb. Pprs, Box 57, no. 216.

[102] The first translation to appear was the *Regulations for the Prussian Infantry* (1754), reprinted as *Regulations for the Prussian Infantry . . . to which is added The Prussian Tactick* (1759); while in the meantime the *Regulations for the Prussian Cavalry* had come out (1757). These three translations were the work of Sir William Fawcett who, as in his 1757 translation of Saxe's *Reveries*, undertook the work only to 'be of assistance' to his 'Brother Officers'. Henceforth during the eighteenth century up-to-date translations of Prussian regulations were always available, as all the advertisements of the booksellers illustrate.

[103] The best of these was the Anon., *New Regulations for the Prussian Infantry: Containing an exact Detail of the Present Field-Service . . . and recent Parts of the Foot-Exercise* (1757). With several excellent plates, and devoted entirely to the study of battalion drill and tactics in the field, this work was of the greatest utility to British officers in the advanced training of their corps. Internal evidence indicates that this was not Fawcett's work.

In 1762 Frederick II's instructions to his generals, written by the King in 1747, were translated into English and published as Anon., *Military Instructions by the King of Prussia* (1762); printed in limited numbers at Berlin in 1753 and captured by the Austrians in 1760, this book had already been printed by the Austrians and the French in 1761. From 1764 through 1785, the London staff kept yearly summaries of the annual Prussian manoeuvres. WO 30/45, MS book.

wrote Saxe[104]—it ranged widely from the raising, training, and petty tactics of his specially designed 'legions', to the major operations of the full army in the field; and at every stage bold new ideas, many of them brilliant and several of them practicable (as Saxe was to demonstrate with success in his campaigns and battles), marked his text, pointing the genius of their author. Free from the conventions of the age and deploring the clumsiness of the unitary army (and especially the static firefights of which so many battles largely consisted), he described a flexible new tactics based on retaining the initiative, on engaging in detail, and (above everything else) on the morale of his soldiers and the speed and handiness of their manoeuvring. Where his ideas were practicable in the armies of the *ancien régime*, the British included, three especially stand out: first, his advocacy of small-redoubts before and within the battle-line to break up the attacks of the enemy and to discourage him from launching major assaults upon your main position, while at the same time permitting you 'to introduce the method of engaging *en détail*, and of attacking in brigades', thus enabling you to fix your enemy's attention at points 'to which you can always send fresh troops';[105] secondly, his stress on the manoeuvrability of the infantry, to be attained by training the troops to march and manoeuvre in close order, to a cadenced step;[106] and thirdly his insistence that officers inspire their men, since morale is by far the most important element in war, where the fate of armies has often been determined by the sudden panic or the sudden bravery of a handful of men.

Capt. Samuel Bever's short, popular guide for young officers, *The Cadet*, was likewise illustrative of the considerable influence

---

[104] Anon. Trans. [Sir William Fawcett], *Reveries, or Memoirs upon the Art of War, by Field Marshal Count Saxe . . .* (1757), v. This translation was reprinted in London in 1759, and again in 1776.

[105] Ibid. 135–6, 149–56, and *passim*.

[106] Marching in step, to a musical cadence, was probably the most widely adopted of the reforms suggested by Saxe (ibid. 15–18); this device made possible speedy and flexible manoeuvring by ranks at close order, and was one of the most significant developments in the drill of the armies of the eighteenth century. On the cadenced step and the British Army, see here, pp. 277–9. In a famous passage, Saxe wrote that 'the manual exercise is, without doubt, a branch of military discipline necessary to render a soldier steady and adroit under arms; but it is by no means of sufficient importance in itself to engage all our attention . . . The principal part of all discipline depends upon the legs, not the arms: the personal abilities which are required in the performance of all manoeuvres, and likewise in engagements, are totally confined to them.' Ibid. 14.

which foreign military works were having at this time.[107] Essentially a collection of thoughts and maxims drawn from the
writings of such prominent captains and theoreticians as
Vauban, Turenne, Folard, Saxe, Santa Cruz, Le Blond, and
Puységur, the aim of *The Cadet* was to distil the best from
foreign-language works and, with a short running commentary,
to make available this material for young British officers who
might otherwise fail to become acquainted with it. Bever's
chapters—most of which were devoted to the duties of each of
the various ranks in the army—displayed a selection of material the choice of which was both judicious and economic.
Though hardly deep, this little collection was a useful introduction of the service to young officers and might also have
stimulated them to further reading.

The first two in what was to be a succession of works on
various aspects of the 'petite guerre' appeared at this time, and
again both were in translation from the French.[108] Both were
excellent, dealing in detail with the considerable variety of the
service likely to befall detached parties. Thus the speedy construction of small redoubts and breastworks; the preparation of
farmsteads, country-houses, churches, and other isolated buildings for defence;[109] the attack and defence of small villages,
street by street and house by house;[110] the blocking of river
fords, and of defiles; and a host of stratagems such as false
attacks, the clever use of obstacles like *abatis* and *chevaux de frise*,
the storming of entrenchments, and night marches, were dealt
with too. Both works were rooted in experience, eschewing

[107] Samuel Bever, *The Cadet. A Military Treatise* (1756), came out in a revised edition
under the same title, in 1762. In 1756 Bever became major of the 46th Foot.

[108] These were Capt. J.-L. Le Cointe's *The Science of Military Posts, for the Use of
Regimental Officers, who frequently command Detached Parties. In which is shewn the Manner of
Attacking and Defending Posts . . .* [and] *the Construction of Field-Forts* (1761); and John
Muller's translation, with additional notes, of the Chevalier L. A. de La Mamie de
Clairac's *The Field Engineer* (1760). A 2nd, revised edition of this latter work appeared
in 1773, again by John Muller. Clairac (whose book was first published in France in
1749, and again in 1757), was 'an Engineer of high Rank in the French Army', as
Muller described him, and had enjoyed 'a long Course of Experience'. Le Cointe
(whose work was published in France in 1759), was a captain in the French horse, and
had served in Piedmont and Flanders under the prince de Conti.

[109] E.g. Clairac on the defence of churches is full of good advice (pp. 41–5).

[110] Le Cointe's description of the detailed preparation of a village for defence is outstanding, as is his discussion of the tactics to be used in attacking such a place (pp.
137–54, 174–80).

theory and dealing in a very practical vein with their subject-matter; and both—Le Cointe's especially—were designed not for trained engineers or senior officers so much as they were aimed at those junior officers who were most likely to find themselves in command of detached forces.[111]

The reform of the English militia and the new vigour introduced into its affairs after the passage of the Militia Acts of 1757–8 was reflected in the appearance of drillbooks devoted to that service; but the best of these books were of use to the officers of the regular army in the basic training of their men too, since the militia drills (on paper) tended to differ very little from the practice of the regular army.[112] Without doubt the most useful and popular such work in the army was William Windham's *Norfolk Militia*, which dealt at length with all five elements of the drill.[113] Addressing itself especially to the procedures by which the men could best be trained, it contained over fifty plates illustrating the manual and manoeuvres; and these were the best plates yet to have appeared in any English drillbook. Another militia officer, Edward Fage, brought out his short but admirable *Regular Form of Discipline* which, like Windham's drillbook, was so clear and well organized in its discussion of basic training that regular officers could hardly but have benefited from it.[114]

There were too, as we have seen, revised versions of Kane,

---

[111] Clairac's was a practical guide but, more than Le Cointe's, it was sophisticated enough to be of use to engineer officers as well as officers from the line regiments. Indeed, Clairac 'considered, that though many have wrote upon the Construction of permanent Fortification, as well as upon the Attac and Defence of Places, yet little had been wrote in regard to the requisite Knowledge of an Engineer in the Field' ('Ed.'). Le Cointe, meanwhile, led off his text with some 35 pages of practical geometry—sufficient for regimental officers otherwise unlettered in engineering, and necessary for a proper basic understanding of the essentials of the 'science' of field-works and defences.

[112] See, e.g., the anonymous *New Military Instructions for the Militia* . . . (1760), virtually a word-for-word copy of the 1758 edition of the *1757 Regulations*.

[113] William Windham and George Townshend, *A Plan of Discipline, Composed for the Use of the Militia of the County of Norfolk* (1759), was rushed to the press late in that year, incomplete; the full edition (with title unchanged) came out at London in 1760. In 1768 the full 1760 edition was reprinted as *A Plan of Discipline for the Use of the Norfolk Militia* . . . (1768). Townshend wrote the dedication only.

In the introduction to his facsimile reprint of von Steuben's *Regulations for the Order and Discipline of the Troops of the United States* (Philadelphia, 1779 (rpt. 1966), R. Riling notes that as many as nine imprints of the *Norfolk Militia* were made in the American colonies between 1768 and 1774.

[114] Edward Fage, *A Regular Form of Discipline for the Militia, As it is Perform'd by the West-Kent Regiment* (1759).

Bland, and Blakeney being printed at this time; and though of limited practical use as regards drill and tactics, the first two of these were still of some value to raw officers as guides to the routine of the service.[115]

Finally, the last of the old profusion of privately prepared manual and platoon exercises came out at this time, the work of George Grant.[116] Grant's platoon was quite impracticable, despite the fact that its preparation had cost him 'a great deal of Pains and Study'; he slurred together too many of the individual motions of the exercise, finishing up with an exercise which still involved more motions than the one that was to be issued by authority in 1764. Grant's little book contained a number of interesting observations on training and tactics, nevertheless; and despite the fact that his text was hardly literate, still these observations may have been of some value to the few who troubled their heads with his written style.

1764–1778

With the conclusion of the Peace of Paris the central authorities in London began once again the preparation of new drill regulations designed to incorporate the considerable tactical experience and change of the past decade. Two new sets of regulations were envisaged from the start and, although they were issued concurrently, the purposes of the two projects were regarded as distinct. On the one hand a new arms exercise was to be prepared and given out, by the King's command, to be practised through the army generally. On the other hand the Horse Guards had a more immediate, particular concern: it planned to regularize the procedure carried out at the spring and autumn reviews of those regiments under its most immediate inspection and control—that is, the regiments doing duty in the kingdom of England. The first of these projects required the preparation and issue of new manual and platoon

[115] Among these, the anonymous *Camp Discipline & Kane* (1757) included much recent material on the encampments of the army, and on such varied topics as pay, honours, clothing, rank, etc., mostly drawn from orders given out by authority over the years *c.*1740–57.

[116] George Grant, *The New Highland Military Discipline, or a short Manual Exercise Explained . . .* (1757). As its title indicates, Grant thought that his manual would be of most use in the Highland regiments, being new-raised corps destined soon to be sent abroad. Grant's book is in facsimile reprint, with an introduction by J. R. Harper, as *The New Highland Military Discipline of 1757* (Ottawa, 1967).

exercises. The second was more complicated, since it entailed the drawing up, the testing, and finally the issuing as regulations not only of orders standardizing the dispositions, the ceremonial, and the drill to be practised by the cavalry and foot at the reviews, but also—and for the first time in the army's history—the issue of a lengthy series of manoeuvres described in detail.

In the event, both projects were to meet with the most notable success; and indeed the success of the second project— that concerning review procedure and manoeuvres—was to be well beyond what had originally been intended, or even envisaged. The new manual and platoon exercises, first introduced in the British Isles in 1764 and issued abroad early in 1766, were to survive as regulation practice throughout the army for the next thirty years; and the new review procedure and manoeuvres, though designed for use only among the regiments in England and first introduced there likewise in 1764, had by 1768 spread abroad unofficially and had come to be followed everywhere as standard practice. Two factors were chiefly responsible for this success: first, the new drill elements were framed and introduced with care and put to trial before being made regulation; and secondly the imperial distribution of the army, with its incident rotation of units to and from England, led to an increasingly widespread acquaintance with, and adoption of, these drill procedures, designed originally only to ease the problems faced by the reviewing officers attached to the London staff.

These various developments emerge clearly when the genesis of the *1764 Regulations* (as the new manual, platoon, review dispositions, firings, and manoeuvres, came eventually to be so called) is studied in detail.[117] Thus, after 'the Party of an Adjutant and 3 Non Commission Officers from Each Regt' assembled at Greenwich early in June 1764 had tested and ac-

[117] With these regulations the old separate section devoted to the simple evolutions was removed as a full element of the drill regimen. The abolition of the old practice— which had survived from the days of the pike and matchlock—of drawing up and exercising in a line on a depth of 6 open ranks, a disposition which led to much filing, countermarching, and doubling of ranks and files, meant that most of the old evolutions need no longer be practised; and the adoption during the 1750s of close rank- and file-intervals, and of marching and manoeuvring in step to a musical cadence, likewise rendered them superfluous. Those few evolutions that were retained were now buried away in the manual exercise and in the manoeuvres.

quired a uniform precision and timing at the new manual and platoon, these exercises were printed at the end of August and issued by the Adjutant-General to all the regiments of cavalry and foot then in the kingdom of England, to be observed henceforth as regulation practice.[118] Three weeks later, on 21 September, the Secretary at War forwarded copies of the same exercises to the Cs.-in-C. in Ireland and North Britain, with the King's directions that all of the regiments under their command be provided with and practise the same.[119] On 13 September, meanwhile, the Adjutant-General sent to all of the foot in England a list—abridged and 'without Explanations' or descriptive plans—of the new manoeuvres tentatively proposed; these were to be practised against the up-coming autumn reviews, scheduled for late October.[120] These 'new' drill manoeuvres were chosen for standardization because they were considered a comprehensive selection from the overall body of manoeuvres then generally practised. Even this limited selection, although comprehensive, was more than a regiment would normally have time to perform at a review; as the Adjutant-General informed the King on 10 October 1764, the reviewing officers 'having directions to Select any which they think most Proper, it will Appear, if the Regiments are Perfect in the whole.' Harvey pointed out that as usual, it was nobody's intention 'to Confine the Regiments to the [manoeuvres] (in their future Discipline) which are Delivered, But to be at Liberty to practice any Others, that may perfect them in all the movements, which Exigencys of Service, or Marchings, may make Necessary, at the same time to be able, to perform all which are Delivered, with the Greatest Exactness.'[121] The last elements were issued on 10 October: on that day an enlarged,

---

[118] WO 4/1044, p. 1, 'June 8th, 1764', and 'August 1764'. The parties at Greenwich were from regiments in England.

[119] WO 4/1044, p. 1, '17th Septem. 1764'; and WO 4/75.B., pp. 216, 220. The new platoon exercise was a slight improvement upon that in use since 1756, reducing the motions from 24 to 21 by streamlining the ramming procedure. It was without doubt the speediest, the easiest-learned, and the most efficient platoon to be issued during the eighteenth century; it survived as regulation practice, unchanged, until 1792, when it was replaced by an inferior exercise. Although a few of the motions in the 1764 platoon were taken directly from the Prussian exercise of the 1750s, it was (like the platoon in the *1756 Regulations* from which it mostly derived) an essentially English production.

[120] WO 4/1044, p. 1, '13 Septem. 1764'.

[121] WO 4/1044, pp. 2–3.

more detailed description of the new manoeuvres was sent out to the English foot, together with directions on the firings and on the new procedure that the foot was to follow when being reviewed; and on the same day all the cavalry in England was issued with the firings, and with directions on the new review procedure to be followed by the mounted arm.[122]

By mid-October 1764, therefore, the horse and foot in England had been provided with the review directions and all the elements composing the new drill, although some of this material was regarded still as tentative. The regiments in Scotland and in Ireland had the new manual and platoon. The Adjutant-General, Col. Edward Harvey, was now able to provide the King with a progress report in which he outlined the stages still to come. Once the reviewing officers had seen the regiments in England perform the new drill and had submitted their review reports, Harvey proposed 'to Receive any Alterations or Additions, which your Majesty may think Necessary'; he likewise proposed, once the reports were in, to settle upon a final set of orders regarding review procedure 'to Lay before your Majesty for your Royal Orders . . . to which all Regiments are to Conform, without Deviation'.[123] The reviewing officers saw the several units in England between 22 October and 12 November, and found them performing the new drill (as Parslow observed) 'surprizingly well for the time they have had to practice'.[124] These were good results, the regiments appearing quite forward after only ten weeks of training; and with the winter now come Harvey was able to settle the revisions that seemed warranted. He accomplished this task to the King's satisfaction, and well in advance of the 1765 reviews he was able to send to the regiments in England the revised drill and review orders.[125] It seems that no more faults were found during the course of the 1765 reviews, since only one slight alteration remained to be made (in the 'method of Drawing up a Batt^n', when on review); and that was given out in February 1766.[136]

---

[122] WO 4/1044, p. 2, 'October 1764', and '10th Octob. 1764'.

[123] WO 4/1044, pp. 2–3. Copies of all drill orders issued so far had, of course, been supplied to the reviewing officers (Majs.-Gen. George Augustus Eliott, John Parslow, and the Duke of Richmond) appointed that season to see all the regiments in England. WO 4/75.B., pp. 269–70, and 4/1044, pp. 1–2.

[124] WO 27/7, *passim*, for their reports.

[125] WO 4/1044, pp. 3–4.

[126] WO 3/24, p. 104.

Thus the several drill elements issued late in 1764 had by the end of 1765 passed through their trial period, and could now be extended by authority, or otherwise. The extension of the arms exercises through the army generally was overdue in any case, what with half of the battalions of marching foot now serving abroad.[127] In January 1766, therefore, the Adjutant-General sent copies of the manual and platoon to the general officers or governors commanding all the forces in Minorca, Gibraltar, the West Indies, and North America, with the King's orders that these 'be Practised without Deviation, by all the Regiments of Infantry in the Service'.[128] These orders were complied with immediately, Gen. Thomas Gage responding from North America, for example, that 'all the Regiments under my Command shall be forthwith acquainted with His Majesty's Order, and be furnished with Copy's of the Book of Exercise.'[129] Meanwhile, provision had long since been made to supply the new review directions and manoeuvres to regiments arriving home in England, in the normal rotation of the service;[130] and at the same time the process of osmosis whereby these directions were to be established and practised elsewhere was already under way. Thus by mid-1766 the rotation of corps between England and Scotland had led to the definite establishment of the full *1764 Regulations* in North Britain;[131] and by the end of 1766 rotation between the British Isles, the West Indies, and North America had led to the introduction of the full *1764 Regulations*

[127] For distribution, see Appendix B.

[128] WO 3/23, p. 3.

[129] C. E. Carter (ed.), op. cit. ii. 347; Gage to Harvey, New York, 30 Apr. 1766.

[130] The directive is in WO 4/1044, p. 39. Between the early autumn of 1764 and the end of 1765, three regiments of foot (the 21st, 22nd, and 35th) had come into England. Of these, the 21st had marched in from Scotland early in 1765, and had been issued the full regulations on 31 Mar. (WO 5/53, p. 159; and WO 4/1044, pp. 3–4); while the 22nd and 35th had both come home late in 1765 from America (where they had been since early 1757 and mid-1756, respectively), and both were issued the new regulations before the year was out (WO 5/53, p. 461; WO 4/1044, p. 2). The regular spring rotation of the horse in Britain brought the 3rd and 4th Dragoons south into England in 1765, and both were sent the new regulations early in the autumn (WO 5/53, pp. 196–200; WO 4/1044, p. 3).

[131] By mid-1766 the single cavalry regiment and two of the five corps of foot, in Scotland, had come in from England carrying the new drill with them; and a third corps of foot was practising it by choice. By early 1767 four of the five battalions in Scotland (the 6th, 7th, 23rd, and 25th) were following the new drill, and so too were both the corps of cavalry (the 10th and 11th Dragoons). In Apr. 1767 the Adjutant-General on the Edinburgh Castle staff bowed to the inevitable, and obtained from Harvey copies

on those stations.[132] Although the Minorca and Gibraltar garrisons remained fixed from early in 1764 until 1768, rotation then began and the full *1764 Regulations* were carried to both those places too.[133] Finally, all the cavalry and foot in Ireland were practising the full *1764 Regulations* by 1768.[134]

The *1764 Regulations* were to remain the standard drill of the army, as a whole, until 1778; and during that period they were often reprinted and were widely available. Indeed no eighteenth-century drill was so widely or so frequently reprinted as were particular elements or the whole of the *1764 Regulations*; and this general availability of the new drill, soon spread abroad by corps coming on to other commands and stations from England and serving among corps already on these sta-

---

of the full horse and foot regulations (WO 4/1044, p. 2). The last Scottish corps to receive the full drill was the 12th Foot, stationed there since 1763; when early in 1767 the 12th marched into England the Adjutant-General in London sent them 'a Copy of what The King Ordered to be delivered to the Several Regts in England Relative to the Exercise' (WO 3/1, p. 37); and early that June the 12th, together with an old English regiment, went through the whole at a review held in Hyde Park before the King, the C.-in-C., and several dignitaries. *London Evening-Post*, (6 June 1767).

[132] At the end of 1764 there were fifteen battalions in North America, none of which had received any part of the new drill. During 1765 and 1766, five of these went home and were replaced by three battalions from England (the 14th, 21st, and 31st) and one from Ireland (the 59th). Of these, the three English corps carried with them the full *1764 Regulations*. In 1767 six new regiments came out from Ireland. Of the fourteen battalions serving in North America by 1772, only two had been there since 1764; three had come out since from England and nine from Ireland. By the end of 1766 not only the new manual and platoon exercises had been printed in America, but so too had the new review directions and manoeuvres, the whole bound together and printed in New York, Boston, and elsewhere.

A similar pattern prevailed in the West Indies, where 5 of the 6 battalions serving there early in 1764 had by the close of 1765 gone home; they had been replaced by three battalions from Ireland and two from England. Of these replacement units, at least one—the 32nd Foot, from England—brought with it the full *1764 Regulations*.

[133] The old Gibraltar garrison was replaced by two corps from England (the 2nd and 12th) and five from Ireland (the 1/1st, 39th, 56th, 58th, and 69th). The old Minorca garrison was replaced by three battalions from England (the 2/1st, 13th, and 25th) and two from Ireland (the 51st and 61st).

[134] It is clear from the 1768 Irish Inspection Returns (WO 27/14) that the full *1764 Regulations* were by that date everywhere in use in Ireland. We have seen that the new manual and platoon exercises were made regulation practice in that kingdom in Sept. 1764; but it is not clear at what point the review directions and new manoeuvres were introduced there. The loss of the Irish army's records (in the burning of the Four Courts in Dublin in 1922) and the absence of Irish Inspection Returns for the years 1765 and 1766 reduce us to speculation. The surviving Irish Inspection Returns for 1767 are laconic (WO 27/11); but it seems likely that the full *1764 Regulations* were in use there in 1767.

tions but as yet practising an older drill, both witnessed and helped occasion its army-wide adoption. Both the British and the colonial militias, as well as the regular regiments, put pressure on the printers for copies; so too did the augmentation of the forces with the coming of the 1775–83 war. The history of the various imprints made over these years illustrates not only the spread of the regulations, but also the tempo of events immediately before the outbreak of fighting, and the requirements of the loyalist Provincial Corps raised in America from 1776 onwards.

The earliest printed version of the 1764 manual and platoon that I have seen was the *New Manual, and Platoon Exercise: with an Explanation. Published by Authority* (Dublin, 1764); this was printed by the 'Printer to the King's Most Excellent Majesty' on the orders of Dublin Castle after receipt of the Secretary at War's letter of 21 September 1764, mentioned earlier. The latest of the many official imprints of these arms exercises appeared as *The Manual Exercise with Explanations as ordered by His Majesty, 1778* (1778); and there were sizable imprints made in the British Isles in 1768, 1770, and 1775.

There were several imprints of the full *1764 Regulations* to appear during these years also. The earliest official copy of the *1764 Regulations* that I have seen was printed in London early in 1766.[135] The latest was a private venture, appearing as Anon., *The General Review Manoeuvres; or, the whole Evolutions of a Battalion of Foot . . . To which is annexed, The Manual Exercise* (1779); several excellent plates illustrating the manoeuvres were included in this version, prepared doubtless for the militia officers then under canvas with their corps in the big camps.

In North America, where so much of the army was to find itself during these years, the earliest known imprint of the full drill is *The Manual Exercise, as ordered by His Majesty in 1764. Together with Plans and Explanations of the Method Generally Practised at Reviews and Field-Days* (New York, 1766), which was certainly the work of Gage's command. A great number of 1764 manual and platoons, and also of the full *1764 Regulations*, were

---

[135] There is in the BL a MS book of hand-coloured plates showing the review dispositions, and each of the manoeuvres (BL Add. MS 28, 856); entitled 'A Plan of a Review, as Performed by the 4th (or Kings Own) Regiment, when Reviewed by His Majesty in Hyde Park, 17th July 1765', this is the earliest full version of the 1764 drill I have seen, and may be compared with advantage with any of the later, printed copies.

printed thereafter in the North American colonies. There were as many as twenty-six American imprints between 1766 and 1780,[136] printed as far afield as New York (in 1766, 1769, 1773, 1775, and 1880), Boston (in 1774 and 1780), Philadelphia (in 1775 and '76), Wilmington, Delaware (in 1775), Providence, Rhode Island (in 1774), Lancaster, Pennsylvania (in 1775), and Newburyport, Massachusetts (in 1774). Needless to say, this outburst of American imprints, *c*.1774–5, boded no good for the British Army; and in the circumstances prevailing by 1774 the sincerity of emulation can hardly have seemed flattering.[137]

Before 1778 only a few additions and alterations were made by authority, which may quickly be summarized. Thus, with the addition of a company of light infantry to each of the battalions in 1771–2 the Adjutant-General sent out a circular with instructions on the disposition of the new company when drawing up in battalion.[138] In May 1772 it was ordered that all the cavalry should henceforth form their squadrons only two ranks deep, thereby abandoning the old practice of drawing up on three ranks which had been followed since the later seventeenth century.[139] During the following three years other measures were taken to simplify parts of the cavalry drill. After tests were conducted at the Adjutant-General's wish in 1773, the cavalry's foot evolutions were abridged; and in the spring of 1774 the cavalry regiments were permitted to dispense at the reviews (as they had no doubt already done in regular training) with many of the old mounted evolutions first regularized in the *1728 Regulations*.[140] In the summer of 1775 Harvey sent all

---

[136] R. Riling (ed.), *Regulations for the Order and Discipline of the Troops of the United States* (Philadelphia, 1779, rpt. 1966), 23.

[137] Printed in the 1774 Boston version of the full *1764 Regulations* was a resolution of the Provincial Congress (held early in the autumn of 1774, in response to the Coercive Acts) that 'the Inhabitants of this Province [Massachusetts] . . . in Order to their perfecting themselves in the Military Art', were to follow this drill. By that date the Massachusetts 'patriots' were collecting arms and training openly; it is safe to assume, then, that the embattled farmer who a few months later fired the shot heard round the world, did so according to King's Regulations.

[138] WO 3/3, p. 48.

[139] WO 3/25, '12 May, 1772'.

[140] The testing was carried on in the 2nd Dragoon Guards and the 2nd Dragoons, both of which were in England in 1773 (WO 3/4, pp. 24, 26). On the mounted evolutions, see WO 3/25, p. 65.

these revisions across to the Irish C.-in-C., observing that 'Reforms are not bro't abt. in a Day'; and at that point they were enacted in the Irish cavalry too.[141]

During this period, meanwhile, the number of private publications coming out continued to increase, reflecting—as had been the case after 1748—the spur given to the military literary world by the great wars of the mid-century. The notable increase in the number of regiments (and hence in the numbers and rate of intake of youthful and inexperienced subalterns) composing the peacetime standing army after 1763, the variety of enemies encountered and theatres recently campaigned in, and the wide imperial dispersal adopted at the war's end, were all factors whose influence is very apparent in the post-1763 private works. And the outbreak of armed rebellion in the American colonies gave a new impetus to publication towards the close of this period.

The need for works addressing themselves to the interior management, training, and discipline of the regiments, and which could serve as texts in the expanded post-war army, was met by several publications of varying quality. For the foot, the best was Capt. Bennett Cuthbertson's *Interior Management*, which reflected a deep knowledge of regimental affairs.[142] Aware that there were no texts available (except for Bland's, now quite outdated) addressing themselves to the establishment and maintenance of good order and discipline in the company or the battalion, Cuthbertson drew up his work to supply that gap; full of admirably organized chapters on all aspects of regimental administration and routine, the book was aimed at the hundreds of subalterns who had nowhere else to find all this material collected together in one place. Included too was a section on the regular exercising and manoeuvring of the battalion which, though brief, was without doubt the best short essay on training to have appeared to date;[143] and Cuth-

---

[141] WO 3/5, pp. 36–7.

[142] Capt. Bennett Cuthbertson, *A System for the Compleat Interior Management and Œconomy of a Battalion of Infantry* (Dublin, 1768). From 1755 to 1768 Cuthbertson had served as adjutant in the 5th Foot, thus acquiring through experience most of his considerable knowledge of regimental management; and this he supplemented by studying 'the Practice of several excellent Battalions', foremost among which was the regime practised in the 20th Foot when under Wolfe's command (pp. viii–xi).

[143] Ibid. 199–219.

bertson added a few pages of suggestions on the training of a light company which, 'though not allowed on the Establishment' at present, he felt sure would be needed against the outbreak of another war.

Addressed to the same topic as Cuthbertson's *Interior Discipline*, but produced in an entirely different format, was the *Instructions for Young Officers*, a collection of daily orders on routine regimental administration and training issued from 1748 to 1756 by James Wolfe, as major and lieutenant-colonel of the 20th Foot.[144] Although the anonymous editor who published these orders made no attempt at organization beyond setting them down chronologically, nevertheless this approach conveyed an immediacy and a realism ideal for young officers fresh from the regulations, or from the more turgid pages of Bland and Simes. Since these orders fairly breathe the admirable spirit of Wolfe and the 20th, not only portraying the details but also capturing the flavour of an extremely well-administered corps, the young officer could hardly but profit from the book.

A considerably larger and more detailed work than either of the above was Capt. Robert Hinde's *Light Horse*, addressed exclusively to the light dragoon regiments.[145] This was a very wide-ranging treatise taking in not only the corps still existing, but also the light dragoon regiments recently disbanded and the light troops that had, during the recent war, been added to the regular dragoon regiments. All aspects of the light dragoon service—interior management, arms, training and drill, clothing, accoutrements, horses, and active service conditions—were dealt with at length; and both Hinde's choice of source material (he often quotes Campbell Dalrymple's *Military Essay*, for example, and various regulations) and his personal commentary (based on his services with the 21st Light Dragoons, 1760–3) were well taken, well organized, and clearly stated. Although concerned especially with the light dragoons, there was much in Hinde's treatise (notably his material on training) that was applicable through the cavalry generally. No cavalry officer could fail to profit from a study of Hinde

---

[144] Anon. Ed., *General Wolfe's Instructions to Young Officers: also his Orders for a Battalion . . .* (1768). Cited under Wolfe, hereafter.

[145] Capt. Robert Hinde, *The Discipline of the Light Horse* (1778).

and, if used in conjunction with Campbell Dalrymple and the current regulations, it left little to be learned about the mounted service.

Among the works addressed to the subalterns with the regiments, the notable quality of Wolfe's orders and of the treatises of Cuthbertson and Hinde stands in sharp contrast to that of the uninspired, but nevertheless bulky effusions of Thomas Simes. Simes, whose works spanned the years 1767–80, was without doubt the most long-winded drudge—and also the most bare-faced plagiarist—who ever served the British Army.[146] In spite of the fact that his books stretch slightly beyond the period at present under consideration, it will be convenient to summarize all of his work here.

Simes's publications represented the most voluminous collection of basic material on regimental administration and daily routine to be prepared by anyone—private or public— during the century. With Bland's old treatise obsolete, and with no work of comparable detail and stature available to fill the gap, it was to Simes perforce that young officers now turned for basic, detailed guidance. But Simes, though prolific, enjoyed an undeserved popularity. Where Bland had been systematic, Simes's books were ill organized; where Bland had been experienced and substantial, Simes was third-rate; and where Bland had been original and had infused his text with judgement, Simes was at best merely derivative and at worst an outright plagiarist.[147]

Of his five books the first three—*The Medley* (1767), *The Guide* (1772), and *The Course* (1777)—were massive but ill-organized compendia of material dealing with all aspects of

---

[146] Simes produced five military works. The earliest was *The Military Medley: Containing the most necessary Rules and Directions for attaining a Competent Knowledge of the Art . . .* (Dublin, 1767). A 2nd, revised edition of *The Medley* appeared at London in 1768. His second work was *The Military Guide for Young Officers . . .* (1772); a 2nd edition of *The Guide* appeared at London in 1776, and a 3rd in 1781. Next came *A Military Course for the Government and Conduct of a Battalion . . .* (1777). *The Course* was followed in 1780 by two works, namely *The Regulator: or Instructions to Form the Officer, and Complete the Soldier . . .* (1780), and his *magnum opus*, entitled *A Treatise on the Military Science, which comprehends the Grand Operations of War . . .* (1780).

[147] Plagiarism was infrequent among English military writers, and Simes's propensities in that direction did not pass unnoticed. Thus John Williamson, in the 2nd (1785) edition of his excellent *Elements of Military Arrangement* (1782), i, p. xiv, was moved to point out publicly that Simes 'has done me the honour . . . to copy almost the whole of my manoeuvres, without informing his reader whence he has taken them.'

regimental administration and routine, together with reprints of all current regulations and reproductions of most of the regular printed administrative forms (such as muster rolls and the like) used throughout the army. All this material was quite useful to young officers; and this (together with the outbreak of war in 1775) accounts for Simes's success. But even his unsystematic compilation of material was marred by the random and oft-repeated addition of chapters dealing with various aspects of active campaigning, most of them cribbed or copied directly from the works of such eminent authorities as Frederick II and Saxe. Nor did these first three publications of Simes differ much, one from another, in their contents; each was essentially a rehash of the volume preceding it, though distinguished by a steadily improving format.

Although his works were heavy-handed affairs, it must be admitted that they served their purpose of providing young officers with a fairly complete catalogue of their duties. Even Harvey, though unimpressed, acknowledged the trouble Simes had put himself to in 'Collecting Several Regulations & Forms of Returns etc & in publishing them together'; and he knew this to be 'of Some Convenience to Young Officers'.[148] But Simes thought that he had accomplished more than the mere 'collecting' which the Adjutant-General acknowledged, the sales success of his publications having turned his head. This led him on to his last two works—one of which was useful and the other a crowning revelation of his vacuity.[149] In *The Regulator* (1780) Simes attempted to outline the duties of all ranks in a regiment and—although still unoriginal in content and fleshed out with the usual mass of administrative forms—he succeeded quite well at this; the format adopted in *The Regulator* was much more logical than that of his previous works, and in consequence the book portrayed rather clearly the internal management, duties, and discipline of the regiment.[150]

[148] WO 3/5, p. 25.

[149] Simes had already made this apparent at the Horse Guards, if not as yet to the general public, when in June 1779 he wrote to Lord Amherst offering to raise and lead '50,000 Moors' for the defence of Gibraltar (WO 34/115, fos. 28–30). See also WO 3/5, p. 25; and WO 34/124, fos. 186–7.

[150] In *The Guide* (1777), 6, Simes had bemoaned the lack of professional qualification in candidates for commissions: as he wrote, 'I hope the time will come soon, when a particular description, by authority, of the duties required from each Commission in the Service, with a general view of every thing an Officer should be acquainted with,

The second of these last works was the *Military Science*, his *magnum opus*; and unfortunately it was his worst effort. Abandoning the drudgery of regimental affairs, he set out to essay the more sweeping, 'sublime' problems posed by the conduct of the strategy and grand tactics of an army in the field. To this end, Simes produced what was little more than an unacknowledged revision of Turpin de Crissé's *Art of War*; and he added to this a lengthy section on the attack and defence of fortified villages lifted (likewise unacknowledged) from the 1761 English translation of Le Cointe's *Science of Military Posts*.

Although his work was uninspired, unoriginal, and repetitive, Simes, because of the great energy he devoted to his task and the sheer volume of his publication, contributed considerably during the later 1760s and the 1770s to the basic schooling of young officers.

The value of a sound education for officers was a subject to which most previous authors had addressed themselves in passing; but now it was taken up in earnest by Lewis Lochée in his *Essay on Military Education*.[151] Convinced that 'in forming the British army, it has been too much the prevailing maxim, that practice is sufficient for the instruction of a soldier', he based his essay on a classic application of the socio-political theories of Montesquieu. Arguing the value of encouraging the cult of honour among the youth of the aristocracy and gentry, Lochée felt that the too-common idea that 'a suit of regimentals will hide all little defects' would give way to a desire for sound military knowledge. It was his belief, further, that all young officers should get a proper education in military matters before joining their regiments, since an honourable and educated officer corps not only would be expert in the field, but would raise the public estimation of the officer's role.[152]

Similar views on the utility of military education were expressed by two other writers, both of whom were themselves officers. Both advocated a more old-fashioned approach to

---

will accompany all Commissions'. *The Regulator* was no doubt devised as this 'particular description', since his insinuation that *The Guide* be used for this purpose had not been taken up. Simes's suggestion was sound.

[151] Lewis Lochée, *An Essay on Military Education* . . . (1773). Lochée was master of a 'Military Academy' in Little Chelsea, which had a fair following in the 1770s; and he was the author of several mathematical works.

[152] Ibid. 18–21.

education than that espoused by Lochée. Lt. John Clarke, in his annotated translation of the *Military Institutions* of Vegetius,[153] stressed the relevance of ancient warfare to modern practice, thinking it to be 'essentially requisite' for officers to be well grounded in its study. All the modern great captains had acknowledged their debt to antiquity; and indeed current drill—'so nearly copied from Antiquity'—and much of modern tactics could be broadened from such study. 'Xenophon, Polybius, Caesar, and Vegetius, will always afford sufficient Employment for a military Man.'[154] Maj. Robert Donkin, meanwhile, argued the same need in a rambling work published in New York during the War for Independence.[155] More especially, Donkin's *Remarks* were aimed at the new modelling of the British Army which, like all other contemporary armies, he felt to be defective in basic organization, recruitment, training, and morale. Basing his views on his studies of the Roman armies of the Republic—the true strength of which lay in discipline, obedience, a love of glory, the confidence that officers and men had in one another, and the spirit of competition between men and between units—he wished to remodel the British Army so that these most excellent military virtues might once again be encouraged. Fostering a sense of honour among the officers and adopting short-term enlistments would help to achieve these ends; and in an army so constituted re-enlistments would be common, while discharged men would flood the countryside spreading tales of the glory and rewards of service.[156]

The recent experience of light infantry, of ranging corps, and of the light legions both in the Americas and Germany was preserved and disseminated in a number of publications after

---

[153] Lt. John Clarke, *Military Institutions of Vegetius . . . With a Preface and Notes* (1768).

[154] Ibid. vii–xi, *passim*. On other translations from antiquity, see above, p. 168.

[155] Maj. Robert Donkin, *Military Collections and Remarks* (New York, 1777). Donkin's text shows him to have been exceedingly well read, but is itself rather slight.

[156] Donkin argued that Britain, as a naval power, had no business in Continental campaigning. He would therefore disband all the heavy cavalry, and retain only eight regiments of light dragoons (four each in Britain and Ireland) for duty in aid of the civil power. He would organize the foot in 100 battalions, each on a peacetime strength of 500 rank and file—an establishment which could be augmented in time of war. He envisaged an imperial army: he would station sixteen of these battalions in Britain, twenty-four in Ireland, ten in the Mediterranean garrisons, and fifty in the Americas. Ibid. 204–10.

the 1763 peace. Donkin's work, noted above, gave to the tactics of the *petite guerre* a lengthy and very sound section clearly inspired by the *Journals* of Robert Rogers and, of course, was an appropriate subject at the time and place where Donkin published.[157]

Maj. Robert Rogers's *Journals* had been published in 1765.[158] Although a straight narrative of the reconnaissance patrols and raids carried out by his corps of Rangers during the North American campaigns of 1755–61, the account was extremely vivid, and conveyed clearly the nature of the continual and often savage *petite guerre* carried out along the frontiers of New France. An invaluable section dealt with rules for training regular soldiers to 'the ranging-discipline';[159] and this, together with the narrative, provided officers with a very clear impression of ranging tactics and of the intelligence value of the ranging service. In short, Rogers's *Journals* conveyed a striking realism and a most consummate professionalism, and any officer reading them would profit greatly should he be assigned to *petite guerre* duties.

A similar, but shorter, narrative of actual operations, this time carried out by regulars taught to fight as true light infantry, was William Smith's *Ohio Expedition*. Describing the brilliant campaign conducted by Col. Henri Bouquet against the Indians of the Ohio country in 1763–4, it had attached to the narrative an excellent appendix (the work of Bouquet himself) describing in detail the equipment, training, and tactics to be used by light infantry engaged with irregulars in an enclosed country.[160] Taken together, the narrative and the appendix provided a fine description of the tactics of a highly trained light corps, invaluable, like Rogers's *Journals*, to the officers of the light companies in each of the battalions of foot.

Yet another excellent work dealing with aspects of the *petite guerre*—this time a full treatise, the best on the subject to appear

[157] Ibid. 222–64.

[158] Robert Rogers, *Journals of Major Robert Rogers: Containing An Account of the several Excursions . . . upon the Continent of North America . . .* (1765).

[159] Ibid. 56–70.

[160] William Smith, *An Historical Account of the Expedition Against the Ohio Indians in MDCCLXIV . . .* (1766), was a reprint of a work which appeared first at Philadelphia in 1765. The London edition had several fine plates illustrating tactical dispositions—as had the French translation published at Amsterdam in 1769. Bouquet's text fills pp. 37–59 of the London edition.

in the eighteenth century—was Roger Stevenson's *Instructions for Officers Detached*.[161] Taking the view that small detachments of regulars and 'partisan corps' (i.e. light legions of the type seen in most European armies during the 1740–8 war and more commonly during the 1756–63 war) could by themselves conduct small operations of the greatest utility to their larger parent armies, Stevenson felt that all officers should be familiar with the tactics of the *petite guerre*. The bulk of his text was devoted to forming a partisan corps and to the duties it would have to perform—reconnaissance, attacking and defending posts, fortifying villages and buildings, raids, ambuscades, and skirmishing.[162] His chapters on the fortification and security of posts,[163] and on their attack and defence,[164] were outstanding; and the whole was clearly stated, making the tactics of the *petite guerre* easily accessible to officers.

Lt. John Pleydell's *Field Fortification*[165] continued and expanded upon the subject taken up earlier in the Clairac and Le Cointe translations—to which, indeed, it owed much.[166] The best work on this subject to date, it nicely complemented Stevenson's work on the *petite guerre* and was, as Pleydell described it, designed for officers of infantry all of whom might upon campaign be obliged to construct redoubts or to defend buildings, villages, bridgeheads, and other posts, all 'without the assistance of an engineer'. The approach was practical, since he realized that the elaborate mathematics and geometry of military engineers were subjects 'too dry for every one to relish'; and indeed there was no need of 'handling the scale and

---

[161] Roger Stevenson, *Military Instructions for Officers Detached in the Field: Containing a Scheme for forming A Corps of a Partisan . . .* (1770). A 2nd, revised edition came out in London in 1779, while the original was reprinted—for obvious reasons—at Philadelphia in 1775. Stevenson was a regimental officer of some experience.

[162] Stevenson had much of his material on minor fortification from Lt. John Pleydell's *Field Fortification*, on which see below. He recommended it to his readers.

[163] Ibid. 28–53.

[164] Ibid. 89–144.

[165] Lt. J. C. Pleydell, *An Essay on Field Fortification; Intended Principally for the Use of Officers of Infantry . . .* (1768). Pleydell, a subaltern in the 12th Foot, claimed that his text was a translation 'from the original Manuscript of an Officer of Experience in the Prussian Service'; but in fact it was almost certainly his own work, the reference to its Prussian origins merely window-dressing.

[166] Parts of Pleydell's work were based closely on Clairac's, although Pleydell expanded greatly upon what Clairac had written. Cf., e.g., the directions for the defence of a churchyard in Pleydell, 94–118, and in Clairac, op. cit. 41–5.

compass . . . [nor] of problems, nor tiresome calculations, in order to learn the art of putting all kinds of posts into a proper state of defence.'[167] Practice, common sense, and study were the essential prerequisites; and Pleydell dealt with the subject in such great detail, and with such ingenuity and inventiveness, that a thorough study of his treatise would prepare any intelligent officer to carry on the defence of posts and field fortifications competently indeed.

Among the works dealing with regular linear tactics published at this time, the foremost was Maj.-Gen. Henry Lloyd's *War in Germany*; one of the most outstanding discussions of warfare to appear during the century, it was unquestionably one of the best pieces of analytical military history to be written in the English language.[168] Dealing in great detail with the campaigns and battles of 1756–9, analysing and criticizing their conduct, Lloyd drew from these studies valuable principles of war.[169] He was at pains to stress the signal importance of study: beyond the understanding of one's duties he felt that knowledge of the history and theory of war, of mathematics, geography, and of the history, political and social constitution, and national character of one's adversaries, was essential for the proper conduct of operations. Any intelligent field or general officer would have profited considerably not only from Lloyd's principles and conclusions, but likewise from his minutely detailed and realistic accounts of battle tactics.

Compared with Lloyd's *War in Germany*, the other works on drill that appeared at this time were second-rate. The anonymous English translation of Leroy de Bosroger's *Elementary Principles of Tactics* had a certain limited following in the British Army, a few corps (as the Inspection Returns illustrate) practising manoeuvres of his invention.[170] Bosroger's ideas—since he was a firm partisan of the column of attack, believing not so

---

[167] Pleydell, op. cit. viii, *passim*.

[168] Maj.-Gen. Henry Lloyd, *History of the late War in Germany; between the King of Prussia, and the Empress of Germany and Her Allies . . .*, i, was first published at London in 1766. A new edition, with both i and ii, appeared in London in 1781. In 1790 a new imprint of i and ii appeared in London.

[169] Notable are his conclusions on Leuthen (i. 138–9) and his concept of a strategic 'line of operations' (ii. 87–95), later influencing Jomini.

[170] Anon. Trans., *The Elementary Principles of Tactics; with New Observations on the Military Art . . . translated by an Officer of the British Army* (1771). The original was first published in Paris in 1768.

much in its physical weight to deliver shock but rather in its moral superiority over the line—were not at any rate in the British tactical tradition; and this was fortunate, since his manoeuvres were over-geometric, and impracticable in action.[171] More immediately useful was the 'German Officer's' *Manoeuvres Upon Fixed Principles*, published in 1766.[172] This small drillbook laid out a series of manoeuvres for the battalion, most of which were described in the *1764 Regulations*, but which were here performed in a fashion more sophisticated than that laid down in the regulations. Although only a well-trained British battalion could have performed them, they were an alternate and a superior system by which the army's new manoeuvres could be carried out.[173] Less useful than the 'German Officer's' work but of more value than Bosroger was Maj. William Young's *Practical Observations*, a lengthy (if light) work describing not only linear drill and tactics in the field, but also field fortification and aspects of the *petite guerre*.[174] Although Young was experienced, having recently served in Germany as major of brigade to 'the Corps of Grenadiers and Highlanders', there was nothing in his work that could not be had more profitably elsewhere.

A final publication appearing at this time was the *Rudiments of War*, a compilation of orders mostly given out in the army since 1702 by the commanders of forces campaigning in Flanders, Germany, and Scotland.[175] Dealing most especially with administrative matters, it touched upon drill only in passing. The *Rudiments of War* was a well-written and extremely useful guide for officers who had not as yet gone on active operations, and its appearance in 1777 was therefore timely.[176]

---

[171] Bosroger, included, e.g. directions on forming 'the wedge', of which there were 'open' and 'full-centre' varieties. These were triangular arrowhead-shaped formations, the leading point of which was to be driven through the enemy's lines! Ibid. 184–5.

[172] German Officer, *Manoeuvres for a Battalion of Infantry, Upon Fixed Principles . . .* (1766). Attached was a series of seventeen excellent plates illustrating the manoeuvres.

[173] Where the *1764 Regulations* relied on filing for most movements, those of the 'German Officer' were better tactically because they preserved a front by marching the lines obliquely; and they were more speedily performed than was possible by filing.

[174] Maj. William Young, *Manoeuvres, or Practical Observations on the Art of War . . .* 2 Vols (1771).

[175] Anon., *The Rudiments of War: Comprising the Principles of Military Duty, in a Series of Orders issued by Commanders in the English Army . . .* (1777).

[176] The bulk of the *Rudiments of War* was taken, often verbatim, from the MS treatise 'British Military Orders', written *c.* 1750 by Lt.-Col. John LaFaussille of the 8th Foot.

1778–1788

By the later 1770s the manual and platoon exercises, the firings, the review procedures, and the manoeuvres, as laid down in the *1764 Regulations*, were still being followed everywhere in the army; additionally, a large number of useful manoeuvres retained from previous practice, or taken from the private drillbooks whether English or foreign, were everywhere in use. The core manoeuvres, however—those of the *1764 Regulations*, which all regiments were to know and practise so that regularity would be assured in the brigades and the line—were by this time in need of wholesale revision, since (as the several private works being published at this time illustrate) the theory and practice of drill and tactics were advancing at a rapid pace.

To attempt to introduce any significant revision in the army's drill regulations at a time when more than half the regiments of foot were away on active operations, in a theatre as distant and as vast as the West Indies and North America, would have been a virtually impossible undertaking; but with the active intervention of the French in 1778 and with the possibility of imminent invasion by an army now known to be very capable and well trained, some revision of the drill practised by that part of the British Army now in the most critical situation—that is, the regiments in England—had immediately to be implemented. In the short term this policy must inevitably result in the practice simultaneously within the army of two different sets of drill regulations; but since the *1764 Regulations* were to be only partially revised (thus easing the problem of standardizing drill everywhere, once conditions became more settled), and since the forces in Britain must at all costs be prepared to meet the thoroughly up-to-date regiments of France, revision was immediately taken in hand.

LaFaussille had not published his work, but occasional references to it in the 1750s indicate that it circulated in manuscript (indeed, in 1752 he sent a copy to the Adjutant-General) (Cumb. Pprs, Pt 4, II, fos. 1–62). It consisted chiefly of orders given out in the army in the Low Countries and Scotland during the campaigns of 1742–8. The anonymous author of the *Rudiments of War*, although he did not acknowledge LaFaussille (d. 1763) by name admitted that he had much of his material from the MS book of an officer who had served as a major of brigade during the Austrian Succession War; he himself added a number of orders of more recent vintage, and rearranged LaFaussille's text and format.

The concentration of troops in the camps formed across southern England during the spring of 1778 presented Amherst and his staff with an ideal opportunity for the speedy and effectual introduction of the revised drill.[177] Early in June 1778 the several general officers commanding the camps were sent by Amherst's staff manuscript copies of a list of nine lengthy manoeuvres, to be given out to the regiments under their command.[178] These new manoeuvres (together with the manual, platoon, and firings laid down in 1764) were practised by all of the foot encamped that summer in England. During the winter following, the new regulations were revised and augmented in light of the summer's experience; and in the spring of 1779 the final revised version of these *1778 Regulations* was issued to all of the foot in England.[179]

The *1778 Regulations* consisted of a detailed description of the disposition of all ranks when drawn up for review, together with a summary of the ceremonial and drill to be performed at reviews. Of the drill elements proper, the manual and platoon laid down in the *1764 Regulations* were retained, and so too were the system of telling off and the firings of 1764.[180] The series of manoeuvres given out in the 1778 camps was repeated in these regulations, but to these were added—for the first time in any British drill regulations, so far as the light companies were concerned—detailed instructions on the movements to be carried out by both flank companies while the body of the battalion was going through the main manoeuvres.[181] Two further refinements never before laid down in regulations were the fixing of the speed of march at the slow and quick step, and orders on the use of the 'musick' and drums when the battalion was manoeuvring.

Despite the fact that the manual, platoon, and firings already

[177] The camps form the subject of Ch. VI of this book.

[178] There are copies in WO 3/26, pp. 12–15, and in WO 34/242, fos. 7–9. Since each of several of these manoeuvres consisted of an involved series of movements, their actual number (as had been the case with the manoeuvres in the *1764 Regulations*) might be thought of as twelve or fourteen.

[179] Copies will be found in WO 3/26, pp. 29–32, 169; and WO 34/258, MP.H/10.

[180] Firing by 'wings' (i.e. half the battalion's frontage), which had not been mentioned in the *1764 Regulations*, was included now. This was no innovation, but rather a belated recognition of practice long since customary.

[181] The flank company manoeuvres were reprinted verbatim in John Williamson, *Elements of Military Arrangement*, i (1785), 150–3.

in use were retained, nevertheless the revised review procedure, the excellent new series of core manoeuvres, and the careful concentration on items of detail all combined to make the *1778 Regulations* a considerable improvement upon any previous practice. Unfortunately however, the peculiar circumstances prevailing at the time these regulations were introduced—and the deplorable condition to which so much of the army had been reduced by 1783—were to have the most deleterious effect upon the success of the new drill. Amherst's writ as 'General-on-Staff', 1778–82, did not run beyond Britain on matters of drill; and his successor Conway (1782–3) took no further drill measures in hand. The *1778 Regulations* were therefore issued only to units in Britain during the American War; and by the end of the war a total of twenty-one battalions had been issued with these, twenty learning the 1778 drill while in the camps of southern England.[182] With the coming of the 1783 peace and the incident reductions and troop-movements, seventeen battalions trained in the new drill survived and were to be found in Britain, Ireland, Gibraltar, the West Indies, and India. But whereas the practice of the *1778 Regulations* was taken up for the first time after 1783 by several corps returning to the British Isles, several of the surviving seventeen battalions already taught the drill abandoned it when they found themselves out of Britain, under new commanders. Thus, after 1783, six of the battalions (the 2/1st, 2nd, 18th, 25th, 50th, and 59th) trained in the *1778 Regulations* in the English camps joined the new Gibraltar garrison; and there, under Gen. Eliott, the *1764 Regulations* were once again made the order of the day. As we have seen, more than half of the battalions in Britain and Ireland during the years 1783–6 had come home in so shattered a condition as to be scarcely capable of performing the 1764 drill, let alone learning anything new. By 1785 only a handful of corps—less than a dozen—were still following the *1778 Regulations* in the British Isles; and by 1786 half of these had given it up. By 1788 only three regiments were attempting it.

---

[182] On corps encamped, see WO 5/60, p. 430–5/64, p. 249, *passim.* The twenty camped battalions were the 1/1st, 2/1st, 2nd, 6th, 10th, 13th, 14th, 18th, 25th, 45th, 50th, 52nd, 59th, 65th, 69th, 72nd, 2/73rd, 75th, 79th, and 87th. The 26th learned the new drill in Britain, but was not encamped. Half of these battalions (the 6th, 10th, 14th, 18th, 26th, 45th, 50th, 52nd, 59th, and 65th) had been wholly drafted in America and had rebuilt themselves in the English camps, following the *1778 Regulations.*

At least thirteen corps returning home after the peace, and in better shape than most, adopted the 1778 drill once settled into Irish or British quarters: thus in Ireland the 4th, 9th, 21st, 24th, 27th, 47th, 48th, and 49th, all home from West Indian or American service, attempted the 1778 drill at their reviews, while in Britain the 7th, 22nd, 35th, and 64th from the Americas, and the 12th home from the wartime Gibraltar garrison, did the same. But their attachment to the new drill was not lasting. Of the corps reviewed in 1788 only the 7th and 35th in Britain and the 69th in Ireland showed the 1778 drill— and then in a modified form.

Thus the uniformity of drill which had been maintained with such unremitting effort for nearly a century past had, by the early 1780s, come undone. From 1783–4 onwards the great majority of regiments—in Britain, Ireland, Gibraltar, India, the West Indies, and the Canadas—were practising a drill regimen the elements of which were disparate.[183] Although the manual, platoon, and firings of 1764 were still being followed by the cavalry and foot, great variety prevailed in review procedure, in the all-important manoeuvres, and in a host of details—length of pace, manner of drawing up, rank- and file-intervals, speed of movement—which collectively ensured that the training and finished drill of the individual corps should vary considerably one from another. In the foot a hotch-potch of manoeuvres characterized the review performances after 1783: many corps practised a combination of manoeuvres, some drawn from the *1764 Regulations*, some from the *1778 Regulations*, and some from the ever-increasing store of customary manoeuvres drawn from a variety of sources; other regiments were practising systems entirely of their own invention; and a few regiments adopted foreign manoeuvres wholesale, throwing regularity off entirely. The situation was most confusing in the infantry, where by the mid-1780s irregularity was the rule; and a few examples, typifying the situation, might be given here. Thus in the summer of 1786 the 63rd Foot, when seen at Glasgow, was found to be following the *1764 Regulations* but including a large number of customary manoeuvres; the 49th Foot meanwhile, seen at Waterford, was following the *1778 Regulations* and adding a fair selection of customary

[183] Cf. the regulations, and the Inspection Returns in WO 27 for these years.

manoeuvres; the 35th Foot, seen at Leeds, drilled 'according to the System they had adopted during their Residence in the West Indies'; and the 7th Foot, at Musselburgh, performed manoeuvres some drawn from customary practice, some from their own invention, and none from any regulations.[184] This sort of variety remained commonplace until the end of the decade. In 1788–9, for example, the 38th Foot at Plymouth did its manoeuvres 'from the Prussian Tactiques' (i.e. from von Saldern's drillbook, on which see below), while the 17th Foot at Chatham followed its own peculiar system and the 34th at Shrewsbury drew its whole repertoire from the customary manoeuvres and nothing from the regulations.[185] By the later 1780s individual corps were in most cases well-enough trained; but few were trained alike beyond the manual and platoon.

In the cavalry the situation was better. Where the manual, platoon, dismounted firings, and dismounted manoeuvres had always been drawn from the currently prevailing regulations, the cavalry had continued to practise such of the mounted evolutions from the old *1728 Regulations* as seemed appropriate, and mounted manoeuvres remained little altered from old practice long since customary. The vogue for 'light' cavalry which set in during the 1760s, however, and continued apace during the 1775–83 war, was a development unsettling to the old system of mounted manoeuvres; and in consequence the cavalry, no longer certain how to proceed, began clamouring for regulation drills.[186] By the mid-1780s official response to these pleas had once again encouraged regularity.[187]

The irregularity which characterized the drill of the army— particularly of the foot—during the years 1783–90 was due to

[184] WO 27/56 and 27/58, Pt. 1.

[185] WO 27/61 and 64.

[186] Complaints on this score began in 1775 (WO 27/35, 2nd Horse and 5th Dragoons), and were repeated in 1778 (WO 27/41, 8th Light Dragoons).

[187] Comparison of the heavy-cavalry manoeuvres shown at all the reviews held from the early 1750s to the early 1790s points up the absence of innovation and the fundamental importance of the practice of customary manoeuvres in that arm. Cf. the manoeuvres of the 3rd Dragoon Guards in 1764, e.g., with those shown by the 10th Dragoons in 1773, by the 11th Dragoons in 1779, and by the 2nd Dragoon Guards in 1785 (respectively, WO 27/7, 27, 42, and 54); these are all typical of current practice. The light cavalry very early on in its career established its own repertoire and stuck to it thereafter. Typical performances were put on in 1769 by the 15th, 16th, and 17th Light Dragoons; in 1780 by the 13th Light Dragoons; and in 1787 by the 15th Light Dragoons (respectively, WO 27/15; 27/17 and 44; 27/59).

four main factors operating coincidentally. The widespread ruin among the battalions coming home after the peace left one-third of the foot disabled until 1785–6;[188] and among these units rebuilding took precedence over regularity. Secondly, there was a general uncertainty—unrelieved by authority—about what in fact constituted the proper regulation manoeuvres. The manual, platoon, and firings as laid down in 1764 were followed, quite properly; but among the many manoeuvres that the regulations of 1764 and 1778 described, and the great many more that customary practice increasingly allowed, there could be no such certainty as to how to proceed. A third factor was the appearance during this period of several private drillbooks drawn heavily from recent French and Prussian theory and practice; these offered tempting alternatives to the current British confusion, and were adopted in several corps. Harmful too, finally, was the absence during these years of a commander-in-chief in London: between Conway's departure in 1783 and the reappointment of Amherst in 1793 the army was left in the hands of civil authority, which saw to its administration but left professional matters to the regiments. The Horse Guards staff alone had no authority to impose regulations; and in consequence (under Sir William Fawcett, now Adjutant-General) they turned to the King, and in 1786 the first steps were taken to restore order.

Restoring regularity, and at the same time preparing a wholly new and sound system of drill which would sweep away the many surviving cobwebs, was not to be the work of a day. The first steps were taken in 1786, when an interim regulation was prepared.[189] Issued in mid-April 'By His Majesty's

---

[188] The condition of these corps was discussed above, pp. 136–7. Entirely typical of them was the 22nd Foot, which in 1783 came home after almost eight years' service in America. In June 1784 the corps consisted of only 160 rank and file, of whom thirty were new recruits; half the firelocks were lost or in bad condition, and only fifty-one men possessed cartridge cases. As Lord George Lennox observed, the 22nd was 'so lately returned from abroad as to be Incomplete for to be Reviewed', and 'tho the whole Strength of the Regiment was Collected, it was not sufficient to form a Division that could act in any shape whatever'. No manoeuvres were even attempted. WO 27/51.

[189] This was issued as *By His Majesty's Command . . . General Regulations and Orders for his Majesty's Forces* (1786). The interim nature of these regulations was clearly spelled out in the text: 'to remove the various Defects in Discipline . . . is a Work, that will require both Time and Perseverance to accomplish—as well as a much more particular and extensive Plan of Reform, and Regulation than the present one:—But, as some

Command' and sent to all the regiments of cavalry and foot serving at home and abroad, these *1786 Regulations* were designed chiefly for the use of the foot. The manual, platoon, and firings, according to the *1764 Regulations*, were left unchanged; the basic training of the recruit (here explicitly addressed for the first time in British regulations), the dispositions to be observed when on review (including definite directions on rank- and file-intervals, length and speed of pace), and the overall review procedure (with detailed orders on the mechanics of marching, wheeling, and the forming of lines and columns), were the subject of this regulation. Although the actual manoeuvres were not laid down, the techniques of movement were standardized. This went a long way towards restoring basic order in the foot's training and in preparing the ground for the introduction of a full regulation drillbook for the infantry.

The spring following, in April 1787, a similar interim regulation was issued to the whole of the cavalry; dealing with the review procedure, the dispositions, and the mounted evolutions and manoeuvres, it once again established the essentials of regularity in the drill of the mounted arm (as of the foot).[190]

Both these interim regulations were quickly put in practice, and thus the ground was prepared for the major drill regulations that were shortly to appear.[191] Meanwhile, several private publications had come out during these years, some of which were to have a notable influence and one of which was to be the basis of the army's regulation drill for the next half-century.

Banastre Tarleton and John Graves Simcoe, lieutenants-

Undertaking of this Kind appears now to have become indispensably necessary, that it cannot be any longer delayed . . . the following General Orders and Instructions, as leading to the Attainment of the important Object in Question [are to be followed]' (pp. v–vii).

[190] This was the *Heads of Review Exercise for a Regiment of Dragoons*, issued under Fawcett's signature of 21 Apr. 1787. It was a summary only (i.e. 'Heads'), since the cavalry, when dismounted, were to follow the *1786 Regulations* already issued.

[191] The mid-April issue of the *1786 Regulations* came too late for their dissemination in Ireland that year before the reviews; but in Britain several regiments were quick to begin their training after them. By 1787 the army everywhere was following these regulations, and continued to do so until they were superseded. WO 27/39, 61, 62, and 63.

The *1787 Regulations*, for the horse, were being practised as early as 29 May in England (WO 27/59 and 27/58, Pt 2). Like the *1786 Regulations*, those of 1787 continued to be followed by all regiments of horse henceforth. WO 27/63, 64, 66, 68, 69.

colonel who commanded the British Army's first true light legions, both published at this time lengthy accounts of the operations of their corps during the late war. Simcoe's *Queen's Rangers*,[192] describing in great detail the terrain and tactics employed by his force on the outpost duty and the *petite guerre*, was without doubt the best narrative account of the operations of a mixed light corps to appear in English during the century. The dedication, the professionalism, and the mutual confidence of officers and men so apparent in this journal, were remarkable; and they cannot have failed to be of assistance to British officers soon to be engaged with French light forces similarly inspired. There was an abundance of excellent material on the training and tactics of light troops, both horse and foot, to be gleaned from Simcoe's work.[193] Much less immediately useful as a guide to the detail of the *petite guerre*, but still a work not to be overlooked on the subject, was Tarleton's *Southern Campaigns*, which appeared at the same time as Simcoe's book.[194] More in the nature of a general history of operations than a detailed account of the conduct of a particular unit, Tarleton's work containted nevertheless a good account of the campaigning of his British Legion—a corps second only to the Queen's Rangers in its successful pursuit of the *petite guerre*.

Where the accounts of Simcoe and Tarleton were most useful only to officers of experience and judgement, John Williamson's *Elements of Military Arrangement* was on the other hand designed particularly for the youthful, inexperienced subaltern.[195] This work was a latter-day *Treatise of Military Discipline*, similarly organized and intended to serve the same purpose; and nowhere among the texts devoted to the routine of the service can developments in drill during the century be more clearly seen

[192] Lt.-Col. John Graves Simcoe, *A Journal of the Operations of The Queen's Rangers, From the End of the Year 1777, to the Conclusion of the Late American War* . . . (Exeter, 1787).

[193] Prefixed to the presentation copy in the King's Library (BL), is a 12-page MS letter addressed by Simcoe to George III, in which he advocates the re-raising of similar light legions, now that the French have them. This letter is itself an excellent summary of the organization, training, and tactics of such units.

[194] Lt.-Col. Banastre Tarleton, *History of the Campaigns of 1780 and 1781, in the Southern Provinces of North America* . . . (1787). Tarleton's work was marred by its attempt to disparage his chief, Cornwallis—which, considering Tarleton's performance at the action of the Cowpens, can hardly be credited.

[195] John Williamson, *The Elements of Military Arrangement, and of the Discipline of War; Adapted to the Practice of the British Infantry* . . ., 2 Vols (1782). Quotations are from a 2nd, revised edition, which appeared in 1785 under the same title.

and appreciated than in the comparison of Bland and Williamson.[196] Aware that the number of books devoted to military subjects had 'of late years been multiplied to an almost infinite degree, so that the bookseller's shelves seem to groan under their weight', Williamson pointed out that there was, even so, still nothing available that would give a young officer a clear and comprehensive description of his duties, and of the regulations according to which the drill should be carried on. What was obviously needed was 'a system of regulations, established by authority, like that among the Prussians, for the exercise, discipline, and whole detail of the service'.[197] In the meantime Williamson supplied the want, and in so far as drill was concerned his text was of the greatest utility. He laid down in detail the manual, platoon, and firings after the *1764 Regulations*; and, aware of the current confusion among the regiments as to what the regulation manoeuvres were, he printed both those of the *1764 Regulations* and of the *1778 Regulations*, together with part of the drill taught in Howe's 1774 light infantry camp (on which, see below). Nor were these the only manoeuvres described in his book: fully aware that 'the number of different [customary] movements has been so multiplied, that some regiments can perform above two hundred', he added a long section dealing with most of the whole stock of the army's customary manoeuvres, including several taken from the Austrian, Prussian, and French services.[198] Williamson's textbook was, then, quite excellent, up to date, and timely; and where the drill of a regiment was concerned it was a trove of material.

Most of the rest of the works appearing at this time were concerned almost exclusively with drill and tactics, illustrating the increasing concern with speed and flexibility on the battlefield which typified European military theory as the century drew to an end. Translations of foreign treatises abounded but,

[196] Like Bland, Williamson dealt at length with the duties of officers at each rank, with the organization and drawing up of a battalion, and with all of the elements of the drill as currently practised in the army. Included too was the routine of guards and pickets, of parades, encampments, garrison duty, campaigning, and even military law. The success of the *Elements of Military Arrangement*, concerned as it was with the basic instruction of officers, underlines the poverty of the works of Thomas Simes.

[197] Ibid. i, pp. x–xi.

[198] For these several manoeuvres, see ibid. i. 133–74. He added a summary of the basic manoeuvres that might be practised with profit by a single company, most useful in an army so subject to long-term dispersal (pp. 117–33).

curiously, it was to be the drillbooks of British tacticians deeply versed in Continental practice that had the most immediate and practical impact. That is not to say that the translations were ignored. The Craufurds' translation of Johann Gottlieb Tielke's *Remarkable Events*[199] was advertised by none other than the Adjutant-General who, in a circular already mentioned, solicited subscribers for a work 'the merit of which is too well known, & too universally acknowledged to require any Comments upon its Excellence from me'.[200] Without doubt the most sophisticated discussion of the relation of ground to tactics—an aspect of tactical thinking now gaining increasing attention, and one which Wellington was to apply so effectively in the near future—Tielke analysed in great detail the battles of Zorndorf (August 1758) and Maxen (November 1759), and used these actions to illustrate the influence of topography.[201]

Another foreign treatise widely known in the army was Isaac Landmann's translation of Maj.-Gen. Friedrich von Saldern's *Elements of Tacticks*.[202] An Inspector-General in the Prussian service from 1763 to 1785, where he enjoyed a considerable reputation as a tactician, von Saldern was chiefly concerned with establishing certain basic, technical principles of foot movement which, when learned, would serve as the basis for performing the most complicated manoeuvres with speed and precision. In his basic principles he was to be followed closely by Fawcett, when he framed the *1786 Regulations*,[203] and later by David Dundas in his celebrated drillbook; and many of these principles were borrowed by Saldern from the

---

[199] Capts. C. and R. Craufurd [trans.], *An Account of some of the Most Remarkable Events of the War between the Prussians, Austrians, and Russians ... And a Treatise On ... the Military Art*, 2 Vols (1787–8). The original German edition had appeared at Freiburg in 1776. Tielke, an officer in the Saxon Army, had previously (at Leipzig in 1769) published an outstanding treatise entitled *The Field Engineer*, translated into English in 1789.

[200] WO 3/27, p. 3.

[201] Tielke attributed Finck's defeat at Maxen to his improper use of ground, which Daun had used with consummate skill.

[202] Von Saldern's *Elements of Tacticks, and Introduction to Military Evolutions for the Infantry ...* (1787), was first published at Dresden in 1784. Landmann was Professor of Fortification and Artillery at the RMA, Woolwich.

[203] In his preface, consequently, Landmann could point out that 'the rules and principles here laid down do not essentially differ from the regulations lately published by royal authority, to establish uniformity amongst the troops of the British army'. Ibid. viii.

best of contemporary French theoreticians and from current Prussian practice. At this basic level Saldern wrought well; but unfortunately for his reputation he was given to constructing the most involved of advanced manoeuvres, difficult enough to perform on the Potsdam parade-grounds and impossible in any battlefield situation; these appeared large in the *Elements of Tacticks*, dimming the excellent metal upon which they were based.[204]

Less noticeable in impact were a Lt. Douglas's translation of the comte de Guibert's *General Essay on Tactics* and Maj. Thomas Mante's translation of Joly de Maizeroy's *System of Tactics*, both of which appeared in London in 1781.[205] Maizeroy's ideas, often confused in their statement, were hardly calculated for success in the British service; and they had little influence on French practice. His denigration of firepower and of the influence of weapons upon tactics rendered his ideas inapplicable, however provocative. Guibert's views—and his essay was widely thought of as one of the most brilliant on its subject in the century—seem on the other hand to have been partly overshadowed and lost sight of because of the influence in Britain of the Prussian school at this time.[206]

Unquestionably the two works whose impact was most widely felt in the British Army of the period were those of Lt.-Col. William Dalrymple and Col. (later Gen. Sir) David Dundas. Dalrymple's *Tacticks*[207] was the fruit of long service experience, of wide reading among the most modern French and German theoreticians, and of four seasons recently spent in the English encampments.[208] It was Dalrymple's concern to standardize the army's manoeuvres and to do so upon sound technical rules of basic movement, aware as he was that of late

---

[204] For a typical jibe at Saldern see P. Paret, *Yorck and the Era of Prussian Reform* (Princeton, 1966), 44. Several British battalions were practising manoeuvres taken from Saldern's drillbook *c.*1789.

[205] Lt. Douglas (trans.)—J. A. H., comte de Guibert, *A General Essay on Tactics. With an Introductory Discourse . . .* 2 Vols (1781). Guibert's work was first published in 1772, and Douglas's translation was of the 1773 Liège edition. Mante's translation of Joly de Maizeroy's *A System of Tactics, Practical, Theoretical, and Historical*, 2 Vols (1781), was of the first, Paris edition of 1766.

[206] R. Glover, *Preparation*, 203.

[207] Lt.-Col. William Dalrymple, *Tacticks* (1781), was reprinted at Dublin in 1782.

[208] Dalrymple, as lieutenant-colonel of the 2nd Foot, 1778–82, camped in 1778 at Coxheath, in 1779 and 1781 at Warley, and in 1780 at Tiptree.

the British Army, compared with foreign armies, had 'not made an equal progress in its Regulations and Tacticks'.[209] The resulting treatise was unique among all the English works that had appeared to date.

The *Tacticks* was unique both in content and in presentation. After devoting a short section to a proposed remodelling of the tactical subdivisions within the British battalion, the rest of the work (dealing with the principles of movement and then with manoeuvres) was laid out in the style of the French military *ordonnances*, proceeding from basic training and moving on to deal progressively with more advanced manoeuvres.[210] The mechanics of movement that he taught (pivot-files, points of bearing, alignments and the like) were quite new to British drillbooks, and Dalrymple advanced them as the basis 'upon which the field discipline of the army might be regulated'; only with these basics could 'an Uniform Tactical System be established, and the whole army trained upon the same plan'.[211]

Dalrymple had a clear grasp of tactics, and each of the manoeuvres he put forward was accompanied not only by excellent explanatory plates, but by descriptions of actual battle situations in which they might be used. He scattered numerous sound tactical observations and principles throughout his work, and let slip no opportunity to advocate constant peacetime training in realistic situations and upon varied terrain. Like Dundas, he felt that the army's service in America during the Seven Years War and the War for Independence had led to a significant decline in the solidity—and appreciation—of British heavy infantry. Three ranks had given way to two, in most battalions, and file intervals were dangerously open; heavy fire and solidity had been sacrificed for the sake of speedy movements. This might suit colonial conditions; but if such dispositions and tactics were attempted in Europe, the British battalions would be crushed by the enemy's heavy infantry and

---

[209] Ibid. viii.

[210] Dalrymple himself pointed out that much of his inspiration came from the *ordonnance* of 1776 for the French infantry.

[211] Ibid. viii. His basic training section covered pp. 18–56, 73–6. These mechanical 'principles' of Dalrymple's were included (in a less sophisticated but more practicable fashion, as was proper) in the *1786 Regulations*; the technical spirit which infuses those regulations is likewise due to the influence of Dalrymple, and had not distinguished previous British regulations.

cavalry (absent, in America). He also regarded current French views on the use of columns for shock action as erroneous: 'In a neighbouring nation, there has been much controversy about formation; I shall venture to say, that our Tacticks must be subservient to the arms, not the arms to the Tacticks; and I am of opinion, that impulsion by close combat, in the manner of the antients, is inconsistent with our present mode of arming.'[212] He thus reaffirmed the traditional British belief in the supremacy of heavy fire; and he went on to support these views by making what can properly be described as *the* classic, reasoned statement of the tactical belief that fire must prevail over shock.[213]

The other of these two most influential works was Col. David Dundas's *Principles of Military Movements*, which came out in 1788 and was to enjoy an immediate success—so much so, in fact, that by 1792 a slightly revised version was to become the regulation drillbook of the army.[214] Dundas's success was due principally to two things: first, he laid bare the extent of the tactical weakness and the irregularity of drill prevailing in the army, the result of the confused profusion of regulations that had come out since the later 1770s,[215] and of the increasingly widespread influence of an unsound tactical doctrine whose origins could be traced to the earlier 1760s; and secondly, he laid down a new system of drill and tactics, the comparative sophistication of which seemed, to the most influential general and staff officers at the Horse Guards and at Dublin Castle, to warrant its immediate adoption throughout the army.

Dundas ascribed the army's drill weakness to four causes, which were mutually contributory. The main problem was the lack of a single fully detailed set of regulations not only dealing with the usual drill elements, but defining also the basic mechanics of movement—the 'principles of movement' of the sort

[212] Ibid. x.

[213] Ibid. 112–14.

[214] Col. David Dundas, *Principles of Military Movements, Chiefly Applied to Infantry. Illustrated by Manoeuvres of the Prussian Troops, and by An Outline of the British Campaigns in Germany, During the War of 1757* . . . (1788). A 2nd edition came out at London in 1795.

[215] Dundas admitted that there were 'many proper and excellent regulations and customs existing in the British service; but it is difficult to know which are obsolete, and which are in force. They are no where collected under one view', and were often lacking in detail. Many regulations (those of 1778 e.g.) 'have been framed at various times [only] to remedy the inconveniences of the day'. Ibid. 15.

described by William Dalrymple and von Saldern. Once a single detailed regulation was given out, laying down the common principles and technique of movement to be taught throughout the army at the level of basic training, regularity in the advanced manoeuvres could easily be achieved. It was Dundas's opinion, secondly, that a system that did not allow for regular peacetime concentrations of regiments for the purpose of brigade training must, in the long run, not only make such manoeuvres difficult to carry out but also encourage the most unrealistic excesses among the isolated, individual regiments.[216] To prove this contention, Dundas had merely to point to the often extravagant review demonstrations put on by corps during the 1770s and 1780s. It was quite common for corps at their annual reviews, *c.* 1770–88, to show the reviewing officers a series of mock movements intended to represent solutions to various tactical problems confronting them. In many cases these representations were quite realistic, and the corps showed themselves well trained; but often the mock situations were such as would never have been encountered by a single regiment upon active service, and a training regimen designed to prepare the regiment to meet such unlikely eventualities was at least impractical and at worst deceptive. Typically, at these unrealistic reviews the battalion would take upon itself the role of a full brigade or wing; the flank companies detached and went through all manner of skirmishing, flanking movements, and assaults, while the battalion-companies broke into penny-packets and, rather than manoeuvring as a solid and steady firing-line, either acted as a reserve to the busy and mobile flank companies or joined with them in rushing about the field. These procedures were hardly calculated to forward the battalion in its essential, proper, and decisive wartime role, that of a component in the larger brigade or line, conforming with its solid, linear manoeuvres; and that, of course, was Dundas's point, for how were dispersed regiments to appreciate their role as cogs in a larger machine, when for years on end in peacetime they were isolated from their fellows?[217] Thirdly,

---

[216] Dundas admitted that a great many corps were individually well trained, but according to different regulations and systems. General officers could hardly manoeuvre large bodies composed of 'such jarring materials'.

[217] Examples of regiments performing in this fashion appear in the returns made every year, *c.*1770–88 (WO 27/18–63, *passim*). See, e.g., the reviews of the 37th Foot

Dundas noted several of the deficiencies in current practice which had developed during the army's service in the Americas where, from 1755 to 1763 and again from 1775 to 1783, a large part of the foot had been involved in operations against enemy forces entirely or virtually bereft of cavalry. Loose formations had resulted, there being no need to look to the means of resisting speedy and prowling horse coming down suddenly upon a flank, or out of the black-powder smokescreen; and this circumstance especially, Dundas wrote, 'has much tended to introduce the present loose and irregular system of our infantry'. Finally, Dundas attacked the fad for light infantry and light tactics which had grown up during the American wars and had further been encouraged by the spread of light troops on the Continent since the appearance of the Grenzer regiments in the Hapsburg service. Although aware of the necessity for good light troops, Dundas believed that the light company had come to play too important a role in the battalion's training; the light infantry had come to seem more useful than the heavy, which was absurd; and its constant place in the limelight at reviews—where too often it acted not in assistance to the body of the battalion, but rather at its expense—hindered the training of the whole regiment.[218]

Such was Dundas's summary of the evils and shortcomings in the army's drill, by the later 1780s. The result he described as 'our very thin and extended order to make more show; an affected extreme of quickness on all occasions . . . the forming and breaking on the move, the easier to cover and conceal lost distances and accidental lines, which otherwise would be apparent . . . the different and false composition of columns' etc. Most corps drilled on a depth of two ranks only, and at open rank- and file-intervals, both of which created weak and irregular lines; in a word, 'all idea of solidity seems lost', and 'our present and prevailing modes are certainly not calculated either

---

at Fort George Ardersier on 1 June 1773 (WO 27/27); of the 19th Foot at Edinburgh on 5 June 1773 (WO 27/27); the 2nd Horse at Thurles on 31 May 1774 (WO 27/32); and of the 7th Dragoons at Inveresk on 21 June 1780 (WO 27/45).

[218] 'The showy exercise, the airy dress, the independent modes which they have adopted, have caught the minds of young officers . . . The battalion [-companies] have been taught to undervalue themselves, almost to forget that, on their steadiness and efforts, the decision of events depends; and that light infantry, yagers, marksmen, riflemen, etc, etc, vanish before the solid movements of the line.' Ibid. 12.

to attack or repulse a determined enemy, but only to annoy a timid and irregular one.'[219] It was these problems that he set out to cure with his principles of movement and his system of manoeuvres.

After an excellent initial discussion of the training of officers and men in the basic principles of movement, Dundas devoted the bulk of his work to the intricacies of battalion manoeuvres and to those of the larger line. Much of his material on the basic mechanics of movement was inspired by current Prussian practice, which was all to the advantage of British drill at this time.[220] His system was no more 'Prussian' than was Guibert's, however, despite his detractors' views;[221] and in his promotion of sound drill mechanics he repeated much that had already been introduced to English readers not only in von Saldern's treatise but in William Dalrymple's of 1781, and by authority in the *1786 Regulations*. Though Dundas's text was lengthy, its contents were no more formidable than those of contemporary French infantry *ordonnances*; he presented his ideas with clarity, and simply; the whole is easily comprehended, his basic principles were few, simple, and clear, and his drill (as events were shortly to prove) required no more than good practice to be properly performed.[222]

1788 AND BEYOND

The regulations issued to the cavalry and infantry in 1786 and

---

[219] Ibid 9–14, *passim*.

[220] Dundas often travelled on the Continent, studying directly the drill of foreign armies—in 1774, for example, touring the garrisons of the Low Countries, the lower Rhineland, and northern France, taking detailed notes on the drill of the Austrian regiments at Brussels, the Prussian battalions at Wesel, and on the large garrisons of Dutch at Maastricht, Namur, Nijmegen, The Hague, and Bergen op Zoom, and of French, notably at Metz and Lille (BL King's MSS 240, fos. 1–30). He also attended the annual Prussian manoeuvres (e.g. in 1785, and again in 1788), an experience he found invaluable; and he acknowledged too the importance of Saldern's treatise in the formation of his ideas. William Dalrymple's drillbook clearly played an important part in Dundas's studies.

[221] For a good overall appraisal of Dundas's drill, and rebuttal of the usual criticisms, see Glover, *Preparation*, 118–21 and *passim*.

[222] Dundas attached to his treatise a 70-page abstract of the whole, for the benefit of regimental officers; it was intended as a guide for training purposes once the contents of the full treatise had been digested. Included in the abstract was a plan or 'form of review, and movements necessary for the practice of a single battalion, and of a small corps'. In this review plan (which was immediately useful, since it followed closely the accustomed pattern of the army's reviews) Dundas reduced his system to eighteen comprehensive manoeuvres, for training purposes.

1787 had been, as we have seen, stop-gap affairs, interim regulations designed only to arrest the rapid deterioration in drill
uniformity. The major new sets of drill regulations thus presaged, and indeed shortly to appear, were to prove to be
extremely successful—more than merely a new codification of
procedure. The *1792 Regulations* for the foot and the *1796
Regulations* for the cavalry were to enjoy a long success in the
army, the *1792 Regulations* surviving as the foundation of
British infantry drill down to the Crimean War. But neither of
these regulations, nor the several rules and orders issued in conjunction with them or as supplements to them, can fully be
appreciated if they are conceived simply as the last in the series
of major drills issued by authority to the eighteenth-century
army: they were rather only an initial part of the general reform of the army conducted under the auspices of the Duke of
York (as Commander-in-Chief from 1795 to 1809, and from
1811 to 1827), as Britain struggled with the changes made
necessary by the unprecedented scale and nature of events in
Europe.

The general reform of the army has been considered elsewhere,[223] and here we need only address ourselves to the
preparation and introduction of the series of regulations that
were to restore the uniformity of the army's drill, ease training,
and see the army through the French Revolutionary and
Napoleonic Wars.

As we observed earlier, it was Dundas's *Principles of Military
Movements* that was to serve as the basis of the new regulations.
At the time of its publication Dundas was well placed to forward his work, since he was himself serving on the Irish staff
and was a friend of that other author and tactician Sir William
Fawcett, the Adjutant-General in London.[224] Dundas's drillbook had also impressed the Marquis of Buckingham (who was
Lord-Lieutenant in Dublin), Lt.-Gen. the Earl of Ross (who
in 1788 was temporary commander of the forces in Ireland, in
the absence of the C.-in-C., Lt.-Gen. Sir William Pitt), and
Gen. Lord Heathfield, a most influential senior general officer

---

[223] Glover, *Preparation*, is best. See also A. Burne, *The Noble Duke of York* (1949).
[224] Dundas was Irish QMG from 1778 to early 1789; and from then until 1793 he
was Irish Adjutant-General, a post more appropriate to his training duties. In 1790
he was promoted major-general.

in London, ex-Irish C.-in-C., and recent victor at the defence of Gibraltar. It was with their support—and to theirs was soon added that of the King and the Duke of York, who was at this time colonel of the Coldstream Guards—that Dundas's drill was tested, revised, and made regulation.

The Dublin garrison was handy and appropriate for the task now taken in hand. In the spring of 1788 the Earl of Ross, working with the Marquis of Buckingham, brought in several weeks ahead of the normal schedule the five regiments told off to form the new Dublin garrison for 1788–9;[225] and these, camped in Phoenix Park together with the five regiments of the old garrison not yet dispersed into county cantonments but held over some weeks for the purpose, were drilled intensively by Dundas to an abridged manuscript version of his drillbook.[226] By mid-summer Dundas's exertions were in 'so fair a way' under 'the Countenance' of Buckingham that Fawcett, paying close attention from London, was planning a meeting with Lord Heathfield in order to draw up a regulation drill based on the abstract Appendix to the *Principles of Military Movements*. 'We must go hand in hand together in the formation of this System', wrote Fawcett to Dundas, hoping (prematurely) that with Heathfield's aid both the Dublin and also the Gibraltar garrisons could serve as 'the Schools for teaching and inculcating the true principles, for the General practice of the whole Army'.[227] By early autumn the Lord-Lieutenant had prepared a series of 'Observations' on that summer's review reports. In it he ordered the Earl of Ross to notify those corps trained in the Dublin system to make no 'Deviations . . . respecting the Manoeuvres and Practice pointed out to them'.[228]

With the reports on Dundas's 1788 experiments favourable, another major step was taken: on 12 May 1789 Lt.-Gen. Sir William Pitt, who by early 1789 had taken up once more his duties as Irish C.-in-C., was ordered by the King to continue

---

[225] Sir R. Levinge, *Historical Records of the 43rd Regiment* (1868), 85. The corps forming the old garrison were the 15th, 16th, 24th, 56th, and 69th of Foot, while the new consisted of the 13th, 27th, 43rd, 58th, and 61st of Foot.

[226] The *Morning Chronicle, and London Advertiser* (21 July 1788) carried a report on the training from a Dublin correspondent.

[227] WO 3/8, pp. 27–8. The Gibraltar garrison was not so employed, in the event.

[228] WO 35/16, pp. 62–5. See also WO 27/63, on the 58th and 63rd.

drilling the Dublin garrison—'a very proper Instrument in your Hands, for correcting those Errors and Abuses, which have crept into his Service, and for introducing that fundamental Reform, which is evidently so much Wanted'—according to Dundas's system; 'and by the Aid of those Experiments, which you will be enabled to make, with such a Body of Troops under your Eye, endeavour to form some fixed and general System . . . for the established practice of His [Majesty's] Whole Army.'[229] Pitt was ordered to carry on this work hand in hand with Dundas, and to report to the King on their progress.

The Lord-Lieutenant, Pitt, Dundas, and the Irish staff now took the bit between their teeth, for not only did they continue the 'Experiments' with the Dublin garrison but on 1 July they printed up and distributed as official drill the *1789 Regulations*, to be observed by all the regiments on that establishment.[230]

The *1789 Irish Regulations* were, in effect, an abridged version of Dundas's *Principles of Military Movements*, dealing at great length with basics (length and speed of pace, intervals, rules for marching, etc.), and with the training of small squads, then of individual companies, and finally of the full battalion. Attention was paid to the instruction of both officers and recruits; included also was a lengthy section (with fine plates) on the advanced manoeuvres of the battalion. A summary description of review procedure was appended; and for training purposes Dundas boiled his system down into a list (with short descriptions) of eighteen comprehensive manoeuvres. As yet, the 1764 manual, platoon, and firings were still followed unchanged.

By mid-November 1789 the progress reports forwarded to London by Pitt had so impressed the King that he ordered Pitt to have those corps destined to form the following year's Dublin garrison practise the new drill well in advance of their arrival at that place—'so that no Time may be lost bringing them forwards'. Fawcett added that, if another year's testing should

---

[229] WO 3/27, pp. 50–1. On 24 May the Lord-Lieutenant received similar orders (WO 3/8, pp. 167–8). This was to a large extent Fawcett's doing.

[230] Properly, *Rules and Regulations for the Field Exercise and Movements of the Army in Ireland* (Dublin, 1789). An improved edition was sent out on 1 Oct. 1789, under the same title. Copies were sent across to Fawcett, who presented one to the Duke of York on 31 July. WO 3/8, pp. 188–9.

show the new drill to be excellent, 'then His M. will then take it into His Royal Consideration how far it may be expedient to extend the Use and Adoption of them still further in his Army.'[231]

The full army in Ireland had, since mid-1789, been following Dundas's Dublin drill as regulation practice; and in April 1791 ('after a full, and very satisfactory Experience of two Years of the new Regulations . . . which have been diligently practised by the Garrison of Dublin'), the King ordered the Lord-Lieutenant 'Officially' to extend 'the said new System of Discipline, throughout the whole Army, in that Kingdom'.[232]

By the beginning of 1792 the new drill was thought ready to be issued generally. In February three Irish battalions embarked to relieve corps long at Gibraltar; and since they carried with them the new drill the Gibraltar command was ordered to 'make . . . Tryal of their modes of formation and movement', and to report upon the same.[233] Meanwhile, Dundas himself had been ordered to London;[234] and early in March a committee composed of Dundas, Fawcett, Col. Fox (of the 38th Foot, a corps very experienced in the new drill), Lt.-Gen. the Earl of Harrington, and the Duke of York, met at 'H.R.H. The D. of Y.'s' under the 'immediate Superintendance and Direction of H.R.H. The D. of York', to discuss the preparation of these regulations for the army generally.[235]

The new *1792 Regulations* were issued, at last, on 1 June 1792.[236] Previously, on 23 March, a long list of general orders had been sent to all corps in Britain laying down several of the basics so that they might lose no time in acquainting themselves

---

[231] WO 3/9, pp. 12–13. That the Irish command and staff had already extended the new drill beyond Dublin, and had made it regulation practice throughout the Irish Army—as was their right, since the King had not disallowed this—was not yet 'officially' recognized in London.

[232] WO 3/10, pp. 8–9.

[233] Ibid., pp. 100–2.

[234] Ibid., pp. 110–11. On 4 Feb. Fawcett informed Dundas: 'I yesterday took The K[ing])s P[leasure] upon the Subject of forming a Small Board of Officers, for the purpose of drawing up from Your General System of Military Discipline, some such Abridgement, as might be fit for the immediate practice of our Infantry on this Establishment.' Ibid.

[235] Ibid., pp. 135–6.

[236] These were, properly, *Rules and Regulations for the Formations, Field-Exercise, and Movements, of His Majesty's Forces* (1792).

with these before receiving the full printed regulations;[237] and additionally, on 20 April wholly new manual and platoon exercises were issued to the army generally, replacing at last the arms exercises practised since 1764.[238]

The *1792 Regulations* (which were sent across to Ireland too, thereby replacing the interim *1789 Irish Regulations* from which they were descended) were by and large a condensation of the 1789 Irish drillbook with added stress put upon the basic training of recruits and upon the drill which dispersed companies could practise. By late June 1792, all the corps in Britain, Ireland, and—where they had been received[239]—on the overseas stations and garrisons, were busily practising the new regulations; and so, on 26 June, the Adjutant-General could inform a correspondent that the corps were all learning the new drill, which 'must of course occupy them pretty close, for some time to come'.[240] Progress was quick, however; and from 23 July to 8 August six regiments (the 10th and 11th Light Dragoons, and the 2nd, 3rd, 14th, and 29th of Foot) formed a special camp on Bagshot Heath near Camberley, under the command of the Duke of Richmond, where they put on a display of manoeuvres and mock combat before George III.[241]

---

[237] A copy is in WO 3/27, pp. 101–6, 'General Orders'.

[238] Printed and issued as *By His Majesty's Command. The Manual and Platoon Exercises* (1792). The new manual was much shorter than the old, striking out many movements now considered as outmoded ceremonial. The new platoon was very little different from that of 1764. The platoon was simplified slightly (for its wording was a trifle ambiguous, in the 1792 version) with the appearance of *The Manual and Platoon Exercises, Etc., Etc.* (1804), which included a précis of the full 1792 drill and also a list of the firings performed by the wings of the battalion acting independently of one another.

[239] Gibraltar was supplied on 8 June (WO 3/10, p. 175). Further afield, the 2/60th when reviewed at Montreal on 1 Sept. was reported drilling 'agreeable to the former Regulations, the Regiment not being yet drilled to the new ones'. The new regulations (or knowledge of them, at least), had arrived there. On 30 Oct. the 4th Foot was seen at Halifax, Nova Scotia, where it was following the new *1792 Regulations*; and so too was the 21st Foot, seen there on 26 Oct. WO 27/72.

[240] WO 3/10, p. 186.

[241] On this camp, see Ch. VI, *passim*. As early as 4 Feb. 1792 the 3rd Foot, in England, had been informed that it was the King's wish to see a battalion 'go through the Exercise and Manoeuvres, ordered last Spring to be performed . . . by the several Regiments which composed the Garrison of Dublin'; and the 3rd, consequently, had been selected to 'proceed without delay to practise the said Exercise'. A copy of the *1789 Regulations* was rushed down to the 3rd; and the lieutenant-colonel of the 38th, a corps trained in the Dublin garrison, was ordered to assist the 3rd in preparing for the royal review. The 3rd was seen by the King and the Duke of York a few weeks later, at Windsor. WO 3/10, pp. 109–10, 124–6.

By the end of the year 1792, therefore, the whole of the regular army had been supplied with the new regulations;[242] and although the confusion and blundering of the next few years were to retard somewhat the full use of the new drill in practice, it was essentially the *1792 Regulations* that saw the British infantry through the later part of the great war against Revolutionary France, and through the whole of the Napoleonic Wars. Revised editions, abridgements, and commentaries were to appear occasionally during the two decades following upon 1792, published both by authority and privately. Official editions (some of them revised) of the *1792 Regulations* were brought out in London and Dublin in 1794, 1795, 1798, 1801, and 1803, all under the same title as the original.[243] From as early as 1795, the Duke of York as C.-in-C. ordered that 'every Officer of Infantry shall be provided with a copy of these Regulations'; and his order was printed in subsequent editions.[244] In 1804 General Orders were issued 'in further Explanation' of the *1792 Regulations*, where certain officers and corps had been observed by the Duke of York to be either misinterpreting, confusing, or deliberately deviating from the prescribed drill.[245]

Most editions of the *1792 Regulations* were, admittedly, lengthy and technical affairs; and so in 1801 a shortened, simplified version was printed by authority for the use of subalterns and NCOs, on the theory that 'unless the training and instruction of Officers and Non-commissioned Officers individually and collectively keeps pace with that of the men, all attempts at improvement must be ineffectual.'[246] Private writers had already anticipated this step; and several of them brought out simplified versions of the review procedure and of

[242] By the end of the year and on into 1793, copies of the new drill were being distributed to the militia too. WO 3/27, pp. 122–4, 161.

[243] One edition, by authority, was printed as far afield as Quebec City, in 1804.

[244] E.g. *Rules and Regulations for the Formations, Field-Exercises, and Movements, of His Majesty's Forces. A New Edition* (1798), iv.

[245] Published as *General Orders and Observations on the Movements and Field-Exercise of the Infantry* (1804). In these (p. 5) HRH directed 'the strictest conformity thereto to be observed in every particular of execution.'

[246] Ibid. 9. This was the first time that any drill publication had been officially and explicitly prepared not only for the officers but for the NCO's as well, the Duke of York 'feeling the propriety and necessity' of such a step. Another edition of this simplified version was published by authority in 1807, with the manual and platoon exercises attached.

the eighteen comprehensive manoeuvres originally abstracted by Dundas and included as an appendix to his *Principles of Military Movements*.[247] The best of these was Smirke's *Review of a Battalion*, first published in 1799 and in its fourth edition by 1806.[248] Concise, handy, and competent, Smirke's little book consisted of a long series of plates—without doubt the finest plates to appear in any British drillbook of the century, a fact which must in itself have accounted for the several reprints: these, with the attached commentary, very clearly illustrated the review procedure and the eighteen most important manoeuvres practised under the new regulations. An equal boon to regimental officers was the *XVIII Manoeuvres*, prepared by Capt. Dominicus and even handier to use than Smirke's book.[249] The *XVIII Manoeuvres* was a pocket reference, with a few pages of text describing the essential principles of movement and with fine little fold-out plans illustrating each of Dundas's comprehensive manoeuvres. These and similar works were all very useful to the officers with the corps; and since the drill regulations of the French infantry, as used throughout this period, were soon available also in an excellent annotated English translation, the foot was now very well provided for.[250]

Meanwhile, the influence of Dundas's drill and the Duke of York's reforms had spread to include the British cavalry. Where the *1786 Regulations* for the foot had been merely interim, so too had the *1787 Regulations* for the cavalry, as we have seen.

[247] This abstract had been reprinted in each edition of the *1792 Regulations*. Cf. the *Principles of Military Movements* (2nd, 1795 edn.), 'Appendix', 57–61, and the *Rules and Regulations for the Formations, Field-Exercise, and Movements of His Majesty's Forces* (1801), 261–8.

[248] Robert Smirke, *Review of a Battalion of Infantry, including the Eighteen Manoeuvres . . .* (1799).

[249] Anon. [Capt. George Dominicus], *General Dundas' XVIII Manoeuvres* (1798). The work was reprinted in 1799. Dominicus was an officer in one of the new patriotic units raised in the City, namely the 2nd Royal East-Indian Volunteers. *East India Kalendar, 1799*, xii.

[250] In 1803 John Macdonald published his translation of the *Ordonnance* of 1791 as *Rules and Regulations for the Field Exercise and Manoeuvres of the French Infantry. With . . . References to the British, and Prussian Systems of Tactics . . .*, 2 Vols (1803). Macdonald made marginal notations throughout, directing British readers paragraph by paragraph to the comparable sections of the *1792 Regulations*, for purposes of comparative study. His copious footnotes were full of sound tactical observations, repeatedly drawing the attention of his readers to the virtues and ills of current British practice *vis-à-vis* these French regulations. Macdonald showed himself one of the most informed and incisive tacticians in Britain; and his later translation from the French, the *Instructions for the Conduct of Infantry on Actual Service . . .* (1807), reaffirms this judgement.

The attention of the authorities, however, had since 1788 been directed almost entirely to the preparation of the new foot drill; and the outbreak of war with France in 1793 caught the cavalry with an as yet unreformed drill for their mounted evolutions and manoeuvres.[251]

Fifteen regiments of cavalry, eleven from the British establishment and four from the Irish, served with the Duke of York's army in the Low Countries during the campaigns of 1793–4, which ended with the disastrous withdrawal of the Austrians and the difficult retreat of the British into northern Germany, seeking to evacuate the Continent.[252] It was while in north Germany in late 1794 and early 1795 that Dundas, now a lieutenant-general and in command of the cavalry, once again took matters in hand by imposing upon all these corps the system of drill that he had used in the 15th Light Dragoons[253] and had modified to correspond (where possible) with the plan and tactical principles of his *Principles of Military Movements*. Dundas had these regulations—'a small, but excellent Collection', as Fawcett described them[254]—which dealt almost exclusively with manoeuvres, printed up in Germany and distributed to the regiments serving there; and a few copies were dispatched to Fawcett.[255]

At the same time that Dundas was attempting to establish a uniform drill among the cavalry regiments in Germany, a set of standing orders (in the vein of those of Molesworth) 'drawn up for the Use & Practice' of the 2nd Dragoon Guards originally, was being prepared for publication by authority in London; these were 'to be forthwith sent to all the Cavalry Corps at Home, to be Observ'd & follow'd by them, till further Orders'.[256] These standing orders—the compilation of Lord Pembroke, of that corps—were delayed in their final preparation because of problems with revisions;[257] and the upshot was

---

[251] Midway through 1792 the King had directed that the new manual and platoon exercises, together with copies of the full *1792 Regulations*, be sent to every regiment of cavalry in the army; these they were to follow henceforth for all their dismounted drill. WO 3/10, p. 193.

[252] Fortescue, iv, Pt 1, 296.

[253] Glover, *Preparation*, 135.

[254] WO 3/14, p. 149.

[255] Ibid., pp. 43, 101, 143, 149.

[256] Ibid., p. 43.

[257] Ibid., pp. 89–90, 100–1.

that both Dundas's cavalry drill and the regulations used in the 2nd Dragoon Guards were, on 1 October 1795, printed together as a single regulation and issued as such to the whole of the British cavalry.[258] Half the text of these *1795 Regulations*, consequently, was devoted to regimental administration, routine, and duties; and however useful in establishing a general system of interior management, this format made these regulations an interim affair in so far as drill was concerned.

Over the winter of 1795–6 Dundas, now returned with the army from the Continent, prepared the text of a more complete cavalry drill; and in the spring of 1796 this was fully tested in a cavalry camp formed near Weymouth, at which Gen. Sir William Pitt again took command with Dundas as his second.[259] Good progress was now made; and on 17 June 1796 the full cavalry drill, the *1796 Regulations*, was finally issued to the whole of the British horse.[260] Like the 1792 foot regulations, the *1796 Regulations* for the cavalry were issued in revised editions and abridgements over the next several years—in 1797, 1798, 1799, and 1808; and (as with the foot regulations) all cavalry officers were ordered by the Duke of York to supply themselves with copies.[261]

The first of the official abridgements of the *1796 Regulations* was prepared in 1798 by Maj. (later Maj.-Gen.) John Gaspard Le Marchant, of the 16th Light Dragoons—and lately of the 2nd Dragoon Guards, where he no doubt had a hand in preparing Lord Pembroke's section of standing orders for the interim *1795 Regulations*.[262] During his service in the Low Countries, 1793–4, Le Marchant had made a study of the superior swordsmanship of the allied cavalrymen; and during the spring of 1795 (part of this time spent at Weymouth camp), he began the

---

[258] These were *By His Majesty's Command. Rules and Regulations for the Cavalry* (1795). The Duke of York's warrant is on Al^r. See WO 3/14, p. 259, for Irish issues.

[259] WO 3/15, pp. 114, 129–30, 146, 153. Camped at Weymouth (where George III attended the trials), were the 1st, 2nd, and 3rd Dragoons, together with the 11th, 15th, and 16th Light Dragoons.

[260] Properly, *Instructions and Regulations for the Formations and Movements of the Cavalry* (1796).

[261] Ibid. (2nd edn., 1797), v.

[262] The abridgement was *An Elucidation of the Several Parts of His Majesty's Regulations for the Formations and Movements of Cavalry* (1798), a handier version of the main cavalry manoeuvres, reaching its 4th edition in 1808. On Le Marchant, see T. H. Thoumine, op. cit. 59.

preparation of a manuscript drill for teaching good swordsmanship (and with it the proper mounted seat) to the British cavalry.
A Board of General Officers approved the manuscript, which
was finished by the following summer; and Le Marchant then
began several months of touring Britain, teaching the new
sword exercise to detachments sent from the several regiments.[263] Late in 1796 his drill was printed and issued to all
corps as regulation practice; and early in 1797 the Duke
ordered every cavalry officer to obtain a copy.[264] The *1796
Sword Exercise* was a brilliant piece of work and a proper
complement to the otherwise complete *1796 Regulations*.

We might add, finally, a note on the specialized training of
light-infantry corps, which got under way just beyond the close
of our period. We noted above that light-infantry companies
had been formed in the battalions serving in the Americas,
*c.*1758–64; and we have seen too that, although these had been
reduced with the coming of the 1763 peace, much of the experience of the light service had been preserved in the army's
customary practice and in the private publications appearing
thereafter. In 1771–2 light companies were once again raised
in all the battalions, this time permanently; and in 1774 the
first specialized schooling of these companies in the discipline
of light infantry proper was held at Howe's Salisbury camp.[265]
It was not until the army experienced the effectiveness of French
light tactics in the 1793–4 Flanders campaigns, however, that
authority was at last stimulated to major efforts, army-wide.[266]
In 1797 printed copies of the short light-infantry drill, taken

---

[263] On its preparation (which included the design, manufacture, and issue of a new
pattern sabre throughout the light cavalry) and on Le Marchant's training tour, see
R. H. Thoumine, op. cit. 40–52. Le Marchant was assisted on his tour by twenty
troopers of the 16th Light Dragoons specially schooled in the new exercise. A similar
tour was carried on in Ireland by one of Le Marchant's subaltern assistants. See also
WO 3/15, pp. 230–1; 3/17, pp. 17–19, 103, 119–20; and 3/29, pp. 121–87, *passim*, on
the tour.

[264] Printed as *Rules and Regulations for the Sword Exercise of the Cavalry* (1796). Containing excellent plates illustrating the trooper's seat, and the various cuts, thrusts, and
parries (mounted and dismounted), this was an admirable drill, clearly described. It
was reprinted several times, including once at Edinburgh in 1803; and a pocket-sized
abridgement or *Explanation of . . . The Six Cuts* came out in 1800 and was reprinted
in 1803.

[265] On which, see pp. 336–7.

[266] The *1792 Regulations* (as had the *Principles of Military Movements*), devoted some
10 pages to the special drill of the light company, but this was scarcely sufficient.

from the *1792 Regulations*, were distributed by the Adjutant-General's office to all corps;[267] and in 1798 there was issued from the Horse Guards a full light-infantry drillbook to be followed henceforth as regulation.[268] A succession of privately published light-infantry studies appeared during the 1790s and beyond; and with Sir John Moore's special training programme in the 1803–4 Shorncliffe camp and the conversion of certain old battalions, some into light-infantry regiments and some into rifle regiments, a true light infantry was at last fully established in the British Army.[269]

ADDENDUM

We have attempted in the present chapter to describe virtually all the drillbooks, regulation or otherwise, available in the English language during our period; and it will be apparent that there was a wide and often rich store of this literature available to the officers of the horse and foot. With that in mind, we think it would be doing less than justice to the 'Military Literary World' of eighteenth-century Britain, were we to fail to mention (if only in a brief sketch) the paramount works among the many devoted to gunnery and fortification; for the mechanical and mathematical professions of the officers of the Ordnance corps, if for the most part abstruse and not immediately relevant to the officers of the army proper, inspired a body of technical treatises some of which were outstanding.

Notable among these were the works of John Muller, 'Professor of Artillery and Fortification' at Woolwich. Two of his publications—*Elementary Fortification* and *Practical Fortification*—dealt respectively with the current theory of the design of major fortifications, and with the practical engineering problems of their construction.[1] A companion study, somewhat less

---

[267] WO 3/31, pp. 28–9.

[268] This was the *Regulations for the Exercise of Riflemen and Light Infantry, and Instructions for their Conduct in the Field* (1798), an official publication translated by Fawcett from the 1797 German work of Col. de Rottenburg. These 1798 regulations were reprinted at London and Dublin in 1803 and 1808.

[269] On Moore's drill and Shorncliffe, see J. F. C. Fuller, *Sir John Moore's System of Training* (1924), and C. Oman, *Sir John Moore* (1953). Fuller's *British Light Infantry in the Eighteenth Century* (1925), is to be avoided, since it is unhistorical, inaccurate, merely a vehicle for his tactical theories of the 1920s.

[1] *A Treatise Containing the Elementary Part of Fortification, Regular and Irregular . . .* (1746) was reprinted in London in 1756, 1774, 1782, and 1799, a clear measure of its

mathematical in its presentation than either of these two works
and therefore comprehensible (and palatable) to the intelligent
regular officer, was his *Attac and Defence*;[2] it was easily the most
important English text addressed to the attack and defence of
major fortresses and fortifications to appear during the eighteenth century; it was (like others of his works) translated into
French and Spanish, it was widely quoted, and it alone would
have assured Muller the reputation of an expert. Not content
with this success, however, Muller not only brought out in 1760
an annotated translation of Clairac's *The Field Engineer*,[3] but in
1757 had published what has since come to be regarded as his
most important work, the *Treatise of Artillery*. This last was a
massive collection of material on the construction of the carriages, beds, and tubes of the guns, howitzers, and mortars used
in the British service, together with sections on artillery ammunition and stores, laboratory works, the crews and teams for
the guns and ancillary equipages, and on the drill, camps, and
marches of the gunners.[4]

Muller, although critical of Vauban and Coehorn, quite
naturally drew on their works; and he was much influenced by
Le Blond, Bélidor, and Vallière.

As learned as Muller (and nearly as prolific) was Lewis
Lochée, whose *Essay on Military Education* (1773) we have
already described. He published two detailed, specialized
works for the officers of the Engineers: the first, his *Military
Mathematics*, was essentially a major text on geometry and
mathematics; while the second, his *Fortification*, illustrated all
aspects of major fortification and was drawn principally from

---

worth. *A Treatise Containing the Practical Part of Fortification* (1757) was reprinted in
London in 1764 and 1774.

[2] *The Attac and Defence of Fortified Places* ... (1747) was brought out in a revised edition in 1756; and the 1756 revision was reprinted in 1770 and in 1791.

[3] On which, see above pp. 206–7.

[4] *A Treatise of Artillery* ... (1757), was reprinted (in revised editions) in 1768 and
1780. Appended to the 2nd, revised edition was a 200-page supplemental essay on ex-
ternal ballistics, which was not included in the 1780 edition and appears to have been
published separately after 1768.

This sort of detailed technical information on the artillery and its service was first
made easily accessible to officers of all arms (artillery included) in Ralph Adye's *The
Little Bombardier, and Pocket Gunner* (1801). A pocket-sized dictionary crammed full of
information, the fine *Little Bombardier* had reached its 8th edition by 1827.

Vauban.[5] More widely useful was his short but excellent
Castrametation, which dealt with the layout of camps and so was
of service to senior quartermasters and engineers.[6]
    There were several other English treatises on these subjects,
of lesser stature. The best foreign works were available in
translation, too. Vauban, the dean of modern military engineers, had written several studies on various aspects of the
science; and some of these appeared in English, in whole or in
part. Abel Swall in 1691 first published his *New Method of
Fortification, As practised by Monsieur de Vauban* . . .; and as late
as 1762 revised editions, abridgements, and extracts were being
taken by English writers from this principal source.[7] Among
the French artillerists, extracts were published in English
translation from the works of Bélidor, Surirey,[8] and Le Blond.[9]

[5] These were *A System of Military Mathematics*, 2 Vols (1776), and *Elements of Fortification* (1780).

[6] *An Essay on Castrametation* (1778).

[7] The best English biography of Vauban, which treats his fortification of places, is
R. Blomfield, *Sebastien le prestre de Vauban, 1633–1707* (1938). The best study of all is
M. Parent and J. Verroust, *Vauban* (Paris, 1971). There is a good bibliographical essay
in G. A. Rothrock (ed.), *A Manual of Siegecraft and Fortification* (Ann Arbor, 1968),
which is a translation (with commentary) of a 1740 Leiden edition of one of his essays.
Rothrock rightly stresses Vauban's theories on the attack, as well as the defence, of
places.

[8] Henry Manningham (trans.), *A Compleat Treatise of Mines. Extracted from the
Mémoires d'Artillerie. To which is annexed* . . . *Bélidor's Dissertation on* . . . *Gunpowder* (1752;
and rpt. 1756). Bernard Forest de Bélidor, who was a professor of mathematics in the
French artillery corps, published several works on gunnery, engineering, and military
mathematics during the 1720s and 1730s, the chief of which was *Le Bombardier françois,
ou nouvelle méthode de jetter les bombes avec précision* . . . (Paris, 1731). A. R. Hall, *Ballistics
in the Seventeenth Century* (Cambridge, 1952), 51, notes that Bélidor had not passed beyond
Galileo in his ballistics theory, neglecting the effect of air resistance; but in the early
eighteenth century only a few authorities had begun to do so, and Bélidor was still
considerd a luminary.

    Pierre Surirey de Saint-Remy's *Mémoires d'Artillerie* appeared in several editions be-
tween 1697 and 1747, each revised to fit contemporary equipment and practice in the
French service. Wide-ranging, excellent technical storehouses, these volumes dealt
(like Muller's *Treatise of Artillery*) with all aspects of ordnance both great and small, and
were considered by contemporaries as the primary works of reference on French
artillery.

[9] An anonymous translation of one section of Guillaume Le Blond's *Elémens de la
guerre des sièges* (Paris, 1743) appeared as *A Treatise of Artillery; or, of the Arms and Machines Used in War* . . . (1746). It was a very slight affair. During the 1730s, 1740s, and
1750s Le Blond had published several fine treatises on contemporary French fortification and siegecraft. His massive *Elémens de tactique* . . . (Paris, 1758), since it is not
innovative but is rather a detailed exposition of the drill of the French horse and foot
early in the Seven Years War, is of much use to historians.

Curiously, none of the major works of the leading French authorities (other than Vauban) was translated in full. Among other foreign works available to English readers, however, two especially fine studies deserve mention. The better of these was Papacino's *Service of Artillery*, translated by Capt. Henry Thomson of the Royal Artillery.[10] Without doubt the most sophisticated, and at the same time most practical, work to appear during the century on the tactical role of the artillery on the battlefield, the *Service of Artillery* with its analytical style, its realism, and its freedom from mathematics was a most compelling and inspiring work, most of it easily comprehensible to regular officers. The other notable foreign treatise was Ens. Edwin Hewgill's translation of Tielke's *Field Engineer*.[11] Addressing the senior Engineer officers attached to the headquarters of an army in the field, Tielke dealt in detail with the whole variety of the services to be expected of them, from laying out encampments to preparing topographical plans of likely fields of battle. Much stress was put on the duty of engineers— with their knowledge of terrain and their cartographical abilities—in reconnoitring in advance of the army.[12]

Among the scientists, finally, the study of exterior ballistics was advanced considerably by Benjamin Robins's *New Principles of Gunnery* (1742), a work of European significance. But the scientific principles (however accurate they might be, and however considerable a scientific advance they were on the ballistics of their sixteenth- and seventeenth-century precursors) of Robins and the other eighteenth-century ballisticians— John Gray and William Starrat, for example[13]—were irrelevant

[10] First published at Turin in 1774–5, *A Treatise on the Service of Artillery in Time of War: Translated from the Italian* . . . (1789), was the work of Maj.-Gen. Allesandro Vittorio Papacino d'Antoni, a general officer in the Piedmontese service and 'Chief Director of the Royal Military Academies of Artillery and Fortification at Turin'. Papacino wrote prolifically on military subjects.

[11] *The Field Engineer; or Instructions upon Every Branch of Field Fortification* . . ., 2 Vols (1789), first appeared at Leipzig in 1769. Tielke was a captain in the Saxon artillery, whose *Remarkable Events* we have already noted above.

[12] In 1802 Isaac Landmann, whose translation of von Saldern we noted above, himself wrote a guidebook (*The Field Engineer's Vade-Mecum*) for Engineer officers serving in the field; and like Tielke he stressed the importance of surveying and sketching from horseback, while reconnoitring. Wellington's staff officers were to use these arts to advantage in the Peninsula.

[13] Who produced, respectively, *A Treatise of Gunnery* (1731), and *The Doctrine of Projectiles, Demonstrated* . . . (Dublin, 1733), the first of which was excellent.

to practice given the technological imperfection of ordnance.[14] Interior ballistics remained a mystery throughout the period; and cannon manufacture remained a craft, not a species of precision engineering in the modern sense.[15]

---

[14] A. R. Hall, op. cit., *passim*; and esp. 8–21, 162–5.
[15] The best study on the subject is M. Jackson and C. De Beer, *Eighteenth Century Gunfounding* (Washington, 1973); and useful too is H. C. Tomlinson, 'Wealden Gunfounding: An Analysis of its Demise in the 18th Century', *Economic History Review*, 2nd Ser. 29 (1976), 383–400. On British artillery, the best study is B. P. Hughes, *British Smooth-Bore Artillery* (1969); and very good too is R. Wilkinson-Latham, *British Artillery on Land and Sea, 1790–1820* (Newton Abbot, 1973).

Chapter IV

Basic Training

The 'basic training' of the private soldier, as it was conducted in the British Army throughout the period under consideration, was laid on in two phases, the first of which—designed solely for recruits—was merely introductory, while the second—aimed at more practised soldiers—was endless; and the term must be understood as embracing both. At the initial introductory phase the new recruit was taught what was variously referred to as the 'material exercise of a soldier' or the 'first Rudiments or Ground Work of a Soldier', whence—having been made familiar with most of the skills that would be required of him in the ranks—he graduated to the exercise of the 'mechanical part of a soldier's business' or the 'mechanical parts of war', which constituted the second phase.[1]

Although the press of war made for some exceptions, characteristic of the initial or 'material' phase of the basic training programme was the care lavished on the instruction of the recruits, who were brought along according to what was called the 'method proportionably gradual' or the 'progressive' method. By this method the recruit was 'drilled regularly through [the] several Classes of Exercise', learning one skill before he was instructed in the next, and so 'carried on progressively' until he was fit to be put into the ranks.[2] Basic to the success of the progressive method were patience and, indeed, kindness on the part of the drill instructors to their newly listed charges; and these were virtues the utility of which the writers of drillbooks, when discussing recruit training, constantly reminded their readers.[3]

---

[1] The phrases are from, respectively, James Wolfe, op. cit. 34; John LaFaussille, in the Cumb. Pprs., Pt 4, II, fo. 3; John Williamson, op. cit. i, p. viii; and William Dalrymple, op. cit. 21.

[2] *1786 Regulations*, 2; and David Dundas, op. cit. 35.

[3] See, e.g., Edward Fage, op. cit. 3, and William Dalrymple, op. cit. 18. Even the Prussian regulations ordered that a similar approach be adopted (*Regulations for the Prussian Infantry* (1759 trans.), 120).

Although the on-going or 'mechanical' phase of basic training was endless, the time required to complete the initial phase could be only roughly estimated because of the great irregularities of unit dispersal both within the British Isles and about the overseas stations and garrisons. As a general rule, recruits taken into the foot regiments stationed in the Mediterranean garrisons, into the corps in the big Irish quarters like Dublin and Cork, and into the Household cavalry and Foot Guards in London and Westminster, were brought along much more rapidly than could be those entertained by the more widely dispersed marching regiments; and recruits taken into the cavalry of the line in both kingdoms (although those in Irish corps found their quarters more settled than those in Britain) had considerably more to learn during their initial training than had simple infantrymen to master. Recruits taken into the additional companies of regiments serving abroad might receive less initial training than others, or they might be put through a 'crash course', depending on the demands being placed upon these companies by their parent corps. Similarly, men who passed through the general recruit depots at Chatham, Tilbury, and Kinsale might get more or less initial training, depending upon the need for replacements abroad. Given this variety, it took from several weeks to a few months for the recruit to acquire some proficiency at the skills that made up the initial phase of his training.[4]

As we shall see, much of the overall training-time available to the army was taken up by basic training; and, since it occupied so considerable a part of the army's time, a detailed summary of the skills taught at that level will be appropriate here, before we turn to an analysis of the significance of the programme. It is clear that by 1715 most of the basic skills taught for the rest of the century had already become established as standard practice in all of the regiments; and it is clear too that these skills were being taught to the recruits, during their initial training, according to the progressive method. According to the lights of the officers immediately in command, the time devoted to individual aspects of training varied from one corps to the next, and so too did the schedule

---

[4] For a more accurate estimate of the training-time of whole regiments, again contemporary, see pp. 294–6.

according to which the various skills were introduced to the recruit as he passed through his initial instruction; but nevertheless these variations were not so significant as to alter the content or the nature of the material taught in the several corps.[5]

During most of his initial training the recruit was instructed individually; and only as he mastered certain aspects of it, or when he had become acquainted with and mildly proficient at several skills, was he attached to small and then increasingly larger groups of recruits, to practise these skills in company and in unison with others.

The recruit was first taught to be 'master of his person', throwing off the carelessness of civilian carriage and adopting the stiff self-possession of military bearing. Next, having learned the simplest postures, he proceeded to the simplest of the evolutions—dressing to his front and flanks, and making the various turns on the spot. Instruction at marching now began; and the greatest stress was put upon marching, naturally enough in an era of linear (and increasingly close-order) tactics. The techniques of movement became steadily more sophisticated as the century wore on, demanding precision, and basic instruction at marching reflected these developments. Until the early 1750s the recruit was taught only to maintain his proper posture and bearing, to take paces either 'long' or 'short', and to step out either 'quickly' when marching in column, or 'softly' when on parade, when manoeuvring, or when advancing in line; and these times and distances were measured only against the scale of what was customarily practised within each regiment. The mid-century was in most respects a watershed in the development of marching technique—and, by direct extension, of manoeuvrability and tactical sophistication. Marching style—that is, the manner in which the legs were lifted and put down—only assumed a regular fashion in the army at the mid-century, after 1748, with the adoption of the 'Prussian step': taken from the stiff-kneed marching style introduced in Prussia during the reforms of Frederick William I's reign, this was to be a notable innovation and was to remain the style after which British infantry performed linear drill until

---

[5] Only with the *1786 Regulations* and those following thereafter did authority seek to impose army-wide uniformity in this matter—doubtless unsuccessfully.

late in Victoria's reign.[6] The Prussian step made for great precision at speed; and indeed a rate of 120 such paces per minute was considered, for the experienced soldier, 'nothing more than an easy walk'.[7] Length and speed of pace were not regulated until the *1778* and *1786 Regulations* took these up; before then, these had been regimental matters, left to the judgement of the field officers and adjutants; but it is clear that there was an informal consensus operating in the army on these important points from at least the mid-century.[8] Having learned to march singly, the recruit then practised marching in unison with others first in a file, then in a short rank, and then in squads composed of increasingly larger numbers; here, marching in step was perfected and the maintenance of proper rank- and file-intervals was taught.

From the Restoration through to the mid-eighteenth century British soldiers performed the evolutions and most of the simpler parade manoeuvres in step and—when deployed in line before the enemy— made minor manoeuvres by closing up the ranks and moving in step, as they did on parade; but on all other occasions marching in step was not attempted and the intervals between the ranks were kept open to avoid confusion, no means of maintaining precision of distance and pace having as yet been devised. Before the introduction of the musical cadence—and thus of the all-important close and regular rank-intervals which that aid made it possible to keep up over lengthy periods, and at speed—marching in step had perforce been performed very deliberately, with an almost funereal solemnity and under the close supervision of the NCOs.[9] It was

[6] William Dalrymple's description (op. cit.), 22, is quite clear; and see also William Windham, op. cit., Pt. II, 20–2; and John Macdonald, *French Infantry Regulations*, i, 21.

[7] William Dalrymple, op. cit. 23 n. 1.

[8] A quick pace was used for manoeuvring in action or trying to gain ground; and a slow pace was used invariably for parades and reviews, and for passing rough ground when advancing in line in action. A third, very rapid pace was used for the bayonet charge. On these, see WO 3/26, pp. 32, 169; WO 3/26, p. 153; and the *1786 Regulations*. Occasional examples of the paces practised in the regiments, before these regulations, appear in the review reports; they indicate that disparity was not great but was noticeable, and also point an informal consensus. Cf. the 1/1st, 18th, and 25th of Foot for 1777, in WO 27/36.

The *1786 Regulations* were the first to attempt to establish a standard pace. Recruits were taught to accustom themselves to a standard pace by practising their marching on long stretches of ground measured off accordingly, and marked with tapes or lines.

[9] On the cadenced step in the British Army, see Addendum to this chapter.

not until the later 1740s that the drums, and more particularly the new fifes, began to be used in some regiments to set a marching cadence; and not until the end of the Seven Years War had marching in step to a musical cadence, with all the tactical advantages that this made possible, become standard practice in the army. Once the great advantages of speed, precision, flexibility, and simplicity which the cadence and the resulting closed ranks made possible had become apparent, however, it was found that the music itself was sometimes a distraction, sometimes (in action) inaudible, and the cadence difficult for the drummers and fifers to maintain. By the mid-1770s, therefore, the musical cadence was not used in the field, but was retained for training purposes: by the music the recruits accustomed themselves to the standard pace and time, now all-important as a foundation of close-order manoeuvres.

Having learned the evolutions, how to march at the various steps both forwards and obliquely, and to wheel and file in small squads three ranks deep, the recruit was next given his firelock; and once familiar with its mechanism, he was slowly taken through the elaborate manual of arms. The greatest stress was put on the manual since it was generally deemed the most important part of the training of the soldier. Taught first to carry his firelock on his shoulder, and then to rest, to order, and to sling the weapon—all rudimentary motions, taught first so that the recruit could continue to practise marching and the evolutions—he then went on to learn the whole elaborate performance of clubbing, securing, presenting, etc., a series which included bayonet drill[10] and the crucial loading and firing motions. Loading and firing were taught to the recruits

---

[10] Bayonet drill was, curiously, rather neglected in the eighteenth century. Buried away in the manual exercise, it was performed in a most unrealistic fashion; and the command in use—'Push your Bayonets!'—betrays both its origin and underdevelopment. Not until 1805, when Capt. Anthony Gordon published his systematic *Science of Defence, for the Sword, Bayonet, and Pike, in Close Action*, was the subject treated in depth by anyone. Many writers lamented this lapse, recognizing the efficacy of the weapon against both horse and foot: e.g. Bennett Cuthbertson, writing in 1768 (op. cit. 210) thought it an 'essential matter, for Soldiers to be perfectly well acquainted with their use', and deplored the fact that British troops in training were seldom even 'permitted to fix them, but on certain occasions'. From Marlborough's campaigns onwards it was the touch-stone of British tactical thinking that heavy fire was all-important; and so it was doctrine perhaps, as much as indifference, that dictated the army's approach. As Campbell Dalrymple wrote (op. cit. 56), 'human nature will always shrink [in the face of heavy fire], and never dare to approach within push of bayonet.'

individually at first, and then in unison with others in increasingly larger numbers; while still practising these motions within the confines of the manual exercise, they used no powder, and the whole was carried on slowly. Before passing on to the platoon exercise, where the loading and firing motions were done much more quickly, the recruit would be taught elementary markmanship.

Virtually all the eighteenth-century (and later-seventeenth-century) drillbooks stressed the importance of at least some target practice;[11] but before 1786 it was only in wartime that this aspect of training could be pursued to any advantage. The quantity of lead shot issued to the regiments in peacetime[12] was quite insufficient for target practice, which was therefore infrequently attempted; the recruits (like the rest of the rank and file) had to be content with firing off blank cartridges, or 'squibs', in simulated platoon fire.[13] This official cheeseparing on the ammunition supplied in peacetime was rectified only in 1786, when issues were greatly increased; but it was possible to justify the policy by sticking to the letter of tactical theory. Since controlled volley fire was considered more important than individually aimed fire—and the peacetime issue of ball is a clear measure of just how much importance was attached to volley fire, over aimed fire—it was upon volley fire in platoon that peacetime training was concentrated. Squibs provided a sufficient degree of realism for this purpose. Poor fire accuracy was to some extent inevitable anyway, given the state of eighteenth-century military arms technology.[14] In 1779 a battalion of the excellent Norfolk Militia, standing on three ranks, fired two volleys at a target 70 yards distant and measuring about $2' \times 80'$, supported on poles. Firing 632 shots, the battalion scored 126 hits, for a score of 20 per cent. In 1755 a

[11] A refrain begun in the *1686 Regulations*, 264, where it was observed that "Tis very necessary for all Captains . . . to practise their men to Shoot at a Mark, which is extream useful.'

[12] On quantities of ammunition issued, see above, pp. 143–5.

[13] When powder was scarce, flints were saved from wear by the use of wood or bone snappers in the jaws of the firelock during mock platoon fire.

[14] On this technological limitation, see A. R. Hall, *Ballistics in the Seventeenth Century* (Cambridge, 1952); see also id., 'Science, Technology, and Warfare, 1400–1700', in M. D. Wright and L. J. Paszek (eds), *Science, Technology, and Warfare. The Proceedings of the 3rd Military History Symposium, U.S.A.F. Academy, 1969* (Washington, DC, 1970), 3–32, *passim.*

section of the Prussian Foot Guards, trying a similar test shoot, scored only slightly better. Better shooting was to be expected from Guards than from militia; but the Norfolk's colonel thought that his results were proof that his men shot very well.[15] A regular marching battalion of British foot (if we can assume them to lie somewhere between the Norfolk Militia and the Prussian Guards) might score 25 per cent hits, in target practice, at 75 yards.[16] Still, marksmen there were—especially among the light companies—who developed their ability by acquainting themselves thoroughly with the peculiarities of their pieces, an activity the opportunity for which was not afforded the majority of British soldiers.[17]

The platoon exercise, like the manual, was taught to a few men at a time, beginning first with a single file and then increasing these numbers. A recruit was taught the exercise in each of the three ranks; and he learned to perform the full loading and firing procedure at top speed and to only four commands. Along with speed, he had to learn to synchronize his reloading motions with those of his comrades in the platoon fire-unit; and in order to ensure his expertise he was put through it endlessly, 'locking up' and kneeling.[18]

Beyond a few other simpler skills—learning the drill signals played by the musicians, perhaps some rudimentary practice with their short hangers or swords,[19] and the handling of grenades by the grenadiers[20]—little else save discipline and

[15] WO 34/114, fo. 123; and P. Paret, op. cit. 14–15.
[16] See also Glover, *Preparation*, 140–1, and C. Ward, *The War of the Revolution* (New York, 1952), i. 44–50, for interesting figures. It has been estimated that in the running fight between Concord and Boston in Apr. 1775 American militia discharged 75,000 rounds in order to hit 247 British soldiers. At Vittoria in 1813 perhaps 459 musket balls were fired by Wellington's army for every French casualty.
[17] On aimed fire, see Addendum to this chapter.
[18] On locking, see Addendum to this chapter.
[19] None of the drillbooks mentions the use of hangers, although they were worn in the battalion companies until 1768 and by the grenadiers until 1784.
[20] No regulations after 1728 carried any special grenade exercise, which until then had been a feature of the drillbooks. The 1735 *Granadiers Exercise* was prepared for the 1st Foot Guards; and the 1722 camps saw paper grenades issued to the troops: both of which indicate their continued use early in the century. There are occasional examples of grenadiers using them at the regimental reviews held later in the century (e.g. by the 2/1st Foot in 1769 and in 1777, and by the 25th in 1777—WO 27/15 and 36). Corps serving in the fortifications—at Gibraltar, at St. Philip's Castle in Minorca, at Charles Fort Kinsale, at Fort George Ardersier, and at Quebec City and Halifax—must

obedience was taught to the men at the basic training level.

It was these skills, then, practised singly and then in combination, that made up the basic training programme of the foot. Most of these same skills were practised by the cavalrymen too, as part of their training for dismounted service; but the concentration in the basic training of the trooper lay, naturally, with the skills peculiar to the mounted arm. The recruits taken by the cavalry were usually men of better character and intelligence than those enlisted by the foot; and they needed to be so because, as the *1755 Dragoon Orders* put it, the trooper had 'a multiplicity of things to do more than a Foot Soldier, and ten times more Arms, Accoutrements, etc', to be master of.[21]

The trooper was first taught how to care for his horse (a task which, for the seven or eight months of the year during which the horses were with the regiments, took up several hours daily) and was made familiar with the many items of his tack. The horses imposed a set of conditions upon the cavalry which circumscribed training in a manner wholly unknown in the foot. For upwards of four months every year, the cavalry regiments had to turn their horses out to grass;[22] and the effect of this upon the cavalry was to oblige them to practise the dismounted drill for a third of the year. During the better part of the year, however, when the horses were with the regiments, the troopers were obliged to devote a good part of every day to cleaning tack and stables and to caring for, and exercising, their mounts—activities which took up about six hours daily in the summer, five and a half hours daily in the winter. In the 5th Dragoons during the 1730s, for example, the daily summer timetable for these duties ran from 5:00 a.m. to 8:00 a.m., and from 5:30 p.m. to 8:30 p.m.; in winter, these duties were carried out each day from 8:00 a.m. to 12:00 noon, from 4:00 p.m. to 5:00 p.m. and from 7:00 p.m. to about 7:30 p.m.[23] Variations on this routine were followed in all the mounted regiments every day.

While familiarizing himself with horse and tack, the cavalry

occasionally have practised handling grenades as part of the tactics for defending the works.

[21] *JSAHR* 23 (1945), 99.

[22] On this, see pp. 292–3.

[23] Molesworth, op. cit. 118–25; and cf. the Standing Orders for the 15th Light Dragoons in J. B. R. Nicholson artt. citt., *passim*.

recruit was also undergoing the 'material' training of the foot soldier; and once through this phase he was taught to ride. Riding instruction was carried on initially in riding houses or enclosures, where the recruits were started upon 'old Horses, that are quiet and ready at their Business'.[24] Once the troopers had acquired their seats at the various gaits and learned to control their animals they began individually, and then in larger groups, to be taught simple and essential mounted evolutions like opening and closing the rank- and file-intervals, wheeling on the flanks or centre of a rank, and passaging.[25] When able to ride, the young trooper was usually assigned a 'recruit horse', which had already been broken by the Riding Master and his rough-riders[26]—and together man and horse advanced, practising the basic evolutions and movements at different gaits.

Once he knew the foot drill and had become a competent horseman, and once his mount had become 'ready at its Business', the trooper was instructed in the use of his firelock (or carbine) and pistols, when mounted.[27] But these of course were secondary arms, and much the greatest stress could now be put upon swordsmanship. Curiously, no manual of military swordsmanship was issued to the army until 1796, when Le Marchant prepared his exercise; but the civilian school would already have provided most of the officers with ample experience of fencing, just as it was a source of many technical treatises on swordsmanship. There is no evidence of a settled style or school —beyond the shape and weight of the blades, of course, those designed for the heavy cavalry being best employed at giving point, and those for the light cavalry for slashing—and before

[24] Molesworth, op. cit. 142–9. The recruits were taught to ride under the direction of the Riding Master and his assistants; and an officer, an NCO, and an experienced trooper usually assisted at the riding house.

[25] The regulation *Standing Orders in Farther Explanation of Regulations for the Formations and Movements of the Cavalry, of the Year 1796* (1799), 346, suggested that the 'principles of all cavalry evolutions, and movements, may, to great advanatage, be practised, and learnt on foot', with the men drawn up in such a manner as to simulate 'the cavalry formations'.

[26] Young 'recruit horses', like raw troopers, were to be brought along carefully and with affection, 'by gentle Degrees, so as never to disgust a young Horse, by being too rough with him'. Molesworth, op. cit. 146. See also Robert Hinde, op. cit. 11–23.

[27] Once again, both man and horse had to be trained, for the horses had to become accustomed to the whirling of the swords, and to the noise and smoke of firearms. On this, see Robert Hinde, op. cit. 26, and Le Marchant in the *1796 Sword Exercise*, 60–1.

the Le Marchant reforms we must draw on descriptions of foreign military training. Thus the *Kürassiers* in the Prussian service were trained to attack, from the saddle, 'Paste-board images, made, and erected to represent an enemy'; and the downward cut delivered with main force while standing in the stirrups was most recommended.[28] Le Marchant's system reduced swordsmanship to sound principles: the troopers were taught six offensive cuts, eight parries to protect man and horse, and a cut-and-guard against infantry. The trooper learned the drill on foot, at a dummy target chalked off against a wall; and later, on horseback, he attacked 'mellons attached to the ends of willow wands', or practised giving the point by thrusting at small metal rings.[29]

It was these skills, then, that constituted the 'material' training of the soldier; but as we observed at the outset, the recruit's introduction to, and individual mastery of, these skills constituted only the initial phase of the basic training curriculum. The second phase, begun immediately upon the conclusion of the first, consisted of endless drill—to the end that the skills acquired in the initial phase should through constant mechanical repetition be honed to a level of perfection verging on the conditioned reflex. Where the initial phase had been relatively short-lived—several weeks to a few months—it was one of the chief peculiarities of the British Army's peacetime training system that much the greatest part of the time available overall, for training of any sort, should be devoted only to the on-going or 'mechanical' phase of basic training. For the private soldier no matter how experienced, drill at the level of the basics was the most constant feature of army life. And it must be emphasized that this endless basic training was carried on at the great expense of more advanced training.

Although there was, as we shall see, an overriding structural factor which largely accounted for the endless practice in the army of the 'mechanical' phase of basic training, there were other important factors that were contributory, if clearly subsidiary. Significant among these was the view—a view not only

---

[28] *Regulations for the Prussian Cavalry* (1757 trans.), 58.

[29] *1796 Sword Exercise, passim.* Le Marchant taught (and stressed the importance of) a secure seat for mounted swordplay. His extremely deep seat (ibid. 65–6) seems inappropriate to strong downward cuts, heretofore the forte of heavy Horse.

popularly conceived but also buttressed by the physiology of the Enlightenment—that 'national character' or temperament was an important factor underlying military potential, a determinant which the tacticians considered when drawing up their schemes. Thus Henry Lloyd, in a lengthy discussion of the subject clearly inspired by Montesquieu, described the 'moral and physical principles [which] formed national characters, whose influence is seen . . . in every army'; and he gave it as his opinion that the English, although they were 'neither so lively, as the French, nor phlegmatick as the Germans', nevertheless were 'somewhat lively and impatient'.[30] Humphrey Bland too noted that most observers regarded English troops as lacking the '*Sang Froid*' of the Dutch, who had a 'greater Proportion of Phlegm in their Constitution than the English, by which their Minds are not so soon agitated as ours'.[31] It was Bland's experience that controlled platoon fire was something that the English were only 'With Difficulty brought to, from a natural Desire and Eagerness to enter soon into Action'.[32] These attitudes were typical; and as late as 1803 John Macdonald, whose appreciation of the fundamental relationship in tactics of mobility, armament effectiveness, and firepower was acute, still stressed the need to fit tactical theory and formations to the peculiarities of national character.[33]

The impression is that a great many officers had an exceedingly low opinion of the humour and disposition of the other ranks in general, in the British Army: and although opinion and prejudice thrived on a plane distinctly lower than that on which were advanced theories of national temper, nevertheless their effect on the training of the troops was quite important. Wellington's pronouncement that the ranks of the army at the end of our period were filled with 'the scum of the earth', 'enlisted for drink', is well known. At the beginning of our period Lt.-Col. John Blackadder of the 26th Foot was using similar words: for him, the army was composed of 'a parcel of mercenary, fawning, lewd dissipated creatures, the dregs and scum of mankind'. Midway through the century, James Wolfe re-

---

[30] Henry Lloyd, op. cit. i E3r–F2r.
[31] Bland, *Treatise of Military Discipline*, 145–7.
[32] Ibid. 67–8, 80.
[33] John Macdonald, *French Infantry Regulations*, i, p. xxv.

marked repeatedly on the 'disobedient and dastardly spirit of the men', whom he described as 'vagabonds that stroll about in dirty red clothes from one gin-ship to another . . . dirty, drunken, insolent rascals'; and referring to their Monongahela behaviour, wondered if 'ever the Geneva & pox of this country' had operated 'more shamefully, & violently upon the dirty inhabitants of it, under the denomination of Soldiers?' More temperate—and more typical—was the opinion held by Lt.-Col. James Murray of the 15th Foot: in 1757 he took it upon himself to add to the men's tricornes 'a Hatband and Tassel a la Hanoverien', advising his colonel that 'tho it may appear to some a little of the coxcomb, I am of oppinion there is no danger of making an English Soldier too much so, on the contrary I have ever found it almost impossible to conquer the Cloonesh Disposition so remarkable in the lower sort of People in this Island.'[34]

If British troops were to be brought to perform their drill properly in the field, both these factors had to be contended with: the clownish disposition of the 'lower sort of people' had to be disciplined, their 'national impatience' bridled and dulled. The sure means of effecting both goals, it was thought throughout our period, was to subject the soldier constantly to the repetition of a set of essential mechanical skills—on-going basic training—thus reducing his natural spirit and encouraging the automaton.

This approach was further reinforced (as Professor Paret has pointed out) by the fact that the principles underlying strategy and tactics were 'mechanistic in character'; only at the close of the century were 'psychological' principles to be deduced. As Kessel put it, the tactics of the period sought to exclude chance in favour of control, rather than attempting to take advantage of uncertainty by encouraging in the men a spirit of initiative or individualism.[35] A complete and docile obedience and automaton-like reflex responses to commands were

---

[34] Blackadder, quoted in R. E. Scouller, op. cit. 253; Wolfe, in R. Wright, op. cit. 418, and in Public Archives of Canada M.G18, L5, vol. 3, pt 2, p. 391; Murray, in Kent RO Amherst MSS 013/4.

[35] Such generalizations are well established; and Paret's summary (in his op. cit. 213–16) of these salient features of eighteenth-century tactics is one of the best available. E. Kessel, 'Die Wandlung der Kriegskunst in Zeitalter der französischen Revolution', in *Historische Zeitschrift*, 148 (1933), 275, is quoted in P. Paret, op. cit. 211.

the touchstone of the other ranks; endless repetition of a few basic skills, together with an iron discipline, seemed to ensure both. Finally, nothing like the wide range of skills needed by the modern private soldier was required of his eighteenth-century counterpart. All these larger considerations, then, contributed to the character of the army's basic training. And a last factor, common to all standing armies since their inception, but one given significant stress in the eighteenth century, was the urge on the part of the officers and NCOs to maintain make-work programmes, to drill the men for its own sake—'to preserve the men from idleness'.

These secondary factors aside, however, there remained one fundamentally significant factor which in itself largely accounted for the army's endless practice of the 'mechanical' phase of basic training—and that overriding factor was the friction of peace. It was the friction of peace that determined the pattern of regimental concentration and dispersal, the pattern of regimental quartering, and the pattern of regimental movements; and the individual regiments subject to these conditions were, as we have seen, commonly to be found in states of considerable dispersal. Each of the component parts of a dispersed regiment—companies, troops, detachments—was small; and for however long the regiment remained dispered nothing more sophisticated than basic training could be attempted. Once the recruit had passed through the initial phase of basic training and had, among his more experienced fellow soldiers, become accomplished at performing his basic skills in the ranks of his troop or company, he had reached a plateau on which his training experience levelled off; and until the day came when his own unit was joined with other troops or companies, his training languished at that level, and consisted solely of endless drilling at the basics just described. The small, dispersed bodies —of fewer than three or four companies in the foot, or fewer than two or three troops in the cavalry, depending upon establishment strengths—simply could not attempt with profit anything more complex than these mechanical basics; numbers, sheer numbers, were an essential prerequisite for the satisfactory and realistic performance of the advanced intricacies of the firings and manoeuvres. Field days, mock fighting, review presentations—even simple technical operations like equalizing the timing and step within the regiment—none of these was possible except in concentration: among the foot, two grand-divisions at the very least and preferably three or all four were essential for proper advanced training; and at the very least one, and preferably all three, of the squadrons forming the cavalry regiment must be concentrated.[36]

We might add too that even when some higher levels of concentration had been achieved within the regiment, time was still devoted to the mechanical phase of basic training: major manoeuvres and complicated firings could not be performed at the drop of a hat, whatever the level or period of concentration might be; while on the contrary, during the whole of the time in which a regiment lay dispersed it was quite impossible to practise anything other than the basics.[37] Thus, endless basic training was a structural feature of eighteenth-century army life, bound to remain so for as long as the friction of peace persisted. The equation was a simple one, part of the very nature of linear tactics performed both in training and in the field by closed administrative units—the regiments—which were also the main permanent tactical units: the more men available in concentration, the more advanced the training that could be attempted.

To a system which stressed so much basic training the importance of the NCOs was naturally great, and they were consequently quite numerous. Their numbers were hardly affected by the war-end reductions of regimental establishments; and despite the fact that the strength of a regiment serving in Ireland might be only one-third that of a sister regiment serving in Britain or abroad, there was no such disparity in the numbers of NCOs. Experienced NCOs—'the nerves and sinews of the corps'—were simply too valuable to be reduced.[38] As establishments varied there were occasionally four, sometimes

[36] The levels of concentration within the regiment, and the levels actually prevailing are pointed out in Appendix A, and on pp. 90–5 above.

[37] The figures on dispersal in Appendix A—essentially, those in the 'M & D' column—are a measure of the time available during which nothing more sophisticated than basic training could be carried on; and as we have pointed out, part of the time represented in each of the other columns would also have been given over to basic training.

[38] John Williamson, op. cit. i. 44. The NCOs were always the subject of special attention in the review reports: e.g. those of the 20th Foot in Oct. 1753 were described as 'Alert in their Duty without the smallest Confusion Noise or Bustle'; and those in

five, and usually six NCOs with each company of foot serving in Britain or overseas, while in Ireland there were usually four or five per company. In the cavalry, the troops of Horse and Dragoon Guards normally had three or four NCOs apiece, in Britain, and two or three in Ireland; while each troop of Dragoons and Light Dragoons in Britain usually had four or five NCOs, while an Irish troop usually had three or four. Despite considerable variations in regimental establishments, the ratio of NCOs to private men was always high: among the Horse, Dragoon Guards, and Dragoons, there was usually 1 NCO for every 7 to 10 troopers; among the Foot Guards, 1 NCO for every 8 to 12 privates was the rule. In the marching Foot—in Britain, the Mediterranean garrisons, and the Americas—there was usually 1 NCO for every 7 to 12 privates; and in the Irish regiments 1 NCO was to be found for every 6 to 8 men.[39] There were more NCOs to private men in the British Army than there were in the Prussian Army.

The NCOs were chosen by the commanding officers of regiments from among their most experienced men, recommended by the captains; the sergeants were 'to carry a good command among the Men' and, in the Coldstream, 'when any Vacancy happens among the Sergeants, the eldest Corporal [was to] succeed on Trial for three Months, and if he does not fulfill the Duty, the next will be appointed.'[40] Corporals in the foot were appointed for their character and long service; and the *1755 Dragoon Orders* declared that a dragoon had to serve 'remarkable well for four Years' prior to being promoted corporal, and corporals had to have three years' service as such before being made sergeants.[41]

As far as the basic training of the young officer was concerned, there was of course no formal provision whatsoever during the eighteenth century; not until 1801, under the re-

---

the 38th Foot in May, 1787, appeared 'very Soldier like, & keep up a strict Discipline'. WO 27/3 and 59.

[39] WO 24/84–558, *passim*. The most striking ratio of NCOs to private men (1 :5) prevailed in the Dragoon regiments in Ireland, 1749–55. Cumb. Pprs., Box 44, no. 124.

[40] Anon., *Camp Discipline & Kane* (1757), 83. See also Clode, ii. 123–4.

[41] *JSAHR* 23 (1945), 103. The 1755 Standing Orders for the Dragoons added that 'No Dragoon shall be made a Corporal merely because he can write a good hand, as has hitherto been the Custom'; the NCOs were to be 'compleat Soldiers and not simple Scribblers'.

forming auspices of the Duke of York, was the Royal Military College founded, and it was several years before the officers trained there began to make a mark in the army.[42] Most young officers, having just purchased their first commissions, joined their regiments with no more experience than that gained from a few guidebooks—those of Bland, Simes, and the rest. Like the other ranks, the officers got their basic training on the job, as it were; and the intensity and quality of that training depended in large measure on the spirit prevailing in each regiment, on the attendance or otherwise of fellow regimental officers to their duties, on the leadership and pressure exerted by the regiment's field officers, and also on the character and inclination of the young officer himself. As we have seen, the great majority of regimental officers were career officers, men who could for the most part be depended upon to learn the basics; and since the young officer's introduction to training was, most often, to the basic training being carried on in the isolated troop or company to which he found himself attached, it was to the basics that he found himself devoting the largest part of his time.

Arrived with his troop or company, the young officer devoted himself to studying the current drill regulations, while at the same time he attended the mounting of guards, parades, and the drills. With the assistance of brother subalterns or of a senior NCO he learned how to perform the manual and platoon exercises of the firelock or carbine,[43] and the great variety of movements, commands, and posts it was the subaltern's duty to learn, to perform, or to occupy when the unit was carrying on its basic training exercises. If he were wise he would refer repeatedly to his primers and keep a commonplace book in his pocket 'ready for any remarks' and containing extracts taken from the regulations.[44] He would also study the

---

[42] There were a very few small private academies in Britain; and a few young men attended these, or better establishments on the Continent. On the early years of the RMC and its origins, see R. H. Thoumine, op. cit. 61–146, and Glover, *Preparation*, 192–6 and *passim*.

[43] In a letter to a young officer, about to set out to join his regiment for the first time, James Wolfe advised that knowledge of the manual would 'readily bring you to understand all other parts of your duty, [and] make you a proper judge of the performance of your men'. R. Reilly, *The Rest to Fortune: The Life of Major-General James Wolfe* (1960), 148–50.

[44] Ibid. 149.

regimental orderly- and records-books, if these were available, to acquaint himself more intimately with the discipline, training schedule, and interior economy of the corps.[45]

It was the young subaltern's responsibility, therefore, to make himself master of the same basic-training skills that were drilled into the men; every officer 'must be taught every individual circumstance necessary to a recruit', first individually and then in 'squads of officers [which] should be occasionally marched and exercised by a field officer'.[46] The series of general orders issued in 1755 enjoined officers 'newly appointed' to 'attend the Parade every morning'; and they were to 'inform themselves of every article of their Duty . . . by asking Questions' of their superiors. All field officers and captains were ordered to 'teach their Subalterns their Duty, and see they do it by fair means, and tell them their faults and omissions . . . and let them know they are not to have their Pay to be Idle.'[47]

Such was the system of basic training practised in the British Army, in peacetime, throughout our period. In wartime the system was either continued in this fashion or speeded up, as the exigencies of the military situation might require. Where the regiments in the field were sometimes sent replacements innocent of all but the most rudimentary instruction, this was a relatively rare and certainly a desperate expedient, since untrained and undisciplined men were a dangerous liability in the era of precise linear tactics, and of murderous close-range volley fire. It was for this reason that drafting was so much resorted to, since it provided the regiments in the field with trained men, whatever its effects might be upon those finding the drafts at home. And it was for this reason too that regiments

[45] 'The regimental books, are those which contain the general orders, regulations, etc., the returns of the regiment, of men inlisted and discharged, proceedings of regimental courts martial, returns of arms, ammunition, cloathing, etc., and all that relates to the operations and oeconomy of the regiment.' (John Williamson, op. cit. ii. 15 n. 17). The reviewing officers made a point of checking to see that corps kept these books up to date, since much relating to training and drill was entered in these from circulars sent out through the Adjutant-General's office.

[46] David Dundas, op. cit. 35. Dundas added, viii, that 'a practical and ready knowledge of the detail, and execution of all possible movements of the troops, ought to be the first and leading study of all ranks'. Most other authors concurred: e.g. Bland, in his *Treatise of Military Discipline*, 115; William Dalrymple, op. cit. 51; Molesworth, op. cit. 162; and Bennett Cuthbertson, op. cit. 203.

[47] *JSAHR* 5 (1926), 198; and *JSAHR* 23 (1945), 104.

serving abroad in wartime formed 'additional companies' at home—companies in which the recruits could be processed through the 'material' phase of their basic training before being shipped abroad.

The practice of the 1775–83 war was typical. From late in 1775 'additional companies' (two each) were formed in the British Isles to feed parent regiments serving abroad. These companies, each commanded by officers taken off the half-pay list and settled in at some promising 'Recruiting Quarters', out-fitted their recruits and sent them to the 'Depots' or 'Stations' —at Chatham for the companies recruiting in England, at Stirling Castle for those in North Britain, and at Charles Fort Kinsale for those in Ireland. Here, subalterns and NCOs detached from the additional companies and under the orders of field officers specifically 'appointed for the purpose of training and exercising the Recruits' assembled at the depots, brought the men along as quickly as possible, drilling them intensively.[48] To speed the process (as the Secretary at War informed the colonels and agents of regiments serving in the American theatre), 'Recruits passed at the several Stations by Field Officers who will have instructions to inspect them, will be deemed as approved by the Regiment.'[49] And then, having been 'disciplined sufficiently to serve in the Ranks on joining their respective Corps in N° America', they were shipped abroad.[50]

The system of basic training practised in the British Army, although it was successful enough in the short-run preparation of the soldier-recruit or the young subaltern, was in the long run often counter-productive and even harmful. Endless drilling in small units, at nothing more sophisticated than the basics, tended to produce a certain myopia among the regimental officers, most especially among the captains and subalterns seldom able to see beyond their own companies or troops. Dispersed, their only resource was to devote themselves to the part of the drill that one or a few troops or companies could practise with profit—the basic skills, the simple evolutions and movements, and, with increasing frequency, the

---

[48] On the supply of arms and ammunition from the Ordnance to these depots, see WO 55/370, 'War Office, 14th November 1776'; 55/417, pp. 274, 279, 288, 290, 298; and 55/418, pp. 55, 71, 124, 132, 164.

[49] WO 4/98, pp. 249–54.

[50] Ibid., p. 249.

manual and platoon exercises. The drill regulations issued to the army before those of 1786 could hardly have been better designed to contribute to the stress on basics, devoted as they were to the most detailed descriptions of the manual and platoon exercises, and the simple evolutions; and thus the regulations—in their style, their context, and in the subjects stressed—took dispersal for granted, assumed it. Not until 1764 did the regulations include anything more sophisticated than the arms exercises, evolutions, the battalion firings, defiling, and forming the square; and not until 1792 was the drill of units larger than the regiment so much as mentioned. Pride of place went to the manual and platoon in all the regulations issued before those of 1778. The stress on the basic elements was reinforced too by their frequent reprinting and reissuing under separate covers, separated from the other, more advanced elements included in their original issue: even the laziest of officers, after all, would need his copy of the manual and platoon. As we observed earlier in our discussion of the trends in eighteenth-century English military publication, the striking frequency with which official and privately produced versions of the manual and platoon appeared, from the very beginning of the century, indicates that these arms exercises had become and remained not only the staple of training but a fetish. Only a few officers—Hawley in 1726, Kane in 1736, Bever in 1756, Cuthbertson in 1768, Hinde in 1778—declaimed against the unrealistic repetition and waste of time involved in 'having [the men] out twice a week to act over that silly thing called Manual Exercise';[51] and where it was 'silly' in the infantry it was 'preposterous' (to use Kane's word) amongst the cavalry.

That a degree of myopia should afflict the captains and sub-alterns is, perhaps, understandable; but this was a myopia which affected not only the officers with the troops and companies but also the greater part of the officers of field and general rank—for it was they who were responsible for each regiment's overall training, they who prepared and sanctioned the regulation drillbooks, and they who reviewed and reported upon the state of training in the corps. The general officers regularly revealed themselves in the inordinate attention they paid to

[51] Hawley, in Sumner, 'Chaos', 93; Kane, *Campaigns*, 109–10; Samuel Bever, op. cit. 49–50; Bennett Cuthbertson, op. cit. 206–7; and Robert Hinde, op. cit. 40.

simple mechanics, even to trifles, in their review reports; and this was a tendency not just of the pedants among the general officers but one which appeared too among the most experienced. An example will suffice. In the reports that he submitted upon the regiments reviewed by him in 1754, Lt.-Gen. James Cholmondeley dwelt upon the intricacies of the manual and the firings to the near exclusion of everything else. Of one regiment, he reported their manual 'very fast and in good time'; their firings, all done 'well', were performed standing, advancing, and retreating, both by individual platoons and by platoons told off in firings; and their vollies were fired 'very well'. With another regiment he was less pleased: they made 'several Mistakes in the Manual'; when firing they did not 'lock well or Level well'; they loaded slowly and the timing of the platoon-fire was off. Cholmondeley's comments, in themselves, were not out of the ordinary; but what was peculiar was that his fascination with the intricacies of the manual and the battalion firings had led him, in the first of these two reports, to praise the drill on foot and in battalion line of a regiment of heavy cavalry, for all the world as if it was an infantry corps as the second of the two reported on actually was.[52]

Endless training at the basics—'tossing of the firelocks', as Campbell Dalrymple contemptuously described it[53]—was in the first instance an activity induced by the physical realities resulting from dispersal. But a training system can only be as good as the broad vision that accompanies it, and unfortunately for the British Army 'tossing of the firelocks' tended to dull the officers as much as it rendered the men docile. Activity induced by necessity came to seem a virtue: the efficacy of smart practice at the basics was overestimated; and the fact that the 'material' and 'mechanical' training of a soldier was undertaken merely in order to prepare him for instruction at advanced drill and tactics was obscured. Hence dispersal, and the training atmosphere that it engendered, lent an unwarranted weight to the value of lengthy basic training; and this could only be at the expense of a sound overall appreciation of advanced training and capability at advanced tactics. Time spent on basic training was time lost on advanced training. In

[52] WO 27/3. These were the 1st Dragoon Guards and the 3rd Foot.

[53] Campbell Dalrymple, op. cit. 165.

consequence, the basic training of the army was counter-productive and—as we shall see below in our discussion of wartime training in the field and of the tactics actually attempted by British regiments in action—it was often pernicious.

ADDENDUM

MARCHING IN STEP

Professor Michael Roberts, in his paper *The Military Revolution, 1560–1660* (Belfast, n.d.), 11 n. 1, quite rightly noted that 'the matter of marching in step needs proper investigation', stressing that the question is a very material one in the history of tactics.

Close scrutiny of the English drillbooks from the Restoration through to the 1760s leads to the conclusions described in our text above. Remarks such as 'The Souldiers must always begin to March with their left foot first, which is observed to conduce most to keep the Ranks even' (*1682 Regulations*, 85–6), are a commonplace in the later Stuart drillbooks, and they remained so until the 1750s; but these remarks are always confined to sections dealing with the simple evolutions, countermarches, and—among the manoeuvres—those occasions when the ranks had been closed up tight prior to wheeling or to advancing a short distance in line, both of which were performed very slowly and with much dressing. Paces were counted out by the men, and music was never used on these occasions to set a cadence. Whenever the rank intervals were opened—as they *had* to be to perform most movements and marches—marching in step was clearly laid aside; and the NCOs, who 'have no place assigned them in Marching', were 'to be moving up and down, to observe that the Ranks and Files be at their due distance' (ibid.), there being no other means known of accomplishing this.

The best and most influential of the early eighteenth-century writers, Humphrey Bland, had no notion of the cadenced step; he drilled and manoeuvred his troops, in his 1727 *Treatise of Military Discipline*, at open rank-intervals just as his predecessors had done. Bland likewise described the slow and careful movements performed in step at the simple evolutions; but when he suggested extending movement made in step to include some others of the evolutions, he admitted that this would 'appear so difficult, that it will deter a great many from attempting it'. He added that the 'common Objection against it, is, that it looks too much like Dancing'; and he felt obliged to argue that with 'Time and Practice' it would come to appear 'easy and genteel' (ibid. 12–13). Nor did the experienced and professional Richard Kane, writing in his *Campaigns* shortly before 1736, conceive of using music to set a marching time— and this despite the fact that he gave over six pages (pp. 115–20) to the proper 'use of the Drum in Action', a 'Thing, hitherto overlook'd by all'. He used it for signals, as did his contemporaries.

The first appearance of the fife in the army—and of the notion of cadenced marching and manoeuvring—was noted by Francis Grose in his *Military Antiquities . . . of the English Army*, 2 Vols (1786–88), ii. 248–9. He wrote:

The fife was for a long time laid aside, and was not restored till about the year 1745, when the Duke of Cumberland introduced it into the guards; it was not however adopted into the marching regiments, till the year 1747: the first regiment that had it was the 19th, then called green Howards, in which I had the honor to serve . . . Fifes afterwards, particularly since the practice of marching in cadence, have been much multiplied.

During the 1750s several references to the slow but steady spread of the instrument can be found: in July 1750, for example, the reviewing officer who saw the 20th Foot in Scotland noted the absence of '3 Drummers at Berwick learning the Fife' (WO 27/1). By the late 1750s and early 1760s experienced and learned observers could still express surprise and excitement upon seeing the efficacy of the cadenced step. During the summer of 1759 William Windham saw the 67th and 72nd of Foot at Hilsea drilling 'to the sound of the fife; keeping the most exact time and cadence'; and, he added, 'The effects of the musick in regulating the step, and making the men keep their order, is really very extraordinary; and experience seems fully to confirm Marshal Saxe's opinion; who asserts, that it is the best and indeed the only method of teaching troops to march well' (*Norfolk Militia* (1759), Pt II, 61). As late as 1763, Lt. John MacIntire in his *Marine Forces*, 172–7, was still obliged to devote many pages to explaining and justifying the new concept of marching in step to fife and drum. 'Marching in *Cadence*', he wrote, 'was followed by the *Romans*, and has been revived by the King of *Prussia*, and is now practised by some of the British Troops' (note 'some', not yet all). McIntire had not only to invoke the Romans and Frederick II to impress his fellow British officers, but Marshal Saxe too, who 'plainly shews the Absurdity of our common Method of marching'. See also Campbell Dalrymple, op. cit. 52–4, and Fawcett's translation of Saxe, op. cit. 15–18. The reduction of rank intervals and the consequent expansion of tactical horizons can be followed in the regulations and private publications of the later 1750s and 1760s.

We noted that the musical cadence, once adopted, became fairly quickly a training aid only. Typical of the difficulties that could result were those seen at a review of the 25th Foot, held at Winchester on 18 June 1777. The reviewing officer noted that the corps's timing was slow (at sixty-four paces to the minute in the slow march, and ninety-four at the quick); and he found that 'the Men got into a run whilst the Fifes were playing a regular redoubled time which did not govern their steps', and that consequently the battalion 'sometimes opened & floated a little' (WO 27/36).

Amherst's *1778 Regulations*, recognizing these problems, laid it down that henceforth all infantry manoeuvres were to be performed by vocal commands only, and that 'Drums should be used as little as possible in manoeuvring of Regiments & Musick [i.e. bands] never'. All subsequent regulations concurred.

AIMED FIRE

It is interesting to note that none of the plates attached to the various drillbooks, illustrating the posture of the soldier at 'Present' and 'Fire', shows him actually taking aim down the barrel of the piece; he is, instead, invariably shown with the butt of his firelock pressed to his shoulder but with his head held erect. Nor do front-rank men, kneeling, support the weight of the piece by placing the elbow on the knee. George Grant, op. cit. 7, noticed this in 1757; and in his drillbook he remarked quite correctly that 'Any Commander that desires His Men to hold up their Heads when they fire . . . was never a Marksman himself; and in such Case, you may set Blind Men a Fireing as a Man that can see.' Writing in 1751, the experienced lieutenant-colonel of the 8th Foot stated that he wished that British troops

were accustomed to take Aim when they Present, no Recruits want it more than Ours, few of them having fired or even handled Fire Arms before enlisted; the explanation of the word Present in the Manual Exercise, is very different in my opinion from what Men shou'd do when Firing at an Ennemy, this gives them a Habit of doing it wrong, and I have room to believe that the Fire of our Men is not near so considerable as it would be, were any pains taken to make them good Marks men. (Cumb. Pprs, Pt 4, ii, fo. 5)

There were no rear sights on the longarms issued to the eighteenth-century army; and the bayonet lug near the muzzle, which served as a guide, was no longer visible once the bayonet was fixed. The directions on 'presenting', in all of the regulations, were no more specific than the plates; at best (as in the *1764 Regulations*) they offered simple and unsatisfactory descriptions. As late as 1807 the wise John Macdonald, in his annotated translation of *Conduct of Infantry on Actual Service*, penned a fifty-page critique of the current British regulations, calling among other things (i, p. lxviii) for the addition of a good section on target shooting.

The value of target practice with ball ammunition was sometimes stressed—although marksmanship was not necessarily the priority. Thus the lieutenant-colonel of one battalion said 'firing ball at objects teaches the soldiers to level incomparably, makes recruits steady, and removes the foolish apprehension that seizes young soldiers when they first load their arms with bulletts' (J. T. Findlay, op. cit. 271). By the early summer of 1757 the 15th Foot, moving towards Barham Downs camp, was profiting from large wartime issues. 'We have three field days every week', reported its lieutenant-colonel, 'Seven rounds of powder and Ball each, every Man has fired about eighty four rounds, and now load and fire Ball with as much coolness and allacrity in all the different fireings as ever you saw them fire blank powder'—and this 'hitherto without the smallest accident' (Kent RO Amherst MSS 013/4).

LOCKING

During the 1720s, the British foot began to 'lock' up their ranks for firing—that is, the front rank knelt down, the second moved slightly to its right, and the third moved a half-pace, thus making of each file an echelon with the firelocks of the two rear ranks levelled through the file interval. Locking was considered important (as witness the repeated comments of the reviewing officers throughout WO 27) because it not only made firing by the rear ranks easier and safer, but made possible the use of narrow file intervals and thereby effectively increased the volume of fire being delivered on any chosen frontage.

Most authorities argue that Marlborough's battalions 'locked' their ranks for firing—most recently, E. Belfield in his *Oudenarde, 1708* (1972), 7; D. Chandler, in his *Marlborough as Military Commander* (1973), 92, and again in his *The Art of War in the Age of Marlborough* (1976), 118–19. The earliest contemporary reference to locking that I have seen, however, was made by Bland in his 1727 treatise. The 'discipline practised in Flanders', which Ingoldsby had Parker introduce into Ireland in 1708–10, did not teach locking but simply had the centre rank stoop low so that the muskets of the rear rank would clear their heads (Cornwall RO DD.RH.388, fos 11, 13, and *passim.*). Marlborough's orders given out through Orkney, as late as 1711, make no mention of locking (BL Add. MS 29, 477). Brig.-Gen. James Douglass, writing in 1728, described Flanders practice as 'ye wholl Body at ye word Make Redy: kneels stoups and Stands', and that no doubt was how Marlborough's men fired (BL Add. MS 27, 892, fos 209–55, *passim*).

Chapter V

Advanced Training: Peacetime

Basic training was directed, essentially, to the practice of the first three elements of the drill regimen—the manual, platoon, and evolutions—and to the necessary attendant skills all of which formed the fundamental building-blocks upon which were grounded the other more difficult elements of the drill. It was these last elements—the detailed firings and manoeuvres—that at various levels of realism and sophistication comprised the advanced training carried on in the regiments in peacetime.

While basic training could be carried on in dispersal, however, advanced training could not be. It was only when the individual troops or companies found themselves in states of concentration sufficient to form squadrons and grand-divisions that practice of the firings and manoeuvres could be attempted; and where it was possible, these elements were practised not only on parade but on field days, on route marches, and in mock fighting where not only the 'hatmen' of the battalion-companies were put through their paces but the flank companies too, acting out their role as satellites to the body of the battalion, practised their specialist duties.

The general dispersal of the army has been our constant theme, to this point. Save for the shakedown days preceding the annual reviews—days during which the troops or companies of the dispersed corps were concentrated in review quarters, there to practise intensively their advanced drill against the up-coming review; or days during which the regiments in the fortifications and the garrison towns gave over their normal routine of garrison duty and called in their outlying detachments—full regimental concentration was, as we have seen, infrequent, and especially so for purposes of advanced training. Although there were considerable limitations on what a mere squadron or pair of grand-divisions could profitably perform, and although they could not hope to approximate many of the more advanced manoeuvres and firings, still whenever possible the officers of the troops and companies come together at these lower levels of concentration were to 'instruct the Men in something useful, and not confine themselves entirely to the Manual Exercise' as was all too frequently done even on these occasions, nor simply to the formal 'Parade of the Profession'.[1]

There was during the eighteenth century a very great increase in the number and complexity of the manoeuvres that a battalion of foot was capable of performing; and concurrent with this development in manoeuvres there was an increasing simplification of the fire-systems used by the battalion. This broadening of the manoeuvres was due not so much to the steady development of new procedures as to the periodic introduction of simple mechanical techniques and refinements—the cadenced step, for example—which made possible major advances over relatively short periods. The movement repertoire of one of the Duke of Cumberland's battalions was only marginally more supple and complex than that known in any of Marlborough's battalions. It was the mid-1750s that marked the great take-off point, so much so that the drill and tactics practised in the army by the mid-1760s differed markedly from that known in the best of the battalions in the great North Brabant camps of 1748. The later 1770s were significant, in their turn, since it was during those years that the influence of the Continental theorists and tacticians was most deeply felt, and the army's practice much up-graded. The mid-1780s marked the beginning of that on-going process of very sophisticated developments which culminated in the *1792 Regulations* and, soon after, in the specialization of Shorncliffe.

The battalion of the early decades of the century was an exceedingly intractable body: movements were deliberate, even ponderous, and carried out according to a system full of difficulties and admitting only the most limited variety. Defiling, marching in the most cumbersome of columns, deploying to a flank, advancing in line, wheeling the line upon a flank, and forming square, these movements exhausted the manoeuvres taught in the battalion before the 1740s. Once the new techniques of the mid-century had been introduced, bringing with them great flexibility and permitting precision at speed,

[1] Bennett Cuthbertson, op. cit. 206.

several dozen new manoeuvres were added to those customarily practised; and most of the technical problems that had attended the older manoeuvres were overcome in the process. With ever-increasing sophistication, the store of practicable manoeuvres had grown by the later 1770s to the point where it was possible for a battalion to perform several score of them. The refinements in technique and the increased stress on uniformity, typical of the later 1780s, capped this process of development, establishing by the last decade of the century a series of regulation manoeuvres which comprehended or formed the basis of nearly any movement likely to be attempted.

Where movement had been limited, early in the century, the methods by which fire was given and controlled were elaborate. Three principles were to guide British musketry throughout the century—the quick development and maintenance of heavy fire, close fire control by the officers, and the preservation at all times of some part of the battalion's firepower; and their application was to give rise broadly speaking to two different systems of fire, one succeeding the other. The first was known as 'platoon-firing', or firing by the 'chequer': the *forte* of Marlborough's battalions, it was in general use until the mid-1750s and remained regulation practice until 1764. The system that replaced platoon-firing was known as 'alternate firing', and it remained in use until well beyond our period. Alternate fire was easier to perform than platoon-fire, but both required the most intensive training, were they to be used in action by the battalion.[2]

Where the trend in foot manoeuvres was towards ever-increasing complexity, nothing resembling this process affected the mounted manoeuvres of the cavalry during the century. Well before Marlborough's campaigns the prestige surrounding the heavy Horse had acted so strongly upon the Dragoons that, despite the fact that they had originally been raised to serve as mobile foot, practice at the foot drill was for them little more

---

[2] 'Alternate fire' consisted of fire given by companies, platoons, or other divisions going from right and left alternately towards the centre of the battalion line; 'platoon-fire' consisted of fire given by platoons grouped into three 'firings', all the platoons in each shooting together according to some prearranged sequence, although they did not stand contiguously in the line. For a more detailed description, see Addendum to this chapter.

than a time-consuming pretence; and despite the fact that the arms, accoutrements, and cobs of the Dragoons were none of them quite the equal of those of the heavy Horse, a caustic critic could observe quite accurately by 1728 that 'the modern Dragoons are better Horse than ever was in England before.'[3] The army was in consequence of this trend bereft of light horse until the Seven Years War—at which point fashion reversed itself, light horse became all the rage, and by the end of the century more than half of the old dragoon regiments had been converted from heavies and several new regiments of light dragoons had been raised.

In so far as mounted manoeuvres went, the cavalry in general had very early in the century reached a level of flexibility, speed, and sophistication which was only slightly improved upon before the *1796 Regulations*. Missile action as an offensive cavalry tactic had all but died out during the Spanish Succession war, shock tactics having supplanted it; it was only partially revived after the mid-century by the light dragoon regiments and troops who used it for skirmishing purposes when covering the manoeuvres of formed cavalry. Shock action —the charge—was very properly regarded as all-important; and the effective delivery of shock depended upon the speed and precision with which the squadrons carried on their man- oeuvres, deploying, forming, and then charging. Its achieve- ment depended not upon a great variety of movements but rather upon a high level of expertise and speed at a more limited number of essential manoeuvres; and the British cavalry throughout the century concentrated less on develop- ing than upon perfecting an already sound and effective body of drill. Like the foot, their success was to be varied.[4]

For the most part, companies or troops which found themselves

---

[3] P. Sumner (ed.), 'Hawley's Scheme for Light Dragoons', *JSAHR* 25 (1947), 63.

[4] Comparison of the cavalry drills described in Ch. III above, and of the drill illustrated in the mass of cavalry Inspection Returns (WO 27) from 1753 to 1800, points this conclusion clearly. It should perhaps be stressed that any significant de- velopment in cavalry tactics, since the troopers used *l'arme blanche* and not missile weapons, depended essentially upon their mobility factor; and the tacticians had already by the early eighteenth century approached the limitations of the horse as a weapon in action. Only with the appearance of a powerful new missile weapon to accompany the cavalry in action—horse artillery—would the effectiveness of cavalry again be modified significantly.

in the lower levels of concentration devoted the bulk of their time to practising those parts of the linear manoeuvres most likely to be required of them when in full regimental strength. Before the appearance late in the century of universal rules and techniques of movement derived from the increasingly 'scientific' schools of tacticians—pivot-files, for example, came in during the 1780s—the squadrons and grand-divisions performed their various marches, wheels by divisions, wheels upon the centre and the flanks of the line, and so forth, all the while concentrating upon the numerous technical devices necessary to perform linear manoeuvres speedily and without confusion. The customs of each regiment counted for much here, as in the speed and length of pace each employed; but it was difficult for dispersed companies and troops to act alike. Because of the 'dispersed condition of quarters, that allow but very little time to practice', a leading British tactician pointed out the very great difficulty of so much as manoeuvring several files in line; he noted that large numbers of foot found it difficult merely to advance in line over rugged ground 'without confusion'.[5] Hence the simplest aids to linear movement—lines of bearing, markers, dressing to the flanks and centre, timing—had all to be assiduously practised, were the troops or companies not to run afoul of one another when they joined in squadron or grand-division, or the squadrons or grand-divisions not to jostle when the full regiment formed. All ranks had to devote a great deal of time and attention to these routine mechanics of manoeuvre, just as they had to practise the manoeuvres themselves; and the greater the number of troops or companies concentrated, the greater the time given over to perfecting these all-important technical aids, without which they could not move as an articulated whole. At the same time, two or three grand-divisions of foot could be told off into platoons or other fire-units, and attempts could be made at orchestrated, synchronized platoon-fire or alternate fire. The cavalry, if numbers were sufficient, might tell off the squadron or squadrons into smaller manoeuvre-units, and practise passing through woods or closed country, charging alternately by divisions supporting one another, extending the front of the line by reducing the depth of rank and forming on the flanks, or skirmishing if they

[5] Campbell Dalrymple, op. cit. 36.

were a light regiment. This was all very prosaic, but common-place; it was the essential stuff of advanced training in peace-time, the most widely practised part of linear drill, and any practice less than perfect would be a threat to the security of the line of battle.

There were of course more useful and sometimes more realistic ways of practising the firings and manoeuvres than what was afforded by parade-ground drilling. Where the num-bers concentrated were sufficient for the purpose (and where waste-land was available, or at least where the local inhabitants were unlikely to complain, both of which were factors seriously affecting the army's advanced training), day 'excursions' on which the men were 'marched some miles into the country . . . and in their progress manoeuvred according to the different situations of the ground', were laid on.[6] Good march discipline was to be maintained on these occasions, 'without the aid of music', and the column 'taken intentionally' across 'Hedges, Ditches, Rivulets, etc'.[7] If the concentrated troops or com-panies were sufficiently adept at their linear manoeuvres, field days were laid on; and 'sham fights' were held on these occa-sions. Field days had the 'advantage to officers, in reducing to reality, in some measure, what they have been practising'. Realism was to be the keynote on field days: squib cartridges were issued, packs were donned, and detachments were sent out to 'form Ambuscades; to take possession of Church-yards, Bridges, Defiles and Heights; that the methods may be shewn, for evading the first, and forcing the others'. Entrenchments and field works were thrown up, attacked, and defended, 'when ground can be obtained'.[8]

The flank companies' specialist training was best conducted, too, in the higher levels of concentration. The grenadiers throughout our period acted either as a tactical reserve to the battalion or formed the head of the battalion column, when

[6] Bennett Cuthbertson, op. cit. 205.

[7] William Dalrymple, op. cit. 60–3 and 205.

[8] Campbell Dalrymple, op. cit. 205–8; and Bennett Cuthbertson, op. cit. 206–7. John Williamson, op. cit. 180, stressed the importance of field days carried on in varying terrain—'varied to every situation in which they may find themselves on real service'. He pointed out that several of the army's customary and regulation man-oeuvres were seldom attempted on regular drill-fields, since they were 'useful only in particular circumstances of ground and position'.

manoeuvring; and when the battalion line was giving fire the grenadier company split into two platoons, one of which stood on each flank until 1771-2, when the left flank position was taken over by the light company. The usual role of the light company during manoeuvres was to skirmish in extended order upon the battalion's flanks or front—a role which the grenadiers practised in most regiments too, from the mid-1760s. Although individual skills such as marksmanship, 'running and leaping', firing independently from cover, and so forth were encouraged, the essential duty of the light infantrymen was to cover the manoeuvres of the hatmen; and in order to practise this most effectively they, like the grenadiers, had to be concentrated with at least a couple of the regiment's grand-divisions.

Field days and excursions into the countryside were always useful, the more so because they were infrequent; but outside the annual concentrations in the review quarters (of which more anon) it was the slow, steady practice of the linear manoeuvres and firings that characterized most of the advanced training activities carried on in the regiments, as was proper. Dundas made the point when he stressed that no matter how large or small the unit might be, marching and manoeuvring should be given pride of place, and were always to be conducted 'on a supposition of lining with other troops, already upon their flanks.'[9] Constantly dispersed, or training only in small bodies, the regiments were apt to forget that their main role in battle would be to conform to the movements of the long solid lines and brigades of which they would form but a part. But since opportunities for this practice came both infrequently and irregularly, depending upon concentration, means had to be found to help maintain some degree of uniformity within the regiment. The officers with the dispersed troops and companies, armed with their copies of the current regulations, could keep their men exercised according to a uniform system: the regulations were of course easily accessible, they were an excellent guide among dispersed units, and all ranks would need to be well acquainted with them when the reviewing season came round. But beyond this there was in fact little that could be done actively to ensure uniformity within a regiment, the diligence of the company officers and a close

[9] David Dundas, op. cit. 59.

adherence by all to the regulation drillbooks being in themselves important but not sufficient. Rotation within the regiment in order to advance the training of outlying detachments by joining them together at the regiment's main quarter was hardly ever allowed by authority; the most frequent—and still, admittedly, only occasional—sort of inter-regimental rotation was the movement of cavalry troops between their quarters, to the end that the whole corps might have the opportunity of using the main enclosed riding house in the vicinity. But save for isolated instances, it was for purposes of relief, not rotation, that exchanges between quarters in a regiment occurred. Thus a regiment serving in a hard-duty area like Cornwall and south Devon, where the duties imposed on outlying detachments were apt to be onerous, was occasionally permitted to relieve such detachments with others found by the body of the regiment lying somewhat more comfortably at Exeter or Plymouth. But only in exceptional circumstances could reliefs be turned to advantage, used for 'equallizing the Discipline' within a regiment. In corps with dedicated officers the field officers, the adjutant, and the senior NCOs would occasionally tour the outlying units in order to 'equalize'. In the 5th Dragoons in Ireland during the later 1730s and '40s, for example the commanding officer and the adjutant toured the regiment's several quarters every three months to see 'that the Men perform their Exercise well, uniformly, and with the same Time between Motions'. Well in advance of the spring reviewing season the Riding Master and his assistants were to go around the quarters, 'employing at least a Fortnight in each Quarter to instruct both Men and Horse'.[10] Good NCOs were normally employed at equalizing a regiment's timing at the manual and platoon, and at marching. In the spring of 1765, for example, all the corporals with The Blues were assembled to learn and perfect their exercise together, 'when they are to return and join the respective Troops to which they belong in order to fully instruct the men.'[11] Even among the Foot Guards, always concentrated in London and Westminster, 'the Drill Serjeants and Corporals of the three Regiments [were] to be exercised together in the Spring . . . that

---

[10] Molesworth, op. cit. 150–60.   [11] WO 5/53, p. 238.

each Regiment may have the same time.'[12] Good NCOs from well-trained regiments were sometimes 'loaned' to others to achieve the same ends.[13] Later in the century, music was used to help maintain drill regularity among the dispersed units;[14] and the attempts made from the later 1770s onwards to regularize length and speed of pace (as in the regulations of 1778 and 1786) likewise contributed to this end.

In consequence, whenever a few companies or troops found themselves together in concentration sufficient to form squadrons or grand-divisions, they had first to devote time to 'equalizing' the mechanics and timing of their arms exercises, evolutions, and movements. Equalizing took time. The experience of three corps—the 11th, 30th, and 32nd of Foot—which came into Dublin in the spring of 1777 to form the new garrison illustrates the problem, and was typical. The companies of each of these corps had been 'widely distributed into County Cantonments, where they were exercised by their respective officers', as was usual; and in that situation it had, as ever, been quite impossible to prevent the dispersed companies from becoming 'accustomed to Time and Motions differing from each other'. Consequently none of these corps, as their commanding officers admitted, was prepared to be seen by the Dublin reviewing officer for at least four to six weeks—the amount of time necessary to equalize 'Time and Motions'.[15]

Since time was always at a premium, and since so much had to be given over to equalizing the drill of troops or companies only recently dispersed and shortly to be dispersed once again, the result was that most of the advanced training conducted in the concentrations of grand-divisions or squadrons tended to be limited in the variety of manoeuvres attempted and to be

[12] See the Guards' Standing Orders of late 1754 in Anon., *Camp Discipline & Kane* (1757), 81.

[13] Thus in Sept. 1767 the 17th Foot came home to England from foreign service in a 'very Indifferent Plight'; and the colonel of the corps 'Expressed his Wishes, that he might have a Serjeant and Corporal with his Regiment, for some Months, from a well Disciplined Corps.' The Adjutant-General wrote to the colonel of the 25th Foot, then in Scotland, asking the 'Favour' of sending down these NCOs to the 17th's quarters in Somerset. WO 3/1, p. 79.

[14] As early as 1761 Campbell Dalrymple wrote (op. cit. 95) that 'The companies before they Joyn, having tunes beaten adapted to the [various speeds of the] march given them to practice by, will obviate great part of the difficulty, when the battalion joins.'

[15] WO 27/37, 11th Foot.

unimaginative or even unrealistic. Attempting first of all to equalize in order that the several units might function smoothly together in line, and then endeavouring to perfect themselves at the regulation manoeuvres and firings, only where time permitted did regiments have opportunity to essay many movements drawn from the larger store of customary manoeuvres— let alone to attempt field days. This was the common lot of the majority of the regiments composing the peacetime army—that is, of the corps stationed everywhere but in the Mediterranean garrisons, in London, and in the Irish garrison-towns. There, in the fortifications and the garrison barracks, the corps were concentrated for as long as they remained on the station— several years at Minorca or Gibraltar, on annual rotation in Ireland, and permanently in London; but, as we observed earlier, it should not be imagined that the situation of the corps in these places (save for the Guards and the Dublin regiments) was much superior to that of their sister-units elsewhere. There were innumerable duties—guards of all sorts, policing, rounds, construction, and (most importantly, in the forts) practice at the specialist attack and defence of the works—and it was to pursue these duties that regiments were principally stationed at these places.[16] It was therefore the army's almost invariable custom, in garrison, to devote two days per week to linear drill; and as often as not the corps concerned merely 'tossed their firelocks'.[17] The regiments quartered in the Irish garrison-towns always kept detachments operating at some distance afield, as we have seen. These factors restricted training-time in the big places, although the problem of equalizing could at least be avoided in this sort of concentration. For the Foot Guards and the Dublin regiments the great utility of St. James's, and especially of Hyde Park and Phoenix Park, was of the greatest importance. The Foot Guards every summer set up

[16] Garrison duty, with its myriad variety of activities, is best described in Bland's *Treatise of Military Discipline*, 148–206. The defence of the works in places like Gibraltar, the Minorcan forts, the Highland forts, and the rest, was the major concern of the training of the corps composing those garrisons; and save for those occasions on which they practised their field drill, the duty of the garrisons does not concern us here since it is properly part of the larger science of siegecraft and fortification.

[17] Most of the drillbooks remark on this timetable: e.g. Molesworth, op. cit. 162; Bennett Cuthbertson, op. cit. 203; and that most detailed record of the activities in any garrison—WO 36/1—covering events in Boston from June 1773 to Jan. 1776.

an encampment in Hyde Park, at which major manoeuvres were conducted; and the Dublin corps often marched out to train on the vast tracts and varied terrain of Phoenix Park.[18] Mock actions—the constantly refought 'battles' of Hyde Park and Phoenix Park—were held by the assembled battalions during the shakedown days preceding the garrison reviews of May and June. It was for these reasons that Dublin was chosen as the testing-ground, during the years 1788–91, for the drill that became the *1792 Regulations*; and Dublin was also singular in that the line foot, horse, and the artillery trained together there on occasion—the only place in the Empire where some modest attempt at inter-arm co-operation was possible in peacetime.

An additional factor, peculiar to the cavalry, needs to be considered here, for it had a significant impact on the advanced training of the entire mounted arm. For upwards of four months per year the troop-horses of the cavalry were nowhere near their regiments, but were 'out at grass'. Just as a racehorse, after too much hard running, can go track-sour and so must be rested out at pasture, so too the cavalry horses, after long autumn and winter months of training (and of a diet made up of too much dry forage), had to be turned out to grass every spring. Out to pasture, resting, grazing on green spring and summer grass (with its rich vitamin A and D content), shoes removed to ease their hooves and to permit them free growth, the horses needed the grass months as an essential tonic.[19] They were also a severe limitation on the training time of the whole of the mounted arm. Although practised troopers would forget few of their riding skills (and the horses even less of their business), still the complicated and difficult manoeuvres of the cavalry would have to be studied long and drilled intensively with the coming on of autumn, and the taking up of the horses from grass. The horses would come back fat and lazy; and a

---

[18] There were permanent butts and field works in Phoenix Park—not to mention resident units of the Royal Artillery with field- and battalion-guns—adding considerably to the variety of the training there (see BL Map, no. 11815.[6].)

[19] 'Grass Guard' detachments from each troop took the horses to pasture and stayed with them all summer. Their duties included not only the obvious riding herd; they must also have a careful eye to the grazing, lest too much lush green grass lead to foundering. It will be appreciated that, in addition, much money was saved on fodder, a scarce and hence an expensive commodity by springtime.

few weeks would be required to get them back up to the mark. The training year for the cavalry, then, was cyclical: an average of about seven or eight months of mounted training, followed by four or five months of the foot evolutions and firings. The long annual separation of the troopers from their mounts must lead one to conclude that the cavalry regiments of the British Army were by their very nature less thoroughly trained than the regiments of foot; and this is a conclusion particularly true of the army in Ireland because of the quartering system practised there. Splendid, well accoutred, imposing, the cavalry of the eighteenth century was both a very powerful and a very frail weapon.[20]

We might illustrate the grass-orders cycle by following all the cavalry in Britain during a typical peacetime year. In 1773 there were in Britain (exclusive of the Household troops) fourteen regiments of cavalry. Twelve of these corps were ordered to turn their horses out to grass early in the month of May, under the care of their 'Grass Guard' detachments; and the horses remained separated from their regiments until mid-September, when they were taken up from grass and returned to their troops. In 1773, then, the horses were gone from the British cavalry for all of four months.[21]

If in the normal peacetime condition of the army the basic training of small numbers could be carried on with little difficulty, and their initial training accomplished relatively quickly, it took a great deal longer to carry out sufficient ad-

---

[20] Lt.-Col. Campbell Dalrymple noted this brittleness, in his *A Military Essay. Containing Reflections on the Raising, Arming, Cloathing, and Discipline of the British Infantry and Cavalry* . . . (1761), 254.

[21] WO 5/58, pp. 188–92, 217, 244–5, 277, 281. The horses of The Blues and of the 15th Light Dragoons were out for a shorter period.

A similar grass-cycle was followed in Ireland. In the 5th Dragoons in that kingdom during the 1730s and '40s, for example, it was 'the constant standing Order, to turn out the Horses to Grass, on every first Day of *May*, and take them in every first of October. But, as many particular Cases may offer', continued the Standing Orders, 'all these are left to the Judgment and Discretion of the Commanding Officers. (For Instance). All Recruit-Horses for the first Year, shall be taken in on or before the first of *September* [i.e. for training].

If the latter Season prove unusually fair; Pasture good and plentiful; Hay indifferent, and scarce: In this Case, the time of keeping out the Horses may be a little enlarged, till the Weather change, or Pasture fall off.

. . . When the Horses are turn'd out, all their Shoes shall be knock'd off; the thin, brittle Edge of the Hoof taken away, and the Hoofs rasp'd thick and round.' Richard, Viscount Molesworth, op. cit. 155–6.

vanced training to render a full regiment 'fit for service', the rating customarily given by reviewing officers to corps that they judged sufficiently well trained to take the field. In the normal routine of the British service, 'fit for service' was a rating that regiments were frequently unable to retain over several years running. Among the pitfalls awaiting corps the most obvious, of course, were the usual wastage and the occasional disasters of active campaigning. Equally harmful could be long service abroad, heavy drafting, the simple ageing of one corps or the infusion of a great many recruits into another, too speedy expansion from cadre strength, or service on board the fleet. We have already seen that in peacetime the regiments, both horse and foot, were invariably below their establishment strengths; and we have seen too that the foot had to recruit at a rate of 1.5 per cent and the horse at a rate of ·9 per cent of their actual strength, *every month*, merely in order to keep up to these under-strength numbers. When corps fell behind in their recruiting, as many always did, they had to cast about for even greater numbers of recruits than normally required; and when they found them, and put them in the ranks after a few weeks of basic training, the performance of the regiment and its efficiency rating must inevitably fall off. The army's manpower problem, as we have seen, was like a revolving door: recruits came in one way as trained men exited another, for whatever reasons among the many likely to operate; and the faster the door revolved in individual corps, so their efficiency declined. This peacetime attrition, which our figures show to have been extremely heavy in the British Army, meant that advanced training took a long time to accomplish; experience of advanced training had to be 'amassed', since progress was slow and back-sliding easy where the personnel was fluid. Most of the old corps had, periodically, to rebuild themselves; and (as with new-raised corps preparing themselves to take their place in the line) this could only be done in settled conditions, with plenty of time available to train in concentration.

There was a general consensus among the senior officers of the army as to the length of time it took to prepare a regiment 'fit for service', once it had fallen behind, just as 'fit' regiments had to train without ceasing. Typical was the judgement made on the 45th Foot which, when seen at Cork in July 1767, had been home less than a year after twenty years' service in North America. Much under strength and full of recruits, the 45th was reported 'not yet disciplin'd, not well appointed, and unfit for service'. A year later, in July 1768, the regiment was seen at Dublin where, up to strength now but with half its men still recruits, it was again reported unfit for service. In May 1769 the 45th was found 'much improved since the last Review'; and with a little care, reported the reviewing officer, it would be 'a Compleat fine Regiment against the Next Year'—which indeed it proved to be. It had taken more than three years of settled conditions in quiet Irish quarters to rebuild the corps, and to make it fit again for active service.[22] Similarly, in April 1773 the 32nd Foot came home to England after nine years' service in the West Indies; and when seen in June at Devizes it was described as 'Totally Unfit for Service'. After more than two years of easy duty in English quarters the 32nd was reviewed at Guildford; and though reported 'much improved . . . and very forward in their discipline' they were judged still to require 'a few Years to be a fine regiment'. By 1776 the 32nd was reported in excellent shape, having taken three years to train.[23] In May 1784 the 63rd Foot was seen at Bury St. Edmunds, home from the American campaigns of 1775–83; the reviewer described 'the very shattered condition' of the corps, which he attributed to 'their having suffered so much, & having been so long, & so much dispersed in America'. A year later the reviewing officer who saw the regiment at Edinburgh reported 'much attention paid to it', and concluded that 'in two years [it] will be a very fine Corps'. Seen at Glasgow in June 1786, the 63rd was reported fit for service.[24] The regiment had taken over two years to retrain. Again, when the reviewing officers saw the 26th and 48th of Foot in 1781—the first drafted a year since and full of recruits, and the second half composed of recruits and in poor condition from foreign service—it was reported that in the case of the 26th it would be 'at least, two years, before it can be returned, fitt for Service', and of the 48th

[22] WO 27/11, 14, 17.
[23] WO 5/58, p. 148–5/59, p. 213, *passim*; and WO 27/27, 34, 35, and 37.
[24] WO 27/51, 54, 56.

that it too would be fit 'in two Years—but scarcely sooner'.[25] In the normal routine of service, therefore, it required from two to three years for a corps to amass sufficient concentration-time during which it might prepare itself fit to take the field.[26] New-raised regiments too generally took two to three years to complete their training, even with the advantage of concentration and camps of exercise.[27] Time spent in the garrison-towns helped only marginally since, as we noted above, the special duties of these places reduced the opportunities for training to two days per week, despite high levels of concentration. The case of the 45th Foot—one of those corps noted above which took three years to render itself fit for service—is typical again. Reported unfit in 1768 and unfit still in 1769, the regiment had spent the intervening year as part of the Dublin garrison. The 49th came home to Ireland after the Seven Years War; and having spent more than fifteen years in the West Indies its condition was deplorable. The 49th too passed the year 1768–9 as part of the Dublin garrison; and although 'vastly improved' during that time the regiment had been unfit for service upon arrival at Dublin and required another year of training still when it left.[28] Likewise the 9th Foot, which came home to Ireland in poor condition after six years' service in the Floridas, served a year with the Dublin garrison, 1772–3; and although 'much Mended' by the experience, it too was unfit for service upon arrival and still unfit on departure.[29] Whether or not a corps spent its time in garrison' or in 'county cantonments', therefore, the two-to-three-year period required for sufficient advanced training applied; the key, as ever, was concentration which provided full opportunity for training.

Thus there was considerable variety both in the concentration-time allowed the regiments and in the levels of advanced training pursued. For virtually the whole army there was, however, an annual and regular opportunity to train little disturbed in full regimental concentration; and for the great majority of the corps this was, in peacetime, the most significant part of

[25] WO 27/47.
[26] There are innumerable examples of the two-to-three-year training period in WO 27.
[27] See, e.g., the new 77th and 81st of Foot, in WO 27/41 and 44.
[28] WO 27/14 and 17.
[29] WO 27/26 and 29.

their advanced-training programmes, colouring the material practised and setting both a goal and a standard against which to measure expertise. All aspects of the army's advanced training were intimately bound together in the reviewing system, to which we refer here; and it is by following the reviewing system in detail that peacetime advanced training can best be described and its efficacy best judged.

Regular reviewing was instituted primarily, of course, in order to ensure that the interior economy and drill of the regiments was kept up and carried on in accordance with the regulations. It was by constant and regular inspection that the central authority was able to oblige the regiments to practise their drill in accordance with its wishes, thus ensuring uniformity; and in this it was largely successful. But reviewing had an important secondary significance in an army subject to such wide peacetime dispersal, since the reviews themselves provided the occasion for carrying on advanced regimental training regularly and intensively.

The system of regular inspection of regiments was introduced by George I in 1716 and made annual from about 1720.[30] As we have seen (pp. 155–6 above), it was the Adjutant-General who was responsible for supervising the system and for co-ordinating the movements and timetables of the regiments and general officers involved; while the copious reports submitted by the reviewing officers were written up and kept at his office for ready reference by the King, by the C.-in-C., and by himself. The system always followed the same pattern. Late in the winter certain general officers were appointed to the London, Dublin, and Edinburgh staffs as reviewing officers for the coming season (the army was reviewed during the spring and early summer, once it had time to shake off the effects of winter rust and before the horses were turned out to grass); and both they and the regiments that each would see were warned of the

---

[30] Fortescue, ii. 51 n. 1; and C. Knight, op. cit. ii, Pt 1, 105. 'Reviewing Orders', i.e. orders to certain general officers to see and report on specified units, appear annually from the early 1720s (WO 26/16). The directions given in these early reviewing orders changed hardly at all later in the century (cf. WO 26/22, pp. 363–7, for 1755 orders, and 26/32, 247–51, for the 1784 orders). Most regrettably, no Inspection Returns (WO 27)—the reports submitted by the reviewing officers—survive before 1753. In SP 41 occasional short reports are met with on regiments before 1753, but they are too laconic to be of much use.

times and places of the impending reviews. The generals so appointed received, soon after, their formal 'reviewing orders'[31] —in effect Royal Warrants authorizing them to perform the duty—which they set about when the particular units they were to see had concentrated and taken up their 'review quarters'. A typical tour of inspection was that made across the south of England in the spring of 1787, by Maj.-Gen. Sir George Osborn; he saw the following units, on the dates and at the places indicated:[32]

> 2 May—one Independent Company of Invalids, at Tilbury Fort
> 3 May—a body of recruits destined for battalions overseas, at Chatham Barracks
> 4 May—17th Foot, at Chatham
> 5 May—three Independent Companies of Invalids, at Sheerness
> 7 May—55th Foot, at Deal
> 12 May—43rd Foot, at Windsor
> 15 May—41st Foot, at Portsmouth
> 16 May—44th Foot, at Hilsea Barracks
> 19 May—33rd Foot, at Taunton
> 22 May—38th Foot, within Plymouth Lines
> 23 May—six Independent Companies of Invalids, at Plymouth
> 24 May—8th Foot, at Plymouth
> 26 May—one Independent Company of Invalids, at Pendennis Castle.

This was but one reviewing officer's tour; normally there were four or five such officers conducting reviews simultaneously in different parts of Britain, and three or four more doing so in Ireland. In 1774, for example, the fourteen regular regiments of cavalry and seventeen regiments of marching foot, in Great Britain, were seen by the five reviewing officers appointed for that season (Lts.-Gen. Sir Adolphus Oughton and the Duke of Argyll in Scotland, and Majs.-Gen. George Preston, William Evelyn, and William Howe in England), while in Ireland the twelve regular cavalry regiments and twenty-nine regiments of

---

[31] These appear annually in WO 3 or WO 26. See, e.g., the series for 1734 in WO 26/18, pp. 143–7, and for 1791 in WO 3/9, pp. 198–207.

[32] WO 27/59, *passim.*

foot serving there were reviewed by Lt.-Gen. Lord Blayney, and Majs.-Gen. the Earl of Drogheda and James Gisborne.[33]

Limited inspections of those few corps in the Americas were carried out from early on too, but at irregular intervals.[34] The same was almost certainly being done at Gibraltar and Minorca, though no early reports survive. Local commanders, not reviewing officers from Britain or Ireland, handled these distant duties. By 1768, however, there were so many regiments serving abroad—the Adjutant-General calculated that in 1769 13,551 rank and file were serving in the battalions overseas, 1,410 more than all those to be found in the marching battalions in Britain and Ireland[35]—that a Royal Warrant had to be issued, laying down guidelines for the full reviews henceforth to be carried out annually on all foreign stations. As in the British Isles, it was felt that regular reviews would 'greatly tend to the Preservation of good Order and Discipline.'[36] Full review reports were coming in from overseas stations by 1770, and continued to do so thereafter.[37]

At review time a regiment's outlying troops or companies were called in for the period of pre-review practice, usually being marched to a group of villages close by one another: in quarters like these, daily concentrations for practice were possible, and reviewing quarters of this sort were usually chosen because a favourite reviewing-ground was close by. The dozens of villages about London served this purpose year after year, with Blackheath, Hounslow Heath, Kew Green, Wimbledon Common, and Hyde Park close at hand. In October 1728, for example, the 3rd Dragoons come down from Yorkshire were quartered with two troops at Hampstead, Highgate, and Kentish Town, a third at Acton and Ealing, another at Hammersmith and Turnham Green, a fifth at Fulham and

[33] WO 27/30, *passim*.

[34] E.g. in Feb. 1729 the Earl of Londonderry, 'Our Captain Genl., and Governor in Chief in & over our Leeward Caribbee Islands', was ordered to inspect and report on Lucas' 38th of Foot, stationed there. WO 26/17, pp. 266–7.

[35] WO 3/1, p. 129.

[36] The warrant and governing instructions were sent in Jan. 1768 to the com̄anders of the forces at Gibraltar, Minorca, Jamaica, Antiqua, Grenada, the Senegal, and in North America. The warrant is in WO 26/27, pp. 474–6, and the Secretary at War's covering letter is in WO 4/83, p. 101. This was all largely the work of Harvey, the Adjutant-General, as is clear from WO 3/1, pp. 129–36.

[37] C. E. Carter (ed.), op. cit. ii. 541–2, 556.

Chelsea, a sixth at Islington and Clerkenwell, another at Kensington, another at Knightsbridge and Hyde Park Corner, and the last at 'St. Giles's Holbourn without the bars & Greys Inn Lane'; Hyde Park was convenient to all of these quarters and, after two weeks of intensive training, the regiment was reviewed there by George II.[38] In June 1728 both Kirke's 2nd and Harrison's 15th of Foot, similarly, were in reviewing quarters near London, the former distributed between Charlton, Blackheath, Greenwich, Woolwich, and adjacent villages, and the latter lying at Eltham, Lewisham, Peckham, Deptford, and Camberwell. Kirke's, long doing the duty about Bristol, had marched in from Wiltshire quarters about Salisbury; and Harrison's came in from quarters about Winchester and Southampton, after a tiring spell in the Cornwall and south-Devon duty area. Both occupied their reviewing quarters for two weeks before being seen on Blackheath by the King. The reviews over, Kirke's was sent upon the Kent coast duty while Harrison's marched north for Chester and environs.[39] The pattern was typical, and did not change for the rest of the century.

Of all the regiments of foot known definitely to have been reviewed in England during the period 1726–9, all but one had been in various states of dispersal for periods ranging close on a year before their review concentrations. The average number of days during which these corps were fully concentrated, at review time, was eleven; the longest period during which any of these foot regiments remained concentrated in review quarters was for nineteen days. Among the cavalry regiments known to have been reviewed during the same period, all had been dispersed for upwards of a year before the review concentrations. Their average concentration time in review quarters was thirteen days; the longest concentration was for twenty-two days. During the five later periods isolated for statistical purposes (Appendix A), there was a slight increase in the average concentration-time of regiments, in review quarters: a working average during the 1720s, '30s, and '50s would be a concentration of two weeks, and of three weeks during the 1760s, '70s, and '80s.

How much time a corps might annually devote to training,

38 WO 5/28, pp. 175–9, 195, 201.   39 WO 5/28, pp. 128–33, 144–6, 150.

when in the lower levels of concentration, and how much time might be given over to training in the pre-review concentrations was to some extent determined by the simple question of the availability of suitable exercising ground. Just as the great fields upon which the wartime encampments were formed had to be hired from private owners, so too had the ground upon which a few companies or troops, or the regiment itself, might wish to stage a field day or otherwise practise its drill, or to appear before a reviewing officer. Wasteland suitable for the purpose seems to have been scarce in England and Ireland (and in Scotland too, by the century's end), a fact which contributed to the popularity of the parks and heaths around London; and save for a few places like the grounds within the defences at Chatham and Plymouth there was literally nowhere else for a regiment to train without first finding the rent-money, or perhaps a patriotic landowner. It being 'not usual . . . to allow a field of Exercise to be hired at the public expence for more than two or three months' per annum, the War Office was obliged for budgetary reasons to allow each regiment no more than 6 to 8 guineas p.a. for the purpose.[40] Nor was it easy to get even this sum from the War Office, as continual complaints show. In June 1784, for example, upon a request for funds from the 11th Dragoons (then headquartered at Canterbury, with detachments upon the Kent coast duty), the Secretary at War replied that the 'strictest œconomy must be observed' in such matters, and would not provide a penny: after all, 'from the number of Detachments ordered upon the Coast, I shall conceive, you can have no great number of Men at head Quarters, & much fewer Horses at this Season'; and furthermore 'common Grounds are the proper places to be made use of Regimental Exercises; & such I make no doubt there must be in the neighbourhood of Canterbury.'[41] In December of the same year the Secretary informed the colonel of the 16th Light Dragoons that ground was to be rented only 'upon extra-ordinary occasions, & when there is no waste Ground that can be used . . . [and] application is to be made at this Office

---

[40] WO 4/135, pp. 158, 227, 299, and 299–484, *passim*. See also WO 4/137, pp. 345–495, *passim*.
[41] WO 4/126, pp. 23–4.

before any expence is incurred'.[42] In May 1792 Lt.-Gen. Lord Adam Gordon wrote to the Adjutant-General, asking him to urge the War Office to grant the same sums for the hire of ground in North Britain as were normally provided for corps in England. In reply, the War Office claimed that it was 'unusual to extend that indulgence to the troops in N° B^n, upon the Supposition, that Ground could be found without being obliged to pay for it.'[43] What sort of ground might be had for this pittance, even when forthcoming, was a subject of constant complaint, and there was much sharp practice by the good citizenry. In 1773 Lt.-Gen. Richard Pierson, who was that season a reviewing officer in Ireland, reported that 'the difficulty of getting proper Ground for the Regiments to Practice, and to be Reviewed on is almost a Universal Complaint in every Quarter of Ireland, and they are generally made to Pay Extravagant Sums for what but ill Answers the Purpose.'[44] In 1786 the 1st Dragoon Guards were reviewed on a 'particularly bad' ground near York—'tho the best the Commanding Officer could procure, having offered a great deal of Money for a convenient Spot without Effect, & was obliged to pay a Great Labour for draining a Moor near the Town, to make it possible for the Regiment to appear.'[45] Although the War Office thought that good ground was easily had in Scotland, nevertheless in May 1770 the 3rd Dragoons had to appear on Musselburgh Links and the 22nd Foot on the links near Leith; again in 1773 we find reviews being held on Musselburgh links, although the wind and sand of the Forth can scarcely have eased training.[46]

Not even traditional grounds long used by the army could be counted upon. When in May 1787 Maj.-Gen. Sir George Osborn saw the 17th Foot, 'they complain'd of want of Ground for Exercising at Chatham—the Old Field of Exercise being

[42] WO 4/127, pp. 511–12.

[43] WO 3/10, pp. 166–7. The militia too suffered from want of this 'indulgence'. In 1759, part of the Warwickshires at Romsey had to use 'first a close belonging to the mayor, then a meadow, then a churchyard. In 1793 the Secretary at War agreed to meet a charge of a guinea incurred by the East Norfolks in hiring a ground at Colchester, and 16s. 6d. for the like at Chelmsford. But he complained of their failure to get his permission first.' J. R. Western, op. cit. 410.

[44] WO 27/29, 57th Foot.

[45] WO 27/56.

[46] WO 27/27; and the *Edinburgh Review* (26 May 1770).

taken from the Troops by the Board of Ordnance.' Osborn commented that 'the Ground with[in] the Lines on which they were Review'd appear'd insufficient for the Drills of the Recruits of the different Regiments, without interfering materially with the necessary exercise of a Battalion Generally Quarter'd at Chatham.'[47]

This contributed not a little to the inefficiency of corps, and was of a piece with the penny-wise cheeseparing on the annual issues of ball ammunition; for the tiniest of savings the training activities were hampered even on those few occasions when major efforts might have been made.

The drill practised at a review invariably followed an established sequence, and this was as true for reviews held abroad as it was for those held in the British Isles. First the regiments of foot (and of cavalry, dismounted) formed battalion line and proceeded to go through the long, slow manual exercise. This was followed by the simple evolutions, and next came the firings by platoons and other divisions standing, advancing, and retreating—the dismounted troopers, needless to say, being much less expert at this than the foot whose proper province it was.[48] Finally, the regiment would proceed to a display of the more commonplace of its complicated repertoire of maneuvres, most of which were chosen from the then current regulations supplemented with a few from the customary practice of the army. In order to carry off these performances it is clear that a great deal of hard practice had to go on during those limited periods when a few grand-divisions or squadrons had found themselves in concentration in the months preceding the reviews; and even more intensive drilling had to be gone through during the weeks in review quarters. It is therefore understandable that some parts of the performances put on by the regiments were often less than perfect, just as the generally good overall proficiency displayed at the reviews reflects extremely well on the industry of the officers and NCOs. It is clear that the corps most often rehearsed beforehand the order

---

[47] WO 27/59.
[48] When the 6th Dragoons were seen at Windsor in May, 1755, they were reported in fine order and fit for service; but when they dismounted and fired in three ranks they succeeded only in churning up the ground close in front of them, since 'the Muzzles of the Firelocks were pointed too low'. WO 27/3.

in which they would show their various manoeuvres, which (though still valuable training) cannot have contributed to tactical realism; the general officers usually preferred the resulting choreographed precision to spontaneity, in any case. Still, most of the firings and manoeuvres shown were those it was generally supposed would be most frequently required on the battlefield, so that review performances were always thought of as simulations, not as parades.

There was always scope for modification in the overall pattern or sequence of a review, should either the regiment's training permit it or the reviewing officer so desire it.[49] The reviewing officer was usually provided by the regiment with a programme before the review; to this he would occasionally suggest alterations, and from it his staff wrote up the returns which were made into fair copies by the Adjutant-General's clerks. This process made it possible for the leading parties concerned to inject more realism into the pre-review training, and into the review itself, than would have been the case had the more straightforward display of the main elements of the drill regulations always been followed. Regiments quite often, in fact, added one or two special tactical simulations to the accustomed sequence of manoeuvres. Thus the 12th Foot, seen at Chatham in 1768, in addition to its regular manoeuvres 'charged to penetrate through the Ennemy's supposed Line', while the grenadiers 'two deep, advanced briskly on the Flanks, & supported [with] a constant fire'. In the review at Newcastle in 1777 the 2nd Foot, advancing in line, detached its light company and two left-flank battalion-companies 'to attack the Enemy in a Wood' and 'Cover the Flank of the Battalion' in a skirmish line. In June 1777 at Clonmell the 8th Light Dragoons skirmished with 'a detached party of the Infantry which had been concealed . . . to cut off their Retreat.' At Gibraltar in March 1777 the 58th Foot, 'supposed to be attacked in a disadvantageous situation', retired to better ground; from its new position the corps was able to detach some subdivisions 'who march under cover and attack the enemy's left flank', thereby prevailing.[50]

[49] See Cumb. Pprs, Box 44, no. 99, pp. 11–12, for an example at the Limerick reviews of 1750.
[50] WO 27/12, 36, 37, and 39.

Reviewing officers, having seen the regiments go through their drill, occasionally ordered them to make speedy dispositions against some hypothetical tactical situation. In August 1771 at Plymouth, for example, Maj.-Gen. James Murray ordered the 6th Foot to assault a stone wall defended by the light infantry.

This was done without hesitation by the Major [Murray reported], By forming three Masked Columns, One upon each flank, and One in the Centre; The Line consisted of a Single rank, By which the Extent of the front was preserved. The Line kept up, in Marching on, a brisk fire upon the Wall or entrenchment to be attack'd, when within a proper distance, The Columns burst out, Attack'd, & carry'd the Entrenchment.

The following day Murray saw the 20th Foot at the same place, and he ordered them to defend a large stone wall; the previous day's admirable attack by the 6th was used as a basis in the precautions taken by the 20th, who consequently 'gained an easy Victory, to the Total destruction of the assaillants'. Later the 20th was ordered to assault the Plymouth barrack square: 'This was done by Investing the Square, Busting open the Gate by a Supposed Petard, entering in Column, & immediately directing the fire of the Column to the Windows, and other Defences within the Square, Which the Defenders would naturally avail themselves of'—all, obviously, excellent practice.[51]

Although they did so infrequently, single regiments sometimes staged very elaborate tactical simulations on their own initiative. That these displays were infrequent reflects, of course, the lack of expertise in the long-dispersed regiments and also the simple difficulty of obtaining near their quarters a piece of ground sufficient for the purpose, as much as it does any lack of imagination on the part of senior officers. However little justice it does to the excellent state of advanced training that some corps were able to attain and display on these occasions, some account of these simulations must be given. In May 1773 at Plymouth the 33rd Foot, divided into two opposing forces, fought a realistic manoeuvre action over the possession of an eminence; and they went through a more involved simulation for the possession of a hill at their 1774

[51] WO 27/21. These manoeuvres can conveniently be followed on BL Map 11.86.

review, this time including the effects of cannon-fire.[52] In 1790 at Portsmouth the 12th Foot, advancing in line, sent forward

the Light Infantry supported by the Grenadiers, and these parties meeting the Enemy began an irregular Fire, [at which the battalion-companies advanced] from the Right of Grand Divisions by Files, as soon as the heads of Columns have advanced a little beyond the Grenadiers and Light Infantry, the Battln. will Form by Files running up, and dressing by the Right, will immediately begin the File firing; the Grenadiers and Light Infantry will extend to Right and Left, and attack the Enemy in Flank . . .[53]

At their 1788 Edinburgh review the 7th Foot fought a mock battle centring upon the possession of a fortified house; and the following year at its review the 23rd Foot, more ambitiously, attempted to 'carry Windsor Castle by a Coup de Main'. The action fought out by the 23rd in the grounds surrounding Windsor Castle was a model of tactical fluidity and expertise.[54] So too was the mock action put on by the 33rd Foot at Gloucester in May 1772. During part of the review the 33rd probed a defended village and wood; later, the battalion

Wheeled to the Left by Companies, & Crossed a Deep & Rugged Valley, the Light Company forming a flanking party on the Right, among some Bushes, & thick Hedges. When the Battalion Gained the Brow of the opposite Hill, the Light Company was Drove in, the Battalion Companies then wheeled to the Right, & rushed down the Hill, to Line a Strong Hedge in the Bottom—where they kept up a brisk & Irregular Fire. On the Retreat beating, the Men run back Independently, to the Brow of the Hill, where they Instantly formed, & fired by Companies . . .[55]

The cavalry too was similarly employed. In April 1775 (to give but one example), the 10th Dragoons at their Newbury review performed two major series of manoeuvres. In the first the regiment divided into halves, one to form the 'ambuscade' and the other to form an 'escort' for the attack and defence of a convoy of wagons upon the march. In the second manoeuvre the regiment again split into halves, one to act as the enemy, the other 'drawn up in a Plain to Attack an Enemy in March thro' a Wood, on its entry into the Open Country'. Both manoeuvres were most realistic, notably the first, since escort duty for

[52] WO 27/27 and 30.   [53] WO 27/66.
[54] WO 27/61 and 64.   [55] WO 27/24.

trains was often performed by the dragoons on campaign.[56]

Save for the Guards, it was exceedingly rare for regiments in Britain to practise their drill together outside the wartime camps of exercise, or on those special occasions when George III saw pairs of regiment in Hyde Park. Of the five instances that I have found of this practice,[57] only on one was really advanced manoeuvring attempted, when early in 1756 Hawley's 1st Dragoons, Wolfe's 8th, and Honywood's 20th of Foot found themselves together at Canterbury, and fought a mock action of some interest. A supposed enemy force (four battalions in line) was 'marked out by stakes of five feet seven inches above the ground, to regulate the movement of the troops, and to guide their levelling [i.e. aiming] well'; and the regiments drew up opposite, the 8th and 20th in line in the centre with one-third of the dragoons on each flank, and the remaining third as a reserve behind the centre. By a heavy fire delivered advancing the English foot ruptured and passed through the enemy's centre, then wheeled outwards to left and right to complete his discomfiture; all the while the dragoons covered the flanks of the foot, while the reserve squadron was kept in hand ready to overwhelm any of the disordered opposing force that might attempt to rally.[58]

Although, as we have seen, the corps composing the big Irish garrisons were usually unable to devote much more of their time to advanced training than were the regiments serving elsewhere, they did nevertheless have the considerable advantage, when reviewing season came round, of concentrating at the garrison town in brigade strength; and so it was possible for these regiments to attempt brigade manoeuvres and large-scale mock actions. In July 1750, for example, Bragg's 28th, Hopson's 29th, Loudoun's 30th, and Otway's 35th of Foot assembled at Limerick and were seen two by two on a near-by common; they manoeuvred together but per-

---

[56] WO 27/33.

[57] In Apr. 1769, and again in Apr. 1770, the 15th and 16th Light Dragoons drilled together on Wimbledon Common (WO 27/15 and 18), and in 1776 the 7th and 10th Dragoons likewise drilled together at Wimbledon (WO 27/33). In Aug. 1771 at Chatham the 7th and 23rd of Foot (plus another unidentified battalion) formed a brigade which manoeuvred as a unit (WO 27/21).

[58] James Wolfe, op. cit. 55–7.

formed nothing extraordinary.[59] There were however more useful concentrations. In May 1768 at Cork the 53rd, 54th, and 58th of Foot manoeuvred together in one and two lines of battle, a useful and realistic rehearsal of linear battle-tactics of the sort that Dundas was later to stress.[60] In 1769, again at Cork, the 40th and 61st of Foot fought a mock battle in the traditional linear style; and among other manoeuvres the 61st, having exchanged volleys with the 40th, 'charg'd with bayonets, threw the 40th into confusion & oblig'd them to break'. The 40th rallied, however, and forming closed column drove through the centre of the 61st.[61] Meanwhile at Limerick the 5th, 38th, and 47th were likewise being reviewed together that year; they performed a rather peculiar deployment to the flanks, from line, which may have impressed the spectators but cannot have been practicable on a field of battle; but, as in all of these cases, the officers concerned could only profit from such rare training experience.[62] A much more interesting affair was held at Charles Fort on Prehan Point, across Kinsale harbour, before Lt.-Gen. Lord Blayney in May 1774. The 33rd Foot, commanded by the Earl Cornwallis, landed on the beach from its boats and moved inland, planning to capture the fort or, if it was found to be garrisoned, to mask it and lay Kinsale under contribution. The 20th Foot sallied forth to defend the place and, after much manoeuvring, took post upon 'Strong ground' where the 33rd was obliged to attack. In the ensuing action both flanks of the 20th were 'forced in upon the Battalion', and the corps was driven back to a new position. There, reinforced by guns from the fort, the 20th took new heart; and the 33rd, seeing that their further progress would be bloody, gave up the design and retired to the boats.[63]

In Phoenix Park two great reviews were generally held annually, in the spring and early summer; at the first the old garrison, about to be relieved and rotated out into county cantonments, was seen, while at the second the new garrison

---

[59] Cumb. Pprs, Box 44, no. 99, pp. 10–17, 44–6.

[60] WO 27/14, 58th Foot.

[61] WO 27/17, 40th Foot.

[62] Ibid., 5th Foot. By a quirk of fate, the 5th, 38th, and 47th were to find themselves acting together again six years later, advancing on the rebels' entrenchments at Bunker Hill.

[63] WO 27/32, 20th Foot.

performed. Thus the regiments composing each year's garrison were reviewed twice in the Park, and each review was preceded by a period of intensive training. The Lord-Lieutenant and the Irish C.-in-C. usually attended, as did the King at London reviews. Since the Dublin garrison was large and was rotated annually, the Phoenix Park reviews gave each regiment of foot on the Irish establishment a regular opportunity of taking part in major manoeuvres; and in the British Army the importance of this can hardly be exaggerated.

The Dublin garrison was usually seen by the reviewing officers in one of two ways: either split into contending forces which fought a mock battle or manoeuvring in united brigades against an imaginery enemy. The mock battles were usually quite complex, with a great variety of tactics being practised. When the garrison manoeuvred as a whole there was a greater adherence to the requirements and limitations imposed by the long, thin line of battle; but this too was of the utmost benefit, even though less fluid. Both sorts of reviews were attempted regularly, and the garrison was usually supported in the field by detachments from the Royal Artillery, which had its own Dublin barracks and was stationed there permanently from 1755.[64]

Before the mid-1760s the Dublin reviews, like those held elsewhere, were fairly rigid affairs despite the numbers of troops involved. In 1750 for example, the garrison (Bligh's 3rd Horse, and St. Clair's 1/1st, Fowke's 2nd, Irwin's 5th, and Hargrave's 7th of Foot) was reviewed in one long line of battle which did no more than show a series of firings, attempting no manoeuvres more difficult than the forming of one great square by the four battalions.[65] By the later 1780s, however, manoeuvring had become a much more complex art, and elaborate tactical displays had become the order of the day. During the period 1768–74, which we might single out for consideration because it most clearly shows the training and reviews of Phoenix Park, both the mock-battle and the brigade styles of reviews were carried on in equal number.[66] How salutary may have been the experience is indicated by the fact that, of the

---

[64] F. Forde, art. cit. 32–8.

[65] Cumb. Pprs., Box 44, no. 99, pp. 7–10; and Anon., *Quarters . . . in 1750* (Dublin, 1750).

[66] Detailed reports on the mock battles will be found in WO 27/14, 5th Foot; 27/17, 45th Foot; 27/29, 9th Foot; 27/29, 42nd Foot; and 27/32, 22nd Foot; and on the

twenty-seven regiments of foot involved during those years, all saw action in the 1775–83 war; twenty-three fought in the Americas, two at Gibraltar, one in Minorca, and one served as marines. By the summer of 1774 all twenty-seven had at least some experience of manoeuvring in large bodies, as part of lines or brigades; and that was more than could be said of any of the infantry or cavalry regiments serving elsewhere. Of the twenty-seven infantry regiments that took part in the elaborate manoeuvres and successful battle of Long Island, in August 1776, seventeen had taken part in these Dublin manoeuvres; and three of the remaining ten had practised mock fights for their review performances in Britain during the 1770s.

We must consider, finally, the pressure exerted by the reviewing system as a whole in promoting regularity in the army's training and drill. In this regard it was of the utmost importance that not only the general officers acting as reviewing officers but also the Sovereign and the Cs.-in-C. personally reviewed units. The Duke of Cumberland, for example, was constantly out reviewing—to the terror of the commanders of the corps concerned[67]—and Lord Amherst spent much time on this duty during the American War, as did Granby during the later 1760s and the Duke of York at the end of our period. Cumberland not only made it his business to review corps passing near London, as they marched from one British duty area to another; he would also ride out to see the pair of regiments returning annually (according to his fixed rotation scheme) from the Mediterranean, once they had landed at Portsmouth, 'refreshed themselves', and begun their long march for North Britain. Thus in 1754 the Duke saw at Reading Manners's 36th and Stuart's 37th come home respectively from Gibraltar and

---

brigade-style manoeuvres in WO 27/14, 45th Foot; 27/17, 27th Foot; 27/23, 5th Foot; 27/26, 9th Foot; 27/26, 28th Foot; 27/32, 24th Foot.

[67] Cumberland was to see Bury's 20th of Foot, of which James Wolfe was lieutenant-colonel, at Reading early in November 1753. The regiment was marching down from Glasgow, and Wolfe was apprehensive all the way. The Duke taking ill, Lt.-Gen. James Campbell reviewed the 20th on 30 Oct. and reported the corps to be in fine order; but Cumberland insisted on having his turn. Although Campbell had thought the 20th to be 'Under the Utmost good Descipline', still Wolfe could fret that 'I wish his Royal Highness's martial spirit would submit itself to his state of health, in which case he wouldn't persevere in his resolution of seeing us.' WO 27/3; and R. Reilly, op. cit. 110–13. Reilly confuses some dates; and he is wrong in supposing the 20th to have escaped the Duke's scrutiny, as is shown in James Wolfe, op. cit. 31.

Minorca.[68] The close attachment of the first two Georges to their army is well known, and needs little further expansion here.[69] George I held many reviews, notably in the big encampments of 1722 and 1723 formed in the south of England. George II saw regiments almost every season on the great heaths and commons round about London.[70] The embarkations for Flanders in 1742 provided George II with an excellent opportunity of seeing many regiments near to the capital. On 27 April 1742, for instance, 'his Majesty attended by a large Train of Noblemen and Persons of Distinction, went from St. James's to Blackheath, and review'd Major-General Howard's [3rd] and Colonel Duroure's [12th] Regiments of Foot'; and the next day the King reviewed Peers's 23rd and William Handasyde's 31st of Foot on Kew Green. 'His Majesty seem'd highly pleas'd with them.'[71] George III was, if anything, even more concerned with reviewing than had been his royal grandfather, a fact oddly ignored by his many biographers. Whenever corps marched near London, passing from one duty area to another, George III, like Cumberland before him, was apt to pounce—so that in July 1770 the Adjutant-General felt it wise to warn the lieutenant-colonel of the 6th Foot that the King 'has in General Rode out to See the Regimts. as they pass near London, most probably H.M. will give a look at the 6th . . . where you will be Seen, I cant pretend to tell, but if I hear will let you know.'[72] Regiments were often concentrated and marched to London purposely to be seen by the King. Early in July 1765, for example, the 4th and 43rd of Foot set out from Chatham, the 4th quartering in Kensington, Brompton, Knightsbridge, and Chelsea, and the 43rd at Paddington, Islington, Tottenham, and Marylebone, against their joint review in Hyde Park before the King on 17 July. The review over, the 4th continued on to Exeter and Tiverton, but the 43rd simply returned to Kent from where it had been bundled for the occasion.[73] The King not only saw regiments at random,

---

[68] WO 5/42, pp. 92, 123–4, 127–8.

[69] The best account is J. Hayes, 'House of Hanover'.

[70] This is made clear, in lieu of surviving Inspection Returns, in the Marching Orders for these two reigns.

[71] *London Evening-Post*, 29 Apr. 1742; and *Daily Post*, 27 and 28 Apr. 1742.

[72] WO 3/2, pp. 67–8.

[73] WO 5/53, pp. 53–391, *passim*. See also L. Cowper, *The King's Own: The Story of a*

as in the case of the 6th just noted, but also prepared part of his reviewing schedule well in advance.[74] George III even had some of the designated corps informed in advance what parts of the drill he wished to see displayed.[75] At all his reviews he was, furthermore, accompanied by a numerous suite—as when in June 1767 he saw the 12th and 13th of Foot in Hyde Park, attended by the Queen, 'their Royal Highnesses the Dukes of York, Gloucester and Cumberland, the Prince and Princess of Brunswick, her Royal Highness the Princess Amelia, the King's sister, the Marquis of Granby, several foreign Ambassadors, and several others of the nobility and general officers'.[76] For the majority of regimental officers this was august company, and every effort at a fine turn-out (which meant intensive drilling to the regulations) would be made—all to the advantage of the service.[77] Were their performances not up to the high standards expected by the King, they soon heard of it: not only did George III make a practice of sending his comments to regiments he had seen himself, but he also read most of the review reports submitted by the reviewing officers.[78] George saw the 23rd Foot at Chatham on 10 June 1772, for example; and although he had the Adjutant-General write 'to Acq^t the Corps, wth His great App[robation]', still the King found fault with the music played by the regiment and ordered them henceforth to conform in this particular to the established practice of the army—this 'not in the least meant, as any Slight to a Corps,

Royal Regiment, i (Oxford, 1939), 217–18, and *London Evening-Post*, 18 July 1765, for details. There is a fine illustrated MS book on this review in BL Add. MS 28,856.

[74] WO 4/1044, p. 61. Thus in the spring of 1766 the Adjutant-General acquainted the colonels of the 1st, 2nd, and 3rd Dragoons, and of the 8th, 14th, 22nd, and 35th of Foot, that HM intended to review their corps that season.

[75] WO 3/1, p. 37. In Apr. 1769 the Adjutant-General informed the colonel of the 15th Foot, that 'When H.M. Reviews a Regt. or Regts., the Comdg. Offr. gives in a proposal as to what particular Exercise he intends to perform. Sometimes Some . . . Evolutions are fixed on, Sometimes other.' WO 3/24, p. 104.

[76] *London Evening-Post*, 6 June 1767.

[77] There was a spirit of competition among the regiments, fostered by these reviews, as is repeatedly apparent in the correspondence of officers: e.g. the lieutenant-colonel of Amherst's 15th Foot, soon to join other corps at Barham Downs in the summer of 1757, wrote that the 15th was 'very ambitious to dispute the Superiority'; and (as he informed his colonel), 'you may with great safety speak for us; we have had an Eye to it, are very desirous of it, and I will agree to the forfeiture of every thing that is Dear to me, if the Regiment does not do Justice to the King, and Honour to you whenever it is employ'd.' Kent RO Amherst MSS103/4, fo. 1.

[78] A great many of the Inspection Returns, after 1760, have 'King' scrawled across their covers in pencil, indicating that George III had read them.

who in every War has done such Service to their Country, but in Conformity to the Principle, which H.M. thinks so necessary, of not having the Estab^d Rules of the Army deviated from.'[79] So closely did George III watch the army! In 1788, after he had read the report submitted on the 45th Foot, the King ordered the Adjutant-General 'to report the deficiencies' to its colonel, 'accompanied with his order to him, to have them made good without delay.'[80] These were minor breaches. If a corps made a bad showing the King's displeasure could be great. When George read the report on the 68th Foot's miserable review of 1767 a detailed, scathing letter was dispatched to the major of that corps: the letter was a shopping-list of complaints, its tone sharp and peremptory. The Adjutant-General, perhaps slightly embarrassed by the tone, added a postscript: 'I Inclose to you an Exact Copy of the Returns . . . Least there shou'd have been any Mistake.'[81]

If the influence of the Kings and of the Cs.-in-C. was of primary importance, that of the proprietary colonels in pushing training and regularity was of considerable importance too. The proprietary colonels usually took an interest, and often a pride, in the proficiency of their units; and whether or not they spent much time with their regiments, they corresponded constantly with their lieutenants-colonel and were often likely to visit at review time. It was part of the duty of the lieutenants-colonel to report to their colonels on the state of their regiments. Since most colonelcies belonged to general officers of great experience—notably under George II—their interest, albeit occasional, might be advantageous in that it kept the field officers up to the mark. The papers of Jeffrey Amherst, for example, who was colonel of the 15th Foot from 1756 to 1768, contain much interesting correspondence between himself and his lieutenants-colonel on the state of training in the unit.[82] Amherst clearly expected proficiency, and this correspondence shows that he got it. The Duke of Cumberland, who was colonel of the 1st Foot Guards from 1742 until late in 1757, paid the closest attention to his regiment; even when on campaign, as

[79] WO 27/24, 23rd Foot; and WO 3/3, pp. 106–7.
[80] WO 3/8, p. 17.
[81] WO 3/1, pp. 107–9. Rebukes like this one are common enough in the letter-books of the Adjutant-General's office.
[82] Kent RO Amherst MSS 013/1–8.

in 1748 and 1757, he was kept minutely informed on the state of the corps in the capital.[83] The administration of another C.-in-C., Ligonier, over the several regiments of which he was colonel, was also close and salutary.[84] Lord Robert Bertie, as colonel of the 7th Foot from 1754 until 1776, drove his lieutenants-colonel hard. After he received a thin and sketchy account of the recent 1764 review of his regiment from Lt.-Col. Richard Prescott, Bertie rebuked him for so summary a manner of conducting such important business; indeed, said his Lordship, this was 'the first time, I ever received a Letter from the Commanding Officer of my Regt. after a Review, that did not give me an Account of the Behaviour of the Regiment: A thing I believe never before omitted by any Field Officer whatever.' Prescott, no doubt squirming, was complaining of old wounds: 'I . . . can Scarcely crawl across the room', he bleated. Further correspondence shows that Prescott made better reports in 1765.[85]

Bertie, if not kept well informed, was at any rate a sound soldier. Wolfe, when major and lieutenant-colonel of the 20th Foot, was constantly troubled by his colonel, Viscount Bury, then a mere youth whose knowledge was slight but whose orders were frequent. In August 1753 Wolfe was complaining that Bury had ordered the 20th's manual changed 'from very quick to very slow, so that at present . . . we are between the two, and can neither do one nor the other as they ought to be done.' 'All the soldiers know', Wolfe added, 'that it is not very material, but some of those that will be present at our review may have other notions.' After this review, Bury ordered Wolfe to speed up the platoon exercise (Cumberland having observed that Pulteney's 13th fired their platoons quicker than did Bury's 20th); as Wolfe put it in Regimental Orders, 'his lordship is very desirous that no regiment should exceed his own in the performance of every part of their duty.'[86]

The reviewing officers, meanwhile, took their duty seriously,

---

[83] In the midst of critical operations against the French army of d'Estrée, the Duke was corresponding with Lt.-Col. Dury about progess the Guards were making with the new manual exercise. Cumb. Pprs, Box 50, nos. 17, 167, 211; and Box 52, no. 64.

[84] See Rex Whitworth, op. cit., *passim.*

[85] Berks RO Downshire Pprs. 039 (Bertie to Prescott, Chislehurst, 13 Nov. 1764; and Prescott to Bertie, Gloucester, 1 Sept. 1764.

[86] Beckles Willson, op. cit. 210, 217–18; and James Wolfe, op. cit. 31.

and they were backed up by the King, the Cs.-in-C., and the colonels. Obedient to their orders to see the regiments go through a display of the whole of their drill—'taking Notice of any defect or Negligence in the Discharge of this part of their Duty; and Strictly Command and enjoin the Officers to Use their utmost diligence and Endeavours to teach and perfect their Men and themselves in the Knowledge and Use of their Arms'[87]—they seldom pulled punches, and often reported at length on corps that they found to be ill disciplined or deviating from the regulations. Typically, in June 1775 Maj.-Gen. Robert Cunninghame reported the 28th Foot (which he reviewed at Limerick) to be 'greatly deficient in its Discipline', despite the fact that the corps was up to strength, well armed and accoutred. 'The Men are slouching and ill set up; They are not Steady and do not know how to handle their Arms.'[88] In 1775 Lt.-Gen. John Irwin, the Irish C.-in-C., reported that the 34th Foot was in poor order, and added the rebuke: 'The Regiment wou'd be fit for Service, if the Officers took as much Pains as the Men.'[89] Late in May 1777 Lt.-Gen. the Earl of Cavan reviewed the 68th Foot at Dublin, reporting as follows: 'This Regiment seemed to require great care and attention. A dissolute Spirit some where prevailed in it, for there were at the time of my Review confined in Prison no less than eight Men . . . [and the 68th] has been no less singular for a daily loss of Men by desertion.' When manoeuvring, nothing was well performed, nor were the men silent, 'there being every moment a buzz of voices heard'. [90] Not only major irregularities, but petty troubles and minor inefficiency were likewise frequently reported. In his October 1754 review of the 4th Dragoons, held at Lichfield, Lt.-Gen. James Cholmondeley found a certain unevenness in their exercises and manoeuvres, the firings 'bad' and their marching in squadron rather poor;

[87] WO 26/22, p. 364.
[88] WO 27/35. The 28th seems to have been behaving in character. The regiment had served in North America, after the peace, until 1767, and had been involved in several fracas. Professor Shy, op. cit. 162, 219–22, 382–3, reviewing its conduct there, concluded that 'it is fairly evident from its record that the 28th—officers and men—was an undisciplined regiment.'
[89] WO 27/35.
[90] WO 27/37. This was the same corps, of which George III had complained so sharply in 1767; and in 1783 the 68th, embarked for Jamaica, mutinied on board their transports at Spithead.

he concluded that the 4th was 'pretty well appointed—not quite perfect in their Discipline, but fit for Service'.[91] As was their duty, the reviewing officers ordered all of these regiments to correct their weaknesses, and did so on all other such occasions.

When occasion required it, the reviewing officers were full of praise for regiments that distinguished themselves by maintaining over long periods high standards of training; and this was deserved praise, considering the difficulties faced most of the time by most of the corps. Regiments of this sort were exceptions, even more so than were the ill-trained and ill-disciplined units just described; for it took not only dedicated officers, a very sound system of interior economy, *esprit de corps*, a low turnover among the rank and file, and good postings, but also a measure of sheer luck to keep one step ahead of the friction of peace for sustained periods. We should note one or two of these corps, if only for the contrast they provide. One such was the 1st battalion, The Royals. The 1/1st Foot was reported in excellent condition at Chatham, in 1777, and it remained in this condition for more than a decade. A reviewing officer who saw them at Dublin, in July 1785, observed that 'This Old Regiment keeps on in its usual Steady Pace.' In May 1786 the 1/1st was again reported a 'Steady slow and sure Regiment, Orderly, and always kept in Strict Discipline'.[92] In June 1789 Maj.-Gen. Patrick Tonyn waxed eloquent at the appearance of the 22nd Foot: 'A Steady and martial Countenance, a spirited & graceful manner, a peculiar exactness in all their Motions, a most complete military Appearance, exhibits the high discipline of this excellent Regiment, proud to distinguish itself . . .'[93] Tonyn devoted similar priase to the 33rd Foot, which he saw that same summer, concluding that 'to report them fit for Service without adding that they are adequate to any active military Service whatsoever, would be too indifferent a representation of their gallant and warlike Deportment.'[94] Such praise was nothing new to the 33rd, which was unquestionably the best-trained regiment in the British Army during the last three decades of our period. In 1769 the 33rd was reported to be in an excellent state of training; in 1772 it was reported 'one of the

[91] WO 27/3.
[93] WO 27/64.
[92] WO 27/36, 27/53 Pt 2, and 27/58 Pt 1.
[94] Ibid.

finest Regiments in His Majesty's Service'; in 1774 Maj-Gen. William Howe found the 33rd's drill and discipline 'Established upon the truest principles, far Superior to any other Corps within my Observation'; and in 1775 the Irish C.-in-C. reported it 'in Perfect good Order'. The 33rd performed admirably during the American War; and by 1787, back in Britain rebuilding, the regiment was again being favourably reported on. In 1788 the reviewing officer who saw them at Windsor reported that 'the Regiment Appears Founded upon the same System as in the Last War . . . likely to retain its usual Discipline.'[95]

It is abundantly clear, then, that the reviewing system functioned very well indeed: it served admirably its primary purpose of enforcing uniformity, and so tying the individual corps closer together; and at the same time it provided the regiments with an annual opportunity—regular, and of known duration—of practising in full and uninterrupted concentration the firings and manoeuvres that constituted the advanced training of the regiment. The system was regular, it was carried out conscientiously, and it was a system with teeth. It ensured that the particularist spirit among the regiments only very occasionally asserted itself in the field of training and tactical doctrine.[96] But however advantageous it was in providing the regiments with an opportunity to concentrate for the purpose of training, it was not of sufficient duration to compensate, in peacetime, for the shortcomings and the irregularity of advanced training as it was carried on during the rest of the year. It was therefore in wartime—by default, and of necessity—that the majority of the regiments composing the British Army were at last given the opportunity to set about intensive and sustained advanced training.

---

[95] WO 27/15, 24, 30, 32, 35, 59, 61, 69. It comes as no surprise that during his 1776 New York and New Jersey campaign, Howe brigaded the 33rd Foot with the Guards.

[96] This conclusion on general regularity of the drill practised in the army during the second half of the century is based on careful examination of the eighty volumes of Inspection Returns (WO 27) which survive for our period. These contain well over 1,000 review reports; and these we have carefully examined and collated against the various drill regulations, and the treatises describing customary practice.

ADDENDUM

PLATOON FIRE AND ALTERNATE FIRE

Although 'alternate fire' was only officially adopted with the publication of the *1764 Regulations*, it had been practised in the best-trained battalions, those with the least doctrinaire field officers, since the mid-1750s. One such corps was the 20th Foot, of which James Wolfe was lieutenant-colonel; and the fire drill practised in the 20th conveniently illustrates the difference between the two systems.

It was Wolfe's duty not only to train the 20th as an effective fighting force, but also to follow the current regulations; and since he thought alternate fire more practical than the regulation platoon-fire—'the impracticable chequer', as he described it (Beckles Willson, op. cit. 368–9)—he was teaching both in the 20th. A Regimental Order of Jan. 1755 ran as follows:

As the alternate fire by platoons or devisions, or by companies, is the most simple, plain, and easy, and used by the best disciplined troops in Europe [i.e. the Prussians], we are at all times to imitate them in that respect . . . [and otherwise] to conform to the established discipline, and to practise all those things that are required at the reviews, to which the knowledge of other matters will be no hindrance. (James Wolfe, op. cit. 34–5)

Figs 1 and 2 show the 20th told off, accordingly.

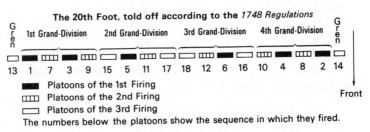

The 20th Foot, told off according to the *1748 Regulations*

| G r e n | 1st Grand-Division | 2nd Grand-Division | 3rd Grand-Division | 4th Grand-Division | G r e n |

13   1   7   3   9   15   5   11   17   18   12   6   16   10   4   8   2   14

■■■ Platoons of the 1st Firing
▥▥▥ Platoons of the 2nd Firing
▭▭ Platoons of the 3rd Firing

Front

The numbers below the platoons show the sequence in which they fired.

Fig. 1.   Platoon-Fire

To perform platoon-fire (Fig. 1), the nine battalion-companies on the 20th's establishment were told off into sixteen platoons, thus breaking up the companies in which the men normally trained and served. The tenth or grenadier company was split in half, the halves separating to stand on each flank of the battalion. These platoons were then told off into three 'Firings', the platoons making up each Firing not standing contiguously but scattered all down the battalion line. Finally, the platoons were numbered. The battalion could now deliver its fire in one of two ways: either by volleys in which all of the platoons in a Firing let fly simultaneously, the second Firing following the first and the third the second, the platoons of each Firing reloading immediately after shooting so that a constant succession of volleys could be delivered; or, if the enemy was less threatening and a less heavy fire was required along the whole of the battalion's front at each discharge, the platoons simply fired one after another according to the sequence in which they were numbered, again spreading their fire widely along the battalion front.

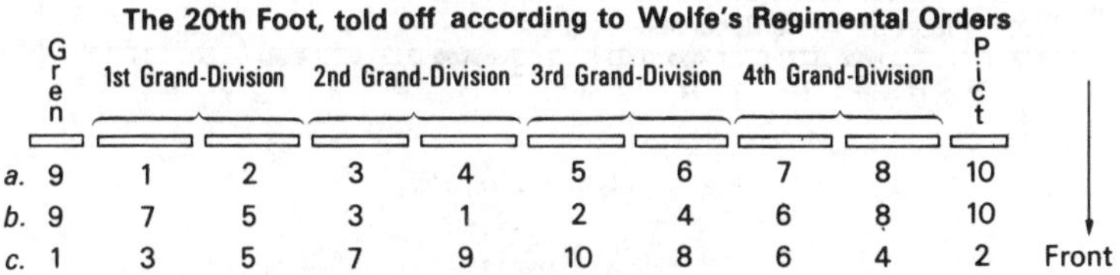

The 20th Foot, told off according to Wolfe's Regimental Orders

		1st Grand-Division		2nd Grand-Division		3rd Grand-Division		4th Grand-Division			
	G r e n									P i c t	
a.	9	1	2	3	4	5	6	7	8	10	
b.	9	7	5	3	1	2	4	6	8	10	
c.	1	3	5	7	9	10	8	6	4	2	Front

The numbers below the subdivisions show the different sequences in which they might fire – *a.* from right to left; *b.* from the centre to the flanks, right and left alternately; *c.* from the flanks to the centre, right and left alternately

Fig. 2. Alternate Fire

To perform the alternate fire (Fig. 2), the means most favoured was to avoid confusing the men by splitting up their parent companies, but rather to turn each company into a fire-unit. These companies (now designated 'subdivisions', their tactical title) were numbered according to the sequence in which it was designed they should fire, one after another— either from right to left, or from the centre of the battalion alternately outwards to the flanks, or from the flanks alternately in towards the centre. The grenadier company was not split but remained in its accustomed place on the right flank, while the left-hand battalion-company—following French practice, and anticipating the light-infantry companies soon to be raised—was designated a 'piquet' company and held its own flank.

The main distinction between these two systems of telling off and giving fire was the absence (in the alternate system) of the big Firings used in platoon-fire. Not breaking up the companies improved the morale of the men, since they went into action in their accustomed units, among officers and men with whom they were well acquainted. The alternate system, finally, was much easier to perform, since the elaborate telling off, the effort of separate platoons to co-ordinate their firing, and the confusion to which the platoon system was subject in battle, were all avoided.

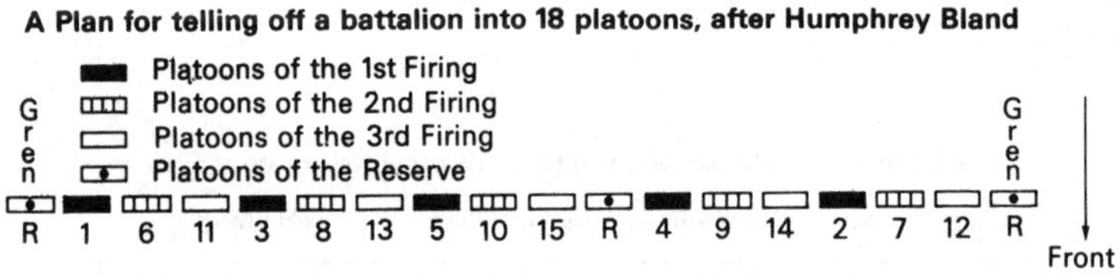

A Plan for telling off a battalion into 18 platoons, after Humphrey Bland

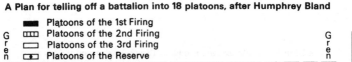

Fig. 3   Platoon-Fire, 1727

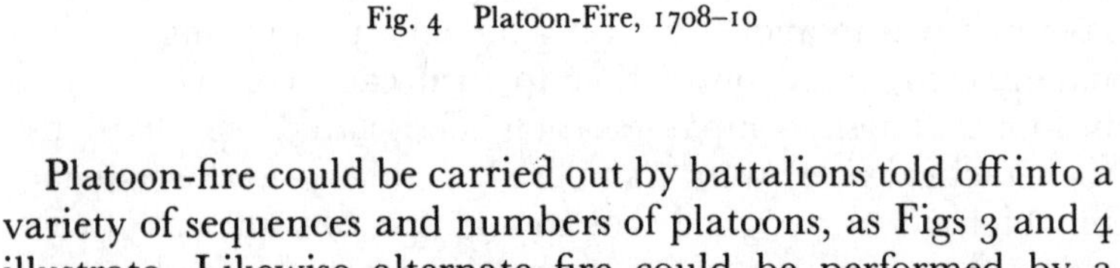

A Battalion told off according to 'the Discipline practised in Flanders', as taught by Parker and Ingoldsby in Ireland, 1708–10

Fig. 4   Platoon-Fire, 1708–10

Platoon-fire could be carried out by battalions told off into a variety of sequences and numbers of platoons, as Figs 3 and 4 illustrate. Likewise alternate fire could be performed by a battalion whose companies (as Wolfe's orders, quoted above, suggest) had been told off into several platoons, giving fire as usual from the flanks to the centre, or from the centre to the flanks.

In his 1727 treatise (pp. 145–7), Bland described the alternate fire already in use among the Dutch; and in so doing he set out the common English objection to it—that there was no fire kept in reserve all down the line at all times, as was the case when the platoons were told off into Firings and then dispersed along the full front of the battalion. By the later 1750s his objection was no longer supported, by which time battle experience (and the success of the Prussians), had shown that husbanding so large a reserve was unnecessary, where alternate fire had cleared the battalion's front and where reloading proceeded fast enough to keep pace with the firing.

Chapter VI

Advanced Training: The Wartime Camps

Despite the fact that all but the rawest of recruits among the mass of private soldiers could be counted upon, at any one time, to be sufficiently well trained in the basic elements of the drill; despite the fact that the central authorities, by means of the regulations and the reviewing system, kept up drill uniformity throughout the army; despite the fact that the majority of the officers serving with the corps were career-soldiers, among whom the field officers, the captains, and the senior subalterns were generally men of lengthy experience of the service; and despite the fact that there was readily available in English a considerable body of military literature; nevertheless it is clear that the majority of the regiments found themselves, on the eve of war, to be quite without, or almost innocent of, experience of large-scale mock action or brigade manoeuvres, to have had inadequate opportunities to conduct the training of the field days and the 'excursions', and to be only just adequately prepared to perform on a parade ground the regulation firings and manoeuvres together with a selection of movements drawn from the army's store of customary practice. These were the inevitable fruits of the peacetime condition of the British Army. Irregular and generally infrequent advanced training carried on in varying levels of concentration, capped by two or three weeks per year of intensive pre-review drill, was not sufficient to overcome the on-going effects of the friction of peace; and the rating 'fit for service' must, within this context, be regarded as expressing a pious hope. Major efforts were required in order fully to prepare a corps; and since peacetime training was bound to be limited it was in wartime—either in the encampments formed at home, or in the cantonments and in the field abroad—that advanced training was at last carried on with realism and with sustained vigour. Granted that the tacticians, the War Office, and all serious general officers recognized the need for the intensive training and manoeuvring of large numbers, it is extraordinary that only the immediate threat of invasion should provide the occasion for such practice. That the concentration of regiments in large encampments—thereby providing the opportunity for such training, itself quite clearly secondary to the overall strategic need for concentrations—was attempted only in emergencies, is eloquent testimony to the difficulties faced by the bulk of the army and its general officers, and to the order of priorities governing the army in peacetime.

Certainly the three most grave military crises faced by Britain during the eighteenth century occurred in 1745 when the French landed the Stuart prince in Scotland and so provoked the greatest of the Jacobite risings, in 1779, when the combined fleets of the Bourbon Crowns lay within sight close off Plymouth, and in 1796, when Bouvet's squadron rode the gale in Bantry Bay. The threat of invasion was the principal strategic weapon France possessed in her rivalry with Britain. France was militarily the most powerful nation in Europe and consequently had little to fear along her coasts, save for the occasional raids which were hardly more than insults; but Britain, the great antagonist, was weak on land. So long as France was able to maintain the threat of invasion, so long as that threat was credible, Britain had to keep a significant part of her land forces at home, a large part of her fleet in the Channel, and had even (as in 1715–16, 1719, 1744–6, and yet again in 1756–7) to import Dutch and German troops to augment the defence forces.[1] In the short term this cost the French little, while it helped to immobilize considerable British resources.

The invasion threat was, fortunately, seasonal. Not only would the Bourbons need to gain temporary naval control of

---

[1] The foreign treaty-troops were always numerous on these occasions, since the threat was serious and the regular army small. In 1715–16 there were 6,000 Dutch foot in eleven battalions serving in Britain; and three Dutch battalions landed in the north of England in 1719, while two battalions of Swiss in the Dutch service sailed up the Thames (J. Baynes, op. cit. 200–1). More Dutch troops came over temporarily in 1744 when the Jacobite invasion fleet was fitting out under Saxe. By early Jan. 1746 there were in Britain ten Dutch battalions, six Hessian battalions, and six Hessian squadrons (Atkinson, 'Jenkins' Ear', 290–5, *passim*). In 1756 there were twenty battalions of Germans in southern England: twelve Hanoverian battalions formed their own camp at Coxheath and eight Hessian battalions encamped by Winchester, both forces with their own artillery, general officers and staffs (Kent RO Amherst MSS 084/6, fo. 1). It will be recalled that some 33,000 Germans served in America, India, Minorca, and Gibraltar during the war of 1775–83. E. Lowell, *The Hessians* (New York, 1874), 20, 299–301; P. Mackesy, op. cit. 62; and P. R. N. Katcher, op. cit. 103–27.

the Channel, but they must do so in the summer or, better, in the earlier autumn; for only then did the winds serve, only by early summer could an army sizeable enough to invade be provisioned (and therefore assembled) in the French and Spanish ports, and only after autumn harvest would an invading army find an abundance of foodstuffs and fodder inland from the beaches.[2]

Although the British did not do so, it was common practice among the French and Prussians to form in peacetime large military encampments in which major reviews and mock combats were held, new tactical doctrine tested, and in which general officers gained invaluable experience of manoeuvring large forces of all arms.[3] The British did not do so in peacetime because of the great expense that camps and manoeuvres entailed; because of popular prejudices against standing—let alone concentrated and encamped—forces; and because, in any case, there were in the towns and along the coasts too few troops to support the civil power, let alone when tied down in one place. To guard against the invasion threat was, however, a different matter; and so it was the British practice in wartime, throughout our period, to form numbers of military encampments, thus concentrating troops at strategic points in the south (and particularly the south-east) of England, largely with a view to defending Portsmouth and London, should an invading force gain a beach-head.[4] Most of the encampments were scattered in an anti-invasion chain extending from the Suffolk

---

[2] A. T. Patterson, *The Other Armada* (Manchester, 1960), 13.

[3] On the French camps, which were notably professional, see R. Villate, art. cit. 237–44 and *passim*. See also J. Colin, *Tactique*; R. S. Quimby, op. cit.; J. Luvaas (ed.), op. cit.; and C. Duffy, *The Army of Frederick the Great* (Newton Abbot, 1974), all *passim*.

Before the Duke of York's reforms at the end of our period there had been only three occasions in peacetime when a number of regiments were drawn together and encamped—in 1722, 1723, and 1792. The camps of 1722 and 1723 were formed in response to Jacobite scares (*HMC Clements MSS* (1913), p. 342), while that of 1792 was formed largely in order to show the King the new drill established by Dundas. In 1774 and 1775 special training camps were set up at Salisbury and Woolwich, respectively; but only seven companies of light infantry were present at the first, while the second was an artillery camp. These camps are noted in passing here (pp. 246, 336–9).

[4] E.g. on operations in England to resist invasion in 1759, see Rex Whitworth, op. cit. 281–312; on the defence arrangements in 1779, see A. T. Patterson, op. cit. 107–32 and *passim*; and see the hypothetical but carefully researched summary of the defence Britain would have been able to mount in 1805, had Bonaparte's flotillas made good their descent on the Kentish coasts, in R. Glover, *Britain at Bay. Defence Against Bonaparte, 1803–14* (1973), 77–102.

coast south across the Thames estuary and west towards Dorset; with the mobile cavalry lying out on the flanks, with the larger concentrations of artillery and foot in Essex, Kent, and the Portsmouth hinterland, and with boats and pontoon bridges linking these forces across the Thames, any likely French descent could quickly be met by small forces, while larger numbers marched hard for the scene. It was, in short, the most appropriate strategic deployment for the small British Army.

As the winds and seasons served the French, so too the British formed most camps in May, June, or early July, and did not break them up until October or early November. Certain principal campsites were used repeatedly, often with very large numbers of troops in them, while other sites were used sporadically and generally held but few men, as circumstances might require. In 1778, for example, there were in Coxheath camp near Maidstone some 17,000 troops (a Dragoon regiment, six battalions of marching Foot, fifteen militia battalions, and three companies of artillery), the whole stretching over some $3\frac{1}{2}$ miles of ground; while in 1782 there were in Bromeswell camp near Woodbridge a scant 100 officers and men of the 22nd Light Dragoons. As the wars progressed, the number of camps being formed during each succeeding summer tended to remain about the same; but with the number of regular regiments available dwindling away as overseas campaigns drew in more men, and as the naval pressure on the Bourbon fleets met with mounting success, the quality of the troops encamped declined as the place of the regulars was taken over by militia. There was admittedly, with naval success, less strategic need for camps in the later stages of most wars—save, of course, for that of 1775–83. Thus few camps were formed after 1741, in the 1739–48 war (the Guards in Hyde Park and at Finchley in 1745, and the concentrations in Scottish camps in 1746–7, were emergency affairs, not regular camps); and there were very few regulars in the camps formed after 1760, during the 1756–63 war. In the 1775–83 war no camps at all were formed until the Bourbons became belligerents in 1778, and by 1780 the regular forces left in British camps were weak and overextended.

Beyond their general strategic location in the southern

counties, other factors of some significance had to be taken into consideration before a particular campsite could be settled upon. The ground had to be fairly flat, free from fences, heavy brush, and other impediments to movement. The place had to be dry and well drained, and consequently not low-lying; there had nevertheless to be adequate fresh water near by.[5] Plenty of wood or furze for fuel had to be close at hand, and forage and provisions must be readily available in the neighbourhood. Good river transport and decent roads were a necessity both for supply and marches. The whole lay-out of the camp, moreover, must be done with a view to sanitation, the armies of the period being unhygienic and the medicines so little effective. Thus in 1780, on the Tiptree Heath site, trenches had to be dug to drain off the water and other effluvia—only one of the innumerable details that had to be looked to if the camp was to be healthy.[6] Not least in importance, finally, was the cost of hiring ground from its private owners.[7]

Camp sites were scouted by Engineer officers, and the Ordnance (which was charged with their routine maintenance and was responsible for the vast stores of camp equipment) kept on file up-to-date site reports. In the spring of 1756, for example,

[5] In July 1740 a 'great Scarcity of Water' at Windsor Forest camp (where five regiments of cavalry, three battalions of foot, and an artillery detachment lay) resulted in the shifting of three cavalry regiments to Datchet, Cobham, and Cricket Hill, distant enough from the camp to be quite inconvenient. WO 5/34, pp. 90–204, *passim*; *London Evening-Post* 15 July 1740; and M. E. S. Laws, op. cit. 6.

[6] On Tiptree, see WO 34/125, fo. 49. Concern with hygiene largely explains the meticulous detail with which the military treatises of the century treated the subject of castrametation. Of the 4,230 men camped at Tiptree in 1780 about 10 per cent were sick by the end of August—a small percentage, the result of proper precautions and camp discipline. WO 34/203, fos. 10–11.

[7] In a report of 1778 on a site near Billericay, it was estimated that twelve battalions might be squeezed on to 100 acres (a battalion in camp normally required 10½ acres, at 700–800 men). In those parts, 100 acres could be hired for £600. Including levelling the site by clearing scrub, and tearing down (and later rebuilding) fences, the Billericay ground could be had for £1,000 per season (WO 30/50, no. 41). Protests from irate farmers are often to be met with in the documents. With the closing of the Winchester camp of 1778, local farmers petitioned for sums: one asked for £84 'damage in keeping 12 Horses out of employment for 21 Weeks during the time of Encampment'; another called for £10 10s. 'damage on 53 Acres seeds where the soldiers exercised'; a third claimed £71 8s. for 'a good live fence grubbed up agt. His Majesty come to review the Camp' (WO 4/104, pp. 325–35). In a plan of the Salisbury camp of 1779, where six regiments of cavalry lay, there appears in the middle of the parade ground 'a Piece of Barley hurdled off'; the troops were to have 'the use of the Ground' only once 'the crop is cleared'—a feature typical in its way of the training of the British Army. WO 34/17, fos. 17–19, enclosure.

Engineer-Director J. Watson surveyed the country between Dorchester and Petersfield, and found seven sites that would serve for encampments. One site, reported Watson, was half a mile to the north-west of Dorchester, lying on 'dry rising Ground, having the Exeter Road in Front, and the River Froom $\frac{1}{4}$ a mile in the Rear'. There was a convenient and 'plentiful Spring of exceeding good water', and 'a great Extent of Ground both in Front and upon the Right of this Camp for 6 or 7 Batt^{ns} and 6 Squadrons to exercise, March, & perform any Movement' upon. There was unfortunately little wood round about, 'the common firing being either Furze or Coal from Weymouth'.[8] This same site was used for a 1757 encampment. A similar report on three Essex sites, made in 1780, described one as too wet but found favour with the others, one of which, used in 1780 and 1781, lay 'on the north part of Danbury Common'; Deputy-Quartermaster-General William Roy reported it a fit place upon which to camp three battalions: it was on dry ground with a fine spring near by, and the ground 'tho covered with Furze Bushes and Roots of Brush Wood', could soon be cleared.[9]

Once the sites had been selected and as occupation by the troops began, vast quantities of equipment and stores had to be dispatched by the Ordnance. The quantity and variety of even simple 'camp utensils'—picks, shovels, kettles, tents, wheelbarrows, etc.—was staggering.[10] Not only had the Ordnance to issue camp utensils and other paraphernalia, but guns, ammunition, stores, and their transport had also to be sent out and maintained. Guns—two light pieces for each battalion encamped, and heavier pieces for battery work in the larger camps—plus all of the ammunition, tools, spares, wagons, and impedimenta which accompanied the artillery in the eighteenth century, had also to be prepared by the Ordnance.[11] Huge artillery parks were assembled at Woolwich and at the

[8] WO 30/54, no. 39; and WO 55/573, pp. 193–200.

[9] WO 34/125, fos. 49–50.

[10] For stores at the camps in 1722, e.g., see WO 55/348, pp. 37–41; for issues in 1740, see WO 53/350, pp. 195–7; for issues in 1781, see WO 53/418, p. 170, and WO 26/31, pp. 45–6.

[11] For an example of the variety and quantity of materials composing a train, see WO 55/351, pp. 311, 316, and 55/352.A, pp. 8–22, on the train sent to Flanders for the campaign of 1744. There are others throughout WO55.

Tower upon the outbreak of war, and then reassembled annually, serving as a pool from which the needs of expeditions,
and of the camps, were met. Finally, ball cartridges—which,
as we have seen, were almost unknown in peacetime—were
made available in the camps in quantities reaching into many
hundreds of thousands, in belated effort to improve individual
marksmanship and battalion musketry. Butts were always a
feature on a campsite.

Once the sites had been determined upon and the Ordnance
storekeepers set in motion, general and staff officers were appointed to the command of each camp and the corps were ear-
marked and informed of impending camp duty. Each camp was
commanded by a senior general officer serving directly under
the orders of the C.-in-C. and the Kings, each of whom took
great interest in the camps. Each senior general officer had
under him (usually) two other generals, who commanded the
'wings' or 'lines' into which British armies were always sub-
divided before the advent of the divisional system in 1809.
Finally there came the brigade commanders. These several
senior officers were assisted by sundry inferior officers appointed to the staff of each camp (serving as ADCs, brigade-
majors, AQMGs, physician and surgeons in the camp hospitals,
etc.); chosen normally by the camp commander from friends,
many of these staff officers came from the regiments actually
serving in the camp.

The regiments selected to encamp were warned well in advance; and as the time drew near each sent to the site its
quartermaster, pioneers, and camp-colour men, who marked
off the ground soon to be occupied by their tent and horse
lines. A typical result was the order of battle at Coxheath
camp in 1778 (Fig. 5).[12]

Between the outside limits of Coxheath and Bromeswell,
mentioned above, there were broadly speaking three sizes of
camps formed during our period, depending upon the number
of troops concentrated.[13] The very largest were eight in number: from east to west (and with the years during which they

---

[12] *General Evening Post* (25 June 1778); and C. Herbert, 'Coxheath Camp, 1778–9',
JSAHR 45 (1967), 148. The county titles indicate militia battalions.

[13] The size and location of the camps, together with the units that camped and the
years of site occupation, were drawn principally from lengthy research in WO 55/3,
5, 34, and 55.

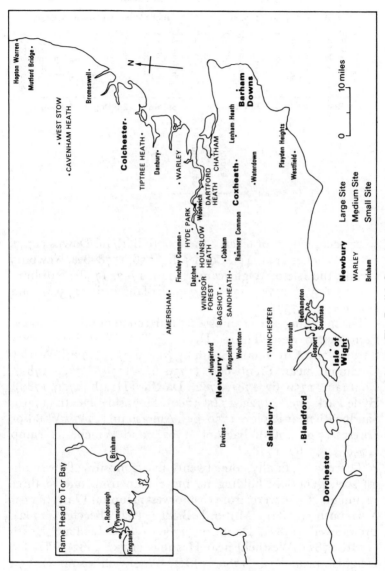

Map 5. The English Campsites, 1722–92

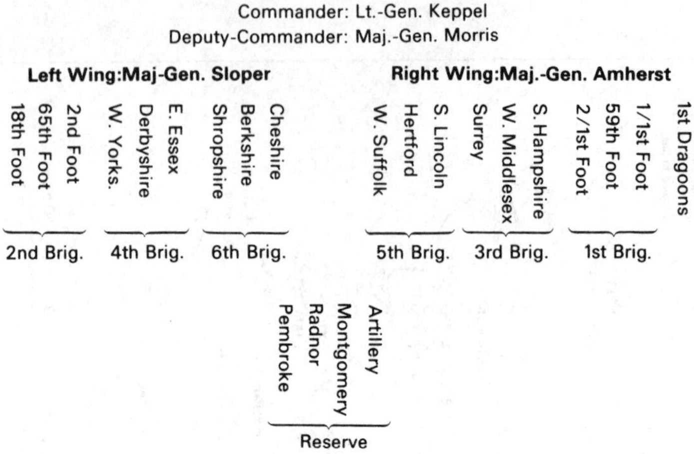

Commander: Lt.-Gen. Keppel
Deputy-Commander: Maj.-Gen. Morris

Left Wing:Maj-Gen. Sloper   **Right Wing:Maj.-Gen. Amherst**

18th Foot	65th Foot	2nd Foot	W. Yorks.	Derbyshire	E. Essex	Shropshire	Berkshire	Cheshire	W. Suffolk	Hertford	S. Lincoln	Surrey	W. Middlesex	S. Hampshire	2/1st Foot	59th Foot	1/1st Foot	1st Dragoons

2nd Brig.   4th Brig.   6th Brig.   5th Brig.   3rd Brig.   1st Brig.

Pembroke	Radnor	Montgomery	Artillery

Reserve

Fig. 5.

were occupied, in brackets), these were Barham Downs (1757, 1760), Colchester (1741), Coxheath (1756, 1778–82), Newbury (1740), the Isle of Wight camp (1740, 1757, 1758), Salisbury (1722, 1757, 1774, 1778, 1779), Blandford (1756), and Dorchester (1757).

The middling-sized camps were thirteen in number, namely, from east to west: Tiptree Heath (1780), West Stowe, near Bury (1778), Cavenham Heath by Newmarket (1779), Warley Common, near Brentwood (1759–62, 1778, 1779, 1781), Chatham (1756–62, 1781, 1782), Dartford Heath (1759, 1780), Hyde Park (1722, 1723, 1745, 1780), Hounslow Heath (1740), Sandheath near Ripley (1759–62), Amersham (1757), Windsor Forest (1740, 1760), Bagshot (1792), and Winchester camp (1756, 1759–62, 1778).

There were, finally, some twenty-five campsites of the smallest sort, generally holding no more than from one to three regiments; these were, from east to west: Hopton Warren, near Yarmouth (1782), Mutford Bridge near Beccles (1782), Bromeswell (1782), Danbury (1780, 1781), Lenham Heath (1781, 1782), Westfield near Hastings (1779, 1782), Playden Heights, near Rye (1780, 1781), Woolwich camp (1775), Waterdown by Tunbridge Wells (1780), Finchley Common (1745, 1780), Ranmore Common (1780), Datchet (1740), Cobham (1740), Kingsclere (1740), Wolverton near Basingstoke (1757), camps at Portsmouth (1780, 1781) and at nearby Bedhampton (1759), Southsea Common (1759), and over at Gosport (1780), a camp at Hungerford (1722), another by Devizes (1740), another near Brixham (1780), and at Plymouth and near-by Roborough and Kingsand each year from 1778 through 1782.

The camps were formed, therefore, during nineteen of the years covered by this study. As we noted above, the invasion threat was seasonal, since men had to wait upon the winds and the crops; and consequently the duration of the camps was relatively constant whether early or late in the century. The troops lay for four months—fifteen to eighteen weeks—in all the camps of 1722, 1723, 1740, 1741, 1757–62, and 1780–2. The infantry camps of 1778 and 1779 lasted for five months, since the invasion threat was greater during those years; while in 1756 the various camps survived from three to six months, what with plenty of Germans available to face the elements (the Hessians at Winchester broke camp only in mid-December). As a general rule, those camps in which only cavalry was to be found broke up about one month earlier than did the infantry camps, since the horses had to be spared; and by late summer the cavalry in all of the camps were turning their horses out to grass.

We might provide a few examples to illustrate the longevity of the camps. In the 1722 Salisbury camp two regiments of Horse, two of Dragoons, and four of marching Foot were under canvas from late May to late September; and three more of Foot joined them in mid-August, come from Hungerford camp and remaining at Salisbury until late September too.[14] From mid-June until mid-October 1740 the whole of the Household cavalry and Foot Guards lay at Hounslow Heath camp, under Sir Charles Wills's command.[15] Similarly at Chatham camp, in 1756, five regiments of marching Foot camped from mid-June to mid-October under Lord George Sackville's command, while over at Blandford two regiments of Dragoons and six of Foot lay encamped only from mid-July to mid-October, under

---

[14] These were the 3rd and 4th of Horse, the 4th and 11th Dragoons, plus Wills's 3rd, Cadogan's 4th, Montague's 11th, and Clayton's 14th of Foot. The later arrivals from Hungerford were Pocock's 8th, Grove's 10th, and Stanwix's 12th of Foot.

[15] SP 41/12, 7 May 1740.

Sir John Mordaunt.[16] At Sandheath in 1759, four regiments of Foot camped from late June until early in November under the Earl of Ancram's command, for nearly nineteen weeks.[17] On Warley Common in 1778, four battalions of marching Foot and eight battalions of militia camped for an average of twenty-one weeks, under Lt.-Gen. Richard Pierson's command, before breaking up early in November; while that same year the four cavalry regiments under Maj.-Gen. George Warde at West Stowe camp, and also another four under Lt.-Gen. James Johnston at Salisbury camp, stayed out for only thirteen weeks, from early July until early October.[18]

The total number of units from the regular army and the artillery that camped during the years covered by this study are listed in Table 10; and it should be emphasized that all militia corps—despite the fact that after the reforms of the mid-1750s they were present in most of the camps, and often in sizeable numbers—are excluded, since their state of training and tactical proficiency (or otherwise) are not our concern here.[19] Compared with the forces regularly encamped by the Prussians and the French—in 1727, for example, there were in four French camps a total of 82 battalions and 131 squadrons; at the Meuse camp in 1733 alone there were 26 battalions and 62 squadrons; at Vaussieux in 1778 there were 44 battalions and

---

[16] At Chatham were Bentinck's 5th, Home's 25th, Loudoun's 30th, Manners's 36th, and Stuart's 37th of Foot; while at Blandford were the 2nd and 10th Dragoons, plus Howard's 3rd, Wolfe's 8th, Skelton's 12th, Amherst's 15th, Kingsley's 20th, and Hay's 33rd of Foot.

[17] At Sandheath were the 5th, 8th, 33rd, and Effingham's 34th of Foot.

[18] At Warley from early June were the 6th, 25th, and 69th of Foot, joined early in July by the new 79th Foot. At West Stowe were the 3rd, 4th, 7th, and 10th Dragoons; and at Salisbury were the 1st, 2nd, and 3rd Dragoon Guards, plus the 6th Dragoons.

[19] The six Marine Regiments are included in the 1740 Isle of Wight camp. The Guards in the camps of 1722, 1723, and 1740 only are included; their annual Hyde Park camps were not really for purposes more serious than 'airing the men' and 'tossing of the firelocks'. The camps of 1780 in Hyde Park and on Finchley Common were not initially formed for training purposes, but rather to concentrate troops to reinforce the Guards and London militia engaged with the Gordon Rioters; some of the regiments in these two camps were drawn in from regular, outlying camps, and are included in the 1780 totals.

Because of the destruction of most records, we know little more about Irish wartime camps than the fact that they were sometimes formed. In 1778 there was a large camp at Clonmell, with two regiments of horse and four of foot, and there was a smaller camp at Kinsale; in 1779 there were small camps at Kilworth, Aghada, and Ardfinnan; and in 1780 Cashell and Kinsale had camps near by.

TABLE 10

YEAR	HORSE	FOOT	ARTILLERY
1722	5 regts + 2 Household trps	13 bns	1 coy
1723	–	9 bns	1 det
1740	10 regts + 6 Household trps	21 bns	3 dets
1741	7 regts	10 bns	—
1756	2 regts	11 bns	—
1757	7 regts	24 bns	3 coys
1758	dets from 9 regts	19 bns	4 coys
1759	—	12 bns + 2 dets	—
1760	—	11 bns	—
1761	—	2 bns	—
1762	—	4 bns	—
1774	—	lt coys from 7 bns	—
1775	—	–	4 coys
1778	9 regts	12 bns	6 coys
1779	11 regts	13 bns	5 coys
1780	—	12 bns	7 coys
1781	2 regts	8 bns	8 coys
1782	5 regts	10 bns	8 coys
1792	2 regts	4 bns	—

trps = troops of cavalry; bns = battalions of foot; dets = detachments from other units; coys = companies; lt = light.

6 regiments of dragoons[20]—these forces seem small; but given the comparatively small number of regiments normally to be found in the whole of England (Appendix B), the British camp concentrations represent major efforts, denuding the countryside of troops.

A typical year's troop dispositions in the camps in Britain is that shown here for 1778:

Warley Common (early July–early November): 6th, 25th, 69th, and 79th of Foot; 8 battalions of militia; 2 companies of the Royal Artillery.

Coxheath (early June–early November): 1st Dragoons; 1/1st, 2/1st, 2nd, 18th, 59th, and 65th of Foot; 15 battalions of militia; 3 companies of the Royal Artillery.

Winchester (early June–early November): 50th Foot; 6 battalions of militia: 1 company Royal Artillery.

Salisbury (early July–early October): 1st, 2nd, and 3rd Dragoon Guards; 6th Dragoons.

West Stowe (early July–early October): 3rd, 4th, 7th, and 10th Dragoons.

Plymouth (mid-June–late October): 13th Foot.

[20] R. Villate, art. cit. 238.

As we noted at the outset, the purpose of the camps (put forth with admirable clarity in the orders appointing general officers to the command of the 1740 camps)[21] was twofold; but for the general and field officers as well as for the tacticians it was the opportunity for advanced training, rather than the larger strategic view that was of primary concern. Indeed the need to form camps for training purposes, come war or peace, was always a constant (if futile) refrain among the military writers: typically, John Macdonald wrote that it would 'be beneficial to discipline were the British army to assemble, annually, in divisions, at certain points, to practise evolutions. This would establish a correctness of division marching, and a skill in executing manoeuvres that would carry our excellent army to a high state of perfection in discipline.'[22] Likewise, Capt. Robert Hinde argued that, 'for the improvement of military knowledge in the cavalry', a few regiments 'might meet and encamp for some little time together, under the direction of a general officer, who should . . . instruct them in the grand manoeuvre.'[23]

Once in the camps, the individual corps quickly set about the task of equalizing the drill of their component troops or companies, since it was to the firings and most especially to the manoeuvres—first by regiment, and then as early as possible in brigades and lines—that camp training was principally to be addressed.[24] Whenever opportunity arose the units went through the full range of firings and manoeuvres that made up the advanced training of individual regiments, while at the same time the camp commanders enforced among them such 'alterations and improvements in the private discipline of corps'—speed of march, length of pace, signals, etc.—as were

[21] These ran: 'Whereas We have thought it Necessary that Our Land Forces which are now dispersed in their several Quarters throughout this Kingdom should be drawn together and be Encamped in Several Bodies to be more Usefull and more Speedily United in Case of Necessity and for the better Instructing Them in Military Discipline . . .' SP 41/12, Secretary at War to Lt.-Gen. Sir Philip Honywood et al., 7 May 1740.

[22] John Macdonald, *French Infantry Regulations*, i. 171.

[23] Robert Hinde, op. cit. 58.

[24] Campbell Dalrymple, op. cit. 165, thought it 'necessary to premise, that the assembling of corps is only for them to act by brigades or in line'; but his precondition —'that every regiment and battalion must be perfect in their discipline before they meet, for the shortness of the time will admit of no tossing of the firelocks'—could hardly be met in the British Army.

necessary to establish that full uniformity among the regiments encamped without which they would be unable to function efficiently and smoothly together. Certain other activities characteristic of active service in the field, but seldom or never attempted in peacetime, were also practised at the regimental level in the camps. Thus battalion-guns—two light, quick-firing brass cannon—were attached to each battalion only when war seemed imminent, or had been declared.[25] Posted on the flanks of the battalion line, these added significantly to the battalion's firepower and were light enough to keep pace with the battalion's movements; manhandled by private men told off to work the drag-ropes while the small detachments of gunners served each piece, they accompanied the foot nearly everywhere on campaign until the very end of the century. The gunners attached to the battalions, of course, learned their business in the Ordnance corps; and the soldiers told off to serve with them as matrosses came under the command of the Royal Artillery subaltern with the guns, and were trained by him in the camps.

In sharp contrast to peacetime training, a great deal of target practice with ball ammunition was carried on in the camps—as indeed it was carried on in all regiments—once war had broken out.[26] At Tiptree Heath alone, in 1780, the 45th Foot and nine militia battalions camped there—some 4,200 men—went through more than 250,000 cartridges with ball; while that same summer Lt.-Gen. Pierson at Dartford Heath camp expected to go through, in a week, the 160,000 ball with

[25] Only at the big annual reviews of the Dublin garrison were battalion-guns attached in peacetime. Outside Dublin, the only example I have found of a regiment practising its drill with these guns attached, in peacetime, occurred in Dec. 1755 at a Rochester review of Stuart's 37th of Foot (WO 27/4); and by that date the army had had its battalion-guns for three weeks, what with war existing in all but name. (See WO 5/42, pp. 472–6 for the mid-Nov. 1755 distribution of battalion-guns to the foot—like augmentations, a characteristic stage in eighteenth-century 'mobilization'.) Very occasionally field pieces—not battalion-guns—might join a regiment on its review day, as happened at the 22nd Foot's review held at Perth in June 1773 (WO 27/27); but such occurrences were the result of unofficial co-operation among regimental officers and local Royal Artillery officers. See also 4th Foot, 1770, and 31st Foot, 1774. WO 27/18 and 30.

[26] In the summer of 1755, with war imminent, the ammunition supplied to the regiments was greatly increased. In May every battalion in Britain was sent sufficient powder for 105,000 cartridges; and in August about thirty-six balls and an extra flint per man were sent to the battalions. WO 55/411, pp. 140–1, 163–4.

which he had been issued and wanted at least 1,000,000—this, for three marching battalions and three of militia. In the Hyde Park camp in 1722, 4,200 men of the Foot Guards were issued 37,000 ball cartridges and 49,000 squibs.[27] Battalion musketry (and individual target practice too, especially among the men of the light companies) was daily practice in the camps; and hence at Coxheath in 1778, for example, the men became 'exceeding expert'.[28]

In the camps, too, the light companies of the several battalions were brigaded, and were able to devote themselves to the specialist activities of light infantry. Several of these companies (which, as we have seen, were formed permanently in British-establishment battalions from 1771, and in those of Ireland from 1772) were assembled at a special camp near Salisbury during August and September 1774, where they were trained by Maj.-Gen. William Howe to a system of skirmishing and speedy manoeuvres designed by him after his experience of the light service during the late North American campaigns.[29] At Salisbury Howe attempted to establish and then to spread through the army a good system of light-infantry drill, which had heretofore been *ad hoc*, established at random; and to train the light companies to a uniform system so that they might function together when joined in composite light battalions on campaign.[30] His system was excellent; it was characterized by endless skirmishing, forward movements in small parties from

[27] On Tiptree, WO 34/203, fos. 10–11; on Dartford, WO 34/126, fo. 194; and on Hyde Park, WO 55/348, pp. 38, 41. In the camp at Beaucaire, in 1753, some 5,000 French soldiers under M. de Crémille burnt 543,000 cartridges; and that was in peacetime. R. Villate, art. cit. 240–1.

[28] *London Evening Post*, 6 Aug. 1778. The reporter claimed that the men 'load and fire with ease five times in a minute'; but he was doubtless watching men using squibs, since such speed with ball cartridges was not possible. The men were apt to be jittery when loading ball—a suspicion confirmed in the 4 Aug. 1778 edition of the same paper, where it was reported that at Coxheath 'Several of the regiments were on Saturday exercised at targets with ball cartridges, and performed exceedingly well; no accident happened except shooting a favourite dog.'

[29] The light companies of the 3rd, 11th, 21st, 29th, 32nd, 36th, and 70th of Foot arrived at Salisbury camp on 6 Aug. 1774, and on 22 Sept. departed for Richmond where, on 3 Oct., they were reviewed by the King. After the royal review the companies rejoined their parent regiments, all in England. WO 5/58, pp. 462–3, 480–1, 491–2.

[30] He failed in this because the events of 1774–5 in Boston overtook the army. The *1778 Regulations*, given out by Amherst, laid down a series of standard light-infantry manoeuvres, as we have seen; but these were not spread beyond the corps serving in Britain at that time. It was not until Moore's system at Shorncliffe spread through the army that a detailed and regular light drill became firmly established.

a two-deep battalion line, by movements carried out either at the quick step or at a run, and by observing both open (4 feet) and extended (10 feet) intervals between the files.[31] In the wartime camps too, after Salisbury, similar training continued, if not to Howe's system.

Although two days per week (according to one regiment) were devoted to the training of individual regiments, it was brigade drill that was properly given pride of place in the camps.[32] Not only were the interests of uniformity served by brigade drill; for as Dundas observed of normal peacetime training, 'speculation only, aided by the practice of small bodies, will often mislead, when applied to the movements of larger ones'.[33] Outside the big peacetime garrisons it was only in the camps that general and field officers enjoyed the opportunity of seeing and handling large forces; and it must be stressed that only in the camps were actual field commands and staffs formed, since in peacetime there was no permanent intermediate command level between the individual regiments on the one hand and the Horse Guards, Dublin Castle, Edinburgh

[31] At Salisbury, sufficient ammunition was issued to provide each officer and man with 90 squibs and 20 ball cartridges, indicating the stress put upon realism in this camp, and on marksmanship among the men (WO 3/4, p. 115; and WO 24/473). The full drill practised by these companies at Salisbury is in NAM MS, no. 6807/157/6, pp. 1–17; and on pp. 19–22 is the description of the review performance put on before George III at Richmond—an extremely realistic display of light tactics, quite the equal of anything practised anywhere else during the later eighteenth century. Interestingly, these companies loaded and fired according to the 1764 platoon exercise, a tribute to its excellence.

[32] An Adjutant-General's circular of 16 May 1795, to the commanding officers of camps, laid down the following rules (which they were to 'Strictly Observe') on the routine of camp life:

'On the Monday, & Friday, in every Week Each Corps is to be exercis'd separately, under the Personal Direction of its own Commanding Officer, practising those parts of the Exercise, set forth in His Majesty's Establish'd Regulations, in which He Himself may find it most defective; or that the Commanding General may think proper expressly to Order.

'On each Tuesday, & Saturday, the Exercising of the Troops, is to be perform'd by Brigades, under the immediate Conduct, & Command of their respective Major Generals.

'On each Wednesday, the Commanding General will take out the whole Line, & make them perform such Movements, Manoeuvres, or other Exercises, as He may think proper.'

Thursday was for rest, with extra drill for awkward or negligent units. The regimen was designed especially 'for the essential purpose of promoting Uniformity in the Discipline of the Troops'. WO 3/28, pp. 89–90.

[33] David Dundas, op. cit. 7.

Castle, or the few colonial governors on the other. This was greatly to the advantage of the general officers, the great majority of whom—excepting only the handful appointed annually as reviewing officers—never manoeuvred so much as a regiment, in peacetime. With full-time realistic training by sizeable numbers at last possible, field and general officers got the much-needed opportunity of seeing and taking part in major manoeuvres which for many of them could, until then, hardly have been more than visions conjured by drillbook plates or distant memories.

In the camps, it was to the manoeuvres that most time was devoted, '*as the feet and not the arms will be exercised*', ran the controlling dictum.[34] Major manoeuvres, mock battles, and large-scale reviews were conducted repeatedly in all camps. As ever, the Hanoverian Kings paid the closest attention; and by so doing they encouraged intensive efforts. Thus George I reviewed the horse in Hyde Park camp on 20 August 1722, 'where His Majesty was pleased to express his intire Satisfaction with the good Appearance the Troops made'; and he travelled on to Salisbury camp next where he reviewed four regiments of cavalry and seven of foot, a particularly large concentration.[35] Later, in September, the news-sheets were reporting that the grenadiers in Hyde Park would soon put on a 'fine Exercise' for the King, since recently 'a great Quantity of Paper Hand-Grenadoes were brought up to the Tower from Woolwich.'[36] George II visited all the main 1740 and 1741 camps. The most senior general officers too held reviews frequently, Lt.-Gen. Sir John Mordaunt, for example holding a 'general review and exercise' of the two regiments of cavalry and six of foot at Blandford camp on 31 August 1756.[37] George III took much interest in the camps: not only did he see Howe's light infantry, fresh from camp, go through their drill and mock fighting in Richmond Park in October 1774; but in July 1775 he attended

---

[34] Campbell Dalrymple, op. cit. 165. By 'arms' he referred, of course, to the manual and platoon exercises.

[35] *Daily Courant*, 22 Aug. 1722; *Weekly Journal or Saturday's-Post*, 1 Sept. 1722; and *London Gazette*, 4 Sept. 1722. See also C. Knight, op. cit. ii, Pt. I, 104. Three battalions which arrived at Salisbury from Hungerford camp came especially for the grand review.

[36] *Weekly Journal or Saturday's-Post*, 22 Sept. 1722.

[37] R. Wright, op. cit. 348–9.

a special demonstration performed by the 1st and 3rd bat-talions of the Royal Artillery, held near Chatham (Townshend, the Master-General, having himself put these artillerymen through their paces a month earlier).[38] On 12 August 1778 the whole of the very large force assembled at Coxheath was re-hearsing for a royal review, the actual event being attended by the King and Queen, escorted by Lord Amherst;[39] and later the King saw the forces at Winchester where a fine series of manoeuvres was gone through—the soldiers (according to an excited local correspondent) being 'emulous in their en-deavours to make a proper appearance on the occasion'.[40] As late as 1792 a special camp was set up at Bagshot, near Windsor, to demonstrate to the King the new system of drill devised by Dundas.[41] The Duke of York, as C.-in-C., was as zealous as had been his predecessors in the business of reviewing camps; and although those formed in the wars against Revolutionary and Napoleonic France are beyond our period, camps of 1793–6 were being used to train the foot in Britain to the new *1792 Regulations*, already established in Ireland.[42]

Formal reviews occupied much less of the time of the corps encamped, of course, than did major marches, manoeuvres, and mock battles. We have space here only to outline these activi-ties. At Winchester camp in September 1778 a fort put up for the purpose was attacked and 'destroyed', and 'a mock en-

[38] Townshend's manoeuvres are in the Kent RO Amherst MSS 095/9A and 9 B; and details of the King's review are in 095/18, 19, and 20.

[39] *General Evening Post*, 15 Aug. 1778; and C. Herbert, art. cit. 142–3.

[40] *General Evening Post*, 22 Sept. 1778. On large-scale reviews at Warley camp, see the same paper for 22 Aug. and 24 Sept. 1778. For Amherst's review there in 1779 see WO 34/114, fo. 48; and for the review of 1781 see WO 34/196, fo. 68. Warley reviews were always sizeable affairs.

[41] WO 3/10, pp. 109–73, *passim*; /27, pp. 116–17; and WO 55/379, p. 123. See also C. Knight, op. cit., ii, Pt I, 245–6. From 23 July until 8 Aug. 1792, the 10th and 11th Dragoons, plus the 2nd, 3rd, 14th, and 29th of Foot, camped at Bagshot under the Duke of Richmond's command. Although it was intended to show the King the new regulation manoeuvres worked up by Dundas and Pitt in the Dublin garrison, the Adjutant-General wrote that Bagshot was planned with the intention 'of shewing His M. . . . a few Corps of Cavalry, Infantry, and Artillery, formed into one Body, the Combined Movements of which, while they gave Satisfaction to His M-y, would at the same time prove an useful Lesson to officers in general; such especially as had never been employed on Actual Service'. WO 3/10, p. 164.

[42] The camps of 1793–4 were essentially staging camps to feed the army in the Low Countries; and there was much confusion too, as the army expanded at this time. For these reasons we have not studied these camps in detail.

gagement . . . was carried on with great dexterity' along with several other 'wonderful manoeuvres'; seven battalions and guns were employed.[43] In August 1778 at Warley Common half the troops defended a wood against repeated assaults by the rest, supported by artillery; and although the attacking force was several times repulsed, their retreat was 'dexterously covered and secured by the light infantry and grenadiers'. A similar attack was laid on a month later at Warley in the presence of Lord Amherst, 'several of the Nobility, [and] British and Foreign General Officers'. Among the many manoeuvres performed by the four regular and eight militia battalions camped there, 'a line of march was . . . formed, and the flanking companies forming upon the right of the line, began a severe firing. The grenadiers and light-infantry companies were detached to force them to quit their position, when a desperate firing ensued, and they drove the enemy from the field.'[44] In the Isle of Wight camp in 1757 the ten regular battalions, two composite battalions of Marines, and the artillery were practising siege warfare, digging entrenchments, and building fortifications.[45] At Kinsale camp in 1778 the light companies of nine battalions were exercised at skirmishing tactics, rather as Howe's companies had been drilled at Salisbury;[46] and in the countryside around Kinsale, meanwhile, very elaborate, realistic, and tactically sophisticated encounters between large opposing forces were carried out: during one such, the leading elements of an advancing 'army', after staging a series of feints which involved clearing a wood and street-fighting in a village, succeeded in gaining a river crossing in the face of much superior forces. Infantry, field artillery, and light cavalry all took part.[47] In 1779 Lt.-Gen. George Lane Parker at Warley sought to introduce more realism by marching his troops through rough country. Lt.-Gen. William Haviland at Plymouth, in 1781, marched seven regiments of foot for a mile in two columns, and then deployed in line of

[43] *General Evening Post*, 22 Sept. 1778.

[44] Ibid., 22 Aug. and 24 Sept.

[45] W. H. Hackmann, 'English Military Expeditions to the Coast of France, 1757–1761', unpubl. University of Michigan Ph.D. thesis, 1969, 33.

[46] C. Knight, op. cit. ii, Pt I, 222.

[47] A summary of these operations (with an excellent 'battle-map'), can be found in the Bucks RO Howard-Vyse Pprs, B/11/5 and 7.

battle. In 1780 the battalions at Dartford Heath marched to Gravesend and crossed the Thames to Tilbury in a day's outing. At Bagshot in 1792 the whole force decamped in the night, and marched in darkness to Farnham where they made camp next day.[48] Coxheath was always a scene of much activity, including route marches and the training of provisional light and grenadier battalions.[49] On 13 July 1778 the Duke of Gloucester saw the many regiments there form columns and march 'to Langley-common, where a mock fight was represented, and all the variety of bush-fighting, ambuscading, assaults, and other military manoeuvres' were performed.[50] Officers and men of the Royal Artillery were present in almost all of the eighteenth-century camps, taking part in joint training; and in the bigger camps not just battalion-guns but mortars and field pieces were assembled, and took part in the mock battles and sieges.[51] The Ordnance also sent down Engineer officers and artificers to prepare field works, and sometimes they took along 'portable Redoubts'.[52]

It will be clear from the foregoing that camp experience was of the utmost service in the advanced training of the regiments; and indeed it could hardly have been otherwise, given a lot as unsettled as that afflicting the peacetime British Army. All the conditions requisite for the serious and effective advanced training of the corps were now present, where for so long they had been denied. Each regiment, in camping, was concentrating; each was able to call together its scattered detachments, troops, or companies not merely for the few weeks of pre-review drill but for several months of the most intensive training, in conditions closely approximating those of actual field service. Ammunition, varied terrain, field equipment, and time, all were plentiful; while dozens of officers with the experience of other corps (and other arms), with different systems of interior economy and customary practices, were close

[48] J. R. Western, op. cit. 411–12; and WO 3/27, pp. 116–17.
[49] Many details on Coxheath training are in C. Herbert, art. cit., esp. 140–3.
[50] *General Evening Post*, 16 July 1778.
[51] M. E. S. Laws, op. cit., *passim*, lists all Royal Artillery units in the camps. In the summer of 1775 a special artillery encampment was formed near Woolwich. See the detailed MS books on gun drill, *c.*1775, in the Kent RO Sackville of Knole MSS 0186/1 and 3.
[52] WO 3/27, p. 116.

at hand. In the camps, furthermore, regiments of the same arm were brigaded, and together they practised the all-important movements of the line of battle and the column of march; while regiments of different arms enjoyed (as did the general officers commanding) the unique training experience of mutual tactical co-operation and support. In the camps the most realistic advanced training, therefore, was carried on intensively for extended periods.

The utility of the camps is clear; and we might best judge the efficacy of camp experience by looking not at corps that came into the camps 'fit for service', but rather at the records of those that came in poorly trained, or otherwise unfit for service. Several examples of corps in this latter condition can be followed, and point the same conclusion. Typical was the 69th Foot which camped at Warley in 1778, at Coxheath in 1779, at Ranmore Common and at Gosport in 1780, before going on campaign late in 1780. Reviewed in Britain in 1777, before camping, the regiment was in good order but half made up of recruits; it was consequently not yet fit for service. Seen at Coxheath late in 1779, it was reported 'well, steady and attentive under Arms, performs what is required of them with precision, and . . . very fit for any Service'.[53] The 30th Foot was in the Dublin garrison in 1777, camped at Clonmell in 1778, and camped again in Ireland in 1779 before sailing for service in the southern colonies and the West Indies in 1781. Reviewed at Dublin late in 1777, the corps was 'dirty', 'slovenly', with the men 'marching very uneven and not compact, always waving from side to side, frequently stragling and flying out from each other'; the manoeuvres and firings were all badly performed; and in short 'This Regiment requires an immensity of care and attention.' Seen after Clonmell camp service, however, the 30th late in 1778 was performing complicated manoeuvres, and was in all respects fit for service.[54] There were other poor corps, suffering from various ills. When Huske's 23rd Foot was seen at Leicester in February 1757, recently returned from the Minorca disaster, it was in a most deplorable condition; yet the regiment was fully restored during the summer and autumn at Chatham camp, and went on to take

[53] WO 27/35 and 42.   [54] WO 27/37 and 41.

part in the epic advance at Minden.[55] When Bentinck's 5th Foot was seen at Salisbury in 1755, it was 'too full of Recruits to be as yet fit for Service'; but by mid-1759 (having camped during the previous three seasons), the 5th was in excellent condition.[56] Bentinck's was an Irish regiment transferred to England in 1755, there to recruit up to the British establishment. When seen in May 1755 it was composed of 420 rank and file of whom half were recruits; by September 1759 it numbered 873 rank and file, almost all of whom were trained soldiers. Other corps followed this pattern, new-raised regiments included. The 79th Foot, raised by the city of Liverpool from January 1778, camped for four months at Warley during the summer and autumn of that year and was deemed fit to go abroad in March 1779—only fourteen months after being raised. The 87th Foot spent the summer and autumn of 1779 at Plymouth camp (it was in fact raised in the camp); and the regiment embarked upon active service early in 1780. The 2/73rd was raised in Scotland in 1777 and spent four months in Kingsand camp during the 1779 season; and soon after it joined the Gibraltar garrison and took part in the epic defence of that place.[57]

Of the twenty-nine marching battalions to camp in England and Ireland between 1778 and 1782, sixteen had been unfit for service upon the formation of their camps; and of these nine were drafted corps, using the camps as concentration centres where they could train and rebuild in ideal conditions.[58] As we noted earlier, eleven of the battalions serving in America were totally drafted there, their officers and NCOs returning home to rebuild the corps anew; and from among these came the nine battalions in question. The 18th Foot was typical of them all. In North America since 1767 and drafted there in 1775, the regiment was at Coxheath in 1778, at Warley in 1779, and at Tiptree in 1780. By the time that the 18th had amassed eight months of camp experience it was reported by a reviewing officer to be in fine condition, well trained and fit for service.[59]

[55] WO 27/4.
[56] WO 27/3 and 6.
[57] P. R. N. Katcher, op. cit., *passim.*
[58] These were the 6th, 10th, 14th, 16th, 18th, 26th, 45th, 50th, 52nd, 59th, and 65th; all but the 16th and 26th camped in England after being drafted.
[59] WO 27/36 and 42.

The 6th Foot was drafted in America late in 1776, and the skeleton sent home. Rebuilding in England, the 6th camped at Warley in 1778, at Coxheath in 1779, and at Playden Heights in 1780—where it was reported fully trained.[60] Inspection reports on the other drafted corps show the same progress; and despite the very great difficulty in obtaining recruits during these years, a problem which slowed somewhat the training of all units, comparison with another drafted corps (the 26th) indicates that the camped corps rebuilt at least a year more quickly than was normally the case.[61]

The efficacy of camp training is clear. But how many regiments actually experienced it? Of the seventy-eight battalions of Foot Guards, marching Foot, and Marines that saw service in the Low Countries and Germany, in Britain, on the French coast, in the Mediterranean, and in the Americas during the 1739–48 war, twenty-four only enjoyed camp training; and of the twenty-three cavalry regiments to see active service in the Low Countries, Germany, and Britain, ten had seen camp service. Of the sixty-eight battalions of Foot Guards and marching Foot that composed the regular army during the war, only eighteen saw camp duty.

During the 1756–63 war, fourteen regiments of cavalry and seventeen battalions of foot served in Germany, arriving in two contingents in 1758 and 1760. Of this foot, all save three battalions had had camp training before embarking, some of the battalions having been encamped during three and four consecutive seasons;[62] and half of the horse regiments had done camp duty before embarking. The regiments sent to North America and the West Indies, where at least forty-six regular battalions saw service at different times during the war, were much less well prepared than those that were sent to Germany.[63]

---

[60] WO 27/42 and 45.

[61] WO 27/47, 49, and 53, Pt 1.

[62] E.g. the 5th Foot camped at Chatham in 1756, at Blandford and the Isle of Wight in 1757, the Isle of Wight again in 1758, and at Sandheath in 1759. The 8th and 33rd of Foot, both of which also served in Germany, likewise spent four summers in the camps before sailing.

[63] These have never been tallied before. Before the outbreak of hostilities, in 1754, the 38th and 49th were already in the West Indies and the 40th, 45th, and 47th in North America. These corps were reinforced from Europe, as follows:

North America: early 1755: 44th, 48th; mid-1755: 35th, 1/42nd; early 1757: 22nd;

Most of them, whether sent out from Europe or raised in America, got their advanced training the hard way, in the field. Since over half of the regiments that crossed the Atlantic during this war came from Ireland, we have no specific details of their previous camp activities; but it is almost a certainty that none of them had, in fact, camped.[64] Of the battalions that came from Britain some were almost raw (the 2/42nd, 77th, and 78th, all Highland corps); and of the others most were recently raised corps formed between 1755 and 1761; most of these had had time in which to prepare themselves 'fit for service', but none save the handful that had gone on the Belle-Isle expedition had any experience of active service.[65] Of them all, only the 3rd, 15th, 34th, 61st, 63rd, 64th, and 72nd had had previous camp experience.

Thus of the eighty-three battalions of Foot Guards and marching Foot that saw service in Germany, Portugal, the West Indies, America, India, the Mediterranean, or upon the

---

mid-1757: 2/1st, 17th, 28th, 43rd, 46th, 55th; late 1757: 77th, 78th; mid-1758: 15th, 58th.

West Indies: early 1759: 3rd, 4th, 2/42nd, 61st, 63rd, 64th, 65th; late 1761: 69th, 76th, 90th, 94th, 97th, 98th; early 1762: 34th, 56th, 72nd.

The following corps were raised either wholly in North America or recruited there on cadres formed in Europe:

from late 1754: Shirley's 50th, Pepperell's 51st

from late 1755: 1/, 2/, 3/, and 4/60th

from mid-1758: Gage's 80th

from mid-1760: Burton's 95th (from South Carolina Independent Coys)

Two ranging corps were raised in America, Rogers's from 1755 and Gorham's from 1761.

It should be noted that there was considerable movement between these two theatres, once the corps had arrived.

When the war began, there were already two coys of the Royal Artillery in North America; by the end of 1758 there were six coys RA in North America, and one coy in the West Indies. In 1760 there were nine coys RA in North America, and one in the West Indies; while in 1762 there were six coys in North America and five in the West Indies. At the war's end, there were eight coys RA in North America, and none in the West Indies.

[64] Camping was of limited value to Irish corps intended for service abroad, before the 1770 change of establishments; for the augmentation of skeletal strengths by great numbers of drafts and recruits, when they departed that kingdom, changed entirely the character of the units and (in the short term) considerably reduced their proficiency.

[65] Not that Belle Isle service gave them much of an advantage. The 90th (raised in 1759), 94th (r. 1760), 97th (r. 1760), and 98th (r. 1761) all came to the West Indies from that place, where the army commander had considered them all to be 'undisciplined and ignorant of their duty'. W. K. Hackmann, op. cit. 173.

French coasts during the 1756–63 war, thirty-three only are known to have experienced advanced training in the camps; and of the fifteen regiments of horse to campaign in Germany and Portugal, seven had seen camp service. Of the 134 regiments of foot that composed the army during the war, only thirty-four saw camp duty.

Not until 1778, when the French became open belligerents, were camps necessary in the 1775–83 war; and consequently of the seventy-nine battalions of foot and two regiments of cavalry that saw service in the West Indies and North America during the war, all save twenty battalions had crossed the Atlantic before the first camps were formed.[66] Of all the battalions to serve in the Americas only nine camped before embarking; and of these six served in the West Indies and only three in North America. Of the total of ninety-eight battalions of Foot Guards and marching Foot and two regiments of cavalry that saw service in North America, the West Indies, the Mediterranean garrisons, India, or on board the fleet, during the war, only sixteen battalions camped before going on active service. Of the 118 battalions of Foot Guards and marching Foot composing the army during the war, twenty-nine battalions saw camp training; and of the thirty regiments of horse, twenty saw camp service.

As the figures given above illustrate, it was always a minority of the regiments composing the army that actually encamped at all. During the 1739–48 war, one-third of the foot and less than half the cavalry camped; during the 1756–63 war, less than a third of the foot camped and only one-quarter of the cavalry did so; and during the 1775–83 war only one-quarter of the foot camped, while as much as two-thirds of the cavalry (the only exception) did so. This was all invaluable experience, for the regiments lucky enough to enjoy it; but since it was not in peacetime but rather in wartime that advanced training was carried on most effectively, most realistically, and most intensively, it was while actually in the field abroad that the majority of regiments were obliged to carry on the business. We shall, therefore, consider that theme in the following chapter.

[66] Of these seventy-nine, the 84th and 105th were raised in North America, and the 99th in Jamaica.

Chapter VII

Advanced Training in the Field

In the routine of peacetime service, extensive concentration time was a luxury seldom afforded the great majority of corps; and so it was in wartime, when the dispersed companies and troops were concentrated in full regimental strength either in the encampments at home or in the field abroad, that the regiments at last enjoyed the opportunity to carry on intensive advanced training. We have seen that, as a rule, less than one-third of the regiments were fortunate enough to spend so much as a single season in the camps before embarking on board the transports for the overseas theatres of operations; and hence it was only when actually arrived in the theatres that the bulk of the army was able to devote itself to sustained advanced training.

The detailed firings and manoeuvres drawn from the regulations and from customary practice were now practised endlessly and vigorously by the regiments both individually and in brigade. We cannot too strongly stress how utterly commonplace this activity was in the field, from at least as early as the campaigns of Marlborough;[1] and it was as characteristic of the army abroad in wartime, as was endless repetition of the mechanical basics typical of the army in peacetime. Advanced training was carried on year-round, as weather permitted: it was done most intensively in the garrisons and cantonments late in the winter and through the spring as the army prepared to take the field with the coming campaigning season; and whenever opportunities arose during the campaigns themselves —as they very frequently did, given the generally slow pace at which operations were conducted—a great deal more was

---

[1] From the beginning of the century we find orders to this effect. Thus a general order given out by Orkney to 'all Commanding Officers of ye British Infantry' in Flanders, in the winter quarters of 1711–12, directed 'All Commanding Officers, to take Care that ye Officers Sarjents and Corp^ls of their Regim^ts be made p'fect in ye Exercise as soon as possible, They likewise to have there Regiments out to Exercise Once a week.' BL Add. MS 29, 477, fo. 13. The *1755 Standing Orders* (p. 194), reflecting the wartime practice of 1742–8, directed that when serving in the field the commanding officers of all corps were to 'exercise their Battalions, at least once a week.'

carried on. Nor was it only regulation and customary drill that corps practised in this fashion. The commanders of armies serving in the field—and, in one or two cases, of expeditionary forces assembling in England—often made additions to, or revisions in, the currently practised drill, in an effort to adapt the corps serving under their command to the peculiar tactical conditions prevailing in specific theatres. At the same time field engineering, the *petite guerre*, ranging service, and the like— activities with which most officers had heretofore been acquainted only in their studies—had now to be practised in earnest, where appropriate.

The regiments had need of this training. Most went to war well trained in the basics but insufficiently trained at the advanced elements of the drill; most went to war with little or no experience of manoeuvring in brigade, let alone in the lines and columns adopted on campaign by the army as a whole; and most went to war not long after taking in considerable numbers of drafts and new recruits, together with a half-dozen or so young and inexperienced subalterns. The peacetime training given the army was insufficient to enable it adequately to perform its tactical role, when first brought before the enemy; and many corps suffered, in consequence, during their initial encounters. Since only a minority camped before proceeding abroad, most were obliged to learn their business on the spot; and it was to require as much as two or three campaigns before the army became sufficiently expert at its business, and thus formidable.

We can illustrate this pattern by studying the performance of the regiments in initial engagements of the wars of our period, and by considering the training carried on during successive campaigns. Initial inadequacy followed by intensive practice was a general pattern, it will be appreciated, wherever the enemy was militarily competent; and such was the case in all the wars of the century save that of 1775–83, where the army was dealing initially with untrained amateurs and so was successful on the battlefield from the outset. Since the wars were so frequent, we cannot of course cover each of the many campaigns, much less in detail; and consequently we have limited ourselves to the key initial actions and successive campaigns of the Austrian Succession and Seven Years Wars. These wars suit our purposes because, between them, they saw the army upon the most widespread and varied service—from Germany and the Low Countries to Scotland, and from New France and New York to the West Indies—and so between them embrace the full range of activities upon which the army was to find itself engaged during our period.

Where the training of the corps was concerned, the same overall pattern was to prevail in the field in both wars, although there were differences in detail. The training carried on over the years 1740–8 was based almost entirely upon the *1728 Regulations*, and on the several orders that had supplemented those regulations; and as we noted earlier (Ch. III), only by the closing years of the Austrian Succession war were some slight departures from this body of regulation drill being made—departures which were to be brought together and themselves made regulation practice at the mid-1750s. Whereas Cumberland in Scotland made slight modifications in the drill and countenanced the minor changes that took place in Flanders, *c*.1746–8, in general he saw to it that the regiments practised their drill quite 'as the Book directs'; and in so doing he was only repeating injunctions given out by all the commanders-in-chief who served during the century.[2] The 1750s, however, were to be years of some change and innovation in the army's drill, stimulated by the experience of the late campaigns and by the study of Prussian and French models; and innovation was to be further encouraged by the tactical demands of those widely flung theatres in which sizeable British forces were to be engaged, during the Seven Years War. The 'fertile geniuses' were to make their appearance in considerable numbers; and their innovations, although seldom more than practical adaptations of the regulation drill to fit specific circumstances, add a dimension to the campaigns of 1755–63 not seen in those of 1740–8. But none of this changed the overall pattern of initial incapacity and intensive practice.

By 1740 the army had passed through a quarter-century of peace interrupted only occasionally and briefly by brush-fire

[2] As early as Marlborough's campaigns, a general order given out in Flanders ran: '[Regimental] Adjutants are constantly to keep to all the Rules and Forms of Discipline and Exercise established by Authority; and on no Pretence whatever are to change, or let fall, any of the said Customs without Orders.' Anon., *Rudiments of War* (1777), 156. This was to be a general refrain in all British armies for the rest of the century.

action against the Spaniards and the Jacobites. Having been dispersed for so long, it was in the English camps of 1740 and 1741, and then in the Flanders cantonments of 1742 and early 1743, that intensive training at the level of the regiment was at last allowed to proceed little disturbed. The immediate results were, however, dismal—a powerful condemnation of the training carried out during the preceding quarter-century, and a graphic illustration of the influence of the friction of peace. During the early years of the new war it was the fire-discipline of the British foot that was found most wanting; and this was remarkable since, as we have seen, it was with the intricacies and the efficacy of the platoon-fire system that the drill-books and the regimental officers of the period had chiefly been concerned.

Dettingen, fought on 27 June 1743, was the first large-scale formal battle in which considerable numbers of British troops were engaged since Sheriffmuir in 1715—or perhaps since Malplaquet in 1709. It is the first of the three main actions in which we shall be considering the performance of the regiments; for those engaged at Dettingen had been out of the British Isles only a year.

At Dettingen the British foot held the left wing of the Pragmatic Army's order of battle, and the British cavalry made up the bulk of the mounted troops present.[3] As the Allied lines advanced to close the 1,000 yards separating them from the French at the opening of the battle, there appeared the first fruits of a quarter-century of peacetime training followed by a year of intensive drill: ragged fire began to erupt here and there from the British battalions, although they were still far beyond effective range. Two officers likened it to a *feu de joie*, as other battalions down the line likewise opened fire, 'tho no Ennemy was at that time almost within Cannon Shot of some Corps which Fired'; it was 'neither directed by officers nor regulated in platoons'.[4] Several battalions 'popp'd at one hundred paces', doing little execution, observed an officer with Peers' 23rd of Foot.[5] Jeffrey Amherst reported that 'our Foot fired too soon &

---

[3] Of the several modern accounts of the battle, the best is M. Orr, *Dettingen, 1743* (1972).
[4] Cumb. Pprs, Pt 4, ii, fos. 4 and 57.
[5] The *Gentleman's Magazine* (July 1743), 381–7, contains several eye-witness accounts.

in too great a Hurry'.[6] James Wolfe, then a young adjutant with Duroure's 12th of Foot, spent much of the day 'begging and ordering the men not to fire at too great a distance . . . but to little purpose. The whole fired when they thought they could reach them, which had like to have ruined us. We did very little execution with it.'[7] When arrived within range, the French cavalry advanced upon the allied foot—prompting the officer commanding one of the English battalions ('who was probably prepossessed with Ideas of Actions collected from books, or Old Soldiers Accounts') to enquire of a general officer standing near by 'whether he shou'd Fire at them by Platoons or Ranks'. The reply was as follows:

Keep your Battalion in a Line with the Regiments on your Right and Left, if you perceive any of them to give way, look Sharp and Guard your Flanks, give great attention to prevent your Men from falling into confusion after they have Fired and are loading again . . . [and] as to Platoon or Rank firing I shall be glad to see you perform either in Action, but I own I never did yet on a Field day or at a Review.[8]

Such a reply may have been realistic, but can hardly have been comforting to an officer trained all his career to attempt controlled fire; but with 'our Men, being then Novices', as Maj. John LaFaussille described them, no more could be expected.[9] And so the firing continued for the rest of the day, some officers in fact quite approving it. Lt.-Col. Charles Russell of the 1st Foot Guards wrote that the infantry

were under no command by way of Hide Park firing, but the whole three ranks made a running fire of their own accord . . . with great judgement and skill, stooping all as low as they could, making almost every ball take place . . . The French fired in the same manner . . . without waiting for words of command, and Lord Stair did often say he had seen many a battle, and never saw the infantry engage in any other manner.[10]

[6] Kent RO Amherst MSS 01/1, 27 June 1743 NS.

[7] Beckles Willson, op. cit. 37. The Austrian foot behaved in this fashion at Guastalla, in Sept. 1734, as an officer recounts in *HMC Clements MSS* (1913), p. 408.

[8] Cumb. Pprs, Pt. 4, ii, fo. 4. Lt.-Gen. Jasper Clayton was referred to.

[9] Ibid.

[10] M. Orr, op. cit. 65. Russell went so far as to observe that, in this manner, not the generals but rather 'our men and their regimental officers gained the day; not in the manner of Hyde Park discipline, but our foot almost kneeled down by whole ranks, and so fired upon 'em.' *HMC Chequers Court MSS* (1910), p. 260.

The running fire which the foot used that day was effective, fortunately, when the lines got within range; but it did not accomplish what Bland, Kane, and the rest saw in the controlled platoon system—that is, it did not keep off the French horse—and so the army courted disaster. The French cavalry broke into the lines of foot—some of them rode through Campbell's 21st and caught Huske's 32nd in the act of forming square (Huske's grenadiers kept them off long enough to complete the manoeuvre)—and most of the left-wing battalions seem to have been obliged to form square, until the British cavalry came to their assistance and restored the situation. Had the French foot closely supported their own horse, the British must have been defeated.

Though the cavalry made a number of timely charges during the course of the battle, their conduct too left much to be desired. When the *maison du roi* was among the British squares, The Blues, the 2nd, and the 8th Horse were sent to drive them off. Over-eager, they broke their order by advancing at a gallop, and then topped off this blunder by firing their pistols rather than falling on with their swords. The 2nd Horse actually collided with The Blues, and both had to fall back to reform.[11] The behaviour of all the cavalry—save for the 3rd Dragoons, who early in the battle sacrificed themselves by attacking the whole of the horse of the *maison du roi*—was thought to be very bad by most officers. 'Our Horse had like to have broke our first line in the confusion', wrote Wolfe.[12] Russell felt that the behaviour of the troopers of The Blues in particular 'was scandalous', adding that 'one general officer had ordered some platoons of his regiment to present and was going to fire upon the latter cavalry, but in consideration of the officers of that corps prevented it.' The Blues, he said, 'fairly one and all faced to the right about and never stood their ground', while the 2nd Horse 'pretty near followed their example' and the 8th Horse 'behaved the least ill, but bad enough'. In short, the cavalry in his estimation had not done their duty: 'our foot did their business for 'em, [and] they may properly be said to be routed and beat by the enemy's horse.'[13] The dragoons seem to have behaved better, though the 4th and 6th Dragoons were twice

[11] M. Orr, op. cit. 59–60.   [12] Beckles Willson, op. cit. 36.
[13] *HMC Chequers Court MSS* (1900), pp. 257, 266–7.

repulsed with loss by the French cavalry. Hawley's 1st Dragoons like Bland's 3rd, performed very well indeed; but neither Hawley nor Bland was likely to suffer anything less from his corps. During the later stages of the battle the whole of the British cavalry, now rallied, launched a series of effective charges—'but not with so much success, tho' they had vastly the advantage by weight of their horses', wrote Maj. Charles Colville of the 21st Foot.[14]

So went the battle of Dettingen, in which all the regiments after a year of advanced training in their Flanders and Rhineland cantonments showed themselves still to be poorly disciplined, tactically clumsy, and as yet inadequately prepared to perform the drill. They were however successful—though it was admitted that their success was due as much to Grammont's folly as to their own prowess.

Stair's forces at Dettingen, though not proficient, had at least the advantage of a year's training behind them; and most of those corps had been in the 1740 and 1741 camps. The regiments that fought at Prestonpans on 2 October 1745, the first engagement of the Jacobite rebellion, were not so lucky. Engaged under Cope at Prestonpans were the 13th and the 14th Dragoons, together with Murray's 46th, Lascelles' 47th, and 5 companies of Lee's 44th of Foot; two companies of Guise's 6th and one of the Black Watch were also present. None of these corps (save the handful from the 6th) had ever been in action. The 13th and 14th Dragoons had been raised in Ireland in 1715, and had been there ever since; only in 1742 had they been brought over to England. The 44th, 46th, and 47th of Foot were all new-raised, raising in Britain early in 1741 and doing duty there since. The Jacobite outbreak found them all in the usual state of dispersal that characterized the normal routine of the duty of Great Britain; and only from late August were they in concentration. 'All the few Troops of this Country are raw', Cope reported in consequence, 'and unused to taking the Field.'[15]

Prestonpans lasted about five minutes.[16] The English line

[14] J. O. Robson (ed.), 'Military Memoirs of Lt.-Gen. The Hon. Charles Colville', *JSAHR* 26 (1948), 118.

[15] R. Jarvis, op. cit. i, 11.

[16] The best account of Prestonpans is to be drawn from the testimony given at the enquiry held later, at the Horse Guards, and published as Anon., *Report of the Pro-*

was drawn up with a dragoon regiment upon each flank and the foot in the centre. There was no second line, and only two squadrons in reserve. The position was a fair one—'There is not in the whole of the ground between Edinburgh and Dunbar, a better Spot for both Horse and Foot to act upon,' said Cope[17] —and since the opposing forces were about equal in numbers the day should have been decided by disciplined volley-fire. The foot drew up 'with Great Spirit, and the utmost Exactness,' testified Col. Peregrine Lascelles, 'in perfect good Order, to attack or receive the Rebels';[18] and that done, said Lt.-Col. Halkett of the 44th, the field officers with the foot proceeded 'to divide into Platoons and Firings', telling off according to the *1728 Regulations*, as was proper.[19] The Highlanders now came rushing down upon the front and right of the English line ('with a Swiftness not to be conceived'); and with that the dragoons stationed upon the right flank, though ordered to advance, 'immediately turned their Backs, and ran off with the greatest Precipitation', said Lt.-Col. Whitefoord of the Train.[20] The panic of the right-flank squadrons immediately communicated itself to those upon the left and in reserve, and they followed suit—indeed, 'all of them so much at the same Instant, that it's difficult to say, which run first', testified Cope.[21] The foot, meanwhile, had attempted to fire into the Highlanders coming down upon them, sword in hand; but they got off only one or at the best two very ragged discharges (hardly volleys). Cope testified—generously—that 'our Foot gave them their Fire'; more accurately Lord Drummore, who was observing the action from behind the English line, testified that 'the Fire of our Foot was infamous, Puff, Puff, no Platoon that I heard', and most other officers concurred.[22] If the foot failed to fire by platoons, they broke and ran in that fashion: Maj. Talbot of the 46th, standing on the left of the line, saw 'the breaking of the Foot, come on regularly, as it were by Platoons, from the Right to the Left', and Maj. Severn of the 47th said

ceedings . . . of the Board of General Officers on Their Examination of Lieutenant-General Sir John Cope . . . Colonel Peregrine Lascelles, and Brigadier-General Thomas Fowke . . . in 1745 (1749). K. Tomasson and F. Buist, *Battles of the '45* (1967), is thoroughly trustworthy; and R. Jarvis, op. cit. i. 3–47, sets the scene in two excellent essays.

[17] Anon., *Report of the Proceedings. . .*, 38.　　[18] Ibid. 65–6.
[19] Ibid. 69.　　[20] Ibid. 50.
[21] Ibid. 41.　　[22] Ibid. 42, 139.

the same thing.[23] To sum up, said Cope, 'the Pannick seiz'd the Foot . . . and they ran away, notwithstanding all the Endeavours used by their Officers to prevent it'; 'the Foot dispersed and shifted for themselves all over the Country.'[24]

Braddock's 1755 expedition against Fort Duquesne was the first campaign of the new war; and the disaster that overtook his forces at the Monongahela, like the events that immediately preceded it, illustrates once again the pattern that so often prevailed in these initial campaigns.[25] The dispositions on the march towards the forks of the Ohio were excellent, as indeed they were on the day of battle. 'There Never was an Army in the World in more spirits than we were,' wrote an officer's batman of the day of battle; and 'So we began our March again, Beating the grannadiers March all the way, Never Seasing.'[26] But none of this availed. Braddock's regiments—the 44th and 48th of Foot, accompanied by some Provincial Companies— had not had sufficient time to train and were, furthermore, caught by the French and Indian irregulars in a difficult tactical situation. Attacked first in front while advancing in column through open woodland, Braddock's advanced party fell back in some confusion upon his van—rather than absorbing the initial shock and thereby allowing the main body to deploy. This confusion was compounded when the main body, coming forward along the woodland trail, became entangled with the disordered van. The French and Indians, meanwhile, moved down both flanks of the British column 'till they had Nigh Inclosed us in', and were soon pouring in from cover a heavy and destructive fire.[27] Some part of the column was sorted out —the colonel of the 44th, reported one witness, 'divided his men and fired some platoons by his own Direction'[28]—but most of the troops simply blazed away into the bush. Confusion slowly gave way to terror, and that to panic; and although the

---

[23] Ibid. 57.   [24] Ibid. 50.

[25] A considerable literature surrounds this expedition, much of it excellent but more of it polemical. The best analysis of the campaign is in K. L. Parker, op cit. 77–139; and without doubt the most carefully researched and balanced reconstruction of the battle is P. E. Kopperman, *Braddock at the Monongehela* (Pittsburgh, 1977). After these, see C. Hamilton (ed.), *Braddock's Defeat* (Univ. of Oklahoma, 1959); and R. L. Yaple, 'Braddock's Defeat: The Theories and a Reconsideration', *JSAHR* 46 (1968), 194–201.

[26] C. Hamilton (ed.), op. cit. 28.   [27] Ibid. 29.

[28] Pargellis, *Military Affairs*, 121.

troops kept up their uncontrolled and largely ineffective fire for over two hours,[29] neither could they be prevailed upon to counter-attack with the bayonet, nor could the officers concert among themselves such a tactic. 'The Pannock was so universal and the firing so executive and uncommon that no order could ever be restor'd', reported an officer;[30] and 'Such was the confusion', said another, 'that the men were sometimes 20 or 30 deep, and he thought himself securest, who was in the Centre.'[31] The result was a bloody defeat and rout.

Whereas the corps caught up in the first engagement of the '45 Rebellion had experienced no previous intensive advanced training on campaign, those that fought in the first of the Pragmatic Army's battles and those with Braddock in the first battle of the Seven Years War had all had some, for what it was worth. We described earlier the manner in which Braddock's regiments were taken from peacetime Irish county cantonments, and their weak cadre strengths built up with drafts and recruits.[32] These corps were sent to America innocent of camp experience; and they were in America only three months before the Monongahela battle. Facing a long and difficult march through a forest wilderness and liable to attack by a nimble and ruthless enemy who employed cover and used the tactics of irregulars, Braddock in the weeks available to him attempted to train his men to deal with the French and Indians. He 'lighten'd them as much as possible', leaving in stores 'their Swords and the greatest part of their heavy Accoutrements'; and he drilled them to form and fight in their accustomed companies, rather than in the platoons where many of the men, told off, would not know their officers. They practised a variety of the alternate fire, using the senior battalion-company in each regiment as a 'Second Grenadier Company upon the left', and leaving the other eight battalion-companies to form eight fire-divisions and sixteen platoons. This was all a very sensible modification of the current drill; and Braddock was pleased to report that the regiments 'behave very well and shew great Spirit and Zeal for the Service.'[33] The corps exercised repeatedly during the few weeks available to them, as the

[29] R. L. Yaple, art. cit. 195, 198.
[30] Pargellis, *Military Affairs*, 99.
[31] P. E. Kopperman, op. cit. 76.
[32] See above, pp. 49–50.
[33] Pargellis, *Military Affairs*, 82–3.

surviving orderly books show: thus at Fort Cumberland camp the 48th, eight weeks before the battle, 'had a Field day', and together with the 44th had another field day a week later.[34] The Duke of Cumberland, in discussions with Braddock before the latter sailed, had stressed that 'the Strictest & most exact Discipline is always necessary, but can never be more so than on your present Service'; this the Duke thought essential 'to prevent any Pannick in the Troops from Indians, to whom the Soldiery not being yet accustomed, the French will not fail to make all attempts towards it'.[35] But a few weeks of intensive training were insufficient to prepare these corps, and Cumberland's warning proved prophetic.

The corps that fought at Dettingen had been on the Continent for a year before that battle, most of which time was spent in Flanders cantonments. No sooner had they arrived in these cantonments but they, like Braddock's regiments, began to practise the advanced elements of the drill. The journals and orderly books kept in the army in Flanders, Brabant, and Germany during the years 1742–8 are filled with daily entries sending corps out to drill or to be reviewed. Typical orders, selected at random, are the following taken from those issued in the brigades quartered at Ghent before Dettingen:[36]

[18 June 1742]: The first Battn. of Guards to march to the place of Exercise next Monday morning at five of clock . . . The 2nd Regt. on Tuesday, the 3rd on Thursday, & Col. Duroure's [12th Foot] on Friday at the same hour & place, & to continue the same weekly.

[6 Sept. 1742]: [Ordered] That Sr. Robt. Rich's [4th] Regt. of Dragoons be under Arms . . . at Seven of clock, at their place of parade, & to go thro' their Exercise both on Foot & Horseback, & that they conform to the book of Exercise establish'd by His Majesty.

[11 Sept. 1742]: Genl. Hawley's Regt. [1st Dragoons] to go out to Exercise tomorrow at the same hour, & to observe the same orders given to Sr. Robt. Rich's Regt.

---

[34] C. Hamilton (ed.), op. cit. 15–16.
[35] Cumb. Pprs, Box 45, no. 103. J. Shy, op. cit. 127–9, makes some interesting remarks on the regulars' fear of forest fighting in the Seven Years War.
[36] Cumb. Pprs, O.B.1, fos. 22, 64, 71.

Dettingen had shown up the unprepared condition of the corps; and so during the twenty-two months between that battle and the next major engagement—at Fontenoy, in May 1745—the army kept to its now established routine of constant, almost daily, practice. Typical once again are the orders given out in the brigades quartered at Ghent during the spring of 1745, of which the following are random examples;[37]

[14 March 1745]: The weather now being warmer, the Corpls. of ye Several Regts. to have as many men out as they can, to perfect them in their marching & manual Exercise. The foot to take their motions from the first Regt. of guards, & the Dragoons from the Royal. The Awkard men to be out every day.

[21 Mar. 1745]: The Several Battns. in Garrison to be under Arms to morrow morning in order to fire four Cartridges pr. Man.

[25 Mar. 1745]: The Corpls. of the Several Grenadier Comps. to perfect themselves in ye grenadier Exercise, from ye first Regt. of guards, & care to be taken that there be no difference, or disparity in ye whole.

[28 Mar. 1745]: Majr. Genl. Howard's [3rd Foot], Huske's [23rd Foot], & Handasydes Regt. [31st Foot] to be out tomorrow . . .

[6 Apr. 1745]: Tomorrow & Thursday the draughts & recruits to burn six Cartridges pr. man.

[11 Apr. 1745]: The Several Regts. of Dragoons to be out . . .

At Fontenoy, on 11 May 1745, the performance of all arms was a marked improvement upon that shown at Dettingen, as was to be expected after so many more months of intensive training. The foot, indeed, performed admirably well; and if they had to be kept on a tight rein while closing the French,[38]

[37] Ibid. O.B.6, fos. 116, 118, 120, 122, 126, 127.

[38] LaFausille, who was at both battles, said that the British foot not only 'threw away their Fire to no purpose' and 'at too great a distance', at Dettingen, but that 'the same would have happened had it not been prevented in time at Fontenoy' (Cumb. Pprs, Pt 4, ii, fo. 4). How the men were prevented from doing so at Fontenoy was described by an officer in one of the foot brigades, who heard its commanding general 'frequently giving directions to the Officers, to tell their Men to preserve their Ranks & keep their line; and to direct them to observe the word of Command, & not to fire till they were order'd.' SP 87/17, fo. 320.

they performed brilliantly when actually come to grips. The controlled volleys were so effective that the *Gardes Françaises* panicked and fled; indeed, even before engaging, the *Gardes* had feared to enter into 'une affaire de mousqueterie' with the English foot, knowing that it would have 'trop d'avantage par sa superiorité'.[39] Several charges were made upon the British front by the French horse, but were broken up by British musketry, none penetrating to within 20 paces of the line. The eventual withdrawal of the British foot was made possible only because they kept up their fire discipline, although under intense pressure; and when the army retreated the British cavalry behaved well too.[40]

By the summer of 1745, then, that part of the army with two or three years' service in the Low Countries was very thoroughly trained at all aspects of the service, which had not been the case in 1742 or 1743; and it was in most respects superior to its Bourbon adversaries.[41]

Late in 1745 a large part of the army was hastily recalled to deal with the Jacobite emergency; but in the Low Countries, meanwhile, the same endless round was kept up in 1745 and 1746 among those corps that had remained there, and was taken up by regiments returning after Culloden to face the French once again. The British regiments that fought at Rocoux in 1746 and at Lauffeldt in 1747 behaved admirably well, being now veteran corps, blooded, used to the rigours of campaigning, and long since completely familiar with, and expert at, the advanced elements of the drill. When the heavily outnumbered British (and Hanoverian) foot covered the withdrawal from Rocoux they 'kept their order as if they had been on a review before His Majesty, at every halt facing where the

[39] J. Colin, *Les Campagnes du Maréchal de Saxe*, iii (Paris, 1906), 111, quoting the comte de Chabannes (who commanded that part of the line struck by Cumberland's battalions).

[40] Ibid. 113; and J. M. White, *Marshal of France. The Life and Times of Maurice, Comte de Saxe* (New York, 1962), 152–64.

[41] This was demonstrated not only at Fontenoy but again, a few weeks later, in the desperate action at Melle. On Melle, which is tactically a most interesting affair, see H. Pichat, *La Campagne du maréchal de Saxe dans les Flandres de Fontenoy (mai 1745) à la prise de Bruxelles (février 1746)* (Paris, 1909), 39–87; and in SP 87/19, see the accounts from Cumberland to Harrington, 19 July 1745 (OS); Moltke to Konigsegg, 9 July 1745; Bligh to Cumberland, 9 and 10 July 1745; and Abercromby to St. Clair, 10 July 1745.

enemy appeared,' wrote Ligonier; 'and let me tell you . . . they must be good troops that will do that.'[42] Lauffeldt was very hard fought, the British cavalry in particular performing well, taking part in one of the largest cavalry encounters of the century, involving some 200 squadrons.[43]

Even so late as 1747 and 1748, intensive training was still a daily feature. Thus in the camp of the brigades composed of Howard's 3rd, Huske's 23rd, Crawford's 25th, and Johnson's 33rd of Foot, typical orders were as follows:[44]

[9 Apr. 1747, Bois-le-Duc]: The Regiments are to form to morrow in Battalions, and afterwards to march by in eighteen Platoons, Grenadiers included . . .

[7 May 1747, Westmael camp]: The 2 Battalions of the first, and the 2 Battalions of the 2nd. Brigade to be under Arms to morrow morning at 8 o'Clock, in order to be review'd by H.R.H. . . . 8 Field Pieces with their proper Officers and Men to joyn them in order to go thro' the fireings.

[22 May 1747, Schilde camp]: the British Artillery will exercise and fire to morrow . . .

A typical corps, Campbell's 21st of Foot, was going through a similar round in its Low Countries' cantonments that year; the lieutenant-colonel of the 21st noted the following in his journal, for example:[45]

[31 Mar. 1747]: The whole Regiment assembled on a moor near the head quarters, and went thro' their exercises.

[14 Apr. 1747]: Yesterday the Regiment . . . went thro' all their exercise. The Duke [of Cumberland] being out riding, the firing drew him that way, and he came unexpected and reviewed the Regiment, which was lucky enough to have his approbation.

---

[42] Rex Whitworth, op. cit. 141.
[43] For the 1746 campaign and Rocoux, and the 1747 campaign and Lauffeldt, see Rex Whitworth, op. cit. 126–67, and J. M. White, op. cit. 179–92, 204–29.
[44] Ipswich and E. Suffolk RO Albemarle MSS 461/99, 9 Apr. 1747; 461/100, 7 May 1747; and 461/101, 22 May 1747.
[45] J. O. Robson, art. cit. 27 (1949), 73–8, *passim.*

[16 Apr. 1747]: Orders came from the Duke that he was to review our Regiment and four more . . .

[28 Apr. 1747]: The Regiment was under arms, and went thro' all their exercise with powder.

[May 1747]: Our Regiment, the Welsh Fusiliers [23rd], Johnson's [33rd], and Flemings [36th] were reviewed by the Duke . . .

Even during the uneventful campaign of 1748 in Brabant, the drilling continued. The Duke of Cumberland, for example, reviewed several corps both British and Allied in July at the 'camp of Nestelroy', near Bois-le-Duc, where on 9 July he saw fourteen squadrons of British dragoons perform an intricate series of manoeuvres. At Eindhoven on 26 September he saw the 2/1st Foot Guards go through the whole of the review exercise, evolutions, and manoeuvres.[46] Lt.-Col. Colville and his 21st of Foot were still hard at it too, among these corps, for on 8 July he noted that 'H.R.H. had another course of reviews of all the Regiments and saw Lee's [44th Foot] and ours on a common about half way betwixt our two quarters . . . All the Regiments had exercise and firing once a week according to orders.'[47] For the regiments on campaign in the Low Countries, therefore, the war ended as it began, practising daily their advanced drill.

Endless training of this sort was typical in regiments campaigning on the Continent; and although they arrived in Germany quite forward in their advanced drill the same round of training was followed by the regiments that served in the Allied army under Ferdinand of Brunswick during the campaigns of 1758–62.[48] Most of these regiments went out from Britain with at least two seasons in the camps behind them; several had spent three seasons in the camps, and a few had spent as many as four. Of the seventeen battalions of foot sent

[46] Detailed plans of these reviews are in the Kent RO Amherst MSS 05/1–8.
[47] J. O. Robson, art. cit. 28 (1950), 79–80.
[48] These corps went out from Britain in two contingents: the first (The Blues; 1st and 3rd Dragoon Guards; 2nd, 6th, and 10th Dragoons; 12th, 20th, 23rd, 25th, 37th, and 51st Foot) arrived in Aug. 1758, while the second (2nd and 3rd Horse; 2nd Dragoon Guards; 1st, 7th, and 11th Dragoons; 15th Light Dragoons; 2/1st, 2/2nd, and 2/3rd Foot Guards; 5th, 8th, 11th, 24th, 33rd, 50th, 87th, and 88th Foot) arrived in the spring and summer of 1760. R. Savory, op. cit. 460–1, 477–8.

to Germany, twelve had in addition to camping already seen some active service on the French coastal raids of 1757 and 1758. Only a few days after disembarking at Emden—although troubled 'by extream long Marches, over very heavy sands, & no water to refresh them'—the soldiers of the first contingent were reported 'all so eager to join Prince Ferdinand before a Battle, that they make no complaints of any fatigue or difficulty.'[49] It was thought best to keep these corps in quiet quarters, however, while they continued their training; and so through the last three months of the 1758 campaign they were not engaged, nor were they drawn from their winter quarters in April 1759 to join in Ferdinand's advance into Hesse, which brought on the battle of Bergen. Only in June were the British regiments brought into the field to play a full part in operations. In the meantime the British had been training intensively, as the orderly books once again illustrate; the following are taken at random from the orders given out in the brigades in Munster:[50]

[14 Feb. 1759]: His S.H. [Prince Ferdinand] permits the regiments to be out to fire when the commanding officer thinks proper . . .

[22 Mar. 1759] Napier's [12th Foot] will have a field day tomorrow.

[3 Apr. 1759]: Stuart's [37th Foot] a field day tomorrow.

[4 Apr. 1759]: Kingsley's [20th Foot] have a field day to-morrow.

[6 Apr. 1759]: Fusiliers [23rd Foot] and Stuart's a field day to-morrow.

[9 Apr. 1759]: Lord George Sackville has ordered three barrels of powder . . . for each battalion, each regiment is to keep 18 rounds per man . . . and may make use of the remainder to practise firings. The Welse Fusiliers have a field day to-morrow.

And so it went until early June. By 4 May the Duke of Richmond could report 'Hume's regiment [25th Foot] very near as good as Kingsley's [20th Foot]', which was to say 'vastly im-

---

[49] SP 87/32, Marlborough to Holdernesse, 9 Aug. 1758.
[50] *HMC Clements MSS* (1913), pp. 431–67, *passim*.

proved'; and 'the Welch Fuzileers and Stuards are steady under arms and march very well.' 'I assure you', he wrote to his brother, 'that the regiments in England must be very *alerte* and take a great deal of pains, or they will not be able to show with these regiments.'[51] Three months after Richmond penned those words, the six battalions trained in the Munster garrison made the epic attack on the battlefield of Minden.

As in the Austrian Succession campaigns, the training was kept up until the end of the war; and orders given out in the spring of 1761, at Paderborn, are typical of this:[52]

[22 Apr. 1761]: the Recruits both of Cavalry and Infantry are to be Drilled and Exercised at Fireings. The Regiments are also to practice the several Evolutions . . . particularly marching and Wheeling . . . and forming quick, after different methods.

[10 May 1761]: Commanding Officers of Cavalry . . . to have their Recruits exercised at Firing, and their Horses the same, in order to tame them as much as possible.

[13 May 1761]: no time [is to] be lost in discipling and perfecting the Battalions by having them frequently out at Exercise.

The Coldstream Guards, at Paderborn, were sent 'out to exercise' on 11, 12, 16, 18, and 26 May, and on 7, 12, and 13 June, within a period of five weeks; and that schedule was typical for the regiments stationed there and elsewhere in Germany.[53]

Wheres there was little action in the colonies after the 1740–2 Cartagena expedition during the 1739–48 war, a great many corps, beginning with those under Braddock, were sent to the Americas during the Seven Years War. As we noted earlier, only a handful of the regiments sent across the Atlantic went out with any camp experience behind them, so that much intensive advanced training had to be carried on in the colonial theatres.

The feeble North American campaigns of 1756 and 1757 are, for our purposes, of little interest: the surrender to Montcalm

---

[51] *HMC Bathurst MSS* (1923), p. 684.
[52] Cumb. Pprs, Pt 4, O.B.8, fos. 8, 15, 17.
[53] Ibid., fos. 17–39, *passim*.

of Shirley's 50th and Pepperell's 51st, besieged at Oswego in 1756, merely underlines the inefficiency of new-raised regiments.[54] Not until the summer of 1757 did considerable numbers of troops reach North America from the British Isles, and owing to the strategic situation it was not until the campaign of 1758 that they could be employed on major operations. The main events of that year were Amherst's siege of Louisbourg, Forbes's advance on Fort Duquesne, and Abercromby's engagement at Carillon. From the training standpoint, Abercromby's seven regular battalions represented a mixed bag. One, the 44th Foot, had been with Braddock and had by now amassed three years' of training time. The rest had seen no action: three (the 27th, 46th, and 55th) had come out without camp duty but had been in America for a year, by mid-1758, and were doubtless quite forward in their drill, while the rest (the 1/42nd, 1/60th, and 4/60th) had been on the scene for two years and may be considered fairly well trained. In the fighting at Carillon they all behaved extremely well, sustaining very heavy casualties while repeatedly storming the French *abatis* and breastwork.[55] At Louisbourg meanwhile, once Amherst's fourteen battalions had made good their landing—a difficult operation, but carried out successfully by picked light and grenadier companies—their ultimate success was assured, given their great numbers and powerful siege train.[56] The careful, methodical march of Forbes's small column on Fort Duquesne —carried out according to the system of the 'protected advance' laid down in Turpin de Crissé's *Art of War*—was a success too, a masterpiece of logistical planning.[57]

By 1759 the forces engaged in North American operations were the equal of the French, the Canadians, and their Indian irregulars. Since Braddock's defeat, the regiments, after ar-

---

[54] On these campaigns, see K. L. Parker, op. cit. 140–213, and Pargellis, *Loudoun*. Pargellis, 141–6, describes these undisciplined and ill-administered corps and concludes that they 'were unfit to belong to an army composed of separate units, each one responsible for its own efficiency.'

[55] The best accounts are in Fortescue, ii, 322–32, and M. Sautai, *Montcalm au Combat de Carillon* (Paris, 1909). Abercromby's journal is in WO 34/76, fos. 154–7.

[56] Amherst's force consisted of the 2/1st, 15th, 17th, 22nd, 28th, 35th, 40th, 45th, 47th, 48th, 58th, 2/60th, 3/60th, and 78th. Of these, only the 15th had had camp training, but most had been in America for at least two years and were by now well trained; indeed only the 2/1st, 17th, 58th, and 78th were in need of further seasoning.

[57] K. L. Parker, op. cit. 252–92.

riving in the colonies, had taken advantage of every opportunity to carry on their advanced training; and the journals and orderly books kept in these corps show that the same endless practice that we have seen going on in the armies serving in Europe was characteristic too of those in America. A few examples of this activity will be sufficient. Thus, when early in June 1757 seven battalions from Ireland and six from New York assembled at Halifax, for that summer's projected siege of Louisbourg, advanced training began immediately; and the following entries illustrate the training going on:[58]

[16 July 1757]: ... the regiments take all opportunities to exercise.

[17 July 1757]: Some intrenchments are erecting on the left of the camp, in order to discipline and instruct the troops, in the methods of attack and defence.

[24 July 1757]: This morning the picquets of the line, with a working party from the army, marched to ... where the intrenchments were thrown up; ... one half carried on approaches, while the other defended; frequently sallying out to obstruct the workmen, when the covering parties attacked, repulsed, and pursued them. ... This is in order to make the troops acquainted with the nature of the service they are going upon ... and is to be continued until farther orders.

[31 July 1757]: This day the trenches were stormed by the picquets; some field-pieces were brought there for this purpose, and every thing was conducted with the greatest regularity.

These activities were aimed especially at preparing the troops for siege warfare; and although the Louisbourg operations were postponed until the following season, specialist training of this sort was invaluable.

It was to the linear, battlefield drill that most training time was devoted, of course, here as in Europe. The orders given out

---

[58] A. G. Doughty (ed.), *An Historical Journal of the Campaigns in North America for the Years 1757, 1758, 1759, and 1760.* i (Toronto, 1915), 34–9, *passim*. This is an edited version of Capt. John Knox's journal of the same title, published in London in 1769. At Halifax were the 2/1st, 17th, 27th, 28th, 43rd, 46th, and 55th Foot, come from Ireland; plus the 22nd, 1/42nd, 44th, 48th, 2/60th, and 4/60th Foot, plus 3 coys of Rogers' Rangers, all from New York.

in Amherst's army in the winter quarters of 1758–9, and soon after in the field as the army moved down the Hudson—Lake Champlain route towards Montreal, are typical. The following are selected at random from that army's orderly books:[59]

[18 Dec. 1758, New York]: the Genl. Commanding in chief orders that the Regiments Should be Exercised twice a Week when the Weather will permit, & that the Commanding Officers will Assemble them by Companies or Batalion as they Judge best.

[22 Jan. 1759, New York]: The Officers Commanding Battalions are to practice their Men at firing Ball, so that every Soldier may be Accustomed to it.

[5 May 1759, Albany]: The Regiments to practice marching by files . . .

[22 Nov. 1759, Crown Point]: The Regiments . . . when the weather permits [will] be assembled for Exercise.

Earlier, we followed a single corps, Campbell's 21st of Foot, going through a typical round of training in the Low Countries in the spring of 1747; and we can do the same with another such, Kennedy's 43rd of Foot, on North American service in the spring of 1759. Typical of the training going on in the 43rd, in garrison at Fort Beauséjour in Acadia, are the following journal entries:[60]

[5 Apr. 1759]: The 43rd regiment are out daily at exercise, though the country still retains its winter habit.

[11 Apr. 1759]: The 43rd regiment are at exercise every morning, and discharge ammunition cartridges; in the afternoon the men are employed in firing at targets, in which they are encouraged by presents from their Officers, according to their several performances.

[14 Apr. 1759]: The 43rd regiment are now making the most of their time in exercising and firing at marks; in short, every man is employed in rubbing off the winter's rust.

[59] Kent RO Amherst MSS 016/1, pp. 1–3, 6–7, 161.
[60] A. G. Doughty (ed.), op. cit. i. 301, 304, 306.

[30 Apr. 1759]: The regiment daily out at exercise, and firing at the target; the Captain of the light infantry spares no pains to form his company, and render them expert for any kind of service.

Late in May Kennedy's joined the forces in Cape Breton, and four months later stood in the centre of Wolfe's line of battle on the Plains of Abraham, taking part in delivering what Fortescue described as 'the most perfect volley ever fired on a battlefield'.[61] As a last example, we might look at the activities of the regiments training under Amherst on Staten Island in 1761, prior to their embarking with Monckton on the Martinique expedition late that autumn. In July and August eleven battalions came in from the quarters which they had occupied during the winter and spring (for the conquest of Canada was complete), and these encamped together on Staten Island across from New York.[62] Here, formed in three brigades, they were drilled intensively under Amherst's direction from late in August until embarking late in November; and in this, once again, they resembled the corps in Europe in the 1747–8 and 1761–2 campaigns, drilling intensively for the last of the war's campaigns just as they had done in the preceding seasons. Typical orders, selected at random from the orderly books, are the following:[63]

[28 Aug. 1761]: Amherst's [15th], & the 1st Royal Highland Battn. [1/42nd] to fire to morrow morning two Rounds of ball, man by man at a Butt . . . The Commanding Officers of the other Regiments will fix on places near their front by the Water side for Erecting butts to fire ball.

[30 Aug. 1761]: The Regimts. are to practice Exercising, drawn up three deep . . .

---

[61] Fortescue, ii. 381. The musketry of the 43rd was excellent, as the above extracts will indicate. When in garrison at Annapolis in the summer of 1758, Capt Knox noted that the officers of Kennedy's 'for their instruction and amusement, fall into the ranks as privates, and practice all the evolutions and firings'. This was admirable. Ibid. 181.

[62] Their winter quarters are in WO 34/74, fo. 6. On the movement of most of these corps down the Hudson to New York, see J. C. Webster (ed.), *The Journal of Jeffrey Amherst . . . in America from 1758 to 1763* (Torronto, 1931), 269–72. The corps that camped on the island, trained there under Amherst, and sailed with Monckton for the Caribbean, were the 15th, 17th, 27th, 28th, 35th, 40th, 1/42nd, 2/42nd, 43rd, 48th, and 3/60th of Foot. The 17th and 27th arrived quite late.

[63] Kent RO Amherst MSS 016/2, *passim*.

[5 Sept. 1761]: The three Brigades[64] to fire four rounds of Ball, by Platoons.

[22 Sept. 1761]: The Regiments that have been reviewed, to be out at Exercise only once a day.

Amherst held a series of major brigade reviews late in September and early in October, at which the corps went through an elaborate series of manoeuvres reminiscent of the best Dublin performances.[65] Among other manoeuvres the battalions of the 1st Brigade, for example, 'marched [forward] by subdivisions in Column', while those of the 2nd Brigade 'passed & forced a bridge, retreated over it, etc.'

It will be evident that target practice was given pride of place in the training carried on in North America by 1758–9, this being one of the fruits of experience in the campaigns against New France. 'Nothing steadys them so much to firing as by firing balls', observed Amherst in the Staten Island camp.[66] It was unfortunate that, with the coming of peace, this lesson should so quickly have been forgotten.

The preceding will be sufficient to illustrate the general pattern of initial inadequacy, followed by endless and intensive practice, imposed upon the regiments by the shortcomings of peacetime training. In order to complete our summary of the training carried on in wartime we have only to consider the revisions sometimes made in, and the additions occasionally made to, the current regulations and customary drill in certain regiments and field forces.

As we noted earlier, innovation and adaptation were more noticeable in the Seven Years than in the Austrian Succession War; innovation was stirred by the lack of success in the Low Countries battles and more so by the fighting in Scotland, and by the mid-1750s innovation had gathered momentum.

We have already described Prestonpans, which lasted five

---

[64] The regiments on the island were brigaded as follows: *1st Brigade:* 15th, 28th, 1/42nd, 2/42nd; *2nd Brigade:* 17th, 35th, 43rd, 3/60th; *3rd Brigade:* 27th, 40th, 48th. The light and grenadier companies formed separate composite battalions. Kent RO Amherst MSS 015/10, 'Troops that form the main Expedition'; and 016/2, 28 Aug. 1761.

[65] J. C. Webster (ed.), op. cit. 273. Detailed summaries of the review performances and manoeuvres of the 1st and 3rd Brigades are in WO 34/100, fos. 56–60, 64–5.

[66] J. C. Webster (ed.), op. cit. 273.

minutes. Falkirk, the second engagement of the Jacobite rising, was hardly more successful.[67] After Prestonpans and Falkirk, matters had to be taken in hand. During the three months that elapsed between Falkirk and Culloden, intensive drilling helped the army to restore confidence in itself.[68] Cumberland busily exercised the forces in Scotland and the North, and sent frequent orders to the commanders of outlying divisions to follow the same regimen. One such was Lord Albermarle who, reporting to the Duke's ADC from Strathbogie on 4 April, wrote:

. . . before I had your letter about exercising ye troops I had seen ye six Batt[s] out and exercise ye Manual & go throw ye Firings, but had not ordered anything more, but gave out this morning H.R.H.'s commands (viz.) one Batt. out every Day, ye Parade to exercise in ye morning, the Pickets at night & ye Recruits and aukward men twice a Day in ye presence of Officers.[69]

Cumberland had laid down a new method of bayonet drill for all to practise, too; but it was so unrealistic as surely to be no more than a morale-booster.[70] All this paid off at Culloden, of course, where the army behaved well. It was upon the platoon fire and bayonets, not upon the cavalry, that Cumberland depended;[71] and the event showed him to be right. Constant drill and minor innovations had sharpened the army: 'Sure never were soldiers in such a temper,' wrote the Duke just after the battle: 'silence and obedience the whole time, and all our manoeuvres were performed without the least confusion.'[72]

After Culloden, there was much training going on in the camps of the Great Glen. Blakeney, who commanded the troops there, was practising a new method 'for a Battalion to Fire Advancing, and retreating', and he sent along to Napier 'a sketch of explanations' for the Duke's perusal; and Cumberland gave out a few modifications in the manual and firings,

---

[67] For Falkirk, see K. Tomasson and F. Buist, *Battles of The '45* (1967), 99–127.

[68] Only three days after the battle Hawley, with the army now at Edinburgh, wrote that 'every wheele is at worke to gett the Engine in motion again. The Foot recover theyr spiritts, they owne to their Officers they all deserve to be hanged, some Regts, have shooke hands and vowel all to dye nexte time'. Ibid. 127.

[69] Cumb. Pprs, Box 13, no. 149, fo. 1.

[70] K. Tomasson and F. Buist, op. cit. 164–5.

[71] E. Charteris, *William Augustus, Duke of Cumberland: His Early Life and Times, 1721–1748* (1913), 247–8.

[72] BM holograph display case, North Library.

though as usual 'all other Parts of the Exercise [were] to be performed as the Book directs without diminution from it'.[73] Here in the 1745–6 Jacobite campaign, then, were presaged some of the alterations soon to be introduced generally as the *1748 Regulations*.

Despite the several sound reforms initiated by Cumberland at the mid-century, and despite his preparation and issue of the *1748*, *1756*, and *1757 Regulations*, there were several intelligent field and general officers who were no longer satisfied either with the platoon-fire system ('Hyde Park firing', as it was derisively labelled), or with the superfluous and elaborate formalism (the 'one–two', as it was contemptuously described) which attended so much of the drill, and of the arms exercises in particular. On the eve of the Seven Years War a few of these officers had taken to training their regiments to perform both the regulation platoon-fire system (to please authority), and the alternate-fire system (which they intended actually to employ in the field).[74] One such officer was Lt.-Gen. Sir John Mordaunt who, when given command of the 1757 Rochefort expedition, took the bit between his teeth and openly proceeded not only to tell off and train his battalions at the alternate fire, but also to cut back on the time spent on the manual and on much of the 'one–two' of the service.[75] Mordaunt's action was to prove a catalyst, for the alternate system was to spread quickly from his 1757 camps at Dorchester and the Isle of Wight to the armies both in Germany and America, and was by 1764 to become regulation practice.

[73] Cumb. Pprs., Box 16, no. 320; and Pt 4, ii, fo. 60.

[74] We described in detail the difference between platoon fire and alternate fire on pp. 318–21 above, where the two systems, as practised in the 20th Foot under James Wolfe's direction, were shown.

[75] Writing to his brother on 9 Sept. 1757, the Duke of Richmond—now lieutenant: colonel commanding the 33rd Foot, and a partisan of these innovations—reported on Mordaunt's activities. 'He has broke through all the absurd regulations that General Napier [Cumberland's appointee] has been puzzling the army with since he has been Adjutant-General. He has abolished the manual exercise both old and new, and draws up all the regiments as Kingsley's [20th] used to do [under Wolfe's direction, as on p. 319 above] . . . and practises no other firing but by companies from right and left; and they practice the same kind of evolutions as Kingsley's used to do and no such absurdities as squares, etc.' *HMC Bathurst MSS* (1923), p. 681. Richmond had served as a young subaltern and captain in the 20th, where he had been befriended and much influenced by Wolfe. As lieutenant-colonel of the 33rd, Richmond was at this time attempting to establish Wolfe's training and drill in that regiment. R. H. Whitworth (ed.), art. cit. 72–6.

We can trace the spread of this innovation from Mordaunt's camps, where it was found effective and well received;[76] but it was only the Kloster Zeven convention and Cumberland's subsequent resignation from all his military appointments, which occurred late in October of 1757, that made this possible. Mordaunt's activities were 'all against orders', contrary to the current drill regulations. There had been hope that Cumberland, as Captain-General, would approve Mordaunt's innovations, and fear only that 'if he listens to those blockheads Napier and Dury . . . we shall return to *one two*'.[77] But Mordaunt's work had been reported to Cumberland in Hanover, and had brought forth a sharp rebuke. The Duke wrote late in August to Barrington, the Secretary at War, with orders to

acquaint . . . all General officers commanding Corps, Sir John Mordaunt not excepted, that I am Surprised to hear that my orders . . . approved & confirmed by His Majesty, are changed according to the Whim & Supposed Improvements of every fertile Genius; and that therefore, it is my positive order, that in the Forming & Telling off of Battalions, they conform exactly to those Standing orders, which they have all received; and that no one presume to introduce new Schemes, without their having been approved of by His Majesty or by my orders.[78]

This was given out by Barrington and Ligonier;[79] but events in Hanover overtook Cumberland, and the innovations were then able to spread.

Of the six marching regiments that formed the first contingent sent to join the army in Germany in the summer of 1758, three—Kingsley's 20th, Home's 25th, and Brudenell's 51st— had been in Mordaunt's encampments; and while training in Munster quarters during the winter of 1758–9 and into the following spring, all six continued to practise telling off and

[76] Kingsley's 20th was already with Mordaunt and, Richmond reported to his brother, 'you have no idea how much it has improved the other regiments'. *HMC Bathurst MSS* (1923), p. 681.

[77] Ibid. It was in fact these very 'blockheads'—Robert Napier and Alexander Dury— who, as Adjutant-General and lieutenant-colonel of Cumberland's 1st Foot Guards, respectively, had assisted Cumberland in the preparation of the current regulations, which Mordaunt was contravening. On their activities in this regard, see above, pp. 199–200.

[78] Pargellis, *Military Affairs*, 398.

[79] WO 4/54, p. 433.

firing according to the alternate-fire system.[80] Again, it was the presence of the 20th Foot that counted for much: the other corps, it was reported, 'have indeed had great advantages in being together with Kingsley's and the Germans.'[81] It was alternate fire that these six corps employed with such extraordinary success soon after at Minden.

Meanwhile, Amherst's army had assembled at Halifax in the spring of 1758 to prepare for the siege of Louisbourg, and Abercromby had taken over the American command from Loudoun. Loudoun, 'whose management in the conduct of affairs is by no means admired', wrote Wolfe to Sackville, 'did adhere so literally and strictly to the one—two and the firings by the impracticable chequer, etc, that these regiments [i.e. the 2/1st, 17th, 22nd, 28th, 35th, 40th, 45th, 47th, 48th, 2/60th, 3/60th, and 78th, already in America under Loudoun's command when Amherst's forces arrived from home] must necessarily be cut off one after another.'[82] Among the regiments newly arrived from England was the 15th Foot, another of those which had camped and trained under Mordaunt; and when in the following 1759 campaign Wolfe himself led ten battalions—including the 15th—up the St. Lawrence for Quebec, it was the alternate firing that was being practised in all of these corps. Typical of these was the 43rd Foot, which had been in garrison in the Bay of Funday posts since coming to Nova Scotia from Ireland, mid-way through 1757. The 43rd, as we have seen, had during these years been following the regulation platoon-fire system, as was natural; but after joining Wolfe's force it was ordered to adopt the new procedure. On 15 July 1759, while lying before Quebec, the regiment was reviewed by Wolfe (who had 'never had any opportunity of seeing the forty-third regiment, before they rendezvoused at Louisbourg'); and Capt. Knox of that corps recounted that 'the method we were ordered to observe did not admit of any confusion, though we fired remarkably quick; our firings were from right and left to the centre, by platoons; and afterwards

---

[80] See the orders of Lord George Sackville, who commanded at Munster—and who was a friend of Wolfe's and in agreement with him on tactical matters, not to mention having himself been proprietary colonel of the 20th from 1746 to 1749—to 'practise chiefly the alternate firing', in *HMC Clements MSS* (1913), pp. 560–1.

[81] *HMC Bathurst MSS* (1923), p. 684.

[82] Beckles Willson, op. cit. 368–9.

by subdivisions.'[83] The 43rd was already well trained, as we have seen; and that they should have found alternate firing to permit them to fire 'remarkably quick' and without confusion is a testament to its utility and superiority. This same alternate fire was doubtless that employed by the battalions on the Plains of Abraham.

There had been another innovation, the work of Amherst himself, introduced early in 1759 in the regiments serving in America; and it was practised both in the forces under his immediate command moving upon Montreal along the Hudson —Lake Champlain route, and in the army commanded by his subordinate Wolfe lying before Quebec. This consisted of a simple and speedy means of reducing the depth of the battalion line from three to two ranks, and of preserving in three ranks the same frontage allowed by the two-deep firing line. Amherst had adopted the thin, two-deep line because (as he informed the men) 'the enemy have very few regular troops to oppose us, and no yelling of Indians, or fire of Canadians, can possibly withstand two ranks, if the men are silent, attentive, and obedient to their officers.'[84] Probably introduced late in January 1759, it was being practised late in May by some of the corps among those preparing at Cape Breton for the up-coming Quebec expedition; and on 9 July the practice was made regulation drill for all units serving in America by a Standing Order of that date.[85] Thus was introduced the thin red line made famous fifty years later by Wellington, in the Peninsula; and its first use in battle was upon the Plains of Abraham on 13 September 1759.[86]

[83] A. G. Doughty (ed.), op. cit. i, 422. See also p. 451, entry for 31 July, where a tactical disposition to fight by companies (rather than in platoons or other divisions which would have broken up the company structure) 'afforded the highest satisfaction to the soldiers [since] this method . . . does not admit of confusion.'

[84] Ibid. 487–8. The absence of cavalry, of course, made such a disposition practicable in America.

[85] Ibid. 348–9, for Cape Breton; and see pp. 487–8 for the Standing Order. The clearest description of the technique by which the rank reduction was effected is in BL Add. MSS 21,661, fo. 80, 'Ordres du G. Amherst pr. la revue'. A short description of this review—put on by the 1/ and 2/42nd, the 55th, and the 77th of Foot at Oswego on 4 Aug. 1760, is in J. C. Webster (ed.), op. cit. 224.

[86] D. Grinnell-Milne, *Mad. Is He? The Character and Achievement of James Wolfe* (1963), 247–55; and see 'General Orders in Wolfe's Army during the Expedition up the River St. Lawrence, 1759', in Anon., *Literary & Historical Society of Quebec. Manuscripts. Series 4* (Quebec, 1875), 35–6 and *passim*.

The last and most significant of the innovations made during these years, in response to the tactical conditions imposed in the field, was the formation of light units—both horse and foot— and the development of specialized equipment, tactics, and training for the light service. In this the British were behind-hand, in comparison either with the Hapsburg forces or with their Bourbon adversaries; and during the Low Countries campaigns of 1742–8 (where corps like the Arquebusiers de Grassin had taken such a toll of British lives, notably at Melle and Fontenoy), and again to a lesser extent during the campaigns in Germany of 1758–62, the British had been obliged to rely on the light forces of their several German allies. By 1759 it had become abundantly clear that Britain herself must raise light troops, and send these to the army in Germany;[87] and so in the autumn of that year Keith's Highlanders (soon after ranked as the 87th Foot) was formed for the purpose and sent out to serve under Ferdinand. In June following another such corps, Campbell's Highlanders (88th Foot) was sent to join Keith's; and together with the new 15th Light Dragoons,[88] which corps arrived in Germany two weeks after Campbell's had landed, these regiments played an important part in the outpost work, ambuscades, and skirmishing of the army.[89]

Whereas in Germany the burden of the light service could be borne by the assorted *Freikorps*, *Jägers*, hussars, and legions of the Hanoverians and Hessians, in America the British had themselves to make a major effort, and to rely on their own resources. The Canadians and their Indian allies were past-masters at the *petite guerre*, while the nature of the country made them formidable; and the forces from metropolitan France— the *troupes de la marine* in particular—showed themselves adept at many aspects of the light service.

Braddock's disaster had pointed the need for specialist units capable of protecting the flanks and the march security of the

---

[87] Single troops of light dragoons had already been attached to each of the regiments of Dragoon Guards and Dragoons, in Britain, in 1756.

[88] As early as 5 Sept. 1759, when Keith's corps was still raising, Granby had written from Germany asking 'that some of the light Dragoons might be sent over, to act in Concert with the Highlanders, as I am confident they would be of the utmost service, on many occasions in this Country'. SP 87/32, Granby to Holdernesse.

[89] For a narrative of their activities, see C. T. Atkinson, 'The Highlanders in West-phalia, 1760–2, and the Development of Light Infantry', *JSAHR* 20 (1941), 208–23.

heavy infantry; and it had shown too the need to devise tactics at which the foot could be trained in order to deal with ir-regulars—'the manner of opposing an enemy that avoids facing you in the open field', it was now clear, 'is totally different from what young officers learn from the common discipline of the army.'[90] Rangers for long-distance scouting were needed too. These requirements were met in several ways. As early as December 1756, the Duke of Cumberland had advised the commander-in-chief in America to 'teach your Troops to go out upon Scouting Parties: for, 'till Regular Officers with men they can trust, learn to beat the woods, and to act as Irregulars, you never will gain any certain Intelligence of the Enemy', nor screen and protect a marching column.[91] Loudoun acted on such advice, and in the training of the four battalions of the new 60th Foot he ordered that

they are then to fire at Marks, and in order to qualify them for the Service of the Woods, they are to be taught to load and fire, lyeing on the Ground and kneeling. They are to be taught to march in Order, slow and fast in all sortes of Ground. They are frequently to pitch & fold up their Tents, and to be accustomed to pack up and carry their necessaries in the most commodious manner.[92]

Loudoun meanwhile increased the number of ranging companies first raised in 1755, and at the same time sent parties of officers and picked men from the regular marching regiments out with the ranging companies, in order to learn the service and carry its principles back with them to their battalions.[93]

Other action was taken with the corps of marching foot. Soon after Braddock's disaster a battalion of Highlanders, the 1/42nd Foot, was dispatched to America; and by the opening of the 1759 campaign three more Highland battalions—the 2/42nd, 77th, and 78th—had all joined the forces there. For the 1758 campaigns each of the battalions of foot in America was ordered to form its own company of light infantry: these were kept up in the regiments until the reductions consequent upon the 1763 peace, and they were often detached from their parent

<hr/>

[90] *HMC Stopford-Sackville MSS* (1910), ii, 2.
[91] Pargellis, *Military Affairs*, 269.
[92] Pargellis, *Loudoun*, 299–300.
[93] Ibid. 304. On the discipline used in Rogers' Rangers, see K. L. Parker, op. cit. 214–40. The series of 'rules for the ranging-discipline' which Rogers prepared for the instruction of regulars attached to his corps, are in Rogers's *Journals*, op. cit. 60–70.

battalions and brigaded in a composite Light Infantry Corps.[94] These light companies were dressed and accoutred for their service—long coatskirts were cut away, small caps were provided, leggings were worn, hatchets and powder horns were supplied—and by the later stages of the 1759 campaign, notably at Quebec, they were putting in good service.

Proper light infantry took more time to train than did the hatmen, not less—which is why the Americans proved to be of little use to the army, and why the army had thus been obliged to form its own rangers and light troops.[95] 'It is not a Short Coat or half Gaters that makes a light Infantry Man,' Lord Townshend was to write to Amherst many years later, 'but as you know, Sir, a confidence in his Aim, & that Stratagem in a personal conflict which is derived from Experience.'[96] This the light infantry companies of the marching battalions had truly acquired by 1763; and their brilliant performance in quelling the 1763–4 Indian uprising led by Pontiac, in which the tactics and the expertise displayed in Bouquet's engagement at Bushy Run stand in such marked contrast to the performance of Braddock's men, eight years earlier, clearly attests this fact.[97]

Such was the training pattern characteristic of the army in the field, in wartime. Hard, intensive training at the advanced elements of the drill was carried on endlessly, and of necessity. Where circumstances were particular, or where the tactical situation proved to be unexpected or peculiar, innovation took place; and wartime innovation sometimes became doctrine after peace was made. But innovation was the exception, where as a rule the majority of corps were busy enough mastering the complexities of their peacetime drill. With the end of a war, the friction of peace once again began its operation among the regiments; and with that the spirit of innovation had to give way to the simple need for uniformity. In the lull after Culloden

---

[94] On these light companies, see A. G. Doughty (ed.), op. cit. i. 303, 306, 379–80; and ii. 281, 337, 347, and 351. See also Kent RO Amherst MSS 016/1, pp. 2–3, 6–7.

[95] Pargellis notes that Loudoun had expected that 'the provincials themselves could serve as irregular troops, until he discovered that the average provincial soldier knew less what to do if he fell into an ambush than a British regular, for he had never been trained, either in the discipline of arms or in frontier warfare.' Pargellis, *Loudoun*, 300–1.

[96] Kent RO Amherst MSS 073/21, fo. 1.

[97] On Bouquet's tactics and Bushy Run, the best study is K. L. Parker, op. cit. 292–342. J. Shy, op. cit. 111–25 and *passim*.

the always inventive Maj.-Gen. William Blakeney (he of the 'Pasteboard images . . . which the Wags of those Days called Puppets') had had time to show to Cumberland, in Kensington Gardens, special 'Performances' of new 'Firings and Evolutions' of his own design. The Duke had expressed his 'approbation'; and Blakeney,

finding that they answer'd with a large Battalion beyond my Expectation . . . made some Progress in writing the Words of Command, Signals by beat of Drum, and the Explanations, to which I design'd annexing very curious Draughts, with the Platoons number'd in such a manner, as to make the whole intelligible to young Officers.

But Blakeney, at this time in command of the forces in Minorca, 'stopt proceeding any further', when after Aix-la-Chapelle the old garrison of that island was replaced by new regiments sent out from the army in Brabant. 'The Officers lately arrived informed me that they had Orders to follow the Discipline they were taught in Flanders last Campaign,' he wrote to the Duke from Mahon in August 1749, 'which I shall take great Care to make them observe Strictly.'[98] Peace, and with it the need to stick to the uniformity of the new *1748 Regulations*, spelled the end of Blakeney's innovations.

---

[98] Cumb. Pprs, Box 43, no. 294, fo. 1.

Chapter VIII

Sea Service and Marines

When in 1726 Lt.-Col. Henry Hawley mused that, 'As we are islanders and have so great a Fleet, should not all the Foot be Marines . . .?',[1] he was expressing a view that was throughout the century a common refrain in the private publications dealing with British military affairs. That all, or at least a significant part, of the army should be organized and trained as marines was a doctrine derived from several factors, among which geography, naval power, mercantilism, trade and the colonies —that is to say, the overall strategic considerations beloved of the 'blue-water' school—loomed large; and that it was a doctrine implemented only partially and fitfully was due to the coexistence of a rival land-service doctrine, somewhat better found and drawn from a different set of strategic considerations.[2] These two opposing points of view—on the one hand the merchantilist, maritime, and colonial strategy, and on the other the European or Continental strategy—presented a dilemma which was always central to the strategic employment of the land forces of the Crown; and the training of those forces reflected the dilemma.

Not only for the Marine corps properly so called but for the regular marching regiments as well, amphibious operations and service on board the fleet, in various capacities, were common activities. The training given these corps was determined to some extent by the nature of the service for which they were intended; and it is with the training of these units for their various duties afloat, and also with the effects of sea service upon the military efficiency of the corps so engaged, that we are concerned here.

The Marines, and the foot shipped as marines, were trained differently in preparation for sea service—especially before

---

[1] Sumner, 'Chaos', 91.

[2] These two schools are best described and assessed in J. S. Corbett, *England in the Seven Years' War. A Study in Combined Strategy* 2 Vols (1907), and in H. W. Richmond, *The Navy in the War of 1739–48*, 3 Vols (Cambridge, 1920). In the former, i. 4–6, 92–4, and 206–9, puts the case most succinctly, while in the latter, i. pp. xiv–xviii is best.

1739–40. The training given the Marines proper, together with their raising and organization, only slowly crystallized around the amphibious role now associated with their title. Marine regiments (the first of which was raised in 1664) had served during the two great wars immediately preceding our period. At the outbreak of the Nine Years War two regiments, Pembroke's and Torrington's, were raised as marines and served as such until being reduced with the Ryswick peace; and in 1698 Brudenell's Marine regiment was raised upon the remains of these two corps while, additionally, Mordaunt's, Seymour's, and Colt's were taken from the land service and converted into marines. All these corps were broken up in 1699, as the fleet was being laid up. With the renewal of war in 1702 seven new marine regiments (Fox's, Holt's, Saunderson's, Allnutt's, Villiers', Donegal's, and Shannon's) were raised, and Seymour's (a regular marching regiment) was converted into a marine corps; but once again, with the Utrecht peace, these regiments were disbanded as they came ashore, a process which had been completed by 1715.[3] At the beginning of our period there was, therefore, a well-established tradition of raising marine regiments for wartime service with the fleet; and well established too was the practice of reducing these corps as the fleet was laid up at the conclusion of a peace, so that there were no marines standing with the peacetime forces until 1763. That they should be raised and broken in this fashion points the primary purpose of their service, and consequently of their training: they were raised and quartered about the principal naval ports in order to provide both an immediate supply and a constant reinforcement of raw seamen—waisters and foremast hands—where the voluntary enlistment and pressing of ordinary and able seamen failed to man the expanding wartime fleet. Whatever their title, the 'marines' raised before 1739 were regarded (and trained) as seamen first, as dockyard labourers second, and as soldiers only third; and indeed these early marine regiments were officially described and specifically designed as 'nurseries for seamen', from which the 'marines'

---

[3] On the careers of these early marine corps, see the summary in WO 55/1810, p. 6; and see also C. Field, op. cit., *passim*, and J. B. M. Frederick, op. cit., *passim*. Of the corps raised as (or converted into) marines in 1702–3, six were converted into regular marching foot regiments during the years 1710 and 1714; and they survived as such, ranking as the 4th, 30th, 31st, 32nd, 35th, and 36th of Foot.

were to be discharged directly into the ships' companies as able seamen, once sufficiently experienced. Although certain of these corps served in amphibious raids (and even on more extensive land service) in Spain during the 1702–12 war, they must all be regarded primarily as sailors in training, serving only part-time as soldiers while learning the ropes.[4]

Not until 1739–40 was this limited conception of the business of marines modified, when ten new regiments (the 1st–10th Marines) were raised. Unlike their predecessors, these were trained both as land soldiers *and* as seamen; none was forced to go aloft (where they would have had to go to acquire the skills of able seamen) and none was expected to become any more competent in working the ship than were ordinary seamen. No longer simply raw hands in red coats to be trained as seamen, nor merely land-soldiers carried on board the men-of-war, the new marines of 1739–40 were schooled in the basics of both services and were thus the first to carry on those joint amphibious duties associated with them since.[5]

Like their predecessors the ten marine regiments of the 1739–48 war were disbanded with the 1748 peace. In 1755, with war looming again, marine forces were raised once more; and although these too were trained for amphibious service both as soldiers and as ordinary seamen, they were raised on an establishment of independent companies copied from the example long since used among their French counterparts, and easier administered when dispersed through the fleet. In the spring of 1755 some fifty unregimented Marine Companies were established and formed into three 'divisions', quartered about the great Chatham, Portsmouth, and Plymouth dockyards; and by mid-1756 these had been increased to 100 companies.[6] With the conclusion of the 1763 peace fifty of these companies were retained as part of the peacetime standing forces, and they survived through to the end of our period.

Both the Marines (especially after 1739) and also the marching foot shipped temporarily aboard the fleet carried on several 'military' duties, amphibious and otherwise. Amphibious

---

[4] H. W. Richmond, op. cit., i. 267–70.

[5] On the definition of the new role see ibid. i. 270–5; and see A. J. Marini, 'Parliament and the Marine Regiments, 1739', *MM* 62 (1976), 55–65.

[6] WO 55/412, pp. 5–10, 58; and C. Field, op. cit., *passim*.

operations were always chancy affairs, subject to hazards not experienced in regular land campaigning and—particularly during the first half of the century—there was often much fumbling and not a little incompetence displayed.[7] Experience eventually bore fruit, however; and for the carrying on of these raids, descents, 'conjunct expeditions', beach assaults or landings, and other combined operations, there had by the later Seven Years War been evolved an elaborate and sophisticated methodology and tactics.[8] The detailed execution of these operations was concerted by the senior officers, both naval and military, with each expedition: and experience, care, and method were brought to bear more often as the methodology of the operations became more generally understood. Overall plans were now laid prior to embarking the expedition, while tactical details (as in the debarkation, landing, and re-embarkation, the conduct of which was once again broadly understood) were settled in conferences held upon arrival at the beaches themselves. Within this overall methodology there

[7] Thomas More Molyneux, op. cit., Pt I, 1–258, *passim*, and Pt. II, 3–8, calculated in 1759 that of the sixty-eight great and small amphibious operations mounted by Britain between 1603 and 1758 (and the majority of these had come between the years 1689 and 1758), thirty had succeeded and thirty-eight had failed. Dividing these operations into 'great' and 'small' (a 'great' operation involved 4,000 or more troops, and a 'small' involved less), he summarized the success and failure rate as follows: '*Great Expeditions*': Succeeded = 7; Failed = 27. '*Small Expeditions*': Succeeded = 23; Failed = 11.'

[8] Quite the best overall description of the conduct of large-scale amphibious operations is D. Syrett, 'The Methodology of British Amphibious Operations during the Seven Years' and American Wars', *MM* 58 (1972), 269–80. Of particular operations discussed in detail, the best articles are N. Tracy, 'The Capture of Manila, 1762', *MM* 55 (1969), 311–23; D. Syrett, 'The British Landing at Havana', *MM* 55 (1969), 325–31; J. M. Hitsman and C. C. J. Bond, 'The Assault Landing at Louisbourg, 1758', *Canadian Historical Review*, 35 (1954), 314–30; and J. C. M. Ogelsby, 'British Attacks on the Caracas Coast, 1743', *MM* 58 (1972), 27–40. Among the larger studies devoted to these operations, those most worth consulting on detailed execution are D. Syrett (ed.), *The Siege and Capture of Havana, 1762* (Navy Records Society, 1970), esp. xiii–xxxv; Sir John Fortescue's classic account of the Cartagena expedition of 1740–1, in ii. 55–79; the Guadeloupe and Martinique expedition of 1759 in M. Smelser, op. cit., esp. 21–6, 46–126; W. K. Hackmann, op. cit., which deals in some depth with the Rochefort raid of 1757 (18–74), the Cherbourg and Saint-Malo raids of 1758 (79–145), and the Belle-Isle descent of 1761 (154–91); and the brilliant reconstruction of the boat-work at Quebec in 1759, in D. Grinnell-Milne, op. cit., *passim*.

Less detailed but useful are Fortescue, ii. 10, 166, on the Vigo raid of 1719 and the l'Orient expedition of 1746; H. W. Richmond, op. cit. iii. 23–38, on l'Orient; R. Reilly, op. cit. 161–2, for a fine contemporary appreciation of the essentials of amphibious warfare; and see *HMC Hastings MSS*, iii (1934), 183–4, for the landing at Kipp's Bay in 1776. Thomas More Molyneux's *Conjunct Expeditions* (1759), remains indispensable for any serious study.

was of necessity much that was *ad hoc*, left to common sense: the sheer variety of this service precluded the formality of Flanders campaigning. Put most simply, it was the burden of the naval officers to get the troops on to the beaches; and only then, as the keels of the landing-boats scraped bottom, did the regimental officers with the Marines and regular marching foot swing into action. Once the army officers took over the conduct of affairs, even as they waded ashore, it was no more than a slight variant of the normal drill and discipline of the land service that was put into practice. Hence, while it is true that these operations were throughout the century a common feature of British campaigning, it is true too that the corps—marching and Marine —can only in the most limited sense be said to have trained especially to carry them on. The soldiers were ferried ashore and there, on the beach, began the land service.

Beyond their normal training in the various aspects and elements of the land-service drill, any 'specialist' training needed by the Marines and regular foot for service as soldiers, afloat, was exceedingly limited. In ship-to-ship combat it was the business of the Marines, and of the marching foot shipped as marines, to line the sides—the poop and the quarterdeck were their usual action stations, being the highest decks from which a clear field of fire was to be had—and to lay down musketry on the tops and upper decks of the enemy alongside. They might also be called upon, in an emergency, either to form a solid line to repel boarders, or to join themselves in boarding the enemy. To perform these duties the soldiers had merely to adapt normal land-practice ('parapet firing' when lining the sides, 'street firing' when defending the stern or any narrow frontage, both normally included in the army's drill-books); and good discipline, fire control, and accurate fire were sufficient to carry on any of these activities. Little more than expertise at the platoon exercise, at bayonet work, and at certain of the firings was required, consequently; and since these were the most common of all training activities both for the marching foot and (in their capacity as soldiers) for the Marines, there was little to be learned by the soldiers in order to perform the duties expected of them in a ship action. Examples of actual training show this. In August 1757, for instance, a company of the 43rd Foot (then in Nova Scotia) was embarked on board the *Success* frigate to serve as marines. Asked to show his men exercising 'in the marine way', the officer commanding the company described their performance as

nothing more than, after firing over the ship's side, to fall down upon one knee, so as to be under cover, and load again; we performed these firings repeatedly for an hour: the men were formed·into three divisions, two upon the quarter-deck, and one upon the forecastle, facing the starboard side of the ship, and then fired, right, left, and center; afterwards several vollies were discharged.

For this display the men of the 43rd 'acquired great applause'.[9] Similarly, when in 1755 the lieutenant-colonel of the 20th Foot, then at Winchester, expected that his men might soon be ordered on marine service, he issued the following regimental order:

As the use of soldiers on board a fleet in an engagement depends almost entirely upon a well directed fire, and as the objects to aim at, vary every instant, the soldiers are to practise to direct their muskets either to the right or left, and to take some particular mark in view before they fire, sometimes upon a level, sometimes above, and sometimes below; they are to fire standing in two ranks, with the lowest men in front.[10]

This was actual practice; and the main treatises dealing with the subject recommended little more. Simplicity was the key: where possible, marines, like the foot, were to learn their drill on land before embarking—'a rolling ship of war in the Bay of Biscay', observed Lt. Terence O'Loghlen, being a 'very improper place to teach the men their firing and evolutions'.[11] O'Loghlen's treatise of 1766 on the training of marines limited itself to drilling the men to perform the parapet firings from the ship's bulwarks (these serving the same function as did parapets in land fortifications), and to taking good aim when in platoon, both forward and obliquely to the flanks;[12] and with that, he

---

[9] A. G. Doughty (ed.), op. cit. i. 52–3.

[10] James Wolfe, op. cit. 39.

[11] Lt. Terence O'Loghlen, *The Marine Volunteer* (1766), quoted in C. Field, op. cit. i. 118–22.

[12] Marksmanship was stressed by all the authors treating sea service. O'Loghlen, op. cit. 120–1, felt that marines 'should be accustomed to fire frequently with ball on board ship at a mark, hung for that purpose at the extremity of the fore-yard arm'; and he thought it a good idea to set a platoon of picked marksmen firing not in volleys across the enemy's decks, but rather as individuals aiming at the enemy's gun-ports. 'Two or three expert men killed at a gun may silence it for half-an-hour.' Likewise Lt. John MacIntire, op. cit. 9, 113, called for constant target practice among marines.

concluded, 'no other firing or evolution should be attempted at sea. It can answer no purpose whatever to puzzle men with impracticabilities.'

Before 1763 Marine detachments, admittedly, often joined their ships with little previous drill of any sort, having only just been raised and embarked on board ships that were themselves still manning and getting ready for sea. In such cases these marines—mere recruits—were first to be taught the use of their arms, without 'worrying about details', since a ship of war could go into action on a sudden. Thereafter they were to be taught the manual and platoon 'in a regular Manner', together with 'every Manoeuvre that can be performed on Board, to give the Men an idea of Land-Service'.[13] Lt. John MacIntire, too, in a simple essay—'Plain Regulations'—wrote that good marksmanship and fire control among marines lining a ship's sides were all-important; and beyond that practice at parapet firing, oblique firing, the street-firing when the enemy lay astern, and bayonet work to repel boarders, were sufficient.

Lastly, both the Marines and marching foot embarked for amphibious operations were put through some simple boat-drill;[14] and if time permitted before embarking an expedition the men were to practise unslinging their firelocks and leaping into the water from the boats, as they came ashore, 'holding their Firelocks high recovered, to preserve their Shot, keeping their Ammunition from the Wet'. Speedily forming and telling off the battalions as they came ashore—the most critical of all amphibious drill—was practised too: but this was no more than what was normally practised on a parade square, any more than sending out flankers and skirmishers was anything new to the men of the grenadier and light companies.[15]

A most important factor in service on board the fleet was the damage thereby inflicted upon the marching regiments so employed. For a marching regiment, any extended service

---

[13] Lt. John MacIntire, op. cit. 1–5.

[14] Ibid. 225. The flat-bottomed boats which came into service *c*.1758, and which were a notable improvement upon the ships' boats normally employed, are described in Adm 95/95, p. 159; in D. Syrett, 'The Methodology of British Amphibious Operations . . .' *MM* 58 (1972), 272–4; in Thomas More Molyneux, op. cit., Pt. I, 211–13, and Pt. II, 58–94; and (somewhat more fancifully) in Joseph Robson, op. cit. 1–9, Plate I.

[15] Lt. John MacIntire, op. cit. 225–8.

afloat for purposes other than simple transport to the landing beaches was prejudicial to its military efficiency: for sea service meant not only wide dispersal among several ships, but dispersal in 'quarters' where the advanced training of the corps was quite impossible. This of course was the normal lot of the detachments of Marines proper, who unlike the regular foot spent half their time serving as ordinary seamen. Marines were trained to their military duties only 'when . . . there is good Summer Weather, and not much of *Ship Duty*'; and that was 'the only Time' when officers of Marines 'should attempt to discipline a Detachment in a regular Manner' for the land service.[16] Since the Marines spent only half their time training as soldiers, and since they customarily served in small detachments which were only infrequently brigaded for short on-shore operations,[17] their military capacity (beyond their simple duty as musketeers in ship-to-ship actions) was much less than what was expected from regular foot; and in their amphibious capacity the Marines were generally expected to do no more than conduct minor raids or support the operations of the regular land forces.

TABLE 11

Rate (+guns)	Marines, 1793	Marines, 1747	Marines, 1741
1st (100+)	113	113	—
2nd (98–90)	103	113	—
3rd (80)	—	91	71
3rd (74)	79	81	42
3rd (64)	57	—	—
4th (60–50)	47	65	37
5th (44–32)	34	55	32
6th (30–20)	24	33	22
Sloops of War	19	23	15

The first two columns show the average number of Marines of all ranks authorized for the various rates of warship, while the figures in the third column give the average numbers actually with the ships of the Channel Fleet in mid-1741.

Figures from WO 26/35, p. 36; WO 55/408, pp. 151–2; and SP 41/3, 14 July 1741.

When marching foot was embarked on board the fleet not as part of an expedition but rather to reinforce (or to serve in the place of) the Marines proper, they became subject to the same

---

[16] Ibid. 2.   [17] See Table 11.

conditions, which made it impossible fully to train the Marine detachments in the land-service drill. During the summer of 1778, typically, the 600 officers and men of the 50th Foot shipped as marines on board Keppel's fleet and, divided among five men-of-war, were engaged in the action with d'Orvillier off Ushant. The 50th came ashore at summer's end, and a year later the corps was found still to be suffering the effects: it marched poorly, its manoeuvres were 'Not always well perform'd', nor was it 'always the most steady and attentive under Arms'. The 50th, reported the reviewing officer, had been 'dispers'd on board the Fleet last summer', a circumstance which had 'impeded it's perfect Discipline'.[18] This was but one marching regiment, it had only been at sea for a few weeks, and it had done no more than line the sides and deliver fire. Much worse could happen to a marching regiment when with the fleet for longer periods or performing different duties. Very lengthy periods of service as marines or, what was much more destructive, the shipping of soldiers to serve as raw sailors in undermanned vessels, were by no means uncommon; and a summary of the more flagrant examples of such usage is instructive.

As we have seen, the last of the Marine regiments raised under Anne had been disbanded by 1715; and in consequence only marching foot was available for sea service during the clashes that occurred with the Spaniards and the Jacobites over the ensuing dozen years. Thus, when Byng sailed for Sicily in 1718 he took out to Minorca on board his fleet four regular battalions; two of these (the 9th and 35th) served as sailors with the ships and, when arrived at Port Mahon, the four battalions there (the 7th, 12th, 27th, and 39th) were shipped as marines, fought at Cape Passaro, and continued in the fleet as marines until 1720.[19] In 1730 the 2nd, 7th, and 14th served several months both as sailors and marines with the fleet sent to the Mediterranean. In mid-1740, when Vernon's fleet lying at Spithead and bound for Cartagena was found to be very short of seamen, the bulk of the 34th and 36th of Foot were turned over to the navy to fill the vacancies; and during the spring and summer of 1741 most of the remainder of these two corps went

[18] WO 27/42.
[19] J. B. M. Frederick, op. cit., *passim*; and Atkinson, 'Early Hanoverians', 138, 141–2.

into the Channel Fleet.[20] In 1741 Haddock's Mediterranean squadron, its crews greatly reduced by sickness, took upwards of 500 soldiers from the regiments at Port Mahon (a 'nursery of seamen' if ever there was one) to eke out the ships' companies.[21] Other corps serving as marines for long stretches at this time were the 39th Foot (from 1744 to 1747), the 29th (from 1740 until 1742), and the 30th (until 1747).[22] During the Seven Years War regular marching regiments were, once again, often shipped for lengthy periods and in damaging capacities. When Byng's ill-starred fleet sailed in 1756 to attempt the relief of Minorca, for example, it was so thinly manned that the 7th Foot had to be put on board to serve as sailors; and the 30th Foot went to sea as marines in 1761 and did not come ashore again until 1763.[23]

During the American War seven corps (the 2nd, 5th, 23rd, 46th, 50th, 79th, and 86th of Foot) served in various capacities afloat, but—as we noted of the 50th above—the service for these units was taxing but not severe, some of them carrying out only short-lived amphibious duties.[24]

By the close of our period the same service pattern continued to prevail. When the 53rd Foot showed up very badly at their Glasgow review in 1791 the major of the corps could wish it reported to Edinburgh Castle that, among other reasons, they had been held back by being 'embarked on board the Fleet to serve as Marines' midway through 1790, and the companies had not been reunited ashore for nearly five months.[25] A great many marching regiments were to serve on board the fleet during the great wars that began in 1793; and although they were merely carrying on a type of service long since a traditional role of British infantry, it remained a service which in many cases seriously harmed their military efficiency, despite the fact that they could perform it with only the slightest modification to the drill in which they had been trained on dry land.

---

[20] WO 5/34, pp. 112–14, 117, 125, 129, 362–4; Fortescue, ii. 61; and H. W. Richmond, op. cit., i. 82–3.

[21] H. W. Richmond, op. cit. 155.

[22] J. B. M. Frederick, op. cit., *passim*.

[23] Fortescue, ii. 293–4.

[24] P. R. N. Katcher, op. cit., *passim*.

[25] WO 27/69.

Chapter IX

Summary and Conclusion

Where the colonial and imperial historians have oftentimes, in passing, noted the dispersal and remarked upon the deplorable condition of those few corps encountered in the overseas stations and garrisons, it has generally been assumed—almost as a corollary—that the great majority of the corps, those more fortunately situated safe at home in Britain and Ireland, must be in infinitely better condition, their situation being unexceptional.

We set out, initially, without questioning this general line of reasoning, commonly held; to essay training, we supposed, would be largely a matter of studying the drillbooks and, once familiar with their contents, of discovering their manner of application by searching the correspondence of officers, the regimental books of the corps, and the orders and directives of the staffs. The levels of proficiency achieved in individual corps could later be checked in the Inspection Returns submitted by reviewing officers.

The assumption underlying this scheme, of course, was that the corps in the British Isles were essentially malleable; that is, that they were inert, passive; more particularly, that they were concentrated and stationary. That the regiments could, with a minimum of fuss, be drawn up on the parade-squares and there exercised at the various elements of the drill, was taken for granted. Time and opportunity, in this scheme, were assumed.

As we became familiar with the drillbooks it became increasingly evident that a very great deal of training, carried on intensively and in high levels of concentration, would be required of the corps were they to master the several elements of the drill; but the Inspection Returns showed quite clearly that a significant proportion of the corps were not by any means so accomplished. Expertise was largely a function of time and opportunity; and opportunity, then, could not have been so freely come by as heretofore assumed. We were obliged at once, in consequence, not only somehow to measure opportunity but likewise to account for its apparent scarcity. In order to determine how, and in what condition, the corps were spending their time, we turned to the Marching Orders; and these set us back on our heels, our initial assumptions going by the board as the movement, duty, and dispersal patterns began to reveal themselves.

As the significance of these patterns became increasingly apparent, so our concern with time and opportunity became primary, where it had been only incidental. For it was around these fundamental patterns that the training of the regiments was arranged; it was according to their dictates that time was apportioned and opportunity occasioned; indeed, such was their influence upon training that much else that required our attention was essentially derivative. Certain other factors meanwhile, the influence of which was important and persistent, if not so essentially significant, drew our attention or suggested themselves; and these too we have considered in their turn, adding their analysis to the overall picture.

Proceeding in this fashion, then, we were able to reconstruct the training milieu in which the corps found themselves; and plainly it bore little resemblance to that supposed milieu previously assumed, or taken for granted. Within the actual milieu, now revealed, neither the physical situation nor the material condition of the corps was at all conducive to a thorough training programme; while from the point of view of training, time was squandered and opportunities were rare. Still, the regiments had operating in their favour several advantages, although it will by now be evident that there were a great many more disadvantages in play to set against these.

In so far as training was concerned, the following were easily the most significant advantages enjoyed by the regiments in the normal round of peacetime service. First, they were issued with and put into practice successive sets of drill regulations, carefully prepared and kept up to date by an informed and competent authority. Secondly, they were subject to a system of regular inspection and review by which deviations and deficiencies in their training and drill would be discovered and, once discovered, ordered remedied or brought into line with uniform practice. Thirdly, they had available to them in the English language a very considerable, wide-ranging, detailed, and often excellent body of privately published military literature, much of which was relevant to their peacetime training and virtually all of which was of benefit to officers in their education for service in the field. And finally, the regiments were trained and led by an officer corps which was careerist, long-serving, notably experienced, and capable.

The importance of these advantages can hardly be exaggerated—not only in their own right but because they were palliative, alleviating the worst effects of the several burdens under which the corps laboured, and not least because they have previously been so little credited. It was because of these advantages, by and large, that most of the corps were kept 'fit for service', most of the time; and if, admittedly, 'fit for service' was an unstable condition, and as a category often expressed a degree of wish-fulfilment or pious hope, still training could not have been carried on without them, and in their absence the condition of the corps would have been grievous.

Where these advantages could shore up or stave off, however, they could not override the baneful influence of the friction of peace. To describe here once again the host of lesser problems afflicting the corps would simply be repetitious: the reader will be aware that the often deplorable condition of the firelocks, for example, the great scarcity of ball ammunition in peacetime, the difficulties experienced in obtaining suitable training-grounds, the weak cadre-strengths of the Irish corps, and the four-month absence of the troop-horses from their regiments, out to grass, were individually hurtful, or worse; and cumulatively, they retarded significantly the training of the regiments. It is rather the major, gnawing problems, the effects of which were most disadvantageous, that deserve repeated emphasis here.

One such was the chronic, two-pronged manpower problem, of which all the corps both at home and abroad were the constant victims. Invariably, too few recruits were available to complete to the establishments, while at the same time there were too many recruits among the men already with the corps. The problem, bad enough in peacetime, was aggravated in wartime to the point where calamity could (and in 1780–3 did) occur. Among all the corps serving in the British Isles from the mid-century down to 1795 it was the normal condition of things in peacetime for the average regiment of foot to stand on only 90 per cent of its authorized establishment, while of its men an average of 16 per cent were recruits; and in wartime these figures fell to 83 and 27 per cent respectively. In the horse meanwhile, the average regiment stood in peacetime on 95 per cent of its authorized establishment, and of its men 9 per cent were recruits; while in wartime the figures fell off to 94 and 19 per cent respectively. There were always a few corps containing even greater percentages of recruits, or standing further below their authorized establishments, or both. Where normal beating up failed, we have seen that inefficient, expensive, and often drastic 'remedial' expedients had to be resorted to—short-term enlistments, bounties, the press, additional companies, and drafting; for wherever they fell below the normal manpower figures, just given, the corps so situated were normally rendered unfit for service.

The manpower problem had a notable effect on the training of the regiments; but the problems raised by the routine movements, duties, and dispersal of the regiments had by far the most significant impact, since these things concerned training in the most fundamental way, determining time and opportunity. The great damage inflicted upon a sizeable proportion of the peacetime army by extended overseas service—where from 1716 to 1739, and again from 1748 to 1755, one-quarter of the corps of marching foot were disposed; and where from 1763 to 1775, and then again from 1783 to 1793, more than one-third of the foot was to be found—can hardly be exaggerated. The many ills of this service could be mitigated only by frequent rotation, to share the burden; but not until halfway through the century was this attempted, and indeed right through to the end of our period there were always corps left abroad for too lengthy stretches. For all intents and purposes we must conclude that at least one-fifth and often as many as one-quarter of the regiments of marching foot, strewn abroad, was perpetually in a low state of interior economy and training and was, consequently, either unfit for service or capable of only the most modest exertions.

The duty of the overseas stations and garrisons, however harmful, fell to the lot of only a minority of the corps. The most grave disadvantage under which the great majority of the corps laboured was the duty of Britain and Ireland, characterized as it was by wide dispersal and constant harassment. There, whenever a march was made, the logistics of movement meant that units spent much time strung out along the roads, and that they did so moreover in a state of dispersal. Action in aid of the civil power, patrols upon the coast duty, and the maintenance of a passive police presence, these were the activities of primary concern to authority when the dispositions of the corps in the duty areas of Britain, and in the police barracks and garrison towns of Ireland, were determined; and just as the resulting quartering patterns effectively dispersed most corps and, in so doing, deprived them of the opportunity of carrying on advanced training, so the pursuit of these activities ate up the time which the corps might otherwise have given over to training.

In an army so situated, whatever training might be carried on was determined almost entirely in accordance with the limited time and opportunity afforded by the routine of service; and this is illustrated by the phases into which the army's training programme was divided.

Basic training was directed essentially to the practice of the first three elements composing the drill regimen—the evolutions and the manual and platoon exercises—and to the necessary attendant skills, all of which formed the fundamental building-blocks upon which were grounded the other more difficult elements of the drill. Its most signal feature was that it occupied so much of that most precious commodity in the British Army—time—thereby reflecting the situation in which the corps found themselves. For the individual regiments subject to the friction of peace were, as we have seen, commonly to be found in states of considerable dispersal; and the small dispersed bodies—of fewer than three or four companies in the foot, or fewer than two or three troops in the horse, depending upon establishment strengths—could not attempt with profit anything more complex than these mechanical basics. Where in its initial or 'material' phase basic training was devoted to inculcating the simple elements and skills, it was both well organized and appropriate; but where in its on-going or 'mechanical' phase it substituted (and rationalized) endless, numbing repetition for what should properly have been only regular refreshment, it was stifling and even counter-productive, affording little scope for creativity or variety; and thus it very often resolved itself into an endless and—as Dettingen and Prestonpans so clearly demonstrated—an ineffective 'tossing of the firelocks'.

It was essentially the detailed firings and manoeuvres, practised in an infinite variety of simulated tactical situations, of varying complexity and sophistication, that constituted the advanced training carried on in the regiments. However imaginative (or otherwise) might be the adjutants and field officers with individual corps, the efficacy of advanced training depended absolutely upon the numbers concentrated and the time available. Men to form the squadrons and grand-divisions, and time for the exercising of these units, were essential where satisfactory and realistic performances were to be attempted; and yet for the majority of regiments neither of these conditions was for long satisfied in the normal routine of peacetime service. What one or two squadrons, or two or three grand-divisions could accomplish, was useful but limited; and save for the weeks in the review quarters (which at least had the advantage of coming regularly each season), regimental concentrations were not common. Field days, day 'excursions', and mock fighting were infrequent; and brigade training was almost unknown. There were, meanwhile, a great many eventualities likely to arise—heavy drafting, service on board the fleet, and so forth—which could seriously retard the military efficiency built up in the corps; and indeed it must be admitted that in the British Army's normal routine of peacetime service it took not only dedicated officers, a sound system of interior economy, *esprit de corps*, a low turnover rate among the rank and file, and good postings which permitted frequent concentration for training, but also a share of luck to keep one step ahead of the friction of peace for sustained periods. 'Fit for service', consequently, was a rating that regiments were frequently unable to retain over several years running in peacetime.

Hence it was not in peacetime but rather in wartime—by default, and now of necessity—that advanced training was carried on most effectively, most realistically, and most intensively. It was only in the encampments at home and in the cantonments and the field abroad that full and lengthy concentration was at last effected, and time and opportunity at last provided. Camp training was excellent: every necessary circumstance now pertained, and everything that had been hard come by (or not come by at all) in peacetime was now available. The drawback was that only a minority of the corps ever managed to camp at all. During the 1739–48 war, one-third of the foot regiments and less than one-half of the cavalry regiments camped. During the 1756–63 war, less than one-third of the foot and only one-quarter of the cavalry camped. During the 1775–83 war, one-quarter of the foot camped and—the only exception—two-thirds of the cavalry. Thus it was while actually in the field that the majority of corps were obliged to carry on the business—which they did, understandably, without let-up season after season. That the regiments should be free to perfect their drill only when arrived in the theatres of operations, almost in the face of the enemy, was to say the least a most extraordinary manner of proceeding.

It is evident that such a programme was woefully inadequate. Most of the training carried on in peacetime, under this programme, was restricted. Only the essentials were well practised. Since time and opportunity were limited, training at the more advanced manoeuvres and tactics could be conducted neither intensively nor vigorously. There was much 'tossing of the firelocks', much 'equallizing'. Many corps were poorly trained; most corps were no better than 'fit for service'; only a few corps—the Guards in London, and the regiments in the big Dublin garrison—were well trained, and they were exceptions proving the rule precisely because they were concentrated and stationary. When crisis, war, or rebellion came, it was in this condition that the army found itself—in need of intensive advanced training, to be carried on by the corps in concentration and undisturbed. But the weaknesses and omissions of years could not be made good in so many weeks, especially not at the eleventh hour—a simple fact illustrated time and again during the earlier campaigns of each of the wars of our period. In these campaigns—those of the years 1740–3, 1755–7, 1793–5—the performance of the corps in action was generally clumsy; while the results of these campaigns were almost invariably dismal. The only exception to this pattern was the string of successes gained in the campaigns of 1775–7; and this was exceptional only because the corps were facing not regular soldiers, but a militarily incompetent adversary innocent of training, buoyed merely by enthusiasm. All this was done at the cost of much blood and much treasure.

Why was so inadequate a training programme suffered to prevail? We noted at the outset of this study that the army had three main roles to play. The performance of its imperial garrison role and, most especially, the pursuit of its police role meant—inevitably—that the army's peacetime preparation for its wartime battlefield role must suffer. We have examined in detail the conditions routinely encountered on peacetime service; and we have seen that it was in the very nature of this service that the corps so engaged should be much preoccupied with civil matters, and much dispersed on that account. It was from these circumstances that the army's training programme was derived; and the inadequacy of the programme was due to the fact that most advanced training was carried on at the convenience of civil requirements, strictly military requirements inevitably taking second place, in these circumstances. Since civil requirements were given precedence over military, the efficient performance of its wartime battlefield role was not treated as the essential and overriding role of the standing army. The army was the guardian of civil order as much as the instrument of foreign policy.

Appendix A

Tables of the Roles and Dispositions of the Regiments in England, Expressed in Time

Although the Quartermaster-General, concerned with logistics, determined the routes of marching troops from the network of roads and halting-places, constitutional law saw to it that no officer of the regular military forces, whatever his rank, had the authority to move soldiers from any one place to another within the Kingdom of England without first receiving due authorization, in the form of written orders, from the civil power. These orders—no matter how urgently the soldiers might be required, nor how few might be the number of soldiers to be moved—had all to be issued by the Secretary at War, at the instance of a responsible Secretary of State. All these Marching Orders—the typical example of which included the date upon which a march was to be begun or concluded, the units that were to perform the march, the units' ultimate destination and place of origin, the reason for the movement, and quite often a route listing each of the daily stages or halting-places to be used for quartering upon the march—were entered in the letter-books at the Secretary at War's office (WO 5);[1] and from these we can plot in the most minute detail all troop movements and dispositions in eighteenth-century England and Wales.

With this great mass of information available, six series of consecutive years were selected at random, and used for statistical 'bores' through the letter-books (Table A1).

TABLE A1

From Spring	To Spring	Total Years
1726	1729	3
1737	1743	6
1751	1756	5
1764	1767	3
1772	1776	4
1786	1790	4

[1] These books were kept up so that the disposition of all troops in the country could be readily ascertained, and so that mileage-rates for cartage—of regimental baggage in wagons legally impressed upon the march, and of military equipment and stores sent from suppliers and government agencies to the regiments—could be assessed and paid. J. R. Western, op. cit.. 360 n. 2.

By recording *every* troop movement made during each of these series, it was possible to isolate and plot the routes and stages used by the army, together with their incidence of use and the reasons for the movements: and at the same time the pattern of quarters emerged.

Tables A2–13, drawn from these series of Marching Orders, are concerned particularly with time—time spent on the march, in aid of the civil power and upon the coast duty, and in various levels of concentration and dispersal. The amount of time spent on these activities, and in these conditions, is expressed in percentages. To arrive at these percentages, a basic unit of measurement had to be established that would represent the smallest appropriate sub-unit of the regiment. The Marching Orders, since they deal in day marches, had themselves provided the day as a measure of time. The 'company/day' for the foot, and the 'troop/day' for the cavalry, suggested themselves, and were used quite as the 'man/hour' is used in manpower and time studies. The method is perhaps best illustrated with a brief example.

Thus, during the period 1737–43 the infantry battalion stood on an establishment of 10 companies. During this same period, Barrell's 4th of Foot spent 1,127 days in England—which is 11,270 company/days. By using the company/day, the amount of time spent by each individual company of Barrell's, performing any task or billeted in isolation or concentration with other companies of the regiment, was computed. When broken into the figures that were the basis for those in the six columns of the tables, we found that 684 company/days were spent by Barrell's in concentration at the level of three grand-divisions, 4,992 company/days either totally dispersed or on the march etc. Reduced to percentages of 11,270, we arrive at the figures in the tables.

The following short forms are employed:

Ft = Foot
D.G. = Dragoon Guards
Dgns = Dragoons
L.D. = Light Dragoons
M & D = Time spent Marching and Dispersed
ACP = Time spent in Aid of the Civil Power
CST = Time spent on the Coast Duty
GDs = Grand-Divisions
Sqn(s) = Squadron(s)
Mon/Yr = Month and Year

Explanatory notes are appended at the end of the tables, where required, and where a few anomalies are dealt with.

TABLE A2: CAVALRY, 1726–9

Regt.	M & D	ACP	CST	1 Sqn	2 Sqns	3 Sqns	In England From Mon/Yr	To Mon/Yr
	(percentage of time spent)							
Blues	82	1	—	16	—	1	Nov. '26–May '29	
2nd Horse	86	—	—	13	—	1	June '26–July '29	
3rd Horse	19	—	—	81	—	—	Oct. '26–Apr. '29	
4th Horse	31	—	—	51	18	—	Jan. '27–June '29	
1st Dgns	81	—	—	19	—	—	Oct. '26–May '29	
2nd Dgns	54	—	—	45	—	1	Jan. '27–July '29	
3rd Dgns	72	—	3	23	—	2	May '28–July '29	
4th Dgns	63	—	—	33	3	1	May '26–July '29	
6th Dgns	66	—	—	30	—	4	Mar. '28–Apr. '29	
7th Dgns	56	—	—	44	—	—	Oct. '26–July '29	
10th Dgns	47	4	—	49	—	—	Oct. '26–June '28	
11th Dgns	51	2	—	47	—	—	Oct. '26–Apr. '28	

TABLE A3: INFANTRY, 1726–9

Regt.	M & D	ACP	CST	2 GDs	3 GDs	4 GDs+	In England From Mon/Yr	To Mon/Yr
	(percentage of time spent)							
2nd Ft	49	1	20	17	4	9	Jan. '27–July '29	
3rd Ft	49	—	—	—	—	51	Oct. '26–May '27	
7th Ft	47	1	—	2	9	41	Jan. '27–July '29	
11th Ft	50	—	—	28	16	6	July '26–Aug. '28	
13th Ft	24	—	—	20	—	56	Apr. '28–July '29	
14th Ft	81	—	3	16	—	—	July '26–Mar. '27	

Table A3—*continued*

Regt.	M & D	ACP	CST	2 GDs	3 GDs	4 GDs+	In England From Mon/Yr	To Mon/Yr
	(percentage of time spent)							
15th Ft	39	2	3	8	12	36	May '26–May '29	
16th Ft	60	2	1	—	22	15	Jan. '27–July '29	
19th Ft	72	—	—	—	16	12	Jan. '27–July '27	
21st Ft	66	—	—	28	—	6	Jan. '27–July '27	
23rd Ft	62	1	—	5	—	32	Apr. '27–July '29	
37th Ft	44	—	—	—	22	34	Jan. '27–July '27	

Table A4: CAVALRY, 1737–43

Regt.	M & D	ACP	CST	1 Sqn	2 Sqns	3 Sqns	In England From Mon/Yr	To Mon/Yr
	(percentage of time spent)							
Blues	49	—	—	46	—	5	Apr. '37–Aug. '42	
2nd Horse	61	—	—	30	—	9	May '39–Aug. '42	
3rd Horse	42	—	—	53	—	5	Oct. '37–May '43	
4th Horse	39	—	—	56	—	5	Apr. '37–May '43	
8th Horse	49	—	—	42	—	9	Apr. '42–Sept. '42	
1st Dgns	42	—	20	32	—	6	Apr. '37–July '42	
2nd Dgns	56	2	13	22	1	6	Apr. '37–July '42	
3rd Dgns	32	—	46	12	—	10	Apr. '39–June '42	
4th Dgns	58	—	29	6	7	—	Apr. '39–June '42	
6th Dgns	42	—	1	50	—	7	May '37–Dec. '41 Apr. '42–Aug. '42	
7th Dgns	36	—	19	39	—	6	Apr. '37–Dec. '41	
10th Dgns	41	—	8	40	—	11	Apr. '41–May '43	
11th Dgns	32	—	4	64	—	—	Apr. '37–May '39 Apr. '41–May '43	

TABLE A5: INFANTRY, 1737–43

Regt.	M & D	ACP	CST	2 GDs	3 GDs	4 GDs+	In England From Mon/Yr	To Mon/Yr
			(percentage of time spent)					
1/1st Ft	49	—	—	—	—	51	Dec. '42–May '43	
(a) 3rd Ft	51	—	34	—	15	—	Apr. '37–Aug. '37	
(b) 3rd Ft	44	7	—	—	4	45	May '40–Apr. '42	
4th Ft	44	1	—	—	6	49	July '39–Aug. '42	
8th Ft	35	—	20	—	45	—	June '39–June '42	
11th Ft	32	2	19	4	37	6	May '36–July '38 May '41–May '42	
12th Ft	52	—	30	—	—	18	May '39–Apr. '42	
13th Ft	71	—	—	—	4	25	Apr. '40–May '42	
14th Ft	91	—	—	—	9	—	Sept. '42–May '43	
15th Ft	11	2	37	1	1	48	Apr. '37–Oct. '40 Dec. '42–May '43	
16th Ft	63	2	17	—	5	13	Apr. '37–Apr. '43	
18th Ft	94	—	—	—	—	6	Sept. '42–June '43	
21st Ft	100	—	—	—	—	—	Sept. '41–May '42	
23rd Ft	62	—	23	—	2	13	May '38–May '42	
(a) 24th Ft	67	2	—	—	4	27	June '39–Aug. '40	
(b) 24th Ft	40	—	—	—	—	60	Dec. '42–Mar. '43	
28th Ft	98	—	—	—	—	2	Apr. '42–Apr. '43	
31st Ft	35	1	—	—	14	50	June '39–May '42	
34th Ft	4	—	9	—	3	84	June '39–July '40	
36th Ft	99	—	—	—	—	1	June '39–July '40	
43rd Ft	41	—	—	—	15	44	Mar. '41–May '42	
45th Ft	41	—	43	16	—	—	Mar. '41–May '42	
46th Ft	33	—	—	—	—	67	Mar. '41–Oct. '42	
48th Ft	11	—	48	40	—	1	Apr. '41–Aug. '42	

TABLE A6: CAVALRY, 1751–6

Regt.	M & D	ACP	CST	1 Sqn	2 Sqns	3 Sqns	In England	
	(percentage of time spent)						From Mon/Yr	To Mon/Yr
Blues	81	1	—	18	—	—	Nov. '51–July '56	
1st D.G.	22	1	14	37	6	20	June '51–Nov. '52 Sept. '54–July '56	
2nd D.G.	38	—	—	44	9	5	Oct. '51–Oct. '54	
3rd D.G.	22	—	37	37	—	4	Sept. '51–July '56	
1st Dgns	19	—	29	33	6	13	Oct. '52–July '56	
2nd Dgns	24	8	4	37	16	11	Sept. '51–July '56	
3rd Dgns	15	—	52	21	4	8	June '51–July '56	
4th Dgns	25	2	22	48	—	3	Sept. '51–July '56	
6th Dgns	28	3	40	24	1	4	May '51–Aug. '56	
7th Dgns	31	10	—	25	12	22	June '51–Oct. '53	
10th Dgns	19	1	33	39	5	3	Aug. '53–July '56	
11th Dgns	22	1	45	15	10	7	Sept. '51–July '56	

TABLE A7: INFANTRY, 1751–6

Regt.	M & D	ACP	CST	2 GDs	3 GDs	4 GDs+	In England	
	(percentage of time spent)						From Mon/Yr	To Mon/Yr
3rd Ft	59	—	—	27	—	14	July '54–July '56	
4th Ft	49	1	47	1	—	2	Aug. '51–Apr. '53	
5th Ft	7	—	—	8	—	85	Feb. '55–July '56	
6th Ft	36	—	29	35	—	—	Aug. '51–Mar. '53	
7th Ft	12	—	—	—	3	85	Mar. '55–Mar. '56	
8th Ft	31	4	—	—	5	60	July '54–July '56	
9th Ft	24	—	—	34	—	42	Mar. '55–Nov. '55	

TABLE A7—*continued*

Regt.	M & D	ACP	CST	2 GDs	3 GDs	4 GDs+	In England From Mon/Yr	To Mon/Yr
			(percentage of time spent)					
11th Ft	48	1	7	23	19	2	Aug. '53–May '55 July '55–Feb. '56	
12th Ft	16	—	—	—	—	84	June '51–Sept. '51 Mar. '55–July '56	
13th Ft	40	—	7	32	—	21	July '52–Apr. '54	
14th Ft	50	1	48	1	—	—	Apr. '51–Apr. '52	
15th Ft	14	1	—	13	13	59	Mar. '55–July '56	
18th Ft	52	2	—	44	—	2	Apr. '55–Nov. '55	
20th Ft	33	6	11	16	23	11	Sept. '53–July '56	
23rd Ft	51	4	32	7	—	6	Aug. '52–Mar. '54	
24th Ft	26	7	46	21	—	—	Apr. '51–Mar. '52	
25th Ft	83	—	—	—	—	17	Oct. '55–July '56	
30th Ft	20	—	—	12	19	49	Mar. '55–July '56	
33rd Ft	43	—	—	4	33	20	Oct. '55–July '56	
36th Ft	88	—	—	—	—	12	Oct. '55–July '56	
37th Ft	25	—	—	5	—	70	Mar. '55–July '56	

TABLE A8: CAVALRY, 1764–7

Regt.	M & D	ACP	CST	1 Sqn	2 Sqns	3 Sqns	In England From Mon/Yr	To Mon/Yr
			(percentage of time spent)					
Blues	58	—	—	23	—	19	May '64–Sept. '66	
1st D.G.	46	2	15	20	—	17	June '64–Apr. '66	
2nd D.G.	18	4	34	21	18	5	Oct. '64–Feb. '67	
3rd D.G.	41	—	—	49	—	10	Oct. '64–Apr. '65	
1st Dgns	18	—	14	58	—	10	Oct. '64–Oct. '66	

TABLE A8—*continued*

Regt.	M & D	ACP	CST	1 Sqn	2 Sqns	3 Sqns	In England From Mon/Yr	To Mon/Yr
		(percentage of time spent)						
2nd Dgns	9	—	29	16	22	24	June '64–Mar. '67	
3rd Dgns	31	6	—	56	—	7	Mar. '65–Feb. '67	
4th Dgns	11	7	16	30	27	9	Apr. '65–Feb. '67	
6th Dgns	15	9	12	36	25	3	Aug. '64–Mar. '65 Apr. '66–Mar. '67	
7th Dgns	34	2	35	32	2	5	Nov. '64–Mar. '67	
10th Dgns	18	2	10	66	—	4	Nov. '64–Mar. '67	
11th Dgns	19	6	27	46	—	2	Aug. '64–Mar. '67	
15th L.D.	60	6	—	27	—	7	Feb. '65–Feb. '67	
16th L.D.	67	2	—	9	—	22	May '64–Feb. '67	

TABLE A9: INFANTRY, 1764–7

Regt.	M & D	ACP	CST	2 GDs	3 GDs	4 GDs+	In England From Mon/Yr	To Mon/Yr
		(percentage of time spent)						
4th Ft	11	2	11	11	5	60	July '64–Mar. '67	
7th Ft	45	—	6	32	12	5	May '64–May '66	
8th Ft	32	18	—	—	29	21	Mar. '66–Mar. '67	
13th Ft	8	7	20	—	26	39	Aug. '64–Jan. '67	
14th Ft	25	—	2	1	24	48	Aug. '64–June '66	
22nd Ft	3	—	22	—	35	40	Sept. '65–Feb. '67	
23rd Ft	31	1	10	21	27	10	Nov. '64–Feb. '67	
32nd Ft	14	—	—	—	—	86	May '64–Oct. '64	
43rd Ft	35	13	17	4	1	30	July '64–Feb. '67	

TABLE A10: CAVALRY, 1772.6

Regt.	M & D	ACP	CST	1 Sqn	2 Sqns	3 Sqns	In England From Mon/Yr	To Mon/Yr
	(percentage of time spent)							
Blues	78	—	—	19	2	1	Apr. '73–Apr. '76	
1st D.G.	49	—	22	24	2	3	Mar. '73–Feb. '76	
2nd D.G.	6	—	21	46	18	9	June '72–Mar. '74 Mar. '75–Apr. '76	
3rd D.G.	20	—	19	24	—	37	Mar. '73–Apr. '76	
1st Dgns	21	3	27	12	10	27	Aug. '72–Mar. '74 Apr. '75–Mar. '76	
2nd Dgns	21	—	17	17	16	29	Apr. '73–Mar. '75	
3rd Dgns	29	1	13	47	5	5	May '72–Apr. '75	
4th Dgns	15	—	32	22	15	16	Mar. '73–Mar. '76	
6th Dgns	24	—	11	44	—	21	Sept. '72–Apr. '76	
7th Dgns	20	—	4	28	14	34	Nov. '72–Mar. '73 Mar. '74–Apr. '76	
10th Dgns	37	—	8	41	—	14	June '72–Mar. '73 Mar. '74–Apr. '76	
11th Dgns	25	—	15	27	—	33	Mar. '73–Mar. '76	
15th L.D.	27	2	—	46	15	10	Oct. '72–Apr. '76	
16th L.D.	23	—	—	45	9	23	Sept. '72–Apr. '76	

TABLE A11: INFANTRY, 1772–6

Regt.	M & D	ACP	CST	2 GDs	3 GDs	4 GDs	In England From Mon/Yr	To Mon/Yr
	(percentage of time spent)							
2/1st Ft	51	—	—	—	9	40	Jan. '76–Apr. '76	
3rd Ft	32	2	33	—	3	30	June '72–Apr. '75	

TABLE A11—*continued*

Regt.	M & D	ACP	CST	2 GDs	3 GDs	4 GDs	In England From Mon/Yr	To Mon/Yr
			(percentage of time spent)					
4th Ft	13	—	—	—	—	87	Mar. '73–Apr. '74	
7th Ft	7	2	24	—	12	55	June '72–Apr. '73	
11th Ft	23	—	8	—	1	68	June '72–Apr. '75	
13th Ft	40	—	—	—	47	13	Dec. '75–Apr. '76	
20th Ft	19	—	12	19	25	25	June '72–Apr. '74	
21st Ft	8	—	30	22	18	22	Aug. '73–Mar. '76	
23rd Ft	9	3	7	—	—	81	July '72–Apr. '73	
29th Ft	2	—	36	—	64	8	Sept. '73–Feb. '76	
30th Ft	28	—	—	—	38	34	Jan. '73–June '73	
31st Ft	20	1	—	—	23	56	May '73–Nov. '75	
32nd Ft	9	—	14	—	39	38	Apr. '73–Dec. '75	
33rd Ft	17	9	15	41	—	18	Sept. '72–Apr. '74	
35th Ft	3	—	—	16	—	81	May '72–Apr. '73	
36th Ft	7	—	10	—	27	56	June '73–Nov. '75	
43rd Ft	28	—	—	—	3	69	Oct. '73–Apr. '74	
66th Ft	24	—	—	—	—	76	Apr. '73–Oct. '73	
67th Ft	23	—	14	—	53	10	June '72–Oct. '73	
68th Ft	30	—	—	—	5	64	Apr. '73–May '74	
69th Ft	66	—	—	32	—	2	Dec. '75–Apr. '76	
70th Ft	14	—	—	37	11	38	Feb. '74–Mar. '76	

TABLE A12: CAVALRY, 1786–90

Regt.	M & D	ACP	CST	1 Sqn	2 Sqns	3 Sqns	In England	
							From Mon/Yr	To Mon/Yr
	(percentage of time spent)							
Blues	70	—	—	28	—	1	Mar. '86–June '90	
1st D.G.	19	1	25	20	25	20	Apr. '86–Mar. '87	
							Aug. '88–May '90	
2nd D.G.	10	—	32	22	11	25	Mar. '86–Apr. '89	
3rd D.G.	21	2	14	35	18	10	Apr. '86–May '88	
							June '89–May '90	
1st Dgns	14	—	35	31	6	14	Apr. '86–Apr. '90	
2nd Dgns	28	1	27	27	7	10	Apr. '86–June '90	
3rd Dgns	21	—	33	28	4	14	Apr. '86–June '90	
4th Dgns	14	3	30	20	12	21	Apr. '86–June '90	
6th Dgns	12	—	32	27	22	7	Apr. '87–June '90	
7th L.D.	20	2	23	29	21	5	May '86–June '90	
10th L.D.	13	—	37	35	7	8	May '86–May '90	
11th L.D.	18	—	33	40	—	9	Apr. '86–May '90	
15th L.D.	23	—	24	36	—	17	Apr. '86–May '90	
16th L.D.	28	2	27	26	3	14	May '86–June '90	

TABLE A13: INFANTRY, 1786–90

Regt.	M & D	ACP	CST	2 GDs	3 GDs	4 GDs+	In England	
							From Mon/Yr	To Mon/Yr
	(percentage of time spent)							
8th Ft	3	—	15	—	14	68	Mar. '86–Mar. '90	
12th Ft	20	—	5	—	—	75	Oct. '87–Mar. '88	
							Feb. '90–June '90	
17th Ft	14	—	18	26	36	6	Aug. '86–Oct. '87	
							Apr. '88–June '90	

TABLE A13—*continued*

Regt.	M & D	ACP	CST	2 GDs	3 GDs	4 GDs+	In England From Mon/Yr	To Mon/Yr
	(percentage of time spent)							
22nd Ft	12	—	4	—	—	84	Mar. '86–Mar. '87 Oct. '87–Mar. '90	
23rd Ft	19	—	7	5	24	45	Mar. '87–Mar. '90	
29th Ft	13	—	8	—	3	76	Oct. '87–Nov. '89	
33rd Ft	10	—	12	—	42	36	Sept. '86–Dec. '89	
34th Ft	9	1	—	—	—	90	Nov. '87–Nov. '89	
35th Ft	15	1	—	—	7	77	Apr. '86–Jan. '89	
38th Ft	3	—	25	—	68	4	May '86–Dec. '89	
40th Ft	28	1	17	31	13	10	Mar. '86–May '89	
42nd Ft	15	—	—	—	—	85	Aug. '89–May '90	
43rd Ft	32	—	—	30	—	38	Sept. '86–Dec. '87	
44th Ft	15	—	—	—	29	56	July '86–Oct. '87 May '88–May '89	
53rd Ft	9	2	—	—	2	87	Aug. '89–June '90	
55th Ft	25	—	7	28	—	40	Sept. '86–Nov. '88	
64th Ft	3	—	14	—	8	75	Aug. '86–Mar. '87	

Notes

[1] The three Regiments of Foot Guards and the Troops of Horse Guards and Horse Grenadier Guards (Life Guards Regiments, from 1788) only very rarely left the London-Westminster area, and so seldom appear in the Marching Orders. For this reason they are excluded from these tables.

[2] A regiment may not have been (in most cases, was not) in England for the whole of one of the survey periods. The dates during which it was present in England (or, in a very few cases, the dates during which the WO 5 entries are clear enough for calculations) are therefore entered in the last column of each table. Thus, during the survey of all troop movements in England during the period 1786–90, for example, the 42nd Foot is entered from August 1789 (when the corps disembarked at Portsmouth, from overseas service) to May 1790 (when it was ordered to march into Scotland).

In a number of cases, two sets of dates are entered for a regiment during one survey period. This indicates that the unit had temporarily left the Kingdom, and returned again. In Table A13, for example, the 22nd Foot is entered from March 1786 to March 1787, and from October 1787 to March 1790. During the intervening period, the regiment had done garrison duty on Jersey and Guernsey.

In two cases (designated 'a' and 'b'), regiments are entered twice in the same list. Each represents a special case. The 3rd Foot, after a normal tour in England, marched into Scotland in the summer of 1737 and did not return to our survey area, England, for three years. The 24th Foot, again after a normal tour in England, was luckless enough to ship with the ill-fated Cartagena expedition of 1740; its pitiful remains, returned home, can hardly be included in the first sequence. The 15th Foot too was on the Cartagena expedition, but came home in much better condition.

[3] Where regiments spent less than ten weeks in England (as occasionally they were met at the very beginning or end of one of our survey periods), they are not included, since their short stay could not be taken as establishing any sort of pattern.

[4] Figures for the Marine Regiments, raising from December 1739 and January 1741, are not included in the tables. They spent little time in England, continually sending detachments to sea on board the men-of-war or (in the case of the original 1st through 6th Marines), were sent *en masse* with the Cartagena expedition shortly after being raised. The Marine Companies raised for service with the fleet in the Seven Years War and kept on foot, thereafter, seldom strayed beyond their navy garrisons and dockyards; and consequently they are not often met with in WO 5, and are not included here.

Appendix B

Annual Charts Illustrating the Distribution and Rotation of the Regiments During Selected Periods

The charts in this Appendix, compiled annually for the years from 1726 to 1729, 1738 to 1742, 1751 to 1755, 1764 to 1767, and 1772 to 1776, show the year-end distribution of all the regiments—Line corps and Guards—composing the regular British Army; and in addition, all the movements made by the corps from one station or garrison to another, during each year, are shown. The world-wide distribution of the army and the patterns of relief or rotation (or otherwise), as described above in Ch. I, (a), appear at a glance.

The following points should be noted:

1. The 41st Foot, or the Invalid Regiment, is excluded here as elsewhere in this study.

2. The three regiments of Foot Guards are considered as forming a total of six battalions before 1760, and seven thereafter. How very small the number of marching regiments serving in England actually was, will be found by subtracting these six (or seven) Guards battalions, always concentrated in Westminster and London, from the total number of battalions shown serving in the whole of England. Thus in 1738, for example, there were only three battalions of marching foot in the rest of the kingdom; from 1750 to 1754, only four.

3. Before 1746 the Household cavalry consisted of six independent Troops—properly, the 1st–4th Troops of Horse Guards, and the 1st and 2nd Troops of Horse Grenadier Guards. The 3rd and 4th Troops were absorbed into the 1st and 2nd in 1746, so that from then until 1788 there existed the 1st and 2nd Troops of Horse Guards, and the 1st and 2nd Troops of Horse Grenadier Guards. Only from 1788 were these several troops amalgamated to form regiments proper—the 1st and 2nd Regiments of Life Guards.

These unregimented Troops always stood on very large establishments, not to be compared with those in the regular line cavalry. For simplicity's sake, therefore, these Troops are considered throughout the charts as forming two regiments of horse, and are so entered.

Distribution and rotation

F – Battalions of Foot

H – Regiments of Horse

NB – North Britain	ENG – England
MIN – Minorca	IRE – Ireland
GIB – Gibraltar	FLN – Flanders
WI – West Indies	NA – N. America

Figures in Roman type show the number of corps on each station or garrison at the end of the year indicated. Figures in italic type, together with the arrows, show the movements of all corps between stations during the same year.

1726:[a]

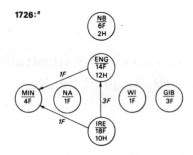

1727:[b]

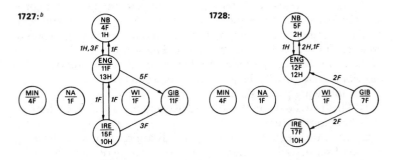

1728:

1729:

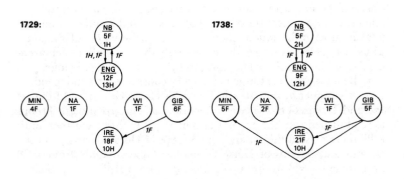

1738:

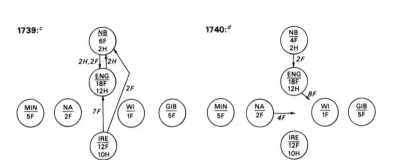

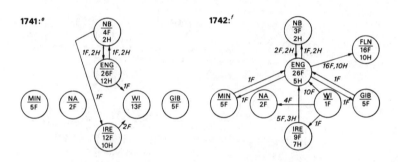

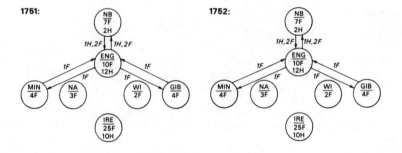

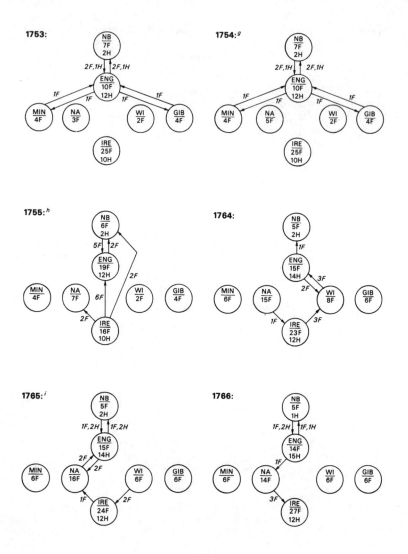

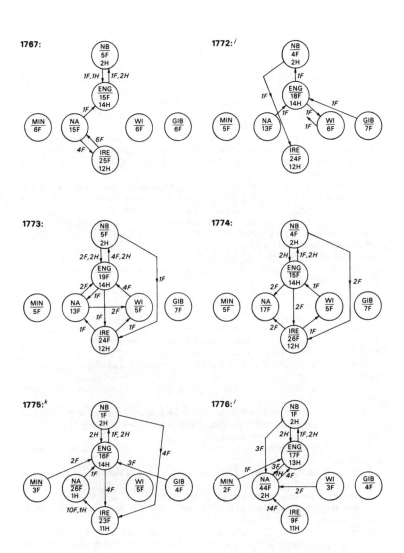

Notes to Appendix B

^a The 26th, 29th, and 39th of Foot crossed to England late in 1726, and in Jan. 1727 sailed from Portsmouth to reinforce the Gibraltar garrison.

^b The 8th, 19th, and 37th of Foot crossed to England from Ireland early in 1727, only to return to Ireland later in the same year, the Spanish threat having passed. The movements of these corps are not shown.

^c The figures for 1739 include neither the 1st through 6th Marines nor Spotswood's four-battalion 61st, all new-raising from late Nov. and Dec. and not yet effective corps. Crawford's 43rd (Black Watch), raised in Oct. 1739, is included, since it was formed from already existing Independent Companies.

^d The figures for 1740 include Gooch's (late Spotswood's) 61st, and the 1st–6th Marines, all now effective; excluded however are de Grangue's 60th and the 7th–10th Marines, new-raising from November and not yet effective. The four battalions of Gooch's from North America, plus the 15th and 24th of Foot together with the 1st–6th Marines, from England, all bound for the West Indies on the Cartagena expedition, are shown still at sea at the year's end.

^e Included in the figures for 1741 are de Grangue's 60th, the 7th–10th Marines, and the 54th–59th of Foot (later renumbered 43rd through 48th), all new corps but effective by mid-1741.

The 2/1st and 6th, from Ireland, and the 27th from England, sent to reinforce the Cartagena expedition, are shown still at sea at the year's end.

^f Richbell's 61st and Battereau's 62nd, new-raising from March, are included in the figures for 1742, since both were effective by mid-autumn. Only remnants of the four battalions of Gooch's survived the West Indies fiasco; they are shown returning to America but the corps did not outlive the year.

^g Shirley's 50th and Pepperell's 51st of Foot, new-raising from Sept. 1754, are included in the totals for 1754.

^h The 52nd–61st of Foot, all raising from Dec. 1755, are not included in this year's totals because they were not yet effective.

ⁱ The 2nd Foot established itself on the Isle of Man in 1765, to deal with the smugglers; and other corps followed in their turn thereafter. I have included Man with the Irish totals throughout the 1760s and 1770s.

^j The 66th Foot sailed from the West Indies late in 1772, and is shown still at sea at the year's end.

^k The 3/ and 4/60th, and the 1/ and 2/71st, new-raising in Britain in 1775, are not included in the year's totals.

^l A composite Guards corps, formed by skimming fifteen men from each of the companies in the three regiments of Foot Guards, was sent to America in mid-1776. It is not shown here.

The 6th, 50th, 59th, and 65th of Foot were drafted in America in 1776, cadres only returning to England to rebuild. I have included these in the English totals for that year.

Appendix C

Table of Regimental Establishments
During Selected Years

The figures in Table C show the establishment strengths of regiments as voted annually by Parliament for service on the various stations and garrisons, both at home and abroad. Most of the figures are for 'Guards and Garrisons', that is the troops allowed to be kept standing in Britain during peacetime; and since, as we have seen, the regiments were invariably under strength, these establishments must be regarded not as actual but as paper strengths.

There are also (p. 421) some examples of establishments for marching regiments of Foot serving in Ireland and overseas, which might be compared with those for their sister regiments serving in Britain.

Establishments are shown by individual troop and company; and beneath these figures the total number of such troops and companies in each regiment is shown.

Certain corps on the British establishment—The Blues, the 2nd or King's Own Regiment of Horse (KDGs after 1746), and the Foot Guards Regiments—had special establishments peculiar to themselves, and these are shown. The six Troops of Household cavalry are excluded, since their inclusion would take up more space than their strengths warrant.

The following short forms are used in the tables:

Dgns = Dragoons
L.D. = Light Dragoons
Ft Gds = Foot Guards
Bn-Coys = Battalion-Companies
Gren Coys = Grenadier Companies
Lt Coys = Light Companies

The figures in the table are taken from the Establishments (WO 24/84–558, *passim*).

The Irish Establishment figures—since there are almost none in WO 24—are taken from various sources, notably the Cumberland Papers, the Inspection Returns on Irish corps (WO 27), and by subtracting figures for augmentations made to Irish corps crossing onto the British establishment.

Notes are appended at the end of the table, where anomalies are dealt with.

TABLE C

'GUARDS and GARRISONS'	1717							1727, 1728, 1729							1733						
	Blues	2nd Horse (KDGs)	Horse (D.G.)	Dgns & L.D.	1st Ft Gds	2nd & 3rd Ft Gds	Marching Foot	Blues	2nd Horse (KDGs)	Horse (D.G.)	Dgns & L.D.	1st Ft Gds	2nd & 3rd Ft Gds	Marching Foot	Blues	2nd Horse (KDGs)	Horse (D.G.)	Dgns & L.D.	1st Ft Gds	2nd & 3rd Ft Gds	Marching Foot
Captain	—	—	—	—	—	—	—	—	—	—	—	—	—	—	—	—	—	—	—	—	—
Lieutenant	—	—	—	—	—	—	—	—	—	—	—	—	—	—	—	—	—	—	—	—	—
Cornet/Ensign	—	—	—	—	—	—	—	—	—	—	—	—	—	—	—	—	—	—	—	—	—
Quartermaster	—	—	—	—	.	.	.	—	—	—	—	.	.	.	—	—	—	—	.	.	.
Sergeant	.	.	.	.	3	3	2	.	.	.	.	3	3	3	.	.	.	.	3	3	3
Corporal	2	2	2	2	3	3	3	2	2	2	3	3	3	3	2	2	2	2	3	3	3
Drummer	.	.	.	.	2	2	2	.	.	.	.	2	2	2	.	.	.	.	2	2	2
Trumpeter	—	—	—	—	.	.	.	—	—	—	—	.	.	.	—	—	—	—	.	.	.
Hautbois	.	.	.	—	.	.	.	.	.	.	—	.	.	.	.	.	.	—	.	.	.
Fifer/Piper	.	.	.	.	.	.	.	.	.	.	.	.	.	.	.	.	.	.	.	.	.
Troopers	37	35	35	.	.	.	.	30	28	28	.	.	.	.	30	28	28	.	.	.	.
Dragoons	.	.	.	35	.	.	.	.	.	.	49	.	.	.	.	.	.	40	.	.	.
Private Men	.	.	.	.	65	65	45	.	.	.	.	60	60	60	.	.	.	.	50	50	50
Troops	9	9	6	6	.	.	.	9	9	6	6	.	.	.	9	9	6	6	.	.	.
Bn-Coys	.	.	.	.	24	16	11	.	.	.	.	24	16	11	.	.	.	.	24	16	9
Gren Coys	.	.	.	.	4	2	1	.	.	.	.	4	2	1	.	.	.	.	4	2	1

	1734						1735						1736					
Captain	1	1	1	1	1	1	1	1	1	1	1	1	1	1	1	1	1	1
Lieutenant	1	1	1	1	1	1	1	1	1	1	1	1	1	1	1	1	1	1
Cornet/Ensign	1	1	1	1	1	1	1	1	1	,	1	1	1	1	1	1	1	1
Quartermaster	1		1		1		1		1		1		1		1		1	
Sergeant	2	2	3	2	3	3	2	2	3	2	3	3	2	2	3	2	3	3
Corporal	2	2	3	3	3	3	2	2	3	3	3	3	2	2	3	3	3	3
Drummer		2	2	2	2	2		2	2	2	2	2		2	2	2	2	2
Trumpeter	1		1				1		1				1		1			
Hautbois	1						1						1					
Fifer/Piper																		
Troopers	30	28	28				30	28	28				30	28	28			
Dragoons				49						49						49		
Private Men			6	6	60	60	59		6	6	70	70	70		6	6	60	60	59
Troops	9	9	6	6			9	9	6	6			9	9	6	6		
Bn-Coys			24	16	9				24	16	9				24	16	9	
Gren Coys			4	2	1				4	2	1				4	2	1	

TABLE C—*continued*

	1741, 1742, 1743, 1744							1749–54							1764–9						
	Blues	2nd Horse (KDGs)	Horse (D.G.)	Dgns & L.D.	1st Ft Gds	2nd & 3rd Ft Gds	Marching Foot	Blues	2nd Horse (KDGs)	Horse (D.G.)	Dgns & L.D.	1st Ft Gds	2nd & 3rd Ft Gds	Marching Foot	Blues	2nd Horse (KDGs)	Horse (D.G.)	Dgns & L.D.	1st Ft Gds	2nd & 3rd Ft Gds	Marching Foot
Captain	1	1	1	1	1	1	1	1	1	1	1	1	1	1	1	1	1	1	1	1	1
Lieutenant	1	1	1	1	1	1	1	1	1	1	1	1	1	1	1	1	1	1	1	1	1
Cornet/Ensign	1	1	1	1	1	1	1	1	1	1	1	1	1	1	1	1	1	1	1	1	1
Quartermaster	1	1	1	1				1	1	1	1				1	1	1	1			
Sergeant			2	3	3	3	3		2	2	2	2	2	3		2	2	2	3	3	3
Corporal	2	2	2	3	3	3	3	2	2	2	2	3	3	3	2	2	2	2	3	3	3
Drummer			1	2	2	2	2		2	2	2	2	2	2		1	1	1	2	2	2
Trumpeter	1	1	1	1				1							1			c			
Hautbois																		1		a	a
Fifer/Piper																					
Troopers	40	38	38					30	36	36	36				28	28	28	28			
Dragoons				59																	
Private Men					71	71	70					48	48	70					47	47	47
Troops	9	9	6	6				9	9	6	6				9	9	6	6			
Bn-Coys					24	16	9					24	16	9					24	16	8
Gren Coys					4	2	1					4	2	1					4	2	1

	1771–4	1779, 1780[b]	1785, 1786, 1787
Captain	1 1 1 1 2 2 1 · 1	1 1 1 1 2 2 1 · 1	1 1 1 1 2 2 1 · 1
Lieutenant	1 1 1 1 2 2 · · 1	1 1 1 1 2 2 · · 1	1 1 1 1 2 2 · · 1
Cornet/Ensign	1 1 1 1 2 2 c · 1	1 1 1 1 2 2 c · 1	1 1 1 1 2 2 c · 1
Quartermaster	1 1 1 1 1 1 1 · 1	1 1 1 1 1 1 1 · 1	1 1 1 1 1 1 1 · 1
Sergeant	· 2 2 2 3 3 2 · 2	· 2 2 3 3 3 · · 3	· 2 2 2 3 3 2 · 2
Corporal	2 2 2 3 3 3 2 · 2	2 2 2 4 4 4 2 · 3	2 2 2 3 3 3 2 · 2
Drummer	· 1 1 2 2 2 1 · 2	· 2 2 2 2 2 1 · 2	· 1 1 2 2 2 1 · 2
Trumpeter	1 · · · c · 1 · d	1 · · · c · 1 · d	1 · · · c · 1 · d
Hautbois	—	—	—
Fifer/Piper	· · · · · · a a ·	· · · · · · a a ·	· · · · · · a a ·
Troopers	28 · · · · · · · ·	28 · · · · · · · ·	28 · · · · · · · ·
Dragoons	· 28 28 · · · · · ·	· 37 37 37[b] · · · · ·	· 28 28 28 · · · · ·
Private Men	9 9 · 6 6 · 47 47 38	9 9 · 6 6 · 60 60 70	9 9 · 6 6 · 47 47 42
Troops	9 9 · 6 6 · · · ·	9 9 · 6 6 · · · ·	9 9 · 6 6 · · · ·
Bn-Coys	· · · · · · 24 16 8	· · · · · · 24 16 8	· · · · · · 24 16 6
Gren Coys	· · · · · · 4 2 ·	· · · · · · 4 2 ·	· · · · · · 4 2 ·
Lt Coys	1 · · · · · · · ·	1 · · · · · · · ·	1 · · · · · · · ·

	Blues	2nd Horse (KDGs)	Horse (D.G.)	Dgns & L.D.	1st Ft Gds	2nd & 3rd Ft Gds	Marching Foot
			1789,		1790		
Captain	1	1	1	1	1	1	1
Lieutenant	1	1	1	1	1	1	1
Cornet/Ensign	1	1	1	1	1	1	1
Quartermaster	1	1	1	1	.	.	.
Sergeant	.	2	2	2	3	3	2
Corporal	2	2	2	2	3	3	3
Drummer	.	1	1	1	2	2	1
Trumpeter	1	.	.	c	.	.	d
Hautbois	.	.	.	.	.	.	.
Fifer/Piper	.	.	.	.	.	a	a
Troopers	28	.	.	.	.	.	.
Dragoons	.	28	28	28	.	.	.
Private Men	.	.	.	.	47	47	37
Troops	9	9	6	6	.	.	.
Bn-Coys	.	.	.	.	24	16	8
Gren Coys	.	.	.	.	4	2	1
Lt Coys	.	.	.	.	.	.	1

MINORCA—Foot

1717: 1 Bn-Coy = 1 Captain, 1 Lieutenant, 1 Ensign, 2 Sergeants, 2
(+1718,   Corporals, 2 Drums, 37 Private Men. Establish-
1727, 1728   ment = 11 Bn-Coys, 1 Gren Coy (of 45 Gren-
and 1729)   adiers).

1748: 1 Bn-Coy = 1 Captain, 1 Lieutenant, 1 Ensign, 3 Sergeants, 3
(+1749–54)   Corporals, 2 Drums, 70 Private Men. Establish-
                 ment = 9 Bn-Coys, 1 Gren Coy.

1768: 1 Bn-Coy = Captain, 1 Lieutenant, 1 Ensign, 3 Sergeants, 3
                 Corporals, 2 Drums, 47 Private Men, + 2 Fifers
                 in the Gren Coy. Establishment = 8 Bn-Coys, 1
                 Gren Coy.

GIBRALTAR—Foot

1718: 1 Bn-Coy = 1 Captain, 1 Lieutenant, 1 Ensign, 2 Sergeants, 2
                 Corporals, 2 Drums, 31 Private Men. Establish-
                 ment = 11 Bn-Coys, 1 Gren Coy (of 37 Grenadiers).

1727: 1 Bn-Coy = 1 Captain, 1 Lieutenant, 1 Ensign, 2 Sergeants, 2

(+1728)   Corporals, 2 Drums, 31 Private Men. Establish-
                 ment=11 Bn-Coys, 1 Gren Coy (of 34 Grena-
                 diers).

1729: 1 Bn-Coy= 1 Captain, 1 Lieutenant, 1 Ensign, 3 Sergeants, 3
                 Corporals, 2 Drums, 50 Private Men. Establish-
                 ment=9 Bn-Coys, 1 Gren Coy.

1748: 1 Bn-Coy= 1 Captain, 1 Lieutenant, 1 Ensign, 3 Sergeants, 3
(+1749–54)   Corporals, 2 Drums, 70 Private Men. Establish-
                 ment=9 Bn-Coys, 1 Gren Coy.

1768: 1 Bn-Coy= 1 Captain, 1 Lieutenant, 1 Ensign, 3 Sergeants, 3
                 Corporals, 2 Drums, 47 Private Men, + 2 Fifers
                 in the Gren Coy. Establishment=8 Bn-Coys, 1
                 Gren Coy.

PLANTATIONS—Foot

1727: 1 Bn-Coy= 1 Captain, 1 Lieutenant, 1 Ensign, 2 Sergeants, 2
(+1728,   Corporals, 2 Drums, 35 Private Men. Establish-
1729)   ment=9 Bn-Coys, 1 Gren Coy.

IRELAND—Foot

1718: 1 Bn-Coy= 1 Captain, 1 Lieutenant, 1 Ensign, 2 Sergeants, 2
                 Corporals, 2 Drums, 35 Private Men. Establish-
                 ment=9 Bn-Coys, 1 Gren Coy.

1727: 1 Bn-Coy= 1 Captain, 1 Lieutenant, 1 Ensign, 2 Sergeants, 2
                 Corporals, 1 Drum, 37 Private Men. Establish-
                 ment=9 Bn-Coys, 1 Gren Coy.

1729: 1 Bn-Coy= 1 Captain, 1 Lieutenant, 1 Ensign, 2 Sergeants, 2
                 Corporals, 1 Drum, 34 Private Men. Establish-
                 ment=9 Bn-Coys, 1 Gren Coy.

1734: 1 Bn-Coy= 1 Captain, 1 Lieutenant, 1 Ensign, 2 Sergeants, 2
                 Corporals, 1 Drum, 34 Private Men. Establish-
                 ment=9 Bn-Coys, 1 Gren Coy.

1739: 1 Bn-Coy= 1 Captain, 1 Lieutenant, 1 Ensign, 2 Sergeants, 2
                 Corporals, 1 Drum, 36 Private Men. Establish-
                 ment=9 Bn-Coys, 1 Gren Coy.

1749: 1 Bn-Coy= 1 Captain, 1 Lieutenant, 1 Ensign, 2 Sergeants, 2
(+1750–54)   Corporals, 1 Drum, 29 Private Men. Establish-
                 ment=9 Bn-Coys, 1 Gren Coy.

1765: 1 Bn-Coy= 1 Captain, 1 Lieutenant, 1 Ensign, 2 Sergeants, 2
(+1766–69)   Corporals, 1 Drum, 28 Private Men. Establish-
                 ment=8 Bn-Coys, 1 Gren Coy.

After 1770 the establishments of the Foot in Ireland were exactly
the same as those of the Foot in Britain.

Notes

[a] As we have seen, fifers began to appear in the Foot Guards and marching Foot during the later 1740s; but they were not allowed (that is to say, not made provision for or paid, as such), until 1764, from which date two fifers were allowed on the strength of each grenadier company. Before that date, some of the drummers in each corps where fifes were taken up learned to play the instrument, and although officially entered as drummers they acted as fifers.

[b] In the figures for 1779 and 1780, the Dragoon establishments only are shown, since the establishments of the Light Dragoon corps differed. These were as follows: 1 Troop = 1 Captain, 1 Lieutenant, 1 Cornet, 1 Quartermaster, 3 Sergeants, 3 Corporals, 2 Drums, 1 Hautbois, 1 Trumpeter, 54 Dragoons. Establishment = 6 Troops.

[c] Although usually excluded in the official Establishments, there were in fact trumpeters serving with the Light Dragoons from 1760 onwards, and with the heavy Dragoons from c.1775. It is however difficult to determine what their role may have been: in 1764, for example, there were (according to Capt. Robert Hinde) both trumpeters and buglers in the corps. He wrote: 'In 1764 His Majesty thought proper to forbid the use of brass side drums in the Light Cavalry, and introduce brass trumpets, so each troop has one trumpeter who when they are dismounted form a band of music, consisting of two French horns, 2 clarionettes and two bassoons and also one fife to a regiment, but when mounted trumpets only are sounded. They use also a bugle horn which is slung over the shoulders of one of the trumpeters and is a signal to assemble the Troops in the same manner as beating to arms formerly' (R. Hinde op. cit., quoted in C. C. P. Lawson, op. cit. iv. 8–9).

Before c.1775, the trumpeters in the heavy Dragoons were part of the 'band of music', and from then on they gave signals in manoeuvring on their trumpets, just as the buglers were doing in the Light Dragoons. The drums continued to be used in the manoeuvres of heavy Dragoons until the end of our period, as is clear from the Inspection Returns.

[d] Buglers, carrying hunting-horns or 'bugle horns', were usually added to the light infantry companies, from their first being raised. Not included in the official establishments, they were most likely the drummers allowed the light companies but taught the bugle in imitation of German *Jägers*.

Bibliography

REFERENCE WORKS

ANON., *The Quarters of the Army in Ireland in 1744*, Dublin, 1744. [I have also used the annual editions of this official Dublin Castle list for the years 1745, 1748, 1749, 1750, 1751, and 1752.]

ANON. RPT, *The Army List of 1740*. *JSAHR* Special Publication, no. 3, 1931.

CANNON, R., *Historical Records of the British Army, comprising the history of every Regiment in His Majesty's Service*. 70 vols, 1835–53. [Individual volumes from Cannon are cited by their proper titles, in the text.]

CLODE, C. M., *The Military Forces of the Crown: Their Administration and Government*, 2 vols, 1869.

FREDERICK, J. B. M., *Lineage Book of the British Army: Mounted Corps and Infantry, 1660–1968*, Cornwallville, New York, 1969.

HIGHAM, R. (ed.), *A Guide to the Sources of British Military History*, 1972.

LAWS, Lt.-Col. M. E. S., *Battery Records of the Royal Artillery, 1716–1859*, Woolwich, 1952.

LESLIE, N. B., *The Succession of Colonels of the British Army From 1660 to the Present Day*, *JSAHR* Special Publication, no 11, 1974.

WHITE, A. S., *Bibliography of Regimental Histories of the British Army*, 1965.

WISE, T., *A Guide to Military Museums*, 2nd rev. edn, Hemel Hempstead, 1971.

PRIMARY SOURCES

Public Record Office, London

WO 1. In-Letters, Secretary at War.
WO 3. Out-Letters, Commander-in-Chief.
WO 4. Out-Letters, Secretary at War.
WO 5. Marching Orders.
WO 17. Monthly Returns.
WO 24. Establishments.
WO 25. Commission Registers.
WO 26. Miscellany Books.
WO 27. Inspection Returns.
WO 28. Headquarters Records.

WO 30.   Miscellanea: Various.
WO 34.   Amherst Papers.
WO 35.   Ireland Miscellanea.
WO 36.   American Rebellion: Entry Books.
WO 55.   Ordnance Miscellanea.
WO 64.   Manuscript Army Lists.
WO 65.   Printed Annual *Army Lists*.
WO 71.   Proceedings, Board of General Officers.
WO 71.   Proceedings, General Courts Martial.
SP   41.   State Papers Domestic: Military.
SP   87.   State Papers Foreign: Military Expeditions.

British Library Manuscripts

Add. MS 21,661.   Haldimand Papers.
Add. MS 22,537.   Carteret Papers.
Add. MS 23,642.   Tyrawly Papers.
Add. MS 27,892.   Douglass Papers.
Add. MS 28,856.   Plan of Review of the 4th Foot, 1765.
Add. MS 29,477.   Military Papers, *c*.1689–1712.
King's MS 239.   Plans of Squadron Evolutions for Dragoons, *c*. 1750.
King's MS 240.   Military Papers of Maj D. Dundas, 1774.

British Library Map Department

Map no. 11.86.   Plan of Plymouth Lines, 1756.
Map no. L1/30a.   Plan of Defences of Kinsale, 1765.
Map no. 11815.(6).   Map of Phoenix Park Dublin, 1789.

National Army Museum. Chelsea

NAM MS 6707/11.   Lt. Hamilton's MS Notebook, *c*.1760.
NAM MS 6806/41.   Papers of George, 1st Marquess Townshend.
NAM MS 6807/6.   Leather-bound MS Notebook, *c*.1745.
NAM MS 6807/157/6.   Maj.-Gen. Howe's MS Light Infantry Discipline, 1774.
NAM MS 6807/205.   Capt. Ellis' Military Commonplace Book, pre-1724.

Berkshire Record Office, Reading

D/ED.039.   Downshire Papers.
D/E.L1.05.   Miscellaneous Papers.

Buckinghamshire Record Office, Aylesbury

Howard-Vyse Papers.

Cornwall Record Office, Truro

DD.RH.388. MS Book, 'Exercise of Firelock and Bayonet . . . appointed by his Excie. Lieut. Genll. Ingoldsby.'

Ipswich and East Suffolk Record Office, Ipswich

Albermarle MSS.

Kent County Record Office, Maidstone

U.269.   Sackville of Knole MSS.
U.1350.   Amherst MSS.

Nottinghamshire Record Office, Nottingham

DDS.49.   Staunton of Staunton MSS.

Cumberland Papers

From this very large collection, I have used not only the general correspondence of H.R.H. William Augustus, Duke of Cumberland, but should like to single out for bibliographical purposes the following:

Pt 4, vol. 2. MS treatise 'British Military Orders . . .', by Lt.-Col. John LaFaussille, *c*.1752.

Box 44, no. 99. MS relation 'Irish Remarks, or Observations on Discipline', by Lt.-Col. Caroline Frederick Scott, 1750.

Pt 4, O.B.1–10. MS orderly books of the Guards Brigade in Flanders, 1742–5, and in Germany, 1761–2.

Historical Manuscripts Commission, Reports

HMC Bathurst MSS (1923).
HMC Chequers Court MSS (1900)
HMC Clements MSS (1913).
HMC Hastings MSS, vol. III (1934).
HMC Stopford-Sackville MSS, vols I and II (1904–10).

Contemporary Newspapers and Periodicals

Daily Courant, 1722.
Daily Post, 1742.
Edinburgh Review, 1770.
General Evening Post, 1778.
London & Country Journal, 1740.
London Evening-Post, 1742, 1756, 1765, 1767, 1778.
London Gazette, 1722.
Morning Chronicle, and London Advertiser, 1788.

Weekly Journal or Saturday's-Post, 1722.
Gentleman's Magazine, July 1743, April 1756.

REGULATIONS

All extant printed regulation drillbooks and orders are listed below, chronologically; the shorthand system by which these regulations were described in the text (ie *1728 Regulations*) s repeated here, for purposes of cross-referencing. All regulations were, of course, anonymously written.

[*1672 Regulations*]
   The English Military Discipline, 1672.
   The English Military Discipline, or the way and method of exercising Horse & Foot, according to the practice of this present time . . . 1680 (another edn of above).
[*1676 Regulations*]
   An Abridgement of th English Military Discipline, 1676.
   An Abridgement of the English Military Discipline. By His Majesties Permission, 1678 (another edn of above).
[*1682 Regulations*]
   An Abridgment of the English Military Discipline. Reprinted by His Majesties Special Command, 1682.
   An Abridgement of the English Military Discipline. Printed by Especial Command for the Use of his Majesties Forces, 1686 (a rev. edn of the above).
[*1690 Regulations*]
   The Exercise of the Foot; with the Evolutions . . . *By Their Majesties Command*, 1690 (rpt 1696).
   The Exercise of the Foot; . . . *To which is added, the Exercise of the horse grenadiers of horse, and dragoons*, Dublin, 1701 (a rev. edn of the above).
[*1708 Regulations*]
   The Duke of Marlborough's New Exercise of Firelocks and Bayonets; Appointed by His Grace to be used By all the British Forces, and the Militia . . . n.d. [*c.*1708].
[*1728 Regulations*]
   Exercise for the Horse, Dragoons, and Foot Forces, 1728 (many times reprinted, the last impression being in 1743).
[*1756 Regulations*]
   A New Exercise, To be observed by His Majesty's Troops on the Establishment of Great-Britain and Ireland, 1756.
[*1757 Regulations*]
   As noted in the text (pp. 199–200 above) there is no known full copy

of these regulations extant. Several reprints of certain elements, and of extracts, appeared as follows:

Manual Exercise As Ordered By His Majesty, For The Year 1758, 1758.
New Manual Exercise, As Performed by His Majesty's Dragoons, Foot-Guards, Foot, Artillery, Marines, And by the Militia . . . Second Edition, 1758.
Ibid. Dublin and Limerick, 1758.
The New Manual Exercise as Performed by His Majesty's Dragoons, Foot-Guards, Foot, Light Infantry, Artillery, Marines, and by the Militia . . . Third Edition, Dublin, 1760.

[*1764 Regulations*]
New Manual, and Platoon Exercise: with an Explanation. Published by Authority, Dublin, 1764 (many times reprinted, the latest before the appearance of the MS *1778 Regulations* being *The Manual Exercise with Explanations as ordered by His Majesty, 1778*, 1778).
The Manual Exercise, as ordered by His Majesty in 1764. Together with Plans and Explanations of the Method Generally Practised at Reviews and Field-Days, 1766 (many times reprinted, the latest of which was the 1780 New York edn.).

[*1786 Regulations*]
By His Majesty's Command . . . General Regulations and Orders for His Majesty's Forces, 1786.

[*1787 Regulations*]
Heads of Review Exercise for a Regiment of Dragoons, 1787.

[*1789 Irish Regulations*]
Rules and Regulations for the Field Exercise and Movements of the Army in Ireland, Dublin, 1789.

[*1792 Regulations*]
Rules and Regulations for the Formations, Field-Exercise, and Movements, of His Majesty's Forces, 1792.
There were many subsequent editions of these regulations, as we noted in the text above (pp. 246–7); and among these a set of supplementary general orders needs particular attention, namely:

General Orders and Observations on the Movements and Field Exercise of the Infantry, 1804.
The arms exercise accompanying the *1792 Regulations* was:
By His Majesty's Command. The Manual and Platoon Exercises, 1792.
A slightly revised edition of this appeared as *The Manual and Platoon Exercises, Etc., Etc.*, 1804.

[*1795 Regulations*]
By His Majesty's Command. Rules and Regulations for the Cavalry, 1795.

[*1796 Regulations*]
  Instructions and Regulations for the Formations and Movements of the Cavalry, 1796.
  An Elucidation of the Several Parts of His Majesty's Regulations for the Formations and Movements of Cavalry, 1798 (an abridged edn of the above).
  The exercise which was soon to accompany the above regulations was:
  Rules and Regulations for the Sword Exercise of the Cavalry, 1796.
  All three of the above appeared in subsequent revised editions (on which, see pp. 250–51 of the text above).
[*1798 Light Regulations*]
  Regulations for the Exercise of Riflemen and Light Infantry, and Instructions for their Conduct in the Field, 1798 (reprints were to appear at least twice).

CONTEMPORARY PRIVATE PUBLICATIONS,
TRANSLATIONS, ETC.

ANON., *The Complete Militia-Man, Or a Compendium of Military Knowledge . . . By an Officer in the British Forces,* 1760.
—— *Commands for the Exercise of Foot, Armed With Firelock Muskets and Pikes; with the Evolutions,* 1690.
—— *Exercise for the Horse, Dragoon, and Foot Forces, upon the Establishment of Ireland. To Which is Added, the Manual Exercise of the Prussian Infantry . . . Now Practised in the Armies of most . . . States in Europe,* Dublin, 1756.
—— *The Exercise of the Foot, with the Evolutions, According to the Words of Command, As they are Explained. As Also The Forming of Battalions . . . in Their Majesties Armies . . .,* 1690.
—— *The General Review Manoeuvres: or, the whole Evolutions of a Battalion of Foot . . . To which is Annexed, The Manual Exercise,* 1779.
—— *Instruction sur l'exercise de l'infanterie, du 29 juin 1753,* Paris, 1753.
—— *Instruction sur l'exercise de l'infanterie, du 14 mai 1754,* Paris, 1754.
—— *Manoeuvres for a Battalion of Infantry, upon Fixed Principles . . . By a German Officer,* 1766.
—— *Memoirs of the Life and particular Actions, of that brave Man, General Blakeney . . .,* London and Dublin, 1756.
—— *The Militia-Man. Containing, Necessary Rules for both Officers and Soldiers . . . Illustrated with . . . different Positions of a Soldier under Arms,* 1740.
—— *A New Military Dictionary; or, The Field of War . . . by a Military Gentleman,* 1760.
—— *New Regulations for the Prussian Infantry: Containing an exact Detail*

of the Present Field-Service . . . and recent Parts of the Foot-Exercises . . ., 1757.

—— *The Proceedings of a General Court-Martial held at the Horse-Guards . . . Upon the Trial of Lord George Sackville. Published by Authority*, 1760.

—— *Report of the Proceedings . . . of the Board of General Officers on Their Examination of Lieutenant-General Sir John Cope . . . Colonel Peregrine Lascelles, and Brigadier-General Thomas Fowke . . . in 1745*, 1749.

——*The Rudiments of War: Comprising the Principles of Military Duty, in a Series of Orders issued by Commanders in the English Army . . .*, 1777.

—— *A System of Camp Discipline . . . and other Regulations for the Land Forces. Collected by a Gentleman of the Army. In which are included, Kane's Discipline for a Battalion in Action . . . Improved*, 1757.

ADYE, R. W., *The Little Bombardier, and Pocket Gunner*. 1801. [This work had reached an 8th, rev. edn by 1827.]

BÉLIDOR, BERNARD FOREST DE, *Le Bombardier françois, ou nouvelle méthode de jetter les bombes avec précision . . .*, Paris, 1731.

BEVER, CAPT. SAMUEL, *The Cadet. A Military Treatise*, 1756; 2nd rev. edn, 1762.

BINNING, CAPT. THOMAS, *A Light to the Art of Gunnery . . . With the most necessary Conclusions for the Practice of Gunnery . . .*, 1676 (rpt 1703).

BLAKENEY, COL. WILLIAM, *The New Manual Exercise, by General Blakeney. To which is added. The Evolutions of the Foot, by General Bland*, Philadelphia, 1746 (several subsequent colonial imprints, in 1747, 1754, 1755, and 1756).

BLAND, GEN. HUMPHREY, *A Treatise of Military Discipline; In Which is Laid down and Explained The Duty of the Officer and Soldier, Thro' the several Branches of the Service*, London and Dublin, 1727; 2nd edn, 1727; 3rd edn, 1734; 4th edn, 1740; 5th edn, London and Dublin, 1743; 6th edn, 1746; 7th edn, 1753; *8th Edition, revised, corrected, and altered to the present practice of the Army*, 1759 (revision by Sir William Fawcett); 9th rev. edn, 1762.

—— *An Abstract of Military Discipline; more particularly with regard to the Manual Exercise, Evolutions, and Firings of the Foot. From Col. Bland*, Boston, 1743 (several subsequent colonial 'abstracts' of Bland appeared, in 1744, 1747, 1754, 1755, and 1759).

BOSROGER, LE ROY DE, *The Elementary Principles of Tactics: with New Observations on the Military Art . . . translated by an Officer of the British Army*, 1771.

BRETON, WILLIAM, *Militia Discipline. The Words of Command and Directions for Exercising . . .*, 1717 and Boston, 1733.

CLARKE. LT. JOHN, *Military Instructions of Vegetius . . . With a Preface and Notes,* 1768.

COLE, BENJAMIN, *The Gentleman Volunteer's Pocket Companion, describing the Various Motions of the Foot Guards, Drawn from an Officer long experienced in ye Military Disciplin . . .,* 1745.

—— *The Soldier's Pocket-Companion, or the Manual Exercise of our British Foot, as now practis'd . . .,* 1746.

CUTHBERTSON, CAPT. BENNETT. *A System for the Complete Interior Management and Œconomy of a Battalion of Infantry,* Dublin, 1768.

DALRYMPLE, LT-COL. CAMPBELL, *A Military Essay. Containing Reflections on the Raising, Arming, Cloathing, and Discipline of the British Infantry and Cavalry . . .,* 1761.

DALRYMPLE, LT-COL. WILLIAM, *Tacticks,* 1781.

DOMINICUS, CAPT. GEORGE, *General Dundas's XVIII Manoeuvres,* 1799.

DONKIN, MAJ. ROBERT, *Military Collections and Remarks,* New York, 1777.

DUNDAS, COL. DAVID, *Principles of Military Movements, Chiefly Applied to Infantry. Illustrated by Manoeuvres of the Prussian Troops, and by An Outline of the British Campaigns in Germany, During the War of 1757 . . .,* 1788; 2nd rev. edn, 1795.

EHWALD, COL. CARL VON, *A Treatise upon the Duties of Light Troops. Translated from the German . . .,* 1803.

FAGE, EDWARD, *A Regular Form of Discipline for the Militia, As it is Perform'd by the West-Kent Regiment . . .,* 1759.

FEUQIÈRES, ANTOINE DE PAS, MARQUIS DE, *Memoirs Historical and Military . . . Translated from the French with Preliminary Remarks . . . by the Translator,* 2 vols, 1735–6.

FREDERICK II OF PRUSSIA, *Military Instructions by the King of Prussia,* 1762 (first English trans. of the *Instructions* of 1748).

—— *Military Instructions From the late King of Prussia to his Generals . . .* Sherborne, 1797.

G[ISORS], M. LE D[UC] DE, *Tactique et manoeuvres des prussiens,* Paris, 1750. (BL entry is under 'D[uc]', incorrectly; it should be 'Comte'.)

GORDON, CAPT. ANTHONY, *A Treatise on the Science of Defence, for the Sword, Bayonet, and Pike, in Close Action,* 1805.

GRANT, GEORGE, *The New Highland Military Discipline, or a short Manual Exercise Explained . . .* 1757; rpt Ottawa, 1967.

GRAY, JOHN, *A Treatise of Gunnery,* 1731.

GROSE, FRANCIS, *Advice to the Officers of the British Army,* 1782.

—— *Military Antiquities respecting A History of the English Army from the Conquest to the Present Time,* 2 vols, 1786–8.

GUIBERT, J.-A.-H., COMTE DE, *A General Essay on Tactics. With an*

Introductory Discourse . . . Translated from the French . . . by an Officer. 2 vols, 1781.

HALY, CAPT. AYLMER, *Military Observations,* 1801.

HINDE, CAPT. ROBERT, *The Discipline of the Light Horse,* 1778.

KANE, BRIG.-GEN. RICHARD, *Campaigns of King William and Queen Anne; From 1689, to 1712. Also, A New System of Military Discipline, for a Battalion of Foot on Action; with the Most Essential Exercise of the Cavalry . . .,* 1745.

—— *Campaigns of King William and the Duke of Marlborough . . . The Second Edition,* 1747.

LA MAMIE DE CLAIRIC. L. A., CHEV. DE, *The Field Engineer . . . Translated from the French, with Observations and Remarks,* 1760; 2nd rev. edn, 1773.

LANDMANN, ISAAC, *The Field Engineer's Vade-Mecum . . .,* 1802.

LE BLOND, GUILLAUME, *A Treatise of Artillery: or, of the Arms and Machines Used in War . . .* 1746 (an anon. trans. of a section of Le Blond's large *Élémens de la guerre des sièges,* Paris, 1743).

—— *Élémens de tactique; ouvrage dans lequel on traite de l'arrangement & de la formation des troupes . . .,* Paris, 1758.

LE COINTE, CAPT. J.-L., *The Science of Military Posts, for the Use of Regimental Officers, who frequently command Detached Parties . . . Translated from the French. By an Officer,* 1761.

—— *Commentaires sur le Retraite des dix-mille de Xénophon, ou, nouveau traité de la guerré . . .* Paris, 1766.

LENS, BERNARD, *The Granadier's Exercise of the Granade, in his Majesty's first Regiment of Foot-Guards . . .,* 1735; rpt 1969.

LLOYD, MAJ.-GEN. HENRY, *History of the Late War in Germany; between the King of Prussia, and the Empress of Germany and Her Allies . . .,* Vol. I, 1766; rev. edn, 2 vols, 1781 (rpt 1790).

LOCHÉE, LEWIS, *An Essay on Military Education . . .* 1773.

—— *A System of Military Mathematics,* 2 vols, 1776.

—— *An Essay on Castrametation,* 1778.

—— *Elements of Fortification,* 1780.

MACDONALD, JOHN, *Rules and Regulations for the Field Exercise and Manoeuvres of the French Infantry, Issued August 1, 1791. Translated . . . with Explanatory Notes, and Illustrative References to the British, and Prussian Systems of Tactics . . .,* 2 vols, 1803.

—— *Instructions for the Conduct of Infantry on Actual Service . . . Translated from the French with Explanatory Notes . . .,* 1807.

MACINTIRE, LT. JOHN, *A Military Treatise on the Discipline of the Marine Forces, When at Sea: Together with Short Instructions for Detachments Sent to attack on Shore,* 1763.

MAIZEROY, JOLY DE, *A System of Tactics, Practical, Theoretical, and*

Historical. Translated from the French . . . by Thomas Mante, 2 vols, 1781.

MOLESWORTH, LT.-GEN. RICHARD, 3rd Viscount, *A Short Course of Standing Rules, for the Government and Conduct of an Army, Designed for, or in The Field. With Some Useful Observations . . .* 1744; rpt Dublin, 1745.

MOLYNEUX, THOMAS MORE, *Conjunct Expeditions: Or Expeditions that have been carried on jointly By the Fleet and Army, with a Commentary on a Littoral War*, 1759.

MULLER, JOHN, *A Treatise Containing the Elementary Part of Fortification, Regular and Irregular . . .* 1746 (rpt in 1756, 1774, 1782, and 1799).

—— *The Attac and Defence of Fortified Places . . .* 1747; 2nd rev. edn, 1756 (rpt in 1770 and 1791).

—— *A Treatise Containing the Practical Part of Fortification . . .* 1757 (rpt 1764 and 1774).

—— *A Treatise of Artillery . . .* 1757; 2nd rev. edn, 1768 (rpt 1780).

PAPACINO D'ANTONI, MAJ.-GEN. A. V., *A Treatise on the Service of Artillery in Time of War: Translated from the Italian . . .*, 1789.

PLEYDELL, LT. J. C., *An Essay on Field Fortification; Intended Principally for the Use of Officers of Infantry . . .*, 1768.

PRUSSIA. KRIEGSMINISTERIUM, *Regulations for the Prussian Infantry. Translated from the German Original*, 1754.

—— *Regulations for the Prussian Cavalry. Translated from the German Original*, 1757.

—— *Regulations for the Prussian Infantry. Translated from the German Original . . . to which is added The Prussian Tactick . . .*, 1759.

REIDE, CAPT. THOMAS, *A Treatise on the Duty of Infantry Officers and the Present System of British Military Discipline . . .*, 1798.

—— *The Staff Officer's Manual; in which is detailed the Duty of Brigade Majors, and Aides de Camp . . . with a Preliminary Essay on the Education of Young Gentlemen Intended for the Military Profession . . .*, 1806.

ROBINS, BENJAMIN, *New Principles of Gunnery . . .*, 1742.

ROBSON, JOSEPH, *The British Mars. Containing Several Schemes and Inventions . . . shewing more plainly, The great Advantage Britain has over other Nations, by being Masters at Sea*, 1763.

ROGERS, CAPT. ROBERT, *Journals of Major Robert Rogers: Containing An Account of the several Excursions he made . . . upon the Continent of North America . . .*, 1765.

S., CAPT. J., *Military Discipline; or the Art of War . . . of Doubling, wheeling, Forming and Drawing up a Battalion or Army into any Figure . . .*, 1689.

SALDERN, MAJ.-GEN. FRIEDRICH VON, *Elements of Tacticks, and*

Introduction to Military Evolutions for the Infantry . . . *By a celebrated Prussian General* . . ., 1787.

SAXE, FIELD MARSHALL MAURICE, COMTE DE, *Reveries, or Memoirs upon the Art of War by Field Marshal Count Saxe* . . ., 1757 (rpt 1759, 1776).

SURIREY DE SAINT-REMY, PIERRE, *A Compleat Treatise of Mines. Extracted from the Mémoires d'artillerie* . . . *By Henry Manningham, Engineer*, 1752.

SIEMIENOWICZ, CASIMIR, *The Great Art of Artillery* . . . *Translated from the French, by George Shelvocke* . . ., 1729 (first publ. in Latin at Amsterdam, 1650; Shelvocke's trans. taken from Chevlet's 1729 Paris trans.).

SIMCOE, LT.-COL. JOHN GRAVES, *A Journal of the Operations of The Queen's Rangers, From the End of the Year 1777, to the Conclusion of the Late American War* . . ., Exeter, 1787.

SIMES, THOMAS, *The Military Medley: Containing the most necessary Rules and Directions for attaining a Competent Knowledge of the Art* . . . Dublin, 1767; 2nd rev. edn, 1768.

—— *The Military Guide for Young Officers* . . . 1772 (rpt 1776); 3rd rev. edn, 1781.

—— *A Military Course for the Government and Conduct of a Battalion* . . ., 1777.

—— *The Regulator: or Instructions to Form the Officer, and Complete the Soldier* . . ., 1780.

—— *A Treatise on the Military Science, which comprehends the Grand Operations of War, and General Rules for Conducting an Army* . . ., 1780.

SMIRKE, ROBERT, *Review of a Battalion of Infantry, including the Eighteen Manoeuvres* . . ., 1799 (in its 4th impression by 1806).

SMITH, CAPT. GEORGE, *An Universal Military Dictionary* . . ., 1779 (rpt Ottawa, 1969).

SMITH, WILLIAM, *An Historical Account of the Expedition Against the Ohio Indians in the year MDCCLXIV* . . ., Philadelphia, 1765 (rpt London, 1766).

STARRAT, WILLIAM, *The Doctrine of Projectiles, Demonstrated and Apply'd to all the most useful Problems in practical Gunnery* . . ., Dublin, 1733.

STEVENSON, ROGER, *Military Instructions For Officers Detached in the Field: Containing a Scheme for Forming A Corps of a Partisan* . . ., Philadelphia, 1770 (rpt 1775); 2nd rev. edn, London, 1779.

TARLETON, LT.-COL. BANASTRE, *A History of the Campaigns of 1780 and 1781, in the Southern Provinces of North America* . . ., 1787.

THOMPSON, CAPT.-LT. GEORGE, *An Abstract of General Bland's Treatise of Military Discipline, Revised by Mr. Fawcett. With the Words of*

Command for the New Exercise, as practised by the Guards; For the Use of the Militia of the County of York, 1760.

TIELKE, CAPT. J. G., *An Account of some of the most Remarkable Events of The War between the Prussians, Austrians, and Russians, from 1756 to 1763: And a Treatise On . . . the Military Art . . . Translated . . .*, 2 vols, 1787–8.

—— *The Field Engineer: or Instructions upon Every Branch of Field Fortification: Demonstrated by Examples . . . in the Seven Years War . . . Translated . . .*, 2 vols, 1789.

TURPIN DE CRISSÉ. LANCELOT, COMTE, *An Essay on the Art of War. Translated from the French . . . by Captain Joseph Otway*, 2 vols, 1761.

VAUBAN, SEBASTIEN LE PRESTRE, MARECHAL DE, *A New Method of Fortification, As practised by Monsieur de Vauban . . .* (trans. Abel Swall), 1691 (several subsequent rpts, reaching the 6th by 1762).

WATSON, J., *A Military Dictionary . . .*, 1758.

WILLIAMSON, BRIG.-GEN. ADAM, *Military Memoirs and Maxims of Marshall Turenne: Interspersed with Others, taken from the Best Authors and Observation, with Remarks*, 1740; 2nd edn, 1744.

WILLIAMSON, JOHN, *The Elements of Military Arrangement, and of the Discipline of War; Adapted to the Practice of the British Infantry*, 2 vols, 1782; 2nd rev. edn, 2 vols, n.d. [*c*.1785].

WINDHAM, WILLIAM, and TOWNSHEND, GEORGE, *A Plan of Discipline, Composed for the Use of the Militia of the County of Norfolk*, 1759; 2nd rev. edn, 1760.

—— *A Plan of Discipline for the Use of the Norfolk Militia . . .*, 1768 (a rpt of the 1760 rev. edn, with a new title).

WOLFE, JAMES, *General Wolfe's Instructions to Young Officers: also his Orders for a Battalion . . .* 1768 (comp. anon.); rpt 1780.

YOUNG, MAJ. WILLIAM, *Manoeuvres, Or Practical Observations on the Art of War . . .*, 2 vols, 1771.

MODERN SECONDARY SOURCES

Books

ALBERT, W., *The Turnpike Road System in England, 1663–1840*, Cambridge, 1973.

ALDEN, J. R., *General Gage in America*, Baton Rouge, 1948.

ATKINSON, C. T., *Marlborough and the Rise of the British Army*, 1921.

ATTON, H., and HOLLAND, H., *The King's Customs*, 2 vols, 1908.

BACQUET, CAPT., *L'Infanterie au XVIIIe siècle; l'organisation*, Paris, 1907.

BAILEY, D. W., *British Military Longarms, 1715–1815*, 1971.

BAYNES, J., *The Jacobite Rising of 1715*, 1970.

BLACKMORE, H. L., *British Military Firearms, 1650–1850*, 1961.

BOUDRIOT, J., *Armes a feu françaises: modèles d'ordonnance*, Paris, 1961–3.

BROOKE, JOHN, *King George III*, 1972.

CARSON, E., *The Ancient and Rightful Customs*, 1972.

CARTER, C. E. (ed), *The Correspondence of General Thomas Gage*, 2 vols, Haven, 1933.

CHANDLER, DAVID (ed.), *Robert Parker and Comte de Mérode-Westerloo: The Marlborough Wars*, 1968.

—— *Marlborough as Military Commander*, 1973.

—— *The Art of War in the Age of Marlborough*, 1976.

CHARTERIS, EVAN, *William Augustus, Duke of Cumberland: His Early Life and Times, 1721–1748*, 1913.

—— *William Augustus, Duke of Cumberland, and the Seven Years' War*, 1925.

CHILDS, J., *The Army of Charles II*, 1976.

CHURCHILL, SIR WINSTON, *Marlborough, His Life and Times*, 4 vols, 1967 (1933).

COLE, LT.-COL. H. N., *Minden, 1759*, 1972.

COLIN, CAPT. J., *Les Campagnes du Maréchal de Saxe*, 3 vols, Paris, 1901–6.

—— *L'Infanterie au XVIIIe siècle. La tactique.* Paris and Nancy, 1907.

COWPER, L., *The King's Own: The Story of a Royal Regiment*. Vol. i, Oxford, 1939.

CUNEO, J. R., *Robert Rogers*, New York, 1959.

CURTIS, E. E., *The Organization of the British Army in the American Revolution*, New Haven, 1929.

DALTON, C., *George the First's Army*, 2 vols, 1910–12.

DARLING, A. D., *Red Coat and Brown Bess*, Ottawa, 1970.

DOUGHTY, A. G. (ed.), *An Historical Journal of the Campaigns in North America For the Years 1757, 1758, 1759, and 1760* [by Capt. John Knox], 3 vols, Toronto, 1915–16.

DUFFY, C., *The Army of Frederick the Great*, Newton Abbot, 1974.

FINDLAY, J. T., *Wolfe in Scotland in the '45 and from 1749–1753*, 1928.

FORTESCUE, J. W., *A History of the British Army*, Vols I–V, 1899–1910.

—— *The British Army, 1783–1802*, 1905.

FULLER, J. F. C., *British Light Infantry in the 18th Century*, 1925.

—— *Sir John Moore's System of Training*, 1925.

GLOVER, R., *Peninsular Preparation: The Reform of the British Army, 1795–1809*, Cambridge, 1963.

GRINNELL-MILNE, D., *Mad, Is He? The Character and Achievement of James Wolfe*, 1963.

HALL, A. R., *Ballistics in the Seventeenth Century*, Cambridge, 1952.

HAMILTON, C. (ed.), *Braddock's Defeat*, Univ. of Oklahoma, 1959.

HAYTER, T., *The Army and the Crowd in Mid-Georgian England*, 1978.

HOGG, O. F. G., *The Royal Arsenal: Its Background, Origin, and Subsequent History*, Vol. i, 1963.

HOON, E., *The Organization of the English Customs System, 1696–1786*, Newton Abbot, 1968.

JAMES, F. G., *Ireland in the Empire, 1688–1770: A History of Ireland from the Williamite Wars to the Eve of the American Revolution*, Cambridge, Mass., 1973.

JARVIS, RUPERT C., *Collected Papers on the Jacobite Risings*, Vol. i, Manchester, 1971.

KATCHER, P. R. N., *King George's Army, 1775–1783. A Handbook of British, American, and German Regiments*, Harrisburg, Penna., 1973.

KENNETT, LEE, *The French Armies in the Seven Years' War*, Durham, NC, 1967.

KNIGHT, C., *Historical Records of The Buffs, East Kent Regiment (3rd Foot) . . . 1704–1914*, Vol. ii, 1935.

KOPPERMAN, P. E., *Braddock at the Monongahela*, Pittsburgh, 1977.

LAWSON, C. C. P., *A History of the Uniforms of the British Army*, 5 vols, 1940–67.

LEVINGE, SIR R., *Historical Records of the 43rd Regiment*, 1868.

LUVAAS, JAY (ed.), *Frederick the Great on the Art of War*, New York, 1966.

McGUFFIE, T. H., *The Siege of Gibraltar, 1779–1783*, 1965.

MACKESY, PIERS, *The War for America, 1775–1783*, 1964.

O'CALLAGHAN, E. B. (ed.), *Burgoyne's Orderly Book*, Albany, N.Y., 1860.

OMAN, SIR CHARLES, *Wellington's Army, 1809–1814*, New York, 1912 (rpt London, 1969).

ORR, M., *Dettingen, 1743*, 1972.

PAKENHAM, T., *The Year of Liberty. The Story of the Great Irish Rebellion of 1798*, 1969.

PARES, R., *War and Trade in the West Indies, 1739–1763*, Oxford, 1936.

PARET, P., *Yorck and the Era of Prussian Reform*, Princeton, 1966.

PARGELLIS, S. M., *Lord Loudoun in North America*, New Haven, 1933.

—— (ed.), *Military Affairs in North America, 1748–1765: Selected Documents from the Cumberland Papers*, New York, 1936.

PATTTERSON, A. TEMPLE, *The Other Armada*, Manchester, 1960.

PICHAT, CAPT. H., *La Campagne du maréchal de Saxe dans les Flandres de Fontenoy (mai 1745) à la prise de Bruxelles (février 1746)*, Paris 1909.

QUIMBY, R. S., *The Background of Napoleonic Warfare. The Theory of*

Military Tactics in Eighteenth-Century France, New York, 1957 (rpt 1968).

RADZINOWICZ, SIR L., *A History of English Criminal Law and Its Administration from 1750*, Vol. iv, 1957.

REILLY, R., *The Rest to Fortune: The Life of Major-General James Wolfe*, 1960.

RICHMOND, H. W., *The Navy in the War of 1739–48*, 3 vols, Cambridge, 1920.

ROGERS, COL. H. C. B., *Weapons of the British Soldier*, 1972.

RUSSELL, J., *Gibraltar Besieged, 1779–1783*, 1965.

SALMOND, J. B., *Wade in Scotland*, London and Edinburgh, 1934.

SAUTAI, CAPT. M., *Montcalm au combat de Carillon*, Paris, 1909.

SAVORY, MAJ.-GEN. SIR R., *His Britannic Majesty's Army in Germany, during the Seven Years' War*, Oxford, 1966.

SCOULLER, MAJ. R. E., *The Armies of Queen Anne*, Oxford, 1966.

SHELTON, W. J., *English Hunger and Industrial Disorders. A Study of Social Conflict during the First Decade of George III's Reign*, Toronto, 1973.

SHY, JOHN, *Toward Lexington: The Role of the British Army in the Coming of the American Revolution*, Princeton, 1965.

SMELSER, M., *The Campaign for the Sugar Islands. 1759. A Study in Amphibious Warfare*, Chapel Hill, N.C., 1955.

STACEY, C. P., *Quebec, 1759. The Siege and the Battle*, 1959.

SYRETT, D. (ed.), *The Siege and Capture of Havana, 1762*, 1970.

THOMPSON, M. A., *The Secretaries of State, 1681–1782*, Oxford, 1932.

THOUMINE, R. H., *Scientific Soldier: A Life of General Le Marchant, 1766–1812*, 1968.

TOMASSON, K., and BUIST, F., *Battles of The '45*, 1967.

TOWSNHEND, SIR C. V. F., *The Military Life of Field Marshal George, First Marquess Townshend, 1727–1807*, 1901.

WALTON, COL. C., *History of the British Standing Army, 1660–1700*, 1894.

WARD, C., *The War of the Revolution*, 2 vols. New York, 1952.

WEBSTER, J. C. (ed.), *The Journal of Jeffrey Amherst, Recording the Military Career of General Amherst in America from 1758 to 1763*, Toronto, 1931.

WESTERN, J. R., *The English Militia in the Eighteenth Century: The Story of a Political Issue, 1660–1802*, 1965.

WHITE, J. M., *Marshal of France. The Life and Times of Maurice, Comte de Saxe*, New York, 1962.

WHITWORTH, REX, *Field Marshal Lord Ligonier. A Story of the British Army, 1702–1770*, Oxford, 1958.

WICKWIRE, F., and M., *Cornwallis and the War of Independnece*, 1971.

WILLSON, BECKLES, *Life and Letters of James Wolfe*, New York, 1909.
WRIGHT, R., *The Life of Major-General James Wolfe . . . Illustrated by his Correspondence*, 1864.
ZWEGUINTZOW, V., *L'Armée russe, 1700–1825*, 4 vols, Paris, 1967–73.

Unpublished Dissertations

BASSETT, J. H., 'The Purchase System in the British Army, 1660–1871', Boston University Ph.D. thesis, 1969.
HACKMANN, W. K., 'English Military Expeditions to the Coast of France, 1757–1761', Univ. of Michigan Ph.D. thesis, 1969.
HAYES, J., 'The Social and Professional Background of the Officers of the British Army, 1714–63', London M.A. thesis, 1956.
PARKER, K. L., 'Anglo-American Winderness Campaigning, 1754–64: Logistical and Tactical Developments', Columbia University Ph.D. thesis, 1970.
SMITH, W. A., 'Anglo-Colonial Society and the Mob, 1740–1775', Claremont Ph.D. thesis, 1965.

Articles

ATKINSON, C. T., 'The Highlanders in Westphalia, 1760–62, and the Development of Light Infantry', *JSAHR* 20 (1941), 208–33.
—— 'The Army Under The Early Hanoverians', *JSAHR* 21 (1942), 138–47.
—— 'Jenkins' Ear, The Austrian Succession War and The 'Forty-Five', *JSAHR* 22 (1943–4), 280–98.
D'ARLINGTON, J., 'The Pattern 1796 Light Cavalry Sabre', *CJAC* 9 (1971), 127–34.
BURTON, I. F., and NEWMAN, A. N., 'Sir John Cope: Promotion in the Eighteenth-Century Army', *English Historical Review*, 78 (1963), 655–68.
DARLING, A. D., 'The British Basket Hilted Cavalry Sword', *CJAC* 7 (1969), 79–96.
—— 'Weapons of the Highland Regiments, 1740–1780', *CJAC* 8 (1980), 75–95.
—— 'The British Infantry Hangers', *CJAC* 8 (1970), 124–36.
FORDE, F., 'The Royal Irish Artillery, 1755–1801', *The Irish Sword*, 11 (1973), 32–8.
FREARSON, C. W. (ed.), '"To Mr. Davenport", being Letters of Major Richard Davenport (1719–60) to his brother during service in the 4th Troop of Horse Guards, 1742–60', *JSAHR*, Special Publication, no. 9 (1968).

GILBERT, A. N., 'Army Impressment During the War of the Spanish Succession', *Historian*, 38 (1976), 689–708.

GRAS, Y., 'Les guerres limitées du XVIIIe siècle', *Revue historique de l'armée*, 26 (1970), 22–36.

GORDON, L. H., 'The British Cavalry & Dragoon Pistol', *CJAC* 5 (1967), 111–18, and 6 (1968), 10–13.

HAYES, J., 'The Royal House of Hanover and the British Army, 1714–1760', *John Rylands Library, Bulletin*, 40 (1957–8), 328–57.

—— 'Leutenants-Colonel and Majors-Commandant of the Seven Years' War', *JSAHR* 34 (1958), 3–13.

—— 'The Purchase of Colonelcies in the Army, 1714–63', *JSAHR* 39 (1961), 3–10.

HERBERT, BRIG. C., 'Coxheath Camp, 1778–1779', *JSAHR* 45 (1967), 129–48.

HITSMAN, J. M., and BOND, C. C. J., 'The Assault Landing at Louisbourg, 1758', *Canadian Historical Review*, 35 (1954), 314–30.

HOGG, MAJ. O. F. G., 'Forerunners of the Army Council', *JSAHR* 11 (1932), 101–48.

McBARRON, H. C., et al., 'The American Regiment, 1740–1746 (The 61st Regiment of Foot, or Gooch's Regiment)', *Military Collector & Historian*, 21 (1969), 84–6.

McDERMOTT, E., 'The Elder Pitt and his Admirals and Generals', *Military Affairs*, 20 (1956), 65–71.

McGUFFIE, T. H., 'The Guards on Police Duty, 1749', *JSAHR* 25 (1947), 185–6.

MARINI, A. J., 'Parliament and the Marine Regiments, 1739', *MM* 62 (1976), 55–65.

MORK, G. R., 'Flint and Steel: A Study in Military Technology and Tactics in 17th-Century Europe', *Smithsonian Journal of History*, 2 (1967), 25–52.

MUSKET, P., 'Military Operations Against Smugglers in Kent and Sussex, 1698–1750', *JSAHR* 52 (1974), 89–110.

NEAVE-HILL, LT.-COL. W., 'Brevet Rank', *JSAHR* 48 (1970), 85–103.

NICHOLS, F. T., 'The Organization of Braddock's Army', *Wm. & Mary Quarterly*, 3rd Ser., 4 (1947), 124–47.

NICHOLSON, LT.-COL. J. B. R., 'The First Standing Orders of the Fifteenth Light Dragoons', *Tradition*, 10 (1965), 2–3; 11 (1965), 30–3; 12 (1965), 30–1; 13 (1966), 30–7; 15 (1966), 28–9.

PARET, P., 'Colonial Experience and European Military Reform at the End of the Eighteenth Century', *Bul. Instit. of Historical Research*, 37 (1964), 47–59.

PICKERING, R. A., 'The Plug Bayonet', *CJAC* 10 (1972), 117–28.

ROBSON, ERIC, 'Raising a Regiment in the War of Independence', *JSAHR* 27 (1949), 107–15.

ROBSON, J. O. (ed.), 'Military Memoirs of Lt.-Gen. The Hon. Charles Colville', *JSAHR* 25 (1946), 54–62; 26 (1948), 117–20; 27 (1949), 2–13, 70–82, 101–6; 28 (1950), 70–81, 101–5.

SCOBIE, MAJ. I., 'The Highland Independent Companies of 1745–47', *JSAHR* 20 (1941), 5–37.

SPAULDING, O. L., 'The Military Studies of George Washington', *AHR* 29 (1924), 675–80.

SUMNER, REVD. P., 'General Hawley's Scheme for Light Dragoons', *JSAHR* 25 (1947), 63–6.

—— 'General Hawley's "Chaos"', *JSAHR* 26 (1948), 91–4.

—— (ed.), 'Standing Orders for the Army, 1755', *JSAHR* 5 (1926), 191–9; 6 (1927), 8–10.

—— (ed.), 'Standing Orders for the Dragoons, *c.*1755', *JSAHR* 23 (1945), 98–106.

SYRETT, D., 'The British Landing at Havana: An Example of 18th-Century Combined Operations', *MM* 55 (1969), 325–31.

—— 'The Methodology of British Amphibious Operations during the Seven Years' and American Wars', *MM* 58 (1972), 269–80.

TRACY, N., 'The Capture of Manila, 1762'. *MM* 55 (1969), 311–23.

VILLATE, R., 'Le mouvement des idées militaires en France au XVIIIᵉ siècle', *Revue d'histoire moderne*, NS 10 (1935), 226–60.

WHITWORTH, MAJ.-GEN. R. H. 'Some Unpublished Wolfe Letters, 1755–58', *JSAHR* 53 (1975), 65–86.

YAPLE, R. L., 'Braddock's Defeat: The Theories and a Reconsideration', *JSAHR* 46 (1968), 194–201.

Index

OTHER TITLES IN THIS HARDBACK REPRINT PROGRAMME FROM SANDPIPER BOOKS LTD (LONDON) AND POWELLS BOOKS (CHICAGO)